CRAIG BR… …pses of *Princess Margaret*, won both the James Tait Black Prize for Biography and the

make us think very seriously about the nature of fame

MARTHA KEARNEY, Chair of the Judges, Baillie Gifford Prize

'It's ingenious, wholly original (not a given, what with the subject matter), absolutely gripping, funny, sad and moving. A complete treat'

INDIA KNIGHT, *Sunday Times Magazine*

'A brilliantly executed study of cultural time, social space and the madness of fame … *One Two Three Four*, by putting the Beatles in their place as well as their time, is by far the best book anyone has written about them and the closest we can get to the truth'

DOMINIC GREEN, *Literary Review*

'It is Brown's feeling for the revolutionary time and his beady eye for the quirks of the story that make the material sing … this kaleidoscopic work makes the familiar story of the world's most famous band zing with freshness'

NICK CURTIS, *Evening Standard*

'Brown is such an infectiously jolly writer that you don't even need to like the Beatles to enjoy his book … And at a time when, like everybody else, I was feeling not entirely thrilled about the news, I loved every word of it'

DOMINIC SANDBROOK, *Sunday Times*

'Craig Brown has completely reinvented biography. He darts in and out of the Beatles' lives, moving backwards and forwards in time, examining not just their characters but also their effect on the world and their obsessive fans and hangers-on. Brown is so funny and so alive to the tiniest, bathetic detail'

HARRY MOUNT, *Spectator*

'Felt like it should be put on prescription to cheer up the nation'

JENNY COLGAN, Book of the Year, *New Statesman*

'The book that has really been getting me through lockdown … just astonishing'

MARK BILLINGHAM, BBC Radio 4, *Saturday Review*

'As a fan of Craig Brown's writing, as well as of the Beatles' music, I was trying to manage my expectations of *One Two Three Four*. I need not have worried. It is not only as affectionately teasing as you would hope, but also as fascinating and funny' NIGEL FARNDALE, *The Times*

'This brilliant writer brings the Fab Four's personalities to glorious life in a book crammed with fascinating facts and intriguing ideas'
CHARLOTTE HEATHCOTE, *Mirror*

'The most entertaining book about the Fab Four ever written'
SAM LEITH, *Spectator*

'Miraculously, Craig Brown's cultural and emotional history … finds new ways into the Greatest Pop Story Ever Told … it's the Beatles book equivalent of the Red and Blue albums: a glorious compendium of Fab Four lore' VICTORIA SEGAL, Books of the Year, *Sunday Times*

'Brown's idiosyncratic style embraces all the funny details of fandom. Nothing in this wonderful book explains how or why this fountain of creativity emerged from these four young men. But their capacity to amaze outlasts them' IVO DAWNAY, *The Lady*

'In a polychromatic cavalcade of chapters of varying length, the man with kaleidoscope eyes conveys what it was like to live through those extraordinary Beatles years' ALAN JOHNSON, *Spectator*

'Even now, when I know I should be spending every spare minute studying a long read about contagion/China/capitalism, I am instead reading Craig Brown's ridiculously enjoyable new biography of the Beatles, *One Two Three Four*. Because, sure, we're living through history. But did you know that Ringo once tried to save money on house repairs by buying his own building company?'
HADLEY FREEMAN, *Guardian Weekend*

'Brown, a perceptive writer and a gifted satirist, makes familiar stories fresh. Along the way he unearths many fascinating tidbits … a fascinating study of the cultural and social upheaval created by the band'

MOIRA HODGSON, *Wall Street Journal*

'The most engaging, most surprising, most thought-provoking and purely enjoyable book I've read in ages. Brown has as many ways to tell a story as the Beatles had to write a song … if you read this book, a splendid time is guaranteed' FRANK COTTRELL-BOYCE, *Tablet*

'Refreshing to read and so loaded down with social observations that I can feel the Fifties and the Sixties crowding in around me as we watch the ascendancy of the strumming schoolboys to complete mastery of the musical universe, universally' JOHN BIRD, *Big Issue*

'One of the best books I've read on any subject in a good while … In much the same way that the Beatles musically recreated, eulogised, and forever preserved the real Penny Lane in song, *One Two Three Four* lets us relive what it was like to happily share the planet for a few years with a band like no other before or since'

MALCOLM JONES, *The Daily Beast*

'A most brilliant mixture of bathos and comedy and deep feeling and British absurdity' TOM SUTCLIFFE, BBC Radio 4, *Saturday Review*

'This marvellous book is a hell of a bargain … An extraordinary story, beautifully told, about four young men who shaped the modern world'

ROGER ALTON, *Daily Mail*

'Craig Brown seems to have invented a new type of biography, which involves leaving out the boring bits, telling funny stories about yourself and indulging in flights of fancy. It works brilliantly. This witty, quick, jolly book about the Beatles is almost unreasonably entertaining'

ROBBIE MILLEN and JAMES MARRIOT, *The Times*

'It reminds one of a sunnier happier time, of youth and optimism … it's been a good solace to me' ROBERT HARRIS, *BBC*

'Delicious genius. Irreverent, yet admiring, ironic, but not snarky'
STEPHEN BAYLEY, Book of the Year, *Spectator*

'Time-play and what-ifs are part of Brown's formidable bag of tricks, deployed to add emotional range and a poignant twist to his comic vignettes. His biographical method – combining fragments, lists, excerpts, quotes and flights of whimsy – is executed as brilliantly here as in 2017's glittering *Ma'am Darling* … Brown's book is an idiosyncratic cocktail of oral history, personal memoir, tourism and biography'
CHARLES ARROWSMITH, *Washington Post*

OTHER BOOKS BY CRAIG BROWN

The Agreeable World of Wallace Arnold

Rear Columns

A Year Inside: Parliamentary Sketches

The *Private Eye* Book of Craig Brown Parodies

Hug Me While I Weep for I Weep for the World: The Lonely Struggles of Bel Littlejohn

The Craig Brown Omnibus

1966 and All That

Fame, Sex, Money, Power: A Beginner's Guide

This is Craig Brown

The Little Book of Chaos

The Marsh Marlowe Letters

Imaginary Friends: Collected Parodies 2000–2004

The Hounding of John Thomas

Craig Brown's Greatest Hits

Welcome to My Worlds!: The Dread Decades of Wallace Arnold

The Tony Years

The Lost Diaries

One on One

Ma'am Darling: 99 Glimpses of Princess Margaret

CRAIG BROWN

One Two Three Four

The Beatles in Time

4th ESTATE • *London*

4th Estate
An imprint of HarperCollins*Publishers*
1 London Bridge Street
London SE1 9GF

www.4thEstate.co.uk

HarperCollins*Publishers*
1st Floor, Watermarque Building, Ringsend Road
Dublin 4, Ireland

First published in Great Britain in 2020 by 4th Estate
This 4th Estate paperback edition published in 2021

1

A catalogue record for this book is
available from the British Library

ISBN 978-0-00-834003-2

Set in Minion Pro
Printed and bound in Great Britain by
CPI Group (UK) Ltd, Croydon

For Frances, Silas, Tallulah and Tom

In five-score summers! All new eyes,
New minds, new modes, new fools, new wise;
New woes to weep, new joys to prize;
With nothing left of me and you
In that live century's vivid view
Beyond a pinch of dust or two;
A century which, if not sublime,
Will show, I doubt not, at its prime,
A scope above this blinkered time.

From '1967', by Thomas Hardy
(written in 1867)

'What a remarkable fifty years they have been for the world … Think what we would have missed if we had never heard the Beatles.'

Queen Elizabeth II,
speaking in November 1997 at a celebration
of her golden wedding anniversary

1

One.

Two.

Three.

Four.

In their neat black suits and ties, Brian Epstein and his personal assistant Alistair Taylor make their way down the eighteen steep steps into the sweaty basement on Mathew Street. Brian finds it 'as black as a deep grave, dank and damp and smelly'. He wishes he hadn't come. Both he and Taylor would prefer to be attending a classical concert at the Philharmonic, but curiosity got the better of them. Four young musicians saunter onto the stage. Brian recognises them from the family record shop he manages: they are the ones who lounge around in the booths, listening to the latest discs and chatting to the girls, with absolutely no intention whatsoever of buying a record.

Between songs, the three yobs with guitars start yelling and swearing, turning their backs on the audience and pretending to hit one another. Taylor notices Brian's eyes widen with amazement. Taylor himself is undergoing one of the most shocking experiences of his life – 'like someone thumping you' – and he is pretty sure Brian feels the same.

After the show, Taylor says, 'They're just AWFUL.'

'They ARE awful,' agrees Brian. 'But I also think they're fabulous. Let's just go and say hello.'

George is the first of the Beatles to spot the man from the record shop approaching.

'Hello there,' he says. 'What brings Mr Epstein here?'

2

Other groups had a front man; your favourite was pre-selected for you. No one would ever pick Hank Marvin over Cliff Richard, say, or Mike Smith over Dave Clark.

But with the Beatles there was a choice, so you had to pick a favourite, and the one you picked said a lot about who you were. For their American fan Carolyn See, there was 'Paul, for those who preferred androgynous beauty; John, for those who prized intellect and wit; George because he possessed that ineffable something we would later recognize as spiritual life; and Ringo, patron saint of fuckups the world over.'

In Liverpool, the twelve-year-old Linda Grant favoured Ringo 'for reasons that are beyond me.' There was, she recalls, 'a real goody-two-shoes at school who liked Paul. George seemed a bit nothing. John seemed off-limits, too intimidating.'

Ringo was the Beatle for girls who lacked ambition. Picking him as your favourite suggested a touch of realism. It went without saying that the others were already taken, but you might just stand an outside chance with the drummer. 'If someone asked who my favorite was I always said, "Oh, I like Ringo,"' remembered Fran Lebowitz, who grew up in New Jersey. 'I liked the personality of Ringo Starr. I still do. He was not, of course, the favorite in my school among the girls. Paul McCartney was far and away the favorite. He was the cute Beatle. So it was probably just a contrarian position to choose Ringo Starr.'

Helen Shapiro was only sixteen but already a major star when the Beatles toured as one of her supporting acts at the start of 1963. Like any other girl, she had her favourite. 'John was married but nobody knew about it at the time so along with a few thousand other girls I had a crush on him … George was the most serious. He would occasionally talk about what he was going to do when he was rich, and try to pick my brains about the financial side of things. I couldn't have been a lot of help. I still wasn't interested in the money. Paul remained the spokesman. Ringo was the quiet one.'

Pattie Boyd met the four Beatles after being chosen to play one of the schoolgirls in *Hard Day's Night*. 'On first impressions, John seemed more cynical and brash than the others, Ringo the most endearing. Paul was cute, and George, with velvet brown eyes and dark chestnut hair, was the best-looking man I'd ever seen.' Unlike millions of other fans, Pattie was able to take her choice a stage further. Reader, she married him.

There was a Beatle to suit every taste. As a fan, you expressed yourself by picking one over the others. Each personified a different element: John fire, Paul water, George air, Ringo earth. Even their friends liked to paint them in primary colours, with sharply contrasting characters, like one of those jokes about the Englishman, the Welshman, the Irishman and the Scotsman. Carolyn See noted how, in *A Hard Day's Night*, they enacted their given personas: 'winsome Paul, witty John, thoughtful George, goofy Ringo'.

The actor Victor Spinetti once told this story about them. While filming *Help!* in Salzburg, he caught 'flu and was confined to bed. 'The Beatles came to my hotel room to visit. The first to arrive was George Harrison. He knocked, came in and said, "I've come to plump your pillows. Whenever anyone's ill in bed they have to have their pillows plumped." He then plumped my pillows and left. John Lennon came in next and marched up and down barking "*Sieg heil, Schweinhund!* The doctors are here. They're coming to experiment upon you. *Sieg heil! Heil Hitler!*" And he left. Ringo then came in, sat down by the bed, picked up the hotel menu and read out loud, as if to a child, "Once upon a time there were three bears. Mummy bear, Daddy bear and Baby bear." And then he left. Paul opened the door an inch, asked, "Is it catching?" "Yes," I said, on which he shut the door and I never saw him again.' Paul was being the pragmatist, as usual. He knew that if he or the others had caught 'flu, there'd be no filming.

Working alongside Brian Epstein, Alistair Taylor observed the different ways the Beatles dealt with their earnings. 'Every month, Brian would issue each of the boys with their financial statements, all neatly and accurately itemised, and sealed in a white manila envelope. They reacted very different. John would instantly crumple it up and stuff it in his pocket. George might have a look. Ringo certainly couldn't understand it and didn't waste any time trying. Paul was the one who opened it carefully and would sit in the corner of the office for hours going meticulously through it.'

As they grew older, the differences in their characters became sharper. It was as though the wind had changed, and each had been stuck with the face he last pulled. Asked to submit ideas for famous figures to include on the *Sgt. Pepper* album cover, George suggested a few Indian gurus, and Paul picked a broad variety of artists, from Stockhausen to Fred Astaire. John's suggestions were more macabre or offbeat: the Marquis de Sade, Edgar Allan Poe, Jesus, Hitler. And as for Ringo, he simply said he'd go along with what the others wanted.

Of course, the Beatles revolved around the contrasting characters of Paul and John. Their recording engineer Geoff Emerick watched the two of them at work. 'They couldn't have been two more different people. Paul was meticulous and organised, he always carried a notebook around with him, in which he methodically wrote down lyrics and chord changes in his neat handwriting. In contrast, John seemed to live in chaos: he was constantly searching for scraps of paper that he'd scribbled hurried ideas on. Paul was a natural communicator; John couldn't articulate his ideas well. Paul was the diplomat; John was the agitator. Paul was soft-spoken and almost unfailingly polite; John could be a right loudmouth and quite rude. Paul was willing to put in long hours to get a part right; John was impatient, always ready to move on to the next thing. Paul usually knew exactly what he wanted and would often take offence at criticism;

John was much more thick-skinned and was open to hearing what others had to say.'

John was brittle, demanding and caustic; Paul emollient, engaging, agreeable. But there were those who detected something single-minded, perhaps even self-serving, beneath Paul's charm. Tony Barrow, who worked as the Beatles' press officer, felt that 'John made the most noise, especially with Epstein. But it was Paul who let John do the heavy lifting when there was a dispute with Brian. Then Paul would finish the persuasion. John would make Brian cry at times, but Paul, more of a politician, would use a quiet influence to get his way. John's bark was worse than his bite. He used the bark to cover up low self-esteem … Paul promised people everything, tickets, gifts, then left it to people like me to fulfil the promises. He wanted to look like a good benefactor, and he was long on promises, short on performance. He was a charmer who was a public relations delight, a man who was master of image-making. He is and was a sheer showman, from his bone marrow to his fingertips. He feeds on the approval of his public.'

Paul was baby-faced, meticulous, perky, diplomatic, energetic, tuneful, ingratiating, optimistic, outgoing, cheery, sentimental, solicitous. John was angular, slapdash, maudlin, difficult, lazy, dissonant, edgy, sardonic, pessimistic, solipsistic, sulky, cool, brutal. Paul considered himself lovable; John believed himself unlovable.

Paul once tried to explain how the two of them had become what they were. 'John, because of his upbringing and his unstable family life, had to be hard, witty, always ready for the cover-up, ready for the riposte, ready with the sharp little witticism. Whereas with my rather comfortable upbringing, a lot of family, a lot of people, very northern, "Cup of tea, love?", my surface grew to be easy-going. Put people at their ease. Chat to people, be nice, it's nice to be nice … Mentally, no one could say much to hurt me, whereas with John: his dad wasn't home, so it was "Where's yer dad, you bastard?" And his mother lived with somebody and that was called "living in sin" in those days, so there was another cheap shot against him. John had a lot to guard against, and it formed his personality; he was a very guarded person … He had massive hang-ups from his upbringing.'

The peculiar power of the Beatles' music, its magic and its beauty, lies in the intermingling of these opposites. Other groups were raucous or reflective, progressive or traditional, solemn or upbeat, folksy or sexy or aggressive. But when you hear a Beatles album, you feel that all human life is there. As John saw it, when they were composing together, Paul 'provided a lightness, an optimism, while I would always go for sadness, the discords, a certain bluesy edge'. It was this finely balanced push me/pull you tension that made their greatest music so expressive, capable of being both universal and particular at one and the same time.

Even as teenagers, they approached their songwriting with a sense of purpose. Paul would bunk off school, and John would join him in the McCartney house in Forthlin Road. Then Paul would open his school notebook, with its blue lines on white paper, and write, 'Another Lennon-McCartney original' on the next blank page, and the two of them would get straight down to composing their next song. Looking back, Paul struggled to recall a fruitless afternoon. 'We never had a dry session … In all the years, we never walked away from a session saying, "Fuck it, we can't write one."'

Sometimes their contributions to the same song were so keenly differentiated that they seemed to be playing up to their caricatures. Paul comes up with 'We can work it out', and John immediately undercuts it: 'Life is very short'. Paul sings 'It's getting better' and John butts in with 'Can't get much worse'. In 'A Day in the Life' it is John, compulsive reader of newspapers, who just has to laugh at the man who's blown his mind out in a car, while it is the happy-go-lucky Paul who wakes up, gets out of bed, drags a comb across his head.

Many of their songs have bright melodies but dark lyrics, or dark melodies but bright lyrics. The words of 'Help!', 'Run for Your Life', 'Misery' and 'Maxwell's Silver Hammer' are all about depression and psychosis, but they are set to jaunty tunes. Deprived of this tug-of-war between the two competing partners, their solo songs often lack that dimension of otherness, with John falling back on self-pity and Paul giving in to whimsy.*

As time went by, their collaboration dwindled, and they composed more and more of their songs separately. But they remained driven by a shared sense of competition; each sought the other's approval. 'It was an ideal match,' wrote the critic Ian MacDonald. 'They laughed at the same things, thought at the same speed, respected each other's talent, and knew that their unspoken urge to best and surprise each other was crucial to the continuing vitality of their music.'

* Fourteen years after the Beatles broke up, Paul told Steve Grant of *Time Out*: 'I know I've lost my edge … I need a kind of outside injection, stimulus, that's not there any more. And remember the edge came from all the Beatles – if Ringo or George didn't like anything, it was out. My stuff has got more poppy without that outside stimulus, but then I've always been more at home with love songs and anthems.' At the same time, John remained frustrated at the relative lack of take-up of his own songs. 'It would sometimes annoy him that Paul's songs were more covered than his,' Yoko told Philip Norman in 2008. 'He'd say, "They always cover Paul's songs – they never cover mine."' In 2019 Paul smiled as he told the BBC journalist Emily Maitlis how cross John would get when he walked into hotel lounges in New York and pianists, seeking to please him, would immediately launch into flowery renditions of 'Yesterday'.

3

Late November 1940

Mary Mohin is thirty years old, and still unmarried. Mary's mother died in 1919, while giving birth to her fifth child, who also died. At the time, Mary was ten years old. Perhaps influenced by this early tragedy, Mary set her heart on becoming a midwife. She achieved her ambition, and more: she is now not only a midwife, but a ward sister.

Jim McCartney is thirty-eight years old, and still unmarried. He was his mother's fifth child, but only the third to live beyond the age of two. He left school just before his fourteenth birthday, and got a good job at a cotton brokers. He is now a cotton salesman, on a decent wage. His main love, though, is playing trumpet with his own six-to-eight-piece ensemble – Jim Mac's Band. They perform all the latest dance tunes; Jim's favourite is 'I'll Build a Stairway to Paradise'.

Excused wartime service because he is deaf in one ear, Jim is attached to the Fazakerley Fire Unit. German bombs have been falling on Liverpool since August; London is the only city to have suffered more devastation.* Somehow, the deadpan Liverpudlian humour sees them through. Over in Arnold Grove, the Harrison family have had their windows blown out, and their leather sofa, which they reserved for special occasions, was shredded by the flying glass. 'If I'd known that was going to happen we could have been sitting on it all these years,' observes Mrs Harrison.

Mary lodges with Jim's sister Gin. Mary and Jim have known each

* Over four thousand Liverpudlians were killed in the Blitz.

other quite well for some years now, though they have never thought of each other in terms of romance.

(a)

Tonight the Nazi bombers fly overhead. Gin and Mary are visiting Jim's mum in Scargreen Avenue when the sirens sound, so they have to stay over. As the bombs fall, Jim and Mary sit and chat for hours. By the time the all-clear is sounded, they feel they are meant for one another. After a brief engagement, they marry on 15 April 1941; just over a year later, Mary gives birth to their first child, a boy. They christen him James Paul McCartney.

(b)

Tonight is quiet. The sirens never sound. As it happens, they will tomorrow night, when Gin and Mary are planning on staying home. So Jim and Mary fail to have their heart-to-heart, and go their separate ways. James Paul McCartney is never born.

4

We had been told to gather outside Liverpool at Speke Hall, described by the National Trust as 'a rare Tudor timber-framed manor house in a most unusual setting on the banks of the River Mersey'. The estate has, the guidebook advises, 'witnessed more than 400 years of turbulent history'.

I was early, so I hung around in the 'Visitor Complex' – a building, not a condition – looking at mugs and scarves and soaps and books about the Tudors. 'A bit of a bookworm? Thumb through our collection of adults' and children's books to find your next great read!'

Before long, a cheery driver called Joe shepherded us onto a minibus, then asked us where we were from. Three of us were from Spain, two from Italy, four from Australia, two from Austria, four from England. A couple of people who had bought tickets were missing, so we waited until two young women came running towards the bus, waving frantically. 'Let's give them a fright,' said Joe, turning on the ignition and setting off. They waved more frantically. 'And now let's see those tears turn to laughter,' said Joe, stopping the minibus and letting them in.

As the minibus left Speke Hall, Joe pressed a button and 'Love Me Do' came bursting from the speakers. 'Whassis rubbish then?' shouted an Australian at the back.

'I can see who'll be walkin' back!' said Joe. 'When he gets off the bus, let's jump 'im!' It was all very merry.

Soon we were in Forthlin Road, the kind of unassuming row of nondescript houses most National Trust members would normally drive through, rather than to.

The National Trust bought 20 Forthlin Road in 1995, on the suggestion of the then director-general of the BBC, a Liverpudlian called John Birt,* who had noticed it was up for sale. Seven years later the Trust also acquired John Lennon's childhood home, 'Mendips', in Menlove Avenue, after it had been bought by Yoko Ono. In a statement around that time, she said: 'When I heard that Mendips was up for sale, I was worried that it might fall into the wrong hands and be commercially exploited. That's why I decided to buy the house, and donate it to the National Trust so it would be well looked after as a place for people to visit and see. I am thrilled that the National Trust has agreed to take it on.'

But it was a decision not welcomed by one and all. Tim Knox, at that time the National Trust's head curator,† declared himself 'furious'. The Trust's usual criterion for taking on a property – that the building should have intrinsic artistic merit – had, he felt, been abandoned in pursuit of shabby populism. 'They're publicity coups – not serious acquisitions,' he said, adding, only half-jokingly, 'Now we're going to take four properties on so Ringo doesn't feel left out.'

Others agreed. 'Architecturally, the house is no more or less interesting than any other arterial, pebble-dashed semi in any other

---

* John Birt, director-general of the BBC 1992–2000. In the summer of 1962 the seventeen-year-old Birt had a holiday job as a bouncer at Southport's Cambridge Hall, where the Beatles were playing two consecutive evenings with Joe Brown and the Bruvvers headlining. After the first concert he and a friend were told to guard the door of the Beatles' Green Room to keep out, in his words, 'a score of emotional and tearful girls of my own age'. One of these girls turned out to be 'the most beautiful girl in Formby. We saw her on the train to school each day. She was in a league of beauty of her own and paid no attention to any of us. No one in my circle had ever spoken to her.' She pleaded with Birt and his friend to let her in to see Paul McCartney. 'My friend said: "We'll let you in to see Paul if you let us have a snog and a feel." She immediately agreed and led us off to some backstairs [sic]. To my shame even at the time, I participated in the encounter despite her inert response. This unedifying experience was soon cut short and we led her back to the Green Room to find that the Beatles had gone. I rushed around in a guilty panic trying to locate Paul and, to my relief, found him at the bar. I retrieved the girl, and took her to Paul, who was with a crowd of admirers. He turned round, recognised me as the bouncer, realised I was there with a purpose and raised his eyebrows questioningly. I explained that I was with someone very keen to meet him and introduced Paul to the apparition at my side. He bowed graciously, and as I departed in embarrassment they were chatting politely to one another.'

† Now the director of the Royal Collection.

middle-class suburb,' observed the design critic Stephen Bayley.* 'Its special value comes from the vicarious, mystical contact with genius. The problem for the Trust's architectural historians is that, since the house was pretty much denuded of its contents, there is no possibility of vicarious, mystical contact with the genius's telly set, kitchen unit or any other artefact that might afford an insight into the inspiration that gave us such a torrent of brilliant words and music. So, they set about faking it.

'The National Trust ... prides itself on its access to expertise. It has some of the world's leading architectural historians on its staff and they went out to buy the stuff to recreate Lennon's home. But when scholarly expertise is focused on junk, in a magical mystery tour of some dingy Liverpudlian dealers, scholarly expertise looks silly. A crap medicine cabinet is admired for its authenticity. The lino is subject to scrutiny worthy of a Donatello relief sculpture. They can find the conical legs of the television set, but not the set itself ... If you are doing the long and winding road of fakery, where do you stop? In the dreamworld of folk memory and fantasy, is the answer.'

The National Trust remains undaunted. 'Imagine walking through the back door into the kitchen where John Lennon's Aunt Mimi would have cooked him his tea,' reads its awestruck introduction to Mendips. It treats the house as a religious shrine, a place of pilgrimage. 'Join our fascinating Custodian on a trip down memory lane ... John's bedroom is a very atmospheric place in which to take a moment with your own thoughts about this incredible individual ...'

Pilgrims to Mendips face rules and regulations stricter than those for the Sistine Chapel. 'Any photography inside Mendips or duplication of audio tour material is strictly prohibited. You will be asked to deposit all handbags, cameras and recording equipment at the entrance to the house.'

---

* Coincidentally, the very same Stephen Bayley who at the age of fifteen wrote the letter to John that spurred him to write 'I am the Walrus' (see page 418).

It can't be long, surely, before one of the faithful witnesses some sort of miracle at Mendips – a blind man sees, a crippled man rises up and walks, a little girl sees John's mother Julia in a vision – leading yet more pilgrims to flock to Menlove Avenue, forming orderly queues for the chance to see the exact spot where Julia met her end.

While our minibus was decanting its passengers, many more were pouring out of a 'Magical Mystery Tour' coach, and behind them, four Germans were stepping out of a black cab. The gateway to 20 Forthlin Road was pullulating with visitors from all over the world, wearing Beatles T-shirts and posing for selfies. The metal sign outside announces 'The proud family home of the McCartney family, Jim, Mary, Paul and Mike. Accessible via the National Trust.'

I started edging towards the front of the queue. I had booked way in advance and paid £31 (including guidebooks) for an official tour of both Beatles houses, and I was worried that people on unofficial tours would creep their way past the guide and elbow their way into Paul's house in my place. Luckily, Joe the driver was standing by, monitoring the chosen few. Our little group marched self-importantly into the front garden of 20 Forthlin Road, and the gates were then satisfyingly closed on everybody else.

Our National Trust guide introduced herself as Sylvia. She conducts 12,000 people a year around Paul's childhood home, twenty at a go, four times a day. Her voice has a hint of Hyacinth Bucket. Standing in the garden, she welcomed us to 20 Forthlin Road. This, she said, was where Paul lived for eight years: 'very important years musically. George Harrison was an early visitor. George would bring his guitar.'

A buzz went around. Stephen Bayley's promise of mystical contact seemed to be taking shape. 'And then when John Lennon started to come down to the house, John would take a short cut through the golf course to get here on his bicycle, taking less than ten minutes through the golf course. And in the room behind you there –' she gestured '– that's where John and Paul sat down and began writing songs together. By the time Paul left here, it was right at the end of 1963, so the Beatles had already got hits in the charts, they were appearing on television. Paul was still coming back though, that was still his bedroom up there, right until the end of 1963. He was the last Beatle to move to London. So when the McCartneys came – sorry, are you recording?'

I froze. I had been covertly recording Sylvia on a mobile phone, but it turned out that she was talking to one of the Australians, standing closer to her. He assured her that, no, he wasn't recording. 'No?' she replied, suspiciously. 'I'm sorry, I just don't like it,' she muttered, before struggling to regain her thread. 'Erm. When. Erm. The McCartneys. So. Erm. When the McCartneys came to live here, erm, these were all council houses, so that means the McCartneys didn't own this house, it was social housing, everybody paid rent.'

Unbeknownst to Sylvia, I carried on recording, slyly holding my phone at a casual angle so as not to excite her attention. It made me feel on edge, as though I were pocketing household products within spitting distance of a store detective.

'Over the years, you can see what's happened. People have bought the houses, and they've changed the doors and windows. When the National Trust got this house, twenty-two years ago now, there were new windows at the front, but the Trust saw that a house across the street still had these original windows, so they did a deal, they got the new ones and we got the old ones back again. So now it looks exactly as it did when Paul and his family lived here.'

We all gazed dutifully at these front windows, marvelling that they now looked just like they would have looked before they looked different. Meanwhile, my phone was recording, and I was growing increasingly worried that Sylvia would notice, and denounce me.

'OK, so if anyone wants a photograph at the front of the house, just give me your phone or your camera. Move to the end of the window so I can fit you in, bunch up a bit for me.' Groups of visitors stood beaming in front of Paul's old front door, or what would have been Paul's old front door if it had been Paul's old front door, which it wasn't. 'Is that everyone? Is that it?'

Sylvia warned us that we were not allowed to take photographs in the house or the back garden. 'There's a special reason here. You'll see inside we've got Mike McCartney, Paul's younger brother's, copyright photographs all around the house. It's lovely to have them. And you'll enjoy them. But he'd take them away if people had photographs of them.'

We moved into the back garden. The National Trust blurb suggests '5 things to look out for at 20 Forthlin Road'. One is described as 'The Back Drainpipe: After Paul's mum died, his father would insist that the two boys were home in time for dinner, if not they were locked out. When this inevitably happened, Paul and Mike would run round the back of the house, climb up the drainpipe, and through the bathroom window, which they always left on the latch for such an eventuality.' Sylvia repeated this anecdote, almost word for word, as we all stared at the drainpipe – or, to be accurate, the replica drainpipe.

'So if when you come in you could hand me your bags and cameras, and if you've got a mobile phone can you switch if off and hand it in, so we don't want to see mobile phones in your pockets.'

With that, Sylvia ushered us inside. Everyone lined up to give her their phones and cameras, as though crossing the border of a particularly nervy country. She then locked them all in a cupboard under the stairs. Disobediently, I kept my mobile phone in my pocket, and immediately regretted it. Throughout the rest of my visit I was terrified that someone would phone me, and the ringing would act as an alarm bell and I would be unmasked and shamed.

We all squeezed into the sitting room, decorated with three different types of wallpaper – 'the McCartney family bought end-of rolls' – none of them original. The brown armchair, chunky 1950s television and corner table were not original either, and nor were the rugs. 'This is the room the McCartneys called the front parlour. The National Trust has recreated it with the aid of photos and family memories,' said Sylvia. In response to a query she said that no, the piano was not original. 'Paul still owns his father's house, and he stays in it when he comes to Liverpool. And that's where the original McCartney piano is. Jim used to play "The Entertainer". Do you know that song – by Scott Joplin? If you think of Scott Joplin and "When I'm 64", you can really tell the influence … Father Jim was a good self-taught musician. Paul followed in his father's footsteps. After a few lessons, he said, "I'll be just like my Dad. I'll teach myself." … He composed "World Without Love" here, and the very beginnings of "Michelle" were written here. And "Love Me Do" – they were sitting here when they wrote it … Paul sat here and wrote "I'll Follow the Sun".' She pointed to a photo of John and Paul on the wall. 'The song they're finishing in this picture is "I Saw Her Standing There" … Another song they finished off was "Please Please Me".'

Every now and then, Sylvia tried to make things personal, beginning her sentences 'Paul told me' – as in, 'Paul told me, "We had some sad years but most of the time we were really happy." Or, 'This was their dining room. Paul told me, "We never ate in here after Mum died."' She added, 'Paul told me, "A lot of people think 'Let it Be' is about the Virgin Mary, but it was about my mother, who would always say "Let it be."' I had read these stories countless times over the years,* but it obviously afforded Sylvia satisfaction to say that she had heard them direct from Paul; and perhaps in the coming years it would satisfy us, too, to say that we had heard them from someone who had heard them from Paul.

We shuffled into the kitchen. 'The quarry tiles have not been changed. All the Beatles have stood on those quarry tiles – though Ringo only twice, as he came late.' We peered down at the sacred tiles beneath our feet. 'The Trust found the original white sink in the garden with plants in it and returned it to its rightful position.' We gazed awestruck at the kitchen sink, imagining young Paul hard at work on the dishes.

Only the tiles and the sink are original to the kitchen, but the experts from the National Trust found feasible lookalikes for the rest: the packet of Lux soap flakes, the Stork margarine, the tea can, the biscuit tin, the wireless, the clothes horse. Photographs of all these items – the

---

* Most recently in the 2018 Paul McCartney *Carpool Karaoke* (50,000,000 views, 70,000 comments), in which Paul says, 'I had a dream in the sixties, where my mum, who'd died, came to me in the dream and was reassuring me, saying, "It's going to be okay, just let it be." And I felt so great, like, it's going to be great … So I wrote the song. But it was her positivity.'

In the *New Yorker* in February 2020, James Corden, who chaperoned Paul around Liverpool for his *Carpool Karaoke*, revealed that Paul had initially been reluctant to return to his family home.'He said, "I haven't been there since I left, when I was twenty. I just feel weird about it."'

domestic equivalents of tribute bands – may be purchased on the National Trust website: photos of a 1950s record player, vacuum cleaner, bread bin, washing tongs, frying pan, kettle, clothes pegs, rolling pin. And everything has been diligently catalogued, like items from the Tower of London. A photograph of a wooden spoon (Date 1960–1962, 260mm; Materials: Wood) is described as 'Historic Services,/ Food & drink preparation, Summary: Wooden spoon, kept in mixing bowl on dresser'.

Alternatively, you can buy a photo of a tea strainer or a doormat or a frying pan or a coat rack or 'Enamel bucket with black rim and handle with wooden grip, date unknown'.

The pride of the collection is surely 'Dustbin: Metalwork, Date 1940–1960, Summary: Metal dustbin with separate lid (plus spare lid in Coal Shed)'. If you were a battered old dustbin, circa 1940–1960, just imagine how proud you would be to end up as a key exhibit in a National Trust property, with 12,000 visitors a year admiring you for looking just like the dustbin into which the McCartney family used to throw its rubbish!

While we were still squeezed downstairs, I became so scared that my phone would ring that I surreptitiously switched it off, and began taking notes instead. 'The lino on the floors is just right,' Sylvia was saying, 'so we managed to track it down, and the cupboard where I put the bags, well, that was where Paul would hang up his jacket and sometimes his leather trousers. Excuse me, you're taking notes. Why are you taking notes?' With a start, I realised that Sylvia was talking to me. 'Who's it for?'

'Me,' I said.

'I'm just checking you're not a journalist.'

'I am. I'm writing a book.'

'Well, I don't like you taking notes.'

'Why not?'

'Well, it's just that a lot of what I say has been told to me by Mike, and it's private information.'

'But you've said you tell it to 12,000 people a year. It can't be all that private.'

'I'm sorry, it's making me uncomfortable. What did you say your name was?'

And so there we were, arguing away in the McCartney front parlour on a very hot day in August. We finally came to some sort of deal that I wouldn't write anything that Sylvia regarded as strictly private, but she kept throwing suspicious glances in my direction. I sensed my fellow visitors edging away from me, as though I had just broken wind.

Eventually we were permitted upstairs. Sylvia led us into Paul's bedroom. On his bed sat an acoustic guitar, strung for a left-hander. Inevitably, this was not the actual guitar. A few records were also on the bed, along with a sketch pad and a copy of the *New Musical Express*. 'We've collected all sorts of things he had in this room. For instance, the bird books – Paul was always a keen birdwatcher.'

'This is strictly private,' she added, looking daggers at me, 'but Paul told me he always liked looking out over these fields, which belonged to the police training college. He liked watching the police horses in the back field.'

It was only later, browsing through the National Trust's colour guide to 20 Forthlin Road, that I chanced upon this passage in Paul's introduction: 'The house looks onto a police training college, and we could sit on the roof of our shed and watch the annual police show without having to pay.'

5

On 6 July 1957, Paul's school friend Ivan Vaughan suggested they go to the church fête at Woolton, where two of his mates would be playing in a skiffle group.

Paul and Ivan looked on as a carnival procession left the church – a brass band, followed by Girl Guides and Boy Scouts and a succession of decorated floats, all led by the Rose Queen and her attendants. At the tail end came the organisers' sole concession to modernity – a teenage skiffle group called the Quarrymen, playing on the back of an open lorry.

Once they had completed a circuit, the Quarrymen jumped off their lorry and set themselves up in a field just beyond the cemetery. Ivan and Paul paid threepence to see them. The first song they heard John sing was 'Come Go With Me' by the Del-Vikings. Paul looked on fascinated, not only by the chords John was playing, but by his ability to make things up as he went along: even then, he couldn't be bothered to learn the words. Using this improvisatory method, John sang his way through 'Maggie May', 'Putting on the Style' and 'Be-Bop-a-Lula'.

Between sets John wandered over to the Scout hut, where he knew his guitar would be safe. Elsewhere, crowds were enjoying a routine by the Liverpool City Police Dogs, while youngsters queued for balloons.

Paul wandered over to the hut with Ivan. He recognised John from the bus, but had never spoken to him: Paul had just turned fifteen, while John was nearly seventeen. Even at that age, John had an intimidating air about him: 'I wouldn't look at him too hard in case he hit me.' So Paul hovered shyly. The group then transferred to the church hall, where they were booked to play another set later. After a while Paul felt bold enough to ask John if he might have a go on his guitar.

Armed with the guitar, he grew bolder still. First, he asked to retune it, and then he launched into various songs, among them 'Twenty Flight Rock' and 'Be-Bop-a-Lula'. 'It was uncanny,' recalled another Quarryman, Eric Griffiths. 'He had such confidence, he gave a *performance*. It was so natural.'

Ever more confident, Paul moved to the piano, and struck up a medley of Little Richard songs. John, too, was obsessed by Little Richard – when he first heard him singing 'Long Tall Sally', 'It was so great I couldn't speak.' And now here before him, a year later, was this kid who could holler just like his idol.

'WoooOOOOOOOOOOOO!'

'I half thought to myself, "He's as good as me,"' said John, looking back on that singular moment. 'Now, I thought, if I take him on, what will happen? It went through my head that I'd have to keep him in line if I let him join. But he was good, so he was worth having. He also looked like Elvis.'

Another band member recalled the two of them circling each other 'like cats'. After a while Paul and Ivan drifted off home; the Quarrymen had another set to play.

Later, John asked his best friend Pete Shotton, who played washboard, what he thought of Paul. Pete said he liked him.

'So what would you think about having Paul in the group, then?'

'It's OK with me.'

Two weeks later, Paul was riding his bicycle when he spotted Pete Shotton walking along. He stopped to chat.

'By the way,' said Pete, 'I've been talking with John about it, and … we thought maybe you'd like to join the group.'

According to Pete, a minute ticked by while Paul pretended to give the matter careful thought.

'Oh, all right,' he replied with a shrug; and with that he cycled off home.

* * *

Everyone has a different version of this first meeting between John and Paul. No two accounts are the same. Some say they met in the hut, others in the hall; some are convinced Aunt Mimi was present, others are equally convinced she was not; of those who say she was, some think she enjoyed the concert, while others remember her tut-tutting all the way through. In 1967 Pete Shotton told the Beatles' first biographer, Hunter Davies, that he couldn't remember Paul making much of an impression on anyone: 'He seemed very quiet.' But sixteen years later, when he came to write his autobiography, his memory had changed: 'John was immediately impressed by what he heard and saw.'

6

Back on the National Trust minibus, we were now on our way to Mendips, where John Lennon lived with his Aunt Mimi. The custodian of Mendips is Colin, who is, as it happens, married to Sylvia. He used to teach English and history, and had retired to Derbyshire. But in 2003 he answered an advertisement for a guide for Mendips, and he has been there ever since.

While I was on the bus between the two houses I worried that Sylvia might have phoned Colin to warn him of trouble ahead, but he appeared unruffled as he welcomed us to the front garden of Mendips. 'Also, welcome from Yoko Ono Lennon. It was Yoko who bought the house in 2002 and then immediately donated it to the National Trust … I hope you enjoy an insight into the formative years of John.'

He pointed to the blue plaque on the front of the house:

'You may have noticed there is no blue plaque on Paul's home. This is because you have to be twenty years dead before they give you a plaque.

'In your mind's eye, remember Paul's home. Well, this house was built in 1933. Paul's was twenty years younger. It was rented, not owned, what they used to call "social housing" – to live here, you would have to have been working class. John's house was in one of the most sought-after neighbourhoods. Lawyers, doctors, bankers lived here. So he was the middle-class Beatle.

'Our researches show that its first owner was Mr Harrap, a banker, and we believe it was his family which called it "Mendips". These are the original windows – it has never been double-glazed. In 1938 George and Mary Smith bought the house; Mary's nephew John came to live with them in 1945. He was raised as an only child.

'Mary Smith – better known as Aunt Mimi – was known for her withering looks,' he continued, 'and she would cast these withering looks on the people who lived on the council estate. She'd call them "common" because they lived in social housing. And so did my mum. And that's because Mimi was a *snob*, and *so was my mum!* They were both SNOBS!'

I was taken aback by the note of anger he had injected into the word 'snobs'. It's not the sort of thing one usually hears from National Trust guides as they glide proprietorially around the stately homes of England. On the whole, they are tweedy types, well-adapted to the demands of snobbery. In fact, many of them would regard Aunt Mimi as something of a role model.

Colin informed us that Aunt Mimi did not like to get her front hall dirty, so she would direct people to the back door. Apparently there is an old Liverpool saying: 'Go round the back and save the carpet.'

'Paul said to me, "I arrived with a guitar on my back and forgot that John had said, 'Paul, don't go to the front door.'" And, for you, too, it has to be the tradesman's entrance ...'

With that, Colin shepherded us into the spacious garden behind the house. While we were shuffling through, I happened to turn round. The Beatles, in their smart grey suits, circa 1964, were leaning over the front gate, pointing at me and grinning.

I took a closer look: they were not the actual Beatles, but replicants, possibly one of the looky-likey groups who had come to Liverpool for that week's International Beatleweek Festival.

Colin led us through the back door, and into the kitchen. Mimi herself renovated it in the 1960s, introducing a shiny new yellow formica worktop and a double-drainer sink, and her refitting was itself refitted by subsequent owners. But with its determination to turn back the clock, the National Trust scoured the country for the type of kitchen items that might just possibly have been in Aunt Mimi's house back then: large jars of pickled onions, tins of baking powder and condensed milk, a bread bin with 'BREAD' on it, a wooden cutting board, PG Tips, Rinzo, Olive Green household soap, a –

'Are you taking notes?'

I looked up. Colin had stopped his spiel and was pointing at me.

'Are you taking notes? Because a lot of what I am talking about is private information.'

Once again I felt as if I had been caught shoplifting, and immediately turned defensive. How could it be private information if he was relaying it to 12,000 visitors a year? He said that he had already written one book about the Beatles, and was gathering material for another. He clearly wanted to ring-fence some of this information for himself. Yet so far he hadn't said anything that I hadn't read countless times.

'Well,' I said, attempting a conciliatory tone, 'tell me when there's something you don't want me to mention and I won't write it down.'

'OK,' he said. 'I don't want you to include anything I say from now on.'

This didn't seem fair. I had, after all, paid my £31 (including guidebooks) to go round the homes of Paul and John, and at no point was I told that I couldn't take notes. In the past I have taken notes on guided tours of Windsor Castle, Cliveden and Petworth House, and the guides have all looked on benignly.

By now I was bristling. Crammed into the little kitchen, everyone else started looking at the floor in embarrassment. It was ridiculous, I thundered, absolutely absurd: this was a public place, a National Trust tour, I had paid my way, the same restrictions didn't apply to any other National Trust house I knew of, and so on and so on. Colin hit back, asking if I'd applied to head office for permission to take notes, and if not, why not, and what he was saying was private information, etc. etc. As our arguments became increasingly circular and tormented, some of the other visitors began drifting off into the next room, forcing Colin to interrupt himself in order to corral them back. '*Could you please stay in this room until I tell you to go!*' he snapped.

Eventually he had no choice but to move on. Subversively, I placed myself at the back of the group and kept writing notes defiantly, but by now I had become so het up that they emerged as indecipherable squiggles. Meanwhile, Colin was prefacing even the most humdrum observations with phrases like 'Strictly between ourselves' and 'Between you, me and the gatepost'.

He told us that Aunt Mimi had taken lodgers (stale buns!) because she needed extra money to send John through art school. 'Considering she herself took in lodgers, it's ironic she called other people common,' he added, meanly. Once more, he called her a snob. Poor Aunt Mimi! I wondered how she would have felt in 1959 had she known that sixty years on, 12,000 visitors a year would be paying £25 a head (excluding guidebooks) to rootle around in her kitchen and be told that she was a snob.

It came as a relief when Colin suddenly announced that we could go upstairs unaccompanied. Free at last from his beady gaze, I poked my head around the door of the upstairs loo. Was this the actual seat that John himself had once sat on, or just a replica? I then went into his bedroom. Three magazine covers were stuck to the wall above the bed, each with Brigitte Bardot in an enticing pose.

Around the time when Mendips was first opened to the public, I watched a TV documentary about Yoko's involvement in the project. She emerged as a controlling figure, stating exactly how she wanted everything to be. Nothing would stop her getting her own way. In one scene, she had even objected to the colour of John's bedspread. 'It was definitely not pink. You know what? I remember John telling me it was green.'

I remember thinking this was one of the most improbable things I had ever heard. But, anxious to butter Yoko up, the National Trust operatives had taken pains to assure her that, yes, of course they would see to it that the bedspread was changed. So it made me very happy to see that the bedspread is still as pink as pink can be. I desperately wanted to point this out to Colin, just to show that I was on the case, but I was fearful that he would have me arrested. Instead, I studied the framed letter from Yoko propped up on the bed. She wrote of how John was 'always talking about Liverpool', and how, whenever they visited the city, they would drive along Menlove Avenue, and he would point at the house and say, 'Yoko, look, look. That's it!'

She went on to say that all of John's music and his 'message of peace … germinated from John's dreaming in his little bedroom at Mendips'. Characterising the young John as 'a quiet, sensitive introvert who was always dreaming', she said that he was 'an incredible dreamer, John made those dreams come true – for himself and for the world'.

She ended by saying that walking into this bedroom today still gave her 'goosebumps', and hoping that for the National Trust visitor it will 'make your dream come true, too'.

* * *

Every year, more pop stars pass from rebellion into heritage. In Bloomsbury, I live in a block of flats which bears a plaque saying that

ROBERT NESTA
MARLEY
1945–1981
SINGER, LYRICIST AND
RASTAFARIAN ICON
LIVED HERE
1972

Elsewhere in London there are plaques of one sort or another to, among many others, Jimi Hendrix, Tommy Steele, Dire Straits, Pink Floyd, the Small Faces, Don Arden, Spandau Ballet and the Bee Gees.

It turns out that Bob Dylan is an enthusiast for visiting sites associated with rock stars. In 2009 he visited Mendips, and was overheard saying, 'This kitchen, it's just like my mom's.' David Kinney, author of *The Dylanologists*, notes that Dylan has also visited Neil Young's childhood home in Winnipeg, as well as Sun Studios in Memphis, where he took the trouble to kneel down and kiss the spot where Elvis Presley first sang 'That's All Right'. Apparently, as Dylan left the studios, a man chased after him and told him how much he loved him. 'Well, son, we all have our heroes,' he replied.

Dylan's own hometown of Hibbing, Minnesota, now offers tours of his old family synagogue, his old school, his old house and the hotel where he had his bar mitzvah. The menu of a Dylan-themed bar called Zimmy's offers Hard Rain Hamburger, Slow Train Pizza, and Simple Twist of Sirloin.

7

Something deeper than music linked John and Paul. Their mothers had died when they were in adolescence: Paul's when he was fourteen, John's when he was seventeen.

When he first met John, Paul had already lost his mother, but John's mother, Julia, was still alive. 'His mother lived right near where I lived. I had lost my mum, that's one thing, but for your mum to actually be living somewhere else and for you to be a teenage boy and not living with her is very sad. It's horrible. I remember him not liking it at all.'

Paul recalled 'a tinge of sadness' in John at being apart from Julia. 'She was a beautiful woman with long red hair. She was fun-loving and musical too; she taught him banjo chords, and any woman in those days who played a banjo was a special, artistic person … John and I were both in love with his mum. It knocked him for six when she died.'

It created a bond between them. Together, the two boys conspired to upend their grief, to turn the wound into a weapon. 'Once or twice when someone said, "Is your mother gonna come?" we'd say, in a sad voice, "She died." We actually used to put people through that. We could look at each other and know.'

There was something more peculiar that linked them, too. In 1997 Paul told his friend and biographer Barry Miles, 'At night there was one moment when she would pass our bedroom door in underwear, which was the only time I would ever see that, and I used to get sexually aroused. I mean, it never went beyond that but I was quite proud of it, I thought, "That's pretty good." It's not everyone's mum that's got the power to arouse.'

One afternoon John ventured into his mother's bedroom. Julia was taking a nap in a black angora sweater, over a tight dark-green-and-yellow mottled shirt. He remembered it exactly. He lay on the bed next to her, and happened to touch one of her breasts. It was a moment he would replay over and over again in his memory for the rest of his life: 'I was wondering if I should do anything else. It was a strange moment because at the time I had the hots, as they say, for a rather lower-class female who lived on the opposite side of the road. I always think I should have done it. Presumably, she would have allowed it.'

John's friends remember Julia as vivacious and flirtatious. The first time Pete Shotton met her, he found himself 'greeted with squeals of girlish laughter by a slim, attractive woman dancing through the doorway with a pair of old woollen knickers wrapped around her head'. John introduced him. 'Oh, *this* is Pete, is it? John's told me so much about you.' Pete held out his hand, but she bypassed it. 'Julia began stroking my hips. "Ooh, what lovely slim hips you have," she giggled.'

Twenty-four years later, in 1979, sitting in his apartment in the Dakota Building, John recorded a cassette tape. At the start he announced, 'Tape one in the ongoing life story of John Winston Ono Lennon.' After rushing through a variety of topics – his grandparents' house in Newcastle Road, Bob Dylan's recent Christian album *Long Train Coming* ('pathetic … just embarrassing'), his love of the sound of the bagpipes at the Edinburgh Military Tattoo when he was a child – he returned, once more, to that recurring memory of the afternoon he lay on his mother's bed and touched her breast.

On *The White Album*,* the song 'Julia' sounds less like an elegy than a love song, full of yearning for someone unobtainable:

> Julia, sleeping sand, silent cloud, touch me
> So I sing a song of love – Julia.

* Officially titled *The Beatles*, it became popularly known as 'The White Album', or occasionally 'The Double White', but never 'The Beatles'. For the rest of this book I will call it *The White Album*.

8

Julia's shifty forty-one-year-old boyfriend Bobby Dykins – 'a little waiter with a nervous cough and thinning margarine-coated hair', in John's words – had lost his driving licence, and his job. Driving drunk along Menlove Avenue at midnight, his erratic movements were clocked by a policeman, who signalled him to stop. But Dykins kept going, turning left when he should have turned right, then mounting the reservation. Asked to get out of the car, he fell to the ground and had to be helped to his feet. The policeman informed him he was under arrest, and made a note of his response: 'You fucking fool, you can't do this to me, I'm the press!'

Dykins was held overnight in a cell, taken to court the next morning, and then released on bail. A fortnight later, on 1 July 1958, he was disqualified from driving for a year and fined £25 – roughly three weeks' wages – plus costs.

Dykins decided that cuts to the household budget were in order; he centred them on the seventeen-year-old John. They could, he said, no longer afford his rapacious appetite; he would have to stay with Julia's sister Mimi. On Tuesday, 15 July, Julia popped round to Menlove Avenue to tell Mimi of these new developments.

Having sorted things out with Mimi, Julia set off for home at 9.45 p.m. Sometimes she would walk across the golf course, but on this occasion she opted for the no. 4 bus, due in a couple of minutes, a hundred yards along on the other side of the road.

As Julia was leaving, John's friend Nigel Walley dropped by, but Mimi told him John was out.

'Oh, Nigel, you've arrived just in time to escort me to the bus stop,' said Julia. Nigel walked her to Vale Road, where they said goodbye, and he turned off. As Julia crossed Menlove Avenue, Nigel heard 'a car skidding and a thump and I turned to see her body flying through the air'. He rushed over. 'It wasn't a gory mess but she must have had severe internal injuries. To my mind, she'd been killed instantly. I can still see her gingery hair fluttering in the breeze, blowing across her face.'

The impact of his mother's death on John was immediate. 'I know what a terrible effect it had on John,' Nigel said, decades later. 'He felt so lonely after it. His outlook changed completely. He hardened and his humour became more weird.' For months, John refused to speak to him. 'Inwardly, he was blaming me for the death. You know – "If Nige hadn't walked her to the bus stop, or if he'd have kept her occupied another five minutes, it would never have happened."'

9

It is June 1957. Paul is a bright grammar-school boy; he has been encouraged to take two of his GCE O-Level exams – Spanish and Latin – a year early.

His father, Jim, keeps pointing out that it's not possible to do your homework and watch television at the same time. Paul argues that it makes no difference. His good marks at the Liverpool Institute seem to support this view. But in truth, his mind is on other things. All he wants to do is play records with his friend Ian James. The two of them go from record shop to record shop. Sometimes they play their guitars together. Revision takes a back seat.

At the end of August Paul's GCE results come through.

(a)

He has passed Spanish, but failed Latin. This means he will not be able to go up a year, as planned. Instead he must remain in the Remove, alongside boys a year younger. Jim is upset. He thinks Paul failed Latin deliberately, because he didn't want to go to university. Paul is also upset. When he goes back to school in September, he hates being in classes with his juniors.

Paul is now in the same year as a little boy he recognises from the bus as a fellow smoker. When he was in the year above, he never really spoke

(b)

He has passed both Spanish and Latin. This means he goes up a year, joining the Lower Sixth with his best friend Ian James. Now and then he sees George Harrison in the school corridors, but Little George is in the year below, and anyway, they don't have much in common. George and Paul occasionally bump into each other on the bus, but there is no reason why Paul would ever introduce him to John; so he never does.

to him. But now that they are in the same year, the two grow close. The boy is called George Harrison.

From the heights of the Lower Sixth, Paul's friend Ian James is baffled by the burgeoning friendship. To him, they have totally different personalities: 'George always seemed a bit moody, morose, whereas Paul was light-hearted – he probably could have been a comedian if he'd wanted, he can tell a tale so well. George was nothing like that. I found it really strange that they were friends.'

Paul is impressed by George's guitar-playing, and introduces him to John Lennon, who is seventeen and no longer at school. John doesn't want to be seen socialising with a fourteen-year-old. He is irritated by the way Little George, as he is known, follows him 'like a bloody kid, hanging round all the time'.

But one day, when John is on the same double-decker, Paul seizes the opportunity to get George into their new band. On the upper deck, Paul tells George to play the song 'Raunchy'. 'Go on, George, show him!' Little George, as they all call him, takes his guitar out of its case and starts to play. John is impressed. 'He's in, you're in, that's it!' The audition is over.

10

On 21 May 1956, Léo Valentin, the Frenchman known as 'Birdman' and billed as 'The Most Daring Man in the World', was crouched in a plane above Liverpool Speke Airport. The author of *Je suis un homme-oiseau* was preparing to leap out wearing wings made from balsawood and alloy. He planned to retire after this one last leap: the £200 he was set to earn from the Liverpool Air Show would help fund his dream of owning a provincial cinema back in France.

'To see a man fling himself into space ...' he once wrote. 'It is a mad action. You want to turn away, but you are fascinated, watching the man who takes pleasure in taunting death.'

An estimated 100,000 spectators were gathered on the airfield below; George Harrison, aged thirteen, and Paul McCartney, just shy of his fourteenth birthday, had cycled there together.

The two boys watched as Valentin hurled himself from the back of the plane. But as he leapt, one of his wings splintered against the plane's door frame. 'We watched him drop and went, "Uh-oh ... I don't think that's right,"' recalled Paul.

Valentin spun around and around, out of control. His parachute failed to open, and then his backup parachute wrapped around him, like a shroud. This made it easier for the crowd below to see the plummeting figure.

'We thought, "Any second now his parachute's gonna open," and it never did. We went, "I don't think he's going to survive that." And he didn't.'

Valentin fell to the ground in a cornfield, 'spreadeagled like a bird', in the words of one spectator.

* * *

In 1964, John Lennon advised the Beatles' press officer, Derek Taylor, against eating the cheese sandwiches at Speke Airport. He had once been employed at Speke as a packer, he told him, and he used to spit in them.

In spring 2002, Speke Airport was renamed Liverpool John Lennon Airport. Along with John F. Kennedy, Leonardo da Vinci and Josef Strauss, John Lennon is one of very few people to have an airport named after them. A seven-foot-high statue of John overlooks the check-in hall, and a vast Yellow Submarine stands on a traffic island at the entrance. The airport's motto is taken from his song 'Imagine': 'Above Us Only Sky'.

11

A Party: 22 Huskisson Street, Liverpool 8 May 1960

All-night parties have become so popular among art students in Liverpool that partygoers are expected to bring not just a bottle but also an egg, for breakfast.

John and his fellow Beatles band member Stu Sutcliffe have been invited to an all-night party at 22 Huskisson Street* by one of their art-school lecturers, Austin Davies. Stu occasionally babysits for Austin and his wife Beryl, who is an actress. John brings his girlfriend Cynthia, and his bandmates Paul and George, both seventeen, tag along, uninvited. The current name of their band is the Silver Beats, but it's still in a process of development.

The party is composed of an odd mixture of guests: in the upstairs room, musicians from the Royal Liverpool Philharmonic Orchestra, still in full evening dress, fresh from playing Tchaikovsky, chat with Fritz Spiegl, their principal flautist; downstairs, art students play Ray Charles's latest single 'What'd I Say' over and over again on the record player.

George can't hear enough of the song. He stands transfixed, knocking back glass after glass of wine and beer, slowly shedding his inhibitions. At one point he spots Spiegl, who has just ventured downstairs, and shouts, 'Hey, Geraldo – got any Elvis?'

---

* By chance, the very same house in which John's mother Julia was living when she married Fred Lennon.

Paul is beginning to enjoy these parties. Always keen to project the right image, he has begun to favour a black turtleneck sweater and to act mysterious, like Jacques Brel. 'It was me trying to be enigmatic, to make girls think, "Who's that very interesting French guy over in the corner?"' He sometimes arrives at parties with his guitar, strumming a French song, singing 'rhurbarbe, rhubarbe'. He has composed a tune to sing along to, but for now it only has one word in French, and that just a name – 'Michelle'.* He can't think of anything to rhyme with it.

The party goes on way past the next morning. Later, Beryl estimates that it lasted three days and three nights. Halfway through the first night, John and his band get carried away, and start singing loudly. Beryl thinks they make a dreadful racket. 'They played almost for two nights. I said it was a disgusting noise. I took the children out.' She walks them down the road to a friend's house, and stays there herself. The next morning she returns to no. 22 to get some clothes, only to find her bedroom door locked. A partygoer tells her that her husband is in there, with a friend. 'That night we separated. We divorced amicably. I never saw the Beatles again.' But she harbours no grudge against the Beatles. In fact, quite the opposite. Forty-eight years later, the acclaimed novelist Dame Beryl Bainbridge talks of those early days with great affection, and picks 'Eleanor Rigby' as one of her Desert Island Discs.†

* Five years later, when Paul and John were harvesting songs for *Rubber Soul*, John suddenly remembered that Paul used to sing a French song at parties. Once again, Paul struggled to think of a rhyme for 'Michelle'. A visiting French teacher, Jan Vaughan, the wife of Paul's old schoolmate Ivan, suggested 'ma belle'. He then asked her to translate 'these are words that go together well' into French, and later sent her a cheque for her contribution. John supplied the 'I love you, I love you, I love you' interlude, after listening to Nina Simone's recently released 'I Put a Spell on You'.

† Bainbridge's other Desert Island Discs were characteristically eccentric, among them 'Two Little Boys' by Rolf Harris, 'Kiss Me Goodnight, Sergeant Major' by Vera Lynn and 'Bat Out of Hell' by Meatloaf.

12

Already well-known as a journalist and editor, and rapidly becoming a household name as a television presenter, Malcolm Muggeridge took a flight from London to Hamburg on 7 June 1961. Two months earlier, he had recorded his distaste for the medium with which he would soon be identified.

> As always deeply distressed by seeing myself on television … Decided never to do it again. Something inferior, cheap, horrible about television as such: it's a prism through which words pass, energies distorted, false. The exact converse of what is commonly believed – not a searcher out of truth and sincerity, but rather only lies and insincerity will register on it.

Having visited the offices of *Stern* magazine, Muggeridge went out on the town. True to character, he took relish in finding it 'singularly joyless; Germans with stony faces wandering up and down, uniformed touts offering total nakedness, three Negresses and other attractions, including female wrestlers. Not many takers, it seemed, on a warm Tuesday evening.'

On a whim, he dropped into the Top Ten Club on the Reeperbahn, 'a teenage rock-and-roll joint'. A band was playing: 'ageless children, sexes indistinguishable, tight-trousered, stamping about, only the smell of sweat intimating animality'. They turned out to be English, and from Liverpool: 'Long-haired; weird feminine faces; bashing their instruments, and emitting nerveless sounds into microphones.'

As they came offstage, they recognised Muggeridge from the television, and started talking to him. One of them asked him if it was true he was a Communist. No, he replied; he was just in opposition. 'He nodded understandingly,' observed Muggeridge, 'in opposition himself in a way.'

'"You make money out of it?" he went on. I admitted that this was so. He, too, made money. He hoped to take back £200 to Liverpool.'

They parted on good terms. 'In conversation rather touching in a way,' Muggeridge recorded in his diary, 'their faces like Renaissance carvings of saints or Blessed Virgins.'

13

Postcards from Hamburg

i

16 August 1960

George is just seventeen years old when he climbs into the cream and green Austin van owned by the band's tubby Welsh manager, Allan Williams. He holds a tin of scones baked by his mother. Before watching her son set off, Mrs Harrison takes Williams to one side. 'Look after him,' she says.

None of the Beatles has ever been abroad. Jim McCartney entertains misgivings, but doesn't feel he can stand in Paul's way. The contract they have just signed gives them 210 deutschmarks a week, or £17.10*s*; the average weekly wage in Britain is £14. 'He's being offered as much money as I make a week. How can I tell him not to go?'

ii

The van is packed with a motley crew. George sits in the back with the other Beatles. Allan Williams is at the wheel, with his Chinese wife Beryl and Beryl's brother Barry sitting next to him. Also on board are Williams's business partner, 'Lord Woodbine', so-called in homage to his devotion to Woodbine cigarettes, and George Sterner, the second-in-command to Bruno Koschmider, the German club-owner with whom the boys have signed a contract.

iii

It's the start of a long journey. There is a five-hour wait at Newhaven, and four hours at Hook of Holland while Williams insists that the Beatles don't require permits and visas because they are students. They stop off in Amsterdam for a short break. John seizes the opportunity to shoplift two pieces of jewellery, several guitar strings, a couple of handkerchiefs and a harmonica. In his managerial role, Williams orders him to return them to the shops, but John refuses.

iv

As they drive through Germany, they sing songs – 'Rock Around the Clock', 'Maggie May' – but when they arrive at the Reeperbahn they are momentarily struck dumb, dazzled by so much neon, and so many open doors through which women can be glimpsed taking their clothes off. But they soon regain their natural ebullience, shouting 'Here come the scousers!' at the top of their voices.

v

Off the Reeperbahn runs Grosse Freiheit. The lights of the strip clubs are being switched on as they arrive, and the prostitutes are beginning to emerge. Still at the wheel, Allan Williams notes that the streets are 'swarming with all the rag-tag and bob-tail of human existence – dope fiends, pimps, hustlers for strip clubs and clip-joints, gangsters, musicians, transvestites, plain ordinary homosexuals, dirty old men, dirty young men, women looking for women'.

vi

Nevertheless, it seems like a dream destination for a band whose achievements in their homeland have bordered on the pitiful. In the autumn they failed to qualify for the talent show *TV Star Search*; in the first three months of this year they had no professional engagements at all; in May they failed an audition to be Billy Fury's backing group. So things are looking up. The people of Hamburg are bored by the lifeless efforts of their home-grown groups: Williams says Germans turn rock'n'roll into a death march. But British bands who have played in Hamburg – Dave Lee and the Staggerlees from Kent, the Shades Five from Kidderminster, the Billions from Worcestershire – have never looked back. The Germans seem to love them all, good, bad and indifferent.

vii

The Beatles are met at the Indra Club by Bruno Koschmider, an unprepossessing manager of an unprepossessing venue, cramped and clammy, with just two customers at the bar. Koschmider shows them to their lodgings. They haven't been expecting much, but what they see confounds even their most meagre expectations. Between the five of them, they are expected to occupy two dark, dank, tiny rooms around the back of Koschmider's grubby cinema, the Bambi Kino. There are no lightbulbs: they will have to make do with matches. The walls are concrete. The first room measures five feet by six. It is furnished with an army-surplus bunk bed and a threadbare couch.

viii

'What the fucking hell!' says John, more used to Aunt Mimi's cosy interior décor. 'Fuck me!' chorus the others. 'Only temporary,' Koschmider reassures them; but he is lying.

This first bedroom is to be shared by John, Stu and George. John and Stu bag the bunk. George, being the youngest, has to make do with the couch.

The second bedroom is exactly the same size, but without a window. There is no means of telling if it is night or day. There are few blankets, and no heating.

Their rooms are a hair's breadth from being en-suite, because the wall is paper thin, and on the other side is a toilet, also used by customers of the cinema. The smells seep through into their rooms.

They have to wash and shave with the cold water from the basin next to the public urinals. George never has a bath or a shower during either of his first two seasons in Hamburg.

ix

It's all a far cry from Las Vegas. Understandably, their natural high spirits are deflated. Their first performance at the Indra is lacklustre. They stand still and chug their way through cover versions of popular hits, while half a dozen punters look glumly on. Koschmider is unimpressed. He hired the Beatles to provide energy; instead they just stand around looking woebegone.

'*Mach Schau*, boys! *Mach Schau!*' he demands. Make show! Make show! It does the trick, and becomes the catalyst for any amount of japes: from now on, the Beatles go all-out to enjoy themselves, strutting and dancing and screaming, hurling abuse at the audience and fighting among themselves.

x

They regularly play the same song for ten or twenty minutes at a time, just for the hell of it. One night, for a bet, they play a single song – 'What'd I Say', by Ray Charles – for over an hour. While the others rag about, Pete remains sombre, drumming as though it were a chore, a bit like washing up.

xi

Pete is also the only one who refuses stimulants. The others are helped in their high-jinks by a smorgasbord of cheap drugs – Purple Hearts and Black Bombers and Preludin, a slimming pill with an active

ingredient* that charges up the metabolism, keeps you wide awake and ensures that you never stop talking. Stu's German girlfriend Astrid Kirchherr is blessed with an in-house supplier: her mother. 'They were fifty pfennigs each and my mummy used to get them for us from the chemist. You had to have a prescription for them, but my mummy knew someone at the chemist.' In time, they toss them back like Smarties, with beer chasers. They even talk of eating 'Prellie sandwiches'.

xii

Unsurprisingly, it is John who pops the poppermost, and to the greatest effect, yelling obscenities, rolling around on the stage, throwing food at other band members, pretending to be a hunchback, jumping on Paul's back, hurling himself into the audience, delighting in calling them 'fucking Krauts' or 'Nazis' or 'German spassies'.

Diplomacy has never come naturally to him. One night he takes to the stage wearing nothing but his underpants, with a loo seat around his head, marching around with a broom in his hand, chanting '*Sieg heil! Sieg heil!*' On another, he appears in swimming trunks. Halfway through 'Long Tall Sally' he turns his back to the audience and pulls the trunks down, wiggling his bare bottom at the audience. Unversed in Liverpudlian manners, the Germans applaud politely.

xiii

Cynthia comes to Hamburg on a visit, and witnesses John so out of his mind on pills and alcohol that he falls about the stage in 'hysterical convulsions'. Offstage, he can be equally feral. He urinates from a balcony onto a group of nuns in the street below. Not that the others are models of sobriety: between numbers, Paul says something rude about Stu's beautiful girlfriend Astrid, who all the band fancy, and Stu duly punches him. Paul fights back, and before long they are grappling onstage in what Paul comes to remember as 'a sort of death grip'. But – *Mach Schau! Mach Schau!* – these spectacles prove popular. They begin to be known locally as the *benakked* Beatles – the crazy Beatles.

---

* Phenmetrazine.

xiv

Hamburg audiences prefer to pick fights with each other, rather than with the band. The waiters – hired from the Hamburg Boxing Academy, so rusty on matters of etiquette – wear heavy boots, suitable for energetic kicking, and carry spring-loaded truncheons in the backs of their trousers, discreetly hidden beneath their jackets. Clubs keep tear-gas guns behind their counters, for use when a skirmish threatens to expand into a riot. In time, the Beatles are allotted the prefectorial duty of making the nightly announcement in German of a ten o'clock curfew for the under-eighteens: '*Es ist zweiundzwanzig Uhr. Wir mussen jetzt Ausweiskontrolle machen. Alle Jugendlichen unter achtzehn Jahren mussen dieses Lokal verlassen.*'*

xv

Bruno Koschmider is no jolly, thigh-slapping *Mein Host*. Kosch by name, Kosch by nature: he patrols his club brandishing the knotted leg of a hardwood German chair. If a customer proves unruly, or is too noisily dissatisfied, he will be bundled into Koschmider's office, pinned to the floor, and beaten black and blue with it.

xvi

In the early hours of the morning, Koschmider's fellow club-owners drop by for a nightcap. They like to send trays of schnapps up to the band, to be downed – '*Beng, beng – ja! Proost!*' – in one. They think it hilarious that this band from England is called the Beatles, which they pronounce 'Peadles', German slang for 'little willies'. 'Oh, zee Peadles! Ha ha ha!'

xvii

The band's japes are not confined to the stage. One afternoon they dare Paul to don a *Pickelhaube* and goose-step up and down the Reeperbahn with a broom for a rifle, while they yell '*Sieg heil!*' They also enjoy

* 'It is twenty-two hours. We must now make a passport control. All youth under eighteen years must now leave this club.'

playing leapfrog in the street. These fun and games prove infectious: Pete Best remembers passers-by joining in, forming 'a long trail of Germans of varying ages all leapfrogging behind us … At some intersections, friendly cops would hold up the traffic to wave us through.'

xviii

In the heart of the Reeperbahn, sex – 'almost limitless sex', in Pete's words – is freely available. 'How could we possibly invite a dame to our squalid digs alongside the cinema urinals, dark and damp as a sewer and about as attractive?' Pete asks, decades later, and then answers his own question. 'But we did, and not one girl ever said no.'

George Harrison loses his virginity at the Bambi Kino, while Paul, John and Pete look on. 'They couldn't really see anything because I was under the covers … After I'd finished they all applauded and cheered. At least they kept quiet whilst I was doing it.'

In these conditions, nothing is private. A fan from Liverpool, Sue Johnston,* receives a letter from Paul in Hamburg. He tells her that one night John ended up with 'a stunning, exotic-looking woman, only to discover on closer inspection that she was a he'. The other Beatles found it hilarious.

Perhaps, in years to come, Pete's description will be the subject of a question in a GCSE mathematics paper: 'For the nightly romp there were usually five or six girls between the four of us … We found ourselves having two or three girls a night each … the most memorable night of love in our dowdy billet was when eight birds gathered there to do the Beatles a favour. They managed to swap with all four of us – twice!' Many of the girls are prostitutes from Herbertstrasse, happy to waive their usual fees for these boisterous young Englishmen. Pete will never forget them: 'I still remember some of their names: Greta, Griselda, Hilde, Betsy, Ruth … The Beatles' first groupies.'

---

* At that time she was going out with Norman Kuhlke, drummer with the Swinging Blue Jeans. She later worked as a tax inspector, and then for Brian Epstein, before embarking on a successful acting career. In 2000 she received a BAFTA for Best TV Comedy Actress.

xix

John is as avid as any of them, but, characteristically, will recall those days of sexual wonder with a mixture of disgust and disappointment.

'I used to dream that it would be great if you could just click your fingers and they would strip off and be ready for me,' he will tell Alistair Taylor. 'I would spend most of my teenage years fantasising about having this kind of power over women. The weird thing is, when the fantasies came true, they were not nearly so much fun. One of my most frequent dreams was seducing two girls together, or even a mother and daughter. This happened in Hamburg a couple of times and the first time it was sensational. The second time it got to feel like I was giving a performance. The more women I had, the more that buzz would turn into a horrible feeling of rejection and revulsion.'

xx

Equally characteristically, Paul will look back on these sexual adventures largely in terms of self-advancement. 'It was a sexual awakening for us,' he tells Barry Miles in 1997. 'We didn't have much practical knowledge till we went to Hamburg. Of course, it was striptease girls and hookers … But it was all good practice, I suppose … So we came back from there reasonably initiated. It wasn't so much that we were experts, but that we were more expert than other people who hadn't had that opportunity.'

14

We assemble by the Star-Club, or where the Star-Club used to be, before it was reduced to cinders in 1983. A tall black sign, like a shiny gravestone, announces 'Star-Club' in diagonal writing, with a picture of an electric guitar below. Beneath the guitar sits a scattering of names from long ago, each set at a jaunty angle, and in a different typeface: 'The Liverbirds Ray Charles The Pretty Things Gene Vincent Bo Diddley Remo Four Bill Haley King Size Taylor and the Dominoes Screaming Lord Sutch Little Richard Johnny Kidd and the Pirates Gerry and the Pacemakers The Rattles The Searchers Brenda Lee The V.I.P.s The Walker Brothers Ian and the Zodiacs Jerry Lee Lewis Tony Sheridan Chubby Checker Roy Young The Lords'.

And there, in the top left-hand corner: 'The Beatles'.

'OK, ze bend voss 300 days in Hemburg. Ze Feb Four in Hemburg only four weeks all other time we hev Pete Best on drums, 60–61 with Stuart, Stuart left ze bend 61 goes to art school dies April 62 in Hemburg 61 Paul change vrom guitar to bass.'

Our tour guide is Peter, a wiry, chain-smoking man in his seventies, his sparse grey hair bound in a ponytail. He rattles through the events and dates at breakneck speed, as though it were a summary of a summary, something he has recited hundreds of times before. Which, of course, he has: he has been guiding the same tour four days a week since 1970.

'Star-Club close 69, then ve hev cabaret for surteen years, in 83 everyzing burned down. One building was at ze front so they rebuild ze back one and where we hed the hall in sixties is beckyard today. Peadles play here April May then November and December 62.'

He has only been going a few minutes, but we are already finding it hard to keep up. It reminds me of a maths lesson, or perhaps a history lesson about the Wars of the Roses, a great jumble of dates and locations.

'Top ect in April, six weeks to May voss menly Gene Wincent, but November Little Richard and December Johnny and ze Hurricanes. Peadles voss one of only four or five bends mostly supporting ze top ects.'

Every now and then he recites an anecdote, but they come unexpectedly, and are often hard to decipher.

'In Germany ve hev Tony Sheridan and the Beat Brothers on "My Bonny" but in England it voss Tony Sheridan and ze Peadles so nobody know Peadles voss sem bend as Tony Sheridan!!!! See some guys, I zink who is zeez guys? I think who is deez English rockers? I sink, oh, shit, voss ze Peadles!!!!!'

We do our best to smile in the right place. Peter leads us into a dingy courtyard, full of litter, and hands around a postcard-sized black-and-white photograph of what it used to look like. It seems to have been just as dingy, but entirely different.

'Dis is picture after ze fire. Here voss stage, here voss hall, stage left to right five metres. Voss a really goot fire!'

We pass the postcard around. Each of us gazes at it, then at the present-day scene, then at the postcard again, as if attempting to work out a puzzle. But nothing fits.

'Here voss zree steps, vun doo zree.'

We look down, pretending to spot three steps. 'OK, you hev your pictures here.' One or two people take photographs of where the three steps would be, were they here, which they aren't.

Peter walks on, and we tag along behind him. As he walks, he zips through another personal anecdote.

'I met John 66, in leather store on Reeperbahn. Zey buy cowboy boots, leather jackets and I voz in ze store when he mek the movie *How I Von dur Var*, I talk to him for ten minutes.'

Someone asks what they talked about.

'So long ago I cannot remember zet von.'

He rushes on, racing through all the bands that played in Hamburg, back in the day.

'OK, so dur sixties was so amezin. Ve hev Jaybirds, voss complete line-up of Ten Years After. Ve hev dur Small Faces. Ten weeks later ve hev Eric Clepton and dur Cream. Ve hev bend called Mendrake Root vit Ritchie Blackmore zey become Deep Purple. Ve hed really goot bend called Ze Earth. On ze vay beck zey change name to Bleck Sabbath. Six months later ve hed Jimi Hendrix here. 6 March 1967 Hendrix play zree days here, Friday, Seturday, Sunday March 67. On ze Monday morning Jimi buy Fender Stratocaster, cost about eleven hundred. On Thursday, he play Monterey, he burn down ze new Stratocaster he buy in Hemburg. He hed not planned to burn down guitar but Ze Who kicked down zeir drums, yeah? So he thought, "Vot cen I do?"

'Now ve go Reeperbahn district.'

We walk towards the end of the street. On the way, he talks about the sort of people who come on his Beatles tours. 'Most English people. Most German not zo interested, maybe older people from East Germany. Ozzervise, Spain, Jepen, South Emerica. Hemburg people is not interested in Peadles. We have Peadlemania museum but after three years it closed. Now, all zey vont is Sex and Crime tours.'

He retains fond memories of the Beatlemania museum. It stretched across five floors, he says, but the exhibits consisted mainly of reproductions of the original items, rather than the items themselves. 'Only original voss contract from Bert Kaempfert with the Peadles, ze rest voss not original. Not original guitars, not original drums. But fifth floor zey hev original signs from ze Star-Club, Indra, all ze signs from the streets. Voss really good museum but not popular enough. I talk to zo many Hemburg people hev not been zere.'

We arrive at a circular paved area, where the street joins the Reeperbahn. It is called Beatles-Platz. Aluminium silhouettes of four figures with guitars and another on drums stand at one edge of the circle, looking rather like outsize pastry-cutters.

'Zis is ze line-up from 1960. We hev John, George, Paul, Pete and there's Stuart on ze right-hend side. On drums is Pete Best, not Ringo.'

He looks disconsolately at the circular area. It's draughty and lacklustre, as unglamorous as can be.

'I don't like zis place but is better zan nothing. We hev it about ten years. You see, it is record label.' We look again, and I can just about make out what he is getting at: in the centre of the circle is a smaller circle, in lighter stone, which could be the label of a giant LP, and two or three metal grooves run around what would be the disc itself, with various Beatles song titles written on them. It's all a bit makeshift.

Someone asks if Pete Best ever comes back. Of all the hundreds of names associated with the Beatles, his is the one that can still darken the atmosphere. 'Pete Best voss in Hamburg four five times, I see him many times, zum people say Pete he's earned nothing but, wideos, dee-wee-dees, they give him lot of money, he really heppy.'

We stare at the songs inscribed on the metal grooves, including 'She Loves You' and 'I Want to Hold Your Hand'. 'In 1964 ze bend voss one veek in Paris, they record two of zeir songs in German language – "Sie Liebt Dich" und "Komm Gib Mir Deine Hand" – you cen listen on YouTube.'

We cross the Reeperbahn. A shop called Tourist Center sports a huge Union Jack as a backdrop to its window display of novelty mugs and cats, dogs and penguins with wobbly heads. I can't spot any Beatles memorabilia, though. Apparently, this was the leather store where Peter encountered John, over half a century ago.

'I voss in the store ven John came in 66. He voss vith ze actor Michael Crarfood and Neil Espinall.' He brings himself up short, suddenly remembering that he has already told us about it. 'Jimi Hendrix stayed zree days in Hemburg in small hotel, March 67. You vont to see?'

He brings out his photographs and sifts through them. One, in black and white, is of Jimi Hendrix and Chas Chandler in a German street. 'All ze buildings are gone now. Jimi ask me, "Vare cen I find the Peadles' places?" and we walk around. I see six concerts with Jimi in March 67. I pick him up outside ze hotel. At end, Jimi give me autograph. He vrite, "To Peter stay kool Jimi Hendrix". Jimi gave me one of his cigarettes. It voss Kool with a K, so ze autograph says "stay kool" vith a K.'

He shows us a building where the Top 10 Club used to be, then whips through one of his hard-to-follow history lessons. 'Zet building voss Top 10 today id is discotheque. Before Top 10 voss a hippodrome, a little bit circus, donkey or a horse walk round – that voss showbiz in the fifties! Peadles played three months first April 61 to end of June six to eight hours every day 35 deutschmarks not a lod of money.' He points to the roof where John, George and Paul once posed for a photograph. '61, ze bend lived under ze roof, zey hev those rooms, one two. 61, Stuart left the bend, Paul changed vrom guitar to bass. Other bends play here – Elex Harvey, Rory Gellegher – but Top 10 Club close 88.'

There is nothing – no sign or statue or plaque – to show that this is where it once was. This makes him cross. 'Hemburg does nothing about Top 10 Club! Nothing about Peadles!'

Also on the Reeperbahn is the police station where Paul and Pete were held overnight, accused of starting a small fire in their apartment. 'Some say it voss con-domes on ze wall, others say it vos some sort of paper. Anyway, zey hev a fire, voss arrested, zen deported, from here ve valk to the Rock'n'Roll door, ten, fifteen minutes.'

On the way, Peter tells us again that since he first showed Jimi Hendrix round in March 1967, he has taken four tours a week, fifty weeks a year. 'Is a lod of tours.' Yet there is precious little to see. Nothing is as it was. Only the police station remains the same. Everywhere else is a memory of a memory, of interest only to the most dedicated Beatles archaeologist.

In 1967, when Hunter Davies first asked the Beatles about their time in Hamburg, they couldn't even remember how many times they had been there. Since then, Beatles historians regularly attempt to reconstruct their lives there, day by day, hour by hour. But in Beatles years, it's as distant as the Dark Ages.

At last we arrive at a vast gate off a street, with a sign in English saying 'Keep Out'. Pete tells us he is not allowed to take us in, but if we go in by ourselves, we should take a snap of the first doorway on the right. It is where John stood for the photo that was later used on the cover of his solo *Rock'n'Roll* album. 'I vish you good luck, ze first door behind the gate, not a problem for you, only for me.' We push the gate and find a gloomy five-storey red-brick building in a poor state of repair. We obediently take pictures of the doorway, but no one really knows why.

Finally, we end up by the Indra, which is still, miraculously, 'Musikeclub Live', but we're not allowed in. A plaque outside says, in German, 'On 17 August 1960 the Beatles performed on the stage of the Indra. It was their first German engagement and the beginning of a great career.'

And so to the Kaiserkeller, with a framed poster of Rory Storm and the Hurricanes outside. 'Von of those guys voss Ringo,' Peter says, and we all try to spot which one. He then shows us a photograph of the seventeen-year-old George with his guitar. 'Voss zold at Bonham auction for two hundred fifty thousand pound including tex and everyzing. Last week at Zotheby, one contrect from Brian Epstein viz ze bend, zet von sold for two hundred thirty-five thousand pound. Emezin!'

We sigh at the idea that so little could have mushroomed into so much.

'But in 62, zey close Kaiserkeller and it voss discothèque.'

15

Their return to Liverpool after a stint of three and a half months in Hamburg was such a sorry affair that they avoided telling their families what had happened.

In brief, they had been tempted away from the Kaiserkeller by a rival club-owner. To exact revenge, the thuggish Koschmider reported George to the police for being under-age, and he was duly deported. On returning home, George felt 'ashamed, after all the big talk'. Koschmider subsequently reported Paul and Pete on the spurious grounds of setting fire to their lodgings, and they too were deported. On 1 December 1960, they arrived back in Liverpool disillusioned and penniless. Ten days later, John followed. Stu remained with Astrid in Germany, a Beatle no more.

The Beatles' fall from grace had been abrupt and painful. John woke Mimi in the middle of the night by throwing stones at her bedroom window. 'He just pushed past me and said, "Pay that taxi, Mimi." I shouted after him up the stairs, "Where's your £100 a week, John?"'

'Just like you, Mimi, to go on about £100 a week when you know I'm tired.'

'And you can get rid of those boots. You're not going out of this house in boots like that!'

Most of their equipment was stranded in Hamburg. They had nothing to show for their time away. Similar groups who had stayed in Liverpool were now several steps ahead of them. The Swinging Blue Jeans were clearly in the lead, headlining a regular 'Swinging Blue Jeans Night' at the Cavern in Mathew Street.

In the three months they had been away, fashions had moved on: everyone was now copying the Shadows, wearing slinky suits, playing instrumentals, performing synchronised dance routines. At first, the individual Beatles were so despondent that they didn't even bother to get in touch with one another: George was unaware that John and Paul had returned. John retired, depressed, to his bedroom at Mendips, refusing to see anyone. While Aunt Mimi grudgingly indulged John's self-pity, Jim McCartney refused to have Paul slouching around the house. 'Satan makes work for idle hands,' he said, telling him to go out and get a proper job. 'This music thing is all right on the side, but Paul, it will never last.' Paul worked briefly for a delivery company, then did donkeywork at Massey & Coggins, a cable-winding firm. The moment his workmates discovered he was a musician, they nicknamed him 'Mantovani'. Being bright and personable, Paul was swiftly earmarked as management material. 'We'll give you an opportunity, lad,' declared the managing director, impressed by his exam results, 'and with your outlook on life you'll go a long way.'

Uncharacteristically, Paul was ready to throw in the towel. After a few weeks John and George turned up at Massey & Coggins. They had been booked for a lunchtime gig at the Cavern, they said, and they wanted Paul to join them. He told them he had a steady job, and was now on £7.10*s* a week. 'They are training me here. That's pretty good. I can't expect more.'

But they persisted, and Paul gave way, bunking off work on 9 February 1961 to play the Cavern at lunchtime. He did the same on 22 February, but it's possible that his employers issued a warning, because when another lunchtime gig at the Cavern was mooted for the following week, he ummed and erred. 'Either fucking turn up today or you're not in the band any more,' snapped John.

What to do? If he chose the Beatles, his father would be furious. If he obeyed his father, and stuck it out at Massey & Coggins, he would have to say goodbye to the Beatles, and any remaining chance of stardom. As usual, John was in no mood for compromise; his intransigence towards Paul may also have been a way of subcontracting his own Oedipal struggles: 'I was always saying, "Face up to your dad, tell him to fuck off. He can't hit you. He's an old man" … But Paul would always give in. His dad told him to get a job, he dropped the group and started working on the lorries, saying, "I need a steady career." We couldn't believe it. I told him on the phone, "Either come or you're out." So he had to make a decision between me and his dad …'

What would have happened had Paul chosen to stay at Massey & Coggins?* Looking back, he is adamant that he had been 'hopeless' at winding coils – 'Everybody else used to wind fourteen a day. I'd get through one and a half, and mine were the ones that never worked' – but it's hard to imagine he wouldn't have mastered the technique. And he had already been fast-tracked towards management. His subsequent career suggests that he possessed the drive, initiative and skills necessary for steering even the most troublesome company through rocky times.

Instead, he bunked off to rejoin the Beatles. A week later he received his wage packet through the post, along with his National Insurance card and his P45.

---

* A decade later, when pop music grew more solemn, Massey and Coggins might have been a winning name for a group, like Loggins and Messina, Gallagher and Lyle, or Crosby, Stills, Nash and Young.

16

A Party:
10 Admiral Grove, Liverpool
8 July 1961

Ritchie Starkey spent his seventh birthday in a coma, having been rushed by ambulance to the Royal Liverpool Children's Hospital. Doctors found he had a burst appendix, and was infected with peritonitis. As he was being wheeled into the operating theatre he asked the nurse for a cup of tea. 'We'll give you one when you come round,' she replied sweetly. But Ritchie failed to come round for another ten weeks. Three times during that first night, doctors told his mother Elsie that they did not expect him to survive. He was to remain in hospital for a year.

Ritchie was back in the same hospital for his fourteenth birthday, in 1954. This time he was admitted with pleurisy, and then developed TB. Convalescing in a hospital in the Wirral, he was taught to knit, to make baskets and to construct a toy farm out of papier-mâché. Every fortnight a music teacher arrived at the ward with a selection of percussion instruments – tambourines, maracas, triangles, tiny drums – and the children were expected to join in, playing 'Three Blind Mice' and 'London Bridge is Falling Down'. But Ritchie stubbornly refused to participate unless he could play a drum. When the teacher left, he would continue drumming on his bedside cabinet, in the absence of anything more drummable. This time he remained in hospital for two years.

But his twenty-first birthday is a much happier affair. Not only has he survived, but he has turned his percussive skills to advantage. He is now the drummer with Liverpool's top band, Rory Storm and the Hurricanes, and he even drives his own Ford Zodiac. Not long ago, he assumed the name Ringo Starr; his drum solos are billed as 'Starr Time'.

Rory Storm and the Hurricanes are playing a season at Butlin's holiday camp at Pwllheli in Wales, but they have one day a week off, so the day after his birthday Ringo drives home for a proper party. So many friends and family have packed into 10 Admiral Grove, his mother's tiny two-up, two-down – Ringo counts sixty-four people in all – that there is a continuous queue to get in. Guests include the Hurricanes, the Dominoes, the Big Three and the Pacemakers, as well as the young Priscilla White, who sometimes takes to the Cavern stage as 'Swinging Cilla', and regularly styles Elsie's hair in return for Spam and chips.*

Ringo is showered with presents, including two rings to add to the three he already wears, and a gold identity bracelet from Elsie, engraved with 'Ritchie' on one side and '21st birthday, love Mum' on the other. From his Auntie Nancy he receives a gold St Christopher medal. It depicts the patron saint of travellers carrying the Christ child on his shoulders across a river. Ringo hangs it around his neck, to keep him safe wherever he goes.

---

* Priscilla White is soon to become Cilla Black, and, under Brian Epstein's guidance, a big star. 'I always reckoned that if I wasn't going to be a singer, I'd be a hairdresser. Elsie was a real character, a surrogate mum to Pat and me and to the other Beatles, and we were forever bumping into each other there. She would cook us all delicious Spam, home-made chips and beans for tea, and she never seemed to mind how often we came round for more or how loud we played the latest records. I thought I did Elsie's hair really well, but, some thirty years later, Ritchie's stepdad Harry told me otherwise: "We didn't say anything at the time," he muttered, "but you used to make a right bloody mess of poor Elsie's hair!"'

17

5 More Postcards from Hamburg

i

On their second stint in Hamburg the Beatles are working at a new venue, the Star Club, for a new manager, Manfred Weissleder, at new lodgings, a lovely clean flat in the Grosse Freiheit. Herr Weissleder tacks on one condition, though: 'I always want you should enjoy yourselves in the Star Club, but if you make shit I send you home.'

Within days, George has been sick on the floor by the side of his bed. The next morning, the unshapely pool is still there, glowering back at him.

The cleaning lady refuses to clear it up, arguing, not unreasonably, that it is not part of her duties. For reasons of his own, George refuses to dispose of it. He has always had this stubborn streak.

ii

The next day, the pool remains doggedly present. The cleaning lady grumbles at the Beatles' general squalor: the smelly socks, the empty bottles, the clothes strewn all over the place. This latest infraction takes their misdemeanours to another level. She goes straight to Herr Weissleder and voices her complaints. Herr Weissleder lends a sympathetic ear. He will take a closer look.

iii

Having examined the evidence, Herr Weissleder rules against George, charging his henchman and bouncer, Horst Fascher, with the job of forcing him to clean it up. Fascher is a former championship boxer. He has also spent time in prison for manslaughter, following a fracas with a sailor. Only the bravest of souls refuse to obey him. John has already fallen foul of him. When John called him a Nazi, Herr Fascher retaliated by marching him to the toilet and urinating over him.

But George, stubborn George, continues to put his foot down, or if not down, at least to one side. No, he says, he is definitely not going to clear it up. Why should he? It isn't his job. For all he cares, it can just stay there. When he needs to get in or out of bed, he simply climbs over it.

iv

The dispute has reached an impasse. The cleaning lady will not clean up the pool of vomit; nor will George. Over the next few days Pete Best observes its sluggish, odoriferous progress with a morbid fascination, watching it 'grow, and grow, mushrooming and taking on a life of its own. Cigarettes were crushed in it, bits of food fed to it, until it assumed the look of a hedgehog.'

The Beatles christen it 'The Thing', and treat it almost like a family pet. Before long, The Thing acquires a local reputation. Pete remembers how 'its fame spread, and people wanted to come and see it'. He estimates it measures roughly six inches in diameter, and it keeps growing upwards, 'like a miniature flower garden'.

As it blossoms, George harbours scary thoughts. 'I'm frightened to sleep in case it eats me,' he confesses.

v

One morning, Herr Fascher pays a return visit, unannounced. He takes one look at the ageing vomit before deciding that enough is enough. He returns with a shovel. 'Don't do it! That's our pet!' yell the Beatles. But their pleas fall on deaf ears. Fascher scoops it up and transports it down the stairs, through the front door and onto the Grosse

Freiheit. The Beatles follow in a mock funeral procession. Fascher finds a bin on the street, and tips The Thing into it.

As for George, he feels he has won a small but significant victory. He kept his word, and refused to back down. Honour has been served.

18

It's late August 1961. Rory Storm and the Hurricanes have come to the end of their summer season at Pwllheli. They were such a success that they have already been invited back next year.

Ringo loves to travel. The Hurricanes were promised tours on the Continent in the autumn, but somehow or other these failed to materialise. Ringo grows fidgety: now might be the time for a bold move, away from the group, away from Liverpool, away from Britain.

He has always been attracted to America, its large cars and country music and blues music and rock'n'roll and westerns. Why not live there? Inspired by Lightnin' Hopkins, he opts for Houston, Texas. Accordingly, he walks into the American Consulate in the Cunard Building in Liverpool and picks up the immigration forms. It turns out he will need to prove that he has money and the promise of a job. Undaunted, he writes to the Houston Chamber of Commerce; in return, he receives a list of local employment agencies. After more to-ing and fro-ing he picks out a job in a factory, thinking he can switch to something else once he gets there.

He's now all set, but what he later calls 'the really big forms' prove a stumbling block. The Americans want to know everything about his family, including their political affiliations. 'Was your grandfather's Great Dane a Commie?' is his way of describing it. These extra forms get the better of him: he simply can't face grappling with them, and eventually he calls it a day.

A few days later, Tony Sheridan asks him to join his backing band for a stint at the Top Ten Club in Hamburg. He doesn't hesitate. He gives Rory Storm twenty-four hours' notice, and sets off for Heathrow, a little nervous before boarding the aeroplane, as it's the first time he has ever flown. But for one or two forms, he might well have been flying on a different plane, in the opposite direction.

19

Halfway through June 1962, Joe Flannery, the manager of Lee Curtis and the All Stars, drops by.

'When are you going to join us, Pete?' he asks.

Pete Best smiles. 'You must be joking. Why would I want to quit the Beatles when we're about to get our big break?'

Flannery stalls. 'Maybe I've jumped the gun. It's just a rumour going the rounds.'

'Why would anyone start a rumour like that?'

Pete is mystified. He has no intention of leaving the Beatles, not after drumming with them these past two years.

The conversation preys on his mind. What rumour? In mid-July he broaches the subject with Mr Epstein. Mr Epstein blushes and stammers. Pete cuts to the chase.

'Look, Brian. Are there any plans to replace me in the Beatles?'

Mr Epstein brushes away his fears. 'I'm telling you, as manager, there are no plans to replace you, Pete.'

That's good enough for Pete. Nothing more is said. Things carry on as usual: each morning, Pete and their road manager, Neil Aspinall, set off in Neil's van with all the Beatles' gear, which is still kept at Pete's mum's huge house in Hayman's Green. They pick up the other Beatles – John, Paul and George – along the way.

On 15 August the group plays two gigs at the Cavern, one at lunchtime, the other in the evening. 'Pick you up tomorrow, John!' calls Pete as he is leaving. 'No,' replies John. 'I've got other arrangements.'

They are to be the last words ever spoken to Pete by any member of the Beatles.

Before Pete leaves the Cavern that night, Mr Epstein says he'd like to see him in his office at ten o'clock the next morning. Nothing odd about that: they often meet to discuss arrangements. Neil drives him in, and drops him off at the NEMS* office. Mr Epstein seems uneasy, blathering away about nothing at all. He asks Pete how he thinks the group is doing. Pete says, 'Fab,' a word not as fashionable as it will shortly become. He senses that something is on Mr Epstein's mind. Who can blame Epstein for his prevarication? He is still only twenty-seven years old, with a background in furniture sales.

Out of nowhere, Mr Epstein blurts out, 'I've got some bad news for you. The boys and myself have decided that they don't want you in the group any more, and that Ringo is replacing you.'

Pete finds it hard to speak. 'Why?'

'They don't think you're a good enough drummer, Pete,' he says. Then he adds: 'And George Martin doesn't think you're a good enough drummer.' George Martin is the producer from Parlophone who auditioned the Beatles. When Pete was out of earshot, he told Brian Epstein

* North End Music Stores, owned at that stage by Brian Epstein's father.

that Pete couldn't keep time, and that he planned on using a session drummer for the actual recording.

Pete says he thinks he's just as good as Ringo, if not better. 'Does Ringo know about this yet?' Ringo is a good friend.

'He's joining on Sunday.'

Mr Epstein continues, briskly, with business. The phone rings. Mr Epstein picks up the receiver, and listens.

'I'm still with him at the moment,' he says, putting the receiver back down. He returns to their conversation. He says that while Pete is still under contract, he'll pay him his current wage – £50 or £60 a week – and he'll also put him in another group, and make him leader of it.

'There are still a couple of venues left before Ringo joins,' he adds, almost as an afterthought. 'Will you play?'

Pete doesn't know what to say, so he says yes. Then he leaves.

As Mr Epstein remembers it, the meeting lasted two hours. Pete thinks it lasted ten minutes.

Neil Aspinall is waiting for him downstairs. 'You look as if you've seen a ghost,' he says. 'They've kicked me out!' says Pete. Neil, who is going out with Pete's mum, says in that case he'll quit too. Pete talks him out of it. 'Don't be a fool – the Beatles are going places.'

Neil drops him home. The minute Pete closes the door, he bursts into tears. He feels like putting a stone round his neck and jumping off Pier Head. He can't face playing another two gigs with the Beatles, and doesn't turn up at the Riverpark Ballroom in Chester that night. 'I had been betrayed, and sitting up there onstage with the three people who had done it would be like having salt rubbed into a very deep wound.'

Only later does he discover that the Beatles were offered a contract with Parlophone a fortnight ago. No one told him about it.

His forthright mother Mona, who helped manage the group before Brian came on the scene, and always calls them 'Pete's group,' immediately phones George Martin in London. The charming record producer assures her that, though he had wanted a different drummer for the recording session, it wasn't up to him whether or not the Beatles kept Pete.

Mona berates Brian Epstein: 'It's jealousy, Brian, jealousy all the way, because Peter is the one who has the terrific following – he has built up the following in Liverpool for the Beatles!' She is sure they got rid of Peter to stop him being the focus of attention, 'with the others just props'.

Whodunnit? As so often with the Beatles, everyone has a different story. In *The Beatles Anthology* – which is, in Biblical terms, the Authorised Version – Paul recalls that after their audition at Abbey Road, George Martin took the other three to one side and said, 'I'm really unhappy with the drummer. Would you consider changing him?' 'We said, "No! We can't!" It was one of those terrible things you go through as kids. Can we betray him? No. But our career was on the line. Maybe they were going to cancel our contract.'

Yet George Martin always claimed to have been baffled by Pete's sacking. He was unimpressed by his drumming, and he had certainly noticed that he was out on a limb from the other three, who all liked larking around. 'But I never thought that Brian Epstein would let him go. He seemed to be the most saleable commodity as far as looks went. It was a surprise when later I learned that they had dropped Pete Best. The drums were important to me for a record, but they didn't matter much otherwise. Fans don't pay particular attention to the quality of drumming.'

But Pete Best always maintained that during his two years as a Beatle, not one of them ever complained about the quality of his drumming: 'Right to the end we were still drinking together and seemingly the best of friends.'

As time went by, John grew increasingly outspoken on this issue, as on so many others.

'We were pretty sick of Pete Best,' he said in 1967. 'He was a lousy drummer. He never improved. There was always this myth built up around him that he was great and Paul was jealous of him because he was pretty and all that crap … The only reason he was in the group in the first place was because the only way we could get to Hamburg, we had to have a drummer … we were always going to dump him when we could find a decent drummer.'

Ringo, too, showed his steel. Thirty years on, he was asked if he ever felt sorry for Pete. 'No. Why should I? I was a better player than him. That's how I got the job. It wasn't on my personality. It was that I was a better drummer, and I got the phone call. I never felt sorry for him. A lot of people have made careers out of knowing the Beatles.'

As in the dénouement of an Agatha Christie, it was the least likely suspect who finally confessed. Many years later, George – quiet, thoughtful young George – came clean. Pete kept calling in sick, he said, so they used to ask Ringo to take his place, 'and every time Ringo sat in, it seemed like "This is it." Eventually we realised, "We should get Ringo in the band full time." I was quite responsible for stirring things up. I conspired to get Ringo in for good. I talked to John until they came round to the idea … We weren't very good at telling Pete he had to go. But when it comes down to it, how do you tell somebody? … Brian Epstein was the manager so it was his job, and I don't think he could do it very well either. But that's the way it was and the way it is.'

> BEATLES CHANGE DRUMMER!
> Ringo Starr (former drummer with Rory Storm & the Hurricanes) has joined the Beatles, replacing Pete Best on drums. Ringo has admired the Beatles for years and is delighted with his new arrangement. Naturally he is tremendously excited about the future.
>
> The Beatles comment, 'Pete left the group by mutual agreement. There were no arguments or difficulties, and this has been an entirely amicable decision.'
>
> On Tuesday September 4th, the Beatles will fly to London to make recordings at EMI Studios. They will be recording numbers that have been specially written for the group.
>
> *Mersey Beat* front page, 23 August 1962

When the news gets out, *Mersey Beat* receives a petition for Pete Best's reinstatement, signed by hundreds of fans. They descend on his family's home. Mo Best remembers her sitting room 'bulging with fans, sighing and sobbing'. These fans also picket Mr Epstein's offices in

Whitechapel. The owner of the Cavern, Ray McFall, provides him with a bodyguard. Ringo receives a poison-pen letter.

The Beatles' next concert at the Cavern is a rocky affair. Pete's fans heckle them, chanting 'Pete is Best!' and 'Ringo never, Pete Best forever!' After half an hour of this, George loses his temper and snaps back. In reply, an aggrieved fan punches George, giving him a black eye. A Pete Best fan called Jenny writes a letter of complaint to George, who answers bullishly, 'Ringo is a much better drummer, and he can smile – which is a bit more than Pete could do. It will seem different for a few weeks, but I think that the majority of our fans will soon be taking Ringo for granted … lots of love from George.'

In time, George is proved right. Fans are fickle. 'I used to love Pete and was heartbroken when they sacked him,' one of them, Elsa Breden, tells the Beatles' biographer Mark Lewisohn over forty years later. 'But it soon passed and it was as if he'd never been there. They were *much* better with Ringo, without a doubt. He gave them that solid backbeat – he's a great rock'n'roll drummer – and he fitted in brilliantly.'

Just six days after Pete's dismissal, John, Paul, George and Ringo are filmed by Granada TV at a lunchtime concert in the Cavern. Pete goes along to watch them. On the way out, Paul's father Jim spots him and exclaims triumphantly, 'Great, isn't it? They're on TV!'

'Sorry, Mr McCartney,' replies Pete. 'I'm not the right person to ask.'

Over the next two years, the Beatles collectively gross £17 million.

For his part, Pete Best joins Lee Curtis and the All Stars. When Lee Curtis goes solo, they change their name to the Pete Best All-Stars. Then one of them leaves, and they become the Pete Best Four. Another leaves, and they become the Pete Best Combo. As the fame of the Beatles grows, interest in Pete fades. 'There was little or no revenue coming in, barely enough to pay my bills, and I reached the stage where I found myself scratching around for enough money to buy a packet of cigarettes. I just couldn't sit back and ignore the fact that I should have shared in the Beatles' success, which I considered to be part of my heritage.'

Pete's wife Kathy works on the biscuit counter at Woolworths. One day in 1967 he waits until she has left for work, goes up to the bedroom, locks the door, blocks any air gaps, places a pillow on the floor in front of the gas fire, and turns on the gas. He is fading away when his brother Rory arrives, smells gas, batters the door down and, screaming 'Bloody idiot!' saves his life.

That same year, Hunter Davies is finishing his pioneering biography of the Beatles. He often tells them tales from his travels, and they are always keen to know what old friends are up to. 'They were mostly interested to hear what had happened, except when the subject of Pete Best came up. They seemed to cut off, as if he had never touched their lives. They showed little reaction when I said he was now slicing bread for £18 a week, though Paul did make a face. John asked a few more questions, but then forgot about it, and they all went back to the song they were recording.'

In 1969 Pete embarks on a career as a civil servant, working in an employment office. For many years his two daughters, Beba and Bonita, have no idea that their dad was once a Beatle.

He is now retired, and, aged seventy-eight, fronts the Pete Best Band. His website, www.petebest.com, promises 'Right from the first beat, you'll be immersed in nostalgia, listening to "the best years" of the Beatles, 1960–62.' The website's tagline is 'The Man Who Put the Beat in Beatles'.

In 2019 the *Sunday Times* estimates Ringo Starr's wealth at £240 million, which makes him the eighth-richest musician in the world. He is a knight of the realm, maintains homes in London, Los Angeles and Monte Carlo, and is married to Barbara Bach, a former Bond girl. Pete Best's old drum kit can be seen in Liverpool's The Beatles Story museum, sad and lonesome, a monument to loss; the tomb of the unknown drummer. On the audio guide, George Martin explains: 'He was probably the best-looking, but he didn't say much and he didn't have the charisma the others had. More importantly, his drumming was OK but it wasn't top-notch, in my opinion. I didn't realise that the boys were thinking much the same thing, and so they took that as the final word, a catalyst, and poor Pete got the boot. I've always felt a bit guilty about that. But I guess he survived.'

20

I arrived at Pete Best's old house in Hayman's Green on the evening of day four of the annual Beatles Week. The basement recreated the old Casbah Club. A very basementy basement, dank, dark and sweaty, it was bursting at the seams with men in their seventies who looked like Bernie Sanders or Bernard Manning. Most wore Beatles T-shirts. A tribute band was tuning up in an authentically sixties manner, saying 'One-two, one-two' over and over again, with no indication that they would ever make it to three.

The Casbah is less a shrine to the Beatles than to Pete Best. Ringo is the great unmentionable. At the entrance, photographs of the Beatles – John, Paul, George and Pete, all autographed by Pete – were on sale for £15. A newspaper cutting with the headline '10,000 SUPPORTING PETE BEST STREET BID' was pinned to a red baize board. It posed an urgent question. In Liverpool, there's a Paul McCartney Way and a John Lennon Drive. So why not a Pete Best Avenue?

Out in the garden, a tribute band from Indonesia, the Indonesian Beat Club, composed of five 'die-hard Beatles lovers', were playing a spirited version of 'My Bonnie', just like Pete and the rest of his band used to do, back in the day. Queuing for a drink, I heard someone mention a Pete Best Fan Club. It is centred around Twitter, where it boasts fifty-three followers. Tweets include 'PETE is the BEST', 'I WANT PETE BEST SO BAAAAAD IT'S DRIVING ME MAD', 'Happiness Is Pete Best!' and the poignant 'MY PETE BEST GENTLY WEEEEEPSSS'.

Flyers near the entrance advertised The Magical Beatles Museum, run by Pete's half-brother Roag, the son of Mona Best and Neil Aspinall.

Its collection includes Pete's Premier drum kit. History in the museum stops in June 1962: it is as though Ringo had never lived. Visitors are greeted by signs saying 'PETE, JOHN, PAUL, GEORGE, STUART'. Roag bills it as 'not just Liverpool's most authentic Beatles museum, but the world's most authentic Beatles museum. My oldest brother Pete Best was the original Beatles drummer with the Beatles from 1960 to 1962. He performed over 1,000 shows and recorded 27 tracks as a Beatle.'

Pete Best's own website announces that 'When not undertaking a variety of celebrity duties, Pete has a busy schedule touring with the Pete Best Band. The Pete Best Band captures the sound of the Beatles in their formative years – the early years for many "was" the Beatles.'

21

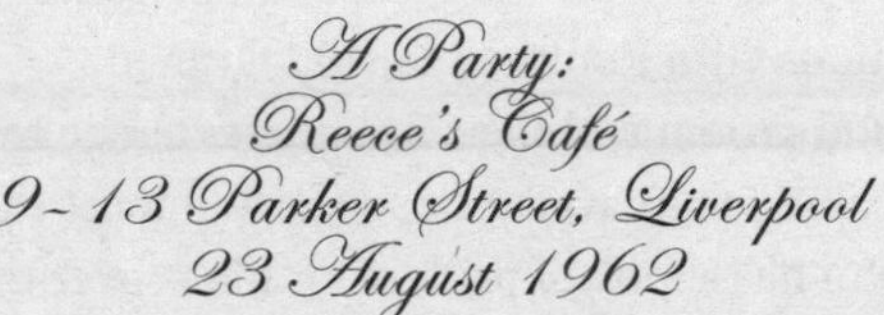

A Party: Reece's Café 9–13 Parker Street, Liverpool 23 August 1962

In July 1962 Cynthia realises she is pregnant. She suspects John will take it badly, so puts off telling him for several days. Eventually, she plucks up the courage. 'As the news sank in he went pale and I saw the fear in his eyes. "There's only one thing for it, Cyn," he said. "We'll have to get married."'

She tells him he doesn't have to; he insists he wants to. The next day, John tells Brian Epstein, who says he doesn't have to go through with it. The Beatles have just signed their first recording contract, and Brian is worried the news will put the fans off. When John tells Aunt Mimi, she accuses Cynthia of wanting to trap him, and says she'll have nothing to do with the wedding.

Recognising that John is serious, Brian takes charge, applying for the emergency licence and booking the register office for the first available date, in a fortnight's time.

On 23 August, Brian, dapper in his pin-striped suit, picks up Cynthia from her bedsit. She is wearing a purple-and-black-checked two-piece suit over a frilly high-necked white blouse, with black shoes and a black bag. Brian takes her in a chauffeur-driven car to Mount Pleasant register office. On the way, he tells her she is looking lovely, and does his best to calm her nerves.

When they arrive, John, Paul and George are already pacing about in the waiting room, dressed in smart black suits. Cynthia thinks they all look 'horribly nervous'. Cynthia's brother Tony and his wife Marjorie are there too.

As the registrar begins to speak, a workman outside starts a pneumatic drill, but they struggle on. The ceremony takes a matter of minutes. They sign the register: John Winston Lennon, 21, Musician (Guitar) and Cynthia Powell, 22, Art Student (School). Now what? Brian suggests they all go to Reece's, round the corner, for lunch. They opt for the cheaper café on the ground floor rather than the more expensive Famous Grill Room on the top floor.

The bride and groom and their five guests queue for soup, chicken and trifle. Alcohol is not available, so they all toast the happy couple with water. John has a look of pride. Cynthia is over the moon: 'A full church wedding with all the extras couldn't have made me happier.'

Brian presents them with a silver-plated ashtray, engraved with the message 'Good luck JOHN & CYNTHIA. Brian, Paul & George 23 Aug 62', as well as a shaving kit in a leather pouch embossed 'JWL', which John will take everywhere. The lunch – fifteen shillings a head – is on Brian, who also announces that he has a bolt-hole in Falkner Street where John and Cynthia can live for as long as they want. Cynthia is so excited that she gives him a hug. Brian looks embarrassed.

That night the Beatles have a gig in Chester, so Cynthia takes the opportunity to make the flat nice. At the gig, John appears out of sorts, losing his temper with the support act and yelling, 'You're doing all our fucking numbers!' He doesn't tell anyone that he's just got married. Even the Beatles' new drummer, Ringo, is kept in the dark.

22

In November 1962 a twenty-two-year-old Sheffield entrepreneur with the unusual name of Peter Stringfellow was casting around for an act for his new nightclub, the Black Cat. Though the Black Cat sounded with-it, it was just the name he gave St Aidan's church hall on the nights he hired it.

Searching through the *New Musical Express*, Stringfellow spotted an advertisement for a group called the Beatles. They seemed to be just what he wanted: at the beginning of October, their song 'Love Me Do' had been his very first record request from a punter; he had been playing it, on and off, ever since.

There was no phone at his parents' house, so he went to a public call box and was put through to the Beatles' manager, a Mr Epstein, who told him that the Beatles would cost £50.

'£50!' replied Stringfellow. 'Excuse me, I pay Screaming Lord Sutch £50, and nobody has heard of the Beatles!'

Epstein replied that, unlike Sutch, the Beatles had a record in the charts. Stringfellow knew that 'Love Me Do' was actually moving down the charts. He said he would think about it.

The next day he called Epstein back, saying he was prepared to pay £50. Epstein said the price had gone up to £65. Stringfellow felt that Epstein was as nervous as he was himself. He sensed that the Beatles were in real demand, and that their success was becoming more than Epstein could cope with. Once again, Stringfellow said he'd think about it.

True to his word, he called back two days later, and said, yes, he could manage £65. Mr Epstein replied that the price had now risen to

£100. 'The Beatles have another single coming out and this will go to the top of the charts,' he said confidently. Stringfellow tried to haggle, but Mr Epstein said he wouldn't take anything less than £90. They finally agreed on £85. Stringfellow was shaken. 'I came out of the telephone in a sweat because I had never paid that amount of money to a band before.'

There was an eerie gap between 'Love Me Do' leaving the charts and the release of 'Please Please Me'. The Beatles seemed to go quiet. Stringfellow began to panic. Had he just wasted all his money?

He placed an advertisement in the *NME* announcing that the Beatles would be playing at the Black Cat in April, and ordered tickets from the printer, each priced at four shillings. Applications came pouring in, even from Scotland, so he went back to the printers and asked them to put up the price to five shillings. By January he had sold over 1,500 tickets, way beyond the capacity of the Black Cat.

He looked around for a larger venue, hit upon the Azena Ballroom, Sheffield's flashiest dance hall, and placed an advertisement in the *NME* announcing the change of venue. By 2 April he had sold two thousand tickets; on the night itself, a further thousand people turned up on the off-chance of getting in.

23

I arrived too late at the International Beatles Week in Liverpool to catch the opening act, Les Sauterelles. They formed in 1962, and according to the brochure, 'soon became the most popular Swiss Beat Band of the sixties. In the hot summer of '68, their single "Heavenly Club" was number one for six weeks in the Swiss Charts.'

Next up were a Beatles tribute band from Hungary called the Bits, followed by the Norwegian Beatles, 'probably the world's northernmost Beatles tribute band', and then Clube Big Beatles from Brazil, who are apparently soon to open their own Cavern Club in São Paulo. Performers on the indoor stage included the Bertils from Sweden, the Fab Fourever ('Canada's Premiere Tribute to the Beatles'), Bestbeat from Serbia, crowned 'one of the thirty most prominent Beatles tribute bands on the planet' by *Newsweek* in 2012, and B.B. Cats, an all-female tribute band from Tokyo who specialise in playing the Beatles' Hamburg repertoire.

There are over a thousand Beatles tribute acts in the world today. Many of them – the Tefeatles from Guatemala, Rubber Soul from Brazil, the Nowhere Boys from Colombia, Abbey Road from Spain – have now been together longer than the Beatles themselves: Britain's Bootleg Beatles and Australia's Beatnix have both been going for forty years.

In the evening, I joined the long and winding queue outside the Grand Central Hall to see the Fab Four from California, one of the most successful Beatles tribute bands in the world. Most of those queuing were around the age of seventy, which would have made them fifteen or so at the height of Beatlemania. The men wore baggy jeans and Beatles T-shirts; the women slacks and generous tops. One or two people were in wheelchairs. At most rock concerts, fans rush to get close to the stage, but when the doors to the Grand Central Hall opened, most people rushed upstairs, to where the seats were.

A depressing man in jeans and a knitted bonnet opened the show, moaning his way through John's passive-aggressive 'Don't Let Me Down', accompanying himself with jerky pyrotechnics on an acoustic guitar. What was I doing there, with these senior citizens togged up in their Beatles gear? With a change of clothes it might almost have been a reunion of Second World War veterans, gathered for a fly-past of Spitfires.

In the 1970s, my parents used to watch a TV programme called *The Good Old Days*. The audience would dress up as Edwardians, the men in straw boaters, fancy blazers and walrus moustaches, the women in feather-rimmed hats and voluminous dresses with high-boned collars. They would gasp adoringly as the high-camp Master of Ceremonies, Leonard Sachs, introduced each music-hall act – tap dancer, conjuror,

barbershop quartet – with a stream of elaborate words: 'Prestidigitational!' ('Oooh!'), 'Plenitudinous!' ('Ahh!'), 'Sesquipidalianism!' ('Oooh!'), and then banged his gavel. At the curtain-call everyone would join in with a sing-song of 'Down at the Old Bull and Bush'. It was what was then known as a trip down memory lane, viewers at home happy to collude in the deception that time could be reversed, and the dead revived.

Was this Beatles revival another quest for the same old thing – dreams of blue remembered hills?

> That is the land of lost content,
> I see it shining plain,
> The happy highways where I went
> And cannot come again.

Such were my maudlin reflections as the Fab Four took to the stage. But then they started to play 'She Loves You', and they sounded just like the Beatles and, to my fading eyes, looked just like them too – Paul arching his eyebrows and rolling his eyes to the ceiling, George slightly dreamy and distant, Ringo rocking his head from side to side, John with his legs wide apart, as though astride a donkey. I was witnessing something closer to a wonderful conjuring trick. One half of your brain recognises that these are not the Beatles: how could they be? But the other half is happy to believe that they are. It is like watching a play: yes, of course you know that the couple onstage are actors, but on some other level you think they are Othello and Desdemona. The drama lies in the interplay of knowledge and imagination. And with the Fab Four, there is another illusion at work, equally convincing, equally transient: for as long as they play, we are all fifty years younger, gazing in wonder at the Beatles in their prime.

24

Helen Shapiro had been asked to leave her school choir because she could never resist jazzing up the harmonies.

So, aged twelve, she formed a group, Suzie and the Hula-Hoops, with her schoolmates Mark Feld,* Stephen Gould and Susan Singer, but they disbanded soon afterwards. Helen liked to hang around the stage door of the Hackney Empire, up the road from her family home, spotting stars like Adam Faith, Billy Fury, Cliff Richard and Lord Rockingham's Eleven. Once, she even managed to get Marty Wilde's autograph.

Aged thirteen, she was determined to become either an air hostess or a singer. This choice was decided for her when her Uncle Harry happened to spot an advertisement for the Maurice Burman School of Modern Pop Singing, where Alma Cogan had once been a pupil. Burman himself had drummed with leading dance bands before the war, and now wrote a regular column for *Melody Maker*. Upon meeting little Helen, he was so excited by her deep, bluesy voice that he waived the fee. Every Saturday Helen attended his school, on the corner of Baker Street and Marylebone Road, and there she learned scales, diction, phrasing and microphone technique.

After six months Burman got in touch with his old friend, the conductor and producer Norrie Paramor. Paramor suggested Helen record a test tape at the EMI studios at Abbey Road. She sang 'Birth of the Blues'. Paramor found it hard to believe that these powerful, poised vocals sprang from a thirteen-year-old.

---

* Who later changed his name to Marc Bolan.

EMI gave Helen a contract. Instead of a percentage, they offered her a penny per single, and sixpence for each twelve-track LP. If she was a success, the amount would rise to three farthings per track, up to a maximum of tuppence a single. 'It all went totally over my head. The people from EMI were all clever businessmen while I was just a young girl who wanted to sing. I never was interested in the financial side of things, until it was too late.'

Helen and her parents thought she should change her name: at that time Jewish performers tended to change their names to avoid anti-Semitism. But Norrie Paramor felt that most people wouldn't twig that Shapiro was a Jewish surname, and it sounded dashing, so they decided to stick with it.

Helen's first single, 'Don't Treat Me Like a Child', was released on 10 February 1961. It seemed to have peaked at a satisfactory number 28 in the charts, but then she appeared on the first edition of the new pop music show *Thank Your Lucky Stars*, and it zoomed to number 4. Helen began to be recognised in the streets.

Her next two songs, 'You Don't Know' and 'Walkin' Back to Happiness', both sold over a million copies, and reached number 1 in the charts. Helen was voted Best Female Act in 1961, and again the following year.

Towards the end of 1962, the promoter Arthur Howes told her about the line-up for her next British tour. 'We're going to put a nice package together for you. We've got Kenny Lynch, Danny Williams. Red Price will be backing you again. Dave Allen is compering, there's a girls' singing group, the Honeys, and a vocal group, the Kestrels. Then we've got this new group, the Beatles. I don't know whether you've heard their record, "Love Me Do"?'

Helen certainly did know about the Beatles: 'They were the funny fellows with the funny hair.'

Her tour kicked off at the Gaumont in Bradford on 2 February. The Red Price Band opened the show, then came the Honeys, the comedian (and compere) Dave Allen, and the Beatles, with Danny Williams ('Britain's Johnny Mathis') closing the first half. After the interval the Red Price Band appeared again, followed by the Kestrels,

Kenny Lynch, Dave Allen again, and finally, topping the bill, Helen Shapiro.

During the sound checks in Bradford, Helen was introduced to the Beatles' bass player, Paul. 'I made some comment about liking "Love Me Do" and he introduced me to the rest of the guys who were really happy because this was their first major concert tour. They'd performed in clubs and ballrooms in Hamburg and Liverpool but never done anything like the pop package and were eager to be onstage.'

At this point, one of them mentioned that they had written a song called 'Misery' for Helen, but it had been turned down on her behalf by Norrie Paramor. Helen apologised, saying she hadn't known about it.

When the Beatles took to the stage, Helen was struck by quite how loud they were. They were used to a noisier crowd. 'They soon cottoned on to the fact that they didn't need to turn the sound up quite so much when people were sitting listening rather than dancing … They had a lot to learn.'

Her management encouraged Helen to travel by herself in a special limousine, to reflect her star status, but she preferred sitting in the coach with the supporting acts. 'I wouldn't have missed it for the world, especially while the Beatles were with us.' Together on the coach, the Beatles would bring out their guitars, and Helen would sing a song like 'The Locomotion'. She remembered how Paul would practise writing his autograph over and over again, and then ask her what she thought of it. On one of these coach rides John and Paul hit upon the idea of running up to the microphone together and singing 'Whoooo!', a routine that within a matter of weeks would be setting off explosions of ecstasy among their fans.

One night Helen let the Beatles into her changing room so they could watch themselves on television for the first time. John was surprised by the way he looked, particularly the odd, jockey-like stance he adopted onstage. They kept nudging one another and commenting. 'Eh, look at that.' 'You look awful.'

As the tour progressed, the Beatles' popularity grew and grew, while Helen's went into decline. By chance, both the Beatles and Helen had

released new singles at roughly the same time – 'Please Please Me' on 17 January, 'Queen for Tonight' on 26 January. As the weeks went by, the status of the famous headliner and the lowly support act switched places. At the beginning of February 'Please Please Me' was at number 33, and 'Queen for Tonight' was nowhere to be seen. By 6 February 'Please Please Me' was number 16, and 'Queen for Tonight' was still nowhere to be seen. On 13 February 'Queen for Tonight' scraped in at 42, while 'Please Please Me' was number 3. By 23 February 'Please Please Me' was number 2 and 'Queen for Tonight' was 33, the highest position it would ever reach: the following week it had slipped to 35. Helen was only sixteen years old, and on the skids: 'I'd been a novelty at fourteen but I suffered from the Shirley Temple syndrome. I'd grown up. Suddenly I was beginning to look a little bit passé in spite of topping the bill.'

One day, reading a music paper on the tour coach, she saw the headline 'Is Helen Shapiro a "Has-Been" at 16?' 'I felt just as if somebody had punched me in the stomach.' In the seat behind her, John Lennon, six years her senior, noticed that she was upset. They had always had a good relationship: like many girls her age, she had a crush on him. He in turn was uncharacteristically protective of her, treating her, in Helen's words, 'like some kind of kid sister'.

'What's up, Helly?'

She showed him the offending headline. John sought to reassure her. 'You don't want to be bothered with that rubbish. You're all right. You'll be going on for years.'

But no amount of reassurance could disguise the truth. Helen Shapiro was to look back on that moment as 'one of those milestones I would pinpoint as the beginning of change; not just for me but for a lot of solo singers. The Beatles were the beginning of a new era, a new wave of groups, the whole Merseyside thing.'

By the end of February, the Beatles had been promoted above Danny Williams on the tour, charged with closing the first half of the programme. For the first time, their music was being drowned out by screams. Helen continued to travel on the coach with the support acts, but, ever conscious of the Beatles' burgeoning star status, Brian Epstein made them travel in their own car, away from the others. They left the tour before the end, off to head their own shows. Helen missed the Beatles: 'Things were never quite the same afterwards.'

After the tour, she continued to record. 'My records were getting better, yet the sales were worse. All during '63 the whole Merseyside thing was growing and growing. London was out, along with solo artistes. The writing was on the wall for anyone who didn't belong to a group, preferably with drums, and lead, bass and rhythm guitars.'

Her next record, 'Woe is Me', peaked at number 35. By October 1963, when she came to release 'Look Who it Is', the Beatles had become the most famous act in Britain: 'She Loves You' was at number 1, and well on its way to selling a million copies.

To help Helen promote her single, the producer of *Ready Steady Go!* suggested she be filmed singing it to the Beatles, who were headlining. It was agreed that she would sing a verse to each Beatle in turn, but as there were only three verses, one of them had to stand aside. They tossed a coin, and the loser was Paul, who went off to a neighbouring studio, where he was charged with picking the winner of a competition in which four girls mimed to 'Let's Jump the Broomstick' by Brenda Lee.

Paul decided that the winner was girl number four, Melanie Coe, aged fourteen, from Stamford Hill in London.

25

On previous shows, the prize had been a date with a pop star, but this time it was just the Beatles' LP, *Please Please Me*. Upon hearing this, Melanie Coe's face fell. 'I thought I was going to have a dinner date with the Beatles, so I was terribly disappointed.' Moreover, Paul McCartney's firm handshake caused her false nails to come loose. 'I don't think I'd ever worn them before, and I wanted to have everything perfect.' But her disappointment was assuaged when the producers, impressed by her natural exuberance, offered her a year's stint as a background dancer, which let her rub shoulders with stars like Stevie Wonder, Dusty Springfield, Cilla Black and Freddie and the Dreamers.

Had she not been picked out by Paul McCartney, might Melanie Coe have been more content with the life of a schoolgirl? Instead she grew restless, and as time went by she started venturing into central London, against her parents' wishes. 'In 1964, I'd say there were three or four discos in London, so you were likely to meet the same people wherever you went.'

On one of these secret excursions she went with a friend from Hamburg to the Bag o' Nails Club in Kingly Street, just off Carnaby Street. As in the Beatles song, she was just seventeen. Her friend had long boasted that she knew the Beatles very well, but Melanie didn't believe her. 'We were sitting down having a drink and in walks John Lennon with his entourage. And she waves to him and he comes over to us. "It's you! Come join us!" And before I knew it, I'm seventeen and I'm at a table with John Lennon! That's how it was!'

Touched by these two encounters, the first with Paul, the second with John, what young girl could have resisted the lure of adult life?

Unfortunately, it wasn't long before Melanie became pregnant. One afternoon she left a note on the kitchen table that she hoped would say more, and left home, off to live with a croupier in Bayswater.

Melanie had been away from home for a week when on 27 February 1967 she saw her picture in the *Daily Mail*, alongside a headline saying:

'A-Level Girl Dumps Car and Vanishes'

On that same day, Paul McCartney also happened to be reading the *Daily Mail*, and his eye was caught by the same headline. The report began:

> The father of 17-year-old Melanie Coe, the schoolgirl who seemed to have everything, spent yesterday searching for her in London and Brighton.
>
> Melanie had her own car, an Austin 1100. It was left unlocked outside her home when she vanished.
>
> She had a wardrobe full of clothes. She took only what she was wearing – a cinnamon trouser suit and black patent leather shoes.
>
> She left her chequebook and drew no money from her account.
>
> Melanie, who has blonde hair and is 5ft 1inch tall, was studying for her A-level examinations. She planned to go to university or drama school.
>
> 'I cannot imagine why she should run away,' her father told reporters. 'She has everything here. She is very keen on clothes, but she left them all, even her fur coat.'

Without realising that Melanie was the very same girl he had picked to win a prize over three years before, Paul was inspired to write 'She's Leaving Home'.

'I started to get the lyrics: she slips out and leaves a note and then the parents wake up and then … It was rather poignant,' he recalled. '… and when I showed it to John, he added the Greek chorus, long sustained notes, and one of the nice things about the structure of the song is that it stays on those chords endlessly.'

John found the Greek chorus – 'Sacrificed most of our lives', 'We gave her everything money could buy' – simple to write: these were the very same complaints he had heard so often from the lips of his Aunt Mimi.

The Beatles recorded 'She's Leaving Home' on the evening of 17 March 1967. By this time Melanie Coe was back home with her parents, who had managed to track her down. She first heard the song soon after it came out on the *Sgt. Pepper* album at the end of May. 'I didn't realise it was about me, but I remember thinking it *could* have been about me. I found the song extremely sad. It obviously struck a chord somewhere. It wasn't until later, when I was in my twenties, that my mother said, "You know, that song was about you."' She had seen an interview with Paul on television and he said he'd based the song on this newspaper article. She put two and two together.

'The most interesting thing in the song is what the father said: "We gave her everything money could buy." And in the newspaper article, my father actually says almost those words. He doesn't understand why I would have left home when they bought me or gave me everything. Which is true; they had bought me a car and they always bought me expensive clothes and things like that. But, as we know, that doesn't mean that you get on well with your parents, or even love them, just because they buy you material things.'

Quite by chance, McCartney had hit another nail on the head: before starting work as a croupier, her older boyfriend had worked in the motor trade.*

---

* The following year Melanie left home again, having married a Spaniard. They broke up after a year, and then she moved to California, intent on pursuing a career in acting and dancing. She enjoyed a brief romance with Burt Ward, the actor who played Batman's young sidekick Robin in the TV series. In 1981 she returned home to look after her mother, who was dying.

26

The Beatles started 1963 playing modest gigs such as the Wolverham Welfare Association dance at the Civic Hall in Wirral (14 January) and a Baptist church youth club party at the Co-Operative Hall in Darwen (25 January). On 4 April, well into spring, they performed an afternoon concert for the boys of Stowe School in Buckinghamshire.

But their popularity was speedily growing. In March their second single, 'Please Please Me', had only been prevented from reaching number 1 in the UK charts by the continued popularity of Frank Ifield's 'Wayward Wind' and, latterly, Cliff Richard's 'Summer Holiday'. But in May 'From Me to You' became their first single to reach number 1, and their debut album, *Please Please Me*, also went to number 1, where it was set to remain for the next thirty weeks.

By the end of that month, they had appeared for a second time on national television, singing 'From Me to You' on the children's programme *Pops and Lenny*, accompanied by Lenny the Lion, the distinguished glove puppet. Furthermore, they had been given a new radio series on the BBC, *Pop Go the Beatles*. The corporation's Audience Research Department estimated that 5.3 per cent of the population, or 2.8 million people, had listened to the first episode, with audience comments ranging from 'an obnoxious noise' to 'really with-it'.

But fame comes with drawbacks. Paul had originally planned to celebrate his twenty-first birthday at the McCartney family home in Forthlin Road, but it soon became clear that fans might prove a hazard. So the McCartneys switched the party to his Auntie Jin's house, across the Mersey in Huyton, where there was plenty of room for a marquee in the large back garden, and privacy was assured.

The birthday party took place on 21 June 1963. Guests included the three other Beatles, John's wife Cynthia, Paul's brother Mike, Mike's two friends Roger McGough and John Gorman, John's friend Pete Shotton, Ringo's girlfriend Maureen, the disc jockey Bob Wooler, Gerry Marsden, Billy J. Kramer and any number of musicians. Paul was particularly delighted when the Shadows came through the door. 'I can't believe it,' he said to Tony Bramwell, who worked for Brian Epstein. He then thought about it for a second, before adding, 'But we're sort of like one of them now, aren't we?'

'Yeah, only bigger,' replied Bramwell, who remembered Paul giving him a doubtful look, 'as if I was pulling his leg'.

Paul's new girlfriend, the seventeen-year-old actress Jane Asher, was also there. They had first met two months before. Cynthia was very taken with her: 'She was beautiful, with auburn hair and green eyes. Also, although she had been a successful actress since she was five, she was unaffected, easy to talk to and friendly.'

Paul's dad Jim played old-fashioned numbers on his piano, and, later, the up-and-coming band the Fourmost took to a makeshift stage. Their bass player Billy Hatton had struck the deal. 'Paul offered to pay us the usual rate for this kind of job, but as we were going to the party anyway, we said we would do it for just one and fourpence halfpenny each.'

As the party progressed, Pete Shotton spotted John in a corner, 'nursing a Scotch and Coke and looking glum as could be'. John seemed pleased to see Pete, and together they drifted into the garden. Over more drinks, John enjoyed pointing out the various pop stars present. 'Cliff Richard might even show up tonight,' he added, before going off to get yet another refill.

Pete set off to find a loo. On his return, everything had changed. 'When I emerged from the WC … the party seemed to have been somehow transformed from a celebration to a wake. Something, obviously, had gone terribly wrong.'

Bob Wooler, the Cavern MC, was lying on the floor, with blood everywhere. Apparently he had been teasing John about his recent holiday in Spain with Brian Epstein, and John had taken his revenge. 'A well-drunk John punched Wooler for taunting him,' recalled Tony

Barrow in his autobiography. Another of Epstein's assistants, Peter Brown, added more detail, saying that 'in a mad rage and obviously very drunk', John had started 'pummelling' an unnamed guest; it had taken 'three men to pull John off, but not before he managed to break three of the man's ribs'.

Tony Bramwell remembered that 'John saw red. He assaulted Bob, breaking his ribs and ending up with a bloody nose himself.' Shotton took it a step further: 'John responded by knocking Bob to the ground and repeatedly clobbering him in the face with, I believe, a shovel. The damage to Bob's visage was so extensive that an ambulance had to be summoned to rush him to hospital.'

In her second autobiography, written forty-two years after the event (she failed to mention the incident in her first), Cynthia Lennon wrote: 'John, who'd had plenty to drink, exploded. He leapt on Bob, and by the time he was dragged off Bob had a black eye and badly bruised ribs. I took John home as fast as I could and Brian drove Bob to hospital.' Cynthia claimed to remember John telling her, 'He called me a queer.' Others, though, have suggested Wooler said something more insidious, like, 'Come on, John. Tell us about you and Brian in Spain. We all know.'

Thirty-six years later, Rex Makin, the Epstein family's solicitor,* gave an account in which he deftly avoided mentioning Brian Epstein or the Spanish holiday, and suggested that Wooler had come on to John: 'Everybody had a lot to drink and John Lennon thought or perceived that Wooler had made a pass at him, whereupon he socked him and broke his nose and gave him a black eye.'

The Beatles' biographers also offer radically different versions of the same event. Hunter Davies, who gave Epstein and the Beatles copy approval for his authorised 1968 biography, wrote that 'John picked a fight with a local disk [sic] jockey,' and quoted John saying, 'I broke his bloody ribs for him. I was pissed at the time. He called me a queer.'

Other biographers have tended to take it a stage further. 'Without warning, John exploded,' wrote Ray Connolly. 'Lashing out, he

* In 1967, Makin was to make all the arrangements for Epstein's funeral. Some credit him with inventing the term 'Beatlemania'.

began to batter Wooler's face and body with both his fists and a stick ... He went berserk, to the extent that when he was pulled off Wooler, the inoffensive and much older man had to be quickly driven to hospital by Brian, where he was treated for bruised ribs and a black eye.'

In his 1981 biography of the Beatles, *Shout!*, Philip Norman described the party as 'a typical Liverpool booze-up, riotous and noisy'. He mentioned that 'John Lennon got into a fight with another guest,' but didn't say who it was, or what the fight was about. Norman was more forthcoming in his 2016 biography of Paul, disagreeing with Connolly that Wooler was inoffensive, and instead describing him as 'notoriously sharp-tongued'. In his account of the fight, Norman had John 'raining punches viciously on Wooler's head and body', but offered no assessment of the injuries. However, in his 2008 biography of John, he stated that Wooler 'suffered bruised ribs and a black eye'.

In his 2005 Beatles biography, Bob Spitz had John beating Wooler 'viciously, with tightly closed fists. When that didn't do enough damage, he grabbed a garden shovel that was left in the yard and whacked Bob once or twice with the handle. According to one observer, "Bob was holding his hands to his face and John was kicking all the skin off his fingers."' According to Spitz, Wooler was taken away in an ambulance with even more injuries: 'a broken nose, a cracked collar bone and three broken ribs'.

Do I hear any advance on a broken nose, a cracked collarbone and three broken ribs? Inevitably, the most excessive bid was submitted by Albert Goldman, the most merciless and hyperbolic of all John's biographers:* 'John doubled up his fist and smashed the little disc jockey

---

* Goldman (1927–94) wrote *The Lives of John Lennon* (1988), in which he portrayed John in a uniquely unflattering light, even going so far as to suggest he was a murderer. Goldman died of a heart attack in an aeroplane on the way to London, following a heated argument with flight attendants about having his seat upgraded. 'Goldman looked like Truman Capote and sounded like Bette Davis,' wrote his *Daily Telegraph* obituarist. 'He was not a modest man: "With the counter-culture," he declared, "I had found a great field that needed a great mind like mine to explore it."'

in the nose. Then, seizing a shovel that was lying in the yard, Lennon began to beat Wooler to death. Blow after blow came smashing down on the defenseless man lying on the ground. It would have ended in murder if John had not suddenly realized: "If I hit him one more time, I'll kill him!" Making an enormous effort of will, Lennon restrained himself. At that instant three men seized him and disarmed him. An ambulance was called for Wooler, who had suffered a broken nose, a cracked collar-bone, and three broken ribs. Lennon had broken a finger.'

All in all, no other event in the lives of the Beatles illustrates more clearly the random, subjective nature of history, a form predicated on objectivity but reliant on the shifting sands of memory.

So a table of the final tally looks like this:

	ASSAULT	EXTENT OF INJURY
TONY BARROW	'Punched Wooler'	No mention
TONY BRAMWELL	'He assaulted Bob'	Broken ribs, bloody nose
PETER BROWN	'Pummelling'	Three broken ribs
RAY CONNOLLY	'He began to batter Wooler's face and body with both fists and a stick'	Bruised ribs, black eye
ALBERT GOODMAN	'… seizing a shovel … began to beat Wooler to death. It would have ended in murder …'	Broken nose, cracked collarbone, three broken ribs. Also, Lennon broke a finger
CYNTHIA LENNON	'He leapt on Bob'	Black eye, badly bruised ribs
JOHN LENNON (1963) to press	'I am terribly upset about this … too far gone to know what I was doing'	No mention of injuries
JOHN LENNON (1963) to Barrow	'He called me a bloody queer so I battered him'	Unspecific injuries: 'He got what he deserved'

	ASSAULT	EXTENT OF INJURY
JOHN LENNON (1968) to Hunter Davies	'I smashed him up'	'I broke his bloody ribs for him'
JOHN LENNON (1980)	'I was beating the shit out of him, and beating him with a big stick'	'I battered his bloody ribs for him'
REX MAKIN	'He socked him'	Broken nose, black eye
PHILIP NORMAN	'raining punches viciously on W's head and body'	Bruised ribs, black eye
PETE SHOTTON	'repeatedly clobbering him in the face with … a shovel'	Extensive damage to face
BOB SPITZ	'leapt on W, beating him viciously with tightly closed fists'	Broken nose, cracked collarbone, three broken ribs

No one seems to doubt, though, that the following day Wooler contacted Rex Makin, who decided to act for both parties, eventually negotiating a £200 payment to Wooler and an apology. Word soon reached the press about the incident. In charge of damage limitation, Tony Barrow got in touch with John, who was bullishly unrepentant. 'He told me gruffly, "Wooler was well out of fucking order. He called me a bloody queer so I battered him … I wasn't that pissed. The bastard had it coming. He teased me, I punched him. Of course I won't apologise."' Barrow then dutifully 'trimmed and toned and spun' this unpromising material, so that the next day's *Sunday Mirror* reported:

> Guitarist John Lennon, 22-year-old leader of the Beatles pop group, said last night, 'Why did I have to go and punch my best friend? … Bob is the last person in the world I would want to have a fight with. I can only hope he realises that I was too far gone to know what I was doing.'

Recuperating in hospital, Wooler received a conciliatory telegram from John: 'REALLY SORRY, BOB. TERRIBLY SORRY TO REALIZE WHAT I HAD DONE. WHAT MORE CAN I SAY?' As it happened, each word had been dictated by Brian Epstein.*

What exactly happened in Spain? Most people agree that when Julian was three weeks old, Brian took the unusual step of taking John on a Spanish holiday à deux. In her first autobiography (1978), Cynthia says that when John asked her if she would mind, 'I concealed my hurt and envy and gave him my blessing.' In her second (2005), her memories have altered; now, when John asks her if she would mind, there is no mention of hurt or envy. 'I said, truthfully, that I wouldn't.'

The implacable Albert Goldman, on the other hand, states that John only got round to seeing his newborn son a week after his birth, and then, 'turning to Cynthia, informed her bluntly that he was going off on a short holiday with Brian Epstein.' In the Goldman version, far from acquiescing, 'Cynthia was outraged by his astonishing news.' Goldman adds that John was indifferent to Cynthia's feelings, saying: 'Being selfish again, aren't you?' He appears to have lifted this version of events from Peter Brown's waspish memoir *The Love You Make* (1983), though it seems unlikely that Brown himself was privy to John and Cynthia's discussion.

So, did they or didn't they? The simple truth is that no one knows, but everyone thinks they know, or at least they want everyone else to think they know. Cynthia covers the matter in two sentences. Pooh-poohing the gossip, she says that after John came back from Spain, 'He had to put up with sly digs, winks and innuendo that he was secretly gay. It infuriated him: all he'd wanted was a break with a friend, but it was turned into so much more.'

* The telegram was sold at Sotheby's in 1984 for £550. In 1980, shortly before he died, John spoke of 'hitting him with a big stick, and for the first time I thought, I can kill this guy. I just saw it on a screen: if I hit him once more, that's going to be it. I really got shocked. That's when I gave up violence, because all my life I'd been like that.'

Of the Beatles' employees, Alistair Taylor and Tony Barrow agree with Cynthia that nothing sexual occurred. Taylor claims that 'in one of our frankest heart-to-hearts John denied it'. 'He never wanted me like that,' he told Taylor, adding, 'Even completely out of my head, I couldn't shag a bloke. And I certainly couldn't lie there and let one shag me. Even a nice guy like Brian. To be honest, the thought of it turns me over.' Barrow says, 'John made it abundantly clear to me that there was no two-way traffic along this route … I don't believe that the relationship between Brian and John became a physical one in Spain or elsewhere. I believe John's version, which was that he teased Brian to the limit but stopped short when they came to the brink.'

On the other hand, Tony Bramwell claims John told him that he finally allowed Brian to have sex with him just 'to get it out of the way'. But Bramwell adds that John may have been lying. 'Those who knew John well, who had known him for years, don't believe it for a moment.' However, Peter Brown begs to differ, painting an unfeasibly vivid picture, as though lifted from an airport novel: 'Drunk and sleepy from the sweet Spanish wine, Brian and John got undressed in silence. "It's OK, Eppy," John said, and lay down on his bed. Brian would have liked to have hugged him, but he was afraid. Instead, John lay there, tentative and still, and Brian fulfilled the fantasies he was so sure would bring him contentment, only to awake the next morning as hollow as before.'*

Pete Shotton was closer to John than the others, and less given to speculation. He writes that when John and Brian went away 'tongues began wagging all over town'. On John's return, Shotton teased him – 'So you had a good time with Brian, then?' – only for John to respond quietly, 'Actually Pete, something did happen with him one night … Eppy just kept on and on at me. Until one night I finally just pulled me trousers down and said to him, "Oh, for Christ's sake, Brian, just stick it up me fucking arse then." And he said to me, "Actually, John, I don't

---

* The memoirs of former Beatles office staff share this strange quality of divine omniscience with the memoirs of royal housekeepers and valets.

do that kind of thing. That's not what I like to do." "Well," I said, "what is it you want to do then?" And he said, "I'd really just like to touch you, John." And so I let him toss me off … So what harm did it do, then, Pete, for fuck's sake? No harm at all. The poor fucking bastard, he can't help the way he is.'

So much for John's associates. Small wonder, then, that his biographers are also divided. Epstein's biographer Ray Coleman insists nothing sexual occurred: 'Since the death of Epstein and Lennon, many with no access to, or observation of, both men in their lifetime have peddled the assumption that Brian and John had a sexual liaison. This is despite the lack of any evidence, despite firm declarations of John's heterosexuality from Cynthia and many other women, and despite the statement by McCartney that he "slept in a million hotel rooms, as we all did, with John and there was never any hint that he was gay".' Coleman argues that Epstein 'would never have risked so profoundly changing his relationship with them, individually or collectively'. He adds that 'Epstein was not a predator,' though there is in fact plenty of evidence to suggest that he was.*

In his biography of John, Ray Connolly judges Pete Shotton to be honest, so believes his claim that John said he had let Brian masturbate him. 'But was John telling the truth? It was well known to those around him that he was keenly heterosexual. But he loved to shock, too. Did he invent a homosexual experience for the fun of it, or, perhaps, did he just exaggerate the incident after Brian made a pass at him? Both are possible. But, equally, as all his life he would be eager to experience anything new, was he curious about homosexuality? When Brian came on to him, did he simply want to know what it was like to be touched by another man?'

Bob Spitz is convinced 'something happened', but is unsure what: 'In the privacy of their room, after an evening of drinking and sporting

---

* Those who have claimed Epstein made passes at them include Pete Shotton, Larry Kane, Pete Best and the Liverpudlian comedian Freddie Starr (1943–2019), who was then singing with a group called the Midniters. Given to exaggeration, Starr is the only one to talk of a struggle: 'I started punching his upper arms, which startled him, because it bloody hurt. He quickly backed off and composed himself.'

about, Brian initiated something that led to physical contact.' Though Spitz peppers the relevant passage with conditionals – '*if* John participated in some sort of homosexual act, *it follows that* …' 'Curiosity *may well* have gotten the better of him …' 'He *may* have been experimenting …' – he concludes on a note of certainty: 'Away from home, in a beautiful resort with a man – certainly a father figure – who was devoted to taking care of him, John was relaxed and open enough to let it happen unconditionally.'

True to form, the relentless Goldman thinks there is no question about it: 'He and Brian had sex.' Quoting Shotton's book as evidence, he argues over the details: 'Brian told Peter Brown the real story: he had given John a blow job. Lennon couldn't afford to acknowledge that sort of intimacy because it would stigmatise him for life.' Yet, as we have seen, Peter Brown was in fact much more circumspect, saying only that Brian had 'fulfilled his fantasies'.

Having already gone too far, Goldman then goes miles further, asserting, on the basis of no evidence whatsoever, that 'John and Brian did not confine themselves to a single sexual experiment in Spain. They were sexually involved for the balance of Brian's life, and their relationship was a *controlling* one, with John playing the cruel master and Brian the submissive slave.'

Philip Norman labels Goldman's book, not unfairly, as both 'malevolent' and 'risibly ignorant'. In his biography of Paul, Norman judges the idea of a sexual encounter between John and Brian possible but not proven, adding that 'Years later, he told a close friend he'd had sex of some sort with Brian, "once to see what it was like, the second time to make sure I didn't like it"'. But in his biography of John, Norman offers a different account, this one from Yoko Ono, with whom he had conducted a series of interviews over three years: 'Years later, John finally came clean about what had happened: not to anyone who'd been around at the time, but to the unshockable woman with whom he shared the last decade of his life. He said that one night during the trip, Brian had cast aside shyness and scruples and finally come on to him, but that he'd replied, "If you feel like that, go out and find a hustler."' Norman adds that 'Afterward, he had deliberately fed Pete Shotton the myth of his brief surrender, so that everyone would believe his power over Brian to be absolute.'*

Perhaps it is best to leave the last word to Paul. 'In an earthquake, you get many different versions of what happened by all the people that saw it,' he observed, decades later, of the Beatles phenomenon. 'And they're all true.'

* Yoko also told Philip Norman that 'from chance remarks' John made, she gathered that he had thought of having an affair with Paul, but Paul had not wanted it. 'Around Apple, in her hearing Paul would sometimes be called John's Princess,' writes Norman. Yoko also told him that she had once heard a rehearsal tape with John's voice calling out 'Paul ... Paul ...' in a strangely subservient, pleading way. 'I knew there was something going on there,' she remembered. 'From his point of view, not from Paul's. And he was so angry at Paul, I couldn't help wondering what it was really about.'

27

The Beatles began 1963 in relative obscurity, and ended it the most famous group in the country. Within another six weeks, they were the most famous group in the world.

As we have seen, at the start of 1963 they were just another jobbing pop group. Their first single, 'Love Me Do', had peaked at number 17. Their first concert of 1963 was presented by the Elgin Folk Music Club at the Two Red Shoes Ballroom in Elgin, Scotland, and was attended by two hundred people. Driving in their van from Elgin to the town hall in Dingwall, they were so cold that they lay on top of one another to keep warm. 'When the one on top got so cold that hypothermia was setting in, it would be his turn to get on the bottom,' recalled Paul. 'We'd warm each other up that way.'

At the time, plenty of other British acts – Adam Faith, Mark Wynter, Jet Harris, and of course Cliff Richard and the Shadows – were doing much, much better.

But when success finally came, it came as a landslide, flattening those ahead. Bands and singers who a few months before might have agreed with some reluctance to employ the Beatles as their warm-up act now found themselves in the humiliating position of opening for them. Within the space of five days in September 1963 they were presented with the Top Vocal Group of the Year award at the Savoy Hotel and headed the bill of The Great Pop Prom at the Royal Albert Hall. Meanwhile, 'She Loves You' was at number 1 in the charts. As they stood in their smart new suits at the top of the steps behind the Albert Hall, Paul felt the sunshine on his face. 'We looked at each other, and we were thinking, "This is it! London! The Albert Hall!" We felt like gods! We felt like fucking gods!'

And this was just the beginning. In October, their appearance on *Sunday Night at the London Palladium* attracted fifteen million viewers. On 4 November they played the Royal Command Performance. Later that month their new single, 'I Want to Hold Your Hand', sold a million copies in the UK before it had even been released – roughly one copy for every fifty people in the country.

By the end of 1964 they had become the most famous young men on earth. In Madame Tussauds, their wax effigies took their place alongside world leaders, mass murderers and members of the royal family. In West Bridgford, Nottinghamshire, four brainy pupils of the Becket Grammar School closed their school concert with a spirited rendition of 'From Me to You' in Latin.* The students of Leeds University elected Ringo Starr their vice-president in preference to a former Lord Chief Justice. Visiting the EMI studios, Sir Malcolm Sargent, the most celebrated British conductor of the day, asked George Martin if he might effect an introduction ('Chaps, Sir Malcolm would like to say "Hello"').

Everyone wanted to meet them. In Hollywood, top movie stars – Edward G. Robinson, Dean Martin, Lloyd Bridges, Kirk Douglas, Shelley Winters, Jack Palance, Jack Lemmon – donated money to charity in order to queue for their autographs. In exile in France, the Duchess of Windsor sang their songs to herself. 'Oh, the Beatles. Don't you just love 'em?' she said to the up-and-coming young interior designer Nicky Haslam, over on a visit. '"I give her all my love, that's all I do-ooo!" Adore 'em. Do you know them? Oh, you are lucky!'

Where did this leave their rivals? For groups like Peter Jay and the Jaywalkers, it must have been hard to stomach. A year before, the Beatles had looked up to them. From the back of the hall, George would gaze at the Jaywalkers as they set up their flashing coloured lights, their flashing drum kit and their exploding cymbals, and he would think of them as 'real big shots'. But now those days were past.

* 'A Me ad Vos'.

Groups that just a short time before had been on level pegging now found it impossible to keep up. The Hollies had formed in 1962, and were having hits by 1963, but by 1964 their achievements seemed minuscule beside the Beatles'. It's not hard to spot a note of resentment in Graham Nash's reminiscences, published half a century later:

> In those days, tweaking a Beatle was like blaspheming the pope. But who the fuck cared? I was getting sick and tired of their holy status, the way they said whatever was on their minds, no matter whom it affected, right or wrong. All of London was in their thrall. And if you didn't know Popes John or Paul, or at least drop their names in conversation, you might as well take the next train back to the provinces, over and out. Keith Richards said it best in *Life:* 'The Beatles are all over the place like a fucking bag of fleas.' They were a great band and I loved their records. Every English group owed them a huge debt, but I had no intention of kissing their asses. Besides, last I looked, the Hollies were holding down places on the same top 10 as the Beatles, so pardon me if you don't like our fucking record but keep it to yourself, if you please.

28

At the close of 1963 the Beatles starred in their own Christmas variety show at the Astoria in Finsbury Park, playing twice a day for fifteen days. In all, a hundred thousand people bought tickets. The show's compere was Rolf Harris, the chummy Australian entertainer whose novelty singles 'Tie Me Kangaroo Down, Sport' and 'Sun Arise', both produced by George Martin, had been top 10 hits. Ten years older than the Beatles, Harris belonged to an older showbusiness tradition, in which professionalism was paramount.

One night, while Harris expounded on the Aboriginal setting of 'Sun Arise' to a restless young audience, John began larking around with a microphone backstage. As Rolf was explaining how some tribes regarded the sun as a goddess, John's grating voice boomed harshly over the speakers: 'I dunno about that, Rolf.'

The audience laughed uproariously. Rolf looked around, but couldn't see where the interruption was coming from. So he persevered, describing how, every morning, the tribes thought the sun's skirts of light were covering the earth.

'Well, of course, you could say that,' John piped up. 'But, then again, I dunno, Rolf! Maybe you're just making it up!'

Ever the pro, Rolf put on a brave face, and emitted a laugh of forbearance. 'But inside,' he later admitted, 'I was seething.'

When the show was over, he barged his way into the Beatles' dressing room and shouted, 'If you want to fuck up your own act, do it! But don't fuck up mine!'

But the Beatles remained unbowed. 'Oooh, Rolfie's lost his rag,' said John, and George joined in: 'Yeah, Rolfie's upset.'

Harris tells the story in his 2001 autobiography *Can You Tell What it is Yet?*, and affects good cheer. 'They started laughing and so did I,' he writes. 'They had such charm that I couldn't be angry with them. At least I'd made my point and they didn't do it again.'

But was he really so conciliatory? In an unguarded moment in 1994, he offered a much less merry version of the event: 'The Beatles mucked about with me. At that Christmas show, they stood off in the wings with a microphone and made silly comments during one of my songs and I came storming off the stage and shouted, "Get some bloody professionalism into you! Jesus! You don't muck around with somebody else's act. Don't ever bloody do that again." I was so angry. And after that they didn't bloody do it again, I can tell you!'

29

Just five days separated the births of John Lennon (9 October 1940) and Cliff Richard (14 October 1940).

By the winter of 1958 Cliff had become a big star, number 2 in the charts with 'Move It'. Meanwhile, John remained a no-hoper, scuttling around Liverpool with his Quarrymen, playing the odd village hall or private function, often for no more payment than a beer and a sandwich.

'Is this boy too sexy for television?' gasped the *Daily Sketch* after Cliff had gyrated a little too suggestively on television's *Oh Boy*. The critic on the *New Musical Express* was even more perturbed: 'His violent hip-swinging was revolting, hardly the performance any parent could wish her children to see.' Before 1963 it was Cliff, not John, who was the rebel, the firebrand, the threat to civilisation. The same evening when Cliff and the Shadows were causing a stir on national television, the Quarrymen were playing skiffle standards at George Harrison's brother Harry's wedding reception in Upton Green.

From 1958 to 1962 Cliff had twenty songs in the top 20, including six number ones. He also starred in two films, *Expresso Bongo* and *The Young Ones*. Small wonder then that John, no stranger to envy, entertained mixed feelings towards him. When the Beatles finally squeezed into the charts with 'Love Me Do' in December 1962, reaching a high point of number 17, Cliff was looking down at them from number 2 with 'Bachelor Boy'. The following month, the *New Musical Express* published its annual readers' survey. In 'Top Acts' Cliff Richard came second to Elvis Presley, with the Beatles a lowly joint 111th. They did better in the more specialist 'British Small Group' category, coming eighth with 735 votes; but the Shadows came first, with 45,951 votes.

Three months later, in March 1963, the Beatles reached number 2 with 'Please Please Me', but they were prevented from reaching number 1 by Cliff, who was already there with 'Summer Holiday'.

But as 1963 rolled on, the tables turned. By the end of that year the Beatles were making Cliff seem old hat. For George Melly, Cliff's erotic twitching was now no more than 'a bent-kneed shuffle, not so much a sexual courtship dance as a suggestion that he'd wet himself'. The Beatles were the future, and Cliff the past. Try as Cliff might, it niggled. In a rare fit of candour, he grumbled about the Beatles' primitivism to a reporter from the *Daily Mirror*: 'All they've done is revert to rock'n'roll. We've played the whole thing down, the screaming and the raving. The Beatles have stoked the whole thing up again.'

That Christmas, the Beatles occupied the number 1 and number 2 slots in the UK charts with 'I Want to Hold Your Hand' and 'She Loves You', while Cliff languished at number 8 with 'Don't Talk to Him'. By now, his fans were drifting off in search of brighter, brasher idols. In the New Year it was revealed that Cliff's own sisters had recently formed a Dave Clark Five fan club.

For five years Cliff had struggled to crack the American market, but without success. In fact, it was Cliff's failure that spurred Brian Epstein to plot the Beatles' American campaign with such meticulous care. 'Cliff went there and he died,' John told the American journalist Michael Braun with pitiless relish as they boarded their plane to Kennedy Airport. 'He was fourteenth on a bill with Frankie Avalon.'

Cliff was in the Canary Isles, completing his third movie, *Wonderful Life*, when he heard the news that the Beatles had achieved the success in America that still eluded him. *Wonderful Life* was released on 2 July 1964, but was overshadowed by *A Hard Day's Night*, released four days later. *A Hard Day's Night* broke box-office records, and was hailed by critics on both sides of the Atlantic for its freshness and originality. In contrast, *Wonderful Life* was called 'a sad little picture' by *Films and Filming*, while the *Sunday Times* described it as 'this bloodsome bore of a film' and 'drivel'. The film was retitled *Swingers' Paradise* for the

American market, but to no avail. At the age of twenty-three, Cliff's film career was over.

Soon after the release of both films, *Melody Maker* published a feature on the shifting tastes of youth. 'I grew out of my Cliff Richard days a couple of years ago,' said a twenty-year-old man. 'When I look back I think how soppy I must have been. Groups now like the Beatles and the Stones have really got something and I can't see me getting tired of them. Not until I'm old, anyway.'

From then on, John occupied such a peak of fame and fortune that he rarely bothered to glance down at Cliff Richard. On the other hand, the slightest allusion to the Beatles played havoc with Cliff's composure. From the mid-sixties he was an 'all-round family entertainer', wholesome and unthreatening, performing in cabaret, in pantomime* and on Saturday-evening television. Deep in his bones, he knew he was no longer 'with-it': 'The success of the Beatles and the Stones had shelved me and the Shadows. We were now the oldsters.' On Saturday, 6 April 1968, while John Lennon was staying with the Maharishi Mahesh Yogi in India, composing songs for *The White Album*, Cliff was bouncing his way through 'Congratulations' in the Eurovision Song Contest, dressed in a light-blue double-breasted suit with frothy white ruffles around the neck and wrists. When the final scores were totted up, it emerged that Cliff had come second to Spain's Massiel singing 'La La La'.

Though he was known for his pleasant, can-do persona and his Christianity, Cliff never quite managed to stifle his indignation towards the Beatles. On Sunday, 19 January 1969 he was singing hymns in an Edinburgh church and talking about his religious beliefs when he snapped, 'The Beatles are very successful artists, and yet they are not successful in life. The Beatles do nothing but chase around the world after a dream, and they must now realise that their Maharishi just

---

* I myself greatly enjoyed Cliff Richard's performance as Buttons in *Cinderella* at the London Palladium in 1966, with Terry Scott and Hugh Lloyd as the Ugly Sisters, Tudor Davies as Dandini, and Jack Douglas as Baron Hardup. The Brokers' Men were played by the Shadows. The speciality act was a baby elephant called 'The Adorable Tonya'. During this same period, the Beatles were recording 'Strawberry Fields Forever' and 'Penny Lane'.

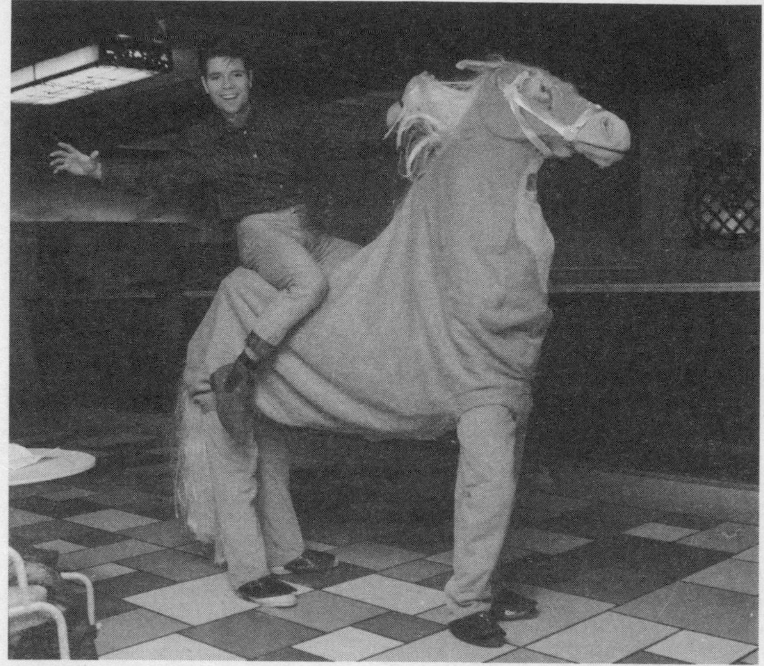

doesn't help them at all. I think they are looking for what Christians have found.'

Almost a quarter of a century later, Cliff could still be rattled by a mention of the Beatles. Interviewing him for *Q* magazine in 1992, Tom Hibbert* asked if he had ever felt jealousy towards them. The vehemence of his reply suggests he had never stopped brooding.

'There was a certain amount of jealousy. It was hurtful to be overlooked so dramatically by the media. But I still sold records by the million, so what the heck? And look at me now. The Beatles don't exist any more, and I was going five years before the Beatles, so no one's ever

* Tom Hibbert (1952–2011) wrote very funny interviews with, among many others, Robert Maxwell, Bernard Manning, Yoko Ono and Sir Jimmy Savile for *Smash Hits* and *Q* magazine. In his obituary of him in the *Guardian*, Mark Ellen wrote: 'Tom was unafraid of silence. He would give his subjects the impression that, despite their obvious successes, they were still somehow shameful underachievers, and then sit back quietly with a cigarette to enjoy the panicked response.'

going to catch me up. I'll always be ahead of everybody. I've just done my thousandth week in the chart and my nearest competitor hasn't reached five hundred weeks in the chart, which means that if that person is to catch me up, I would have to stop recording now and they'd have to have a record in the charts every week for the next five years. It's not possible. I'm well ahead … And another thing: when it came to rebellion, we were far more the rebellious crowd. The Beatles were accepted by royalty, they were accepted by all the high society. The Shadows and I never were. So we had one up on them.'

30

One day, it struck Ringo Starr that he would never be able to go back to being plain Ritchie Starkey.

He was with his family at his auntie's house in Liverpool, when some of Ringo's tea spilt into his saucer. He was shocked by what happened next.

'Everyone's reaction was, "He can't have that! We have to tidy up!"'

In the old days, he would have been left to clear up his own mess. But not any more. Now they were treating him differently, as though he were a superior outsider, and not one of them. It felt, he said, 'like an arrow in the brain': 'Suddenly I was "one of those", even within my family, and it was very difficult to get used to. I'd grown up and lived with these people and now I found myself in weirdland … Once we'd become big and famous, we soon learnt that people were with us only because of the vague notoriety of being a "Beatle". And when this happened in the family, it was quite a blow.'

There was no way back. Any complaint would serve only to reinforce their attitude. 'I couldn't stand up and say, "Treat me like you used to," because that would be acting big-time.'

31

'Please Please Me' is going down in the charts, crossing paths with 'From Me to You' on the way up. Meanwhile, the Beatles are appearing in a variety concert at the Royal Albert Hall, 'Swinging Sound '63', along with Del Shannon, Lance Percival, Rolf Harris, Shane Fenton and the Fentones, the Springfields and George Melly.

In an interval between rehearsals, they meet Jane Asher in the Green Room. At the age of sixteen, Jane is already something of a showbiz veteran: her first starring role was *Mandy* in 1952, and then she starred opposite Jack Warner as the Little Girl in Hammer Horror's *The Quatermass Xperiment*. Since then she has appeared in *Alice in Wonderland*, *The Prince and the Pauper*, *The Adventures of Robin Hood*. In the theatre, she was the youngest ever Wendy in *Peter Pan*. Recently she has become a household name as a regular panellist on TV's *Juke Box Jury*.

Jane is attending the variety concert on behalf of the *Radio Times*: a reporter and a photographer are there to record her reactions. The Beatles are in awe of her, perhaps Paul most of all: 'We had a photo taken with her and we all fancied her. We'd thought she was blonde, because we've only ever seen her on black-and-white telly doing *Juke Box Jury*, but she turned out to be a redhead. So it was: "Wow, you're a redhead."'

Their Royal Albert Hall concert proves to be a milestone, the first time an audience has screamed with quite such abandon. Later, fans climb on the roof of their car and block its way. The police eventually manage to clear a path, and the Beatles and their friends drive off, without really knowing where they are going. They usually end up at the Ad Lib Club, just off Leicester Square, but George, the shyest of the four, worries that hundreds of fans will already be on their way there. Accompanying them, the journalist Chris Hutchins suggests they all go to his place on the King's Road. He then immediately regrets it, wondering how the four Beatles, Shane Fenton* and Jane Asher will all be able to squeeze into the tiny bedsit, and where they will sit, given that there aren't enough chairs.

The problem is solved by everyone sitting on the carpet. But then another problem presents itself: John finds a bottle of amphetamines and starts swallowing them, washing them down with the Mateus rosé provided by Hutchins. Charged up, he becomes aggressive towards Jane. For John, thwarted sexual attraction can sometimes shrivel into spite. First, he talks about their adoring fans.

JOHN: Yeah, the group the fans love so much they want to tear us to pieces.

JANE: (laughing) Oh, John. You're such a cynic. Admit it, you adore the attention!

JOHN: Sure I'm a cynic. What we play is rock'n'roll under a new name. Rock music is war, hostility, conquest. We sing about love, but we mean sex, and the fans know it.

HUTCHINS: The fans think you're decent, clean-living chaps.

JOHN: It's just an image, and it's the wrong one. Look at the Rolling Stones. Rough as guts. We did that first and now they've pinched it.

RINGO: You can't blame them for that.

JANE: The fans have to dream that one day they might marry a Beatle.

JOHN: Yeah, but only those who haven't reached the age of puberty. I give some girl an autograph and she wants my tie or some hair. Then she wants to have sex. Then she tells me she's only fifteen. Jailbait. Is there any more booze?

* Born Bernard Jewry, he changed his name to Shane Fenton, and later to Alvin Stardust.

HUTCHINS: (pouring the last of the wine into John's empty glass) That's the last of it. I wasn't expecting company.

JOHN: OK, there's no more booze. Let's talk about sex. Jane, how do girls play with themselves?

JANE: (shocked but cool) I'm not going to talk about that!

JOHN: You're the only girl here and I want to know. How do you jerk off?

HUTCHINS: There's only one jerk here.

JOHN: Oh fab! No booze, no birds, insults from the host … what kind of rave is this? Bleedin' marvellous. I'm going in search of some crumpet. Call me a taxi.

JANE: (crying, comforted by George) You know, John, you can be very cruel sometimes.

JOHN: (standing at the front door) It's the beast in me.

Around this point, Paul ushers Jane out of the room, and away from John. They sit on a bed together, and chat about food and books. They get on to Chaucer's *Canterbury Tales*, which they were both taught at their respective schools. Off the cuff, Paul quotes from the 'General Prologue': 'Ful semly hir wympul pynched was.' Jane, a former pupil at the sophisticated Queen's College in Harley Street, seems much more impressed by this than by Paul's status as a pop idol, and Paul is equally impressed by her order of priorities. As the evening draws to a close, Paul volunteers to drop Jane home. Before they say goodbye, he has decided that this is the girl for him. On the doorstep of the Asher family home in Wimpole Street he asks for her phone number, and Jane happily gives it to him.

32

They became boyfriend and girlfriend, and Jane's parents gave Paul his own little bedroom on the top floor of 57 Wimpole Street, next to Jane's brother Peter's room. Paul was to live there, as part of the Asher family, for the next three years, his bedroom filling up with the fruits of his extraordinary career: eventually he was to stow his gold records under his bed, and his MBE on a shelf, alongside two drawings by Jean Cocteau. It was at Wimpole Street that Paul received a letter from the Beatles' accountant in 1965 informing him that, at the age of twenty-three, he had become a millionaire.

The Ashers were a remarkable family in every way: remarkably accomplished, remarkably civilised, remarkably welcoming. At the age of eight, Peter Asher had appeared opposite Claudette Colbert and Jack Hawkins in the film *The Planter's Wife*, and at ten, opposite Cecil Parker and Donald Wolfit in *Isn't Life Wonderful*. Jane's younger sister Claire had acted in the BBC's long-running radio soap opera *Mrs Dale's Diary*. Their mother Margaret was a professor at the Guildhall: back in 1948 she had tutored George Martin in the oboe.

Just like Paul fifteen years later, Martin had relished his visits to the Asher home, with all its comfort and erudition. Despite his upper-class persona (the legacy of wartime service with the RAF, during which 'we were taught important military details like how to hold a knife and fork correctly') he had been brought up in a three-room flat in Drayton Park with no kitchen, no bathroom and a toilet shared with three other families. Coming from such an impoverished background, he had been tantalised by the glimpse of a more agreeable life offered by the Ashers of Wimpole Street. And now, Paul, in his turn, was to be tantalised. Everything seemed touched by culture. In the hall of no. 57 hung an engraved portrait of Alfred, Lord Tennyson, a distant relative of Margaret Asher; the glass-fronted bookcase in the dining room contained a rare 1926 first edition of *Seven Pillars of Wisdom*, brought into the family by Margaret's father, the Hon. Edward Granville Eliot, who had been Lawrence of Arabia's solicitor.

Jane's father, Dr Richard Asher, was a pioneering endocrinologist who in 1951 had named and identified Munchausen's Syndrome, the mental disorder that drives individuals to fabricate symptoms of illness. He was also a skilled and witty writer: an article by him in the *Lancet* in February 1951 begins: 'Here is described a common syndrome which most doctors have seen, but about which little has been written. Like the famous Baron von Munchausen, the persons affected have always travelled widely; and their stories, like those attributed to him, are both dramatic and untruthful. Accordingly, the syndrome is respectfully dedicated to the Baron, and named after him.' Inevitably, the title 'Munchausen's Syndrome' was criticised by the po-faced for being inappropriately light-hearted.

Dr Asher's articles in the *British Medical Journal* remain a joy to read – funny, alert, aphoristic, self-deprecatory, sparklingly clear – and they indicate the breadth of education Paul would have received in his conversations with him. In 'The Dangers of Going to Bed', Asher argues against the medical consensus that staying in bed was the surest route to recovery: 'Look at a patient lying long in bed. What a pathetic picture he makes! The blood clotting in his veins, the lime draining from his bones, the scybala stacking up in his colon, the flesh rotting from his seat, the urine leaking from his distended bladder, and the spirit evaporating from his soul.' He then undercuts himself by saying, 'I have painted a gloomy and unfair picture: it is not as bad as all that.' Later in the same article, he speculated as to the reasons why confinement caught on: 'Too often a sister puts all her patients back to bed as a housewife puts all her plates back in the plate-rack – to make a generally tidy appearance.'

Another of his articles in the *BMJ*, carrying the incendiary title 'Why are Medical Journals so Dull?', argues against stodginess and obscurity in favour of lucidity and precision: 'A poor title dulls the clinical appetite, whereas a good title whets it. I have called this article "Why are Medical Journals so Dull?". I do not claim this title is specially good, but it is better than "A Study of the Negativistic Psychomotor Reactions induced by Perusal of Verbalized Clinical Material".'

It's easy to see how Paul would have revelled in such cheery cut-and-thrust. The whole Asher family involved themselves in discussions around the table, alive with erudition and curiosity and fun. 'They would do things that I'd never seen before, like at dinner there would be word games,' Paul told Barry Miles. 'Now, I'm bright enough, but mine is an intuitive brightness. I could just about keep up with that, and I could always say, "I don't know that word."' He remembered an argument over dinner between Dr Asher and his son Peter, Paul's contemporary, over when the tomato was first introduced to England. This was not the sort of topic they discussed in Forthlin Road. Throughout his years with the Ashers, Paul was treated not as a pop star, but as one of the family: 'It was very good for me, because in their eyes I wasn't just the Beatle.' The atmosphere at Wimpole Street also appealed to his competitive spirit: 'I often felt the guys were sort of partying, whereas I was learning a lot; learning an awful lot.' In her music room in the basement, Margaret Asher taught Paul how to play the recorder – he plays it on 'Fool on the Hill' – though her attempts to teach him how to read music were soon abandoned.

His intellectual curiosity was stimulated. 'I don't want to sound like Jonathan Miller going on, but I'm trying to cram everything in, all the things I've missed,' he told the journalist Maureen Cleave in 1966. 'People are saying things and painting things that are great, and I must know what people are doing … I vaguely mind people knowing anything I don't know.' He read Jung and Huxley, watched plays by Alfred Jarry and Harold Pinter and listened to avant-garde composers like Stockhausen and Luciano Berio.

Sometimes Jane would take Paul to stay with family friends out of town. 'This was another rather upper-class thing: going for the week-end to the country … It was the first time I'd seen people leaving a book by your bedside for you to read. I was quite impressed by their choice of books. It was the assumption that you were reasonably intelligent that I liked. They didn't talk down.'

Inevitably, Beatles fans would linger outside the house, ready to pounce. While Paul was away filming *Help!*, Jane's father set himself the task of plotting an escape route for him. He climbed out of a back window and scaled his way along to the house next door, then tapped on a window to explain Paul's peculiar problem to the occupier of the neighbouring flat. On Paul's return to London, Dr Asher was thus able to present him with a secret route through to New Cavendish Street. 'I used to go out of the window of my garret bedroom, onto a little parapet. You had to be pretty careful, it wasn't that wide, it was only a foot or so, so you had to have something of a head for heights. You'd go along to the right, which was to the next house in Wimpole Street, number 56, and there was a colonel living there, an old ex-army gentleman. He had this little top-floor flat, and he was very charming. "Uh! Coming through, Colonel!" "Oh, oh, OK, hush-hush and all that!" and

he'd see me into the lift and I'd go right downstairs to the basement of that house. There was a young couple living down there and they'd see me out through the kitchen and into the garage.'

If I could be any Beatle, at any time, I would be Paul in his Wimpole Street years, living with Jane, cosseted by her family, blessed by luck, happy with life, alive to culture, adored by the world, and with wonderful songs flowing, as if by magic, from my brain and out through the piano: 'I Want to Hold Your Hand', 'I'm Looking Through You', 'The Things We Said Today', 'And I Love Her', 'We Can Work it Out', 'Here, There and Everywhere', 'Yesterday'.

But nothing lasts. On Christmas Day 1967, Paul and Jane announced their engagement; seven months later, in reply to a chance question from the TV chat-show host Simon Dee, Jane announced that it was all over: 'I haven't broken it off, but it is broken off, finished. I know it sounds corny, but we still see each other and love each other, but it hasn't worked out. Perhaps we'll be childhood sweethearts and meet again when we're about seventy.'

Over fifty years on, they both remain discreet about the break-up, speaking about it in nothing but the most general terms, leaving others to speculate. Some suggest Jane caught Paul in bed with an American woman called Francie Schwartz.* While Jane was away acting, Paul and Francie had been together in his new house in St John's Wood. 'There were fans waiting at the gate as usual and they tried to warn Paul that Jane was approaching. But Paul thought they were joking,' recalled Alistair Taylor. According to Taylor, Jane broke up with Paul, rather than vice-versa, and refused to take him back. Though Paul, a master of self-possession, has said 'I don't remember the break-up as traumatic really,' and 'I got cold feet,' elsewhere he has admitted, 'It was shattering to be without her.' Others remember the shock he suffered. Taylor, who thought Jane 'the most adorable woman you could expect to meet', recalled Paul being 'absolutely devastated … he went completely off the rails. "I had everything and I threw it away," he would say.' His hairdresser, Leslie Cavendish, noted that 'he seemed

* Who later wrote a kiss-and-tell book called *Body Count*.

heartbroken to me. He'd stopped shaving his beard, hardly ever left the house and began taking more drugs.'

One or two of their acquaintances claim to have seen it coming. Marianne Faithfull never felt they were a natural fit: 'I always thought Jane and Paul were very tense. I do remember very clearly an evening at Cavendish Avenue where she wanted the window shut and he wanted the window open. That really was like a Joe Orton play. It was fucking great. I sat there all night watching Jane get up and close it, and Paul open it and … nothing was said. And quite soon after they split up, which of course I could have told anyone they would.' But she fails to offer a reason why Jane would have wanted the window open. Might it have been to release the fumes of marijuana that were the necessary accompaniment to any visit by Mick and Marianne?

33

Before going onstage at the Majestic Ballroom, Newcastle upon Tyne, John and Paul seized the time to write a song.

On 26 June 1963 the two of them were sharing a twin-bedded room at the Royal Turk's Head Hotel.* Paul reached for his cigarettes. 'We must have had a few hours before the show, so we said, "Oh, great! Let's have a ciggy and write a song!"'

The lyrics of their previous singles – 'Love Me Do', 'Please Please Me', 'From Me to You', 'I Saw Her Standing There' – all revolved around a single person, but Paul now resolved to do something different.

'It was Paul's idea,' recalled John. 'Instead of singing "I love you", we'd have a third party.' This signalled the way their different approaches to songwriting were to develop: Paul's towards a third-person narrative, rather like a miniature short story, and John's more autobiographical.

> You think you've lost your love
> Well I saw her yesterday-ay

One young man is talking to another about a girl who may or may not have left him. The two men are, consciously or unconsciously, versions of the two composers – Paul optimistic, self-confident, never short of advice, and John, primed to cause hurt – 'she said you hurt her so' – while in retreat from his own sense of guilt. Like so many subsequent Lennon/McCartney songs, its energy comes from this intermingling of the dark and the sunny.

---

* Later renamed the Rainbow.

The Beatles had the next day free, so John and Paul went back to Liverpool. This gave them the chance to complete their new song in Forthlin Road, while Paul's dad Jim sat in the next room, smoking and watching television.

At this stage John and Paul were both magpies, lifting whatever took their fancy from other people's songs: the 'woo woo' came from the Isley Brothers' 'Twist and Shout'. John, in particular, was fond of these whoops and hollers, noises below or beyond words: when he heard Elvis Presley singing 'All Shook Up', his first thought was that he had never heard 'uh huh', 'oh yeah' and 'yeah, yeah' all in the same song before.

After a while, the two of them burst into the living room. 'Dad, listen to this. What do you think?' Then they sang him their new song: 'She Loves You'.

'That's very nice, son,' said Jim, one of the old school. 'But there's enough of these Americanisms around. Couldn't you sing, "She loves you, yes, yes, yes"?' John and Paul failed to take this advice seriously. 'We collapsed in a heap and said, "No, Dad, you don't quite get it."'

Four days later, the Beatles went to the EMI studios in Abbey Road to record their new song. They arrived early, in order to pose for a new set of pictures in the alleyway behind the studio. By now, wherever they went they were attracting fans. One thing led to another: the fans who were already waiting outside telephoned their friends to tip them off, and those friends told more friends, and so forth. Before long, this mass of girls somehow managed to break through the front door and to rush around the building in search of their idols. 'It's a bloody madhouse out there,' said Neil Aspinall as he entered the studio.

Meanwhile, placing the song sheets on the music stands, the EMI recording engineer Norman Smith* glanced at the lyrics. 'I thought, "I'll just have a quick look. 'She loves you, yeah, yeah, yeah; She loves

---

* While working at EMI, Norman Smith (1923–2008) produced Pink Floyd's 'See Emily Play', as well as their first four albums. He later became briefly famous as the gravelly-voiced Hurricane Smith, whose single 'Don't Let it Die' reached number 2 in the charts in 1971.

you, yeah, yeah, yeah; She loves you, yeah, yeah, yeah."' I thought, "Oh my God, what a lyric. This is going to be one that I do not like."'

George Martin, calm as ever, ran John and Paul through their new song, with George Harrison joining in on the choruses. 'I thought it was great, but was intrigued by the final chord, an odd sort of major sixth, with George doing the sixth and John and Paul the third and fifths, like a Glenn Miller arrangement. They were saying, "It's a great chord! Nobody's ever heard it before!" Of course, that wasn't quite true.'

In fact, much of John and Paul's early inventiveness as songwriters sprang from a kind of blissful ignorance. Neither could read music, or had ever had formal lessons. This meant they tended to come across chords by chance. Their early songs reflect the innocent wonder with which they chanced upon the source of all music, as if for the very first time.

With the marauding fans dispersed from the building, the recording session could begin. It occurred to recording engineer Geoff Emerick that the excitement generated by the invading fans helped to spark a new level of energy and invention in the band's playing, not least from Ringo and George. Hearing the song performed, Norman Smith, having been sceptical, immediately got the point of it: 'When they started to sing it – bang, wow, terrific. I was up at the mixer jogging around.'

Emerick, too, was enthralled: 'There was a level of intensity in that performance that I had not heard before and have rarely heard since. I still judge that single to be one of the most exciting performances of the Beatles' entire career.'

'She Loves You' was released on 23 August 1963. Within a month it had sold three quarters of a million copies in Britain, making it the fastest-selling record ever. It was to remain in the top three for eighteen weeks, and in the charts for thirty-one weeks. For many, fans and foes alike, it remains the quintessential Beatles song. The words to which Jim McCartney had objected – Yeah! Yeah! Yeah! – have become emblematic of the Beatles phenomenon: either callow and inarticulate, or fresh and liberating, depending on your outlook. In Europe, the Beatles were commonly referred to as 'the Yeah-Yeahs'.

For conservatives who preferred the world to stay the same, 'She Loves You' acted as an alarm call; for Marxists, it symbolised Western decadence. 'Is it truly the case that we have to copy all the dirt that comes from the West?' asked the East German leader Walter Ulbricht in a speech to his party. 'I think, Comrades, with the monotony of the yeah yeah yeah or whatever it is called we should make a stop.'

For once, America was slow to pick up on a new trend. Released in the States on 16 September, 'She Loves You' sold barely a thousand copies in its first few weeks, and failed to hit the charts. At the cutting-edge Café Wha? in Greenwich Village, the hard-boiled folk singer Steve De Naut first heard it in October. His then girlfriend, Vicky Tiel, remembers him marching into her apartment and – 'Listen to this, baby' – placing it on the record player. 'Steve and I started to make love. At the point where it changes beats, he stopped in the middle of having sex. "Listen to this!" he said. The music went down to another beat. He said, "Nobody fucking *does* that! That's *no*! And the 'yeah, yeah, yeah'? That's fucking *no*! Nobody *does* that!"'

Vicky couldn't understand what Steve was getting at. 'It's a new type of music,' he explained. 'I've never heard anything like it. And it's fantastic.' He then added, more despondently: 'I'm finished. It's over. It's over for all of us.'

34

John Lennon and Ringo Starr were born in 1940, when the words *blitz*, *paratroops*, *call-up* and *quisling* came into being, as well as the verb *to scramble* in its new meaning of 'to make a speedy take-off'.

Other neologisms of 1940 heralded a bold new unstuffy age of American goods and trends: *beefburger*, *crew-cut*, *holiday camp*, *mobile home*, *nylons*, *telly*, *super-duper*, *youth club*. Many were born of inventions: *jeep*, *plutonium*, *radar*. Some, like *telly*, were chummy abbreviations for recent inventions now so widespread that they felt like old friends. Others, like *extra-sensory perception*, emerged from a closer study of what had always been there, or – viewed from another angle – what had always been not there.

The following year, 1941, the term *welfare state* was coined, as were *disc jockey*, *boogie*, *cheesed-off*, *Terylene*, *sunbathe*, *straight*, in its meaning of 'conformist', and *knockers* meaning breasts. It was also in this year – the year between the births of John and Paul – that the word *teenager* made its first appearance.

Paul McCartney was born in 1942, when *spaceman*, *office block*, *napalm* and *sixty-four-dollar question* first appeared, along with the abbreviations *PR* and *preggers*. George, the youngest Beatle, was born in 1943, when *bobby socks*, *disposable*, *paper towel*, *pizzeria*, *double glazing* and *falsies* were coined. *Squarebashing* also made its debut that year, and, perhaps as a sort of cosmic counterbalance, so did *group therapy* and *free expression*. In England, Barnes Wallis invented the *bouncing bomb*, and in Switzerland, Dr Albert Hofmann combined Lysergic Acid with Diethylamine to create *Lysergic Acid Diethylamide*, later to become known as *LSD*.

Most people date the origin of the Beatles to 1957, when the fifteen-year-old Paul introduced himself to the sixteen-year-old John. Many of that year's new words and expressions were centred around youth: *Frisbee, skiffle, sexpot, scooter, pop art, bonkers, backlash, Hell's Angel, flick knife, diminished responsibility, consenting adult, role model, angry young man*. A long-playing record began to be known as an *album*. In the USA, female traffic wardens were nicknamed *meter maids*. The adjective *fab*, an abbreviation of fabulous, was first heard that year, though it wasn't to become widespread until 1963, more often than not preceding the number four.

It was also in 1963 that another word associated with the Fab Four came into being. On 5 October 1963 a young concert promoter called Andi Lothian was in Glasgow's Carnegie Hall when onto the stage came the young group he had booked. For him, the audience reaction called to mind the relief of Mafeking: 'absolute pandemonium. Girls fainting, screaming, wet seats. The whole hall went into some kind of state, almost like collective hypnotism.' Amidst the mayhem, a startled reporter from Radio Scotland yelled, 'For God's sake, Andi, what's happening?' From out of nowhere, a new word popped into his head. 'Don't worry,' he yelled back, 'It's only … *Beatlemania*!'

35

Towards the end of 1963, the sanity of the younger generation was being called into question. 'Many young people these days complain that adults tend to condemn them,' wrote one irate newspaper reader. 'But when one sees the disgusting behaviour now occurring up and down the country under the name of "Beatlemania" it is impossible not to draw certain conclusions.'

A columnist in York's *Evening Press* echoed this sentiment: 'Ask any teenager in York and they could name the four Beatles. Now ask those same teenagers for the names of a few other well-known personalities. The Secretary General of the United Nations, for example, or even our own Prime Minister. The answers, in many cases, will not slip so easily off the tongue. Such is fame. Such is our sense of values in the modern world.' That same columnist, the aptly-named John Blunt, decried 'the howling, screaming, bustling, shoving, fighting mobs which collect whenever they make an appearance'.

Throughout the Beatles' tour of the UK, reporters struggled to describe the sound of thousands of adolescents screaming at the top of their voices. 'I have not attended the mass torture or execution of 5000 assorted farmyard animals,' wrote the *Newcastle Journal*'s reporter Rodney Pybus. 'But I imagine the noise they would make would be very similar to that which forced my fingertips deep into my ears.' Other newspapers roped in tame psychologists to dig deeper in the hope of uncovering the source of this mayhem. 'This is not really hysteria. Hysteria is pathological. It is a disease,' concluded Professor John Cohen, the head of the Psychology Department at Manchester University. To the central question – why do the girls scream? – he drew a blank: 'You might as well ask a flock of geese why they fly and flap their wings.' At the Beatles' concert in the Southend Odeon on 9 December, a policeman armed with a noise meter recorded the screaming at 110 decibels, the equal of a sustained artillery barrage.

The American journalist Michael Braun accompanied the Beatles to the Cambridge Regal on 26 November. At that same venue the previous March the group had supported 'America's Exciting' Chris Montez and 'America's Fabulous' Tommy Roe. But now it was they who were being supported by others. Fans had been queuing in the streets outside the Regal since 10.30 a.m. By 6 p.m. the line was already half a mile long. Hours before the show, the Beatles had met the police at an agreed spot a mile away, to be smuggled into the theatre in the back of a police van.

When I was a child, whenever we went to the cinema in Dorking, or the pantomime in Leatherhead, 'God Save the Queen' would be played before and after each show. As if by magic, the audience would rise from their seats and stand to attention until the patriotic strains were finally exhausted. When the National Anthem was played at the start of the Beatles' Cambridge show, Michael Braun witnessed not a hint of rebellion. But then again, there were plenty of unscream-at-able support acts to get through before the Beatles were due on, among them Peter Jay and the Jaywalkers, the Vernon Girls and the Brook Brothers. But the second the Beatles were announced the audience burst into high-pitched screams that continued right up to the strumming of the final chord of 'Twist and Shout'. 'Some girls are now waving handkerchiefs,' wrote Braun. 'Others are sitting in a foetal position: back arched, legs folded under, and hands alternately punching their thighs and covering their ears. Most of the boys just keep their hands over their ears.'

Braun watched a girl in an aisle seat crying every time the lights went up and down. At the end, after 'Twist and Shout', she stood on her seat screaming and crying until the National Anthem began to play over the house speakers. At that moment, in common with all the other girls, she stopped screaming and stood stock-still. But the second it drew to a close – Gar-aar-ard Say-aay-aayve the Quee-eee-eeen! – they all started screaming again.*

This peculiar pattern was repeated throughout the Beatles' tour of Britain. Stewards at these shows tended to be middle-aged and hard-done-by, temperamentally ill-suited to extracting enjoyment from youthful exuberance. At the show in Leicester's De Montfort Hall on 1 December, police and stewards were supplied with cotton wool to protect their ears. The fifty-nine-year-old Ray Millward complained that he had been kicked and punched by a delirious female fan: 'We used to get a lot of hysteria with Cliff Richard, but this beats everything. I had a shoe and an umbrella thrown at me. One girl fought like a wildcat. I had to force her arm behind her back to get her to sit down. She was scratching, kicking and screaming.' Jelly babies – which, in an offhand moment, the Beatles had said they enjoyed – were now being hurled at them from every corner, even though the group had publicly protested that they would prefer it if they weren't. Misunderstanding them, some girls started throwing full boxes of chocolates instead. Autograph books, a doll and a giant panda were also hurled. Despite this pandemonium, the fans still stood stock-still for the National Anthem, a godsend from the Beatles' point of view, as it gave them plenty of time to make a speedy getaway through the stage door to their waiting Austin Princess. Meanwhile their fans remained inside, rooted to the spot out of respect for Her Majesty.

That November, as the Queen Mother, Princess Margaret and Lord Snowdon arrived at the Prince of Wales theatre for the Royal Command Performance, they were greeted by crowds chanting 'We Want the Beatles!' At that moment, it must have dawned on them that, like so many other long-established groups that year, they too had just been downgraded to a support act.

---

* While writing this book, I have had nights when I have been kept awake as this or that Beatles song played over and over again in my brain. When it has been some particularly repetitive song – 'Yellow Submarine', say, or 'All Together Now' – I found that singing an opposing 'God Save the Queen' in some other part of my head proved the only way to drown it out. The trouble with this method, though, is that you are left with a song even more annoying than those it has replaced.

Taking his seat in the audience, Brian Epstein was nervous. Could he trust John to behave? The day before, John had worked out a cheeky joke for introducing their final song, 'Twist and Shout': 'For our last number, I'd like to ask your help. Would the people in the cheaper seats clap your hands. And the rest of you, if you'd just rattle your jewellery.' It was already slightly edgy, but in the dress rehearsal John had made it a good deal edgier by saying 'rattle your *fucking* jewellery'. To Epstein's relief, when the big moment came John omitted the expletive, and even added a chummy thumbs-up to show it was only a joke. In their black ties and evening dresses, the audience burst into laughter and applause.

After the show, the Beatles were presented to the Queen Mother. Or – given society's new priorities – was it the Queen Mother who was presented to the Beatles? She had, she said, very much enjoyed herself. And where would they be performing next? Slough, came the answer. 'Oh, that's near us,' she replied.

The next day's newspapers were full of the Beatles. Devoting an editorial to their triumph, the working-class *Daily Mirror* welcomed the revolution:

> Fact is that Beatle People are everywhere. From Wapping to Windsor. Aged seven to seventy. And it's plain to see why these four cheeky, energetic lads from Liverpool go down so big.
>
> They're young, new. They're high-spirited, cheerful. What a change from the self-pitying moaners, crooning their lovelorn tunes from the tortured shallows of lukewarm hearts.
>
> The Beatles are whacky. They wear their hair like a mop – but it's WASHED, it's super clean. So is their fresh young act. They don't have to rely on off-colour jokes about homos for their fun …
>
> Youngsters like the Beatles are doing a good turn for show business – and the rest of us – with their new sounds, new looks.
>
> *Good luck Beatles!*

On perpetual guard against the new and unseemly, the *Daily Telegraph* condemned the delirium. 'This hysteria presumably fills heads and hearts otherwise empty,' argued the author of an anonymous editorial. 'Is there not something a bit frightening in whole masses of young people, all apparently so suggestible, so volatile and rudderless? What material here for a maniac's shaping! Hitler would have disapproved, but he could have seen what in other circumstances might be made of it.'

On their return to Leicester a year later, in October 1964, the Beatles attempted to execute their usual trick, rushing offstage and into their car while the National Anthem was playing. But in that brief period, the mores of society had changed: this time, a group of sixty or seventy fans failed to stand to attention, preferring to run out of the theatre and swarm around the Beatles in their car, hammering on the roof and windows. Discombobulated, the driver lost his nerve and careered into another car, but still the fans hammered away, forcing the Beatles to wait for the police to come and free them.

36

The sudden arrival of the Beatles came as a shock to many in the old guard of showbusiness.

Marlene Dietrich, star of *The Blue Angel* (1930) and *Blonde Venus* (1932), was sixty-one years old when she agreed to appear in the 1963 Royal Variety Performance. Her international stature seemed to guarantee her the role of star of the evening.

In July 1963 the impresario Bernard Delfont was asked by his sixteen-year-old daughter Susan to book the Beatles for the show. Delfont was nonplussed: 'I had never heard of them … when I asked what they did, she said they were somehow – well, you know – different.'

Soon afterwards, he heard that someone in his organisation had booked them for a Sunday performance at the Princess Theatre, Torquay. He immediately phoned the theatre manager.

> 'How's business?' I asked the manager.
>
> 'We've sold out,' he said. 'There are fans sleeping on the street, waiting for returns.'
>
> That was good enough for me. I made the booking.

By November, the Beatles' fame had eclipsed Dietrich's. As the big day drew closer, Delfont noticed how much this upset Dietrich, who felt that all the kudos should be hers. 'I anticipated a clash of temperament, but I should have known that Miss Dietrich would not stoop to a vulgar brawl,' he recalled. 'Instead, she fought back with all the subtle ruthlessness of Lady Macbeth.'

During rehearsals, Delfont's sister Rita noticed Dietrich behaving 'petulantly and selfishly', hogging more than her fair share of the time available. When she had finished, all the photographers swept down to the front of the stalls. 'Not now, darling!' she ordered. 'Come back in an hour when I've got my make-up on!' It had simply not occurred to her that they were there for the Beatles.

The cameras flashed away as the Beatles rehearsed for their allotted period. 'By the time Marlene returned, now resplendent in a sequined gown and wearing full make-up, there wasn't a photographer in sight,' recalled Rita Delfont.

The photographers returned for photocalls just before the show. Once again, the Beatles were the centre of attention, but each time they struck a new pose Dietrich would miraculously appear, elbowing her way into the frame. 'The boys, who were still a little unsure of themselves, accepted the intrusion as a compliment. Not so the production team, who recognised scene-stealing when they saw it.'

Nevertheless, she made quite an impression on Ringo: 'I remember

staring at her legs, which were great, as she slouched against a chair. I'm a leg-man. "Look at those pins!'"

Dietrich herself finally warmed to the group. 'They are so SEXY!' she remarked to Brian Epstein after the curtain went down. 'It was a joy to be with them. I adore these Beatles. They have the girls so frantic for them. They must have quite a time!'

Four years later, the Beatles repaid the compliment by placing Marlene Dietrich among the chosen few on the cover of *Sgt. Pepper*.

37

In the basement of the Ashers' house in Wimpole Street was a little room where Margaret Asher would teach her pupils how to play the oboe. It contained a sofa, an upright piano and a music stand. When Margaret wasn't in need of the room she let Paul use it to write his pop songs.

One day in mid-October 1963 John dropped by. The two of them went down to the little room in the basement and sat together on Mrs Asher's piano stool. Brian Epstein had told them that their next, most important task was to compose a song to crack the elusive American market. Up to now, their hit singles in Britain – 'From Me to You', 'She Loves You', 'Please Please Me' – had all flopped over there.

Doodling about, they came up with the line 'Oh, you-ou-ou got that something'. Paul hit a chord to accompany it. 'That's it!' said John. 'Do that again!'

After an hour or so, Paul went upstairs and put his head around the door of Peter Asher's bedroom. 'Do you want to come and hear something we've just written?' he asked. Peter accompanied him back downstairs, and together Paul and John played him their new song, 'I Want to Hold Your Hand'.

'What do you think?' asked Paul.

'Oh, my God! Can you play that again?' said Peter. As he listened to it for a second time, he thought: 'Am I losing my mind, or is this the greatest song I ever heard in my life?'

* * *

A day or two later, John and Paul took 'I Want to Hold Your Hand' along to the Abbey Road studios. They were speedy workers: in the same session they recorded 'I Want to Hold Your Hand', its B-side, 'This Boy', their first Christmas message for their fan club, and half of 'You Really Got a Hold on Me'. As if this were not enough, Paul left halfway through to go out to lunch with a girl who had won first prize in a 'Why I Like the Beatles' essay competition.

These were busy days. Over the next three weeks they packed in an appearance on *Thank Your Lucky Stars*, a tour of Scandinavia, the Royal Command Performance ('rattle yer jewellery'), concerts in Cheltenham, Sheffield, Slough, Leeds and Northampton, and a trip to Dublin.

On 9 November they were driven in their Austin Princess to East Ham, where the crowds outside the Granada cinema were so wild that even the Beatles' food had its own police escort.

Before they went onstage, George Martin put his head round the door and called for silence.

'Listen, everybody, I've got something important to tell you all. I have just heard the news from EMI that the advance sales of "I Want to Hold Your Hand" have topped a million.'

Everyone cheered. 'Yeah, great,' said John, never slow to spot the cloud blocking a silver lining. 'But that means it'll only be at number 1 for about a week.'

'I Want to Hold Your Hand' was released in Britain on 29 November 1963, little more than six weeks after John and Paul had composed it in an hour in Margaret Asher's basement room. Two weeks later it reached number 1, knocking 'She Loves You' down to number 2. Contrary to John's prediction, it was to remain at number 1 for another four weeks, and was in the charts until the end of April, by which time their follow-up single, 'Can't Buy Me Love', had already topped the charts for three weeks.*

---

* 'Can't Buy Me Love' surrendered its number 1 slot to another Lennon/McCartney composition, 'World Without Love', sung by Peter Asher and his friend Gordon Waller, jointly known as Peter and Gordon.

'I Want to Hold Your Hand' was not released in America for another month, and then only after a notably random chain of events. A Washington disc jockey had been given a British copy by an air hostess, and played it over and over again on his show, prompting top-forty stations in Chicago and St Louis to follow suit. At this point, Capitol Records recognised its potential, and released it as a single on Boxing Day 1963. Within a week it had reached number 43 in the US charts; it seemed likely to climb higher.

38

At three in the morning on 17 January 1964, the Beatles were in their palatial suite at the George V Hotel in Paris, having just played the first of a series of concerts at the Olympia Theatre. As they sat around in their pyjamas and dressing gowns, Brian Epstein came in, clutching a telegram.

'Boys,' he said, 'you're number 1 in America!' For once, even John was thrilled. Their road manager, Mal Evans, witnessed their elation. To him they were 'just a bunch of kids, jumping up and down with sheer delight'.

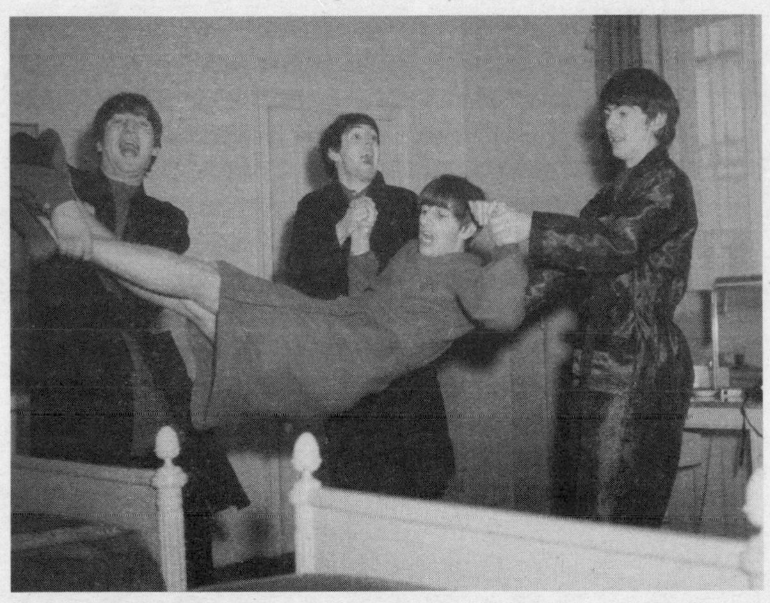

Ringo was cock-a-hoop: 'We couldn't believe it. We all started acting like people from Texas, hollering and shouting Ya-hoo.' Paul climbed onto Mal's shoulders and demanded a piggyback ride. There to cover their tour, the photographer Harry Benson suggested they stage a celebratory pillow-fight. 'That's the stupidest thing I've ever heard,' said John. A second later he picked up a pillow and whacked Paul on the back of the head, and then all four of them leapt onto the vast Empire bed and started walloping one another with pillows. In their pyjamas and dressing gowns, they continued their merry japes, picking Ringo up and – 'One, two, three, four!' – throwing him into the air. Would they ever again be so deliriously happy?

39

It had all happened so fast. Exactly a year before, on 17 January 1963, they had been playing the Cavern and the Majestic Ballroom, Birkenhead. A year before that, on 1 January 1962, they had been turned down by Dick Rowe of Decca Records, on the grounds that 'groups of guitars are on their way out'.

And now they had cracked America. In the first three days of its US release, 'I Want to Hold Your Hand' sold a quarter of a million copies. It went on to sell five million.

The poet Allen Ginsberg was in the Dom, a 'hip hangout' in New York's East Village, when he first heard the song: 'I heard that high, yodelling alto sound of the OOOH that went right through my skull, and I realised it was going to go through the skull of Western civilisation.' To the amazement of his fellow intellectuals, the portly Ginsberg got up and danced around.

When Brian Wilson of the Beach Boys heard it, 'I flipped. It was like a shock went through my system.' The current Beach Boys single, 'Be True to Your School', had the chorus:

> Be true to your school now
> Just like you would to your girl or guy
> Be true to your school now
> And let your colors fly.

In that instant, Wilson realised that the Beatles had rendered him antique. He was two days younger than Paul, but now felt like an old-timer: 'I immediately knew that everything had changed.'

For the past six months the Beach Boys had been the most popular group in America. But from now on they would be obliged to live in the shadow of the Beatles. To make matters worse, the Beatles were signed to Capitol, the same label as the Beach Boys. The very same executives who had been giving the Beach Boys all their attention now couldn't stop talking about the Fab Four. 'The Beach Boys had been it for two years, but now people thought the Beatles were the future. And loyalties ran thin at Capitol,' recalled their promoter, Fred Vail.

The following April they recorded 'Don't Back Down'. Unlike their other songs, it had an air of doom about it: 'The girls dig the way the guys get all wiped out … When a twenty-footer sneaks up like a ton of lead'. It was to be the Beach Boys' very last surfing song.

In Freehold, New Jersey, a fourteen-year-old boy was sitting in the front seat of his mother's car when the song came on the radio. He felt time stop, and his hair standing on end. 'Some strange and voodoolike effect' took hold of him, 'the radio burning brighter before my eyes as it strained to contain the sound'. They reached home, but he didn't go in. Instead, he ran straight to the bowling alley on Main Street, rushed to the phone booth and called his girlfriend Jan.

'Have you heard the Beatles?' he asked.

'Yeah, they're cool,' she replied. He then rushed to Newbury's, a store with a minimal record section. 'I Want to Hold Your Hand' wasn't in stock, so instead he bought a single called 'My Bonnie', apparently by 'The Beatles with Tony Sheridan and Guests'. 'It was a rip-off. The Beatles backing some singer I'd never heard of … I bought it. And listened to it. It wasn't great but it was as close as I could get.'

He instantly set his heart on a guitar displayed in the window of the West Auto store on Main Street. When the summer came, his Aunt Dora paid him to paint her house, and he bought the guitar with the money he earned: 'That summer, time moved slowly.' He lived for every release by the Beatles. 'I searched the newsstands for every magazine with a photo I hadn't seen and I dreamed … dreamed … dreamed … that it was me … I didn't want to *meet* the Beatles. I wanted to *be* the Beatles.'

Over half a century on, Bruce Springsteen still believes that hearing 'I Want to Hold Your Hand' that day in his mother's car changed the course of his life.

In Chicago, the ten-year-old Ruby Wax was standing in a record shop when the B-side of 'I Want to Hold Your Hand' came blasting out.

'Over the speakers the Beatles were singing "Well, she was just seventeen", and all of my organs lit up into red alert. This was the most exciting sound I had ever heard – it was a Big Moment. No one man since then has ever switched the "on" button like they did.'

Over the next few weeks, Ruby plastered her bedroom wall with Beatles posters, which she then ritually licked. She collected Beatles magazines, pens, records, sunglasses, clocks, socks and stickers. 'I would turn up the sound of my Beatles records to eardrum-shattering levels and weep and moan and scream out my love.' She would even call the telephone operator in Liverpool just to hear her say 'Hello' in a Scouse accent. 'Then I'd become so overwhelmed I'd have to hang up.'

Serving a ten-year sentence in McNeil Island Corrections Center, Washington State, the petty criminal Charlie Manson kept hearing 'I Want to Hold Your Hand' playing on the radios circulating among the inmates.

According to his biographer, Manson was impressed by the music, but far more impressed by the adulation the Beatles were receiving: 'Charlie always yearned for attention; now he decided that fame was what he really wanted. If these four Beatles could have it, why couldn't he? … Charlie started telling anyone willing to listen and also those who weren't that he was going to be bigger than the Beatles.'

From that point on, Manson spent his time in McNeil hunched over a guitar. Whenever his mother Kathleen came visiting he would tell her, with an almost manic insistence, that one day soon he too would be famous.

40

In January 1964 the Ronettes came to London to headline their first British tour, supported by a local group, the Rolling Stones.

On their first night a party was thrown for them by the Radio Luxembourg disc jockey Tony Hall at his home in Green Street, Mayfair, just down the road from where George and Ringo were living.

John, George and Ringo were already there when the Ronettes came in. The Ronettes were aware of the fame of the Beatles – since their arrival they had heard of little else – but had still not heard their music. For their part, the three Beatles were mustard-keen on the Ronettes, with their lusty, yearning voices and shapely bodies.

As the Ronettes entered, John, George and Ringo made a beeline for them, and showered them with praise. 'You've got the greatest voice,' George told Ronnie Bennett, the lead singer. 'We loved it the first time we heard you.' Generally thrifty with his compliments, John was similarly effusive. 'Fuckin' great,' he said.

'They kept telling us how much they loved our long black hair, and how our whole look blew them away,' remembered Ronnie. 'And we weren't exactly having a bad time ourselves.'

They all started dancing to records by the Ronettes – 'Be My Baby', 'Baby, I Love You', 'I Saw Mommy Kissing Santa Claus'. Over the course of the evening the three girls enjoyed teaching the Beatles the latest dance moves from America: the Pony, the Jerk, the Nitty-Gritty. Usually a reluctant dancer, John proved eager for tuition from Ronnie. 'Every time we'd start to dance, John would come over and say, "I don't know if I've got this one yet, Ronnie. I may need some extra instruction." It didn't take me long to figure out that he liked me.'

At the same time, George was making it clear that he was similarly taken with Ronnie's elder sister, Estelle. 'We were young and in a foreign country, so we decided to forget our boyfriends back home and have some fun,' recalled Ronnie, whose highly-strung boyfriend, the record producer Phil Spector, was safely back in America.

As the night wore on, George and Estelle disappeared from the dance floor, and Ronnie agreed to let John take her on a tour of the house. She was impressed: 'There were antique vases and fine art in every room.' Upstairs, John began trying all the door handles. It dawned on Ronnie that he was after a hidey-hole. 'John finally found one door open, so we walked in, but it was so dark we didn't even notice that George and Estelle were already in there, sitting on the bed. "Oops! Sorry guys!" I said.' They eventually found an empty room. Together they sat on a window seat, gazing out over a view of 'this fairy-tale land of lights and towers that seemed to go on forever' as the mood became more intimate.

'What's all this like for you?' asked Ronnie.

'Well, there's a draught, and this window seat is killing my bum.'

'That's not what I meant. I mean being famous.'

'Oh, I see. Serious stuff. I'll need a smoke for this, then.'

They talked about fame. John remembered sitting in cafés with the other Beatles, fantasising about the future. 'We'd sit there with our jam butties and tea, saying, "When we get our record contract, everything's going to change. We'll have limousines and chauffeurs, and we'll never have to eat another jam butty as long as we live!" Then we got our record contract, and you know what's 'appened?'

'Nothing really changed?'

'Nope. Turns out we were right – everything did change. We got our limousines and our drivers, and now we've gone right off jam butties. If I even think of them I want to heave up.'

All this talk made Ronnie wonder whether John was 'one of these heavy brain people, just like Phil'. She could also tell that John liked her 'for more than just my voice. When he leaned over and started kissing me, I have to admit he made me forget about Phil for a few seconds.'

Professionally, Ronnie had often sung about kissing – 'I'll make you happy, baby, just wait and see. For every kiss you give me, I'll give you three' – but so far she had taken things no further. 'I know it might seem hard to believe now, but I hadn't done much more than kiss a guy on the lips until then, and that included Phil. Romance was everything, and sex was still a mystery. But the way things were going on that window seat, it didn't look like it was going to stay that way for long.' As they kissed, John started 'moving his hands around in places I didn't even know I had'. He then put them around her waist, and tried to edge her towards the king-sized bed, but at that moment Ronnie's thoughts turned to Phil, and she suddenly dug her feet into the rug, causing

John to topple over onto the floor. 'Do you think we could go back down to the party?' she asked.

Estelle and Ronnie embarked on a series of double dates with George and John. Ronnie was intrigued by how starstruck the two Beatles were, always wanting to know more about American singers and musicians: 'Tell us about the Temptations! … What's Ben E. King really like?'

One night, George and John collected Estelle and Ronnie from the lobby of the Strand Palace Hotel. Caught off-guard, John made the mistake of asking their mother, who was accompanying the girls, if she would like to come too. Her enthusiastic response came as a bitter disappointment. 'Dinner? Oh, that sounds fun. Let me get my purse.'

The evening proved awkward, not least for Ronnie. 'How can you say anything with your mother sitting around? And the worst part was that she didn't say a word the whole time. She just kept staring at us through the whole meal.'

Decades later, her mother confessed to Ronnie that she didn't care for the way 'these big grown men were really liking my little girls … I thought, "Well, what kind of a life am I going to have now?"' It was, she thought, 'the most hurtingest night of my life'.

Towards the end of the month, Phil Spector arrived in town. Ronnie knew his presence would spell the end of their fun: he was bound to refuse to go clubbing, and would certainly never let her go out without him. Phil never said anything, but Ronnie sensed that he didn't like the way she had been spending so much time with the Beatles: Phil could be tricky that way.* At the same time, on their UK tour Keith Richards

* And how! In 1968, soon after their marriage, he gave her a car for her twenty-fifth birthday, but insisted she drive it only when accompanied by him – or if he was unavailable, by a life-sized inflatable plastic replica of him, with its knees bent in a permanent sitting position. 'Now nobody will fuck with you when you're driving alone,' he explained triumphantly. Year upon year, Phil's jealousy increased. He trapped Ronnie in their house, surrounding it with barbed wire and guard dogs, and confiscating her shoes to prevent her from running away. Furthermore, he threatened to have her murdered if ever she tried to escape. 'I'm completely prepared for that day,' he told her mother. 'I've already got her coffin. It's solid gold. And it's got a glass top, so I can keep my eye on her after she's dead.'

of the Rolling Stones had fallen in love with Ronnie: 'Keith used to say, "Oh, we would have great babies because you have that black, thick hair and I have black, thick hair."'

On 5 February Tony Hall threw another party at his Green Street flat, this time for the Beatles, who were set to embark on their first US tour. 'It was a very sweet evening,' recalls one person there that night, 'because the Beatles, as big as they were at that time, had no idea what was about to hit them when they went to America, so they were very apprehensive.' Everyone danced along to Martha and the Vandellas' 'Heat Wave', and Ronnie joined in the singing at the top of her voice.

'Ronnie was the bird everyone wanted to shag' remembered Tony Calder, a music PR. 'Everybody was salivating over this incredible little thing.' Meanwhile, he saw Phil Spector 'getting very wound up about the attention everybody was paying to Ronnie. You could feel the sexual tension, every guy in the place looking at her. Because she was exotic. And she was American!'

Phil's jealousy rocketed still further when he heard from Ronnie's mother that John had invited the Ronettes to fly to America with the Beatles. Ronnie hadn't had the nerve to tell Phil about their generous offer, so she had asked her mother to broach the topic.

'You know, Phil, it might be good publicity if the girls went back on the jet with the Beatles.'

'No, I've already bought their tickets.'

The Ronettes flew back to New York the next day, without the Beatles. Phil told Ronnie he would make his own way back.

41

Ronnie was back home with her mother and sister in Spanish Harlem, watching TV coverage of the Beatles arriving at JFK, when she happened to recognise a familiar figure on the screen: 'I almost fainted when I looked at the TV and saw Phil Spector following the Beatles out of their plane. I wanted to strangle him!'

Having wheedled his way on board the Beatles' plane, Spector had proved a tricky passenger. 'He's as mad as a hatter,' observed Ringo. '… We realised how crazy he was because he "walked to America". He was so nervous of flying he couldn't sit down, so we watched him walk up and down the length of the plane all the way.'

By the time their plane touched down in New York, 'I Want to Hold Your Hand' was number 1 in the *Billboard* charts. And the pre-orders for merchandise were rolling in: half a ton of Beatles wigs were following them to America, as well as 24,000 rolls of Beatles wallpaper.

After a press conference at the airport the Beatles were driven to the Plaza Hotel,* and shepherded past thousands of fans who were screaming 'We want the Beatles!'

John and George took the trouble to leave the names of the Ronettes with hotel security. Ronnie and Estelle were ushered upstairs, together

* In her autobiography Ronnie states that it was the Warwick Hotel, but on their first visit to the US the Beatles stayed at the Plaza, transferring to the Delmonico on their next visit, in August of that same year, after the Plaza, upset by the mayhem, refused to have them back. Nor does she mention the presence of John's wife Cynthia, even though Cynthia had flown out with him. Albert Goldman, one of John's least reliable biographers, states boldly that 'As soon as Cynthia's back was turned, he hustled Ronnie into an adjoining bedroom.' It is possible that Ronnie has got her dates muddled, and John's failed seduction took place at the Delmonico. The Beatles didn't stay at the Warwick until 1966.

with their cousin Nedra, the third member of the group, and Nedra's boyfriend Scott. For once, Phil Spector had taken his eye off the ball: while Ronnie was out having fun, he was busy in the studio.

The Beatles had an entire floor of the hotel to themselves. Every surface groaned with sandwiches and alcohol. 'We're prisoners up here, so they have to feed us well,' explained John. In every room there was a television switched on, but with the sound turned down. Record players were dotted about, with singles scattered all over the floor. 'I love America,' said John. 'People here just bring you anything you want.'

Estelle and Ronnie sat on the floor with George and John, playing records and chatting. As it grew dark, Ronnie noticed that many of the original visitors had started to leave, and a whole lot of new guests were arriving, most of them young ladies with very short skirts: 'You didn't have to be a genius to figure out that a whole new kind of scene was about to start.'

Mal Evans was going around the remainder of the first batch of guests telling them that it was time to go. 'Don't worry, Scott's with us,' said Ronnie. 'We don't know him, Ronnie,' replied John. 'He's got to leave.'

In that case, said Estelle, she was leaving too. She tried to encourage Ronnie to come with her, but, as the group's name suggests, Ronnie was always the most forward of the Ronettes: 'If weird things were going to happen up there, I didn't want to miss them.'

The remaining guests started flocking into one of the bedrooms. John grabbed Ronnie's hand. 'C'mon, don't you want to see what's so interesting?'

The bedroom was, to Ronnie's eyes, abnormally crowded. Everyone had gathered around in a circle; a man was standing on a chair taking photographs of whatever was going on in the centre. When people spotted John with Ronnie, they made way for them.

Ronnie looked on aghast. 'It was the most amazing thing I'd ever seen. This girl was lying on the bed, and one of the guys in the Beatles' entourage was having sex with her – right in front of all these people … And from the look on her face, she didn't seem to mind being used as entertainment at a Beatles party, even though none of them were even taking part. I guess it was enough to just be in the same hotel suite as them, as if that gave her something to tell her grandchildren.'

The man and woman kept at it, 'having sex every which way', while the photographer snapped away. For Ronnie, it was an education. She was still a virgin, and furthermore, she always made a point of keeping her underwear on in bed, just to be on the safe side. Though she knew the basic details, 'I didn't know the first thing about doing sixty-nine, or any of these other variations. This was 1964, when you couldn't even get films with that stuff on them – and here was an actual girl having naked sex in every different position! That was a scene I'll never forget.'

She was so nonplussed by the goings-on in front of her that she couldn't help emitting – 'Oh my God!' – involuntary exclamations. Before long, John leaned over and whispered, 'Ronnie, could you do that a little quieter, please.'

As the floorshow continued, John helped himself to the only armchair in the room, and encouraged Ronnie to sit on his lap. His excitement was all too tangible: 'I may have been dumb back then, but I knew when it was time to get up off a guy's lap.' She left the room.

John followed her, and they went into his bedroom. He pointed to the Manhattan skyline, and asked if she remembered the time they looked out of the window in London. Then Ronnie sat down, and John stood behind her, rubbing her neck with his hands.

Ronnie said she had to tell him something. Not now, he said. She said she must. He said he knew all about her and Phil – 'I just thought you and I might have something too.' Ronnie stood up. She loved talking to him about music, she said, 'but sometimes a guy can seem more like a brother than a boyfriend. And that's the way I think of you. I adore you, John. But not the way you want.'

As she left the room, John slammed the door behind her. But when he phoned her the next day, he behaved as though nothing had happened. Was she free that evening? The Beatles wanted to get away from it all, and to try some real New York food.

And so the three Ronettes enjoyed a quiet night out with the four Beatles at Sherman's Barbecue in Harlem, on 151st and Amsterdam. In future, whenever Ronnie dropped by Sherman's, the manager would greet her with a smile. 'I remember you! You're the little girl that brought the Beatles!'

42

In Britain, the success of the Beatles was comparatively gradual: they hoved into view. But in America, they arrived with the sudden impact of a tidal wave. One minute, silence; the next, everywhere the Beatles.

For most of 1963 the Beatles were famous in Britain, but unknown in America. Both Brian Epstein and the group themselves were wary of mistiming their first appearance there. Having seen what happened to Cliff Richard, they were determined not to make the same mistake. 'Lots of British artists had been across the Atlantic and died a death,' noted Epstein's personal assistant, Alistair Taylor. 'Cliff Richard invaded the United States and nobody noticed.'

It so happened that on the morning of 31 October the lugubrious chat-show host Ed Sullivan touched down at Heathrow Airport, following a talent-scouting tour of Europe. He was immediately struck by thousands of screaming girls crowded onto the roof of the Queen's Building. Might it be the royal family? He put this suggestion to one of the girls, but she just burst out laughing. Finally he asked an airport official, who replied, 'It's the Beatles.'

Sullivan was quick off the mark. He contacted Brian Epstein with a view to getting them on his show. With the spectre of Cliff fresh in his mind, Epstein had already planned to make his American campaign invincible: everything – marketing and record deals, concerts and promotion, press and TV – would be in place before the band arrived. So at the beginning of November he flew to New York for a series of business meetings, one of them with Ed Sullivan's producer and son-in-law, Bob Precht.

Precht definitely wanted the Beatlcs, but only as a novelty item, a curiosity from England. Epstein, on the other hand, was determined that they should appear as stars, topping the bill. The deal Epstein finally negotiated was a brilliant compromise – the Beatles would top the bill on two consecutive shows, but for the negligible payment of $7,000. Precht saved money – they both knew that Epstein would be making an operating loss of about $50,000 – and the Beatles would get the platform they craved: two weeks headlining America's most popular show. And by the beginning of 1964 the deal was looking good for Ed Sullivan too: when the Beatles finally touched down in America on Friday, 7 February, 'I Want to Hold Your Hand' was already number 1 in the charts, with 'She Loves You' at number 21 and rising.

Their screaming fans precede them, pressed five deep against the windows of the terminal building at Kennedy Airport. As the plane door is opened, the screams drown out the sound of the jet engines. After their press conference at the airport the Beatles are escorted to the Plaza Hotel by four New York City Police cars and two motorcycle outriders, sirens wailing. At the Grand Army Plaza they are greeted by fans ten feet deep, many of whom have been waiting since dawn.

In a housing complex in Philadelphia, the fitfully employed Joe Queenan Sr learns from the *Catholic Standard and Times* that the Beatles are wholly unsuitable for children. To his thirteen-year-old son, Joe Jr, it is as though his father believed that 'their sole purpose in life was to corrupt the youth of America and lead them down the road to rack and ruin'.

Joe Sr refuses to let Joe Jr and his three sisters watch the group's appearance on *The Ed Sullivan Show*. He gives all four children advance warning that he will be commandeering the family's tiny black-and-white television on each of the nights on which the Beatles are due to appear. 'It was as if he were inviting us, nay, encouraging us, to slip rat poison into his lager,' recalls Joe Jr.

* * *

At the Beatles' rehearsal in the afternoon, the audience, mainly teenage girls, are reasonably quiet as they sit gazing at the empty stage; but when Ringo's drums are rolled onstage, they all start to scream.

The rehearsal starts with Ed Sullivan instructing the audience to pay attention to all the other fine performers, not just the Beatles. 'Because if you don't, I'll call in a barber.' After this little quip, he returns to his usual portentous self. 'Our city – indeed, the country – has never seen anything like these four young men from Liverpool. Ladies and gentlemen – the Beatles!'

A reporter from the *New York Herald-Tribune* compares the noise that erupts from the audience to 'that terrible screech the BMT Astoria train makes as it turns east near 59th Street and Seventh Avenue'.

Backstage, Brian Epstein corners Sullivan. 'I would like to know the exact wording of your introduction,' he says.

Sullivan replies, 'I would like you to get lost.'

An hour later, Sullivan returns to the stage to practise his warm-up. 'Listen, kids,' he says, 'there are other talented performers on this show, so clap for them too.' Just to be sure, he makes them rehearse their clapping. They are obedient. And so they should be: though the theatre seats seven hundred, over 50,000 requests for tickets were received for tonight's show.

'We'll be going on in eight minutes,' he announces, to low groans: eight minutes is an eternity.

Eight minutes later – a trumpet fanfare. The glossy curtain rises to form an arch. 'Good evening, Ladies and gentlemen! Tonight, live from New York – *The Ed Sullivan Show*! Tonight, *The Ed Sullivan Show* is brought to you by Anacin, the headache remedy with a special combination of ingredients to relieve pain, to relax tension, soothe irritability – *Anacin!* And by Pillsbury, makers of light, fluffy Pillsbury refrigerated biscuits and a complete line of fresh foods in the dairy case. And now –' a roll of drums '– here he is – Ed Sullivan!'

Head down, eyes darting to and fro, Sullivan enters, sombre and shifty, looking like the shady brother of Humphrey Bogart. 'Thank you very much,' he says, putting his hands up and then swiftly bringing them back down, to make the audience stop applauding. He takes a nervous look to his left, then scratches his nose with the back of his hand. Once again he signals the audience to shut up; he shows no trace of a smile.

Finally, hush descends. 'You know, something very nice happened and the Beatles got a great kick out of it,' he says, in an oddly offhand way. His hands are in his pockets. 'We just received a wire, *they* did, from Elvis Presley and Colonel Tom Parker, wishing them a tremendous success in our country, and I think that was very nice.' In fact, this is not strictly true: Colonel Parker sent the telegram without Elvis's knowledge.

There is yelling. 'Now this –' Sullivan clears his throat. 'Now this –' he clears his throat again. More yelling. He holds up a forefinger, shakes it, the irate headmaster, then looks down at his shoes. 'Now this, this particular series, we've had many exciting acts on the stage. Thanks to our little Italian cook, Topo Gigio. Thanks to Belgian Singing Nun, Sister Soeur Sourire. To Milton Berle … and last Sunday, of course, the never-to-be-forgotten teaming on our stage of Sammy Davis and Ella Fitzgerald. Now tonight the whole country is waiting to hear England's Beatles. And you're gonna hear them – and they're tremendous ambassadors of goodwill – after this commercial. Now, if you're a person who has to be shown, here's a really big brute from all-new Aero Shave!'

After the commercial break, we return to Ed Sullivan, who looks as if he's going to announce a fatal car accident. 'Now, yesterday and today our theatre has been jammed with newspaper men and hundreds of photographers from all over the nation, and these veterans agree with me that the city has never witnessed the excitement stirred by these youngsters from Liverpool who call themselves the Beatles. Now, tonight you're gonna twice be entertained by them – right now, and again in the second half of our show. Ladies and gentlemen' – an extravagant wave of his arms – 'the Beatles!'

Screaming, screaming and yet more screaming. The camera cuts to the audience – virtually all girls between twelve and fifteen years old.

'Close your eyes and I'll kiss you,' sings Paul, waggling his head, raising his eyes to the ceiling. Next to him, George taps his toes. Ringo looks happy. John, to the right, appears detached, perhaps even slightly bored.

Close-ups show tearful girls, screaming and holding their heads as if they might otherwise fall off. They all remain firmly seated: perhaps they are obeying pre-show instructions from the fearsome Mr Sullivan.

Paul seems at home – jigging about, shaking his head from side to side. Throughout the show, it is clear that he is the Beatle in the driving seat.

The camera moves in on Ringo, who can obviously see a monitor, because he now smiles even harder, prompting a huge yell from the audience.

'All my loving, I will send to you-ou-ou!' When George and John go 'ooo' everyone screams some more. John permits himself a quick smile. The most abrasive of the Beatles, he is also their most nervous performer.

George, who was suffering from a high temperature this morning, launches into a twangy country-and-western guitar solo. What big eyebrows he has!

A girl of twelve bounces up and down in her seat, clapping, screaming, running her hands through her hair, up and down, up and down.

The song comes to an end; they all take deep bows, and then Paul launches straight into 'There were bells, on a hill, but I never heard them ringing' – the cheesy ballad from *The Music Man* – 'till there was you.' A subtitle appears on-screen beneath his head saying 'PAUL'. Then – to more screams – a close-up of Ringo ('RINGO'). Ringo grins, seems to say something to himself, and laughs. And then George, who bursts into his first big smile. Finally John, whose close-up comes with the caption 'SORRY GIRLS, HE'S MARRIED'. The screams for him are more subdued, but he smiles nonetheless.

The song ends. Another deep bow, and then straight into: 'She loves you, yeah, yeah, yeah!' Everything comes alive. There is scarcely a child who isn't screaming and clutching her head, as though on a particularly scary rollercoaster.

'She said she loves you' – a close-up of Ringo, grinning and nodding his head – 'and you know that can't be ba-ad. WOOOOOOH!'

The four of them shake their heads with amazing vigour, the starting pistol for the most frantic screams so far. John, legs wide apart and arched, jogs up and down. His microphone is on the blink, so his voice is barely heard throughout the evening, which makes him seem more of a backing singer, even when he is singing lead.

By now, everyone in the audience is clapping along. Most of the girls are sporting old-fashioned side partings and sweaters topped with strappy dresses.

'YEAH, YEAH, YEAH, YEAH, YEAH, YEAH, YEEEEAAAAAH!'

It's over. Screams galore. Cut to Ed Sullivan applauding. He is smiling, or very nearly smiling, but with the ends of his mouth turned down. He puts his hand up for silence.

'Now, you promised!' he barks, reminding the girls of his talking-to before the show began. They hush, but not entirely; there is excited chatter in the background as he continues, in his eat-your-greens tone: 'They'll be back in the second half of the show after you've enjoyed Georgia Brown, the star of *Oliver!*, Tessie O'Shea, one of the stars of *The Girl Who Came to Supper* – but right now, a word about Anacin.'

A hundred miles away, the thirteen-year-old Joe Queenan Jr has managed to bypass his father, slipping around the corner of the block to the television of his more merciful Uncle Jerry. He is amazed by what he has just seen: 'To this day I believe my life as a sentient human being, and not merely as my parents' chattel, began at that moment.'

In El Cerrito, California, the Fogerty brothers, Tom and John, are watching *The Ed Sullivan Show* with their friends Doug Clifford and Stu Cook. They immediately think of forming a quartet, just like the Beatles. 'Wow, we can do that. If these guys from England can come out and play rock'n'roll, we can do it.' They can't lay their hands on Beatle wigs, so they wear Three Stooges wigs instead.*

The thirteen-year-old Tom Petty, watching the show on the family television in Gainesville, Florida, thinks, 'There is a way out … You get your friends and you're a self-contained unit. And you make the music.' Within weeks, groups are playing in garages all over his neighbourhood.

Chrissie Hynde, aged twelve, is the daughter of a Yellow Pages manager. She watches *The Ed Sullivan Show* on her family television in Akron, Ohio. She will never forget it: 'It was like sex, but without the sex. I remember exactly where I was sitting. It was amazing. It was like the axis shifted … It was like an alien invasion. If you were a little virgin and didn't want to grow up like I didn't, didn't want to enter the adult world like I didn't, it gave you some kind of new avenue of sexuality. It could be more cerebral. You didn't have to actually touch the person's acne.' Going into Harvey S. Firestone High School the next day, Chrissie notices that all the boys have combed their hair down over their foreheads, so she does the same: 'I could never set my hair in rollers again. I combed it out straight and cut my bangs.'

In Baltimore, thirteen-year-old Greg Kihn follows suit. On the Friday he'd left school looking like Dion. On the Monday he returns to class with his hair ungreased and brushed forward: 'That's how quickly it happened.'

---

* The Fogerty brothers' band was to develop into Creedence Clearwater Revival.

For the little Wilson sisters in Bellevue, Washington – Ann, thirteen, and Nancy, nine – it's as if a lightning bolt has struck them: 'It was a huge event, like the lunar landing … Right away, we started doing air-guitar shows in the living room, faking English accents and studying all the fanzines.'*

Billy Joel, fourteen, is watching with his family on Long Island: 'They looked like these working-class kids, like kids we all knew. And John Lennon had this look when he was on Ed Sullivan like: *Fuck all of you. This is total bullshit to me*.' Billy knew his destiny then and there: 'I said at that moment, "I know these guys. I can relate to these guys. I am these guys. That's what I want to do. I want to do that. I want to be like those guys. This is what I'm going to do – play in a rock band."'

Ed Sullivan reappears, looking as though he might benefit from a couple of Anacin himself. 'Now here …' There is a buzz of chatter from the audience. Ed drops his voice to a bass. '*Quiet!*' he snaps, then, perhaps surprised at his own irritability, flashes a quick lizardy smile. 'Here's a very amusing magician we saw in Europe and signed last summer – Fred Kaps!'

In white tie and tails, the Dutch magician doggedly goes through his routine. When Kaps finishes his act, Sullivan fails to signal his approval by inviting him over for a congratulatory handshake. Instead, he waves in his general direction. Next come the cast of the Broadway production of *Oliver!*, headed by Georgia Brown, singing 'As Long as He Needs Me', then 'I'd Do Anything', accompanied by the seventeen-year-old English actor Davy Jones.†

They are followed by an impressionist, Frank Gorshin, who rattles through Dean Martin, Marlon Brando and Burt Lancaster to effortful laughter. And so to another ad break, for New Pillsbury Quick Refrigerated Dinner Rolls. 'Nothing says lovin' like something from the oven – and Pillsbury says it best!'

---

* The Wilson sisters later rose to fame with the band Heart.

† Hearing the screams that greeted the Beatles, Davy Jones thought to himself, 'I'd like a little bit of this action.' Two years later, he successfully auditioned to become the lead vocalist of the Monkees.

'England's wonderful Tessie O'Shea' takes to the stage, a plump, chirpy, white-haired lady, rather full of herself, in a long sparkly dress and white fur stole. 'Oh hello, good people, how do you do?' she sings in her introduction. 'It's wonderful to be here to sing to you, but darlings, please don't ask me what the songs will be – I like a bit of everything, well, you know me!'

The young audience, having patiently sat through the Dutch conjuror, the cast of *Oliver!*, the impressionist and the fat lady on the banjo, have never been more desperate for the Beatles. Instead, Sullivan introduces comedy duo McCall and Brill, who perform a wordy sketch involving a series of aspirant actresses trying to impress a Hollywood agent. The only real laugh they get is from a topical joke they added just before they came on: 'My little girl is waiting outside. You know, she used to be one of the Beatles.' 'What happened?' 'Somebody stepped on her!'

Sullivan fails to thank them. At last, after a commercial for Pineapple Lemon Parfait from Pillsbury, the moment has arrived. 'Ladies and gentlemen, once again – THE BEATLES!' For the first time, Sullivan's smile seems wholehearted.

'She was just seventeen – you know what I mean!' sings Paul, to an audience largely composed of young girls who probably have no idea what he means. But they couldn't care less: by now they are all screaming their heads off.

George looks much more cheerful, but it is Ringo whose close-up seems to prompt the loudest cries. Perhaps through a trick of perspective, John looks a bit too wide and chunky, as though he is in a hall of mirrors. 'Woooh!' The four of them all shake their heads at once, prompting the girls to go berserk. 'Oh yeah, I'll tell you somethin', I think you'll understand …' The camera zooms in on a girl in winged glasses, chewing gum, bouncing up and down in her seat, clasping her hands together, as if in prayer, while radiating pure delight. 'I can't hide! I can't hide! I can't hide!' Behind her, a portly grey-haired man in horn-rimmed specs and a bow tie manages a pained smile, but you can tell he wishes it were over.

And it is. Screams pile upon screams. Paul, George and John are joined by Ringo, who jumps down from his elevated platform and skips behind them. Ed Sullivan shakes each of them by the hand. You can see George saying 'Thank you!' He waves to the back row, and the others join in. Even Sullivan is smiling. They mouth 'Thank you' as they leave the stage. Sullivan wants to say something, and signals for silence. 'All of us –' he begins, but the screaming continues. 'All of us. All of us –' He holds up his hands. 'All of us on this show want to express our deep appreciation to the New York Police Department for its superb handling of thousands of youngsters who cluttered Broadway and 53rd Street ready to greet the Beatles under the command of Deputy Chief Standford, and our deep appreciation of the newspapermen, magazine writers and photographers who have been so darned kind to the Beatles and to us.'

It should be over, but for some reason it isn't. 'And now, ladies and gentlemen, a very fine novelty act – Wells and the Four Fays!' An all-singing, all-dancing troupe of acrobats trot on, performing cartwheels and contortions in time to the music.

And it's still not over. 'Before I tell you about next Sunday's show starring Mitzi Gaynor and the Beatles, right now – here's a real treat from the folks at Pillsbury!'

Sullivan, the severe headmaster, permits himself just a hint of goodwill. 'You've been a fine audience, despite severe provocation.' A quick lizard smile. 'Next Sunday, our show originates at Miami Beach from the Deauville Hotel … Next Sunday's show stars Hollywood's Mitzi Gaynor, the Beatles –' More screams, which continue at such a pitch that they drown out his announcement of the other acts. 'We'll also have the winner of the Liston/Clay fight at Miami Beach, which plays host to President Johnson on February 27th.' And, in closing: 'Now I'm delighted, all of us are delighted, and I know the Beatles on their first appearance here have been very deeply thrilled by their reception here. You've been fine. Now get home safely – good night!'

Then, as the closing credits roll: 'Tonight *The Ed Sullivan Show* has been brought to you by Pillsbury, where the good things you bake always begin with the best – Pillsbury's best. And by new Aero Shave – Keeps Drenching Your Beard Through the Shave.'

43

Many American teenagers watch the Beatles on *The Ed Sullivan Show* against a noisy backdrop of snorts and harrumphs. In New York, twelve-year-old Sigrid Nunez has to contend with her mean uncle mocking their looks, their voices, their every movement. Some parents call them faggots. Others take the ultimate stand and switch their televisions off. 'You call that music?' Sigrid's friend's father shouts. 'And when do you think was the last time those creeps had a bath?'

But not every member of the older generation is against them. Billy Graham watches *The Ed Sullivan Show* in order to, as he puts it, 'gain a better understanding of the youth of today'. For the first time, America's most celebrated evangelist breaks his own rule to avoid television on the Sabbath. After all, he has to know what is going on. He concludes, not unfairly, that 'The Beatles are a product of our time. They represent the restlessness and the longing of young people today for something off-beat, something different.' Later, in Omaha, he advises a packed audience: 'Watch the kids' reaction to the Beatles and you'll know that man is an emotional creature.'

In New York, Jamie, Alexander and Nina Bernstein, aged from twelve to two, keep an eye on their forty-five-year-old father Leonard. Barely three months ago, on the day after the assassination of President Kennedy, he conducted the New York Philharmonic playing Mahler's Resurrection Symphony for a televised memorial. For Leonard, as, in a different way, for Billy Graham, the Beatles represent a vision of the future: 'I fell in love with the Beatles' music (and simultaneously, of course, with their four faces-cum-personae) along with my children, two girls and a boy, in whom I discovered the frabjous falsetto shriek-cum-croon, the ineluctable beat, the flawless intonation, the utterly fresh lyrics, the Schubert-like flow of musical invention and the Fuck-You coolness of these Four Horsemen of Our Apocalypse … Together we saw it, the Vision, and heard the same Dawn-Bird, Elephant-Trump, Fanfare of the Future.'

The following morning, over breakfast in their suite at the Plaza Hotel, the Beatles sift through their reviews. Conservative commentators compete with one another to voice the most vehement disdain. The *New York Times* carries two reviews, neither appreciative. 'The Beatles' vocal quality can be described as hoarsely incoherent, with the minimal enunciation necessary to communicate the schematic texts,' writes the music critic Theodore Strongin. The TV critic, Jack Gould, calls their performance both 'a sedate anti-climax' and 'a fine mass placebo'.

Under a front-page headline, 'Beatles Bomb on TV', the *Herald-Tribune* says: 'The Beatles apparently could not carry a tune across the Atlantic but were saved by the belles in the audience.' Their reviewer condemns them as '75 per cent publicity, 20 per cent haircut, and 5 per cent lilting lament', and 'a magic act that owed less to Britain than to Barnum'.

The *New York Daily News* offers a mixed response: admiration, stupefaction, incomprehension. 'Not even Elvis Presley ever incited such laughable lunacy among the screaming generation. The Presleyan gyrations and caterwauling, in fact, were but luke-warm dandelion tea compared to the 100-proof elixir served by the Beatles.'

'Just thinking about the Beatles seems to induce mental disturbance,' notes George Dixon in the *Washington Post* a week later. Like many other commentators, he can't stop going on about how they aren't worth going on about. 'They have a commonplace, rather dull act that hardly seems to merit mentioning,' he writes, 'yet people hereabouts have mentioned scarcely anything else for a couple of days.'

The viewing figures offer no comfort to the critics. Seventy-three million Americans tuned in, the second-largest viewing figure in the history of commercial television. The first came eleven weeks earlier, following the chilling words 'News just in of shots fired in Dallas.'

In many people's minds, the two events will always be linked: the assassination of JFK was winter; the Beatles are spring. Years later, Joe Queenan Jr, now a successful writer, is convinced the link is valid: 'I have always believed that the Beatles' stupendous success in America was directly related to JFK's death. I remember reading this theory years and years after the fact and thinking, "Yes. Here is one theory about pop culture that is not stupid or obvious." The Beatles helped heal America … Some musicians heal ethnic groups. Some musicians heal nations. The Beatles healed an entire planet.'

44

From the *Billboard* Hot 100 for the week of 4 April 1964:

1. 'Can't Buy Me Love' – The Beatles
2. 'Twist and Shout' – The Beatles
3. 'She Loves You' – The Beatles
4. 'I Want to Hold Your Hand' – The Beatles
5. 'Please Please Me' – The Beatles

Also:

31. 'I Saw Her Standing There' – The Beatles
41. 'From Me To You' – The Beatles
46. 'Do You Want to Know a Secret' – The Beatles
58. 'All My Loving' – The Beatles
65. 'You Can't Do That' – The Beatles
68. 'Roll Over Beethoven' – The Beatles
79. 'Thank You Girl' – The Beatles

Two songs about the Beatles also made the Hot 100 that week: 'We Love You Beatles' by the Carefrees, and 'A Letter to the Beatles' by the Four Preps.

45

Once the Beatles' *Ed Sullivan Show* was all over, one or two of the performers couldn't bear to remember it.

For Charlie Brill and Mitzi McCall, it had all started so well. They were a sophisticated young comedy duo, striving to make their mark. They had, in their own words, been 'sitting at home, starving' in Los Angeles, when their manager called. 'Guess what?' he said. 'I got you on *The Ed Sullivan Show*.'

They let out a yell. This was the biggest show in America, miraculously able to transform jobbing performers into national stars.

They immediately set to work honing a routine. 'We rehearsed and rehearsed and we fine-tuned it … and we told everybody, in fact I think I sky-wrote it over Hollywood: "We're on *The Ed Sullivan Show*. Yippeeee!" We were on our way!' They were excited, too, by the chance to meet some of their idols: they had been tipped off that two big musical theatre stars, 'Two Ton' Tessie O'Shea and Georgia Brown were on the same bill, along with the impressionist Frank Gorshin. Someone also mentioned this new pop group they'd never heard of, from England.

On the way to the studio, Charlie and Mitzi were still finessing their routine when their cab came to a halt. The streets had been cordoned off, with thousands of people queuing around the block. They couldn't understand why.

Low on the bill, they were shown to the worst dressing room. In the corner was a soda machine for the use of one and all. Presently, they were called for a dress rehearsal. After it, a voice came over the loudspeaker: 'McCall and Brill, Mr Sullivan's office, please!' So they went downstairs, and were shown in. 'And there he was! Ed Sullivan! He was sitting on the chair getting made up and I looked at the man who could make our entire careers!' Sullivan had been observing their rehearsal, and he was not pleased. 'The piece of material you're doing is too sophisticated for this audience,' he said. 'It's going to be mainly fourteen-, fifteen-, sixteen-year-old girls in the audience tonight, and kids.'

In an hour's time they were going to be live on television, and here was Mr Sullivan ordering them to change a routine they had been fine-tuning for weeks! Determined not to panic, they got down to work.

Suddenly, there was a knock at the door. 'And there was this guy standing there with funny hair and granny glasses,' recalled Charlie, 'and he said, "Givvuzza coagluv," And I said, "This guy wants a glove or something, I'm not sure what he wants." And he started to laugh, and he said, "No – *givv uzz a coag luv*," and he pointed to the Coke machine. And I said, "Oh – *yeah*! Come in!" And he said, "Can you give me a dime, 10 cents?" And I said, "Oh, I gotta buy you the Coke as well. Whaddya think, we're made out of money, kid?"'

The young man took the Coca-Cola, then sat down on the sofa in their dressing room and started chatting away. 'While he's talking to us, he takes out a pen and a napkin and he's drawing me. He's looking at me and he's drawing some pictures of me and Mitzi on napkins.'

Eventually the show began, and the young man was onstage with his group. They were singing 'Close your eyes and I'll kiss you', but neither Charlie nor Mitzi could hear them. 'Honest to God, the screams all through were so loud I never got a chance to hear what they sounded like. I never heard or saw such bedlam in my life! And when they finish, the screams keep going on!'

McCall and Brill were the last act before the reappearance of the Beatles in the second half of the show. Before they came on, there were screams from the audience, who thought the Beatles were next. Undaunted, the two of them launched into a jaunty satirical routine in which Charlie played a casting director while Mitzi, an energetic mimic, played a succession of different women, from a stage mom to a method actor. Each of their gags was met with silence.

'We were up there for two years … We didn't know what we were doing. We didn't know if we'd finished the act or not finished the act. The band leader had the punchline, and he played it – Ta-da!'

They now reckon it was the worst three minutes of their lives. In fact, they had bombed so badly that when they came offstage the other performers looked away. Meanwhile, the Beatles were singing 'I Saw Her Standing There' and 'I Want to Hold Your Hand', and the screams were unabated.

After the show, Frank Gorshin took the couple out to Sardi's and tried to comfort them. 'Don't worry,' he said. 'This is not the end of your lives.' But they were so downhearted and embarrassed that they couldn't face returning home to California. Instead they headed south to Florida, for a week's break.

In Miami, they were walking to their car one night when a limousine pulled up alongside them. Inside were the Beatles, there for a second appearance on *The Ed Sullivan Show*, which was being recorded at the Deauville Hotel. John Lennon remembered them from their dressing room, and cheerfully introduced them to Paul, George and Ringo.

'What are you doing here?' he asked.

'Escaping from you,' they replied.

Back in Los Angeles, their agent failed to call them for six months. Eventually their careers got back on track, but they would never forget the day that had held such promise, and delivered such disappointment.'We were in the midst of greatness. We didn't know it,' says Charlie. For the rest of the sixties they couldn't help but wince every time they heard the Beatles. And it was still only 1964: an awful lot of wincing lay ahead.

46

And there were other, more grievous casualties too. In the eleven-week period between the Kennedy assassination and the Beatles' appearance on *The Ed Sullivan Show*, the *Billboard* chart had been dominated by a most unlikely record: a young Catholic nun from Belgium, singing a hymn to St Dominic in French.

In September 1959, twenty-five-year-old Jeanne-Paule Marie Deckers, the daughter of a *patissière*, entered the convent of the Missionary Dominican Sisters of Our Lady of Fichermont, to become Sister Luc-Gabrielle.

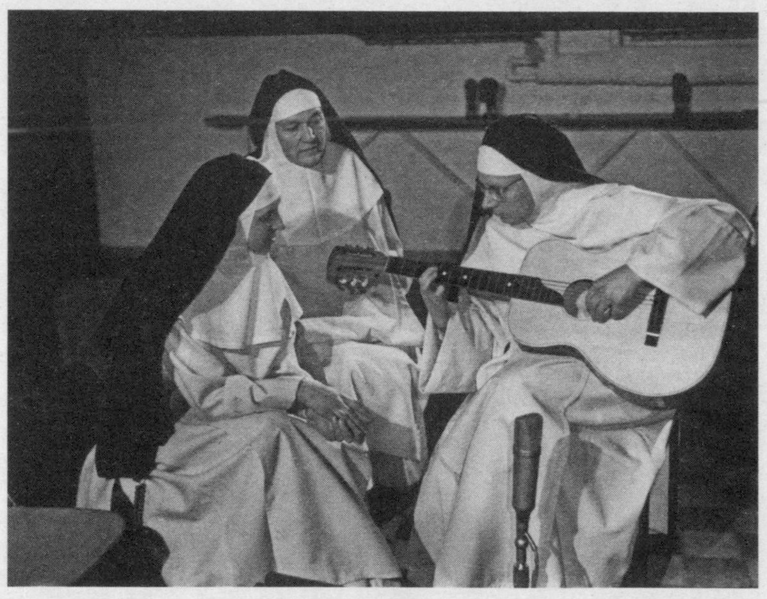

Permitted an acoustic guitar, she would occasionally perform her own songs to her fellow nuns. Her superiors were so taken with her singing that they encouraged her to record an album, to be sold as a souvenir to visitors to the convent.

Sister Luc-Gabrielle recorded it at the Philips studios in Brussels in 1961. The studio engineers passed the album to the record company executives, who persuaded the convent to release the track 'Dominique' as a single, and Sister Luc-Gabrielle to change her name to 'Soeur Sourire', or 'Sister Smile'.

The song became a hit in Belgium, then in Europe, then in the United States. The charts have always been a mixed bag, but 'Dominique' is without doubt the first and only single about the thirteenth-century founder of the Dominican order, sung in French, to have become an international hit.

> Dominique-nique-nique went about simply,
> A poor singing traveller.
> On every road, in every place,
> He talks only of the Good Lord,
> He talks only of the Good Lord.

Sister Luc-Gabrielle, now nicknamed 'the Singing Nun', was an unlikely pop star. The money she earned from the records went straight to her convent: 'My superiors wanted to protect my personal religious life, and I was kept away from the whole world of the song, the spectacle, and so on. In a way it was good. My superiors feared that I would become haughty.'

On his talent-scouting trip to Europe, Ed Sullivan had visited the convent at Fichermont, filming the heavily bespectacled Sister Luc-Gabrielle strumming her acoustic guitar and singing 'Dominique'. She became one of his most popular novelty acts ever, more popular even than the cheeky puppet Topo Gigio and the dancing bear from the Moscow State Circus.

After the assassination of President Kennedy, the American public took to the innocent, hopeful sound of the Singing Nun. Within a week her album, *Her Joys, Her Songs*, elbowed 'Louie Louie' by the Kingsmen out of the way to reach number 1 in the charts. There it remained from December through January.

But with the arrival of the Beatles, and the release of *With the Beatles*, the chart career of Sister Luc-Gabrielle ground to a halt. After a world tour, she retreated to the convent, where she heard the news that 'Dominique' had won a Grammy for Best Gospel or Religious Song, and that her album had sold two million copies.

In 1966 Debbie Reynolds starred in the title role of a feature film called *The Singing Nun*, but by now Sister Luc-Gabrielle had grown notably less docile, describing the film as 'absolutely idiotic'. Around this time she left the convent and reverted to her old nickname, 'Jeannine' Deckers. Set on pursuing a singing career, she released a succession of singles, but they were too radical for her fans to swallow. The first, a protest song against the Roman Catholic Church's attitude to birth control, was called 'Glory be to God for the Golden Pill'; the next was the unusually morose 'Sister Smile is Dead'. Neither played to her strengths.

Later, in the 1970s, her similarly downbeat album *I Am Not a Star in Heaven* also flopped. By now she was living with a woman, though they shared a vow of celibacy, and had transformed their living room into a chapel. Realising that her career as a chart-topper was over, Deckers became a teacher of handicapped children. In the early 1980s she was pursued by the Belgian authorities for $63,000 of back taxes earned on her records. But she had nothing: not unreasonably, she argued that the convent, having taken most of her royalties, was liable for any tax. In an attempt to raise money she re-recorded 'Dominique', this time to a heavy disco beat, but it failed to catch on.

In April 1985 Deckers and her companion Annie Berchet, or 'Sister Annie', committed suicide together in their shared flat in Wavre, near Brussels. 'We are going together to meet God our Father,' read their joint suicide note. 'He alone can save us from this financial disaster.'

47

Staying in Miami for their second *Ed Sullivan Show* appearance, the Beatles were approached by Harold Conrad, the publicist for the World Heavyweight Boxing Championship. He wanted photographs of them with either the champ, Sonny Liston, or the upstart no-hoper Cassius Clay, who would be challenging him in Miami in a week's time. Bookies were quoting odds of 7–1 against Clay; the *New York Post* was predicting the fight would be over in eighteen seconds.

John showed no hesitation: 'Clay's not going to win. He's a big mouth. The other one is going to kill him. We want him.'

But Liston had no interest in being photographed with what he called 'those skinny little bums'. He'd gone with Harold Conrad and Joe Louis to watch the Beatles recording *The Ed Sullivan Show*. Halfway through, he'd turned to Conrad and said, sniffily, 'Are these motherfuckers what all the people are screaming about? My *dog* plays drums better than that kid with the big nose!'

It was the British photographer Harry Benson, desperate for a shot combining the two biggest news stories of the moment, who persuaded the Beatles to court the no-hoper: 'I go to the Beatles and I say, "This man's very colourful and he's young and good-looking and I'll see what I can do."'

Clay agreed to meet the Beatles at the Fifth Street Gym on 18 February. The Beatles were joined by Robert Lipsyte, a twenty-six-year-old cub reporter from the *New York Times* who was covering the fight because the veteran sports reporters considered it beneath them: they were convinced they would have to spend their time hanging around outside Mount Sinai Hospital, waiting for the latest report from Intensive

Care. Nor did they like the loudmouth Clay; they were irritated by his cockiness, his verbosity, the way he danced about in the ring.

The Beatles arrived on time, annoyed that they had been cajoled into the project. Lipsyte witnessed their surly entrance: 'These four little guys were being herded up the stairs and they were cursing with British accents, and apparently these were the Beatles. They were very angry – they didn't want to pose with Clay, he was a loser.'

Ringo, in particular, felt they were wasting their time. 'Let's get the fuck out of here,' he said. Lipsyte heard one of them saying, 'That stupid wanker is going to get knocked out in the first round.'

The contempt flowed in both directions. When Ferdie Pacheco, Ali's personal physician, set eyes on the Beatles, he was equally dismissive: 'They were street kids from Liverpool, sunburnt like lobsters. They looked so small and pitiful.'

Clay was nowhere to be seen, but suddenly the dressing-room door burst open. His frame filled the doorway. 'Hello, Beatles!' he said. 'Let's go and make some money!'

Benson persuaded them all into a boxing ring as Clay took control: 'The four couldn't get a word in edgeways. They were like little lambs.' They pretended to fight, four against one. Clay held Ringo in the air, called Paul 'pretty boy', and lined them up, tapping Ringo on the chin and making them collapse like dominoes. They did whatever he told them to do. At one point he made them pose lying flat on the floor. Then he said, 'Who's the greatest?' and they chorused 'You are!' All the photographs make them look weak and tiddly next to Cassius Clay: they barely come up to his shoulder.

After a while, Clay and the Beatles started chatting about music and boxing, as well as the money they were all going to make.

'You're not as dumb as you look,' said Clay.

'No,' replied John. 'But you are.'

It was a risky reply. Clay checked to see John was smiling, and decided it was only a joke.

After a few minutes they said their goodbyes, and the Beatles were led away. Once they had gone, Clay turned to Lipsyte and said, 'Who were those little sissies?'

On 25 February 1964, Cassius Clay beat Sonny Liston in six rounds. Liston left the hall in tears, his arm in a sling, while Clay hollered, 'I want everybody to bear witness! I am the greatest! I shook up the world! I am the greatest thing that ever lived!'

Clay was twenty-two years old, a little younger than Paul, a little older than George. Veteran sports writers smelled something unpleasant in the air. The gruff columnist Jimmy Cannon was particularly steamed up. 'Clay is part of the Beatle movement,' he wrote. 'He fits in with the famous singers no one can hear and the punks riding motorcycles with iron crosses pinned to their leather jackets and Batman and the boys with their long dirty hair and the girls with the unwashed look and the college kids dancing naked at secret proms held in apartments and the revolt of students who get a check from Dad every first of the month and the painters who copy the labels off soup cans and the surf bums who refuse to work and the whole pampered style-making cult of the bored young.'

For many of the older generation, Cassius Clay and the Beatles were auguries of impertinence, dirtiness, disrespect, and everything else that was dragging the world downhill. Yeah, yeah, yeah: what kind of language was that?

48

Yeah, yeah, yeah: a *Newsweek* critic focused on those three little words – or rather, one little half-word, repeated – to convey everything he hated about the Beatles: 'Musically they are a near disaster, guitars and drums slamming out a merciless beat that does away with secondary rhythms, harmony and melody. Their lyrics (punctuated by nutty shouts of "yeah, yeah, yeah") are a catastrophe, a preposterous farrago of Valentine-card romantic sentiments.'

In the *National Review*, the conservative iconoclast William F. Buckley penned a diatribe under the title 'Yeah, Yeah, Yeah, They Stink': 'Let me say it, as evidence of my final measure of devotion to the truth: The Beatles are not merely awful, I would consider it sacrilegious to say anything less than that they are godawful. They are so unbelievably horrible, so appallingly unmusical, so dogmatically insensitive to the magic of the art that they qualify as crowned heads of anti-music, even as the imposter popes went down in history as "anti-popes".'

But young people felt differently. Roz Chast was coming up to her ninth birthday when she first heard it. 'That song provided my first inkling that there was another world out there, one that did not include my parents, my relatives, my neighbours, my teachers or my classmates – a world of carefree and attractive young people who did not worry about illness or money, and who did not care about homework or why one was not popular ... What was it about "She Loves You" that felt like an anthem of liberation? Perhaps it was that chorus of "Yeah, yeah, yeah", or maybe it was that thrilling "Wooooo!", or maybe it was the Beatles themselves. I'd never seen anything like them.'

Later that spring, Roz was staying with her parents at a hotel in Puerto Rico when she paired up with another little girl. One day the two families went out driving together. While the parents chatted away, the two girls began to sing 'She Loves You' as loud as they possibly could, though they were shaky on most of the words, except for 'Yeah, yeah, yeah!' and 'Wooooo!'.

'More than fifty years later, I still remember how thrilling that was. I don't recall any of the grown-ups getting particularly mad at us. They were just baffled. This was us, this kind of music. Not for them. And that was OK with us.'

In the third grade, Roz found herself close to the bottom of the social pecking order. The four most popular girls in the school dressed up in Beatle suits, Beatle boots and Beatle wigs, and played cardboard guitars. They sang 'She Loves You' and went 'Woooo!' and shook their heads.

'When I think about "She Loves You", and how much I loved that song, how new it sounded, and how happy it made me feel to hear it, I think about how much it represented the mirage of a possible future, one that was more joyful and more interesting than my lonely and borderline-grim childhood with its homework and tests and mean girls and stupid boys and parents who worried about everything and got angry over nothing.'

Joe Queenan had never heard anything like it. Before 'She Loves You' came blaring through his sister's transistor radio in Philadelphia, 'I had no interest in music, period. Until that moment, I viewed music as an annoyance at best, and at worst as a punitive child-rearing device.' His parents played Frank Sinatra, Tony Bennett and Perry Como. 'When the Beatles showed up, we felt the way the French must have felt when the GIs swarmed into Paris in August 1944 … The Beatles held out hope that life might actually be worth living, that popular culture need not be gray, predictable, sappy, lethal.' For him, that moment he first heard 'She Loves You' signalled 'the first time in my life I heard a song that seemed to speak directly to me and not to adults … I still think it is the greatest song ever written. For me, it is and always will be the song that changed the world. I love that song. I absolutely love it. And with a love like that, you know you should be glad.'

49

In Reseda, California, sixteen-year-old Pam Miller was so besotted with the new arrivals that within the privacy of her schoolgirl diary she turned herself into a Liverpudlian. On 10 February 1964 she wrote: 'Paul you are gear. Really Fab. Say chum, why are you so marvellous, luv? The most bloomin' idiot on earth is me, cause I'm wild over you chap.'

From then on she posted Paul a poem every day, sealed with a kiss. As February rolled into March, her diary entries grew more intimate:

> 2 March 1964: It is 2:21 am at Paul's house. He's sleeping. I'm glad. I wish I could see him sleeping, I really do. I wish I could be *with him* sleeping (just kidding). I hope he read my poem before he closed his beautiful brown eyes.

Pam was perhaps rather more forward than other Beatles fans of her age. One of her particular treasures was a bubble-gum card of Paul – a photograph of him playing his bass guitar on a hotel bed, with his legs apart. She studied it close-up: 'You could actually see the shape of his balls being crushed by the tightness of his trousers. I carried that card around with me in a little gold box with cotton covering it like it was a precious jewel.'

Virtually every day, on her local radio station KRLA the disc jockey Dave Hull, 'the Hullabalooer', would deliver an update on the state of Paul's relationship with his new girlfriend. Pam listened with growing resentment of the young lady she came to call 'the creepy freckle-faced bow-wow, Jane Asher', or simply 'Pig-Face'.

Pam covered her bedroom with Beatles merchandise. Her three best friends were also Beatles fans. Each had her own favourite. Stevie loved Ringo: 'I've got to meet Ringo or my whole life will be completely empty. Oh, I'm suffering so. He's my love and I love him. Oh, God, please don't let my Ringo be taken away!'

Linda loved John. Together, Pam and Linda would *be* Paul and John. They spoke to each other in Liverpudlian accents, pretending to go to parties and to eat in expensive restaurants. Pam had a reel-to-reel tape recorder, and would make up little plays, taking all the parts herself. In all of them, Jane Asher would die. But in her letters to Paul, she was the soul of tact:

> Dear Paul, Your fans will always love you. Personally, I will never stop. Since hearing about your engagement to Jane Asher, I'll have to love you in another way, all of my own.

Pam's friend Kathy was in love with George. It so happened that Kathy's father had a pal who worked at the Hollywood Bowl, where the Beatles were due to play in August. Luckily, this pal managed to wangle them four tickets. Pam framed hers, hung it on her bedroom wall and started counting down. In her diary entry for 3 June she wrote: 'There's an actual day this year that is called August 23rd! It comes in 83 days!!'

With twenty-one days to go, the four girls went to see *A Hard Day's Night*. It was everything Pamela hoped it would be. 'The Beatles are the greatest actors alive,' she told her diary.

On 23 August she wrote: 'Day Of All!! Tonight I saw Paul. I actually looked at his lean slender body and unique too-long legs. I saw his dimples and his pearly white teeth. I saw his wavy, yet straight lengthy hair, I saw his doe-like eyes … and they saw me. Maybe it's fate that brought him to our sunny shores … for I am here too.'

50

Dear George.

Lots of people ask me if I think the Beatles will become American citizens after their stay but I know you well enough to say that you love your home (Liverpool) best, don't you, George? But of course! Oh well … I hope I can come to your birthday party as I must talk to you, George, before I go bonkers. My friend at school went to your party last year. You came with the others to pick her up at her house. It was funny, really, 'cause Paul used her 'lav' and she would'nt [sic] let her mum clean the 'lav' out until – months later, it was. It started to smell so it had to be cleaned after long last. But it was funny, 'cause she was always up in that toilet.

Emma P.
Harrisburg, Pennsylvania

Dear, darling Beatles,

To think that I, Harriet Watts, live on the same planet with the Beatles, breathe the same air as the Beatles, see the same sun, moon, and stars as the Beatles.

Oh! It's just too much!!

Fondly and Forever,
Harriet W.
Atlanta, Georgia

Dear Beatles,
I told my Mother that I can't imagine a world without the Beatles, and she said she could easily.

Loyal forever,
Lillie K.
Fairbanks, Alaska

Dear Beatles,
I have 826 pictures of the Beatles, and am just beginning.

All my love,
Diana A.
New York City

Dear Beatles,
We have started a Beatle fan club.

So far we have two members. I am club President and Winifred is Vice President in charge of new members.

Your fans,
Gloria J. and Winifred Z.
Oakland, California

Dear Beatles,
Please dedicate your next song to me.

If you do, it will be a terrific seller, because I have loads of friends, and they will all buy the record.

Your fan,
Irma S.
Raleigh, North Carolina

Dear Beatles,
Please call me on the Telephone. My # is 629-7834

If my mother answers, hang up. She is not much of a Beatle fan.

With love from,
Maxine M.
Cleveland, Ohio

Dear Beatles,
I am a loyal fan. I have every one of your records and I don't even have a record player.

Love, Donna J.
Portland, Maine.

Dearest, sweetest Beatles,
I have Beatle pictures all over my room. I have Beatle pictures over my bed. I have Beatle pictures over my desk. I have Beatle pictures in my closet. I have Beatle pictures over my bookcase.

My mother hopes you are just a fad.

Love from a Beatle fan – all the way!
Stella J.
Chicago, Illinois

DEAR BEATLES
DO YOU THINK THAT YOU COULD SING AT OUR SCHOOL DANCE ON MAY 15?

THE REASON IS NOBODY EVER SANG AT OUR SCHOOL DANCE, EXCEPT MARSHA GOLDMAN, WHO IS IN GRADE 10.

MARSHA SINGS OK BUT SHE ALWAYS FORGETS THE WORDS.

PLEASE SAY YES.
LOVE,
JOAN G.
ST. PAUL, MINNESOTA

Dearest John,
I would like a lock of your hair. Also, a lock of hair from George, Paul, and Ringo. You know you have plenty of hair, so you can spare one lock each for me.

With love,
Sylvia M.
New York City

P.S. Please write the name of the person on each lock, so I will know who the lock of hair belongs to, as it is hard to tell when it is not on a person's head.

51

At their first American concert, at the Washington Coliseum, the screaming was so piercing that a police officer was driven to block his ears with bullets. Straight afterwards, the Beatles were guests of honour at a reception at the British embassy, where the hysteria took on a different form.

They were welcomed by the ambassador, Sir David Ormsby-Gore.

'Hello John,' he said, as he put out his hand.

This gave rise to a standard piece of Beatles horseplay. 'I'm not John,' said John. 'I'm Charlie. That's John.'

'Hello John.'

'I'm not John,' said George. 'I'm Frank. That's John.'

'Oh dear. I'll never get these names right. My wife is much better at remembering names.'

Ormsby-Gore then led them through into the embassy's ballroom, heaving with men in dinner jackets and women in evening gowns, all peering at the Beatles with a peculiar mixture of excitement, curiosity and disdain.

'There were a lot of Hooray Henrys there, and we had never really met that kind before,' recalled Paul. John escaped into a neighbouring room in search of a drink, only to find himself buttonholed by a British diplomat: 'We were wondering whether we might prevail upon our guests to participate in our rather small but not insignificant raffle?'

John hesitated.

'Come along now! Come and do your stuff!' snapped someone else from the embassy. Always the least biddable Beatle, John insisted on finishing his drink first, adding, 'I'm not going back into that crowd.'

'Oh yes you are! Come on, come on!'

'Come along now!' chorused a young woman in a ballgown.

John turned to Ringo. 'I'm getting out of here.'

Ringo calmed him down. 'Let's get it over with.'

Presently, the Beatles pulled the winning raffle tickets out of a hat. Afterwards, a tipsy lady put her arms around Paul. 'And which one are YOU?'

'Roger.'

'Roger what?'

'Roger McCluskey the Fifth.'

Later, asked what she thought of the Beatles, she replied, 'Monstrous.'

The Beatles were soon surrounded by yet more guests asking for autographs for their children or grandchildren. Watching John, one said in a stage whisper, 'Look, he can actually write!'

It was a remark designed to be heard by its victim. The other Beatles froze, and so did Brian Epstein: it seemed to them perfectly possible that John would reply with his fists. Instead, he simply refused to sign, even when an embassy official pressed a piece of paper into his hand and barked, 'You'll sign this and like it!'

Ringo, being more compliant, kept signing away. While he was signing, a mystery assailant took out a pair of scissors and began to snip away at his hair.

With each new telling, the incident was to take on the texture of a parable.

Ringo was convinced the offender was a man. As he remembered it, when challenged, the man had replied, 'Oh, it's OK, old chap … bullshit, bullshit.' Peter Brown, on the other hand, was convinced that 'a woman in an evening gown produced a pair of cuticle scissors from her evening bag and before he could stop her, snipped off a lock of his hair as a souvenir for her daughter'. This version was confirmed by a reporter from *Newsweek*, who claimed that 'a matron whipped out scissors, snipped off a lock of Ringo's hair', adding that she then 'disappeared in the crowd'.

John thought 'some bloody animal cut Ringo's hair. I walked out of that swearing at all of them, I just left in the middle of it.' But Paul was pretty sure that there was more than one perpetrator, and all four Beatles had been targeted: 'I remember girls wanting to cut bits off our hair, which was not entirely on – so there were a few elbows in gobs.'

In his autobiography George Martin blamed 'the full quota of chinless wonders', saying they 'behaved abominably. They would approach the boys with an off-hand, "Oh, which one are you?" and one actually got a pair of scissors and snipped off a piece of Ringo's hair while he was talking to someone else.'

The American journalist Michael Braun, trailing the Beatles around for a book, was sure it was 'a British debutante' who had withdrawn 'a pair of nail scissors from her purse'. Their authorised biographer, Hunter Davies, claimed that 'Several elderly ladies, with glasses of drink in their hands, accosted the Beatles and demanded autographs.' But Davies thought it was a single 'young lady guest' who 'started snipping off locks of Ringo's hair'. In *The Beatles Diary: An Intimate Day by Day History*, Barry Miles added extra colour: 'The British community, arrogant debutantes and aristocrats, disgraced themselves, and one woman even snipped off a lock of Ringo's hair just behind his left ear. John pushed all the autograph seekers away saying, "These people have no bloody manners."'

It was Cynthia Lennon whose memory proved the least forgiving. In her first autobiography, *A Twist of Lennon* (1978), she described the episode in terms of class warfare: 'The true-blue British high society abroad treated them like freaks, as only the upper-class British at their worst could do. Scissors were produced by their hosts. "Oh which one are you? I'm sure you won't mind will you, darling, if I cut a little of your hair to send home to my daughter in boarding school." Not bloody likely, Missus. That was it. They left. Protocol or no protocol they weren't going to stand for that.'

It was a man, or a woman, or women, either young or old. At any rate, most of the witnesses agreed that whoever did it was British, and posh.

Epstein led the Beatles away, with John swearing. As they were leaving, Lady Ormsby-Gore said, 'Thank you so much for coming. I'm sorry about all that down there. It can't have been much fun for you.'

Ringo turned to Sir David and asked, 'And what do you do?'

In the car back to their hotel, Epstein assured the Beatles that he would never again force them into attending an official function.

Foreign Office officials publicly denied that any such manhandling had taken place, repeating Sir David's assurances that 'The suggestion they were manhandled by anyone is untrue.' Back in London, a Conservative MP, Joan Quennell, wrote to the Foreign Secretary, Rab Butler, asking if it was true that 'the young British entertainers known as the Beatles were manhandled by British officials'. Mr Butler replied stating that, on the contrary, the Beatles' manager had written to Lady Ormsby-Gore 'thanking her for a delightful evening'.

52

The mystery was solved forty years later, when a fifty-eight-year-old Canadian woman named Beverly Markowitz confessed to the *Oshawa Times*.

In 1964 Beverly had been living with her parents in Silver Spring, Maryland, and dating a local disc jockey. Though she had heard 'I Want to Hold Your Hand' a couple of times on the radio, it had made little impression: 'I just thought it was another rock'n'roll band with a cool hairdo. They were all cute, though.'

Beverly's boyfriend had managed to buy tickets to the Beatles' first American concert, at the Washington Coliseum, and she had agreed to come along: 'He told me that the Beatles were going to be really big.' After the show he told Beverly that the Beatles would be at a party at the British embassy. Why didn't they try to crash it? Beverly was reluctant: 'We were in the parking lot. It was cold. It was snowy. It was late and dark and everything, and I had to get home or my dad was going to kill me.' But her boyfriend wouldn't take no for an answer. After all, they looked the part: 'I had a dress and heels on. My hair was all done up, and my date was in a suit.' Finally, she agreed.

It was much easier to get into the embassy than they had imagined: 'This white-haired drunk guy walked out, and when he went back in, we just walked right in with him. We got to go past the press and the velvet rope and right into the party.'

But the Beatles were upstairs, in a roped-off area. It was getting late. Beverly asked her boyfriend to take her home, but 'he said we weren't going anywhere until the Beatles came down.'

So they waited, and soon the Beatles came downstairs. Beverly approached them and asked for their autographs. 'They were all very nice, except for John. He wouldn't sign anything for anybody at all. I kept saying to him, "What is the matter with you?" Very arrogant.'

Her boyfriend still refused to take her home, even though she insisted her father would be furious. 'I kept saying, "Let's go, let's go, let's go," and my boyfriend just didn't want to leave. I couldn't figure how to get out, so I thought we'd just get thrown out.'

She worked out that the quickest way to be ejected was to cut some hair off a Beatle. She picked Ringo: 'He's kinda short, and I had on heels, so I could kind of get to him easier than the taller ones … I pulled out those little scissors from my purse. I just went clip, clip, clip, clip, clip all around the side, and he didn't feel it at first.'

Beverly remembered Ringo turning round and grabbing her by the shoulder. Just as she planned, she was immediately thrown out of the embassy, and returned home bearing a lock of Beatle hair.

Shortly afterwards she taped Ringo's hair into her autograph book, where it remains to this day, alongside his autograph.

Others were to find the process of harvesting Ringo's hair less irksome. Back in England, a thirteen-year-old Beatles fan, Katie Riggins, and a friend wrote letters to the mothers of Ringo and George asking for something belonging to their boys. Nearly a year later, Katie received a lock of Ringo's hair through the post, accompanied by a letter from Freda Kelly, the Beatles' Northern Fan Club secretary, saying that Mrs Starr wanted her to have it. Her friend received a similar envelope, containing George Harrison's old toothbrush.

53

For Christmas 1964, when I was seven, my brothers and I were given Beatles wigs by our parents. At that time, a factory in Bethnal Green was manufacturing 30,000 Beatles wigs a week, to be sold in shops for 30 shillings a head. But those were quality wigs, made of fabric: ours were 7/6*d*, and made of the same thin, moulded plastic as cheap masks, so brittle and sharp-edged that they were painful to wear: if you tilted your head upwards, the bottom edge would cut into the crook of your neck, and if you turned your head to the side, it would scrape the skin behind your ears.

Nor did these 'wigs' look at all like hair. In fact, they could have doubled as Frisbees. That same year, Santa also put a Beatles Magnetic Hair Game in my Christmas stocking. It turned out that it wasn't really a game at all, in that it had no rules or even instructions. It simply consisted of four outlines of the Beatles' heads, a magnet, and hundreds of little black iron filings. What little game there was involved using the magnet to move the iron filings into place, so that each Beatle would be left with something vaguely approaching a Beatles haircut, or what a Beatles haircut might have looked like if the Beatles had been stricken with alopecia. Fifty-five years later, in the spring of 2019, I noticed the very same Beatles Magnetic Hair Game, in good condition, advertised for £1,250.

Before I ever heard their music, all I knew about the Beatles was their hair; that, and their 'yeah, yeah, yeahs'. Everyone talked about their hair, and in families these talks would often end in rows, the younger generation being strongly for, and the older generation just as strongly against. The rows even brewed in the Beatles' own families.

'That hair, it was the very limit, the absolute end,' John's Aunt Mimi complained after watching one of their first TV appearances, on *Thank Your Lucky Stars* on 13 January 1963.

At the end of that year, Field Marshal Montgomery, 'Monty', became the first person to mention the Beatles' hair in a parliamentary debate. Speaking in the House of Lords in support of young men undergoing National Service – 'Look how well they fought in Malaya, in Korea and against the Mau-Mau' – he ended his speech with the words, 'In closing, I should like to say one thing: that if it is decided to have National Service, it may even result in the Beatles having to get their hair cut.' A few weeks later, on 9 December, the Labour MP Emrys Hughes answered Montgomery's point.

> MR EMRYS HUGHES: I do not know why they should get their hair cut. I do not understand that that argument is likely to bring young men into the Army at present. Why should a soldier need to have his hair cut in a certain way? Why should not soldiers be allowed

to wear beards? [Laughter.] My hon. and learned Friend the Member for Northampton (Mr. Paget) laughs. I have myself been asked why the young man who wants to join the Army is told that, if he goes into the Army, he will have to cut off his beard, whereas if he joins the Navy he can keep his beard.

Not for the first or last time, an argument about the Beatles' hair reeled off into an argument about everything else:

LORD ROBERT GROSVENOR (Fermanagh and South Tyrone, Ulster Unionist): Is the Hon. Gentleman aware that some soldiers are allowed to wear beards?

MR EMRYS HUGHES: I was not aware of that. If the Hon. Member wishes to develop that point later, I shall be very pleased indeed to have expert information upon this point.

MR REGINALD PAGET (Northampton, Labour spokesman for the Royal Navy and Army): If my Hon. Friend is interested in a reason, the traditional reason why soldiers are precluded from wearing beards is that a beard is a convenient thing to get hold of when you are cutting somebody's head off, and that occurs much more rarely in ships.

The origin of the Beatles' haircut is generally dated to the afternoon of 12 or 13 October 1961 at 29, rue de Beaune, Paris. John, the most well-to-do of the group, had been given £100 – £2,000 or more in today's terms – for his twenty-first birthday by his Aunt Elizabeth. He had decided to spend it on a holiday in Paris with Paul. At this time both of them wore their hair slicked back, with quiffs, in the manner of Elvis.

Arriving in Paris, they looked up an old friend from Hamburg, Jurgen Vollmer, and hung around with him. Vollmer wore his hair in a fringe, as a reaction to, in his words, 'the bourgeois horrors in Hamburg'. Calculating that it might give them more pulling power with the fast girls of the Left Bank, John and Paul wanted their hair like Vollmer's, though 'his was actually more coming over to one side', recalled Paul. 'A kind of long-haired Hitler thing.' In his garret room at the Hôtel de Beaune, Jurgen agreed to style it. First he cut Paul's hair, then John's. The next day, when the concierge spotted all the hair clippings on the floor, he let out a yell.

This may have been the first time that John and Paul adopted their 'moptop' hairdos, but where did the style itself originate? Stu Sutcliffe's exotic German girlfriend Astrid Kirchherr has sometimes claimed the credit, though on other occasions she has denied it: 'All that shit people said, that I created their hairstyle, that's rubbish! Lots of German boys had that hairstyle!'

She had certainly cut Stu's hair into a fringe six months earlier in Hamburg. Pete Best remembered both John and Paul poking fun at it. 'This was going too far, we all thought, and fell about, pointing to the fringe.' Suitably embarrassed, Stu combed it out, but according to Best he let it reappear over the course of the next few days, at which point George copied it.

Astrid herself traced its origin back two thousand years or more, claiming to have copied it from Jean Marais' haircut in Jean Cocteau's *Le Testament d'Orphée* of 1960, 'which I am certain was inspired by the ancient Greeks'. But the most dogged of all Beatles sleuths, Mark Lewisohn, casts doubt on this claim, having unearthed a photo of Jurgen Vollmer with the very same haircut in 1957, nearly three years before the release of Cocteau's film.

Though the hairstyle's lineage may be lost in time, its impact on the world is undeniable. As Pete Best asked, 'Who would ever have foreseen that Astrid's simple experiment with Stu would eventually result in half the male population of the world getting in on the act, and some worried nations like Indonesia even going so far as to pass laws making Beatle cuts illegal?'

John and Paul arrived back in Liverpool on 15 October. Neil Aspinall was in charge of picking them up for their next gig: 'We went to collect John, and his hair was down. But it was when we went to collect Paul that we realised something was going on, because not only was Paul's hair down as well, but he *skipped* out of his house – in that way he does – pointing at his hair and generally unable to be subtle about it. His hair was different and we had to notice it.' Paul remembered everyone saying, 'Eh, your hair's gone funny,' to which he and John replied, 'No, this is the new style.'

And so it turned out to be: in the fifties, young men in Britain wore their hair swept back, larded with hair cream, thinking it looked moody and metropolitan. The Beatles' hair, combed forward and unsculpted, was boyish, cocky and bright. Within two years their hairstyle had become a symbol of a new decade of freedom and youth, with the result that, in certain institutions, it was outlawed. In November 1963 the headmaster of Clarks Grammar School in Guildford issued a ban on Beatle haircuts. 'This ridiculous style brings out the worst in boys,' he thundered. 'It makes them look like morons. If I find the ban is being disregarded I shall write to all the parents asking them to support me.' But an anonymous 'senior boy' reacted grumpily to the injunction. 'The ban will not go down well with most boys,' he told the *Surrey Advertiser*. 'I think it is stupid. The Beatles are great and I see nothing wrong with their style of haircut.'

Within a few months the craze had spread to America. On 7 February 1964 the writer Tom Wolfe witnessed the arrival of the Beatles in the US: 'When they arrived at Kennedy, I could see all the boys running down the halls combing their hair forward. That's when the sixties really began.' George Martin remembered watching fully grown men walking down 5th Avenue in Beatles wigs: 'It was just madness.' Twenty thousand Beatles wigs a day were being sold in New York alone, costing $2.98 each.

Around that time, the fourteen-year-old Bruce Springsteen entered the record section of Newbury's store in Freehold, New Jersey, and clapped eyes on *Meet the Beatles*. It was, he still believes, 'the greatest album cover of all time ... All it said was *Meet the Beatles*. That was exactly what I wanted to do. Those four half-shadowed faces, rock'n'roll's Mount Rushmore, and ... THE HAIR ... THE HAIR. What did it mean? It was a surprise, a shock. You couldn't see them on the radio. It is almost impossible to explain today the effect of ... THE HAIR.'

Bruce's immediate reaction was to have his hair styled like the Beatles'. He knew the consequences: 'The ass-whippings, insults, risks, rejections and outsider status you would have to accept to wear it.' When his father saw what he had done, 'his first response was laughter. It was funny. Then, not so funny. Then, he got angry. Then, finally, he popped his burning question: "Bruce, are you queer?"'

Most of Bruce's contemporaries proved every bit as unforgiving. But one or two others were, like him, prepared to brave the taunts of the world for the sake of the Beatles. And so they soldiered on, ships against the storm: 'I ignored the insults, avoided the physical confrontations as best I could and did what I had to do … each sunrise held the possibility of a showdown.'

Twenty years earlier, Frank Sinatra had attracted his own 'Sinatramania'. Girls had gone crazy at his concerts, screaming the house down. Back in 1962, the composer Jule Styne had declared that Sinatra had 'defeated rock'n'roll', but this prediction now seemed premature. Aged forty-nine, Sinatra had no single in the charts, and just the one album, at number 10. In contrast, the Beatles had the top five singles, and the top two albums. Sinatra found it hard to stomach. 'He genuinely hated rock'n'roll, hated the Beatles … He had nothing but contempt,' noted the Sinatra family friend Rock Brynner, then aged seventeen.* Whenever the Beatles came on the radio or television, Sinatra would make his children switch them off. 'Long hair drove him batty,' recalled his valet George Jacobs. 'He didn't care how good the new music was … to him it was all one big excuse to take drugs.'†

* * *

---

* Rock Brynner (1946–), son of Yul Brynner. Historian, academic, co-founder of the Hard Rock Café.

† Whether out of familiarity or expediency, Sinatra eventually came round to the Beatles, recording both 'Yesterday' and 'Something', which he described as 'the greatest love song of the last fifty years' (though he misattributed it to Lennon and McCartney). In the summer of 1968 he also agreed to perform a one-off recording of 'The Lady is a Tramp' for Maureen Starkey's twenty-second birthday. The revised lyrics included the lines 'She married Ringo, and she could have had Paul/That's why the lady is a champ.' The master recording of the single was destroyed, and only one copy now exists, though its whereabouts are unknown. It has since been described by Daniel Finkelstein in *The Times* as 'the rarest and most valuable record ever made'.

By the end of 1964, all but the most stalwart British opponents of the Beatles' hairdos had run up the white flag. In December of that year, Earl Mountbatten of Burma, Chief of the Defence Staff, former First Sea Lord, last Viceroy of India, asked the head of his private staff, William Evans, to obtain a box of Beatles wigs for his grandchildren. The managing director of the manufacturing company drove to Mountbatten's Hampshire home, Broadlands, with a special presentation set. 'Mountbatten pranced around in a wig throughout Christmas Day,' recalled Evans. A year after criticising their hairdos in the House of Lords, Field Marshal Montgomery performed an about-turn, declaring that he looked forward to inviting them down to his country house 'to see what kind of fellas they are'.

But more oppressive regimes sought to outlaw Beatles hairstyles. In July 1964 President Sukarno of Indonesia announced that his government would no longer permit 'a hair style a la Beatles' on the heads of the country's youth: 'A few days ago there came to these parts some confused young men from England called "the Beatles",' he declared at an assembly. 'Their hair reaches down to their eyebrows ... Young men, if there are any among you who imitate them, beware! I will issue an order to the police throughout Indonesia, if there is an Indonesian youth who imitates, has his hair "Beatled", hold him, shave him completely bald ... Are the police here or not? Make a note, make a note of my order!'

In the Soviet Union, Beatles records were banned, long hair on men was outlawed, and anti-Beatle propaganda was rife. In 1966 a news programme on the lone, state-run TV channel featured a series of grotesque photographs of the group and their screaming fans, backed by a commentary that mixed horror with sarcasm:

> Pop quartet the Beatles – look how elegant they are! But when they started their career they were performing onstage just wearing swimming trunks with toilet seats on their necks! Then they met a kind fairy – London dealer Brian Epstein. This London fairy understood that these gifted guys could be real cash earners. Struck down with psychosis, the fans don't hear anything any more.

> Hysterics, screams, people fainting! Demolished concert halls and fights are the usual finale of a concert. It's a world consisting of four walls covered with the photos of four singers with long hair.

There followed images of extreme poverty in the Deep South, of teenagers dancing wildly and of members of the Ku Klux Klan with burning crosses, all contributing to a portrait of Western indifference to social injustice.

> Keep on dancing, lads, don't look around! You don't really want to know what's happening! Keep on going, louder and faster! You don't care about anyone else!

Mikhail Safonov was a schoolboy in Leningrad when Soviet radio played 'A Hard Day's Night' as an example of a capitalist song about the relentless pursuit of money. It was the first time he had ever heard the Beatles. Initially, he was unmoved, but before the end of 1965 he had become caught up in a particularly perilous form of Beatlemania. He and his school friends would copy Beatles records and exchange them on the black market. All over the Soviet Union, young fans like Mikhail would write out Beatle lyrics and pass them around, learning English from them. The most rebellious liked to switch the names of Lenin and Lennon, even though discovery could cost them any hope of further education. One school staged and broadcast a show trial of the Beatles, with a prosecutor railing against them as 'Bugs'. At the end of the trial they were found guilty, in their absence, of antisocial behaviour. But this verdict was set to backfire: 'The more the state persecuted the Beatles,' recalls Mikhail, 'the more they exposed the falsehood and hypocrisy of Soviet ideology. And in attacking something the whole world had fallen in love with, they isolated themselves even more. It made us more doubtful that our beloved country was right after all.'

Mikhail's nickname at school was 'Ringo', because he aped his hairstyle. Having won a silver medal at school, he was obliged to go to the Palace of Culture to collect it, his banned Beatle hair glued down and parted with sugar and water to replicate an approved cut. But as he was leaving, a group of policemen spotted its true length and chastised him for being a long-haired deviant, setting him free only after he had shown them his silver medal.

As an adult, Mikhail became a senior researcher at the Institute of Russian History in St Petersburg. Looking back, he believes that 'Beatlemania washed away the foundations of Soviet society … One could argue they did more for the destruction of totalitarianism in the USSR than Solzhenitsyn and Sakharov.'

Strange though it may seem, this view has been confirmed by both Mikhail Gorbachev and Vladimir Putin. When Paul visited Moscow in May 2003, to perform a concert in Red Square, he had an audience with President Putin, who told him that hearing the Beatles as a boy growing up in the Soviet Union was 'like a gulp of freedom'. On the same visit, former president Gorbachev told Paul: 'I do believe the music of the Beatles taught the young people of the Soviet Union that there is another life.'

As the Beatles' hair inched downwards, past their collars, across their ears and over their shoulders, hair on other heads followed suit. For young people, long hair came to symbolise freedom, even happiness. 'If my hair seems a little on the long side it's because the idea became implanted in my brain at a very early age: long hair equals happiness. And that's from the Beatles,' says the cellist Steven Isserlis, who turned nine years old at the end of 1967.

When 'Penny Lane' was released at the beginning of that year, many of his regular customers expected Harry Bioletti, whose barber shop it immortalised, to be filled with delight. 'Oh dear me no!' he protested. 'I did the Beatles' haircuts when they started up and became the Quarrymen. But I've taken their pictures down. Such hair is bad for trade. I'm not disloyal, but business is business. I encourage plenty off the top in my shop.'

Our village barber in Surrey had a cartoon stuck on the wall next to his mirror. It showed two men standing next to each other in a public urinal, one with long hair, the other with short hair.

'Blimey! You gave me a start!' exclaims the short-haired man. 'I thought you was a girl!'

A popular joke of that time involved a young man going into his local barber shop and saying that he'd like a Beatles haircut. The barber then gives him a short-back-and-sides.

'But the Beatles don't have their hair cut like that!' protests the young man.

'They would do if they came in here,' comes the reply.

During the mid to late sixties it was hard to keep up with the Beatles and their hair, particularly if one took their moustaches, beards and sideburns into account. September 1968 marked the fifth time in four years that the technicians at Madame Tussauds felt obliged to update the Beatles' waxworks to allow for their ever-changing appearances; three months later Paul grew a beard, and they had to start the process all over again.

By then the Beatles' personal hairdresser, Leslie Cavendish, had become a celebrity in his own right. Having started off in the trade washing hair for Vidal Sassoon, he was now photographed and interviewed in fashionable magazines, and invited to all the best parties. He went on to write an autobiography, *The Cutting Edge*, full of details about the way each of the four would react to his styling. Oddly enough, it was Ringo he found the least approachable, 'the only Beatle … who didn't want you to forget that he *was* a Beatle,' whereas Paul was always easy-going and appreciative. George had the thickest head of hair, 'at least twice as thick as Paul's,' but barely spoke while it was being cut, beyond offering 'a polite word of thanks' when it was over. John was tricky – 'perhaps the worst client I ever had to handle' – because he was a terrible fidget. '"Could you please keep your head still, John?" I'd ask, again and again, as patiently as I could. John would briefly acknowledge me, nodding his head as if he'd understood, but the mere fact of nodding demonstrated he hadn't quite got the message.'

Latterly, John would have his haircuts supervised by Yoko Ono:

> Frankly, I couldn't grasp half of what Yoko was going on about, but then again, neither could John. In fact, he was becoming increasingly exasperated by her:
>
> 'I don't understand what you're trying to say!' he'd complain, shaking his head dangerously. 'I just don't understand!'
>
> 'You don't understand because you don't listen,' Yoko would answer playfully, as if he were a stuck-up little boy – which perhaps he was. Amazingly, this only seemed to turn him on more. John was normally the dominant character in any conversation. And yet here, for the first time, I saw this fierce little lady completely in control of their dialogue.

Being the only part of the Beatles' bodies that could be chopped off and removed without causing alarm, their hair was particularly coveted by fans and collectors. In 1966 a German barber, Klaus Baruch, gave John a short-back-and-sides in preparation for his role as a soldier in the film *How I Won the War*. It made headlines around the world: 'LENNON ACTS WITHOUT LOCKS'. 'BEATLE SEVERS MOP TOP'. 'SHORN LENNON: TOP CHOPPED'. So determined was Brian Epstein to prevent the precious hair clippings falling into the hands of souvenir-hunters that he deputed Neil Aspinall to supervise its incineration.

But it now appears that Mr Baruch retained a few locks as a nest-egg for his retirement. Fifty years on, a four-inch lock of Lennon's hair from this trim was placed on sale by Heritage Auctions of Dallas. 'This is the largest lock of John Lennon's hair ever offered at auction,' said the auctioneer, Gary Shrum. It eventually sold to Paul Fraser from Bristol for £35,000, three times the estimate. At the time of writing, Paul Fraser Collectibles is offering 'a guaranteed genuine half-inch strand of John Lennon's hair – exceptional provenance – acquired from barber Klaus Baruck in Berlin' for £399. The brochure adds that this single strand of hair is 'presented on a display sheet ready for framing'.

54

Dear Ringo,

There is only one Ringo, and there is only one Winifred Henderson.

Isn't it about time that the one and only Ringo and the one and only Winifred Henderson got two – gether at last!

Love and stuff,

Winifred H.

Bayonne, New Jersey

Dear Ringo,

what did you do before you were a Beatle? were you an ordinary person?

love,

Janet L.

Miami, Florida

Dear Ringo,

You have the nicest smile of all the Beatles. Are those your real teeth?

I hope you don't mind my asking.

Sincerely,

Evelyn M.

Salt Lake City, Utah

Dear Ringo:
I named my new dog after you, and he is the proudest dog on the block.

with love,
Susie P.
Winston-Salem
North Carolina

Dear Ringo,
YOU ARE THE HANDSOMEST MAN IN THE WORLD, EXCEPT FOR MY FATHER.

MY FATHER IS HANDSOME TOO, IN AN OLD WAY.

Love,
Norma A.
Denver, Colorado

55

These days, Ringo is a byword for good luck, but his early life was riddled with misfortune. The Starkey house was a two-up, two-down in a very rough part of the Dingle, where they are traditionally rumoured to 'play rag-tag with hatchets'. The house had no bathroom, and an outside toilet. His father left home when Ringo was three years old. 'We were working-class, and in Liverpool when your dad left you suddenly became lower-working class.' At school he was placed in the C-stream, where he was regarded as unexceptional – or, to quote one of his reports, 'honest, cheerful, and willing and quite capable of making a satisfactory employee'. But he was in hospital for two years from the age of thirteen, so his education effectively stopped then: had it not been for the efforts of the daughter of a neighbour who taught him to read, he would have been functionally illiterate.

Aged fifteen, young Ritchie Starkey went straight from hospital to a job as a messenger with British Railways, but after six weeks he was sacked for failing his medical. For a while he worked as a waiter, and then his stepfather found him a job as an apprentice pipe-fitter: 'I started to be an engineer but I banged my thumb the first day. I became a drummer because it was the only thing I could do.' He lacked both vanity and any trace of self-pity. Despite all his misfortunes, he refused to believe that as soon as you're born, they make you feel small. In a radio interview in 1966, Brian Matthew breezily asked him: 'Would you say on the whole that you've had a fairly easy life?'

RINGO: I've had an easy life. Never been hungry. Never been cold. Y'know, I've had a good life. I wouldn't change any of it. This bit's much better, but still it wouldn't bother me to go through all the rest again.

MATTHEW: Are you from a big family or a small family?

RINGO: I'm the only child.

MATTHEW: Oh, well, there you go.

RINGO: People say, 'Oh, you're an only child, you must've been spoilt,' but my mother went out to work and she was the only one getting any money, so I suppose that's why I only asked for little things, not big things. They may have seemed big but they weren't really.

It was always rumoured that Pete Best was sacked from the Beatles because the others were jealous of his good looks. If so, what someone once referred to as a bus-driver's face was Ringo's passport to fame and fortune.

He was not the best-looking or most charismatic or most musical or most interesting of the Beatles, but somehow this made him an essential part of the group's mix. He was the Horatio figure, the Dr Watson, the Tommy Atkins who in his plodding, selfless, reliable way may be a few steps behind the rest, but is always there to stop them going over the edge.

'Why don't you ever say anything except "I'm the drummer"?' John asked him irritably, in front of a journalist, as they were touring Britain in 1963.

'I don't like talking. It's how I'm built,' replied Ringo. '… I don't mind talking or smiling, it's just I don't do it very much. I haven't got a smiling face or a talking mouth.'

In narrative terms, he serves as a workhorse among prize ponies, the honest-to-goodness, plain-speaking character to whom others can relate. Of the four Beatles, he is the only one who could be described as a bloke. 'Ringo is not the world's most inventive drummer,' observed George Melly, 'but he IS lovably plain, a bit "thick" as a public persona, and decidedly ordinary in his tastes. He acts as a bridge, a reassuring proof that the Beatles bear some relation to ordinary people.'

In May, 1963, when the Beatles were just taking off, Ringo went into their fan club's office and asked the secretary, Freda Kelly, if she would deal with his fan mail. Freda was reluctant: 'Get your mum and dad to do it. All the other parents do,' she said.

'Me mum doesn't know what to put,' Ringo replied, adding, 'Anyway, I don't get a lot.'

Feeling sorry for him, Freda said, 'All right, bring it in, but just this once.' She remembers him arriving the next day 'with one of those small poly bags that tights come in – that was all his mail, stuffed inside. Paul got two feet of mail, but Ritchie only had that small sack, with ten letters in it.'

To this day, jokes are made about his lowly position as the runt of the Beatles litter. In an episode of the cartoon *Family Guy*, three girls sit in a bedroom talking about their favourite Beatle. The first two declare their love for Paul and for John. 'You know what? I'm in love with Ringo!' says the third girl. At this point, Ringo appears outside the bedroom window, at the top of a ladder, and asks her to repeat what she said. The girl suddenly becomes hesitant: 'I don't know what I said.' But Ringo is not to be deflected. 'It sounded like you said you were in love with Ringo,' he says.

'Um. Um. I don't think so.'

'I'm pretty sure you said "I'm in love with Ringo." Well, here I am!'

He opens his arms wide and beams.

At this point the first girl asks, hopefully, 'Are John and Paul out there?' Ringo replies, 'No, just Ringo!' and all three girls look downcast.

But over the years Ringo has had the last laugh. In America, more so than in Britain, he gathered a sizeable following of his own fans. Characteristics that appeared run-of-the-mill in Britain seemed to strike Americans as remarkable, even exotic. Phil Spector wrote and produced a song, 'Ringo, I Love You', for the singer Bobbie Jo Mason,*

---

* A pseudonym disguising the sixteen-year-old Cherilyn LaPiere: Spector favoured all-American names for his female singers. LaPiere was shortly to become more famous as Cher. 'Ringo, I Love You' failed to chart. Some attributed its failure to Cher's deep voice: apparently, many radio producers feared that the person yearning to hold Ringo tight was a man.

who sang of dreaming about Ringo holding her hand, and running her fingers through his hair. A single by the Young World Singers, released during the 1964 US presidential elections, was called 'Ringo for President'.* As Brian Epstein once noted: 'America discovered Ringo.'

And Ringo continues to pop up in the intimate reminiscences of models, singers and actresses. A few years ago I was browsing through the memoirs of Christine Keeler† when I came across this passage in her chapter 'Lust and Marriage':

> I kept going to the Ad Lib and one night ended up dancing with Ringo Starr. The Fab Four were the biggest thing in the world and we were great curiosities on the dance floor. Which is why we ended up in bed together the next morning, the morning Freddy turned up unexpectedly for a reconciliation. If it had been anyone else but a Beatle I think he might have bashed Ringo about. As it was, he was so taken aback when he saw it was Ringo in bed with me that he did nothing, just stood there gawping. Ringo made a break for it – and broke my banister as he went. He got married for the first time a week later.

In his memoirs, the NEMS director Peter Brown notes that Ringo was the 'last Beatle to settle down with one girl', and furthermore, that 'with his big puppy eyes and self-effacement, he seemed an easy target for every blonde bombshell who could get near to him', among them the glamour model Vicki Hodge.‡ In the memoirs of Chris O'Dell ('the remarkable story of an ordinary woman who lived the dream of millions'), several pages are devoted to the former Apple employee's affair with Ringo in the early 1970s: 'It was as if two wires suddenly connected, sending an electrical jolt of attraction right through me. In

* In Britain, a raucous cover version by Rolf Harris failed to chart.

† The call girl whose affair with the Secretary of State for War John Profumo was said to have led to the downfall of the Conservative government in 1964.

‡ Who also boasted of flings with, in alphabetical order, Prince Andrew, David Bailey, John Bentley, John Bindon, Yul Brynner, Elliott Gould and George Lazenby.

that instant, Ringo wasn't just a friend, he wasn't just a Beatle – he was a man. A very desirable man … We comforted each other at a time when we both needed comforting. He was good to me, and always, always kind, and just being with him made me happy. I wanted it to last, but I knew it wouldn't …' In 1981 Ringo married the former Bond girl Barbara Bach.

Somehow he possessed the happy knack of turning misfortune to advantage. He had been born left-handed, but his grandmother – his father's mother – had forced him to use his right hand. Such brutal coercion can lead to lifelong problems, but in Ringo's case it meant that he tackled a right-hand drum kit with the thwarted instincts of a left-hander, which gives his drumming the idiosyncratic style that countless Beatles tribute acts still find hard to duplicate.

His drumming was never flash: he was content to let it pass unnoticed, at the service of the song. In all his years as the Beatles' recording engineer, Geoff Emerick found his character dull – 'I honestly don't remember having one memorable conversation with Ringo' – but he was often struck by the galvanising effect his drumming had on the group's creativity: 'It could get incredibly boring and depressing hearing them play the same song for nine or ten hours at a stretch, especially if it was getting worse and worse as they got more drugged and went off into tangents. Interestingly, during those long jam sessions Ringo would most often be the one to take them in new directions – he'd get fed up doing the same beat all the time and he'd change it, which sometimes sparked a musical change from one of the others.'

Like many musicians, Graham Nash feels that Ringo's drumming is undervalued: 'Ringo plays a heartbeat, which is a sound I love. It's one of the secrets of great drumming, because, in life, everything starts with a heartbeat. Your mother's heartbeat is the very first thing you hear when you are conceived, and that sets the rhythm for the rest of your life … The heartbeat is the most important part of music if you want to connect on a personal level. And it's very subtle … He's an incredible drummer, one of the most underrated. And the Beatles were very lucky to get him.'

He was always unassuming. 'Ringo is a lovely boy,' Brian Epstein said to his solicitor, Nat Weiss. 'One of the great assets of him is that even though he's the least talented he's not uptight about it.' This may sound patronising, but it was undoubtedly well-meant: with three competitive songwriters, the group grew increasingly combustible – a fourth might have created an explosion.

Alone of all the Beatles, Ringo possessed no talent for composing. But one day, in a sudden flash of inspiration, the germs of a song entered his head, as if from nowhere. He worked on the song for three hours, and presented it to the other three the next day. After an awkward silence, they felt obliged to point out that it had already been written and recorded by Bob Dylan.

Nor was he much of a vocalist, though the others were happy to maintain a touching tradition of giving him one song to sing per album. During the recording of *Sgt. Pepper*, Emerick watched as Ringo struggled through 'With a Little Help from My Friends'. Appropriately, given that it was a song about friends helping you hit the right notes, John, Paul and George gathered round him, 'silently conducting and cheering him on as he gamely tackled his vocal duties'. But when it came to sustaining the final high note he grew self-conscious, and lost his nerve. 'It's OK, just put your mind to it. You can do it,' said George. 'Just throw yer head back and let 'er rip!' Finally he succeeded, and the others all cheered, toasting him with their Scotch and Cokes. The next day, as the rest of them added their backing vocals, 'Ringo sat up in the control room … beaming like a proud papa.'

He is the personification of the adage 'Dogged as does it.' Against all the odds, he carries on, come what may. Before playing to 10,000 people at the Forum in Montreal in 1964, the Beatles received news of a plot by anti-Semites to kill Ringo. Ringo reacted by pointing to a gap in their logic: 'The one major fault is that I'm not Jewish.' However, the authorities took the threat seriously, and feared that behind his drums onstage he was, quite literally, a sitting target. For his part, Ringo faced the threat with his usual sang-froid, his only concession being to adjust his cymbals to a 45-degree angle, in the hope that they might deflect a bullet. Throughout the concert a plain-clothes policeman sat beside him. Drumming away, Ringo couldn't stop thinking about this bodyguard: 'If someone in the audience has a pop at me, what is this guy going to do? Is he going to catch the bullet?' Before long, he couldn't stop smiling. 'I found this was getting funnier and funnier all the time, and the guy just sat there.'

Ringo is buoyant; no matter what happens, he bobs back up. He is the common man for whom providence keeps coming up roses, the triumphantly untragic hero, raised higher and higher by his flaws. There is a scene in *Help!* in which he escapes from a yacht by diving overboard into the ocean. It was filmed in the Bahamas with a camera mounted on a raft positioned a hundred yards away. Meanwhile, the area was surrounded by nets to keep sharks at bay. Victor Spinetti watched as Ringo kept leaping overboard for take after take, only to be picked up and hoisted back onto the yacht, shivering.

> 'Oh V-vi-vic,' he said as, once more, the hairdresser dried his hair, 'd-d-do I have to do this a-g-gain?'
>
> 'Why?' I asked him. His answer stunned me.
>
> 'I c-c-can't swim.'

56

On page 598 of James Boswell's *Life of Johnson*, an unnamed clergyman puts in the briefest of appearances. Boswell and Dr Johnson are in the middle of an argument about the best sermons in English when 'a Clergyman, whose name I do not recollect' pipes up with a suggestion. Johnson slaps him down – 'They were nothing, Sir …' – and the unnamed clergyman is never mentioned again.

One hundred and twenty-five years after Boswell recorded the incident, the essayist Max Beerbohm lamented the way this curt dismissal by Dr Johnson was now all that anyone would ever know of this anonymous clergyman: 'Fragmentary, pale, momentary; almost nothing; glimpsed and gone; as it were, a faint human hand thrust up, never to reappear, from beneath the rolling waters of time …'

Jimmie Nicol makes the same sort of fleeting appearance in the story of the Beatles. In the 420 pages of Hunter Davies' pioneering biography of the group he appears nowhere at all, and he pops up just twice in Bob Spitz's 983-page biography, on pages 506 and 507, his Christian name mis-spelled as 'Jimmy'. The Beatles' own vast *Anthology* allots him a single entry, on page 139. In Philip Norman's 400-page *Shout! The True Story of the Beatles*, he merits three passing mentions, all in the same brief paragraph:

> In June they toured Scandinavia, Holland, the Far East and Australasia. Ringo Starr was having his tonsils out and missed three-quarters of the journey; in his place sat Jimmy Nicol, a session drummer small and obscure enough to scotch any rumour of permanent change. Nicol drummed with them until Melbourne,

where Ringo rejoined: history from then on relates nothing further on Jimmy Nicol.

Fragmentary, pale, momentary; almost nothing; glimpsed and gone: such is the fate of Jimmie Nicol. Until June 1964, his career had been up and down, but largely down. He had drummed on 'Giddy-Up-a-Ding-Dong' by Colin Hicks & His Cabin Boys,* but it had failed to chart. He then briefly joined Tony Sheridan and the Wreckers, before leaving them to play with Vince Eager and the Quiet Three.† They toured Britain in 1960, on the same bill as Eddie Cochran and Gene Vincent. Cochran took a shine to them and promised to take them back to Los Angeles at the end of the tour; but on 17 April 1960 Cochran was killed when his taxi crashed on the outskirts of Chippenham.‡ Having lost their mentor, Vince Eager and the Quiet Three were forced to stay in Britain, playing a summer season in Great Yarmouth instead of flying out to Los Angeles. Subsequently, after a row over money with their manager/promoter Larry Parnes, Eager and the band broke up, leaving Jimmie once more high and dry.

Going it alone, he formed Jimmie Nicol and the Shubdubs, but their ska version of 'Humpty Dumpty' failed to take off. In early 1964 he

---

* Colin Hicks was the younger brother of Tommy Steele. He had been a cabin boy on a Cunard cruise, returning in autumn 1957 to find his elder brother famous. Colin looked like Tommy, and sounded like him too: he would later ascribe his failure to crack the charts to this insuperable resemblance.

† Vince Eager was born Roy Taylor, but was given a fresh name by his manager, Larry Parnes. Known by some as 'Parnes, Shillings and Pence', Larry Parnes made it a rule to select stage names for his protégés, among them Billy Fury (born Ron Wycherley), Marty Wilde (Reginald Smith), Dickie Pride (Richard Knellar), Lance Fortune (Chris Morris), Johnny Gentle (John Askew), Georgie Fame (Clive Powell) and Tommy Steele (Thomas Hicks). One of the few to mount a successful resistance to Parnes's compulsive name-changing was Joe Brown, who refused to go by the name Parnes had allotted him: Elmer Twitch.

‡ The first policeman on the scene of the crash was a young cadet called Dave Harman. Back at the station, he began strumming on Cochran's Gretsch guitar, which he had rescued from the wreckage, and found he had an aptitude for music. Consequently he left the police force, changed his name to Dave Dee and formed Dave Dee, Dozy, Beaky, Mick and Tich. Between 1965 and 1969 the group spent more weeks in the UK singles chart than the Beatles.

drummed on 'Beatlemania', a cut-price album of Beatles' cover versions, and then he drummed for Georgie Fame's backing band, the Blue Flames, by night, and worked in a music store during the day.

On the afternoon of 4 June 1964 he was sitting at home in Barnes, south-west London, when the telephone rang. 'Hello, is Jimmie Nicol in please? This is George Martin calling. What are you doing for the next four days? Ringo is ill, and we want you to take his place on the Beatles' tour. Would you mind going to Australia?'

Who would have said no? Martin told Jimmie to come to the EMI studios at 3 p.m., adding, 'The Beatles want to run through some numbers with you.'

Earlier that day the Beatles had been posing for photographs to mark the beginning of their first world tour when Ringo had begun to vomit. Rushed to University College Hospital, he was diagnosed with tonsillitis and pharyngitis. Brian Epstein told the other three that they would need a replacement. George, never the most pliable of the Beatles, put his foot down: 'If Ringo's not part of the group, it's not the Beatles. I don't see why we should do it. I'm not going to go.'

Epstein talked them through the economics of cancelling a world tour, whereupon George, always beady about money, immediately changed his mind. They now had twenty-four hours to find someone who could drum, and who looked, however fleetingly, like a Beatle. As it happened, their first two choices – Raye Du-Val of the Blue Notes and Bobby Graham of Marty Wilde's Wildcats – had prior commitments, but after a friendly phone call from Paul, Georgie Fame agreed to release his new drummer.

At Abbey Road, Jimmie successfully drummed his way through 'I Want to Hold Your Hand', 'She Loves You', 'I Saw Her Standing There', 'This Boy', 'Can't Buy Me Love' and 'Long Tall Sally'.

'Right then, you're in,' said John.

That evening, two women arrived at Jimmie's house: a hairdresser, ready to give him a new Beatle fringe, and a wardrobe lady, carrying Ringo's Beatle suit, which would need to be altered overnight for this taller, burlier new Beatle.

The following day, John, Paul, George and Jimmie flew to Copenhagen, where they were booked into the Royal Hotel, staying in the same suite of rooms President Khrushchev had occupied a fortnight before. Meanwhile, Ringo lay in his bed at University College Hospital, feeling sorry for himself: 'It was very strange because I wasn't well and they'd taken Jimmie Nicol and I thought they didn't love me any more. All that stuff went through my head.'

But Ringo's cloud was Jimmie's silver lining. 'The day before I was a Beatle, not one girl would even look me over. The day after, when I was suited up and riding in the back of a limo with John Lennon and Paul McCartney, they were just dying to get a touch of me.'

His first concert as the Beatles' new drummer got off to a shaky start. 'He was sitting up on this rostrum, just eyeing up all the women,' recalled Paul. 'We'd start "She Loves You" – "1, 2," and nothing. "1, 2," still nothing.' But he soon got the hang of it.

For the next ten days Jimmie was treated as a full member of the Beatles, appearing alongside John, Paul and George at press conferences, grinning broadly and laughing at all their jokes. However, film footage shows that he himself contributed little in the way of banter. Asked in Holland how he feels about his first two shows with the group, he replies, 'Sweat was rolling off my cheeks in buckets.' But the rest of the questions – 'Do you wear something on your head when you go swimming?' 'Do you do it for the money?' are directed at the others, with George struggling to explain the pun within the name of the Beatles through a Dutch interpreter.

In Hong Kong, the Beatles' press officer, Derek Taylor, introduced them as 'John, Paul, George and Jimmie Nicol', at which the first three hooted and whistled in his support.

'Mr Nicol, how do you feel being rushed into this vast world of publicity all at once?' asks a reporter.

'It's a most exciting experience,' replies Jimmie.

'Correct!' chorus John and George.

Even now, photographs of the Beatles taken during their ten-day tour can bring the viewer up with a jolt: it is as if a random tourist has thrust his head through the hole of a 'Picture Yourself as a

Beatle' stand at a funfair. He leaps out at you, an intruder in a family album.

On their flight from Hong Kong via Darwin to Sydney, Jimmie sat next to John. The two of them seemed to hit it off, and it even crossed Jimmie's mind that if he played his cards right, he could be in with a chance of replacing Ringo on a permanent basis.

At their first press conference in Sydney, the three regular Beatles batted away questions with their usual chirpy banter.

'What do you expect to find here in Australia?'

'Australians.'

'Have you been practising up your Australian accents?'

'No, cobber, not at all.'

As the conference progressed, the chain-smoking Jimmie was put on the spot.

'How about you, Jimmie? You haven't said anything. How do you feel, Jimmie, being in with the Beatles – a new talent – standing in for Ringo?'

'It's a good experience, man.'

'How is Ringo?'

'Erm, he's much better. He joins them on Sunday.'

'What do you do then?'

'Erm, I go back to London and they're fixing up a band for me, and I do some television.'

The spotlight swung back on John, Paul and George, who were better equipped to answer the more general questions. But, noticing Jimmie's silence, one reporter asked, 'Have you got an agreement that Jimmie mustn't speak?'

'Ask him a question,' said George.

'I can't answer questions that, erm, I don't know anything about.'

'What's the group you play with in England, Jimmie?'

'Well, I've played with a lot of groups in England. Just before I left, I was playing with a rhythm and blues band …'

'Does Brian Epstein manage you?'

Jimmie thought for a few seconds. 'Nobody … No, he doesn't.'

The other three all laughed at his hesitant response.

'You'd know it if he did!' said John.

Three hundred thousand people packed the streets to welcome John, Paul, George and Jimmie to Adelaide, where they were greeted by the lord mayor and honoured with a civic reception in the town hall. Out on the balcony in front of the cheering crowds, each of the Beatles was introduced in turn. A noticeable drop in temperature came when Jimmie's name was called, and even one or two boos.

At the press conference, one reporter observed: 'There's more people here than came to see the Queen.'

'I should think so,' said George. 'She didn't have any hit records.'

'Jimmie, do you think that Brian Epstein is going to wave his magic wand at you sometime and include you as a fifth Beatle?'

'That I don't know.'

'What's it like being thrust in with the Beatles?'

'It's the end, you know!' By this he meant 'It couldn't be better,' though it now carries a hint of doom.

Throughout his time as a Beatle, Jimmie was in two minds about the man he had been hired to replace: 'Until Ringo joined us in Melbourne, I was praying he would get well. At the same time, I was hoping he would not come back. I was having a ball.' But in public, he remained sunny.

'Jimmie, you've got your final performances tonight and then Ringo arrives tomorrow.'

'Yeah, that's right. I'm looking forward to meeting him.'

'And then it's all over for you. What's going to happen? I hear you may not be going back to England?'

'Not for a little while, no. I fancy going back to Sydney.'

At the end of the Beatles' final concert in Adelaide, Jimmie's very last show as a Beatle, Paul publicly thanked him for standing in as their drummer. He then added that Ringo would be returning the next day, and the audience burst into rapturous applause.

Ringo and Brian Epstein flew from London to Melbourne, arriving just before the others, who were flying from Adelaide. Up to a quarter of a million fans surrounded their hotel, screaming 'We want the Beatles! We want the Beatles!' The police called in the armed services, but they failed to prevent Ringo having clumps of hair pulled from his head as he rushed from his car to the hotel. The other three Beatles were then smuggled into the hotel through the back door, along with Jimmie. Once they were all inside, John, Paul and George were reunited with Ringo, and Ringo and Jimmie shook hands.

The five Beatles were escorted onto the hotel balcony. 'Hello everybody, how are you?' Paul said over a loudspeaker. 'Hello, hey!' added Ringo, and the crowd went wild. Jimmie joined in the waving, but said nothing. Sensing a bit of comical argy-bargy was in order, Ringo grabbed Jimmie's neck and performed a mock-strangling for the camera.

At the press conference in the hotel ballroom, Jimmie sat at one end of the table. He was asked if he would be forming a new band, but no one seemed particularly interested in his reply. 'I don't know yet,' he began. 'Until I get back …' Then John started to interrupt and Ringo signalled for Jimmie to be quiet. Feeling unwanted, Jimmie began drumming his fingers on the table. It was to be the last time he ever drummed with the Beatles.

That evening, Brian Epstein issued strict instructions that no one was to leave the hotel: if they wanted to have fun, they must have it in their suite. While John, Paul, George and Ringo had a party, Jimmie disobeyed orders and slipped out onto the streets. Realising he had absconded, Epstein despatched Mal Evans and Derek Taylor to look for him; they eventually tracked him down to a bar.

'You mustn't be on the streets,' said Taylor. 'You can't come into a bar.'

'What are you talking about? I'm not a Beatle any more.'

'You're a Beatle until we put you on the plane.'

Evans and Taylor settled his bill, and marched him back to the hotel.

The next morning, before his former bandmates had woken up, Jimmie was escorted to the airport by Brian Epstein. The atmosphere in their car was, he felt, a little testy. Was Epstein still cross about his behaviour the night before?

There were no fans at the airport, and no press or television. Sitting alone, he was spotted by a journalist who happened to be passing through. The journalist asked him what his plans were.

'Well, I hope to do something that I want to do,' he replied. 'Now there's a possibility that I might be able to do something.'

Before bidding him farewell, Epstein presented him with a gold watch, inscribed 'To Jimmie, with appreciation and gratitude – Brian Epstein and the Beatles'. He also gave him an envelope containing £500 for ten days' work. Jimmie then climbed the steps of the plane, giving a parting wave to a solitary cameraman. As the plane left the runway, he ceased to be a Beatle. He never spoke to any of the Beatles again: 'After my part of the Beatles' tour ended, I went back to England on my own. None of the Beatles ever phoned me after that. No phone call.'

For a few weeks, he felt the warm afterglow of celebrity: one or two people recognised him in the street, and when he went to watch Shirley Bassey performing at the Talk of the Town, she told the audience he was there, and asked him to stand and take a bow.

What next? In his position, which of us would not have felt, deep down, that, with a little bit of luck, all this fame and fortune, fun and adoration, might last forever?

At first, Jimmie seemed to have the wind behind him. Alert to his new-found fame, Pye Records re-released his ska version of 'Humpty Dumpty', slyly crediting it on the label to 'Jimmy Nicol now with the Beatles'. The *Daily Mirror* ran headline 'Jim Plans to Rival Beatles', on top of a story in which he was quoted as saying he wanted to make Brian Epstein wish he'd made him a permanent Beatle. Georgie Fame had kindly kept his place in the Blue Flames open, but, bucked by his new celebrity, Jimmie felt he could do better, and told him he was moving on.

Luck seemed to be on his side. It so happened that, three days after Jimmie's return, Dave Clark, the vocalist-drummer of the Dave Clark Five, was rushed to hospital with a duodenal ulcer, just when his band had been booked to top the bill for a three-week summer season at the Winter Gardens in Blackpool. This time, rather than simply step in for the drummer, Jimmie was invited to replace the entire band with one of his own. Understandably, he felt glad all over. 'I just can't find words to describe how I feel about taking Dave's place,' he told the *Daily Mirror*. 'One week, you're drumming away with the biggest group in the world. Then you hear they want you to take over from the second-biggest group.'

Within two days he had re-formed his earlier group, the Shubdubs, and they were on their way to Blackpool. Needless to say, a few of the supporting acts at the Winter Gardens – among them comedian Dick Emery and trumpeter Eddie Calvert – were put out by the news that Jimmie was now topping the bill. 'Most of the cast were bemused that we had come from nowhere to top the bill, due to Jimmie's sudden leap to fame,' recalled a Shubdub.

It was while Jimmie Nicol was in Blackpool that things began to go wrong. A rush-released follow-up single, 'Husky', failed to make the charts, despite an appearance by the band on *Ready Steady Go!*. Jimmie had a three-single contract with Pye; after the failures of 'Humpty Dumpty' and 'Husky', it was vital that his next single was a hit, or he would be dropped.

For this crucial record, Jimmie chose to revive an old blues song from the 1930s, 'Baby Please Don't Go'. Little did he know that another band, Them, had recorded the very same track for Decca, with two unknowns – Van Morrison and Jimmy Page – on vocals and lead guitar, and a song called 'Gloria' on the B-side.

The version by Them went to number 10; the Shubdubs' vanished without trace. From that point on, Jimmie's life seemed to go into free-fall. Pye refused to renew his contract; his wife filed for divorce. Undaunted, he bought himself a brand-new Jaguar, but within a fortnight the police had issued him with court summonses for four motoring offences.

He continued to pay each of the other five Shubdubs £26 a week, even though they were getting little work, and he himself was playing solo in bars for only £10 a week: 'I borrowed everywhere because I believed that one day there would be a turning point.' But the turning point never came. At the beginning of 1965 the Shubdubs' trumpet player decided to call it a day; soon the others followed suit.

Jimmie then formed a seven-piece group – the Sound of Jimmie Nicol – and somehow managed to convince Decca that an upbeat version of 'Oh My Darling Clementine', renamed 'Sweet Clementine', had all the ingredients of a hit. In pursuit of this dream he borrowed £3,000 to equip his band. They made their debut at the Chelmsford Corn Exchange on 3 April 1965, but failed to attract a single review.

Failure craves a reason. Jimmie developed a theory to explain his fall from grace: obviously, Brian Epstein had turned against him, punishing him for his rebellious behaviour on that last night in Australia; Epstein had clearly put pressure on promoters to blacklist him. No one could see the logic behind this theory – why would Epstein do such a thing? – but the scepticism of others served only to fuel Jimmie's burgeoning sense of conspiracy.

In April, George Harrison took the trouble to come to a performance by the Sound of Jimmie Nicol. Between sets, he asked a waiter to take a drink to Jimmie, but Jimmie sent it back. 'I declined the offer,' he explained later. 'I do have my self-respect. I will not be bought by anyone.' By now, he was finding hurt everywhere.

'Sweet Clementine' proved a flop, and Decca dropped Jimmie. He could no longer afford to pay the band. At the same time, he split up with his manager. On 30 April 1965, while the Beatles were filming *Help!*, he was declared bankrupt, his debts of £4,066 far surpassing the £50 in his bank account.

The *Daily Mail* ran the headline 'The Rise and Fall of the Fifth Beatle'. In the accompanying interview, Jimmie complained that 'standing in for Ringo was the worst thing that ever happened to me. Up to then I was feeling quite happy, turning over 30 to 40 pounds a week. I didn't realise that it would change my whole life. Everyone in show business said I couldn't miss. I was the hottest name there was. But after the headlines died, I began dying too. No one wanted to know me any more.' Quizzed about his future, he replied, 'The future? Nothing. There's nothing for me now.'

Ringo Starr read this maudlin interview while he was filming the scene in *Help!* in which he fails to notice someone cutting out the floor around his drum kit, and tumbles through the hole. 'I didn't think he could fail,' he said. 'No one did.' The following week Jimmie was taken to court by his ex-wife, who was seeking £30 in maintenance arrears.

For his part, Paul McCartney tried to lend a helping hand, persuading Peter Asher, brother of Jane, to hire Jimmie for a brief tour with his duet Peter and Gordon. Jimmie then moved to Gothenburg, where he played with a Swedish band, the Spotniks. He eventually went with them to Mexico City, where they were employed as the house band at the Alameda Hotel. Like the Beatles, Jimmie experimented with drugs in the second half of the sixties, though with notably less aplomb: one night he fell off his seat while attempting to play drums for the Spotniks, and was asked to leave.

Teaming up with a musician called Eddie Quinn, he then formed

Los Nicolquinn, an awkward combination of their two surnames. Together they performed one of his songs, 'I'm Lost', which came with a gloomy lyric about being 'badly beaten up'. The chorus consisted of the title, sung over and over again.

He remarried in Mexico, but his new wife soon grew tired of his endless complaints that Brian Epstein had ruined his life. One day he took off his Beatles commemorative watch and smashed it to bits. The marriage was to last barely a year.

And so the decades rolled by. Jimmie made an experimental movie called *Gas*, in which he can be seen drumming his hands on a naked woman; he formed a band called Blue Rain; he recorded a version of 'Jumpin' Jack Flash'. Returning to London in the mid-1970s, he abandoned music for the building trade. By now he had become too forgotten a figure even to feature in round-ups of forgotten figures.

Philip Norman's book *Shout!*, with its single disobliging reference to Jimmie, was published in 1981. Three years later, the Official Beatles Fan Club of the Netherlands tracked him down and persuaded him to attend their convention in Amsterdam. During a question-and-answer session, Jimmie claimed that the Beatles had forced him to pretend he was Ringo Starr: 'They did not want to admit, even though it was black and white in the press, that there was anybody else playing drums except Ringo.'

Since then, sightings of Jimmie Nicol have been few and far between. In 1988 there were unconfirmed rumours that he had died, but it emerged that they had been put about by Jimmie himself. In 2005 a reporter from the *Daily Mail* caught up with him in London, but he refused to say a word. In Mexico, his former wife continues to believe that he never recovered from his ten days as a Beatle: 'Jimmie was affected for his entire life because of his experience with the Beatles. He didn't get to stay with the Beatles. He thinks he failed because of that time with them. He was frustrated. So maybe his whole life has been frustrating, from being the Fifth Beatle. I think it affected his mental health.'

At a record convention in Utrecht in 2011, a Dutch record collector spotted Jimmie Nicol, or someone who looked like him. 'I went up to the man and said, "Are you Jimmie Nicol? The drummer?" … He signed his name – Jimmie Nicol – on a piece of paper, but then headed off without saying a word.'

57

Eric Clague was a postman. Every day throughout 1964 he used to deliver a sack of fan letters to 20 Forthlin Road, Liverpool, where Paul McCartney was brought up, and where his father still lived.

'At the height of the Beatles' fame, I used to deliver hundreds of cards and letters to the house,' Clague recalled thirty-four years later. 'I remember struggling up the path with them all. But of course they just reminded me of John Lennon and his mother.'

Six years before, Clague had been a junior constable in the Liverpool Police Force. On 15 July 1958, while off-duty, he was driving a Standard Vanguard sedan along Menlove Avenue when a forty-four-year-old woman stepped into his path. He braked, but too late: his car hit the woman, hurling her into the air.

In the kitchen of her home in Menlove Avenue, Mimi Smith and her lodger Michael Fishwick heard a screech of brakes and a thud. They looked at each other, but didn't say a word. In Fishwick's words, they 'just ran like hell'.

An ambulance arrived, but there was nothing to be done. Mimi's younger sister Julia was dead. 'When I ran across the road and saw her, I knew there was no hope,' Mimi remembered.

At that time Eric Clague was a learner driver, and was not supposed to be driving alone. An internal police inquiry was followed by an inquest. Clague insisted he had been driving at 28 mph in a 30 mph zone. Though this was contradicted by an onlooker, the jury chose to believe him. Mimi was furious: 'The coroner seemed to be bending over backwards to help this man who'd killed Julia.' A verdict of misadventure was returned, and Eric Clague was exonerated.

Mimi waved her walking stick at him. 'I got so mad … that swine … If I could have got my hands on him, I would have killed him.' John's friend Nigel Walley, who was present at the inquest, remembers Mimi screaming 'Murderer!' at Clague, before being hushed by the ushers.

Clague was suspended from duty, and resigned from the police force shortly after. He then took a job as a postman, which is how he came to be making daily deliveries to the Allerton district of the city.

His identity remained a secret until February 1998, when he was tracked down by a reporter from the *Sunday Mirror*. Up until that moment he had told no one of his involvement in the death of Julia Lennon.

'I have been haunted by this for all these years,' Clague told the reporter. 'Hardly a week goes by when I don't think about it. Ever since the Beatles became famous I have been expecting this to come out. To be honest I've been dreading it. It's not something I like to think about. At the time, I thought of sending the family my condolences, but I thought it would only make matters worse. They were very angry and upset by what had happened, naturally so, I suppose. I remembered how the family had blamed me and I wanted to tell them that there was really nothing I could have done. Mrs Lennon just ran straight out in front of me. I just couldn't avoid her. I was not speeding, I swear it. It was just one of those terrible things that happen. I read later how his mother's death had affected John Lennon terribly. I feel desperately sorry about that. But, as I say, it was just an accident.'

After the Beatles became world famous, Clague had read in a newspaper that John's mother had been killed by a car in Menlove Avenue. 'I put two and two together and realised that it was his mum that I had killed. Everything came back to me and I felt absolutely terrible. It had the most awful effect on me. The Beatles were everywhere, especially in Liverpool, and I couldn't get away from it. My postman's round took me to Forthlin Road, where Paul McCartney used to live. At the height of the Beatles' fame I used to deliver hundreds of cards and letters to the house. I remember struggling up the path with them all. But of course they just reminded me of John Lennon and his mother. It is something I have always kept deep inside. I haven't even told my wife and children. I suppose I will have to now.'

58

The dislikes of Noël Coward were legion, spanning most of the twentieth century and much of the nineteenth. They included Gilbert and Sullivan ('I HATE Gilbert and Sullivan'), Tallulah Bankhead ('a conceited slut'), Marilyn Monroe ('silly bitch'), Arthur Miller ('lacking humour to an alarming degree'), Mrs Alexander Woolcott ('that dreadful blouse she wore made me feel quite ill and she squinted vilely'), Oscar Wilde ('a silly, conceited, inadequate creature'), Neville Chamberlain ('bloody conceited old sod'), the Duke of Windsor ('I've known for years that he had a common mind and liked second-rate people'), Mandy Rice-Davies ('squalid, conceited nasty little slut') and Samuel Beckett ('I would rather play bingo every night for a year than pay a return visit to *Waiting for Godot*'). So it should come as no surprise that 'the Master', as he was known, had little time for the Beatles.

When the Beatles first met Coward, on Saturday, 6 June 1964, it all seemed to go swimmingly. They were introduced by the flamboyant bouffant-haired singer Alma Cogan, famous for her novelty records 'I Can't Tell a Waltz from a Tango' and 'Never Do a Tango with an Eskimo', who had, in turn, first encountered them backstage at the London Palladium. Alma had taken a particular shine to Brian Epstein; there was even talk of marriage. So it was perfectly natural that she should invite Brian and the boys along to the frequent showbiz parties she threw at her swish apartment in Stafford Court, on Kensington High Street.

There the Beatles mixed with mainstream showbiz types, most of them top-of-the-range family entertainers: Danny Kaye, Frankie

Vaughan, Ethel Merman, Sammy Davis Jr. Paul, in particular, thrived in such company: 'We were on the cusp of the change-over between showbiz styles ... They were all a little older than us, probably ten, twelve years older than us, but they were great fun, very confident showbiz people who welcomed us into their circle.'

He regarded these parties, like so much else in his life, as an education: 'I saw a documentary about John Betjeman, who said that when he got out of college there was a country house to which he was invited. And he said, "There I learned to be a guest." And that's what was happening to us at Alma's flat. There we learned to play charades, and we started to do it at our own parties. It was just a little learning curve.'

6 June 1964 was a typically hectic day for Noël Coward. He lunched with Vivien Leigh ('she was fine and gay') at her home, Tickerage Mill

in Sussex, and from there he motored to Brighton to pop in on Vivien's former husband, Sir Laurence Olivier, and his new wife Joan Plowright. In the evening it was back to London to dine with Terence Rattigan and Robin Maugham, and then on to Alma Cogan's birthday party, shortly after midnight.

Alma introduced Coward to John and Paul. He found them 'pleasant young men, quite well behaved and with an amusing way of speaking'. But he thought no more about them: his social whirl scarcely allowed time for cogitation. The next day he lunched with 'the dear Queen Mother at Clarence House. She was more enchanting than ever.'

Did he, perhaps, feel threatened by the Beatles? By 1964, Coward was part of the old guard. He was born in 1899, and took his first role on the West End stage back in 1911, at the age of eleven. Though his background was not so very different from the Beatles' – his father was an impoverished piano salesman – he swiftly assimilated into high society, readily adopting the mannerisms and accents of the English upper classes. Small wonder, then, that the current rise of working-class culture held so little appeal for him. 'I wonder how long this trend of dreariness for dreariness' sake will last?' he sniffed after emerging from John Osborne's play *Look Back in Anger* in 1956.

In his style and outlook, Coward was a far cry from the Beatles. His singing voice was clipped and refined, his songs crisp, witty, knowing and polished. The three words least likely to emerge from his mouth were yeah, yeah and yeah.

Coward made the mistake of relaying his encounter with John and Paul, in derogatory terms, to David Lewin of the *Daily Mail*. It never occurred to him that Lewin would quote him in print complaining that the Beatles were 'totally devoid of talent. There is a great deal of noise. In my day, the young were taught to be seen but not heard – which is no bad thing.'

A year later, on 11 June 1965, Coward was upset to read that there were MBEs for the Beatles in the Queen's Birthday Honours List. 'It is, of course, a tactless and major blunder on the part of the Prime Minister,' he confided to his diary. 'And also I don't think the Queen should have agreed. Some other decoration should have been selected to reward them for their talentless but considerable contributions to the Exchequer.'

A fortnight later, he happened to be in Rome for the wedding of the Italian Princess Torlonia, which he attended with Merle Oberon. Finding himself with time on his hands, he went to the Teatra Adriano, where the Beatles were playing. It seems more than likely that he was the only sixty-six-year-old man in the audience.

It proved to be an unusually raucous and ramshackle concert, possibly owing to the fact that the theatre was half empty, giving the Beatles licence to fool around. While Ringo was singing 'I Wanna Be Your Man' Paul contracted a fit of the giggles and had to leave the stage; George, unamused, scowled in his direction. On his return to the stage Paul's microphone toppled over, which set John laughing, though George remained irritated.

But not half so irritated as Noël Coward, who spent most of his time with his fingers in his ears. 'I had never seen them in the flesh before,' he wrote in his diary. 'The noise was deafening throughout and I couldn't hear a word they sang or a note they played, just one long ear-splitting din.' Nevertheless, he decided to go backstage to see them afterwards, only to be met by Brian Epstein, 'who told me they had gone back to the hotel and would I go there'.

Coward was duly received at the hotel by Epstein and the band's publicist Wendy Hanson, who gave him a drink then scurried off to get them, but returned saying they had been upset by his remarks in the *Daily Mail* a year before.

'I thought this graceless in the extreme, but decided to play it with firmness and dignity,' recalled Coward. 'I was told that the Beatles refused to see me because that ass David Lewin had quoted me saying unflattering things about them.' At this point, either Epstein or Wendy Hanson – the memories of Coward and McCartney differ on this – decided to try them again.

'Brian came and said, "Noël Coward would like to meet you boys,"' remembered Paul. 'We all said, "Oh, fucking hell, no! No, no, no. I'm going to bed." … Brian said, "You can't! You just can't!"' Ringo also remembers that it was Epstein who tried to persuade them: 'Brian came to us and said, "Noël Coward is downstairs and he wants to say 'hi.'" Ringo captures the general mood of the group: "'Fuck off!" We wouldn't see him. I mean, "Sod off, Noël."'

But Epstein persisted. Finally Paul, ever the diplomat, agreed to appear as their representative.

'I asked Wendy to go and fetch one of them and she finally reappeared with Paul McCartney,' wrote Coward, 'and I explained gently but firmly that one did *not* pay much attention to the statements of newspaper reporters. The poor boy was quite amiable and I sent messages of congratulation to his colleagues, although the message I would have liked to send them was that they were bad-mannered little shits.'

Coward died in 1973; his private diaries, containing these reminiscences, were not published until 1982. 'He said some not too pleasant things about us …' Paul observed to Barry Miles in 1997, 'so fuck him anyway.'

But Coward had reserved even harsher words for the Beatles' fans there that night: 'It was like a mass masturbation orgy, although apparently mild compared with what it usually is. The whole thing is to me an unpleasant phenomenon. Mob hysteria when commercially promoted, or in whatever way promoted, always sickens me. To realise that the majority of the modern adolescent world goes ritualistically mad over those four innocuous, rather silly-looking young men is a disturbing thought. Perhaps we are whirling more swiftly into extinction than we know. Personally I should have liked to take some of those squealing young maniacs and cracked their heads together.'

59

How else to describe the sound of Coward's 'squealing young maniacs'? In February 1965 Eleanor Bron travelled back with the Beatles from Nassau to Heathrow, having completed the Bahamian shoot for *Help!*: 'I was not prepared for the noise when we walked out onto the tarmac. It was Trafalgar Square with the volume up, beyond imagination – the sound of millions of starlings startled into the air. But the starlings were girls, when I looked back, very very young ones, who covered the airport buildings. Wherever you could see, wherever they could see, wherever they were allowed, and elsewhere, oozing and easing themselves in where they were not; waving banners and arms, pushing and heaving, in great danger I imagine of falling over the edges, wriggling and ceaselessly squealing – a high sighing hopeless poignant sound, unrequitable.'

From a film-maker's point of view, there were some advantages to the screaming. Clive Reed, the first assistant director of *Help!*, was responsible for making sure the Beatles got to the set on time. He found he was able to monitor how far away their car was by the decibels of the screams. 'He'd say, "They're just by the roundabout," or "They're just coming over the bridge,"' remembered the director of photography, David Watkin.

Ronnie Spector and her cousin Nedra were in the audience at Shea Stadium. Afterwards, they were climbing into their companion's Bentley when a group of fans recognised them and assumed that the Beatles were in there too. 'We had just enough time to slam the doors shut before the kids were climbing all over our car, screaming and yelling and bouncing it back and forth … There were at least a hundred teenagers screaming outside our car. They were pounding on the windows with their fists, and the ones on top of the car were kicking at the glass with their heels. Being trapped in a car while a mob of kids tries to beat their way in is about the most terrifying thing you can imagine. We looked out the window and all we could see were fists and feet. It reminded me of the little sparrows who kept throwing themselves against the door in that Alfred Hitchcock movie *The Birds*.'

The screaming was uncontrolled, and uncontrollable. In November 1963, two hundred women working at a cotton mill in Accrington went on strike after their foreman banned them from listening to the radio programme *Housewives' Choice*: he was sick of the way they would start to scream the moment a Beatles song came on.

But other fans, less flighty, were able to locate their inner off-switch. The jazz singer George Melly took his little daughter to the Beatles' Christmas show at Hammersmith in 1964. Before it began, he heard two girls behind him discussing whether to scream at the supporting acts, or to save it up for the Beatles. 'They decided to save it, and then, when the Beatles did come on, they quite calculatedly covered their ears and let rip.' The forceful sixty-nine-year-old Lady Christabel Ampthill, escorting a grandchild to the same concert, couldn't contain

her irritation with a screamer. Prodding at her with her umbrella, she bellowed, 'You know, my dear, it's only the plain girls who scream.'

The twelve-year-old Linda Grant couldn't stop screaming, though she didn't know why: 'I didn't understand why you had to scream, but it was what you did. It was mandatory. There was this cult-like element to it.' At the Seattle Center Coliseum in August 1964, the screaming kicked off well before the Beatles appeared. The reporter Larry Kane noted that by the time Jackie DeShannon was launching into her final song, 'The screams were at such a pitch that for the first time on the tour I had to hold my hands over my ears and grasp my tape recorder between my elbows. Actual pain had set in. And it was just beginning ... I could see abject fear in the eyes of Paul McCartney. Paul always had an upbeat look, but his lips pursed and his brows tightened in signs of obvious tension ... The combination of noise, onrushing fans, and jellybeans flying randomly about the small stage made me feel that I was in the middle of a psychotic ward with fourteen thousand crazies.'

Dr Bernard Saibel, supervisor of the Washington State Division of Community Services, was stationed in the same audience, an unlikely figure in horn-rimmed spectacles, studiously jotting his psychological observations in a notebook, ready to write a report. 'BEATLEMANIA ANALYZED – Frightening, Says Child Expert' ran the headline in the next day's *Seattle Daily Times*.

> The experience of being with 14,000 teenagers to see the Beatles is unbelievable and frightening ... The hysteria and loss of control go far beyond the impact of the music. Many of those present became frantic, hostile, uncontrolled, screaming, unrecognizable human beings.
>
> ... The externals are terrifying. Normally recognizable girls behaved as if possessed by some demonic urge, defying in emotional ecstasy the restraints which authorities try to place on them.
>
> ... The music is loud, primitive, insistent, strongly rhythmic and releases in a disguised way (can it be called sublimation?) the all too tenuously controlled, newly acquired impulses of the teen-ager.
>
> Mix this up with the phenomena of mass hypnosis, contagious

> hysteria and the blissful feeling of being mixed up in an all embracing, orgiastic experience and every kid can become 'Lord of the Flies' or the Beatles.

Later, in Vancouver, Larry Kane witnessed 'a riot, pure and simple', with girls trampled in the rampage, and medical crews racing around in all directions. 'When the victims were retrieved, they bore the signs of Beatles-induced combat – bloody lips and noses, bruises, welts, abrasions and contusions.' By the end of the evening 135 people had been treated for injuries, including broken limbs and trauma to the head.

Touching down in Houston the following year, the Beatles' plane was surrounded by fans while its engines were still running. Some managed to climb onto the wings, and crawled towards the portholes, waving at those inside. In Dallas, young fans walked from the airport to the Beatles' hotel, many of them in tears. One clutched a bunch of grass in her hands, screaming: 'Ringo! Ringo walked on this grass!'

At their concert the following night, when they started playing 'I Saw Her Standing There' one young fan, Carol Bedford, 'lost control completely. My hands were stretched over my head.' Hoping to calm the crowd down, the Beatles played the slower 'This Boy', but to little effect: 'During this song, a policeman nearly lost his life. He was blocking my view of Ringo and I raced to push him over the balcony.' Fortunately, Carol's boyfriend managed to hold her back.

When the Beatles came to Chicago in August 1965, twelve-year-old Ruby Wax's mother bought tickets for both the afternoon and evening shows at the White Sox Stadium: 'I loved Paul the most – I was ready to give myself to him but first I had to look like Jane Asher. I had to straighten my hair, so I plugged in the iron. No one told me you were supposed to put a cloth between the iron and your hair – most of my crispy hairs dropped out, leaving a couple of burnt knots on my scalp. In the end, four remaining hairs jutted out from beneath my plastic John Lennon hat.'

At the afternoon concert she screamed along with all the other girls, but for the evening concert she hatched a cunning plan to meet the Beatles in person. Having noticed that they exited through a dugout in the stadium, she calculated that it was the route to their dressing room. So she waited until they finished their first song, then nipped into the dugout. Ruby arrived in a shower area, but to her annoyance 'four other fat, sad, hairless, girdled girls' were already there. Together, they found somewhere to hide. 'Before getting into the shower stall, I went around touching the toilet lids because I believed they had Beatles germs on them. Then I joined the fat losers, and we stood in that shower stall for God knows how long – we didn't know how much time went by, as we were panting with excitement.'

After a while, they noticed that the screaming had stopped. Hesitantly, they emerged from the shower and looked around for the Beatles, but they were nowhere to be seen. 'The stadium was empty and dark, there was silence only broken by my mother's voice shouting, "Vooby, vooby ver are you?"'

Newspapers of all stripes employed psychiatrists to come up with theories to explain this curious phenomenon. In Britain, Dr David Holbrook reported to readers of the *New Statesman* that 'The Beatles are a masturbation fantasy, such as a girl presumably has during the onanistic act – the genial smiling young male images, the music like a buzzing of the blood in the head, the rhythm, the cries, the shouted names, the climax.' In the more racy *News of the World*, the newspaper's 'resident psychologist' declared, 'the girls are subconsciously preparing for motherhood. Their frenzied screams are a rehearsal for that moment.' Holbrook felt that the craze for hurling jelly babies at the Beatles was probably symbolic too.

Driving with the Beatles to the premiere of *Help!* in Piccadilly Circus, Victor Spinetti was taken aback by the screaming maelstrom. As their limousine edged through the crowds, John said, 'Push Paul out first! He's the prettiest!' But George's was the first door to open. A girl reached in and tore madly at his hair. Spinetti compared it to a scene from *The Bacchae*: 'Two thousand years ago, its author, Euripides, could tell you all about Beatles fans, only his hero had not just his hair but his arms and legs pulled off.'

In Panama City, Florida, a fundamentalist preacher detected the devil at work. 'What can we learn from the Beatles in the light of the

Bible?' he asked his congregants. He suggested that the group had emerged from 'the slums of Liverpool' as 'the apocalyptic minions of Satan'. Furthermore, 'demonic, evil powers' were at work in their music, as described in 1 Timothy 4:1: 'Now the Spirit speaketh expressing, that in the latter times some shall depart from the faith, giving heed to seducing spirits, and doctrines of devils.' He reported that his own daughter had fallen under Satan's spell: 'I watched my Christian daughter dance, frenzied, to Beatle music and rock'n'roll records for five months,' he declared. Her frenzy came to an end only when 'the Lord condemned her in a still voice'.

Even the most sophisticated found themselves succumbing to the general hysteria. In February 1964, George Martin and his wife Judy were sitting with the audience to watch the Beatles' first US concert, in Washington, DC. In the seat next to him, a teenage girl was busy bouncing up and down.

'Aren't they just great?' she said. 'Aren't they just fabulous?'

'Yes,' Martin replied, in his understated way. 'Yes, they certainly are.'

'Do you like them too, sir?'

'Yes, I do rather.' All the while, he thought she must be wondering what this old gentleman was doing there. Then, as the Beatles started to play 'I Want to Hold Your Hand', Martin surprised himself: 'Judy and I just found ourselves standing up and screaming along with the rest. This may sound daft, but it was exactly the same screaming that adults do at football matches … it was all too easy to scream, to be swept up in that tremendous current of buoyant happiness and exhilaration.'

60

At that same Washington concert, a thirteen-year-old girl called Jamie stood close to the stage, clutching a plastic bag containing jellybeans, ready to throw at the Beatles.

Jamie was hanging around in the auditorium after the show when a friendly policeman handed her a crumpled piece of paper he had picked up from the stage: a set list scribbled by John, beginning with 'Roll Over Beethoven' and ending with 'Long Tall Sally'.

Without thinking, Jamie tucked the piece of paper into her plastic bag, where it joined a handful of jellybeans still unthrown. For the next thirty-odd years the bag mouldered in a cupboard, but in 1995 Jamie, now a mother, needed money to help pay for her teenage daughter's education, and remembered the smeary set list. Accordingly, she sent it to auction, where it was bought by a collector for $5,000, though it would now be worth something closer to $40,000.

The price of Beatles relics, even the least noteworthy, continues to soar. In 2016, an unused ticket for that Washington concert fetched $30,000. Even a set of four tiny squares of white bedlinen, each square measuring half a centimetre by half a centimetre, cut from sheets slept in by the Beatles when they stayed at the Whittier Hotel in Detroit on the night of 6 September 1964, sold for £595.

A single red brick mounted on a silver plaque with the inscription 'This is to certify that this is one of 5,000 bricks which Royal Life have salvaged from the original Cavern Club, Mathew Street, Liverpool England' was sold in Los Angeles for £896 in 2019. Item 83 in the same auction was billed as 'an overtime requisition form for G.T.H. Hipson, who was employed at Ringo Starr's Sunny Heights, Weybridge, home, with the last week ending on April 30, 1967. Starr signed the form "R. Starkey" when it was passed for payment on May 4, 1967. Attached is a The Beatles Limited petty cash claim form that is also dated May 4, 1967.' The pleasure afforded by the ownership of this wonderfully obscure item may be hard to pin down, but a collector was nevertheless prepared to pay £384 for it. Other items included a sheet of paper listing John's high-school detention records from 28 October 1954 to 9 January 1955 – 'Reasons for detention include "chatter ad nauseam", "talking repeatedly", "noise" and "eating again"' (£3,125), a June 1967 quarterly telephone bill totalling £12.91, addressed to Mrs M.E. Smith (Aunt Mimi) and signed 'in blue pen' by John (£1,024), and a ticket stub for the 7 December 1963 BBC recording of *Juke Box Jury* on which the Beatles appeared (£437).

These were some of the more affordable lots. An early, smudged draft of John's letter to the Queen announcing the return of his MBE sold for £19,200; a baseball signed by all four Beatles before their last US concert for £56,250; a New Zealand autograph book containing the autographs of all four Beatles as well as Brian Epstein, Jane Asher, Pattie Boyd and Helen Shapiro for £10,240; and a modest 1964 announcement (17x22 inches) declaring that the Blenheim Lounge of Liverpool Airport 'will be closed in the interest of public safety' for a Beatles press conference, signed by the group, sold for £31,250.

Over the years, grander items of Beatles memorabilia have fetched infinitely more: in 2005, Madame Tussauds discovered the wax heads of John, George and Ringo featured on the *Sgt. Pepper* album cover, which had been lost for nearly two decades, and auctioned them for £81,500. In 2018, Sotheby's sold the 'Apple Corps Ltd Dissolution of Contract, signed by all four Beatles' for $118,750. John's copy of the abandoned 'butcher' cover for the album *Yesterday and Today*, featuring the band in butchers' smocks with dismembered dolls, signed by John, Paul and Ringo, sold for £179,200. But these were a snip compared to the $790,000 paid in 2015 for copy 0000001 of *The White Album* ('very clean and fresh with very minor abrasions').

Musical instruments associated with the Beatles are perhaps the most valuable relics of all: at that same sale in 2015, a skin from the drum kit played by Ringo on *The Ed Sullivan Show* sold for $2.1 million, while a guitar played by John fetched $2.4 million. At Bonham's in 1997 a guitar commissioned by Paul but never played by him was sold to a bidder from Tokyo for £126,000.

A group photograph signed by all four Beatles would currently fetch £29,500. By comparison, a colour photograph of all three members of the Apollo 11 space crew – Neil Armstrong, Buzz Aldrin and Michael Collins – would fetch only £10,000, roughly the same as a signed photograph of John Lennon. A signed photograph of Neil Armstrong, the first man on the moon, might go for £3,000; signed photographs of Winston Churchill and John F. Kennedy are currently on sale for £1,750 and £3,000 respectively. Signed photographs of President Trump go for around $1,000. Paul McCartney's autograph is £2,950, which makes it currently the most valuable of any living person.*

When someone dies, their autograph gains in value, death having limited the stock. It is in the macabre nature of idolatry that an autograph associated with the death of the idol is the most valuable of all: in 2011, the *Double Fantasy* album cover signed by John Lennon for his killer, Mark Chapman, sold at auction for $532,000.

* Annoyingly, I have lost the autograph Paul gave me circa 1972. I spotted him and Linda sitting towards the back of the auditorium before a concert at the Victoria Palace theatre by the group Grimms, of which his brother was a member. The only item I could find for him to sign was a photograph of Roxy Music, signed by the group, which I was carrying from the previous day. Paul obligingly wrote 'And me too – Paul McCartney' on the top right-hand corner.

61

New Facts on the Fab 4
From *Fabulous* magazine, 1965

1. John flew to Hong Kong wearing pyjamas.
2. John is a cat-lover.
3. Ringo spent much of his childhood in a Cheshire hospital.
4. John used to envy his cousin Stanley's Meccano set.
5. Brian Epstein hesitated a long time before taking Ringo as a replacement for Pete Best.
6. George is afraid of flying.
7. George has bought a bow and arrow.
8. Pattie Boyd didn't like the Beatles before she met them on the set of *A Hard Day's Night*.
9. John's father was a singer on pre-war Atlantic liners.
10. Ringo's stepfather, Harry Graves, sings Beatles songs at family parties.
11. The Beatles never visit a barber.
12. Paul washes his hair every day.
13. The Beatles turned down the offer of an appearance on the 1964 Royal Variety Show.
14. Ringo cannot swim, except for brief doggie paddle.
15. Brian Epstein made the Beatles have their hair cut short after he signed them in 1962.
16. They are never photographed with their hair 'up'.
17. Paul ate corn flakes and bacon and eggs at a champagne and caviar luncheon in London. Music publisher Dick James was host.

18 The Beatles didn't want to go to Australia without Ringo when he was ill. But Brian persuaded them to change their minds.
19 Paul has a mini as well as an Aston Martin DB4.
20 George's personal Christmas card was a photograph of him scowling at a cameraman.
21 John never saw an audience properly until Dundee in Scotland. Then he wore contact lenses.
22 An American firm wrote to the Beatles asking if they could market the Beatles' bathwater at a dollar a bottle.
23 They refused the offer.
24 Their road manager, Mal Evans, was once a bouncer at the Liverpool Cavern Club.
25 Neil Aspinall, their other road manager, was given a Jaguar last Christmas – a present from the Beatles.
26 Paul drinks coffee for breakfast. The other three drink tea – even in America.
27 Ringo had his new clothes designed by a woman, Caroline Charles.
28 Jane Asher bought Paul a record player for his Aston Martin.
29 Brian Epstein says, 'America discovered Ringo.'
30 Paul believes he is not a very good guitarist.
31 None of the Beatles drinks Scotch and Coke. They now dilute the occasional spirit with lemonade.
32 John told an American journalist that US fashions were five years behind the UK.
33 The Beatles never really liked jelly babies. They just said they did for a joke.
34 They carry a crate of pop in the trunk of their Austin Princess.
35 Their new chauffeur, Alf Bicknell, used to drive for David Niven and Cary Grant.
36 Burt Lancaster has sent Ringo a set of pistols. They became friends in Hollywood.
37 Burt let them use his home for a showing of *A Shot in the Dark*.
38 Edward G. Robinson and his grandchild twice joined the queue to shake hands with The Beatles at their Hollywood garden party.

39 So did Mrs Dean Martin and her five children.

40 The Beatles have no pockets in their trousers and only two side pockets in their jackets. Paul designed them.

41 All they carry on them in the way of money is a few banknotes.

42 John has bought his mother-in-law a house near his own in Surrey.

43 None of The Beatles wears undershirts.

44 Paul wants to buy a farm.

62

Mary Wood's Tale

I was about eleven years old when the Beatles came to power. We lived in Larne in Northern Ireland. One of the pop magazines was very big – twice the size of A4 – and had full-page headshots of the Beatles. I didn't particularly like the shots of John, Ringo and George, but I pinned them up anyway, as I felt it would be disloyal to Paul if I didn't. Paul's face was right next to my head when I was in bed. I cherished it, but then I cut it around the face and sellotaped it onto my teddy bear's face so it could sleep next to me. Before long, it started crumbling to dust.

The Beatles were a game-changer as regards what type of men one fancied. It was simply that they had long hair. Other men in those times all had short hair – moreover, short hair with dandruff. The longer, softer style was just more flattering. I suppose they were girly men.

And that was the point. Recently, someone told me that there is a period of latency when a young girl just daydreams about men but doesn't actually want to have sex with them, and that's why so many boyband members are effeminate. It's a 'moony adolescent' period where you think about romance and idealise the object of your passion, but don't actually want the fantasy spoiled by the reality of going on a date with them.

My father was a doctor, a GP. My dream was that Paul, somehow, would have a minor injury and would have to call at our house for my father to stitch it up. My father would decree it would be best if he went to bed for a couple of days to recover, and since he would be recognised if he went to a hotel, he should stay in our house, in a pop-up hospital ward for one. I would help to nurse him. So then it would only be a matter of time before we got engaged.

The trouble was that Paul didn't come to Northern Ireland very often. But in November 1964 he came and my Aunt Sheila bought tickets for me and my sister and our cousins and we went to the King's Hall in Belfast. The four Beatles came onstage and they held their instruments but any tunes would have been totally drowned out by the mass hysteria of the audience. The hall erupted into screaming and moaning. I just mimed screaming, to fit in. Have you tried screaming? It's not at all easy to do for more than two ten-second bursts. You don't get anywhere and it just wears out your voice. You should try it. We couldn't hear a word anyway, and I don't know if the Beatles were even bothering to play or just miming.

One thing put me off Paul, though. He was pouring with sweat and he wiped the sweat on his clothes. Despite this I genuinely, at the back of my mind, thought I was going to marry him. I felt it in every fibre of my being. It was the reason I didn't work for my A-Levels. I reckoned that anyway I wouldn't have time to go to university or have a career as I would be constantly on tour with Paul. The fact that I was going to marry Paul informed my behaviour in general, but I didn't tell anyone, obviously, because it was a kind of religious thing, a secret between me and God.

The day I turned eighteen I got on a plane to London. I had left school and done my A-Levels. I got bad grades. I knew Paul lived in St John's Wood, so I went to the nearest tube station. I thought it would require some sleuthing, but no, the man behind the counter of the tube station told me the exact address, and, armed with an *A to Z*, I walked towards it.

I had imagined that I would just stand outside his house and sooner or later Paul would come out and, seeing me, invite me in, and then he would fall in love with me and the engagement would be announced within a few days and that would show my parents that I knew best about my life plans. That would put them in their place.

But when I got to the house I was amazed that there were about twenty to thirty other girls there. How come there was a sense of camaraderie when we were all competing for the same prize? I don't know. Perhaps it was part of that moony adolescent thing, and we didn't actually want to set up home with Paul, we were just in love with the idea of it.

The other girls said that Paul wasn't even inside the house anyway. So why were they standing outside crying and moaning and pushing letters through the railings? I think there were railings.

Shortly after that he got married to Linda, and I was genuinely thrown, like one of those men who go to Cirencester Agricultural College to train to run their estate, and then the estate is sold and they are left washed-up without a role in life, fit for purpose but with no ability to demonstrate their fitness. So I had been cheated of my destiny by Linda.

63

The Rolling Stones were among those attending the premiere of *A Hard Day's Night* on 6 July 1964, in the gracious presence of HRH Princess Margaret and Lord Snowdon.

Outside the London Pavilion, two hundred policemen were restraining 12,000 fans chanting 'Beatles! Beatles! Beatles!' The band had still not grown accustomed to such hullabaloo. Approaching Leicester Square in the back of their chauffeur-driven car, John looked out of the window and asked Brian Epstein, in all innocence, 'Is it a Cup final or something?'

The Beatles' arrival was accompanied by what one onlooker called 'an immense throaty roar', followed by a massed chorus of 'Happy Birthday to You'. Ringo, the oldest Beatle, would be celebrating his twenty-fourth birthday the following day.

Once the Beatles were safely inside the cinema, a clean red carpet was rolled out by the theatre manager and his staff, just in time for the arrival of the royal party. On the day of their wedding, in May 1960, Princess Margaret and Lord Snowdon were possibly the most adored people in Britain, perhaps even the world. At that time, up in Liverpool, the Silver Beetles had just failed their audition to support Billy Fury on his northern tour.

But four years on, the crowds made it quite clear which of them inspired the most adoration. After all the mayhem surrounding the Beatles, the arrival of the royal couple seemed a terrible anti-climax, the cheers for the princess and her husband pitiful compared to those that had greeted the band.

As Princess Margaret and Lord Snowdon walked into the auditorium, a detachment of trumpeters heralded their arrival with a fanfare, and the Metropolitan Police Band launched into a stately rendition of 'God Save the Queen'. The audience stood keenly to attention, and so did the Beatles. But Mick Jagger and the Rolling Stones, sitting in the seats immediately behind the Beatles, refused to budge. Alistair Taylor, Brian Epstein's personal assistant, was appalled. 'Of course, John is seen as the great rebel but he wasn't really like that. In fact, he was the first on his feet when the first bars of the National Anthem were played, and all the other boys stood up. So did everyone else, except for the Rolling Stones. They sat sprawled out as an arrogant gesture of defiance. John was definitely not impressed.' Forty years on, Taylor still found it hard to contain his outrage. 'I suppose they thought they were making a point, but they were guests of the Beatles that night and I believe they should have shown more respect.'

After the film, the Beatles were presented to Princess Margaret. Cynthia Lennon had made a special effort. She was wearing a full-length sleeveless dress in black and beige silk from Fenwicks, along with a black Mary Quant chiffon coat, bordered with black feathers. At John's urging she wore her hair up, to make herself more like Brigitte Bardot. In common with the other Beatles, John wore a dinner jacket and black bow tie. In his first book, *In His Own Write*, published just three months before, he had referred to the royal couple in his punning way as 'Priceless Margarine and Bony Armstrove', but he now seemed cowed in their presence. 'When it came to meeting royalty in the flesh John was as much in awe as the rest of us,' Cynthia was to recall. 'He was so pleased and proud that the princess had come to see the film that his anti-establishment views flew out of the window and he stood red-faced as she spoke to him.'

'How are you coping with all the adulation?' asked the princess. Cynthia was unimpressed by such a drab question, and found the princess's conversation 'clipped and superficial'. Attempting to draw his wife in, John said, 'Ma'am, this is my wife Cynthia,' but the princess offered her only the most cursory of glances. 'Oh, how nice.'

The reception at the Dorchester was attended by the princess and her husband, though they were due to leave before dinner for another appointment. Brian Jones and Keith Richards of the Rolling Stones had not been invited, but had somehow got in, provocatively underdressed in turtleneck shirts. 'Isn't this the greatest party crash of all time?' smirked Jones. The night before, they had appeared on *Juke Box Jury*: the morning's newspapers described them as 'rude', 'anthropoid', 'boorish' and 'charmless'.

The party was an uneasy mix of the old and the new, the young and the old. As a creaky dance orchestra struggled through a selection of tunes from the top 10, an elderly woman in a ballgown buttonholed John.

'You're simply darling,' she said.

'Can't say the same for you, love,' he replied.

Meanwhile, Princess Margaret and Lord Snowdon were clearly enjoying themselves, and stayed much later than planned. This, in turn, meant that dinner had to be postponed. Unaware of the protocol, George Harrison approached the film's producer, Walter Shenson, and asked, 'When do we eat?' Shenson told him that dinner could not be served until the departure of the royal couple. At this, George strode across to the princess and said bluntly, 'Ma'am, we're starved, and Walter says we can't eat until you leave.'

'Come on, Tony. We're in the way,' replied the princess, taking orders from the youngest of the Beatles. This might be seen as a pivotal occasion in British social life, the moment a princess scuttled away on the orders of a Beatle; for the first time, but not the last, royalty deferred to celebrity.

As the reception drew to an end, everyone grew more relaxed. Brian Jones and Keith Richards were surrounded by begowned and bejewelled autograph-hunters, and Jones was happily signing away. At this point, the orchestra struck up the National Anthem. True to form, Jones ignored it, and carried on signing. 'Stop it! Stop it!' hissed an elderly woman in a diamond necklace. In reply, Jones stopped signing, picked up a woman's scarf from a nearby table, wrapped it around his neck and, in time to the slow drudge of the music, executed a pastiche of a burlesque dancer.

When the orchestra reached the final chorus, John Lennon found his anti-establishment attitudes boosted by champagne and shrieked

'Go-o-d save the Cream!' On the way out, he spotted the old woman in the ballgown to whom he had been so terse earlier in the evening. 'Good night, Mrs Haitch! We'll dance again some Somerset Maugham!' he yelled, punningly. Nothing like this had ever happened at the Dorchester before; the times they were a-changin'.

64

Afterwards, John, Paul and Ringo went with Brian and Keith to the Ad Lib Club, just around the corner in Leicester Place. Paul left comparatively early – they had to mime on the next day's *Top of the Pops* – and Ringo, now the Birthday Boy, left shortly after 4 a.m., having stayed up to look at the film's reviews in the early editions of the newspapers: 'I got all the papers at four in the morning, drunk out of my mind trying to read them. But I couldn't focus.' This was a shame, as the reviews were full of superlatives, with the *Daily Mail* comparing them to the Marx Brothers.

John was clearly in for the long haul, draining Scotch and Cokes one after the other. 'His hand gripped his glass as if he were trying to crush it,' noted one observer. 'His eyes seemed hard, sharp and unsmiling. His upper lip sometimes curled as he talked, displaying hard white teeth.'

The more the night wore on, the fonder John grew of the two Rolling Stones present. 'I love you. I loved you the first time I heard you,' he said. But, even when drunk, he never plunged so deeply into sentimentality that he was unable to haul himself back out. 'But there's something wrong with you, isn't there? There's one of you in the group that isn't as good as the others. Find out who he is and get rid of 'im.'

The talk turned to music: Jones and Richards argued that the Stones played genuine rhythm and blues, while the Beatles just played commercial pop. This was a sore spot for John; he abruptly changed the subject.

First, he looked at Jones. 'Your hair makes it,' he said. Then he looked at Richards. 'Your hair makes it,' he said. Then he turned to absent friends. 'But Mick Jagger. You know as well as I do that his hair doesn't make it.'

And so it went on.

John said, 'In another year, I'll have me money and I'll be out of it.'

'In another year,' said Brian, 'we'll be there.'

John took a philosophic drag on his cigarette. 'Yeah,' he said, 'but what's *there*?'

The Beatles and the Rolling Stones were always being treated as rivals. They had first met just over a year before, at the Station Hotel in Richmond, Surrey. At that point the Beatles were far ahead, topping the bill on a nationwide tour, while the Stones were still playing in pubs.

In the first week of May 1963 George Harrison was judging a talent contest at the Liverpool Philharmonic Hall, and found himself on a panel with Dick Rowe, who was already widely known as The Man Who Turned Down the Beatles. Rowe told George that he was still kicking himself for that mistake. Graciously, George replied that he had probably been right, as they'd done a terrible audition.

Sensing Rowe's disappointment with the talent on show at the Philharmonic, George tipped him off about a great new group who played every Sunday in Richmond. Within days, Rowe had offered them a contract. Ever competitive, the Beatles were distressed that the Stones had negotiated a better deal with Decca than they themselves had with EMI. They soon began to worry that the underdog was becoming the overdog. From then on, there was always an edge to their friendship. One day, John and Paul were emerging from Dick James's* office on Charing Cross Road when they heard Mick and Keith shouting at them from a passing taxi. The two Beatles cadged a lift, and as the four of them travelled along, Mick said, 'We're

* Dick James (1920–86), music publisher of the Beatles. Originally a singer with Henry Hall's Dance Band, his most celebrated performance was the theme to the popular TV series *Robin Hood*, with its rousing chorus, 'Raarbin Hood, Raarbin Hood, riding through the glen, Raarbin Hood, Raarbin Hood, with his band of men …' James was known for his stinginess. For Christmas 1964 he gave the Beatles a bottle of Brut aftershave each.

recording. Got any songs?' John and Paul thought of one straight away. 'How about Ringo's song? You could do it as a single.' And so, from this chance encounter, the Rolling Stones gained their first top 20 single, 'I Wanna Be Your Man'.

In some ways, John helped to fuel his own fears that the Stones were a more authentic version of the Beatles, the Beatles freed from Sunday best. Mick Jagger sang 'wanna', while John sang 'want to'; the Beatles were happy to settle for holding hands; the Stones aimed to go the whole hog. The rough, bluesy insolence of the Stones reminded John of the Beatles before they had been buffed and polished by Brian Epstein. In hip circles it had become fashionable to regard the Beatles as soft, pretty and artificial, and the Stones as tough, bullish and real.

John was increasingly riled by the comparison. 'John went bananas about all the publicity the Stones were getting for being rough,' recalled Bill Harry, editor of *Mersey Beat*. 'He knew the Stones were middle-class boys from the Home Counties, not leather-jacketed Teds at all. While the Beatles had been swearing and whoring it in Hamburg, they had been attending trendy schools. John hated it. He really hated it.'

Before long, music fans felt they had to support either the Beatles or the Stones, as though they were rival football teams, or warring countries. It made men feel more manly to prefer the Stones, and women more raunchy. Somehow, the Beatles' most vociferous supporters only made matters worse. 'This horrible lot are not quite what they seem,' Maureen Cleave wrote of the Stones in the *Evening Standard* in March 1964. '… They've done terrible things to the music scene, set it back, I would say, about eight years.' But some of her complaints against the Stones seemed closer to compliments: 'Just when we'd got our pop singers looking neat and tidy and, above all, *cheerful*, along come the Rolling Stones, looking almost like what we used to call beatniks … They've wrecked the image of the pop singer of the sixties.'

A couple of days later, in a bold headline, *Melody Maker* asked, 'WOULD YOU LET YOUR SISTER GO WITH A ROLLING STONE?' To which Maureen Cleave replied, a week later: 'But would you let your daughter marry one? Parents do not like the Rolling Stones. They do not want their sons to grow up like them; they do not want their daughters to marry them.'

She went on to associate the Beatles with the very same morés John had striven so hard to reject: 'Never have the middle-class virtues of neatness, obedience and punctuality been so conspicuously lacking as they are in The Rolling Stones. The Rolling Stones are not the people you build empires with: they are not the people who always remember to wash their hands before lunch.'

The divide continues to this day. Men and women now in their seventies and eighties proudly declare, 'Actually, I always preferred the Rolling Stones,' as though it were proof of their raw integrity.

John's fixation with the Rolling Stones lasted for years to come, not least because people like him tended to prefer groups like them. At the same time, he resented them as copycats who stole ideas from the Beatles. After the Beatles released 'Yesterday', the Stones recorded 'As Tears Go By'. Hearing from their shared engineer, Glyn Johns, that one of the Beatles' new songs was to be called 'Let it Be', the Stones decided to call their new album *Let it Bleed*, and so forth. Shortly before the Beatles split up, John was still complaining of their plagiarism: 'I would just like to list what we did and what the Stones did two months after on every fucking album and every fucking thing we did. And Mick does exactly the same. He imitates us. You know, *Satanic Majesties* is *Pepper*!' "We Love You", man, it's fucking bullshit! That's "All You Need is Love".'

Like rival Elizabethan households, Britain's two most illustrious groups operated a delicate rivalry, its wheels oiled by deference from the upstart towards the grandee. From George Harrison's perspective, 'Mick Jagger was always lurking around in the background, trying to find out what was happening. Mick never wanted to miss out on what the Fabs were doing.'

Jagger lived in Marylebone Road, a walk across Regent's Park from Paul's house in St John's Wood. They would meet from time to time, but it was Jagger who would always come to McCartney, not vice versa. 'I don't remember him coming to us,' Marianne Faithfull, Jagger's then girlfriend, says of Paul. 'Mick always had to come to his house, because he was Paul McCartney, and you went to him. Paul never came to us. I was always very curious about how Mick saw him, how Mick felt about him. It was always fun to watch. There was always rivalry there. Not from Paul, none at all. Paul was oblivious, but there was something from Mick. It was good fun. It was like watching a game on the television.'

In some ways, the two bands were mirror images of one another: Paul and Mick the savvy front men, always with an eye on the prize; Ringo and Charlie the older, unflappable blokes on drums; John and Keith the rogues, the hard men, the undeceived; and Brian and George the other-worldly ones, nursing resentment at their exclusion by the top dogs.

Beneath his brittle façade, John was scared by life. Nicky Haslam, who knew him and liked him, describes him as 'a wuss'. Sensing this vulnerability, Keith Richards would goad him. Like many bullies, John dreaded being bullied. He would try to get his dig in first, but unlike him, Richards was impregnable. On one occasion John told Keith that his guitar solo in the middle of 'It's All Over Now' was 'crap'. Keith remained unruffled: 'Maybe he got out the wrong side of the bed that day. OK, it certainly could have been better. But you disarmed the

man. "Yeah, it wasn't one of my best, John. Sorry. Sorry it jars, old boy. You can play it any fucking way you like.'"

In the early days, Richards enjoyed telling John that he wore his guitar too high. 'Got your fucking guitar under your fucking chin, for Christ's sake. It ain't a violin.' 'Try a longer strap, John. The longer the strap, the better you play.' 'No wonder you don't swing, you know? No wonder you only rock, no wonder you can't roll.' As time went by, he would note with satisfaction the furtive but steady descent of John's strap.

65

We last encountered sixteen-year-old Pamela Miller* in 1964, when she saw the Beatles at the Hollywood Bowl. In her diary, she wondered if fate had brought Paul to America 'for I am here too'. But within a year she had met a boy called Bob, who converted her to the Rolling Stones. When Pamela told her old Beatle friends Kathy and Stevie of her new passion, they reacted badly:

> 5–9–65
> Dear Pam, I suppose you are wondering why Linda, Stevie and I acted the way we did after school yesterday. The main reason is because you are a phony person. You better watch out before you become completely friendless. Why on earth could you even start to like Mick over Paul? … Pam, you try to be strange, but you aren't. You are just being a loser. Nobody likes you when you act the way you do … You were always so enthusiastic about the Beatles and now you're a Rolling Stones fan. I don't see how you could pick them over the Beatles unless … you were being a phony all that time. The Stones are dirty and sloppy and they repugnate me. When I think back to how you used to sign your name 'Paul n Pam', I can't believe you're the same girl. I don't hate you, but frankly, I don't like you much.
> Kathy 'n' Stevie

---

* From this point on she would style herself Pamela, not Pam. Her tastes broadened still further: her future conquests were to include, in alphabetical order, Woody Allen, Chris Hillman, Mick Jagger, Waylon Jennings, Don Johnson, Keith Moon, Jim Morrison, Jimmy Page, Gram Parsons and Noel Redding. Under her married name, Pamela Des Barres, she wrote two entertaining memoirs, *I'm With the Band: Confessions of a Groupie* (1987), from which this letter is taken, and *Take Another Little Piece of My Heart: A Groupie Grows Up* (1992).

66

The greater their success, the more the Beatles fell prey to chancers and charlatans.

Six months older than John Lennon, Jeffrey Archer arrived in Oxford in October 1963, having enrolled on a one-year course for a diploma from the Oxford Department of Education. In later years he was happy to be described as a graduate of Oxford University, though his qualifications for enrolment consisted only of three O-Levels and a diploma from the International Federation of Physical Culture, a bodybuilding club run from an office block in Chancery Lane.

By now, he had embarked on a lifelong career in self-promotion. On his arrival at the offices of the Oxford student magazine *Cherwell*, he announced that, with its aid, he would raise £500,000 for Oxfam. 'It will be the biggest story you've ever had. But I need your help.'

The editor of *Cherwell* arranged for Archer to meet the universities correspondent of the *Daily Mail*. Over a drink at the Union, Archer ran through his plan, and asked if the *Daily Mail* would back it. 'Very unlikely,' came the reply.

'Would it help if I managed to bring in the Beatles?' added Archer.

According to Archer, he then telegrammed Brian Epstein 'and asked for an interview, and signed it on behalf of eight thousand students at Oxford, having of course had the blessing of the Vice-Chancellor and the Proctors'.

Epstein was wary of allowing the Beatles to give their blessing to this sort of charitable fund-raising, believing it would make it harder to refuse anyone else. Though they had received no reply from him, *Cherwell* ran a front-page headline, 'A Million Pound Beatle Drive', which the national press duly covered. Archer then elbowed his way backstage at a Beatles concert, and persuaded them to pose for a photo putting money into collection tins while they held a poster saying 'WANTED £1,000,000'.

On seeing the photograph, Epstein was livid. 'He was absolutely spitting blood about it,' recalled Pat Davidson, Oxfam's press officer. 'He didn't want to speak to anyone from Oxfam. He was furious.'

At this point, Archer explained to Epstein that it might gravely damage the Beatles' reputation if they withdrew from the project. At the same time, he promised Epstein that he would arrange an agreeable lunch for the Beatles to meet the new university chancellor, the former prime minister Harold Macmillan. Impressed by the idea of such a get-together, Epstein was, however reluctantly, persuaded. 'It's not clear, however, that Archer had actually booked Macmillan when he made the promise to Epstein,' writes Archer's canny biographer Michael Crick. 'But he was certainly confident that he could.'

Such is the power of PR, or myth, or both, that many people continue to believe that, thanks to Jeffrey Archer, the Beatles once had lunch

with Harold Macmillan. But such a meeting never took place. Archer claimed to have arranged this lunch in late February 1964, but when he rang to confirm, he discovered that they were in Florida, and all set to meet Cassius Clay. So Macmillan had lunch alone with Jeffrey Archer, gloomily complaining that, without the Beatles, the event was like '*Hamlet* without the ghost'. Or the ghost without Hamlet, he might more accurately have said.

On the Beatles' return, Archer fixed a date for them to be photographed at Oxford University alongside their autographed poster. This time it was Harold Macmillan who cried off. But on 5 March 1964, John, Paul, George and Ringo dined at Brasenose College. The dean remembered John being 'asleep most of the time' and Ringo 'monosyllabic', but on the other hand George and Paul were full of beans. In fact, the dean considered Paul so 'quick and intelligent that he could easily have been an Oxford undergraduate'. Over dinner, George turned his nose up at the smoked salmon, and asked a waiter, 'Have you any jam butties?' 'I'll trade you an autograph for a jam butty,' replied the waiter, and the deal was done.

After dinner, Sheridan Morley, a student at Merton College,* found himself standing next to Ringo Starr in the Brasenose urinals. 'He asked if I knew this Jeffrey Archer bloke. I said everyone in Oxford was trying to work out who he was. Ringo said: "He strikes me as a nice enough fella, but he's the kind of bloke who would bottle your piss and sell it."'

---

* Later a theatre critic.

67

As 1963 drew to a close, the *Evening Standard* concluded, '1963 has been the Beatles' year. An examination of the heart of the nation at this moment would reveal the name Beatles engraved upon it.' By now, politicians of all parties were recognising the importance of mentioning the Beatles. It proved they were modern, democratic and on-the-ball. In February 1964, while the Beatles were away on their first US tour, the Conservative prime minister Sir Alec Douglas-Home told the annual conference of the Young Conservatives that they were 'our best exports'. He praised their 'useful contribution to the balance of payments', adding, 'If any country is in deficit with us I only have to say the Beatles are coming ... Let me tell you why they have had a success in the United States – it is because they are a band of very natural, very funny, young men.'

Soon politicians were vying with each other to garland the Beatles with superlatives. As the general election loomed, Conservative parliamentary candidates were advised to drop the Beatles into their speeches as often as possible. It was almost as if their name had become a spell, with magical powers to transform the old into the young, and the fuddy-duddy into the with-it.

The Labour Party leader, Harold Wilson, was not to be outdone. A crusader for the modern, the classless and the go-ahead, and a Merseyside MP to boot, he pooh-poohed Douglas-Home's elderly, aristocratic attempts to appear young and trendy, poking fun at 'these apostles of a bygone age trying to pretend they are with-it by claiming the Beatles as a Tory secret weapon'. Wilson insisted that the Conservative government 'would not hesitate, if there were votes in it,

to appoint Paul and George, Ringo and John, collectively to Washington to run the embassy'.

Knowing that the Beatles would be receiving the Variety Club 'Show Business Personalities of 1963' award, Wilson telephoned Sir Joseph Lockwood, the chairman of EMI, to suggest that 'as a fellow Merseysider', he would be the ideal person to make the presentation.

And so it happened that, on 19 March 1964, at a packed luncheon at the Dorchester Hotel, the leader of the opposition delivered a speech in praise of the Beatles.

> This is a non-political occasion so I'll stay non-political. Unless I'm tempted. I said that yesterday, and I was. But there were attempts recently by a certain leader of a certain party – and wild horses wouldn't drag his name from me – to involve our friends the Beatles in politics. And all I could say, with great sadness as a Merseyside Member of Parliament, which I am, was that whatever other arguments there may be, I must ask, is nothing sacred, when this sort of thing can happen? So to keep out of politics, I just repeat to you what the *Times* musical correspondent said referring to this music as

> distinctly indigenous in character, most imaginative and inventive examples, and I'm sure the *Times* music correspondent spoke for all of us when he said of our friends the Beatles that harmonically it is one of their most intriguing, with its 'chains of pandiatonic clusters' (laughter).

Wilson then bustled about with a proprietorial air as the Beatles came up for their awards.

> WILSON: One at a time! There's yours! And there's yours!
>
> GEORGE: Ladies and gentlemen, Mr Barker, Mr Dobson (laughter), and the press, I'd just like to say it's very nice indeed, especially to get one each, because we usually have a bit of trouble cutting them in four.
>
> WILSON: (keen to nose in, and to show he knows which Beatle was which) And now Paul.
>
> PAUL: Thank you very much for giving us this silver heart. But I still think you should have given one to good old Mr Wilson.
>
> WILSON: Ringo …
>
> RINGO: Anyone who knows us knows that I'm the one who never speaks, so I'd just like to say thanks a lot.
>
> JOHN: I'd just like to say the same as the others – thanks for the Purple Hearts.
>
> RINGO: Silver! Silver!
>
> JOHN: Sorry about that, Harold! We'd like to sincerely thank you all, and we've got to go now because the fella on the film wants us and he says it's costing him a fortune.

Some weeks later, Edward Heath, recently promoted to President of the Board of Trade, joked that the Beatles were now making so much money that they were 'propping up the entire national economy'.

Wilson's Labour Party entered the October 1964 general election under the self-consciously 'pop' campaign slogan 'Let's Go with Labour'. On polling day the Beatles were filmed for the TV news programme *North-East Newsview* sitting around a table in a hotel in Stockton-on-Tees, smoking cigarettes and pouring themselves tea from a silver pot. They were, as usual, light-hearted and wisecracking. The only comments to border on the political came from George, who was upset by the demands of the taxman.

Q: Have you in actual fact had time to vote yourselves?
PAUL: No, we missed it actually. We ...
JOHN: We were having dinner at the time.
JOHN AND PAUL: (laugh)
Q: I think Paul has aspirations to become prime minister. Have you still got those ideas?
PAUL: No. Not a politician. It's a hard life, you see. It's a hard day's grind.
RINGO: (narrating) ... he said, in a merry voice.
PAUL: (to the interviewer) Like a cigarette?
Q: No, I don't smoke at all. Thank you.
RINGO: They're [cigarette prices] going up, you know.
GEORGE: We'll have to give those up soon.
PAUL: We'll have to give these up.
RINGO: (lights Paul's cigarette) Aye! None of these luxuries!
JOHN: Don't tax THEM, Harold.
RINGO: It's bad enough as it is.
...
Q: During the last few weeks, the Grimond group and the Home group and the Wilson group have been edging you off the papers. Have you been envious of all these groups?
GEORGE AND JOHN: No.
PAUL: No. We sell more records and things than they do.
GEORGE: The situation looks pretty Grimmond, doesn't it!
BEATLES: (laugh)
RINGO: That's a good'n.
PAUL: No, you know. Good luck to 'em.
Q: Have any political parties contacted you and said, 'Would you say publicly you'd vote for us?'

JOHN: Oh, no.

GEORGE: No, 'cuz then the others don't buy the records.

Harold Wilson led Labour to victory at the election, becoming the youngest prime minister in 150 years. Decades later, another Labour prime minister, Gordon Brown, contended that 'the Beatles helped Labour win in 1964'. As an exceptionally young history undergraduate at Edinburgh University in the late sixties, he had argued with his lecturers that 'the 1964 and 1966 elections were won on a wave of enthusiasm for change and that no one illustrated this mood better than the Beatles. Without their fame, Harold Wilson might have struggled to popularise his theme: creating a vibrant, dynamic Britain free from the stuffy establishment living in the past … There was no better example of his theme that Britain was changing than the Beatles, who I and millions of other teenagers first followed from 1962 – young, unconventional, from the north, and awash with new energy.'

The president of the United States took more convincing. On the Beatles' first American tour, at the start of 1964, Lyndon Johnson's sixteen-year-old daughter Luci pleaded with her father to invite them to the White House.

'All our country was just peppered with pain,' she recalled half a century later, 'and so it occurred to me that, being the daughter of the president of the United States, I might be able to have every adolescent's dream come true: the Beatles to my house. So I got extremely excited about it and went to my father and asked if we could have the Beatles come. I was dumbfounded by his response. He said that this was the time for our family to be getting down to work. We couldn't be all about "yeah, yeah, yeah". He didn't tell me not to play their records and he didn't tell me not to dance to them. But he sure as heck said they weren't coming to the White House. Period. End. Closed subject.'

But by the summer of that year, President Johnson had changed his mind. Like everyone else, he craved their light. Before the Beatles' second American tour the White House press office put out feelers to Brian Epstein: would they consent to being photographed laying a wreath on President Kennedy's grave in Washington, alongside President Johnson? On behalf of the Beatles, Epstein politely but firmly declined.

68

As the years rolled by, even politicians with the most meagre interest in the Beatles felt obliged to drop their names, just to show they were in touch. On 11 October 1969, celebrating her tenth anniversary as an MP, Margaret Thatcher spoke at her Finchley Conservative Association Ball. Over the past ten years there had, she said, been many changes in society: 'In 1959 we had not heard of the Beatles or David Frost, there was no permissive society and no hippies.' Though she was probably unaware of it, the previous week John and Yoko had been recording 'Don't Worry Kyoko (Mummy's Only Looking for Her Hand in the Snow)', the B-side of the Plastic Ono Band's 'Cold Turkey', just a few miles away, in Abbey Road.

'But some things have not changed,' she continued. 'Right is still right and wrong is wrong … It is the good news which should be broadcast, and in Finchley there is a lot of good news.' She then paid tribute to the Finchley Chrysanthemum Society for 'producing bigger and better blooms'.

Eighteen years later, Mrs Thatcher was preparing to fight her second general election as prime minister. Keen to harness the skittish youth vote, her aides lined up an interview with *Smash Hits*, a magazine with an estimated readership of 3.3 million, its average reader being fifteen years old.

A week before the interview, Mrs Thatcher's aide Christine Wall wrote her a briefing note, suggesting topics that the interviewer, Tom Hibbert, might raise. They included 'any pop star/film star heroes you had as a youngster', 'your feeling about today's stars' and 'your position on drugs'.

Under the heading Points to Make, Ms Wall advised: 'It is worth mentioning that a degree of teenage rebellion is part of growing up,' and 'Teenagers have long been anti-establishment whatever the political persuasion of the Government of the day,' adding that 'You may not enjoy the interview. Mr Hibbert may ask superficial questions which betray a lack of understanding. The challenge of the interview will be for you to demonstrate that just because you are not part of the pop scene, you are still in touch with youngsters and understand their needs ...'

On the morning of the interview, she handed Mrs Thatcher a further memo:

> PRIME MINISTER
> YOUR INTERVIEW WITH SMASH HITS
> You asked for some examples of contemporary and past popular music. Here are some suggestions:
>
> CURRENT POP CHARTS
> At Number 1 and 2 in the singles charts at the moment are two American 'soul' songs both hits in the sixties and now hits again 20 years later. At No. 1 is 'STAND BY ME' by BEN E. KING. At No. 2 is 'WHEN A MAN LOVES A WOMAN' by PERCY SLEDGE ... I attach the latest Top Ten chart list.
>
> Music from the Andrew Lloyd Webber musical 'PHANTOM OF THE OPERA' continues to do well in the charts. The soundtrack album is at No 1 in the LP charts and the single 'MUSIC OF THE NIGHT' sung by MICHAEL CRAWFORD is now at No 34 in the singles charts after being in the top ten ...

A bizarre paragraph reminded Mrs Thatcher that 'Two of the most recent BIG BAND HITS are "PASADENA" by the TEMPERANCE SEVEN in the 1960s and "THE FLORAL DANCE" by THE BRIGHOUSE AND RASTRICK BRASS BAND in the 1970s.' Punk was also mentioned. The only other musical phenomenon to be accorded its own briefing note, seventeen years after they had split up, was:

> THE BEATLES
> Probably the two most famous BEATLES songs amongst many hits are YESTERDAY which has been recorded by hundreds of people including FRANK SINATRA AND ELVIS PRESLEY and ALL YOU NEED IS LOVE which was performed live in front of 64,000,000 people on TV in 1968.

When the big day came, Mrs Thatcher did her best to show that her finger was on the pulse of youth. Having offered Hibbert a glass of water ('It's Malvern Water. British! We only serve British!'), she rattled through most of the points on the memo, even mentioning 'When a Man Loves a Woman', big bands, and punk ('I know we have got the punks. The punks spend a lot of time and money on their appearance').

When Hibbert asked if she would have been very upset if her children had formed a pop group, she replied, 'No, I should not have been at all upset … I would have been much more concerned if they did not do anything. Mark did, as a matter of fact learn the guitar.' He was not particularly good at it, she added, 'but he had quite a musical sense, and they all listened to – heaven knows, we had all the latest pop records – there were the Beatles in our time you see, and they are very interesting and they are just coming back because their songs were tuneful. I remember "Telstar", lovely song, I absolutely loved it.'

'Telstar', Hibbert politely pointed out, was not by the Beatles but by the Tornados.

'The Tornados, yes, then we had Dusty Springfield, but the Beatles I remember most of all. They had to have this thing on all day, I said [to her children], "The pair of you, did you have to listen to that?" but it became part of the background.'

On 31 May 1990, six months before being squeezed from office, Margaret Thatcher paid a visit to Abbey Road, to celebrate the eightieth anniversary of the EMI studios. While there, she posed for photographs, playing the drums in the studio and walking across the famous zebra crossing on the road outside. 'I loved the songs of the Beatles,' she told journalists. 'They were sheer genius both in the way they performed and in some of the songs they wrote.'

But five years into her retirement, she had grown less enamoured of the Beatles' influence. In her autobiography she complained of 'a whole "youth culture" of misunderstood Eastern mysticism, bizarre clothing and indulgence in hallucinatory drugs'.

'I found Chelsea a very different place when we moved back to London in 1970,' she continued. 'I had mixed feelings about what was happening. There was vibrancy and talent, but this was also in large degree a world of make-believe. A perverse pride was taken in Britain about our contribution to these trends. Carnaby Street in Soho, the Beatles, the mini-skirt and the maxi-skirt were the new symbols of "Swinging Britain". And they did indeed prove good export earners. Harold Wilson was adept at taking maximum political credit for them.

The trouble was that they concealed the real economic weaknesses which even a talented fashion industry and entrepreneurial recording companies could not counter-balance. As Desmond Donnelly remarked, "My greatest fear is that Britain will sink giggling into the sea.'"

69

A Party:
Mr Brian Epstein. At Home.
Buffet Supper 9.30 p.m. Informal Dress.
15 Whaddon House, William Mews
Knightsbridge, London SW1
12 August 1964

Brian Epstein is throwing a party to launch the Beatles' second tour of the United States: thirty performances in twenty-four cities in thirty-two days, covering 22,441 miles.

Invitations have been posted to a variety of stars, including Cilla Black, Peter and Gordon, the Searchers, Tommy Steele, Mick Jagger, Keith Richards, Lionel Bart, Dusty Springfield and Alma Cogan. Three cutting-edge disc jockeys have also been invited: Alan Freeman, Pete Murray and Brian Matthew.

Epstein has roped in his interior decorator, Ken Partridge, to help with the ambience. Partridge erects a marquee on the roof, complete with french windows, so guests can look out over the city. The floor is raised, and covered in cherry-red sisal carpeting. There is a bandstand big enough for a small orchestra, plus a dance floor. The centre pole of the marquee is covered in Spanish moss, and intertwined with seven hundred carnations in the shape of a palm tree. The entire structure has taken five days to erect.

Brian is determined to keep it tasteful. 'I don't want any gimmicks,' he says.

'You mean you want white tablecloths, silver candelabra, white flowers?' says Partridge.

'Perfect.'

'Pink-and-white-striped?'

'Yes, I want all that.'

On the big day, Partridge is adamant that no one goes up on the roof before the party. But, late in the afternoon, Brian tells him his mother is downstairs. 'She's just back from the hairdresser, and she'd love to come and see it.'

'No,' says Partridge.

'Please.'

'Well, all right. Just this once.'

Queenie Epstein is ushered upstairs. She takes one look at all the carnations, half red and half white, and is horrified. Combining red and white is unlucky, she insists. This is one of a number of superstitions she harbours: she is also convinced that birds pictured on curtains will bring bad luck.

'What are we going to do?' Brian asks Partridge, adding, 'It must be changed! We can't have any bad luck just before the boys leave on tour!'

'What are we going to do? Nothing,' replies Partridge. But then he asks Pam Foster, who is in charge of the flowers, to come up with a solution. She nips down to Harrods, a few hundred yards away, to buy a quantity of red ink. Back at the flat, she pours the ink into a bucket, then removes the white carnations from the various displays and dips them all in it.

The guests arrive. The rooftop dinner is sumptuous. Tony Barrow considers the word 'buffet' inadequate to describe 'the spectacular display of food on offer, from fillets of beef to slices of duck, from chilled lobster to all manner of other seafood delicacies and baskets laden with exotic fruits'.

Everything is going swimmingly when there is a small commotion at the front door. A woman in a mink coat insists that she and her escort have been invited, yet they are not on the guest list. 'This is awful,' she tells the doorman.

Upstairs, Ken Partridge is told of the commotion below. 'Who is this woman?' he asks. He goes downstairs, to be confronted by 'this little woman in a pink coat'. She tells him, 'We met Brian with Li in a restaurant and he asked us to come along.' Partridge recognises her. 'Judy Garland!' he exclaims delightedly. 'Please come in! You're my guest!'

Like many fractured souls, Brian Epstein is a big fan of Judy Garland. He ran into her the previous night at the Caprice with Lionel Bart, or 'Li', and asked her to come and meet the Beatles. Stupidly, he forgot to add her name to the guest list.

Judy passes through the downstairs room, which is now deserted, and according to Partridge looks as if a bomb has hit it: 'Everybody had gone upstairs and there were hundreds of dirty glasses, cigarette butts, everything around.'

'Oh my God, I'm late,' says Judy.

'No, they're on the roof.'

'What are they doing on the roof?'

'Well, they're not jumping off. They're having dinner.'

Partridge ushers her upstairs, and places her next to Lionel Bart. Cilla Black notices that Judy has made no attempt to disguise her recent injuries: 'The first thing we all noticed was that both her wrists were covered in white bandages.'

'Hold my hand,' Judy tells Partridge. 'I'm so frightened.' As he moves his hand in her direction, she stubs out her cigarette on the back of it.

'I've never burned anybody before,' insists Judy.

'I shall treasure it for the rest of my life,' Partridge replies stoically.

Brian comes over to greet her, and the older members of the party gather round admiringly. Judy begins to relax, and after dinner is over, seems happy to mix with the other guests. The younger types – the Stones, the Searchers – don't really know, or care, who she is. She encountered the Beatles three weeks ago, when she joined them in *The Night of a Thousand Stars* at the London Palladium, alongside Gloria Swanson, Merle Oberon, Laurence Olivier and Zsa Zsa Gabor. She had gone to the Palladium straight from a nursing home to which she had been admitted after having suffered cuts to her arms and wrists – sustained, or so she insisted to the press, while struggling to open a metal trunk with a pair of scissors. The actress Hayley Mills, aged sixteen, had been standing backstage next to the Beatles when Garland took to the stage in a red sequined sheath dress with long sleeves: 'There was tremendous applause and then there was a lull before she started to speak or sing. And in that lull, you suddenly heard John's voice yelling out, "Show us your wrists, Judy!" I don't think she heard. I do hope she didn't hear.'

Tonight, John makes no attempt to renew his brief acquaintance, but Paul engages Judy in a conversation about Lionel Bart's new show, *Maggie May*. Looking across the room, Tony Barrow considers that Judy looks 'pale, weak, ill at ease and a million miles from the effervescent personality we'd seen so many times on the cinema screen'. Nevertheless, amidst the general melee, he observes her 'bouncing off the walls and gabbling away to her host'.

At one point, Brian spots his grandmother buttonholing Judy. After Judy has moved on, Brian asks what they were talking about. 'How to make chocolate cake,' replies Judy.

Judy potters off in search of the lavatory, and fails to reappear. Cilla Black is just leaving when Brian approaches in a panic.

'Judy's been in the bathroom for at least fifteen minutes.'

'So? Women are not like guys, Brian,' she replies. 'They take a while in there.'

Five minutes later, Cilla is saying goodnight to Ringo when Brian hurtles over again. 'She's still in there,' he hisses. 'We can't have her committing suicide here. Go in and get her, Cilla.'

'Oh God!' replies Cilla, who is beginning to worry. 'You want me to go in there and see if she's slashed her wrists again?'

'*Please*, Cilla.'

Outside the lavatory, concern is growing. One or two guests have tried rapping on the door, but to no avail. At last, Judy emerges. Tony Barrow notes that she is 'perspiring profusely', but otherwise perky.

Around midnight, the police arrive: neighbours have been complaining about the noise. Summoned to deal with them, Alistair Taylor picks up an unopened bottle of champagne. Brian asks him what he is doing with it. He explains that it is a peace offering for the police. 'Oh no you don't,' says Brian. 'If anybody's going to give away my wine it's going to be me.' He snatches the bottle from Taylor's hands and stomps off. But then he thinks better of it.

'Alistair,' he says, 'give this champagne to the police with my compliments, and in future please make sure you ask me personally before you shower my hospitality on outsiders.'

Later, after Judy has left, Brian and Lionel Bart hatch a plan to present her in the West End, but nothing comes of it.

At this moment, Judy Garland has a little under five years left to live, and Brian Epstein exactly three years, two weeks.

70

On 28 August 1964, as the Beatles struggled to make their way through the crush in the lobby of the Delmonico Hotel on Park Avenue, Ringo found himself trapped in a crowd of girls. One of them tore his shirt open; another grabbed at the gold St Christopher medal he had been given by his Auntie Nancy.

Ringo only realised it had disappeared once he had extracted himself from the scrum, and by then it was too late. When the Beatles arrived at their suite at the Warwick Hotel for a live interview, it was clear that Ringo was upset. 'What's the matter?' asked the WABC disc jockey 'Cousin Brucie' Morrow, who was to conduct the interview. 'You don't look too good.'

'Somebody grabbed me St Christopher's medal,' said Ringo mournfully. He had worn it, night and day, ever since his twenty-first birthday, a year before he joined the Beatles; small wonder he associated it with good luck.

The interview was being broadcast live. Outside in the street, six thousand fans were glued to their transistor radios to hear what was being said in the room above.

Cousin Brucie had a bright idea. 'I went on the air and said to the kids: "Look, somebody must have found Ringo Starr's St Christopher medal." I didn't say "took it" or "stole it", I said, "Somebody must have found it." I said, "Look, if you return it you will not be in trouble and you'll come up here with Cousin Brucie and you'll meet Ringo and he'll give you a kiss." Well, of course, the place went crazy, and you heard them outside – WAAAGH! – through the windows. There were thousands of them.'

Other radio interviews repeated the sad tale of the lost St Christopher, along with Ringo's promise to reward whoever found it with a kiss. The fans proved wily. Within an hour, the shops of Manhattan had sold out of St Christopher medals, and an equal number of calls had been received from girls claiming to have found Ringo's. One of them was answered by Cousin Brucie himself. 'Cousin Brucie, my name is Mrs McGowan, and my daughter Angela found Ringo's St Christopher medal. Is she in any trouble?'

But was she telling the truth? Her fear that her daughter might be in trouble suggested she was. When Angela said it had come loose from Ringo's neck when she tore his shirt in the Delmonico Hotel, Cousin Brucie knew he had found the culprit.

'I knew right away that I had a tremendous news piece, and I didn't want anybody else to get it. "Stay right where you are," I said. "I'm going to send a car for you."'

The next day, with television cameras whirring, Ringo was interviewed by three different reporters, who towered over him with their microphones. Then Angie McGowan was introduced to him by Cousin Brucie.

'Angie, sweetheart, this is your idol, this is Ringo.'

Angie, a pretty brunette, stepped forward, gave a little curtsey, and returned the St Christopher to its owner.

'It's very small,' said Ringo, 'but it means a lot.'

'Sorry about your shirt,' said Angie.

'I can buy another shirt, but I can't buy another one of these.'

Ringo gave Angie the promised kiss, whereupon three of her friends stepped forward, and he kissed them too. Angie kissed him again, with her hand to his head, and Ringo signed an autograph for her. Cousin Brucie reported that the girls were kissing him again, off camera. 'He's still kissing Angie; what is going on over there!?'

Meanwhile, Ringo tucked his St Christopher into his jacket pocket, just to be on the safe side.

71

Penelope Fitzgerald identified the social message Evelyn Waugh wished to convey as: *I am bored; you are frightened.*

The same might be said of Bob Dylan. Though unlike Waugh in most other respects, his presence can be intimidating, his disdain curbed only by indifference.

This was never more true than in the summer of 1964. Dylan had recently established himself as the most hip, most gritty, most forceful performer on the planet. Yet the title of most popular belonged elsewhere.

Like most people in America, Dylan first heard the Beatles in January 1964. They had soon become unavoidable. 'We were driving through Colorado, we had the radio on, and eight of the top 10 songs were Beatles songs … "I Wanna Hold Your Hand", all those early ones,' he recalled.

Dylan immediately recognised that they were not purely a commercial phenomenon, bound up with screaming girls: 'They were doing things nobody was doing. Their chords were outrageous, just outrageous, and their harmonies made it all valid … I knew they were pointing the direction of where music had to go.'

The meeting between these two musical superpowers was brokered by a journalist called Al Aronowitz. While the Beatles were staying at the Delmonico, Dylan was at home in Woodstock, in upstate New York. Aronowitz took a call from John Lennon, with whom he had become chummy.

'Where is he?'

'Who?'

'Dylan.'

'Oh, he's up in Woodstock, but I can get him to come down.'

'Do it!'

That evening, Dylan and Aronowitz dutifully pushed their way through the fans outside the hotel, accompanied by Dylan's tour manager Victor Maymudes, who doubled as his dope-carrier. In the hospitality suite on the Beatles' floor, Derek Taylor was busy entertaining some lesser celebrities, including the disc jockey Murray 'The K' Kaufman, the Kingston Trio and Peter, Paul and Mary, but Dylan and his entourage were a cut above, so they were ushered into the Beatles' suite without further ado.

They had just finished their room-service dinner when Dylan arrived. Brian Epstein acted as greeter: 'I'm afraid we can only offer champagne.' Dylan said he'd prefer cheap wine, but having established his no-nonsense credentials, gruffly agreed to make do with champagne.

The introductions were tentative. 'Bob and the Beatles all needed room to swashbuckle,' Aronowitz recalled, 'but nobody wanted to step on anybody else's ego.'

At once, the talk turned to drugs. The Beatles offered Purple Hearts, but Dylan declined, suggesting marijuana.

'We've never smoked marijuana before,' confessed Epstein.

'But what about your song? The one about getting high?' said Dylan.

'Which song?' asked John.

'You know – "I get high! I get high!"'

John was driven to correct him, pointing out that the chorus to 'I Want to Hold Your Hand' is not 'I get high', but 'I can't hide'. How, John wondered, would marijuana make them feel?

'Good,' said Dylan. He began to roll a joint, but was unexpectedly cack-handed.

Aronowitz looked on in despair. 'Bob hovered unsteadily over the bowl as he stood at the table while he tried to lift the grass from the baggie with the fingertips of one hand so he could crush it into the leaf of rolling paper which he held in his other hand. In addition to the fact that Bob was a sloppy roller to begin with, what Bob had started drinking had already gotten to him.'

There were roughly twenty policemen stationed in the corridor outside, while waiters kept popping in and out. Dylan, Aronowitz and Maymudes felt that somewhere more discreet was required, so everyone crammed into one of the bedrooms.

Dylan lit the first joint, and passed it to John, who, always more cautious than he liked to appear, passed it on – 'You try it!' – to Ringo. It was, Aronowitz noted, an act that 'instantly revealed the Beatles' pecking order. Obviously Ringo was the low man on the totem pole.'

'He's my royal taster,' explained John, confirming Aronowitz's suspicions.

Ringo was unsure what to do, so Aronowitz talked him through the correct procedure: inhale deeply, hold it in your lungs for as long as possible, exhale. But he failed to add, 'then pass it on'. As it became clear that Ringo considered the joint his to keep, Maymudes got down to rolling some more. Within minutes they had one each, and everybody was puffing away.

Paul was underwhelmed. 'For about five minutes we went, "This isn't doing anything," so we kept having more.' Suddenly, Ringo started giggling. It proved infectious. 'His laughing looked so funny that the rest of us started laughing hysterically at the way Ringo was laughing hysterically. Soon, Ringo pointed at the way Brian Epstein was laughing, and we all started laughing hysterically at the way Brian was laughing.'

Aronowitz remembered Epstein saying, 'I'm so high I'm on the ceiling,' over and over again. Then he started looking at himself in the mirror, saying 'Jew, Jew …' It was, thought Paul, 'as if he was finally sort of talking about the fact – "Oh, I'm Jewish. I forgot."'

Later that evening, the British journalist Chris Hutchins returned from an evening out with Neil Aspinall. He was unlocking the door to his bedroom when Aspinall whispered, 'Come and look at this.'

The two of them crept into the Beatles' suite. 'Seated on five chairs arranged in a line were the Fab Four and their manager Brian Epstein, all stoned. Every now and again, a man standing at one end of the line would push the closest Beatle off his chair and, in domino effect, each would knock the next one off, ending with Brian, who would collapse to the floor laughing helplessly, setting the others off. It was a surreal scene, made more bizarre by the fact that the man doing the pushing was Bob Dylan.'

Presently, Paul convinced himself that he had discovered the meaning of life, and started bustling around the suite looking for a pencil and paper to jot it down before he forgot. 'I suddenly felt like a reporter, on behalf of my local newspaper in Liverpool. I wanted to tell people what it was.' He instructed Mal Evans to follow him around the suite with a notebook, to inscribe his words of wisdom. Whenever the telephone rang, Dylan would answer it with the words, 'This is Beatlemania here.'

The Beatles rang through to Derek Taylor in the suite next door, telling him to join them. Taylor found Epstein 'reeling around, holding a flower', telling him that 'I MUST try it, this wonderful stuff that made everything seem to float upwards'.

'We've been turned on,' explained George. For the next quarter of an hour Taylor encountered 'a smoky, murky muddle of unfamiliar expressions' – 'turned on', 'stoned', 'way out' – peppered with the more commonplace 'incredible', 'wow', 'man', 'fab' and 'gear'. It was clear to him that Bob Dylan was top dog, 'thin and beaked, with the beady-eyed gaze of a little bird'.

The effect of Dylan's visit on the Beatles was deep and long-lasting. Two months later they recorded 'She's a Woman', which included John's line 'Turn me on when I get lonely'. By the time they came to film *Help!* in February 1965 they were, according to John, 'smoking marijuana for breakfast … it was all glazed eyes and giggling all the time'. The following June they recorded 'It's Only Love', which included the very words Dylan had misheard: 'I get high'.

From then on, drugs references in their songs kept tumbling out – 'riding so high', 'find me in my field of grass', 'because the wind is high, it blows my mind'. Most of them passed unnoticed at the time: only years later did Paul confess that his jaunty, upbeat 'Got to Get You Into My Life', with its tender, loving lyrics 'I need you every single day of my life' and 'When I'm with you I want to stay there', was in fact an ode to pot. By the time they came to record *Sgt. Pepper*, tracks free of drugs references were thin on the ground.

Like so many fans, John took steps to turn into his hero. His voice grew more rasping, his attitude more sarky, his lyrics more opaque. Years later, he told the photographer David Bailey about these replicant instincts. 'He said to me, "Y'know, when I've discovered someone new, I tend to become that person. I want to soak myself in their stuff to such an extent that I have to be them." When he first found Dylan, he said, he would dress like Dylan and only play his kind of music, till he kind of understood how it worked.' During one recording session, George Martin had to ask John if he could try to sound less like Bob Dylan. 'He wasn't doing it deliberately. It was subconscious more than anything.'

Dylan seems to have enjoyed the Beatles' company. Their friendship blossomed in a haze of dope. But there was never any question as to who was the master, and who the servants. Marianne Faithfull witnessed the Beatles greeting Dylan after they watched him perform at the Royal Albert Hall on 27 May 1966.

'Dylan went into the room where the Beatles were sitting all scrunched up on the couch, all of them fantastically nervous. Lennon, Ringo, George and Paul, Lennon's wife Cynthia and one or two roadies. Nobody said anything. They were waiting for the oracle to speak. But Dylan just sat down and looked at them as if they were all total strangers at a railway station. They were frozen in each other's company. It wasn't so much a matter of them being so cool as the fact that they were too young to be genuinely cool. Like teenagers, they were afraid of what others might think.'

Their subservience surprised her. 'I thought, Jesus, how could anyone ever have thought these scared little boys were gods?'

72

The Beatles phenomenon came as a surprise to composers still working in the classical tradition. What to make of it all?

Some tried to grin and bear it. 'I don't think the Beatles are by *any* means a wholly *bad* influence,' said Benjamin Britten, retreating into litotes for an interview with Radio Finland in 1965. 'I think they're charming creatures. I don't happen to like their music very much, but that's just me. I think it's very natural that light music should exist; but if a person likes the Beatles, it doesn't by any means preclude their love of Beethoven. Everything I read about the Beatles gives me great pleasure. I also think they're *frightfully* funny.'

Aaron Copland, sixty-three years old when the Beatles burst on America, approved of them, though in a slightly mystified sort of way. Their music, he said, 'has an unanalyzable charm. It's very hard to say what they do, but the result has a fascination about it. It is immediately recognizable and it sticks in the mind.' Later, he came to recognise their unearthly grip on the zeitgeist. 'If you want to know about the sixties, play the music of the Beatles.'

By and large, classical music critics were just as keen to prove they were not fuddy-duddy. In the *Sunday Times*, Richard Buckle called the Beatles the greatest composers since Beethoven; in the *New York Review of Books*, Ned Rorem compared them to Schubert; in *The Listener*, Deryck Cooke attempted to convey the full majesty of 'Strawberry Fields Forever' by elevating it to a branch of Higher Mathematics: 'It has a first nine-bar section divided into one-and-a-half, two, two, one-and-a-half and two, the penultimate bar being in 6/8 instead of 4/4, quaver equalling quaver. After a delaying six-beat major phrase harmonised by the tonic chord ("Let me take you down, 'cos I'm going") the tune plunges fiercely on to the flat seventh, harmonised by the minor seventh on the dominant, for a solidly rhythmic beat phrase ("*to* Strawberry Fields").'

Writing in *The Times* on 27 December 1963, William Mann had famously praised a song he misnamed 'That Boy' for its 'chains of pandiatonic clusters'. He went on to note that 'they think simultaneously of harmony and melody, so firmly are the major tonic sevenths and ninths built into their tunes, and the flat submediant key switches, so natural is the Aeolian cadence at the end of "Not a Second Time" (the chord progression which ends Mahler's Song of the Earth'.

By now, Mann had the wind behind him. 'Those submediant switches from C major into A flat major,' he continued, 'and to a lesser extent mediant ones (e.g. the octave ascent in the famous "I Want to Hold Your Hand") are a trademark of Lennon–McCartney songs … The autocratic but not by any means ungrammatical attitude to tonality (closer to, say, Peter Maxwell Davies's carols in "O Magnum Mysterium" than to Gershwin or Loewe or even Lionel Bart); the exhilarating and often quasi-instrumental vocal duetting, sometimes in scat or in falsetto, behind the melodic line; the melismas with altered vowels ("I saw her yesterday-ee-ay") which have not quite become mannered, and the discreet, sometimes subtle, varieties of instrumentation – a suspicion of piano or organ, a few bars of mouth-organ obbligato, an excursion on the claves or maracas …'

Ever the ingrate, John refused to thank Mann for his appreciation. 'He uses a whole lot of musical terminology,' he complained to an interviewer. 'And he's a twit.'

It was left to the wayward Canadian classical pianist Glenn Gould to mount a full-blown counterattack on the Beatles. Gould refused to go along with the prevailing notion that they were a breath of fresh air, the natural heirs to Schubert, and so forth.* Instead, he described their

* Gould was a non-conformist in other ways too; he made many a rock star appear strait-laced. As a child, he kept a pet skunk. He refused to wear tails for public performances, preferring to appear in scruffy clothes and mismatched socks, with his shoes often held together by rubber bands. He liked to play on a low chair, sitting just fourteen inches from the

music as 'a happy, cocky, belligerently resourceless brand of harmonic primitivism'.

As the Beatles' music developed, Gould disapproved of their pretension more than their primitivism – or rather, he saw the one as a cover-up for the other: 'After all of the pretension has been cut away and after all the faddish admiration … has been removed, what you really have left is three chords.' To him, these three chords were 'ultrasimplistic', but the group counterfeited complexity by topping off their little ditties with what he called 'piles of garbage'. For Gould, 'The Beatles seem to want to say, "We are going to show you that it is possible to work with a minimal harmonic structure and to so becloud the issue that that's what we're doing that you're going to think it's new and it's different and whoopee!" And all of this electric garbage – I mean, you don't necessarily get it good by adding a sitar.' It was this sense of a cover-up that made Gould particularly dislike those Beatles songs that others regarded as their most advanced. For him, their apparent sophistication was no more than an elaborate deceit, artificially manufactured with knobs and switches; he even went so far as to liken 'Strawberry Fields Forever' to 'a mountain wedding between Claudio Monteverdi and a jug band'.

Those in search of true simplicity would be better off looking elsewhere: 'Now, if what you want is an extended exercise in how to mangle three chords, then obviously the Beatles are for you; but, on the other hand, if you prefer to have the same three chords unmangled – just played nicely – then Tony Hatch* is your man.'

---

ground, so that his knees were higher than his buttocks. On many of his recordings of Bach he can be heard humming along and making odd clucking sounds. He gave up concert performances at the age of thirty-one, describing live audiences as 'a force for evil'. He also disliked bright colours, sunny weather, shaking hands, Mozart and Italian opera. On the road, his motoring skills were particularly quirky: he liked to drive with his legs crossed, dummy-conducting from a score open on the passenger seat. He couldn't see anything wrong with it. 'It's true that I've driven through a number of red lights on occasion,' he once protested. 'But on the other hand, I've stopped at a lot of green ones and never gotten credit for it.'

* Born 1939. Composer of hits like 'Downtown' and 'Don't Sleep in the Subway' for Petula Clark, and later the catchy theme tunes for, among others, *Emmerdale Farm*, *Crossroads* and *Neighbours*.

The music critic Fritz Spiegl – who we last encountered bumping into a tipsy George at Beryl Bainbridge's Liverpool party in May 1960 – went even further. He argued that the Beatles had done more damage to music than any other four people in history. They did this, he said, by offering instant bliss without effort. Their music lacked the reserve that characterises all good art; it held nothing back.

Within the literary world, opinions on the Beatles were also divided – largely, though not exclusively, along lines of age. The buttoned-up English poet Philip Larkin (b.1922) recognised the Beatles' sociological importance, while not particularly enjoying their music. In one of his most quoted poems, 'Annus Mirabilis', he declares that:

> Sexual intercourse began
> In nineteen sixty-three
> (which was rather late for me) –
> Between the end of the 'Chatterley' ban
> And the Beatles' first LP.

Larkin's attitude to the Beatles changed with the years. By nature a fan of trad jazz, he was always feeling left behind. In December 1963 he noted that their second LP, *With the Beatles*, 'suggests that their jazz content is nil, but that, like certain sweets, they seem wonderful until you are finally sick'. After his death in 1985 it emerged that he had once nursed a craving for at least one of their sweets, having bought his lady friend Maeve Brennan a copy of 'Yesterday' before playing it over and over again to himself, in a fashion verging on the obsessive.

By 1967 Larkin was feeling a pang of nostalgia for their early records. What had all that wealth and acclaim done to them in the meantime? Listening to 'A Collection of Beatles' Oldies', in March 1967, he thought it would 'prove admirable demonstration material for Marx's theory of artistic degeneration: WEA lecturers please note'. Four months later, the release of *Sgt. Pepper's Lonely Hearts Club Band* confirmed that they had taken off in the wrong direction. 'The Beatles, having made their name in the narrow emotional and harmonic world of teenage pop, are now floating away on their own cloud. I doubt whether their own fancies and imagination are strong enough to command an audience instead of collaborating with it.'

Larkin's curmudgeonly friend Kingsley Amis was less mealy-mouthed. 'Oh fuck the Beatles,' he wrote to Larkin on 19 April 1969. 'I'd like to push my bum into John L's face for forty-eight hours or so, as a protest against all the war and violence in the world.' Amis had personal reasons for his dislike. 'I met Lennon a couple of times. The first time he was being nasty to his wife, the English one not the Nip, the second time she wasn't there and he was just generally offensive. No breeding, what?'

The most furious condemnation of the Beatles came from Paul Johnson, writing in the *New Statesman* in February 1964. 'The Menace of Beatlism' was a bracing riposte to a speech made by the Conservative government's minister of information, William Deedes, to the City of London Young Conservatives. Deedes had cannily noted that the Beatles 'herald a cultural movement among the young which may become part of the history of our time ... For those with eyes to see it, something important and heartening is happening here. The young are rejecting some of the sloppy standards of their elders ... they have discerned dimly that in a world of automation, declining craftsmanship and increased leisure, something of this kind is essential to restore the human instinct to excel at something and the human faculty of discrimination.'

That these remarks should have passed unchallenged by Young Conservatives infuriated the thirty-five-year-old Johnson. 'Not a voice was raised to point out that the Emperor wasn't wearing a stitch,' he thundered. He felt that it was only because the Beatles were earning over £6 million a year that they had gained the approval of the moneyed classes: overnight, they had become part of the export trade, and electorally valuable.

Johnson had seen the signs coming: 'Of course, our society has long been brainwashed in preparation for this apotheosis of inanity.' Writers of distinction could now be spotted 'squatting on the bare boards of malodorous caverns, while through the haze of smoke, sweat and cheap cosmetics comes the monotonous braying of savage instruments'.

Johnson compared the teenagers of 1964 with his own generation twenty years before: 'At sixteen, I and my friends heard our first performance of Beethoven's Ninth Symphony; I can remember the excitement even today. We would not have wasted 30 seconds of our precious time on the Beatles and their ilk.'

He ended his piece on a note of optimism. Cells of resistance were springing up. Teenagers 'who flock around the Beatles, who scream themselves into hysteria, whose vacant faces flicker over the TV screen, are the least fortunate of their generation, the dull, the idle, the failures . . .'

'The Menace of Beatlism' prompted more letters of complaint than any other article ever published in the *New Statesman*. Many readers worried that Johnson had grown old before his time; one even suggested he try ingesting monkey glands.

73

Q: What will you do when the bubble bursts?
JOHN: Get jobs.

Press conference, Los Angeles, 23 August 1964

Q: What will you do when the bubble bursts?
JOHN: Count the money.

Press conference, Cincinnati, 27 August 1964

Q: Have you fellas given any thought to what you're going to do when the bubble breaks, so to speak?
PAUL AND GEORGE: (laugh)
JOHN: Well, we're gonna have a good time.
GEORGE: We never plan ahead.
Q: How about your retirement or buying into a big business …
John: We already are a big business, so we don't have to buy into another one.
Q: Well, I'm talking about if this business should wane slightly.
GEORGE: We'll start planning when it starts to wane, but at the moment we'll just let it go on as it is.
PAUL: Anyway, yeah. We've never made plans for anything, so there's no real reason to make plans now.

Press conference, Chicago, 5 September 1964

Q: It's assumed that you will sing for quite some time yet, but what do you plan to do after …
GEORGE: … the bubble bursts.

PAUL: Nobody's made any plans, but John and I will probably … (laughs) Ooo, we have this one every day, you know. John and I will probably carry on songwriting. And then George will go into basketball.

GEORGE: Or rollerskating. I haven't decided yet.

Press conference, Kansas City, 17 September 1964

Q: Fred Paul from KAXK. First of all I'd like to say Hi to you all again, it's really good to see you. I'd like to ask a question that you've never been asked before.

JOHN: Oh no.

Q: What are you going to do when the bubble bursts?

Press conference, Los Angeles, 24 August 1966

I came back to my publisher and told him that I had the exclusive contract to be the Beatles' biographer, and he said, despondently, 'Oh … the bubble's going to burst. This is 1967, we know everything that we could possibly want to know about the Beatles, and they'll disappear soon.'

Hunter Davies, new introduction to his 1968 authorised Beatles biography (1996)

74

At 10 p.m. on Saturday, 21 August 1965, a week into their second full North American tour, the Beatles set off from Minneapolis to Portland, Oregon, in an Electra plane.

Among those travelling with them was Larry Kane, covering the tour for the top 40 music station WFUN Miami. After he had eaten, Kane pushed his seat back and dozed off, only to wake up with a start. 'My eyelids popped open in reaction to what appeared to be a bright light off the wing. Was I dreaming? I looked and looked again. My adrenaline surged. I swallowed hard. There, in front of my eyes, was a fire, racing out of the right engine on the wing.'

Kane ran to the front of the plane and thumped on the door to the flight deck, but was met with no response. The plane was on autopilot, and the pilot and his co-pilot were at the back of the cabin, hobnobbing with Paul and John. Kane rushed towards them, screaming, 'There's a fire in the right engine!' Immediately, everyone on the plane began to panic.

Each of the Beatles acted in his own different way. Ringo simply stared at the fire. Paul tried to act cool, but Kane noticed that he was biting his lip. George ran to the back, saying, 'Beatles and children first.'

John, on the other hand, could not hide his terror. He looked at the fire, said, 'Oh shit, oh shit, oh shit,' ran to the emergency door at the back, and began tugging at the handle. Kane grappled with him, pulling his hands off and pushing him away, saying 'Are you crazy? You'll get us all killed.' At that point they were flying at a height of 22,000 feet.

But John was not to be put off by logic. He charged at the door again, but the burly Mal Evans stood in his way.

By now the pilots had returned to the cockpit. Over the intercom came the announcement that they were close to Portland, and that they could rely on the remaining engines to get them there safely. 'What a bunch of rubbish!' yelled John, with his eyes tight shut.

Half an hour later the plane landed at Portland, to be greeted by firefighters, who covered it in a sea of foam. Kane remembered everyone on board sighing 'Oh God' and 'I'll never fly again.' But two days later they had to board another plane to take them to Los Angeles, where they were due to meet Elvis Presley. As they boarded, Ringo chirped up, 'Let's stay alive in '65.'

Eight months later, an Electra plane operated by the same charter service crashed in Ardmore, Oklahoma, killing seventy-eight soldiers on their way home from training, and five crew members, three of whom – the pilot and two engineers – had been with the Beatles on their hazardous flight to Portland.

75

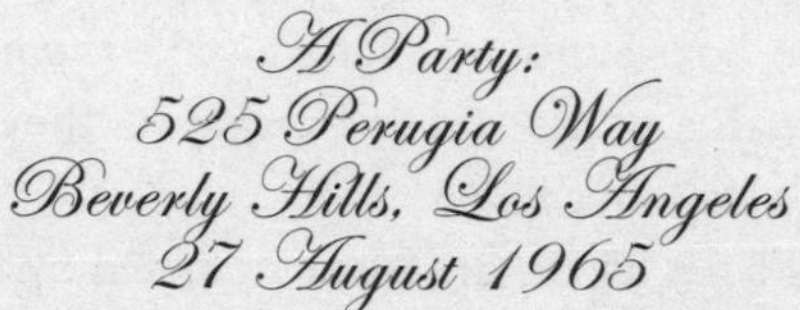

The party arrangements have been lengthy and fraught; almost closer, in their withdrawals, stand-offs and concessions, to negotiations for a peace settlement.

Which is, in a way, what it is. The brash young Beatles are in the ascendant. Elvis Presley was once the talk of America, but now it is all Beatles, Beatles, Beatles. They have stolen his thunder. Until the spring, Elvis's career was in the doldrums, with no top 10 single since 1963. His movie career, too, is adrift: his last, *Tickle Me*, set in a beauty parlour, was barely noticed. But the Beatles can do no wrong. They have just premiered *Help!*, which seems set to repeat the success of *A Hard Day's Night*. Three days ago, Hollywood's crème de la crème – Rock Hudson, Jack Benny, Jane Fonda, Groucho Marx, James Stewart – attended a party in their honour, and even queued for autographs.

At the beginning of the month, Elvis's manager, Colonel Tom Parker, invites Brian Epstein to his New York office to hammer out a deal. They sit on chairs made from elephants' feet and finalise arrangements over pastrami sandwiches and root beer. The colonel calls the shots. The Beatles will come to Elvis, not the other way round; no cameras or tape-recorders will be permitted; and no publicity of any sort. In turn, Epstein insists that there must be extra security on the gates.

John makes his own demands, saying he doesn't even want the colonel or Epstein to be at the meeting: 'If both sides start lining up teams of supporters it will turn into a contest to see who can field the most players.' But over another business lunch, beside the pool of the Beverly Hills Hotel, Parker insists he will attend, so Epstein demands parity. Before long, the numbers have increased: as Elvis invites more of his self-styled 'Memphis Mafia', the Beatles invite their roadies Neil and Mal, their press officer Tony Barrow, and their driver Alf Bicknell, as well as Chris Hutchins from the *NME*, who helped Epstein gain an entrée with the colonel.

When the big day comes, there are nerves on both sides. 'Before the Beatles arrived that night, Elvis and I were in his bathroom doing his hair,' recalls one member of his entourage, Larry Geller. 'Elvis was unusually quiet, even pensive, as he drummed his fingers on the marble ledge.' In their limousine on the way there, Barrow notices the Beatles growing tense. They are, after all, about to meet the man who has long been their idol. 'Do you think the colonel has bothered to tell Elvis we're coming?' asks John.

The Beatles and their entourage are led into a vast circular room, lit in red and blue. In a red shirt with bolero sleeves, Elvis stands in the centre of a ring of twenty people. His wife Priscilla stands beside him. 'Her black bouffant towered above her head and she was heavily made up with thick black mascara, midnight-blue eyeliner, red blusher and Heartbreak Pink lipstick,' noted Chris Hutchins. 'She was wearing a figure-hugging cream jacket with long pants and there was a jewelled tiara on her head.'*

For a few seconds, silence falls as the English and American gangs face each other. Priscilla Presley senses their nervousness: 'You could hear a pin drop when they walked in … I was amazed at how shy they were … they were speechless, totally speechless, truly like kids, meeting their idol. Especially John – John was shy, timid, looking at him. I mean, I really believe he just couldn't believe he was actually there with Elvis Presley.'

Priscilla finds the atmosphere 'a little bit awkward because they kept looking at him, not really saying anything and not really sitting down, just staring at him'. She remembers Elvis saying, 'Guys, if you're gonna just stand around and stare at me, I may as well do my own thing.' He sits down, and the Beatles sit cross-legged on the floor around him. 'A chair for Mr Epstein,' says the colonel, and people rush forward with a selection of them.

They talk about touring; George tells Elvis about their plane catching fire on their flight to Portland on Monday. Elvis says one of his aircraft engines once gave out over Atlanta. Meanwhile, the two managers huddle in a corner; Brian is keen to organise UK concert dates for Elvis, but the colonel has a rule not to mix business with pleasure. Instead, he announces to the room, 'Ladies and gentlemen, Elvis's private casino is now open for your pleasure. Brian, let's play roulette.'

The two managers go through to the casino as Elvis picks up a bass guitar and starts playing along to songs on his jukebox. A television is

---

* Or so Hutchins wrote in the notes he secretly maintained over several visits to the loo. Others remembered differently: Paul had Priscilla wearing 'a purple gingham dress and a gingham bow in her very beehive hair'; Neil thought it was 'a long dress and a tiara'; George was convinced it was 'some sort of tight cream top with long flimsy trousers to match'; and Tony Barrow was equally sure that it was 'a full-length lime-coloured gown'.

on, with its sound turned down. Occasionally he picks up a remote control to switch channels. It is the first remote control Paul has ever seen. 'He was switching channels and we were like, "Wow! How are you doing that?"'

Elvis calls for more guitars for the Beatles, and they join in. Paul chats to him about playing bass. The conversation is a little desultory, until John sharpens it up. 'Why have you dropped the old rock stuff?' he asks Elvis, adding that he'd loved his early records, but didn't like the more recent ones. Elvis says he'll soon be making rock records again. 'Oh, good,' says John. 'We'll buy them when you do.' Elvis is nonplussed: he has grown accustomed to everyone telling him what he wants to hear. Later, John says he spotted a slogan saying 'All the Way with LBJ'. John regards LBJ as a warmonger. Was this what prompted his putdown of Elvis?

They all go back to their jamming, this time 'I Feel Fine'. Ringo has no drums, and feels under-used drumming on a table with his fingers, so he drifts off to play pool with the roadies.

John puts on a comical Clouseau voice, saying, 'Zis is ze way it should be … ze small homely gathering wiz a few friends and a leetle muzic.' Elvis looks baffled. After a while, the songs run dry and they all join the others in the games room. The colonel is more forthcoming than his client. John is amused by his swashbuckling stories of his early life as a carnival showman: how he wrestled with a lion, how the dancing chickens danced only when he placed them on an electric plate. 'He's an amazing character, a real hustling showman,' John tells Hutchins later. 'But Elvis – what a total anti-climax HE was. He seemed to be completely out of his head. Either he was on pills or dope … whatever it was, he was just totally uninterested and uncommunicative.'

Colonel Parker signals the end of the party by handing out presents of Elvis records to one and all. He also gives the four Beatles little covered wagons that light up when you push a button. He tells Brian Epstein he is going to buy him a cocktail cabinet. Brian says he is going to ask Harrods to send the colonel a Shetland pony, as a memento of his days in the circus.

As they are ushered out the front door, Elvis says, 'Don't forget to come and see us again in Memphis if you're ever in Tennessee.'

Still adopting a comical voice, John shouts back, 'Zanks for ze music, Elvis! Long live ze King!' Then he asks Elvis to join the Beatles at their place in Benedict Canyon the following night.

'Well, I'll see. I'm not sure I'll be able to make it or not,' replies Elvis.

On the way back, John describes the party as a total non-event: 'I can't decide who's more full of shit, me or Elvis Presley.'

Once the Beatles are safely out of sight, Elvis goes back into the house and draws Larry Geller to one side. What really blew his mind, he says, is the state of their teeth. He can't understand why, with all their money, they haven't had them fixed.*

---

* Five years later, on 30 December 1970, on an impromptu visit to the White House, Elvis tells President Nixon that 'The Beatles had been a real force for anti-American spirit ... The Beatles came to this country, made their money, and then returned to England where they promoted an anti-American theme.' Present at the meeting, the White House counsel Egil 'Bud' Krogh noted that, while the president nodded in agreement, he also 'expressed some surprise'. Early the following year, Elvis expresses similar misgivings on a tour of the FBI building in Washington: 'Presley indicated that he is of the opinion that the Beatles laid the groundwork for many of the problems we are having with young people by their filthy unkempt appearances and suggestive music,' reads an official memo.

76

Even Beatles need dentists. To become the Fab Four, their teeth needed as much tweaking as their hair and clothes, perhaps more.

John Riley was the son of an upstanding south London police constable. He had studied cosmetic dentistry at Northwestern University Dental School in Chicago before setting up a practice in Harley Street. He is said to have possessed a quality rare, and perhaps dangerous, in a dentist: charisma. 'He was the sort of man that if he walked in the room, you'd feel his presence even before you saw him,' observed one of his clients. By the early 1960s he had become one of the most fashionable dentists in town, much sought after by figures in showbusiness and the arts, including all four Beatles.

George's teeth needed particular attention: photographs from the Cavern days reveal them as uneven and rickety. Through the latter part of 1963 and into 1964 he became such a frequent visitor to Riley's clinic that the two men struck up a friendship of sorts, sometimes going out clubbing together. In February 1965 the Beatles even invited Riley to the Bahamas to keep them company while they were filming *Help!*. Yet Pattie Boyd never felt entirely comfortable in his presence, particularly when lying back on his dental chair with her mouth wide open. To be a dentist in Swinging London may have seemed like an anomaly, but it was the ideal profession for someone who regarded teeth as mere stepping stones to other, more potent, areas of the human body. Pattie wondered if he might have taken advantage: 'No matter what he was going to do in our mouths, he would give us intravenous Valium. All of the Beatles went to him and we took it for granted that this was what happened – no one questioned it. We would go into a deep sleep and wake up not knowing what he had done. I watched him trying to revive George once by slapping his face. It was sinister – he could have been doing anything to us while we were out.'

In April 1965 Riley and his girlfriend Cyndy, whose job was to hire the bunny girls for the Playboy Club, invited John and Cynthia and George and Pattie over for dinner at his home in Bayswater. 'We had a lovely meal, plenty to drink,' Pattie recalled.

As dinner came to an end, George and Pattie got up to leave, explaining that they were planning to see Klaus Voorman and his new band playing at the Pickwick Club, just off Leicester Square.

As Pattie remembers it, Cyndy then said, 'You haven't had any coffee yet. I've made it – and it's delicious.' So they sat down and drank their coffee. Then John made another move to leave, explaining that Klaus was due on soon.

'You can't leave,' said John Riley.

'What are you talking about?'

'You've just had LSD.'

'No we haven't.'

'Yes you have. It was in the coffee.'

According to Pattie, John was 'absolutely furious'. He had read about this comparatively new drug in *Playboy* magazine. 'How dare you fucking do this to us!'

In great waves, the LSD took effect. Cyndy thought time had stopped, and as if this weren't bad enough, that they were all going to drown. 'The *Bismarck* is sinking! The *Bismarck* is sinking!' she shouted, over and over again. Pattie felt strongly that she didn't want to stay there: 'I wondered if the dentist, who hadn't had any coffee, had given it to us hoping the evening might end in an orgy.' George entertained similar suspicions: 'I'm sure he thought it was an aphrodisiac. I remember his girlfriend had enormous breasts and I think he thought that there was going to be a big gang-bang and that he was going to get to shag everybody. I really think that was his motive.'

The four guests insisted on leaving. Riley said they shouldn't drive, and offered to drive them himself. They refused, and the four of them squeezed into Pattie's Mini and set off. Pattie was convinced it was shrinking: 'All the way the car felt smaller and smaller, and by the time we arrived we were completely out of it.'

They stumbled into the lift at the Pickwick Club, then became convinced that the little red light in it was a raging fire. When the doors opened they emerged screaming into the club. John Riley had followed them in his car. He sat at their table, and turned into a pig.

Pattie was discombobulated: 'People kept recognising George and coming up to him. They were moving in and out of focus, then looked like animals.' They left the Pickwick and walked to the Ad Lib, in Leicester Place: 'On the way I remember trying to break a shop window.' As the lift doors opened there, they crawled out and bumped into Mick Jagger, Marianne Faithfull and Ringo. 'John told them we'd been spiked. The effect of the drug was getting stronger and stronger, and we were all in hysterics and crazy. When we sat down, the table elongated.'

After heaven knows how long, they made their way home, with George driving 'at no more than ten miles an hour' all the way back to Esher. John couldn't stop cracking jokes; LSD is the ideal drug for those addicted to puns, as it turns everything into something else, then back again.

The LSD took eight hours to wear off. Cynthia remembered the four of them sitting up for the rest of the night 'as the walls moved, the plants talked, other people looked like ghouls and time stood still'. For her, it was 'horrific, I hated the lack of control and not knowing what was going on or what would happen next'.

George and Pattie vowed never again to visit John Riley. No one wants a groovy dentist, any more than they want a sybaritic bank manager or a butter-fingered brain surgeon. But while Pattie and Cynthia felt that the whole experience had been very frightening, George saw it as a revelation: 'It was if I had never tasted, talked, seen, thought or heard properly before. For the first time in my whole life I wasn't conscious of ego.' And John loved exactly what Cynthia loathed: the lack of control, the unexpected weirdness of everything. Within weeks of that first trip, he would be dropping acid every day.

77

On a pretty regular basis, Omega Auctions – 'proud to be one of the top auction houses worldwide for music memorabilia' – auction items associated with the Beatles. In March 2019, for instance, they took £3,600 at auction for a Quarrymen business card, £2,640 for a programme for the 1963 Northwich Carnival and Gala ('where the Beatles crowned the Carnival Queen') and £48,800 for Paul McCartney's English Literature schoolbook.

The catalogue for their sale on 5 November 2011 included a more peculiar item:

> JOHN LENNON TOOTH – this truly unique piece of memorabilia, a tooth of John Lennon's, was given to his housekeeper, Dorothy (Dot) Jarlett during her employment as housekeeper at his Kenwood home in Weybridge, Surrey. Dot was employed at Kenwood approximately

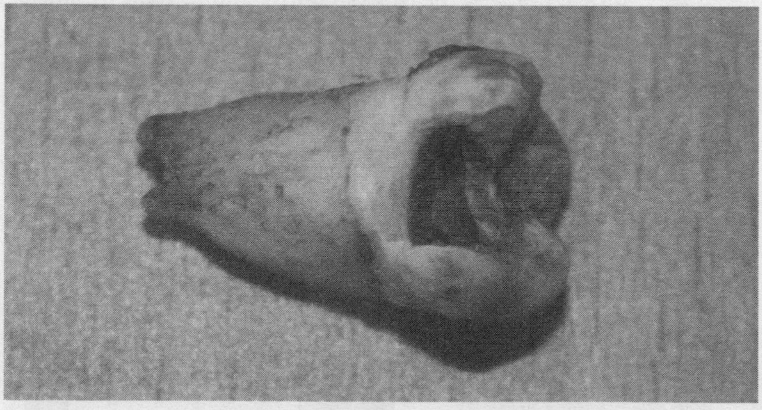

> between 1964 and 1968. John had a warm relationship with Dot and her family, often referring to her as 'Aunty Dot' and even naming his dog Bernard after Dot's husband. John was to give many gifts to Dot and her family over the years, some of which have previously been sold by the family through Sotheby's. The tooth, being such a rare item, has been kept in the family until now and comes with a sworn legal affidavit by Dot Jarlett attesting to the authenticity of the item. The tooth was given to Dot as a souvenir for her daughter who was a huge Beatles fan. The tooth is discoloured and contains an obvious cavity.
>
> Estimate: £10,000–£20,000

'It was by far the most weird and wonderful item we have ever had submitted to us,' recalled the auctioneer, Paul Fairweather. 'It was a very tense bid towards the end, and a huge cheer rang out when the final bid was made.'

The successful bidder was Dr Michael Zuk, a dentist from Alberta, Canada, who paid £19,000.* At the time, Dr Zuk said he planned to display the tooth in his surgery, before taking it on a tour of dental schools.

It might seem strange, or at any rate unusually zealous, for any dentist to spend so much money on a discoloured tooth in order to take it on tour. But in fact Dr Zuk had another, more crafty, plan in mind.

'I am looking for people who believe they are John Lennon's child and have a claim to his estate and hopefully I can legitimise their claim,' he announced seven years later. 'John was a very popular guy who was having sex with lots of women, and I doubt birth control was on his mind. I would ask anyone who is participating to sign a commission agreement which would mean if they were related they would pay my company a percentage of their inheritance, like a finder's fee.'

Dr Zuk said he planned to extract DNA from the discoloured tooth; in the event of a match he would seek a settlement from Lennon Inc.,

* By chance, a year earlier Sir Winston Churchill's set of false teeth had sold for £15,200.

which had recently recorded an annual income of £10 million from holdings of £400 million. He recognised that Yoko Ono Lennon would, in all likelihood, express 'huge concern' at any such claim. On an earlier occasion, when he publicly suggested cloning John Lennon from the tooth, he had received a stiff letter from her solicitor.

He added that he was searching for men or women in their fifties, born at a time 'when young women were throwing themselves at the Fab Four'. He had, he explained, already been contacted by a woman who claimed to be the daughter of John Lennon, but her claim had been based only on anecdotal evidence. 'I want to hold off testing until I have a small group of hopefuls, or one with a very high supporting story.'

Now based in New York, Dr Zuk confessed to purchasing the tooth as a businessman rather than as a fan. It was, he said, 'a business opportunity. I bought the tooth not because it's a stinky rotten tooth. I was thinking, "How can I turn this into something which pays for itself?"'

78

On the morning of Saturday, 12 June 1965, Tony Benn, the radical Postmaster General, picked up his *Daily Mirror*. The headline read: 'Now They've Got Into the Topmost Chart of All'.

It seemed that the Beatles were to be appointed Members of the British Empire in the Queen's Birthday Honours. Never before had any pop star come close to such an award.* A truffle-hound for conspiracies, Benn could sniff an establishment plot: 'No doubt Harold [Wilson] did this to be popular and I expect it *was* popular – though it may have been unpopular with some people too … But the plain truth is that the Beatles have done more for the royal family by accepting MBEs than the royal family have done for the Beatles by giving them.'

Benn's cabinet colleague Barbara Castle was similarly sceptical. 'Over coffee at the Welsh table I sounded out the boys about the Beatles' MBEs,' she wrote in her diary. 'The reaction was wholly unfavourable, the word "gimmick" being prominent. The ploy of Harold's seems to have boomeranged … He seems to have a streak of vulgarity which is also part of his strength.'

The Beatles themselves had received the news by post. 'Paul was looking through the pile of fan mail in our dressing room a few weeks back and he came across this envelope that had "From the Prime Minister" written on it,' George told a press conference on the day of the announcement. 'It must have been there at least a couple of days.

* Awards for popular entertainers were at that time few and far between: George Robey, 'the Prime Minister of Mirth', was appointed a CBE for his charity work in 1919. Gracie Fields (1938), George Formby (1946) and Stanley Holloway (1960) all received OBEs.

He opened it and the letter said that he was being considered for an award and would he sign the enclosed form. We all said, "We wish we had one," then dived through the rest of the mail and found that we did have one – one each!'

When a reporter asked what they were planning to do with their medals, they each reacted according to character.

'Hang it on the wall,' said George.

'Tuck it around my neck,' said Ringo.

'Keep it in a safe place,' said Paul.

'I think I'll have mine made into a bell push so that people have to press it when they come to the house. Or I'll take it to an antique dealer and find out what it is,' said John.

The other 182 recipients of MBEs that year were not natural bedfellows of the Beatles. They included Thomas Arthur Bish, executive engineer in the Telephone Manager's Office at the Nottingham General Post Office; William Boggon, manager of the Ravensworth Ann Colliery; Edwin Cuthbert Cory Crapp, head of the Supply Section in the Conference, Services and Supply Department of the Diplomatic Administration Office; and Charles Edwin Puddle, the aptly-named head gardener at Bodnant Garden in Denbighshire. Apart from the Beatles, the only MBEs for anyone in the public eye were awarded to Robert Dougall, the newsreader, and Louis George Martin, an Olympic weightlifter.

It was perhaps inevitable that a number of previous recipients of honours were to take personal offence. Hector Dupuis, a Canadian MP, complained that he was being placed 'on the same level as vulgar nincompoops'. Richard Pape, a wartime escapee, returned his Military Medal to the Queen, protesting that 'The Beatles' MBE reeks of mawkish, bizarre effrontery to our wartime endeavours.'*

---

* In 1953 Pape had published a book about his wartime exploits, *Boldness Be My Friend*. 'Unique among the escapers of the Second World War, Richard Pape was neither an officer nor a gentleman,' wrote his literary agent Anthony Blond in Pape's obituary, following his death in 1995. 'A red-headed Yorkshireman, his frame bulged with unofficer-like qualities; he was brutally drunk, murderous, treacherous and sly.' Blond successfully negotiated a contract for Pape's memoirs: 'When we sent the contract to Pape in South Africa – he was a natural unreconstructed hard-line Boer, who regarded me as a nigger-loving, wimpish Jew – he got out of his car and went to shoot his wife. Luckily, he missed.'

Most aggrieved of all was Colonel Frederick Wagg, who had served in the armed forces during both world wars. Colonel Wagg returned no fewer than twelve military decorations and cancelled a £12,000 bequest to the Labour Party, declaring that 'Decorating the Beatles makes a mockery of everything this country stands for. I've heard them sing and play and I think they're terrible.' His outspoken comments gave rise to a mountain of counter-complaints sent to him by Beatles fans. A message on one envelope saying 'WAGGY WILL PAY THE POSTAGE' did nothing to calm Colonel Wagg's temper.

Before the ceremony itself, the Beatles were surrounded by their fellow MBE recipients asking for autographs. 'They were all nice,' observed Paul. 'But one fellow said, "I want it for my daughter, but I don't know what she sees in you!"' During the ceremony, he recalled, 'The man shouted out, "George Harrison, John Lennon, Paul McCartney and Ringo Starr!" The word "Starr" was the cue for us to walk forward, left foot forward. It was just like a show.'

The Queen asked John, 'Have you been working hard recently?' Like many of her subjects when confronted by Her Majesty, John went blank. 'I couldn't think what we've been doing, so I said, "No, we've been having a holiday," when actually we've been recording.'

She then asked them all, 'Have you been together long?' Ringo replied, 'Yes, many years. Forty years.' And together, Ringo and Paul chorused: 'We've been together now for forty years and it don't seem a day too much.'

According to Ringo, at this moment a 'strange, quizzical look' came over Her Majesty's face.

'Did you start it all?' she continued.

'No, they did,' replied Ringo. 'I joined last. I'm the little fellow.'

'It's a pleasure giving it to you,' she said.

'But that's what she said to everybody,' George told the press conference afterwards. 'Then we bowed and we walked towards the Queen, then we walked back and bowed, and then we walked away.'

'She was just like a mum to us,' added John.* 'She was so warm and sweet. She really put us at ease.'

Over the years, Paul's memories of his visit to the Palace remained much the same: a mixture of amazement and amusement, in roughly equal measure. 'For four Liverpool lads it was, "Wow, hey man!" It was quite funny. But she was sweet. I think she seemed a bit mumsy to us because we were young boys and she was a bit older.' George and Paul both wore their MBEs on the *Sgt. Pepper* album cover. Ringo, being more conservative, obeyed the instruction that came with the medal, which specified that it was on no account to be worn in public.

A photograph taken immediately after the ceremony shows John holding up his medal. There is a guileless smile on his face, and not a trace of his usual ironic detachment. Pete Shotton remembers him as 'genuinely thrilled'. When John next visited his Aunt Mimi, he pinned the medal to her chest, saying she deserved it more than he did. For the next four years it was to take pride of place on her mantelpiece.

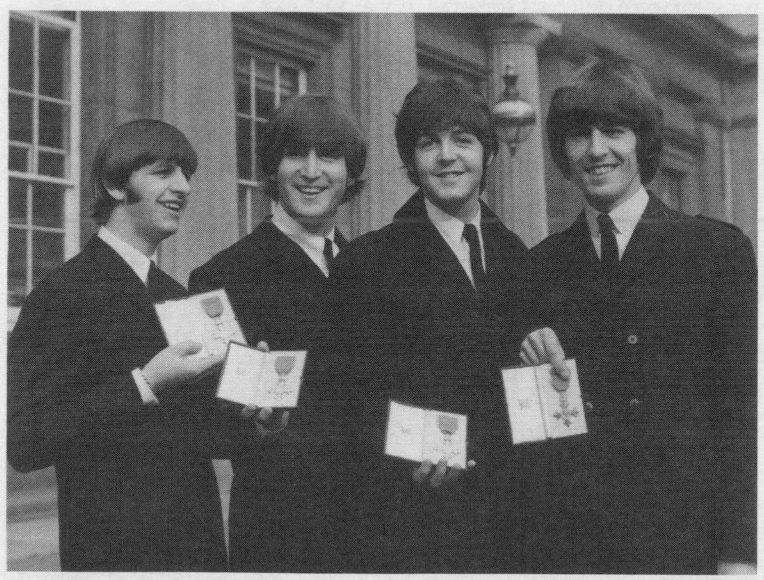

* In fact the Queen was only fourteen years older than Ringo and John: thirty-nine compared to their twenty-five.

79

A short, blurry black-and-white newsclip shows the Beatles climbing the steps of an aeroplane through an arch emblazoned with the message 'BOAC welcomes the BEATLES'.

Two oddities date it to 7 June 1964. First, the Beatle at the back is taller than Ringo, but he is definitely not George, who is three steps up, or John, two steps up, or Paul, who is alongside him. When this unidentified Beatle turns round to wave to the crowds, it turns out to be our poor old friend Jimmie Nicol, who stood in for Ringo when Ringo went down with tonsillitis.

But there is also another person walking up those steps with the group: a matronly figure in an old-fashioned hat, like a figure out of a Giles cartoon. For a split-second she half-turns, beaming. It is Aunt Mimi, who had been invited by John to join them on their flight to the Antipodes, where she had relations.

George judged this trip his favourite. 'I remember them saying, "Return to your seats because we're approaching Hong Kong," and I thought, "We can't be there already." We'd been sitting on the floor drinking and taking Preludins for about thirty hours and so it seemed like a ten-minute flight.'

Aunt Mimi would have known nothing of this particular variety of in-flight entertainment. Had she got wind of it, she would not have been amused, but John was clearly on best behaviour. Interviewed during the flight by an Australian journalist called Bob Rogers, he is a little sleepy and tongue-tied, but unusually polite.

'John, have you ever been interviewed 34,000 feet above sea level before?'

'Er … no. Definitely not.'

'How are you enjoying the trip?'

'Not bad. It's a bit long, y'know. But they're looking after us well.'

'Is this the longest trip you've made?'

'I don't know.' He scrunches up his eyes, as if trying to work it out. 'Yes. It is, isn't it?'

In a voiceover, Rogers says, 'John Lennon's famous Aunt Mimi, who brought him up in Liverpool, was also on board. It was Lennon's way of saying Thank You.'

Aunt Mimi is much more outgoing than John. She has made an effort, with a string of pearls around her neck and an elaborate hat consisting of lots of flowers bunched together. She is a good-looking woman, with high cheekbones, and, despite her sourpuss reputation, merry almost to the point of bubbliness.

Rogers introduces her. 'Mrs May Elizabeth Smith of Woolton, just outside of Liverpool, better known as Aunt Mimi, the lady who brought John Lennon up from a boy.'

'Yes, that's right.' She looks very proud.

'What sort of boy was he?'

'A lovable rebel.' She laughs out loud, and grins.

'A lovable rebel. Did he get into trouble?'

'Not real trouble, just mischievous, you know.'

'Did you think he was going to become a star such as this in the music world when he was a boy?

'No. Not in the music world at all. But I always felt he would do something with his writing and drawing.'

The only other filmed interview with Aunt Mimi was to take place seventeen years later, in 1981, a year after John's death. Southern TV's James Montgomery* conducted it at Mimi's seaside house, 'Harbour's Edge', which John bought for her in 1965.

'… now, for the first time, his aunt Mimi Smith has opened the door of her home in Dorset to talk of an extraordinary friendship that

---

* Later to marry model, actress and *Men Only* columnist Fiona Richmond, star of, among others, *Let's Get Laid* (1977), *From Here to Virginity* (1981) and *Tell Tale Tits* (1987).

existed between them and lasted until his death just a year ago. John Lennon bought this house, which looks over Sandbanks Bay, for his Aunt Mimi sixteen years ago …'

Montgomery and Aunt Mimi are seen sorting through old snapshots of the young John. Mimi is wearing a smart black suit with a white silk shirt, and a silver brooch.

Now aged seventy-five, she remembers buying John his first guitar. 'Well I battled against it for quite a long time. I didn't want him wasting his college time and missing lectures by *wasting his time playing the guitar*.'

Exasperation creeps into her voice, as though, in some parallel universe, her feckless nephew is still nagging her for his first guitar, and she is still trying to steer him onto the straight and narrow.

'Whereas his training would last, these things *come and go*, they're playing their guitar one week, everyone's clamouring for them – then they disappear, and *nobody ever hears of them again*. And then what was I going to do if I had a boy of twenty-one thrown back on my hands, *qualified for nothing*?!?!' Her voice rises and trembles on the word 'nothing'.

Montgomery asks Aunt Mimi if she can remember when John got his first guitar.

'He was a bit like yourself, a soft-soaper.' A flash of her nephew's combative flintiness. 'And he picks me up, and, you know' – here she performs kissing gestures and noises – 'kisses me on the cheek. "Mimi, can I have a guitar?" And he *hadn't any money to get a guitar*. There was only me who could buy him one! And I remember we went to Liverpool and we went into a guitar shop and they were all over the place, and I didn't know anything about them so he chose one and it was *seventeen pounds*!'

'How surprised were you that the Beatles went on to achieve worldwide fame and success?'

'I knew they had something – but *nobody expected this*. It was a shock to them, too.'

She talks of the days when John would come to visit her at her new house by the seaside. 'He'd nip down weekends. Suddenly there'd be a whirlwind, and he'd come in. It was usually when the pressure was getting a bit much and he'd come down here and do cartwheels on the beach.' She laughs and smiles. 'By himself, nobody else there.'

After he'd gone to live in America, they would talk on the telephone once or twice a week, 'about current affairs, how the pound was going up and down, that sort of thing. Another time, he'd be reminiscing about his childhood. The funny things – I was always chasing him, you know.' She gives a throaty chuckle. 'I knew what he was up to before –' She pauses, clearly visualising the young John. 'What he could *not* make out was how I knew when he was up to something!' She carries on laughing, obviously enjoying the memory.

'What about the antics he got up to – the famous love-in with Yoko Ono? Did you talk to him about that?'

'I certainly did. I just found him, telephoned him, and said, "That's enough! Thank you! We've had enough! Keep that lot for the music hall!"' She giggles. 'And that was the end of it.'

'So he listened to you, then?'

'Well, though he rebelled, and said, "I'm not going to do as you tell me," he always did! … When he'd been naughty, I'd ring him up and I'd say, "Don't have me come to New York!" And then he'd say, "You're just being grumpy." So as soon as he said that, down goes the phone, you see. And then I'd wait for about half an hour and he'd get friendly with me again.' She puts on John's voice: '"Hello, is that you, Gertie? Never mind, Gertie."' She roars with laughter.

'Did he give you many presents?'

'Honestly, the place is full of presents – beads, pearls, *everything*! I could have had anything in the world. But I'm just one of those people who's rather spartan, and I don't want anything.'

The camera focuses on John's framed Silver Heart from the Variety Club of Great Britain sitting on the mantelpiece, presented to him by Harold Wilson in 1964.

'What do you think of all these stories that have been published about him since his death? … Stories about his private life, his sex life?'

'I've never heard anything like it in my life! … I think they're sick, depraved people, obsessed with sex, craving for attention.'

'When was the last time he phoned you?'

'The night before he was murdered. Two hours. And he would say, "I'll be seeing you soon Mimi, I can't wait to see you," and then of course at five o'clock the next morning it came over the overseas news, and honestly, if I thought he was dead I don't think I could go on. I don't think of him as dead.'

'Of all the songs that John played and sang, was there a favourite one that you enjoyed?'

'Well I don't know. I think "A Hard Day's Night" is not so bad at the present time!' Once again, she laughs her throaty laugh.

80

On YouTube, that brief interview has attracted over half a million views, and over a thousand comments, almost all of them fond: 'What a grand lady.' 'National treasure Rest in peace.' 'What a caring, grounded soul. She gave a legend love and a bit of discipline and wings to grow. Heaven bless the Mums and Aunties of the world.' 'I believe if there had been no Mimi there would not have been the John Lennon who we came to love and therefore no Beatles.' 'Aww, a lovely lady. I know he had difficulties during childhood, but he was lucky to have someone so kind-hearted RIP.'

Yet two women who knew her well – John's first wife Cynthia, and his half-sister Julia Baird – have written damning portraits of Aunt Mimi. Julia – the daughter of John's mother (also called Julia) and her waiter boyfriend Bobby Dykins – nurses a particular antipathy to her mother's elder sister. Aunt Mimi had, says Julia, an 'obsessive need to control the lives and actions of those around her'. In her memoir, *Imagine This: Growing Up with My Brother John Lennon* (2007), she accuses Aunt Mimi of 'the greatest possible hypocrisy', claiming that in 1956, at the age of fifty, this prim, upstanding woman embarked on an affair with a lodger twenty-six years her junior. The accusation of hypocrisy is due to Mimi's appearance of propriety and the apparently sly means by which she eased John away from his mother, complaining to social services that a couple living in sin were not to be trusted with a child. According to Julia, Aunt Mimi's last words, spoken to a nurse, were 'I'm terrified of dying. I've been so wicked.' Though, to be fair, the same nurse has been reported elsewhere as saying they were much sunnier: 'Hello, John.'

Cynthia Lennon was no more forgiving. 'She loved to fuel the image of the stern but loving aunt who provided the secure backdrop to John's success,' she writes of Aunt Mimi in one of her two autobiographies. 'But that wasn't the Mimi I knew. She battered away at John's self-confidence and left him angry and hurt.' Cynthia portrays Mimi as very la-di-da: 'Mimi's manner was almost regal. She spoke without a hint of Scouse and I thought John must have adopted his working-class Liverpool accent as a rebellion against her. Early on it became apparent to me that Mimi was something of a snob; she was middle-class with upper-class aspirations, and one of her favourite words was "common". She used it to condemn most of John's interests and friends – including, I suspect, me.'

Far from accepting the idea that Aunt Mimi gave John 'wings to grow', Cynthia portrays her as trying to clip them: while the other families encouraged the Beatles to go to Hamburg, Mimi 'did everything she could think of to stop John going'.

On John's arrival back from Germany, he presented Cynthia with a chocolate-brown leather coat from C&A Modes: 'I felt so gorgeous in it I couldn't wait to show it off.' They both dropped round to Aunt Mimi's with a chicken for lunch, but she showed no gratitude: 'Mimi saw the coat and heard that John had bought it for me and she hit the roof. She screamed at John that he'd spent his money on a "gangster's moll" and hurled first the chicken, which she grabbed from me, then a hand-mirror, at John. "Do you think you can butter me up with a chicken when you've spent all your money on this?" she screamed.' Cynthia remembered John leaving by the back door. '"All she cares about is fucking money and cats," he said.'

During the Beatles' residencies at the Cavern, Jim McCartney often dropped by to hear them, and George's mum, Louise, was also a frequent visitor, cheering them along. But it was definitely not Aunt Mimi's scene. According to Cynthia, she put her head round the door only once, to see where John had been wasting his time. Louise Harrison called over to her, 'Aren't they great?'

'I'm glad someone thinks so,' Mimi shouted back. 'We'd all have had lovely peaceful lives but for you encouraging them!'

She was filled with horror at the smell and the noise. 'Try as I might, I just couldn't get near the stage,' she complained to Hunter Davies. 'If I could, I would have pulled him off it.'

After the show, she forced her way into the Cavern's squalid dressing room. 'Very nice, John,' she said sarcastically, leaving soon afterwards. 'Her abrupt departure hurt John,' recalled Cynthia. 'He'd have loved her to be proud of him.'

In 1962, John played Aunt Mimi the Beatles' first single, 'Love Me Do'. Her reaction was uncompromising: 'If you think you're going to make your fortune with that, then you've got another think coming.'

When John finally plucked up the courage to tell Aunt Mimi that he and Cynthia were getting married, 'She screamed, raged and threatened never to speak to him again if he went ahead with it.'

Everyone is agreed that Aunt Mimi was a snob. They take note of her collection of Royal Worcester dinner plates, her leather-bound collected works of Sir Winston Churchill, and the gardener she employed. Mimi objected to George's thick Scouse accent, but she

didn't approve of Paul either, blaming him for tempting John into the unseemly world of rock'n'roll. 'She would always refer to me as "Your little friend"', says Paul. 'I'd look at her, she'd smile. I'd know what she'd done. I would ignore it. It was very patronising, but she secretly quite liked me, she sort of twinkled, but she was very aware that John's friends were lower-class. She was the kind of woman who would put you down with a glint in her eye, with a smile, but she'd put you down all the same.'

In those early days, Aunt Mimi refused to allow George or Paul to cross her threshold. 'He [Paul] used to come to my front door. He'd be on his bike, which he'd lean against the fence. He would look over at me with his sheep eyes and say, "Hello, Mimi. Can I come in?" "No, you certainly cannot," I'd say.' One day Aunt Mimi appeared to relent, telling John that if George came round, she would be prepared to let him in. 'He arrived with a crewcut and a pink shirt. I threw him out. Well, it wasn't done. I might have been a bit old-fashioned, but schoolboys dressing like that! Up till John was sixteen, I always made sure he wore his regulation school blazer and shirt.'

After the Beatles became world famous she would rail against John for assuming an exaggerated Scouse accent. After all, she had brought him up to speak the Queen's English. To a thirteen-year-old Beatles fan who wrote saying she had seen John on television, she replied, 'When he came home, I said, "John, what's all this about, what's happened to your voice?" … He didn't really talk like that. I brought him up properly, not to talk like a ruffian.' While the other Beatles' relatives remained awestruck by their celebrity, Aunt Mimi always treated John as Brian's mother treats her son in *Monty Python's Life of Brian*: 'He's not the Messiah. He's a very naughty boy!' On the release of *Two Virgins*, with its cover photograph of John and Yoko naked, she made her feelings all too clear: 'It would have been all right, John, but you're both so ugly. Why don't you get somebody attractive on the cover if you've got to have someone completely naked?'

Soon after embarking on his relationship with Yoko, John took her to meet Aunt Mimi in Poole. It was never going to be the easiest of introductions. Aunt Mimi told James Montgomery about the encounter: 'He came in all bright and breezy – typical John – and she followed behind. I took one look at her and thought, "My God, what is that?"

'Well, I didn't like the look of her right from the start. She had long black hair, all over the place, and she was small – she looked just like a dwarf to me. I told John what I felt while she was outside, looking across the bay. I said to him, "Who's the poison dwarf, John?"

'… Well, I didn't know what it was all about. I wondered who it was. And he said, "It's Yoko." I didn't think anything of it, you know. But I did say, "What do *you* do for a living?" She said, "I'm an *artist*." I said, "That's very funny, *I've* never heard of you!"'

While John was in the loo, Aunt Mimi informed Yoko that she had always brought him up to have good manners, and that was why he always stood up when a woman came into the room. On his return, she warned him of what happened to the Duke of Windsor, the former King Edward VIII. The duke had been remarkably popular, she said, but the public had gone off him when he married Mrs Simpson. 'He lost his popularity, and John, you'd better know that.'

Mimi remembered John brushing her little homily away. 'He laughed it off, but he knew I didn't like her and he knew I was a good judge of character. I couldn't see what he saw in her and I thought it was wrong and nothing good would come of it.'

81

But another argument, equally strong, can be made in favour of Aunt Mimi. After all, she lies in the grand tradition of Great British Aunts: bossy, demanding and fearsome, unabashed upholders of the social fabric, capable of reducing even the most recalcitrant nephews to jelly. 'It is no use telling me that there are bad aunts and good aunts. At core, they are all alike,' observes Bertie Wooster. 'Sooner or later, out pops the cloven hoof.'

Pete Shotton recalled John's childhood obsession with Richmal Crompton's *Just William* books, which are choc-a-bloc with aunts, most of them forbidding, in both senses of the word. They range from Aunt Jane, 'tall and prim and what she called "house proud"', to Great-Aunt Augusta, who lives by the adage 'There's no joy like the joy of duty done.' With his pals Ivan Vaughan and Nigel Whalley in tow, John led a gang called the Outlaws, just like William's. 'I used to live *Alice* and *Just William*,' he recalled. 'I wrote my own William stories, with me doing all the things … After I'd read a book, I'd relive it all again. That was one reason why I wanted to be the gang leader at school. I'd want them all to play the games that I wanted them to play, the ones I'd just been reading.'

His Outlaws would get up to all sorts of pranks and japes, some playful, others verging on the delinquent. They would pinch apples, ride up Penny Lane on the bumpers of the tram cars, spend money intended for the church collection on bubblegum, smash street lamps with stones, shoplift cigarettes, and pull girls' knickers down. At the school fête, John and Pete set up a dartboard decorated with their teachers' faces. On another occasion, they made dog collars out of old cereal packets and dressed up their classmates as vicars. To make money, they stole school-dinner tickets and sold them around school.

The influence of William is tangible, and may well have infected the Beatles. 'The Beatles made me laugh immoderately, the way I used to laugh as a child at the *Just William* books,' recalled Maureen Cleave, the journalist who knew them best in their early days of fame. 'Their wit was just so keen and sharp – John Lennon's especially. They all had this wonderful quality – it wasn't innocence, but everything was new to them. They were like William, finding out about the world and trying to make sense of it.' William's Outlaws, like John's, were always on the lookout for fishy ways to make their fortunes. In *William's Double Life* (1929), when the Outlaws try to raise money, they are disappointed by the poor response from their various aunts and uncles:

> 'I went round to them ALL,' said Ginger mournfully, 'an' my Aunt Emma she said, "Certainly not, after your ball comin' in through my landin' window like it did last week," an' my Uncle John said, "Cert'nly not after you goin' over my lawn with your scooter the way you did yesterday," an' my Aunt Jane said, "Cert'nly not after you chasin' my dear Pussy as I saw you last week," an' my Uncle George said, '"Cert'nly not after you throwin' stones up at my walnut tree like I saw you doin' yesterday," an' my Uncle John said, "Cert'nly not after you climbin' my rose pole an' breakin' it" …'

In *Just William* (1922), William puts one of his scariest aunts to good use. He arrives in her room to find his imposing Aunt Emily has fallen asleep, and that 'She lay in her immense stature in a blouse and striped petticoat, while from her open mouth issued the fascinating sounds.' Seizing an opportunity for commerce, William then places a sign on her door saying:

FAT WILD WOMAN
TORKIN NATIF
LANGWIDGE

and charges the neighbouring children tuppence to see her. 'They stood in a hushed, delighted group around her bed. The sounds never ceased, never abated. William allowed them two minutes in the room. They came out reluctantly, paid more money, joined the end of the queue and re-entered.'

William extends the exhibit to incorporate Aunt Emily's dressing table, posting notices such as 'FAT WILD WOMAN'S TEETH' and 'FAT WILD WOMAN'S HARE'. But suddenly Aunt Emily comes to life.

> She sprang up and, seizing him by the shoulders, shook him till his teeth chattered, the tinsel crown fell down, encircling ears and nose, and one of his moustaches fell limply at his feet.
>
> 'You wicked boy!' she said as she shook him. 'You WICKED, WICKED, WICKED BOY!'

John and his gang once constructed a makeshift raft from old planks, but it tipped over, casting them into a murky pond teeming with frogs. In an attempt to dry his clothes so Aunt Mimi wouldn't know what they had been up to, John built a bonfire, but it got out of hand and the fire brigade arrived with sirens blaring. It could just as well have happened to William.

Called to see the deputy head, Mr Gallaway, on charges of misbehaviour, John and Pete were told to stand behind him while he got out the Headmaster's Punishment Book. To amuse Pete, John put out a hand and tickled Mr Gallaway's bald pate. Thinking it was a fly, Mr Gallaway kept swatting his head. 'This subtle play of hands continued for several minutes,' Pete recalled, 'until both of us were doubled up with suppressed laughter – to the point that John (as was his wont in such desperate situations) literally pissed himself.' When Mr Gallaway asked what the puddle was, John replied, 'I think the roof's leaking, sir.' Pete exploded with laughter, but once again John saved the day. 'Bless you, Pete!' he exclaimed, adding, for Mr Gallaway's benefit, 'He's been sneezing all day, sir. He has a dreadful cold.'

Mimi was strict with John. Whenever word got back to her about his bad behaviour, she would send him to his bedroom without any supper. Only once did she beat him, having caught him stealing money from her handbag. But these punishments had little effect. 'I was coming down Penny Lane one day and I saw this crowd of boys in a ring, watching two boys fighting,' Aunt Mimi recalled. '"Just like those common Rose Lane scruffs," I said ... Then they parted and out came this awful boy with his coat hanging off. To my horror it was John. John always liked me telling him that story. "Just like you, Mimi. Everybody else is always common."'

To the end of his life, John stayed in constant touch with Aunt Mimi, perhaps because she was the only person on the planet who could see through his nonsense. In 1968 Hunter Davies observed that of all the Beatle parents, 'Mimi is probably the only one whose relationship has not really changed. She still in many ways treats John as she's always done, whereas with the others there is a hint of hero worship, almost reverence. Mimi still criticizes John's clothes and how he looks, as she did when he was a teenager. She tells him when he's looking fat and not to spend too much. Mimi even doesn't care for the way John speaks. She says he won't speak properly, never finishing sentences. "John's always been a bad speaker. And he's getting worse all the time. I often can't understand what he's talking about. His mind's jumping all over the place."'

In turn, John's devotion to Aunt Mimi transcended all his fads and his failings, and all her rantings against them, justified and unjustified. As a child he could bear her reprimands, and even her occasional praise, but he hated it when she ignored him. 'Don't 'nore me, Mimi,' he would say. When he grew up, and all the rest of the world started paying him attention, he still needed to be sure that Mimi wasn't ignoring him. To the end of her days, Mimi kept a plaque in pride of place on her mantelpiece, given to her by John, and engraved with one of her grumbles from his adolescence: 'The guitar's all very well, John, but you'll never make a living out of it.' For both of them, her admonishment had become a source of pride. To the end of his days, John wrote a long letter to her once a week, signed 'Himself'. In their monthly phone conversations he liked to tease her into a furious response by exaggerating his Scouse accent. In New York he developed a craving for items that reminded him of his childhood with his Aunt Mimi. She dutifully posted him her Royal Worcester tea service, along with his Quarry Bank school blazer and stripy school tie: 'I sent him parcel after parcel of stuff.'

John kept urging Aunt Mimi to abandon Dorset for an apartment in the Dakota. The uncompromising tone of her reply must surely have pleased him, as it was so entirely in character: 'You'll never catch me over there. I have never liked Americans. And you shouldn't be there either, it's no good for you.'

'He comes to see me as often as he can,' she told Davies in 1968. 'He sat up on the roof for four days in the summer. I ran up and down getting drinks for him. He never shows much emotion. He finds it hard to say sorry. But one night he said that even if he didn't come down to see me every day, or every month, he always thought about me at some time every day, wherever he was. That meant a great deal to me.'

In 1979 John wrote a long, nostalgic letter to his cousin Leila – 'I thought of you a lot this Xmas – the shadows on the ceiling as the cars went by at night – putting up the paper chains …' He ended it with a reference to Aunt Mimi: 'I'm almost scared to go to England, 'coz I know it would be the last time I saw Mimi – I'm a coward about Goodbyes.' For her part, Yoko thought that when John sat down with a cup of tea in their apartment at the Dakota, stroking a cat, 'he always looked just like Mimi'.

Every Christmas when John was little, Mimi would take him to *Puss in Boots* at the Liverpool Empire. One year it was snowing, and John went in his Wellington boots. When Puss first came onstage, John stood and piped up, 'Mimi, he's got his Wellington boots on! So have I!' Everyone in the audience turned to him and smiled.

In December 1963, after a year in which the Beatles had, in the words of the TV host Alexander Kendrick, transformed the country into 'Beatleland, formerly known as Britain', they brought their Christmas show to the Liverpool Empire. Aunt Mimi stood at the back, having turned down John's offer of a seat in the front row.

'I was very proud of course to see him playing on the stage at the Empire. It was the first time I realised what an effect they had. They had mounted police to keep the crowds back … It was very exciting. But I couldn't help thinking all the time: "No, he's not really a Beatle. He's the little fellow who once sat upstairs with me and shouted, 'Mimi, he's got his Wellington boots on!'"

82

Compared to the other three, John was Lord Snooty. In 1950s Liverpool, his family was regarded as posh by the teenage George and Paul. Unlike them, John lived in a privately-owned semi-detached house that had a name – 'Mendips' – not a number. As if this were not smart enough, it overlooked a golf course. John had an aunt not an auntie, and not just any old cat but a Siamese cat, as well as one relative who was a dentist in Edinburgh and another who worked for the BBC. He also had an uncle who taught Paul handwriting and English at the Liverpool Institute.

Paul was impressed. 'John had an Aunt Harriet, and Harriet was not a name we came across, especially when they called her Harrie! We never knew women called Mimi, which is very sophisticated, very twenties and thirties, very jazz era. So it was Harriet and Mimi. I can imagine them with long cigarette-holders. It was like Richmal Crompton's *Just William* books to me ... So John was a particularly attractive character in that kind of world.' Even now, when Paul speaks of John's comparatively well-to-do childhood, there is a slight element – 'So there!' – of reverse snobbery about it. It is as if, after all these years, he still feels the need to counter John's claims of poverty. 'John lived just the other side of the golf course, literally and metaphorically. People don't realise how middle-class he was. It's a very fancy neighbourhood ... In fact, John once told me that the family had once owned Woolton, the whole village.' In *The Beatles Anthology* he goes a few steps further, saying, 'To us, John was *upper* class ... It's ironic, he was always very "Fuck you!", and he wrote the song "Working Class Hero" – in fact, he wasn't at all working class.'

In an interview John gave shortly before his death, he acknowledged that he had never really been a Working-Class Hero: 'I was a nice clean-cut suburban boy, and in the class system that was about half a niche higher-class than Paul, George and Ringo, who lived in council houses. We owned our own house, had our own garden, they didn't have anything like that. So I was a bit of a fruit compared to them, in a way. Ringo was the only real city kid. I think he came from the lousiest area … I was always well dressed, well fed, well schooled, and brought up to be a nice lower-middle-class English boy, you know?' In middle age he had come to think that it was being middle class, not working class, that had made the Beatles different. After all, George, Paul and John were all grammar-school boys. 'Up until then all rock'n'rollers … had been black and poor: rural South, city slums. And the whites had been truckers, like Elvis. But the thing about the Beatles was that we were pretty well educated and not truckers. Paul could have gone to university. He was always a good boy. He passed his exams. He could have become, I don't know – Dr McCartney. I could have done it myself if I had worked. I never worked.'

On first becoming famous, both Paul and John took care to overplay their Scouse accents. When Paul arrived home after the Beatles' first TV appearance, his younger brother Michael asked him, 'Why did you talk like that on the TV? It sounded like George gone wrong.' Among his Liverpudlian contemporaries, Paul was teased for having risen a notch up the social scale by passing his 11-Plus and going to the Liverpool Institute. 'There weren't many other kids from the Institute living round our way. I was called "college pudding". "Fucking college pudding" they said.'

This did little to staunch the flow of snobbery that greeted their early success. While the Beatles were away on a brief tour of Scandinavia in October 1963, the Lord Privy Seal, Edward Heath MP, was heard to say that he found it hard to recognise what they said as 'the Queen's English.'* On their return to London, the group were asked to comment

---

* The son of a Kent builder, Heath had altered his own accent, and was teased for his idiosyncratic vowels, not least by Monty Python's Flying Circus, who released a spoof educational disc called 'Teach Yourself Heath.'

on this hoity-toity remark. John put on a theatrically posh accent: 'Ay can't understend Teddy saying thet et awl, reyaleh, I can't understend Teddy!' Then he smiled, looked at the camera and said, in a rather more menacing way, 'I'm not going to vote for Ted.'

PAUL: Oooh!
Q: But you're not going to change your accent for the Lord Privy Seal?
JOHN: (swinging into an exaggerated Scouse accent) Ah, no lak will keep lak the same kand of thing like, won't we? Yeah thaz right.
PAUL: Oh, aye! Yes!

To another reporter, Paul said, 'And I bet half the people who voted for him didn't speak the Queen's English either.' Later, Heath tried to make amends, bafflingly hailing the group as 'the saviours of the corduroy industry'. Who knows? Perhaps corduroy represented Mr Heath's outer limit of modishness.

* * *

Six months later, the Beatles were filming *A Hard Day's Night*. The American director Richard Lester, who had lived in England for a decade, was intrigued by their impact on the British class system. 'I think they were the first to give a confidence to the youth of the country, which led to the disappearance of the Angry Young Man with a defensive mien,' he told his biographer. 'The Beatles sent the class thing sky-high; they laughed it out of existence and, I think, introduced a tone of equality more successfully than any other single factor I know. Eventually it became taken for granted that they were single-handedly breaking Britain's class system without the benefit of an education or family background.' Yet even he couldn't resist adding a corrective: 'They were, of course, much more middle-class than most people admitted.'

Filming *Help!* in the Bahamas in February 1965, Eleanor Bron went with the Beatles to a smart party in Nassau, ostensibly held in their honour.

She was put off by what she saw. The Beatles were, she felt, simultaneously patronised and scorned. The 'swells of the island' were 'able to contain neither their curiosity nor their middle-aged spleen at seeing these four "uneducated", "lower-class" youngsters (products of the Welfare State) succeed. Who knows what manoeuvres they must have gone through for the privilege of being able to assemble at this scandal of a dinner given in honour of these mere boys, just so that they could turn their noses up at them; or – if they could thrust themselves close enough – to insult them personally, down their noses, with snide remarks; requesting autographs for "demented" granddaughters. And if they could not get close, watching from afar with pouchy eyes for proofs of callowness, social solecisms and unacceptable accents, so that they could relay these to the world, and their sense that they have been cheated – the shockingness of what the world is coming to.'

Her fellow actor Victor Spinetti took a similar view. 'We were driven to the home of the minister of finance. The guests, Government House officials and their wives, sipped at their drinks and milled about in a group, carefully preserving, I noticed, a gap between themselves and the Beatles. From their vantage point, they stared at the boys and talked, not to them but about them. "Which one is Ringo?" I heard a voice call out.

"'I think it's that one, the one with the big nose," came a drawled answer as they all continued to stare. One of them, a woman, left the group and wandered across to George.

"'Is that hair real?" she asked, and, without waiting for an invitation, tugged it. "Oh yes," she said, turning in astonishment to the others. "It is." These people were looking at the Beatles as if they were prize polo ponies, except that for them, prize polo ponies would have been more interesting.'

They were all led into dinner. Each place setting was laid with row upon row of gold cutlery and a variety of glasses. Ever mischievous, the Beatles played up to the roles assigned to them by the dignitaries. 'Oooh, what are those?' they asked. The po-faced wife of the governor turned to her husband and murmured, 'They don't know their knives and forks.'

Such was the all-pervasive nature of the British class system that there were booby traps even within the bosom of the family. Forty years after his mother's death, Paul told Barry Miles of a moment in his childhood that continued to be 'a strange little awkwardness for me'. He had, he said, once chastised his mother for saying the word 'ask' with a long 'a'. 'She pronounced it posh. And I made fun of her and it slightly embarrassed her. Years later I've never forgiven myself. It's a terrible little thing. I wish I could go back and say, "I was only kidding, Mum."'

As we have seen, John's Aunt Mimi looked down on the young George Harrison for having what she referred to as a 'low Liverpool voice'. 'You always seem to like lower-class types, don't you, John?' she said.

With the Beatles' fame came status. They entered the celebrity class, which has long maintained a sort of non-aggression pact with the upper class. At the height of their success, George spoke proudly of what he had learned from his privately-educated wife, Pattie Boyd. 'The natural thing when you get money is that you acquire taste,' he told Maureen Cleave in 1966. 'I've got a lot of taste off Pattie. You get taste in food as well. Instead of eggs and beans and steak you branch out into the avocado scene. I never dreamt I would like avocado pears. I thought it was like eating bits of wax – fake pears out of a bowl – when I saw people shoving it down.'

In their journey up the social ladder, the Beatles were sometimes obliged to learn the ropes. Looking back on her marriage, Pattie remembered that George's family 'held their knives like pens, and "tea" consisted of cold ham or pork pie, tomatoes cut in half, pickled beetroot and salad cream, with sliced white bread. They had it at six o'clock, and later in the evening there was tea and biscuits.'

Some credited the Beatles with fracturing the class system. In her novel *A Word Child* (1975), Iris Murdoch – a tremendous Beatles fan – pictured her narrator listening to four young men from disparate backgrounds chatting around a kitchen table. 'Here at any rate class no longer existed,' he reflects. 'The Beatles, like Empedocles, had thrown all things about.'

The Beatles arrived on the scene after a series of plays and novels – *Look Back in Anger* (1956), *Room at the Top* (1957), *Saturday Night and Sunday Morning* (1958), *The Loneliness of the Long Distance Runner* (1959) – had focused on English working-class youth. But while these works portrayed young men stuck at the bottom of a merciless hierarchy, or forced to adapt if they want to rise, in *A Hard Day's Night* and *Help!* the Beatles threw off any such shackles to create a world of their own; they are cheerful and self-confident, scorning any pressure to conform.

In both films they subvert expectations of how working-class lads should behave. One scene in *Help!* shows the four Beatles arriving at a traditional working-class terrace in a chauffeur-driven Rolls-Royce. Two old dears, played by Dandy Nichols and Gretchen Franklin, wave at them from the other side of the street.

'Lovely lads, and so natural. I mean, adoration hasn't gone to their heads one jot, has it?'

'Just so natural, and still the same as they was before they was.'

Each Beatle enters a different front door. The camera follows them inside, only to reveal not four little houses but one big luxurious pad, filled with all the fashionable accoutrements of the sixties high life – sliding bookshelves, fitted carpets, leather sofas, trendy lighting, even a Wurlitzer organ that rises from the ground. It's a sweet joke, and one that gleefully subverts the dictum that the proper way to deal with success is to not let it change you. The Beatles stand for fun and enjoyment, for doing whatever you want, regardless of your background. Unlike Jimmy Porter and Joe Lampton, they are neither angry nor cowed: they are free.

83

When we talk about the Beatles, we talk about ourselves.

At the end of August 1966 the *Saturday Evening Post* published 'The Monarchs of the Beatle Empire', a piece by the British journalist James Morris.* In it, Morris saluted the Beatles for liberating Britain from class. To twenty-first-century ears its tone may hint of Lady Bracknell, but its sentiments remain radical. First, he described the arrival of these 'four young roosters from the north' into 'a country so long hag-ridden by class'. When Morris had been to Liverpool, somebody had complained that 'They're all grammar-school boys really,' but for Morris this was by the way: 'the point is that they have managed to make the whole subject of personal origins, so long an obsession of the English, irrelevant to themselves'. In the past, the regional character in England was always exploited for comic purposes, but the Beatles had just carried on regardless: 'They have simply ignored the old English social divisions and effortlessly stormed the barricades of custom.'

Morris confessed that he was not their biggest fan: 'I still, to be honest, don't awfully like the look of them – which is to say, I don't like their faces, just as I don't happen to like caraway seeds or Rubens.' But he was attracted to the Beatles for their 'absolute aloofness to old prejudices and preconceptions, their brand of festive iconoclasm'. Their glory lay in their detachment from Britain's imperial grandeur. They are New Men, 'the British emancipated at last from the White Man's burden'. Morris proclaimed 'an inescapable sense of holiday in England today – a springy, frothy sense of release'.

---

* Educated at Evelyn Waugh's old school, Lancing College, and Christ Church, Oxford.

He then touched on what many people thought of as their androgyny, the product of long hair, pretty faces and skinny frames. They had thrown aside all the old tenets of manliness: 'Children are said to love them because they don't know whether they are boys or girls.' They were, he said, 'minstrels of … emancipation' who had 'expressed something that most of us in England have instinctively felt – that the old values really did need a cheerful dust-down. Why *should* we be manly? Why *should* life be quite so real, quite so earnest? Why should we stiffen our upper lips? Who says so? *Why?*'

Though he never mentioned it in the piece, two years before, James Morris had embarked on a prolonged course of pills derived from the urine of pregnant mares. In his autobiography, *Conundrum*, written many years later, he chronicled his transformation 'gradually from a person who looked like a healthy male of orthodox sexual tendencies, approaching middle age, into something perilously close to a hermaphrodite, apparently neither of one sex nor the other, and more or less ageless'. This initial treatment led him to full sex reassignment surgery in 1972, at which point James became Jan.

84

A week after the Beatles' civic reception in Liverpool Town Hall on 10 July 1964, John bought his first property. From now on, he too had somewhere to rattle his jewellery.

'Kenwood' is a mock-Tudor mansion situated on the St George's Hill estate in Weybridge, Surrey, bang next to the golf course. It cost the twenty-three-year-old John £20,000, at a time when the average house in Britain sold for £3,400. He added a swimming pool – 'Nothing like I ordered,' he complained – and countless luxuries and further embellishments – two eighteen-foot sofas, a marble fireplace, a sunken bathtub, a jacuzzi in the master bathroom. These cost a further £40,000. For all its eccentricities, this was the bourgeois dream.

Each day, vans from the smartest stores delivered unimaginable quantities of merchandise: telephones and tape-recorders, a gorilla fancy-dress costume, a suit of armour, a jukebox, a pinball machine, a vast altar crucifix and five televisions, which John liked to keep turned on, but with the sound down.

He had two large attic rooms knocked together to make room for twenty different Scalextric model racing car sets, complete with landscaping. 'If you're going to do something, you might as well do it properly,' he told a friend.

He bought books galore, including leather-bound editions of Tolstoy and Oscar Wilde, and the complete *Just William* series, along with more specialist and unexpected works such as *Forty-One Years in India* by Field Marshal Lord Roberts and *Curiosities of Natural History* by Francis T. Buckland.

The dining room, covered in purple velvet wallpaper, sported a long white table surrounded by a dozen antique chairs. The kitchen contained any number of cutting-edge gadgets, none of which John was able to operate. Cynthia was similarly bamboozled, but managed to master the waffle machine. Tired of eating just waffles, John asked his interior designer, Ken Partridge, to send someone down to teach Cynthia how to work the other appliances, though he himself never bothered to learn.

The garden was filled with furniture and statuary, much of it covered in psychedelic colours after John and his friend Terry went wild with the spray paints. Later, a giant boot, eight feet high, from the film *Help!* stood at the bottom of the garden. Four garages, all in a row, provided shelter for three shiny new cars – a Rolls-Royce, a Mini Cooper and a Ferrari.

For most of his life, the only space John had had to himself was his cosy little bedroom in Mendips. It is understandable, then, that rather than expanding into Kenwood's twenty-seven rooms, or parading around its impressive gardens, he spent most his time confined to the modest sunroom, scrunched up like an embryo on a tiny yellow sofa which had, naturally enough, been a gift from Aunt Mimi.

In those days, John only had to imagine more possessions and – Hey presto! – they would appear overnight. A standing order with Hamley's toy shop supplied him with every new board game the moment it was issued.

He found his staff harder to manage. He liked his amiable daily, Dot Jarlett, but she got on badly with the cook, whose handyman husband wouldn't stop flirting with the guests. Before long, the cook's daughter left her husband and moved into the staff flat with her parents, but she then started making passes at John. Meanwhile, household items kept disappearing. The never-ending episodes of pilferage and squabbling upstairs and downstairs gave Kenwood something of a psychedelic Swinging Sixties Downton Abbey feel. In a later episode, Cynthia was informed by a nosy neighbour that John's smelly, chain-smoking chauffeur Jock was living in the back of the Rolls-Royce. 'I was hopeless when it came to standing up to people,' admitted Cynthia. Eventually, Brian Epstein took control, sacking the cook, her husband and the chauffeur.

Though decorated and furnished as a fun palace, Kenwood soon became the setting for an Ibsen drama, forgotten figures emerging from the fog of the past, set on sabotaging the future. By now, John was one of the four richest and most famous and most liberated young men in the world; but he was also a husband, a father, a nephew and a son. And a son-in-law, too: from the start, he was at daggers drawn with his forceful mother-in-law, Lillian, who had moved down from Liverpool to live in nearby Esher. Lillian liked to spend her days busying herself at Kenwood, or rootling around antique shops and auction houses for bits and pieces she judged would contribute to the interior decoration. Though the beneficiary of John's largesse – he had not only bought her a house, but also paid for its upkeep, and gave her an allowance – Lillian remained convinced that her daughter had married beneath her. For his part, John found it easier to pretend that Lillian wasn't there. One visitor remembered seeing her 'flopped on a couch, stuffing glacé fruits into her mouth', while John 'passed through without comment'.

And ghostlier figures than Lillian would also come knocking. One day, when Cynthia was alone in Kenwood, she opened the door to a stranger, 'a tiny man with lank grey hair, balding on top'. The man introduced himself as John's long-lost father, Fred, a claim confirmed at first sight: 'He looked as unkempt and down-at-heel as a tramp – but, alarmingly, with John's face.'

Cynthia said she was expecting John back in an hour or two. She told Fred he was welcome to wait, introduced him to his grandson, Julian, and gave him a cup of tea and cheese on toast. Their conversation proved stilted, but they soon found a shared pursuit: when the fifty-two-year-old Fred mentioned that his hair was a mess, Cynthia offered to cut it for him.

For some reason John had failed to tell Cynthia that, just a few weeks before, he had met his father for the first time in seventeen years. John had been six years old when Fred had tussled with Julia over which of them would look after him. Fred had been gone to sea for four years, working as a ship's steward. On his return to England he had smashed a shop window and stolen a mannequin. Having been arrested while waltzing with the mannequin, he had been imprisoned for six months.

From prison he wrote to Julia's sister, John's Aunt Mimi, asking her to help him regain a role in John's life. Mimi's response had been severe: 'You have made an absolute shambles of your life and have brought shame and scandal upon your family. If you have a shred of decency left in you I advise you to go to New Zealand alone and put your past life behind you. Surely you don't want your son to know you've been in jail?'

By 1963, Fred was working as an itinerant washer-up in hotels and restaurants. He had given up any hope of seeing his son again until a fellow worker at the Moore Place Hotel in Esher pointed out that the leader of the Beatles was called Lennon, and looked just like Fred.

Fred despatched a series of letters to John, but they went unanswered. In time he contacted a reporter from the *Daily Sketch*, who, sensing a cracking story, engaged in negotiations with Brian Epstein for a meeting between long-lost father and famous son. At last, on 1 April 1964, the two met at the NEMS offices in Monmouth Street.

John's first words to Fred were testy, to say the least: 'What do you want, then?'

Fred replied that he didn't want anything. 'I told him that he got his talent from me,' he told the *Daily Sketch*, adding, with familial tactlessness, 'I don't want to sound boastful, but I was doing what John is doing twenty-five years ago – and better!' In his seafaring days, Fred had entertained his fellow crew members with selections from the musicals: for his showpiece, he would black up his face to deliver a tearful rendering of Al Jolson's 'Little Pal'.

After fifteen minutes or so, Fred and John were interrupted by Epstein, on the pretext of an engagement at the BBC. The meeting had been awkward, but not disastrous.

John can surely be forgiven for harbouring mixed feelings towards his father. From that moment on, his relationship with Fred would swing between love and hate, interspersed by long periods of surliness. He seems to have recognised similarities in their characters which, had providence worked in a different way, might have set him on a similar path. 'I don't really hate him now, the way I used to,' he told Hunter Davies. 'It was probably Julia's fault as much as his that they parted. If it hadn't been for the Beatles, I would probably have ended up like Freddie.' At the time, Davies thought this an unlikely scenario, but he came to recognise the truth in it: 'It is hard to imagine John fitting in with a proper job, or office hierarchy, or even managing to make a living as an artist or designer, not of course that he had passed any of his art college exams. He would have become bored far too quickly. So he might well have ended up as a bum.'

Fred managed to establish some sort of patchy relationship with John, who appreciated his cocky, rackety, rebellious side, and recognised in his more forgiving moments that Fred – who had himself been brought up in an orphanage – was the victim of circumstances. 'He's all right. He's a bit wacky – just like me,' John told Cynthia; and he said much the same to Pete Shotton: 'He's good news. A real funny guy – a loony just like me.'

Their future relationship was fitful and explosive, their reconciliations often ending in arguments, requiring fresh reconciliations. When things were going swimmingly, Fred made a habit of putting his foot in it. Chatting about music one day, John asked Fred which of his own compositions was his favourite. 'I think all your songs are bloody great,' he said. 'But I've always had a special affection for "Penny Lane".'

Fred's interest in John was not wholly paternal. 'Now, it's back to finding some work. John has his thousands and I've got four shillings,' he told a reporter after their first meeting. 'But I'm still the happiest bloke alive.' But the temptation to capitalise on their relationship proved irresistible. First, he sold his life story to *Titbits* magazine for £200, and then in 1965 he recorded a dreadful single, half-sung, half-spoken, 'That's My Life'. 'I've been an entertainer all my life,' he explained to the press.

He had high hopes for the song, but it failed to sell. Like many unsuccessful artistes before him, Fred looked around for someone to blame, and found Brian Epstein. There may even have been some truth in this: in her autobiography, Cynthia says that John 'was furious at his father's blatant jump on the bandwagon of his own success', and 'asked Brian to do anything he could to stop it. Whether Brian did or not I don't know, but the record never made it into the charts.' Together with his new-found manager, Fred dropped round at Kenwood at eleven o'clock one evening, ready to demand an explanation, but John was not in a welcoming mood. 'Fuck off!' he shouted, before slamming the door in his father's face.

Yet the two continued to keep in touch, and John financed Fred's existence, albeit on a modest level, giving him a one-bedroom flat in Kew and £10 a week. While employed washing dishes at the Toby Jug Hotel in Tolworth, Surrey, Fred became engaged to a student called Pauline, thirty-five years his junior. He then turned up at the door of Kenwood with Pauline, asking if John and Cynthia might give her a job and somewhere to live. Once again, Kenwood became a setting for family melodrama. 'She lived with us for a few months, but it was a nightmare,' recalled Cynthia. 'She was constantly in tears and arguing with her mother over Alf [Fred]. She slept in the attic, and we'd hear her screaming down the phone and sobbing up there.'

For her part, Pauline did not take to John: 'His table manners were the most atrocious I had ever witnessed. He said little, but as he munched I noticed him sizing me up with those penetratingly suspicious eyes that were to become quite familiar to me during my stay at Kenwood.'

One evening, Pauline and Fred went out to a nightclub in Kew, where they bumped into Cynthia, all by herself. According to Pauline, 'Freddie was deeply shocked to find John's wife clubbing without a suitable escort, and he treated her to a lecture on the subject of wifely duties … I was furious with him for offending Cynthia.' But perhaps he had also offended Cynthia in another, less seemly way. Pete Shotton remembered that 'Freddie exhausted the limits of even John's tolerance when he attempted to seduce his daughter-in-law. Cyn was so distraught that John threw his father out of the house, and refused ever to see him again.'*

With so much drama going on, it is perhaps not surprising that John sought refuge in 'Sunny Heights', just down the hill.

---

* John's relationship with his father finally came to an end in 1970, when Fred wrote to him mentioning that he was planning to write his autobiography. An Apple secretary asked Fred and Pauline to come to Tittenhurst Park on John's thirtieth birthday, 9 October. Kept waiting in the kitchen, they were greeted by an irate John, saying, 'I'm cutting off your money and kicking you out of the house … Get out of my life – get off my back!'

It emerged that John's post-Beatles 'primal scream' therapy had triggered violent feelings against his father. 'Have you any idea of what I've been through because of you? Day after day in therapy, screaming for my daddy, sobbing for you to come home!' According to Pauline, John also repeatedly described his mother as a 'whore'. Grabbing his father's lapel, he said, 'As for your life story, you're never to write *anything* without my approval. And if you tell anyone what happened here today … I'll have you killed.' This threat worried Fred so much that he gave a statement of their conversation to a solicitor, with instructions that it be made public if he should 'disappear or die an unnatural death'.

85

Ringo had bought his very own mock-Tudor residence on the same swish estate a year after John bought Kenwood. He then hired a building company to undertake extensive renovations. These soon got out of control. Thinking to reduce costs, and hoping for a sound investment to fall back on when the famous bubble burst, Ringo then bought the building company. But he was no businessman: he bought the property for £37,000, spent a further £53,000 on it, and then sold it four years later for £47,000. Neither did his new building company ever get off the ground. When asked what went wrong, he replied, 'No one wanted to buy the houses we put up.'

But it was all good fun while it lasted, and John and Cynthia would pop by whenever they needed cheering up, which was most of the time. Unlike Kenwood, which rapidly became a museum for exhausted enthusiasms, Sunny Heights* was, as its name suggests, a fun palace, its jollity undimmed by angst or self-pity. As well as adding a whole new wing, a workroom and a home cinema, Ringo installed his own pub, the Flying Cow, in the front room, complete with mirrored walls, sporting prints and a psychedelic light show. He relished playing mine host from behind the bar, pulling the beer taps and pressing the buttons on the fully operational till. The Flying Cow also boasted a dartboard, and a pool table specially flown over from America. 'It was always party time at the Starkeys,' recalled Cynthia. 'Ringo was gregarious and

* The original owner of the house had called it 'Haleakala', the name of the massive volcano that forms the larger part of the Hawaiian island of Maui. 'Haleakala' means 'House of the Sun', so when a Mr Pope bought the property in 1948 and changed its name to 'Sunny Heights', he wasn't being quite as radical as it might appear. So now you know.

fun-loving, a clown and a joker with an infectious laugh. Together, he and Maureen made an irresistible double act, both extrovert and uninhibited.'

Sunny Heights was, in many ways, more lavish and luxurious than Kenwood. Finding John's five televisions a little meagre, Ringo installed a television and two telephones in every single room. For some reason he hated seams, so he ordered a chocolate-brown Wilton carpet to be woven in one huge stretch for the main living room. But he was soon to discover that there is no clear correlation between luxury and happiness, and that, more often than not, the one is a substitute for the other. Drawing Ringo's portrait on a spare wall, the caricaturist Gerald Scarfe* noticed that many of the rooms in Sunny Heights were

* Later to marry Jane Asher.

completely empty: 'I thought coming from a two-up-two-down house he didn't know what to do with them.' When Ray Connolly visited Ringo there in March 1968, he found him bewildered by choice. 'I've got a friend in Liverpool called Roy,' Ringo told him. 'You know, he's a joiner, and he's only got about thirty records, but he gets so much pleasure from them. Yet I've got a cupboard here with about five hundred LPs, and when I want to play one I have to close the cupboard again because I don't know which one to put on any more … I suppose I get bored like anyone else, but instead of having three hours a night, I have all day to get bored in. Even this house was a toy. In Liverpool, I'd always lived in a four-roomed house and the height of my ambitions was a semi in Aigburth. Sometimes I feel like I'd like to stop being famous and get back to where I was in Liverpool. There don't seem to be so many worries in that sort of life, although I thought there were at the time. But I had to come here to realise that they counted for very little.'

86

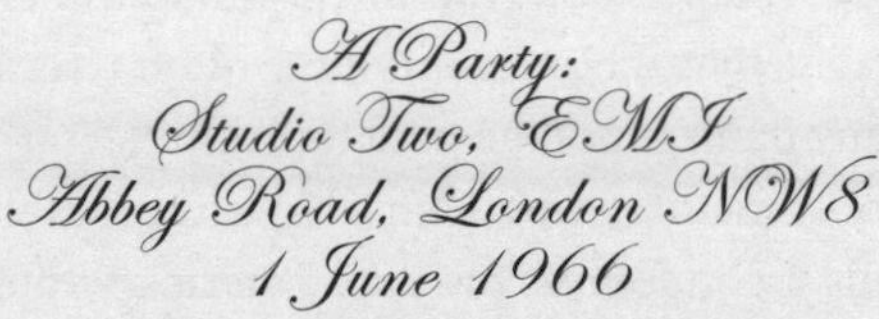

The Beatles have already taped a rhythm track for 'Yellow Submarine', along with Ringo's unsteady vocals and his meandering, mock-poetic introduction* ('And we will march to free the day to see them gathered there, from Land o'Groats to John o'Green ...'). But it is essentially a singalong song, so in the evening they invite a few party-loving friends to join them in Studio Two, among them Pattie Boyd, Mick Jagger, Brian Jones, Marianne Faithfull, and the Beatles' faithful chauffeur Alf Bicknell.

As they enter, the Beatles' engineer, Geoff Emerick, realises that they are all what he euphemistically describes as 'distinctly in a party mood'. From the look of them, he suspects that at their dinner beforehand 'more than food was being ingested'. Though he himself has never tried pot, he has been around enough musicians to recognise its aroma: 'We were sometimes aware of the funny smell in the studio after the Beatles and their roadies snuck a joint off in the corner, though I doubt very much if the straitlaced George Martin knew what was going on.'

The studio rapidly transforms into the ultimate Swinging Sixties party, with women in mini-skirts and flowing blouses, and men in purple bell-bottoms and fur jackets. Emerick suspects they are unlikely

---

* Later junked.

to stay still – 'There was no way I was going to try to contain that lot!' – so he gives them all handheld microphones on long leads.

John says he wants to sound as though he's singing underwater. He tries gargling and singing at the same time, but ends up choking. So he changes tack, insisting on a tank being brought into the studio so he can stick his head in it.

By now, George Martin is adept at dealing with John's excesses, and tries to dissuade him. But John is insistent. Emerick suggests a compromise: why not get John to put the microphone underwater? George Martin is worried that the microphone will be wrecked, and warns Emerick that any damage will be paid for by him.

They look for something with which to waterproof the microphone. Mal Evans finds a condom in his bag. Emerick wraps it around the microphone, and then dips the finished product into a milk bottle filled with water. They are about to start recording when the bossy studio manager, Mr Fowler, puts his head around the door to check that nothing is amiss.

Emerick knows that if Mr Fowler spots the microphone in the milk bottle he will be sacked on the spot. But John is quick-witted: the second he sees Mr Fowler, he grabs the apparatus and hides it behind his back.

'Everything all right, lads?' asks Mr Fowler.

'Yes, sir, Mr Studio Manager, sir, absolutely smashing, sir,' says John, to the sound of suppressed giggling from everyone, including George Martin.

The recording goes ahead, but the underwater sound is unsatisfactory, and is soon abandoned. On with the party!

The Beatles raid an oversized cupboard in the studio, known as the Trap Room, a treasure trove of odds and ends: thunderstorm gadgets, old hosepipes, a football rattle, wartime hand bells, chains, gongs, wind machines, whistles and hooters. The beautiful people grab what they can, and amidst much merriment and clinking of glasses, the sing-song begins. You can hear the yelps and hollers of the partygoers on the record, during the second verse, the most voluble coming from the previously softly-spoken Pattie Boyd.

Soon everyone squeezes into the tiny echo-chamber at the back of the studio. Once again, Emerick detects 'the faint smell of "incense"'. While the partygoers clank and giggle and rattle and hoot, John puts on a Goon-style voice and says, 'Full steam ahead, Mr Bo'sun! Full steam ahead!' The evening ends with Mal Evans marching around the studio, banging on the big bass drum strapped to his chest, and everybody else straggling behind him, whooping and hollering and dancing the conga.

87

A 'Pre-Opening Celebration' for Sibylla's discothèque in Swallow Street, Mayfair, was thrown at the club's premises on 21 June 1966. In a feature in *Queen* magazine, Cathy McGowan, the presenter of *Ready Steady Go!*, enthused that 'a more glittering line-up of guests could hardly be imagined'.

The discothèque's prospectus stated that membership would not be based on the old class divisions of 'breeding, schooling and wealth'; the new requirement was more modern, though just as inexact: 'hipness'.

Interviewed by Jonathan Aitken,* the co-owner Kevin Macdonald said that he and his partners had brought together 'the new aristocracy in Britain … the current young meritocracy of style, taste and sensitivity … the top creative people; the top exporters; the top brains; the top artists; the top social people'.

The guest list† was published in the next issue of *Queen*, under the heading 'How Many Swinging Londoners Do You Know?'

David Bailey, photographer
John Barry, composer
Jane Birkin, actress, wife of John Barry
Jacqueline Bisset, actress

---

* Aitken (1942–) is the author of, among many other works, *The Young Meteors* (1967), a collection of profiles of the young and fashionable, and *Nixon: A Life* (1993), a sympathetic portrait of the former US president. He became a Conservative MP in 1974. In 1999 he was convicted of perjury and perverting the course of justice, and sentenced to eighteen months in prison. Twenty years later, in June, 2019, he was ordained as an Anglican priest.

† Here abbreviated.

Pattie Boyd, Beatle wife
Michael Caine, actor
Leslie Caron, actress
Julie Christie, actress
Mike d'Abo, singer, soon to join Manfred Mann
Nigel Dempster, gossip columnist
Terry Donovan, photographer
Peregrine Eliot, aristocrat
Alan Freeman, disc jockey (shareholder)
Nicholas Gormanston, Anglo-Irish aristocrat
Celia Hammond, model
Anita Harris, singer
Bruce Higham, property developer (major shareholder)
Terry Howard, photographer (major shareholder)
Mick Jagger, Rolling Stone
Brian Jones, Rolling Stone
John Lennon, Beatle
Paul McCartney, Beatle
Kevin Macdonald, copywriter (major shareholder)
Cathy McGowan, presenter, *Ready Steady Go!*
David Mlinaric, designer
Andrew Loog Oldham, Rolling Stones manager
Jane Ormsby-Gore, daughter of UK ambassador to the USA
Sir Mark Palmer, founder, 'English Boy' model agency
Lance Percival, entertainer
Sir William Pigott-Brown, National Hunt jockey, principal shareholder
Alexander Plunket Greene, fashion entrepreneur, husband of Mary Quant
Mary Quant, fashion designer
Michael Rainey, fashion designer, 'Hung On You', husband of Jane Ormsby-Gore
Keith Richards, Rolling Stone
Edina Ronay, designer and actress
Maureen Starkey, Beatle wife

Eric Swayne, photographer, former boyfriend of Pattie Boyd
Gordon Waller, singer, Peter and Gordon

Writing in the *Daily Express* that year, Robin Douglas-Home, a Scottish aristocrat, recognised that London's 'privileged class' was now 'actors, pop singers, hairdressers, and models'. Times, he said, had changed. 'If a 14th Earl with a grouse moor and George Harrison with Pattie Boyd walked together into a restaurant and there was only one table left, who would be given the table? Well – if the head waiter had any sense – obviously George and Pattie.'

But pockets of resistance remained. On New Year's Eve 1966, George was refused admission to Annabel's, the smart nightclub in Mayfair, for not wearing a tie. In her autobiography, Lady Annabel Goldsmith, after whom the club had been named, recalled the incident with thinly-disguised relish: 'On 31 December 1967' (she was in fact a year out) 'the Beatle George Harrison arrived at the blue and gold canopy, intending to see in the New Year in style. With him were his wife, Pattie Boyd, his manager Brian Epstein and his friend, the rock star Eric Clapton. Heavily bearded, wearing a polo-necked sweater and a thick scarf, he was astonished to be refused entry by the doorman. Insulted at being offered a shirt and tie when the dress code was not being met, Mr Harrison reminded the doorman that in his opinion Annabel's needed the Beatles rather more than the Beatles needed Annabel's. "I don't think this is the case nowadays or ever was in the past," was the doorman's reply, and the Harrison party saw in the New Year at the nearby Lyon's Corner House.'

88

We are on the Mop Tops Tour of Liverpool. 'So that's the Roman Catholic cathedral. It has four bells – Matthew, Mark, Luke and John. But Beatles fans call them John, Paul, George and Ringo! When I told that to an American tourist the other day he said, "Ringo? That's a good name for a bell!" I said, "I make the jokes, mate!"'

We walk around the corner to what was once the Oxford Street Maternity Hospital, but is now part of the university. A rival guide has beaten us to it.

'Good day, Sunshine!' says the rival guide to our guide, and then adds, 'Here comes the sun!' Our guide, Stevie T, chuckles effortfully, then waits for his rival to go away before walking us to the plaque by the front door.

To Julia Lennon, née Stanley, a son
John Lennon
(1940–1980)
born here in the former
Liverpool Maternity Hospital
6.30 p.m. 9 October 1940

He tells us of the Nazi bombing of Liverpool that took place that same week. 'But there was no bombing on 9 October. John must have been singing "Give peace a chance"!' In Liverpool, everything returns to the Beatles.

He drives us to the other end of Hope Street, to Gambier Terrace, a beautiful 1830s terrace close to the Anglican cathedral.

'Now, you all know your Beatles. Rod Murray – does that name ring a bell?'

We act as though it's on the tip of our tongues.

'Well, it's impossible to remember everything, isn't it?' he says, with an air of forbearance. It's Beatles Week in Liverpool, and levels of Beatles expertise are disarmingly high. I've been reading about the Beatles non-stop for a year, but compared to most of the fans I've barely reached intermediate level.

Rod Murray was, it turns out, one of the Dissenters, an arty group distinguished by its refusal to play any music. John and Stu Sutcliffe lived in Murray's scruffy first-floor flat in Gambier Terrace in early 1960. John said it was just like a rubbish dump. Stevie T allows time for photographs of the front door that John used to walk in and out of.

Back in the minibus, Stevie T talks of the various Beatles tours he has been on. 'I went with the Beatles team to Manchester. The trouble was – nothing there. None of the places they went to exist any more. There's a lovely fellow there who does rock'n'roll tours of Manchester – Stone Roses, Oasis, all the rest of 'em. Now, what's 'is name? Wilde. Paul Wilde. That's it!'

I ask him whether his children are keen on the Beatles. 'They're not all that interested in music, to be honest. Mind you, the other day I heard my younger son playing music in his room. So I went in, and do you know what he was playing? Barry White! BARRY WHITE!' I shake my head sympathetically.

We drive to Toxteth. Stevie T parks near no. 9 Madryn Street, Ringo's grandparents' house, where Ringo was born. In 2005, Liverpool City Council ruled that Madryn Street and ten neighbouring streets were to be demolished. Following an outcry from Beatles fans, it was announced that no. 9 would be saved. It was to be dismantled brick by brick and stored until a suitable site could be found. There were even plans to reconstruct it in the Museum of Liverpool, but they fell through.

We walk round the corner to 10 Admiral Grove, where Ringo lived with his mother from the age of six. I ask Stevie T if Ringo bought his mother a smarter house when he became rich and famous. 'He bought her a lovely bungalow in Gateacre. She stayed there to her dying day, but she never liked it. Too posh for her.'

No. 10 is painted pink and white, like a party cake. A middle-aged businesswoman, Jackie Holmes, bought it recently for £70,000. She also owns 9 Newcastle Road, Julia Lennon's old home, and 25 Upton Green, where George once lived. No one seems to know what she plans to do with her purchases.

A rival tour is busy peering through the windows of no. 10, so we have to wait our turn for a snoop. There is not much to see: the front room is entirely bare. Stevie T fills in the hiatus with an anecdote. 'The house only had an outside toilet, by that wall at the back. The only place for Ringo's fans to sit was on the wall. When he walked to the outside toilet, they'd all scream, so whenever he wanted to go to the toilet, the whole of Liverpool would know.'

'And so on to our next moptop-tabulous tour destination!' It's the lake in Sefton Park. We gaze at it from the road. This, says Stevie T, is where Fred Lennon first met Julia. In the distance, we can just about make out the top of the Palm House. 'It was in a terrible condition. George gave them half a million towards restoring it, but he didn't want anyone to know.'

Clearly, a Liverpool by-law requires any building associated with the Beatles, however tangentially, to display a statue or plaque. There is a Beatles statue at Pier Head, and a further eight Beatles statues are in the Cavern Quarter, including one of John Lennon outside the club itself and one of Eleanor Rigby – by Tommy Steele, of all people – in Stanley Street.

The statue of John at Liverpool John Lennon Airport was unveiled by Yoko Ono in 2002. Plaques abound, too. You can find plaques to Bob Wooler, their first manager; to Mal Evans, their roadie; to the Quarrymen and to the Dissenters. A plaque between a tattoo parlour and a tattoo removal parlour on Rodney Street reads: 'THIS PLAQUE COMMEMORATES THE BIRTH HERE OF BRIAN SAMUEL EPSTEIN BORN 19 SEPTEMBER 1934 + DIED LONDON 27 AUGUST 1967'. There are further plaques on the Cavern Club, the Casbah Coffee Club, the Grapes pub, all the Beatles' individual homes, and the Grosvenor Ballroom, where they used to play. With the benefit of hindsight, it might have been less time-consuming to place plaques on the handful of buildings in Liverpool with no Beatles associations.

Stevie T walks us to the Sefton Park Hotel, billed as 'located in a former Beatle's home, offering comfortable accommodation, a warm welcome and great food and drink'. The plaque by the entrance reads:

STUART SUTCLIFFE
THE
FAMILY HOME OF
STUART SUTCLIFFE
1961–1970

This claim seems a little fanciful, as everyone knows that Stu died very young, before the Beatles took off. Later, I check out the dates. Stuart Sutcliffe died from a cerebral haemorrhage in Hamburg on 10 April 1962, having been in Germany for most of 1961 and 1962. Admittedly, he was in Liverpool from 20 January to 27 March 1961, but that was before his family moved to Sefton Park. This leaves just a handful of days in August 1961, when he returned from Hamburg for hospital tests, and a few more days in February 1962, when he came back to see his mother, who was recovering from an operation.

Not to worry! The hotel dining room is decorated with photos of Stu and the Beatles, Stu and Astrid, Stu and John. The wordy inscription above a framed copy of Stu's birth certificate reads: 'Stuart's sudden death in Hamburg is part of Beatles folklore, a poignant story of a young man whose promising career as an artist/musician was tragically cut short, but Stuart's importance to the Beatles as one of the founding members and a close friend of John Lennon is legendary.'

Back in the minibus, Stevie T announces that next week he is off to Bangor in Wales with a group of Beatles fans from Sweden. They plan to look round places visited by the Beatles when they stayed in Bangor for two nights in August 1967, for a seminar by the Maharishi. 'I'm just going for the ride, not for work. Should be a lorra fun.'

'Guess where we're going next?' he says, pressing a button on the dashboard. Out through the speakers comes 'Penny Lane'. We halt by a street sign saying 'Penny Lane' and wait for other tours to move on before taking a closer look. This sign, says Stevie T, is not original. 'The minute the song came out, they were all stolen. Eventually the council stopped replacing them. This meant there were Penny Lane signs everywhere in the world – except for Penny Lane!' The current sign, firmly affixed to the wall, is covered in fans' signatures. A sheet of Perspex has been stuck over it ever since Paul McCartney came up to Liverpool with James Corden for his *Carpool Karaoke* in 2018 and added his modestly-sized autograph.

We stop off at St Barnabas church hall, where Paul served as a chorister, and the Beatles used to play from time to time. It's now a pub. 'Make a lovely photo, them hanging baskets. Fun question: what famous musician once lived in that flat up there? You'll never guess! No? No? Put you out of your misery – Freddie Mercury! Yes, Freddie Mercury! Unbelievable!' As we set off, Stevie T points at an elderly man in the car park. 'Look! Over there! That's LEN GARRY! And that woman next to him, that's his wife!' We try to look excited. Sensing that we haven't a clue who he's on about, Stevie T informs us that Len Garry was one of the original Quarrymen.

Penny Lane is rich in buildings mentioned in the song – the barber shop, the bank, the shelter in the middle of the roundabout – but they are drabber than expected. The barber shop is still there, now called Tony Slavin, but instead of the barber showing photographs, he is subject to them: every tourist in the city is busy snapping a selfie against the shopfront. 'John, Paul and George all had their hair cut here,' says Stevie T proudly. I think of asking him why Ringo never did, but the question evaporates in my mouth. The famous 'shelter in the middle of the roundabout' now has a sign saying 'Sgt Pepper Bistro', but it is boarded up, with no bistro in sight. It emerges that a Mr Ray Maatook bought the former tram stop in 2004, with exciting plans to develop it as a 'Beatles-inspired bistro', but it has remained empty ever since.

What about the banker who never wears a mac in the pouring rain? Where's the bank? 'There used to be three banks claiming the title,' says

Stevie T. 'But there's only one left, the TSB. D'y'see it over there? So they have the claim to fame.'

We talk about Len Garry. Surely some of those Quarrymen wish they'd stuck it out, and become Beatles? If the group had been John, Paul, George and Craig, and I'd decided to leave them for a proper job, I would still be bristling with envy and resentment. 'No, no, I don't think so,' says Stevie T thoughtfully. 'Well, maybe Chas Newby. You see, Chas was good-looking – just like Paul. He played bass – just like Paul. He was left-handed – just like Paul.' I try to nod knowingly, hoping that Stevie T won't twig that I have no idea who Chas Newby is.

Later, I look him up. Chas Newby was not, as I had imagined, an actual Quarryman, but he filled in for Stu Sutcliffe for four gigs in December 1960. John then asked Chas to go back to Hamburg with them, but he opted for university instead. He went on to become a maths teacher in Droitwich. In retirement, at the age of seventy-five, he joined the Quarrymen for the very first time, having missed the bus well over half a century earlier.

'Here's a question for you. Great final question for *Who Wants to Be a Millionaire?*! What name did George Harrison sometimes use as a pseudonym?' We look blank. 'Wanna know the answer?' Stevie T parks his minibus and points at the street sign. 'Arnold Grove!' We are standing outside no. 12, the birthplace of George Harrison. 'Two up, two down. Six in the house, no bathroom. When they wanted a bath, they got the tin bath off its peg, and put the kettle on.'

We stare at the front door. We stare at the top windows. We stare at the bottom windows. We take photographs. I feel a little sheepish. 12 Arnold Grove is not operated by the National Trust: it is the home of Kathleen Hughes, a retired carer. Mrs Hughes complained to the *Daily Telegraph* in 2015 that she was 'sick to death' of tourists: 'The tour taxis come zooming up the street and in the summer there are hundreds of them every day. At the weekend, they are turning up constantly, even as late as two o'clock in the morning. I live on my own … It's horrible having strangers sticking their faces in my window and knocking at all times of the day … I'm really fed up of it and so are my neighbours, especially with these cruise ships coming into Liverpool bringing hundreds of coaches of tourists outside my door. The whole Bayern Munich football team came to see the house once, and they were all sticking their faces in the window. Frankly, it's getting out of hand.'

We steal away. Next stop Woolton, and Strawberry Fields, where once again Stevie T vents his irritation with his rivals. 'You'll find some tour guides pointing to that tree over there, or that one, or that one, and they say, "That's the tree in the song, where John says, 'No one I think is in my tree.'" Well, it drives me mad! They're daft! I mean, he's not talking about an ACTUAL tree! He said he always felt special and different growing up. That's what "no one else is in my tree" means! Yet they still go on pointing to this tree or that! Drives me hopping mad!'

In 2000 the original wrought-iron gates were stolen, and sold to a scrap-metal dealer. Two days later the dealer started entertaining suspicions, and went to the police. The originals are now in storage, and the present gates are replicas.

We drive on to St Peter's church. The churchyard is pullulating with other guides, so Stevie T walks us across the road to St Peter's church hall, which has yet another plaque:

IN THIS HALL ON 6th JULY 1957
JOHN & PAUL
FIRST MET

This plaque comes with a plaque of its own, the second one in metal, and much more wordy than the first, suggesting it had been dictated in a pub towards closing time:

> The Quarrymen featuring Eric Griffiths, Colin Hanton, Rod Davies, John Lennon, Pete Shotton and Len Garry performed on the afternoon of 6th July at St Peter's Church Fete. In the evening before their performance in this hall, Ivan Vaughan, who sometimes played in the group, introduced his friend Paul McCartney to John Lennon. As John recalled … 'that was the day, the day that I met Paul, that it started moving'.

We take photographs of the hall, and the plaque, and the plaque's plaque. As we walk back towards the churchyard, I notice that Stevie T is taking care to avoid the other guides.

'Do you have a friendly rivalry with them?' I ask him.

'Not friendly,' he replies. Tension creeps into his voice. 'A lot of them don't know what they're talking about.' He takes us into the churchyard. 'See, come over here. Look at this!' We gaze at a gravestone to John Mackenzie, 'who died September 16th 1915, aged 73 years'.

'These other guides, they just stand there spouting rubbish. They say that's Father Mackenzie from "Eleanor Rigby", and then they encourage everyone to take photographs of the gravestone. And you ask me why I don't like them! Do you want to know the true story? Do you? Well, I'll tell you the true story. The true story is that the real Father Mackenzie had nothing to do with that Father Mackenzie. The real person wasn't called John, he was called Tom. And he wasn't a priest, but a guy who used to introduce the Beatles onstage who they nicknamed "Father Mackenzie". In fact, he was ex-army, and they say he was always darning socks. Does that remind you of something – yes, "darning his socks in the night when there's nobody there" – are you with me? So please, please, I beg of you, don't tell me that John Mackenzie was the original Father Mackenzie. Drives me hopping mad!'

89

Doctrinal differences have led to schisms among Beatles historians quite as fierce as those that beset the early Christian Church. Behind and a bit to the left of John Mackenzie's gravestone another gravestone commemorates various other members of the Rigby family, including, roughly halfway down, Eleanor Rigby. Stevie T complains that rival guides encourage people to believe that this is the famous Eleanor Rigby. 'It's a lovely romantic story. Only trouble is – it's just not true!'

Stevie T has faith in those Beatles theologians who believe that Paul took the name 'Rigby' from a wine-shippers in Bristol, and 'Eleanor' from Eleanor Bron. Paul himself has confirmed this version of events on a number of occasions, but that has done nothing to stifle the voices of the dissenters.

Lionel Bart once declared that 'Paul always thought he came up with the name Eleanor because of having worked with Eleanor Bron in the film *Help!*, but I am convinced he took the name from a gravestone in a cemetery close to Wimbledon Common where we were both walking. The name on the gravestone was Eleanor Bygraves. He then came back to my office and began playing it on my clavichord.'

The nominative etymology of Father Mackenzie has been subject to similar schisms. Pete Shotton remembered being in the room when Paul named the priest in his new song 'Father McCartney'. Shotton recalled saying, 'Hang on a minute, Paul. People are going to think that's your poor old dad, left all alone in Liverpool to darn his own socks.' He then said, or claimed to have said, 'Give us that phone book, then, and I'll have a look through the Macs.' First he suggested 'McVicar', and then, when that didn't fit, 'Mackenzie'.

However, in a 1966 interview with Hunter Davies in the *Sunday Times*, Paul, who suffers from a forgivable tendency to place himself centre-stage, recalled that it was he, not Pete, who looked through the telephone directory in search of an alternative Mac: 'I went through the phone book and got the name Mackenzie.'

Thirty-one years later, in 1997, Paul told Barry Miles of false Father Mackenzies popping up in his life, along the lines of false Anastasias. 'A man appeared, who died a few years ago, who said, "I'm Father Mackenzie." Anyone who was called Father Mackenzie and had any slim contact with the Beatles quite naturally would think, "Well, I spoke to Paul and he might easily have written that about me."'

There are divisions, too, over who composed the song – Paul or John or both of them. In *Melody Maker* in 1971, John claimed to have written 'at least 50 per cent' of it. By 1972, in an interview with *Hit Parader*, this had risen to '70 per cent'. Later that same year, talking to Ray Connolly, he increased it to '80 per cent'. A week before he died in 1980, he was less specific about percentages but equally proprietorial, claiming to an interviewer from *Playboy* that 'The first verse is his [Paul's] and the rest are basically mine.'

But those who were present when the song was composed remember John's contributions as negligible. Even his most loyal friend, Pete Shotton, reckoned they were 'virtually nil'. When Paul couldn't think of an ending, Pete had been 'seized by a brainwave. "Why don't you have Eleanor Rigby dying?" I said, "and have Father Mackenzie doing the burial service for her? That way you'd have the two lonely people coming together in the end – but too late."'

Then John spoke up for the very first time, just to put his friend down: 'I don't think you understand what we're trying to get at, Pete.' Pete felt humiliated. 'All I could think of to say was "Fuck you, John."' With that, the composing session came to an end. But when Pete heard the record for the first time, he felt 'over the moon' that Paul had gone along with his suggestion. 'Perhaps, I reflected, it was *John* who hadn't understood what we were getting at.'

Why would John have so exaggerated his contribution to 'Eleanor Rigby'? Perhaps it was simple envy. Of all the Beatles' songs, its lyrics have been the most extravagantly praised, and by all the right people. On its release, George Melly said, 'Pop has come of age,' and Jerry Leiber said, 'I don't think there's ever been a better song written.' 'Eleanor Rigby' was taken up by poets, including Allen Ginsberg, who claimed to have played it to Ezra Pound, who, he said, 'smiled lightly'. Thom Gunn compared it to Auden's ballad 'Miss Gee'. Karl Miller included it in his anthology *Writing in England Today*. James Fenton remembers Auden listening to it 'in search of something to be influenced by'. More recently, the novelist and critic A.S. Byatt praised the lyric for displaying 'the minimalist perfection of a Beckett story'. Its appeal is wide-ranging: over the years it has been chosen as a Desert Island Disc by, among others, the cosmologoist Professor Carlos Frank, the actress Patricia Hayes, the American mezzo-soprano Cathy Berberian, the Armenian balladeer Charles Aznavour and the former Chancellor of the Exchequer Geoffrey Howe.

One Beatles theologian, Erin Torkelson Weber, author of *The Beatles and the Historians* (2016), offers another reason for John's dubious claims. In an interview with *Playboy* in 1971, the Beatles' dodgy business manager, Allen Klein, admitted that, in his attempts to cultivate John through flattery, he had taken care to 'remind' him of his authorship of 'Eleanor Rigby', assuring him that he wrote 60 or 70 per cent of the lyric. 'He just didn't remember until I sat him down and had him sort through it all.'

Torkelson pins John's misattribution to Klein's persuasiveness. 'It appears that in his efforts to become Beatles manager and gain Lennon's approval, Klein may have convinced the songwriter that he had written lyrics actually by McCartney.'

90

Fame came with advantages. One quiet Sunday, the singer songwriter Donovan was sitting in his flat in Maida Vale when the doorbell rang. Paul had arrived, with his acoustic guitar.

They smoked a joint or two. Paul played Donovan two songs he was working on. One of them was about a yellow submarine, and the other went:

> Ola Na Tungee,
> Blowing his mind in the dark with a pipe full of clay –
> No one can say …

In time, Ola Na Tungee would transmute into Eleanor Rigby, and his mind in the dark with a pipe full of clay would turn to rice in the church where the wedding had been. But for the moment, Paul was just fiddling around.

Before long, the doorbell rang again. Donovan went to answer it. A young policeman told him that there was a car outside; it was parked illegally, at an odd angle, the doors open, with its radio still on.

Paul joined them at the door.

The policeman's eyes lit up. 'Oh, it's you, Mr McCartney. Is it your car, sir? A sports car?'

Anyone else would have been faced with a reprimand and a parking fine. Instead, the policeman offered to park Paul's car in a more suitable spot. Paul thanked him, and handed over the keys. A few minutes later the policeman returned, to tell him that everything was now in order.

As he handed over the keys he saluted, allowing Paul to return to his guitar, and Ola Na Tungee.

91

Paul changed 'Ola Na Tungee' to 'Daisy Hawkins', but it didn't scan properly, so he changed it again, this time to 'Eleanor Rigby'. Half a century on, Colin Campbell, Professor of Sociology at York University, was to devote an entire book to an analysis of the lyrics of 'Eleanor Rigby':

> As we have seen, Paul seemed to envisage Eleanor Rigby as picking up rice after the wedding was over, having 'missed the wedding'. In other words she turned up for the wedding but was too late to take part in the celebrations. This suggests that the reason she picked up the rice was in order to have something to connect her not just with weddings in general, but this wedding in particular, one in which she had intended to participate. So should we really think of her as a wedding guest? In which case presumably this picking up rice is not something that she does on a regular basis. It is simply that she wishes to have something to remind her of this wedding. But then if she is a guest but has missed the service would she not now be on her way to the reception? Or has she missed that as well?

… And so on. But, as with many Beatles songs, the lyrics have been misheard as well as misinterpreted. Some hear 'all the homely people'. Later in the song, the words after 'Father Mackenzie' are sometimes taken to be 'Darling it sucks in the night when there's nobody there'. At the same time, Eleanor Rigby 'picks up her eyes from the church where the wedding has been'.

And what's this song? 'Take the back right turn!' 'Pay per bag right turn!' When the songwriter Bobby Hart first heard it in 1966, he imagined the Beatles were singing 'Take the last train!' By the time he realised it was 'Paperback Writer', it was too late: the wrong words had lodged in his brain. Three months later, he was trying to write a debut single for the the Monkees. Asked by their management for something that sounded like the Beatles, he composed a song from the misheard line. 'Take the last train to Clarksville', it began, and it took the Monkees to number 1 in the US charts.

Everyone has a different Beatles songbook nestling in their heads, because everyone hears different words to different songs. Deep down, I still think that John is singing 'Kangaroo days, ah!' in 'Across the Universe'. Maybe it's because I first heard the track on the World Wildlife Fund charity album, *No One's Gonna Change Our World*,* which had a photograph of a panda on the cover, and liner notes by, of all people, the Duke of Edinburgh. In fact John was singing the no less obscure 'Jai Guru Deva'.†

When 'Penny Lane' was released, many American fans, ignorant of Britain's charity Poppy Day, were left wondering why a pretty nurse would be selling puppies from a tray. The other side of the single was also subject to misinterpretation. Elvis Costello's manager, Jake Rivera, long thought that on 'Strawberry Fields Forever' John sang 'Living is easy with nice clothes'. Additionally, he thought Paul liked the girl in 'And I Love Her' because 'She gives me everything, and tender veal'. Others heard it as 'And I love fur' because 'She gives me everything, internally'. And what of the orthodontist? 'And in my orthodontist, she is standing right in front me'.

Even the simplest Beatles lyric is open to mishearing. 'And when I get home to you, I find a broken canoe'. 'I don't care to march for

---

* It was an unlikely location for a Beatles premiere. The album was subtitled 'The Stars Sing for the World Wildlife Fund'. Other tracks included 'Cuddly Old Koala' by Rolf Harris, 'When I See an Elephant Fly' by Bruce Forsyth, 'I'm a Tiger' by Lulu, 'Wings' by the Hollies, 'The Python' by Spike Milligan and 'Land of My Fathers' by Harry Secombe.

† Literally, 'Glory to the shining remover of darkness.'

money'. 'Friday night arrives without a fruitcake'. 'Michelle, ma belle, Sunday monk, he wants to ban odd socks, to ban odd socks'. 'There beneath the goose and bourbon skies'. 'But if you go carrying picture of German cows'.

From sense to nonsense; from nonsense to sense. For years, I thought I was mishearing the words of 'Come Together'. They seemed like nonsense, from the first line – 'You come all flat up' – to the last. When I finally got round to reading the lyrics, it turned out that the first line was 'Here come old flat top', which really makes no more sense than 'You come all flat up', and perhaps rather less. Two lines on, I was relieved to find that what I had always taken to be 'Jew Jew eyeballs' – John was no stranger to anti-Semitism – was written as 'joo joo eyeballs', though heaven knows what *they* are. Other lyrics that I had always imagined I had misheard – 'Joe jam football', 'walking finger', 'he back production', 'oh, no sideboard' – weren't all that off-track: they're actually 'toe jam football', 'monkey finger', 'he bad production' and 'Ono sideboard'.

Like searching for human faces in a cloud, those who look hard enough for a particular meaning will eventually find it. Some were convinced that each verse of 'Come Together' contained a description of a different Beatle – George, the holy roller; Ringo, the shooter of Coca-Cola; Paul, the good-looking one who's so hard to see. But, as was so often the case, this interpretation never occurred to the song's composer.

John's love of nonsense can be traced back to the time he learned to read and write. Aunt Mimi remembered that from an early age his spelling had been notably offbeat: 'Chicken pox was always chicken pots. He went on holiday to my sister's in Edinburgh once and wrote me a card saying *Funs are getting low.*' As a child he was captivated by the works of Edward Lear and Lewis Carroll, reciting 'Jabberwocky' over and over again to his friends: *''Twas brillig, and the slithy toves/ Did gyre and gimble in the wabe …*' For the rest of his life John responded gleefully to puns and wordplay, relishing the way that, through the simple act of altering a letter, sense could so easily be nudged into nonsense.

'You should say what you mean,' the March Hare went on.

'I do,' Alice hastily replied; 'at least – at least I mean what I say – that's the same thing, you know.'

'Not the same thing a bit!' said the Hatter. 'Why, you might just as well say that "I see what I eat" is the same thing as "I eat what I see"!' …

Alice felt dreadfully puzzled. The Hatter's remark seemed to her to have no sort of meaning in it, and yet it was certainly English.

Paul reckons that 'Strawberry Fields Forever' and 'I am the Walrus' both sprang from John's obsession with 'Jabberwocky': '"I am he as you are he …" It's thanks to "Jabberwocky" that he could do that …' His childhood friend Pete Shotton remembered that 'From a very early age, John's ultimate ambition was to one day "write an *Alice*" himself.'

Every evening the twelve-year-old John would work furiously at pastiches of Carroll and Lear, scribbling them into an exercise book before transferring them to a hand-written newspaper he called 'The Daily Howl'. Items included a weather report – 'Tomorrow will be Muggy, followed by Tuggy, Wuggy and Thuggy' – and a parody of *Davy Crockett*, 'The Story of Davy Crutch-Head'. He was also clearly influenced by *1066 and All That*, the popular mock-history book by two schoolmasters, W.C. Sellar and R.J. Yeatman, in which half-remembered facts are tossed and turned, replicating the internal muddle of a schoolboy's mind, so that past and present, fact and fiction, the silly and the solemn are transformed into a jumbled version of the truth: 'The gun powder plot was an awful thing it is still done on the 5th Nov. Guy Fawkes chose the 5th Nov because it was Fireworks Day. Guy Mitchell, the singer, claims direct descent from Guy Fawkes.' Reading this, Sellar and Yeatman would have recognised John as one of their own.

John loved to listen to the relentless, unstoppable punning of the Goons on the wireless, imitating them in class the next day. He spent the money he had been given for his sixteenth birthday on two 78rpm records. One was Elvis Presley's 'Hound Dog'; the other 'The Ying-Tong Song' by the Goons, with its B-side of 'Bloodnok's Rock'n'Roll

Call', 'featuring Major Denis Bloodnok, Roland Rockcake and His Wholly Rollers'.

The Goon scripts were all written at a frenzied pace by Spike Milligan, a manic depressive who lived his life at the mercy of puns, the willing victim of the twisted logic they both reflected and fanned. At the height of his success, Milligan was writing the third series of the Goons when he experienced a complete mental breakdown: 'The madness built up gradually. I found I was disliking more and more people. Then I got to hating them. Even my wife and baby.' Soon, he began to believe that only by killing his fellow Goon Peter Sellers would his mind correct itself. Accordingly, he went round to Sellers' house and walked straight through a glass door, cutting himself all over and ending up in the isolation ward of a mental hospital, bound in a straitjacket.

'Before becoming the Beatles' producer, George Martin, who had never recorded rock-n-roll, had previously recorded with Milligan and Sellers, which made him all the more acceptable,' John reminisced in the *New York Times* in 1973, while reviewing *The Goon Show Scripts*. 'Our studio sessions were full of the cries of Neddie Seagoon, etc., etc., as were most places in Britain.' In the same piece he argued, accurately, that *The Goon Show* was more original and revolutionary than John Osborne's *Look Back in Anger*. Looking back on his schoolboy newspaper 'The Daily Howl', he acknowledged that 'it seems strangely similar to *The Goon Show*'.

Were the jokes Milligan cracked – those manic, relentless, unstoppable jokes – an escape from the trap of depression? Or were they part of that trap – the little lumps of cheese beneath the coiled spring? Whenever he sensed the world was not mad enough, his brain found ways to make it madder. And there was a degree of megalomania to his comedy: he wanted the world, and everyone in it, to bow before his jokes. If they refused, he gave them hell. Performing onstage with the Goons in Coventry in 1954, he grew increasingly furious at the lacklustre response of the audience. Finally he snapped, screamed 'I hope you all get bombed again!', left the stage and locked himself in his dressing room. When his fellow Goons finally managed to prise the door open they found Milligan standing on a chair with a noose around his head, trying to hook the other end of the rope around a pipe overhead.

The pun is a kind of verbal schizophrenia, in which a word points in two ways at once, meaning two entirely different things at the same time. Shakespearian characters tumble into a world of puns when they begin their descents into madness. In his *New York Times* review John described the *Goon Show* scripts as 'a conspiracy against reality. A coup d'état of the mind.' The same might be said of his own incessant punning.

A psychological phenomenon known as Forster's Syndrome is named after the German surgeon who first described it. Dr Forster had been removing a brain tumour when he observed a singular phenomenon. As he manipulated certain areas of the brain, his patient would burst into a manic flight of puns, the sound of one word echoing but also distorting that of its predecessor, turning it into something more savage and brutal. All the words the patient uttered had something to do with knives and butchery – and this black humour came, as Arthur Koestler put it, 'from a man tied face down on the operating table with his skull open.'

The pun can also arise from aggression, a revenge for being mocked or patronised. It is a covert way of establishing superiority in a hostile environment, of ordering the world according to one's own whim. The pun slips madness into language: what is the Freudian slip, if not a pun?

Lennon had a facility, bordering on a compulsion, for puns. Perhaps being asked to choose between your mother and your father splits your mind and your emotions in a pun-like way. The pun allows you to say two things at once. Like the Freudian slip, of which it is a more conscious variant, it might be defined as saying one thing when you mean a mother.

When he first became friends with Paul, John would show him the pun-based jokes he had typed out the night before, many of which he was later to include in his pun-titled book *In His Own Write*.* 'We

* One copy of which he inscribed to a fan, 'To Sheila, with love and dressed fishes.'

would sit around giggling, just saying puns really, that's basically what it was. In the early owls of the Morecambe. I remember "a cup-o-teeth" was one section that was in the typewriter when I was around there.'

The name of the Beatles now passes unquestioned. Even though beetles established themselves on this planet roughly 300 million years before their Liverpudlian counterparts, it is beetles, not Beatles, whose spelling we instinctively query. The group's name is itself a pun, 'the worst and most glorious band name in all of rock'n'roll history', as Bruce Springsteen once put it. John and Stuart Sutcliffe had been trying to think of an animal name, along the lines of Phil Spector's Teddy Bears or Buddy Holly's Crickets. They came up with 'the Lions' or 'the Tigers', before hitting upon 'the Beetles'. With characteristic perversity, John liked the idea of naming his band after such a low life-form, and then he converted it into a pun, to incorporate 'beat'.

From the early days of the Beatles, his long letters to fans are riddled with puns, many impenetrable. One, written in 1961 or 1962 to a Norwegian girl called Lindy Ness, begins, 'I am typing this one fingered lettuce to you,' and goes on to warn her of 'the evil temptations which confront a jung girl in a forrid country'. Other puns in the same letter include 'condiment' for continent, 'debb and duff' for deaf and dumb, 'thy kingdom come thy Wilbur Dunn', and 'suffer little chilblains to come over me'. What can Lindy Ness – who he calls Sad Ness – have thought?

After a show at the Rialto cinema in York in November 1963, the American journalist Michael Braun recorded the banter between the four Beatles. 'One more ciggy and I'm gonna hit the sack, "hit the sack" being an American thing we got off Gary Coople as he struggled along with a clock in *Hi, Goons*,' says John, adding, 'But I never really liked "sack", it's, uh, something you put potatoes in over here.'

'The whole thought of hitting the sack,' says Paul. 'It's so – so dirty, and it can mean a lot of things.'

'You can sack Rome,' says John, 'or you can sack cloth – or you can sacrilege, or saxophone, if you like, or saccharine.'

Five years later, Victor Spinetti worked with John on the stage adaptation of *In His Own Write*. He was amazed by John's facility with puns:

'During work on the play at the Mamounia, I noticed that something was missing. Over my shoulder I said, "I need a Queen's speech here, John." Without hesitating, he grabbed a sheet of cardboard from a shirt Cynthia had just bought and wrote:

> My housebound and eyeball take great pressure in denouncing this loyal ship in the blue corner, two stone three ounches, and he was sitting on the lav at the time.

'"Will that do?" he said, shoving it over to me. He hadn't paused. He hadn't crossed anything out.'

The Beatles albums *Revolver* and *Rubber Soul* had punning titles, and so did John's first two books, *In His Own Write* and *Spaniard in the Works*. In some passages, the puns are so ubiquitous as to be claustrophobic:

> Azue orl gnome, Harrassed Wilsod won the General Erection, with a very small marjorie over the Torchies. Thus pudding the Laboring Partly back into powell after a large abscess.

Authority figures of the time have their names fed into the pun machine, only to emerge eviscerated: Selwyn Lloyd, Harold Macmillan, Ted Heath, LBJ, Emmanuel Shinwell and Princess Margaret are transformed into 'Seldom Loyal', 'Harrassed Macmillion', 'Head Teeth', 'LBW', 'Emmanuel Shitwell' and 'Priceless Margarine'.

Once the Beatles had finished recording *Sgt. Pepper*, they gathered in Studio Two of Abbey Road to listen to the end result, right up to the final thunderous piano chord of 'A Day in the Life'. All four of them were delighted, but then John and Paul had the idea of squeezing in something extra, on the inner part of the disc where the needle ends up going round and round.

The engineer, Geoff Emerick, remembered John saying, 'Let's just put on some gobbledegook, then bifurcate it, splange it, and loop it.' They then nipped back into the studio, and spoke whatever nonsense came into their heads. Emerick played the tape back to them, and they chose a snippet of Paul saying, 'Never needed any other way.' This meant that listeners with primitive record-players would hear 'never-needed-any-other-way-never-needed-any-other-way-never-needed-any-other-way' ad nauseam, until they were driven to reach out and turn it off.

In those days of few distractions, some Beatles fans liked to place the stylus at the end of side two, then turn the record anti-clockwise by hand, in order to hear the same words in reverse. To many people, 'never-needed-any-other-way' backwards sounded just like 'Will-Paul-be-back-as-Superman,' a phrase that offered further encouragement to those who were already convinced that Paul was dead. But other people heard other things. Some heard 'The corned beef there is super, man,' or 'We're parking our Kings Super van,' while others were convinced that the original message was not 'Never needed any other way' but the saucier 'Never could see Annie's u.' These issues continue to engage Beatles fans with time on their hands. On YouTube, a film of the *Sgt. Pepper* LP going round and round on a turntable, first clockwise, then anti-clockwise, has attracted more than 200,000 views, and seven hundred comments, most of them arguing, with varying degrees of passion, for their own interpretation of the words, forwards and backwards, backwards and forwards, sense into noise, noise into sense.

92

On 29 August 1966, the Beatles closed their set at the Candlestick Park baseball stadium in San Francisco with 'Long Tall Sally', an old Little Richard number that had been part of their repertoire from the very start. 'See you again next year,' said John as they left the stage. The group then clambered into an armoured car and were driven away. It was to be their last proper concert.

Their American tour had been exhausting, sporadically frightening, and unrewarding. Their brief tour of the Philippines the previous month had been even more gruesome. The haughty first lady, Imelda Marcos, felt that the Beatles had snubbed her by failing to attend a party in their honour, and had consequently instructed thugs to jostle and kick them as they tried to navigate the departure lounge at Manila Airport. 'I have never been so terrified in my life,' said George. 'We will never go back there.'

By this stage their delight in their own fame had worn off. They were fed up with all the hassle of touring, and tired of the way the screaming continued to drown out the music, so that even they were unable to hear it. Having been shepherded into an empty, windowless truck after a particularly miserable show in a rainy St Louis, Paul said to the others, 'I really fucking agree with you. I've fucking had it up to here too.'

'We've been telling you for weeks!' came the reply.

On their flight back to England, George told Tony Barrow, 'That's it. I'm not a Beatle any more.' Like the others, but perhaps more so, after 1,400 shows he was sick to death of playing live: at the age of twenty-three, he had had enough.

John, too, was despondent. 'He was very depressed about everything,' said a journalist who sat with him on the plane. 'He felt there was no point in doing anything, since it wouldn't last very long anyway.' As the years rolled by, John allowed his view of these days of touring to curdle into self-pity. Five years on, he was to describe them to Eric Clapton as 'night after night of torture'.

For the first time in years, the four of them were able to take a break from being Beatles. With three months free, they could do what they liked. Ringo chose to relax at home with his wife and new baby. John went to Europe to play Private Gripweed in Richard Lester's film *How I Won the War*. George flew to Bombay to study yoga and to be taught to play the sitar by Ravi Shankar. This left Paul to his own devices.

For a while, he enjoyed himself in London, immersing himself in the counter-culture, as the avant-garde was then briefly known. By now he was one of the most famous men in the world. Even as a member of an audience, or a visitor to a gallery, he was always the centre of attention. So at the beginning of November he decided to conduct a little experiment: what would it be like to be normal?

Paul's pursuit of anonymity had its showy aspect. It was almost as if he were acting not acting, or being ostentatiously incognito. His first stop was a company called Wig Creations, who dutifully measured his upper lip and gauged the exact colour of his hair in order to produce a false moustache, and provided him with two pairs of fake spectacles fitted with clear lenses. By slicking his hair back with Vaseline and donning a long overcoat, Paul found he could wander unrecognised.

Suitably togged up, he set off on a solo motoring holiday in France. Looking back on that jaunt, he pictured himself as just another humble traveller. 'I was a lonely little poet on the road,' he said, though few poets in history have been able to cruise around the Continent in a brand-new Aston Martin DB6.

Paul and his Aston Martin were transported to France by an exclusive air-ferry service operating from a little airport in Kent. On arrival he glued on his moustache, donned his overcoat and his glasses, jumped into his sports car, and headed off for Paris.

Once there, he wandered around by himself, filming bits and pieces, employing experimental filming techniques he had picked up from New Wave cinema and Andy Warhol. Sometimes he stayed in his hotel room writing a journal. At dinner he sat by himself, jotting down notes. He wanted to 'retaste anonymity. Just sit on my own and think all sorts of artistic thoughts like, I'm on my own here, I could be writing a novel, easily. What about these characters here in this room?' It's easy to forget that he was still only twenty-four years old, with his life ahead of him.

After Paris he embarked on a leisurely drive towards the Loire, filming as he went. 'I was looking out of the hotel window in one French city and there was a gendarme on traffic duty. There was a lot of traffic coming this way, then he'd stop 'em, and let them all go. So the action for ten minutes was a gendarme directing the traffic.' After shooting this scene he rewound the film and shot more footage, so that the one was superimposed over the other, the cars appearing to pass through the gendarme like ghosts.

Upon reaching Bordeaux, he felt a hankering for the night life. Still in disguise, he turned up at a local discothèque, but was refused entry. 'I looked like old jerko. "No, no, monsieur, *non*" – you schmuck, we can't let you in!' So he went back to his hotel and took off his scruffy overcoat, his moustache and his glasses. Then he returned to the disco, where he was welcomed with open arms.

By now, he had begun to recognise the shortcomings of anonymity. 'It was kind of therapeutic, but I'd had enough. It was nice, because I remembered what it was like to not be famous, and it wasn't necessarily any better than being famous. It made me remember why we all wanted to be famous; to get that thing.' Reflecting on his brief retreat from celebrity, he felt happier with his lot. Fame, success and money may well have their shortcomings, but they are still a lot better than their alternatives.

Before setting off on his jaunt, Paul had arranged to meet Mal Evans under the Grosse Horloge in the centre of Bordeaux, reckoning that by then he would be in need of company. The two of them drove to Madrid, then down to Cordoba and Málaga, vaguely thinking they would hook up with John. But when Paul discovered that John had already left Spain he abandoned his plans, phoning Brian Epstein to send someone from London to drive his car home. Epstein also booked Paul and Mal Evans flights to Rome, then on to Kenya, where they went on safari, with a night at Treetops Lodge in Aberdare National Park.

Paul flew from Nairobi to London on 19 November, ready to record the Beatles' new album on the 24th. On the flight back with Mal, he was thinking about his recent assumption of another persona, and wondering if the Beatles might benefit from something similar. 'With this alter-ego band, it won't be us making all that sound, it won't be the Beatles, it'll be this other band, so we'll be able to lose our identities in them.' But what would they call themselves? While he was wondering, their in-flight meals arrived, complete with packets marked 'S' and 'P'.

'What's that mean?' asked Mal, before answering his own question: 'Oh, salt and pepper.'

'Sergeant Pepper,' said Paul, without thinking.

93

In the early hours of the morning, John, Paul and George were working on 'It's Getting Better' in Abbey Road. Looking down from the control room, George Martin noticed something wrong. John was sitting down, and George and Paul had their hands on his shoulders.

Martin pressed the intercom button. 'What's the matter, John? Is it something you ate?'

George and Paul laughed. John said, 'No, it's not that. I'm just having trouble focusing.'

'Do you want to be driven home?'

'No.'

'OK. Come up here.'

Slowly, John climbed the stairs to the control room. Then he looked up at the ceiling.

'Cor, look at the stars, George.'

Martin looked up, but saw only ceiling.

A few minutes before, John had dipped into his discreet little art-nouveau Liberty pillbox. Meaning to take some uppers, he had taken a tab of LSD by mistake. George Martin was from another generation; he had no idea about hallucinogens. 'How about a spot of fresh air, John?'

But where to go? Outside, the usual array of fans were hanging around, ready to pounce. Martin thought that the roof would be the best place. 'Come on, John, I know a way up the back stairs.'

Paul and George began clowning around, singing old numbers in silly voices, unaware that Martin was taking John up to the roof.

Martin and John walked around for a while. It was a lovely night, with very bright stars. 'Aren't they fantastic?' said John.

John sensed that Martin was looking at him in a funny way. At that moment he realised that he had accidentally taken LSD.

'Don't go too near the edge, there's no rail there, John,' said Martin. There was a drop of ninety feet to the pavement below.

After a while, Martin returned to the control room alone.

Paul asked, 'Where's John?'

'I left him up on the roof, looking at the stars.'

'Ah, you mean like Vince Hill?' joked Paul – Vince Hill's rendition of 'Edelweiss', from *The Sound of Music*, was challenging their 'Penny Lane'/'Strawberry Fields Forever' single for the number 2 slot in the charts.* Paul and George started singing 'Edelweiss' at the top of their voices.

'Edelweiss! E-del-weiss! You look happy to gree-ee-!'

Suddenly it struck them that John, high on LSD, was in great peril. Together, they hurtled up the stairs and brought him back down. Then they all decided that this was a good time to end the session, and Paul took John back to his house, close by.

For some time John had been badgering Paul to try LSD, but Paul, naturally cautious, had kept putting it off. But now he made a snap decision to take some. 'John's on it already, so I'll sort of catch up.'

The pair of them stayed up all night, hallucinating together. 'And we looked into each other's eyes, the eye-contact thing we used to do, which is fairly mind-boggling. You dissolve into each other … And it was amazing. You're looking into each other's eyes and you would want to look away but you wouldn't, and you could see yourself in the other person. It was a very freaky experience and I was totally blown away. John had been sitting around very enigmatically and I had a big vision of him as king, the absolute Emperor of Eternity. It was a good trip.'

* 'Release Me' by Engelbert Humperdinck remained, resolutely, at number 1.

94

At 8 p.m. on 10 February 1967, forty-two classical musicians, most of them middle-aged, assembled in Studio One at Abbey Road. On the instructions of the Beatles, they had donned full evening dress, for which they were to be paid a little extra.

The musicians included the violinists Henry Datyner, forty-four, who had won first prize in the 1944 Geneva International Music Competition, and Erich Gruenberg, forty-three, who had been the leader of the Palestine Broadcasting Corporation Orchestra from 1938 to 1945, and had since led the Stockholm Philharmonic Orchestra, the London Symphony Orchestra and the Royal Philharmonic Orchestra. The leader of that evening's orchestra was David McCallum, sixty-nine, who had led the London Philharmonic Orchestra.

On arrival, the musicians found the studio decked out in brightly coloured balloons. They were then ordered to don a selection of comical masks, party hats, rubber noses, bald wigs, clip-on breasts and gorilla paws. 'Here you go, mate, have one of these,' said Mal Evans, handing them out.

'Most of the musicians seemed taken aback,' recalled Geoff Emerick. 'One of them even rudely slapped Mal's hand aside.'

David McCallum sat motionless in his clown's nose, while Erich Gruenberg held his bow in a gorilla's paw.

Next to arrive were a hand-picked selection of beautiful people, or the Beatles' 'way-out friends', as George Martin, also decked in evening dress, preferred to dub them. They included Mick Jagger and Marianne Faithfull, Keith Richards, Donovan, Pattie Boyd, Mike Nesmith of the Monkees, and Graham Nash of the Hollies. Having drifted in, they wandered around the orchestra handing out party novelties, sparklers, joints and, as Martin put it, 'God knows what'. As was customary on such occasions, pretty bubbles filled the air. Unusually, Brian Epstein was in the studio too, nervously surveying this bizarre clash of cultures. For Geoff Emerick, the session marked a transition: 'The lines between classical and pop music were blurring, and even though many of the orchestral players were disdainful of contemporary music, they could see the writing on the wall.'

The four Beatles arrived last of all, Paul in a tweed overcoat, John in a smart blue velvet suit and bright red tie, his face adorned with a Zapata moustache and extravagant sideburns. They were all, noted Emerick, 'in a decidedly jolly mood … as if they had started the party several hours earlier'. Like royalty, they 'wandered around bestowing their attention on one subject, then the next'.

Already discombobulated by the fancy dress and party novelties, the orchestra were now obliged to take instructions on how to play their own instruments. Between them, Paul and George Martin had decided that the twenty-four-bar bridge between John's 'I read the news today,

oh boy' section and Paul's 'Woke up, got out of bed' section should be filled by individual orchestra members playing the lowest to the highest notes in an unsynchronised slide.

Apart from a shared start and finish, there was to be no coordination, no sense of unity, none of the usual orchestra teamwork. 'I want everyone to be individual,' Martin told them. 'It's every man for himself. Don't listen to the fellow next to you. If he's a third away from you, and you think he's going too fast, let him go.'

Gruenberg, who had delivered the first Russian performance of Benjamin Britten's violin concerto in Moscow, appeared disgruntled. 'All we want you to do is some free-form improvisation,' Paul chipped in.

'Not completely free-form, Erich,' said Martin, encouragingly. 'I'll be conducting, and there is a score of sorts. But we need each musician to play on his own, without listening to those around him.'

Emerick wandered around adjusting the microphones as Gruenberg passed on these outlandish instructions to his baffled colleagues. 'For a moment you could hear a pin drop. Then the murmuring began. "Do *what*??" "What the bloody hell … ?"'

'They all looked at me as though I were completely mad,' recalled Martin. Emerick sensed that 'The general response wasn't so much outrage as dismay. The musicians knew they were there to do a job; they just didn't like what they were being asked to do. These were forty of the top classical musicians in England, and they certainly hadn't spent decades honing their craft in order to be told to improvise from their lowest note to their highest … It wasn't exactly dignified, and they resented it.'

But Martin, a natural optimist, felt that they eventually came round to it. At first they 'thought it was all a stupid giggle and a waste of time', but in the end 'they were carried into the spirit of the party just because it was so ludicrous'. The session ended, unexpectedly, with a spontaneous burst of applause from everyone in the studio, including the orchestra. Had it dawned on them that they had just participated in the creation of something extraordinary? Perhaps they were simply relieved.

Twelve days later, the Beatles recorded the long, booming piano chord that ends 'A Day in the Life'. For this, EMI dogsbodies moved five different keyboards into Studio Two: two Steinway grand pianos, a Steinway upright piano, a Wurlitzer electric piano and a spinet. John, Paul, Ringo, Mal Evans and George Martin each stood by a keyboard, and when Martin called out 'One, two, three – go!' they hit the chords as hard as possible. Soon after they had finished, George Harrison arrived with Dave Crosby of the Byrds. 'Nice of you to turn up, George,' said John shirtily. 'You only missed the most important overdub we've ever done.'

'A Day in the Life' lasts 5 minutes 34 seconds. It had taken, in all, thirty-four hours to record. Four years earlier, the entire recording of the Beatles' first album, *Please Please Me*, was all done and dusted in a day.

95

During that same week in January in which the Beatles began recording 'A Day in the Life', Joe Orton was contacted by Walter Shenson, the producer of *A Hard Day's Night* and *Help!*. Would he be interested in rewriting a script for the Beatles?

Orton – the most fashionable, witty and shameless young playwright of the day – tried to play it cool. 'Well, I'm frightfully up to my eyes in it at the moment. I'm writing my third play.'

'I'd certainly love to have you take a look at this draft,' said Shenson. 'I've discussed it with the boys, I mean I mentioned your name to

them. They didn't react too much, I must say. But I think I can persuade them to have you.'

Orton had just been taken down a peg or two. 'Yes,' he replied. 'Please send the script over and I'll read it.'

He found it dreary, but with scope for improvement, particularly as Shenson had said that the Beatles wanted to make it more challenging. In his diary Orton wrote: 'Already have the idea that the end should be a church with four bridegrooms and one bride ... but albeit in such a way that no one would object. Lots of opportunities for sexual ambiguities ...' He felt there were opportunities, too, for rehashing old material from a rejected novel he had written with his boyfriend, Kenneth Halliwell.

Over lunch, Walter Shenson told him that the Beatles had been thinking of doing a remake of *The Three Musketeers*.

'"Oh, no," I said. "That's been done to death."

'"Brigitte Bardot wanted to play Lady de Winter," he said.

'"She's been done to death as well," I said.

'"Oh, heh, heh, heh, boy!!" he said. "You certainly are quick."'

Orton got to work on a new script, with the provisional title of 'Up Against It'. By the end of the day he had completed the first two pages. He was ruthless in offloading a lot of old material onto the Beatles. 'I'm not bothering to write characters for them,' he confided to his diary. 'I shall just do all my box of tricks – Sloane and Hal – on them. After all, if I repeat myself in this film it doesn't matter. Nobody who sees the film will have seen Sloane or Loot.'

The next day, Walter Shenson phoned to say that Brian Epstein was 'delighted' he was on board. 'You'll be hearing either from Brian or Paul McCartney. So don't be surprised if a Beatle rings you up.'

'What an experience. I shall feel as nervous as I would if St Michael, or God was on the line.'

'Oh, there's not any need to be worried, Joe. I can say, from my heart, that the boys are very respectful of talent. I mean, most respectful of anyone they feel has talent. I can really say that, Joe.'

A week later, someone from Epstein's office invited him to 'meet the boys' the following Wednesday. Orton's report of his visit is characteristically comical: 'a youngish man with a hair-style which was way out in 1958, short, college boy, came up and said, "… I'm Brian Epstein's personal assistant." It crossed my mind to wonder why the English have never got around to finding a perfectly respectable word for "boy-friend". "I'm afraid there's been a most awful mix-up. And all the boys' appointments have been put back an hour and a half." I was a bit chilly in my manner after that. "Do you want me to come back at six?" I said. "Well, no. Couldn't we make another appointment?" "What guarantee is there that you won't break that?" I said. "I think you'd better find yourself a different writer." This said with indifferent success, though the effect was startling. He asked me to wait a minute and went away to return with Brian Epstein himself.

'Somehow I'd expected something like Michael Codron.* I'd imagined Epstein to be florid, Jewish, dark-haired and overbearing. Instead I was face to face with a mousey-haired, slight young man. Washed-out in a way. He had a suburban accent. I went into his office. "Could you meet Paul and me for dinner tonight?" he said. "We do want to have the pleasure of talking to you." "I've a theatre engagement tonight," I replied, by now sulky and unhelpful. "Could I send the car to fetch you after the show?"'

Orton arrived at Epstein's Belgravia house ten minutes early, and walked around to kill time. When he rang the bell, an old man appeared. 'He seemed surprised to see me. "Is this Brian Epstein's house?" I said. "Yes, sir," he said, and led the way to the hall. I suddenly realised that the man was the butler. I've never seen one before … He took me into a room and said in a loud voice, "Mr Orton." Everybody looked up and stood to their feet. I was just introduced to one or two people. And Paul McCartney. He was just as the photographs. Only he'd grown a moustache. His hair was shorter too. He was playing the latest Beatles record "Penny Lane". I liked it very much. Then he played the other side – Strawberry something. I didn't like this as much.'

They chatted, and agreed that the film should not be set in the 1930s. Later, they went down to dinner. 'The trusted old retainer – looking

* Theatre producer (b.1930), knighted in 2014.

too much like a butler to be good casting – busied himself in the corner. "The only thing I get from the theatre," Paul M. said, "is a sore arse."' Paul added that *Loot* was the only play he hadn't wanted to leave before the end.

'"I'd've liked a bit more," he said. We talked of the theatre. I said that compared with the pop-scene the theatre was square. "The theatre started going downhill when Queen Victoria knighted Henry Irving," I said. "Too fucking respectable."'

The two men talked of drugs, magic mushrooms and LSD. '"The drug not the money," I said. We talked of tattoos. And after one or two veiled references, marijuana. I said I'd smoked it in Morocco. The atmosphere relaxed a little.'

After dinner, they watched a television programme. 'It had phrases in it like "the in crowd" and "swinging London". There was a little scratching at the door. I thought it was the old retainer, but someone got up to open the door and about five very young and pretty boys trooped in. I rather hoped this was the evening's entertainment. It wasn't, though. It was a pop group called the Easybeats. I'd seen them on TV. I liked them very much then.'

At this point the French photographer Jean-Marie Périer arrived, bearing a set of photographs for the cover of *Strawberry Fields Forever*. 'Excellent photograph,' judged Orton. 'The four Beatles look different in their moustaches. Like anarchists in the early years of the century.'

Orton engaged an Easybeat in conversation, 'feeling slightly like an Edwardian masher with a Gaiety girl', before deciding it was time to go home. 'I had a last word with Paul M. "Well," I said, "I'd like to do the film. There's only one thing we've got to fix up." "You mean the bread?" "Yes." We smiled and parted. I got a cab home.'

The next day Orton spoke to his agent, Peggy Ramsay. '"We should ask 15,000 pounds," I said, "and then if they beat us down, remember no lower than 10,000. After all whether I do it or not is a matter of indifference to me." Peggy agreed. She said she'd ask 15 and try to get 12 and a percentage. "If they won't pay us 10 they can fuck themselves," I said. "Of course, darling," Peggy said.'

Leaving Ramsay to sort out the contract, Orton got down to the writing, unashamedly plundering his unpublished novel *Head to Toe* for most of the action. He thought it 'might have been designed with the Beatles in mind', though even in 1967 he was probably overestimating their appetite for decadence.

Within a fortnight he had almost completed his script. After a vague suggestion from Epstein that they might get Antonioni to direct the film, Orton heard nothing more from either Shenson or Epstein; both failed to return his calls. A livid Peggy Ramsay described Epstein as 'an amateur and a fool'. In his diary, Orton condemned him as 'a thoroughly weak, flaccid type'.

After some time, he was informed that 'Up Against It' was being returned to him. 'No explanation why. No criticism of the script. And apparently, Brian had no comment to make either. Fuck them.' But in his heart, he knew full well why they had turned it down. 'By page 25, they [the Beatles] had committed adultery, murder, dressed in drag, been in prison, seduced the niece of a priest, blown up a war memorial and all sorts of things like that. I can't really blame them, but it would have been marvellous.'

Within a week, the producer Oscar Lewenstein purchased Orton's rejected script for £10,000. On 9 August a chauffeur arrived at Orton's Islington flat to drive him to Twickenham Studios for a meeting with Lewenstein and the Beatles' old film director, Richard Lester. When there was no answer he telephoned Lewenstein, who told him to try again. Finally he looked through the letterbox, and saw the naked body of a bald man lying flat on the hallway floor.

The police found two corpses: Kenneth Halliwell on the floor, and Joe Orton on the bed, bludgeoned to death with a hammer. Orton's brilliant success had exacerbated Halliwell's already heightened sense of failure. After killing Orton, he had swallowed twenty-two Nembutals, washed down with a can of grapefruit juice.

At Joe Orton's funeral in the West Chapel of Golders Green Crematorium they played 'A Day in the Life', which had been Joe's favourite track. Some thought it too quiet; others disapproved of the way all the psychedelic references had been spliced out, on the un-Ortonesque grounds of good taste. On the way out of the chapel, one of the mourners pointed out that the booming piano chord at the end sounded just like the lid of a coffin being banged shut.

96

The further they travelled, the more they looked back. They were Pied Pipers, leading their generation in a conga along untrodden paths; but they were also the little boys at the end of the line, filled with longing for the world they had left behind.

After the Beatles finished playing the Liverpool Empire in December 1963, John went to his Aunt Harrie's house, and rootled through his old bits and pieces. His school friend Pete Shotton looked on in amazement as John sorted through old books and drawings: 'It seemed to me that John, at a glittering crossroads of his life and career, was grasping instinctively for the mementoes of his childhood – as if these reassuringly familiar objects might somehow ease his transition into an unknowable future.'

At the age of twenty-four, John was perplexed by the complexities of adulthood, and yearning for days gone by. 'When I was younger, so much younger than today'. Aged twenty-five, he sang wistfully of the 'places I'll remember all my life'. At twenty-six, his great eulogy to childhood, 'Strawberry Fields Forever', juxtaposed the hallucinogenic and the nostalgic, like an acid trip in a nursery. Paul has described the Salvation Army garden on which it was based as a form of utopia, John's 'secret garden … there was a wall you could bunk over and it was a rather wild garden, it wasn't manicured at all, so it was easy to hide in. The bit he went into was a secret garden like in *The Lion, the Witch and the Wardrobe*, and he thought of it like that, it was a little hideaway for him where he could maybe have a smoke, living his dreams a little, a getaway. It was an escape.'

Some of Lennon and McCartney's darkest songs exhibit the ruthlessly jaunty quality of nursery rhymes. Bungalow Bill goes into the jungle with his gun and kills animals; Maxwell murders his victims with a silver hammer. John's solo song 'My Mummy's Dead' has the same tune as 'Three Blind Mice', whose tails are chopped off with a carving knife.

When Kenneth Tynan was working on the stage version of two of John's books for the National Theatre, he set himself the tricky task of trying to explain what they meant to a bemused Laurence Olivier. 'John's poems are all about the beginning of things,' he said. 'The first awareness of cinema, of books, or poetry. Through that, we get a whole picture of his childhood in Liverpool.' He then remembered something the Maharishi had said about 'that absorption that comes when children are playing and they're nowhere else'.

For his part, Paul had been brought up on family sing-songs. It gave him pleasure to write music that his father might have played 'a long, long time ago'. The Beatles' surreal TV film *Magical Mystery Tour* was regarded as almost incomprehensibly adult by most viewers at the time, but it was largely formed of random memories of childhood. 'I've had this idea,' Paul told his assistant Alistair Taylor when he was wondering what to film. 'Do they still do mystery tours on buses?' For all its progressive wackiness, it was a trip into the past, dotted with scenes from the Beatles' childhoods – brass bands, sing-songs on coaches, Busby Berkeley dance routines, men with knotted hankies on their heads, tug-of-wars at village fêtes – all viewed through the distorting mirrors of dreams or LSD or both. The Beatles embarked on the filming with the capriciousness of children. Paul once phoned Taylor at two in the morning saying, 'I want a dozen midget wrestlers by tomorrow.' The film looks ramshackle because that's what it was: ideas that had occurred overnight would be filmed the next day. One morning John said to Paul, 'God, I had the strangest dream.' 'Come on, then,' replied Paul. 'Remember it and we'll film it.' John said he had turned into a waiter and had been shovelling spaghetti over someone. 'Fantastic!' said Paul. 'That's on!'

On its release in May 1967, *Sgt. Pepper's Lonely Hearts Club Band* was hailed as a vision from the future. Timothy Leary, allergic to understatement, declared, 'John Lennon, George Harrison, Paul McCartney and Ringo Starr are mutants. Evolutionary agents sent by gods, endowed with mysterious powers to create a new human species.' Even the more nuanced Kenneth Tynan considered it 'a decisive moment in the history of Western civilisation'.

But it is as much an exercise in playing about with the past: a wallow in nostalgia, embroidered with quaint brass bands and fairground paraphernalia. Hippies loved to spot references to dope and LSD in the album, but Paul's grandfather Joe, the tuba-player in his workplace* company band, would have spotted just as many allusions to Edwardian circuses and music halls. The title track looks back twenty years to when 'Sgt. Pepper taught the band to play'; 'Getting Better' is based in school; in 'She's Leaving Home', the runaway girl's parents 'sacrificed most of our lives'; 'Being for the Benefit of Mr Kite' celebrates the good old days, when a splendid time was guaranteed for all; in 'Good Morning Good Morning', John decides to 'take a walk by the old school', and finds 'nothing has changed it's still the same'. Even in the most outwardly progressive of the tracks, 'A Day in the Life', John sees a film in which 'the English army had just won the war'; and 'When I'm Sixty-Four' extends the reach of nostalgia into the future, with Paul looking forward to the time when he can look back on a golden past.

* Cope Bros & Co. They manufactured tobacco products – snuff, cigarettes, pipe tobacco, cigars.

97

Figures on the cover of Sgt. Pepper's Lonely Hearts Club Band

Fred Astaire, dancer
Mahavatara Babaji, guru
Aubrey Beardsley, artist
The Beatles, in person and in waxwork
Larry Bell, sculptor
Wallace Berman, artist
Issy Bonn, comedian
Marlon Brando, film star
Bobby Breen, singer
Lenny Bruce, comedian
William Burroughs, author
Lewis Carroll, author
Stephen Crane, author
Aleister Crowley, author, occultist
Tony Curtis, film star
Marlene Dietrich, singer, film star
Dion, singer
Diana Dors, actress
Bob Dylan, singer songwriter
Albert Einstein, physicist
W.C. Fields, comedian
Sri Yukteswar Giri, guru
Huntz Hall, actor
Tommy Handley, comedian

Oliver Hardy, comedian
Aldous Huxley, novelist and philosopher
James Joyce, author
Carl Jung, psychologist
Stan Laurel, comedian
T.E. Lawrence (Lawrence of Arabia)
Richard Lindner, artist
Sonny Liston, boxer
Dr David Livingstone, explorer
Karl Marx, economist and philosopher
Merkin, artist
Max Miller, comedian
Tom Mix, film star
Marilyn Monroe, film star
Sir Robert Peel, prime minister, founder of the police
Edgar Allan Poe, author
Tyrone Power, film star
Simon Rodia, sculptor
George Bernard Shaw, playwright
Terry Southern, author
Karlheinz Stockhausen, composer
Albert Stubbins, footballer
Stuart Sutcliffe, former Beatle
Shirley Temple, child film star
Dylan Thomas, poet
Johnny Weissmuller, actor
H.G. Wells, author
Mae West, film star
H.C. Westermann, sculptor
Oscar Wilde, author and playwright
Sri Paramahansa Yogananda, guru
Timothy Carey, actor (obscured by George Harrison)
Sophia Loren, actress (invisible behind the Beatles' waxworks)
Marcello Mastroianni, actor (invisible behind the Beatles' waxworks but for his hat)

Proposed but not used:

Mahatma Gandhi, political activist (dropped following pressure from Sir Joseph Lockwood, head of EMI)

Leo Gorcey, actor (dropped after asking $400 for his image)

Adolf Hitler (requested by John, but dropped as too controversial)

Jesus Christ (requested by John, but dropped as too controversial)

98

If you were twenty in the summer of 1967, San Francisco was the only place to be. But I was ten, and boarding at a Roman Catholic prep school called Farleigh House, in Farleigh Wallop, a few miles from Basingstoke. My friend Miller tried wearing a flower in his hair, only to be told by Major Watt to take it out at once. Major Watt was rumoured to be a Nazi spy. Someone had seen him in the school grounds late at night flashing secret messages to the Germans with a torch.

Gentle people were few and far between. Our new history master, Mr Wall, wore pink socks and had a slapdash, bohemian air about him, but he left under a cloud after dropping his trousers when someone enquired as to what colour his pants were. Gentleness, flowers, and even hair were in short supply.

I was studying hard for my confirmation. Why did God make me? God made me to know him, love him and serve him in this world and be happy with him forever in the next. In our confirmation classes we took a peculiar delight in cross-questioning Mr Callaghan on the fine points of Roman Catholic theology. It always came back to the same old desert island. 'Sir, sir, sir! But what if you were stuck on a desert island, and there was a baby who was dying, and the baby hadn't been christened, sir, and there was no water about, sir. Would you be allowed to use your spit, sir? Would you be allowed to use your *pee*, sir?'

We had two Masses a week, on Wednesdays and Sundays, and two Benedictions, on Tuesdays and Fridays. Every Benediction, we would sing a hymn called 'Tantum Ergo':

Tantum ergo
Sacramento
Veneremur cernui
Et antique
Documentum
Novo cedat ritui

I sang it twice a week for five years. None of us ever asked what it meant, and I still don't know. Sacraments, venerate, antique, documents … but its meaning didn't matter. Its sound was its meaning; its absence of meaning was its meaning. Latin was God's first language, and its meaning floated direct to heaven on a cloud of incense pouring out of a thurible swung with such vigour by the seniors that the new boys in the front row would often disappear, coughing and spluttering, in an unholy fog.

'Lady Madonna' came out halfway through the next spring term. I have a vivid memory of hearing it coming from a radio belonging to builders who were patching up the school swimming pool. Its title represented the perfect amalgam of the two essentials of a private Catholic education in Britain, suggesting that the Virgin herself was an aristocrat.

But what did it all mean? Why would Lady Madonna have to worry about making ends meet?

'Lady Madonna' was followed by 'Hey Jude' and 'Instant Karma'. Pop music was moving away from meaning, and closer to the language of 'Tantum Ergo', forcing sense to make way for something more mysterious.

At Boy Scout camp we sang 'Gin gan gooly-gooly-gooly-gooly watch-a, gin gan goo, gin gan goo'. In maths, we drew Venn diagrams. The Beatles sang 'I am the Walrus' ('goo-goo-ga-joo'). On Ash Wednesday we heard the priest repeat, 'Remember man that thou art dust and unto dust thou shalt return' over and over again as he rubbed ash onto our foreheads. On holy days of obligation we all went to visit priests' hidey-holes in Catholic stately homes. I often wondered whether groups with Latin names, like Procul Harum and Status Quo, were Catholic too. And behind it all, 'Tantum Ergo' was our soundtrack.

My reverence for the faraway heaven of San Francisco was never at odds with my reverence for what in another hymn we called 'Faith of Our Fathers'. I remember feeling a sharp sense of shock on first glimpsing the heading at the top of the music master's sheet music for 'While Shepherds Watched Their Flocks'. It simply said, 'Sox'.

Fifty or more years on, I make my living from parody, easing sense into nonsense, translating the words of others back into their original gibberish. I find 'Tantum Ergo' has lodged in my head, a dissident group of my brain cells forming a chapel choir, singing it at full blast at impromptu moments. And at other times I find the choir in my head singing,

> *Friday night arrives without a suitcase*
> *Sunday morning creeping like a nun*

or

> *Semolina pilchard*
> *Climbing up the Eiffel Tower*
> *Elementary penguin singing Hare Krishna …*

or

> *There's nowhere you can be that isn't where you're meant to be*

and my imagination keeps returning to Farleigh House, Farleigh Wallop, Basingstoke, Hampshire. Or perhaps it has always been stranded there, and I am the boarder who never came home.

99

At the dawn of the Summer of Love, Brian Epstein informed George Martin of his bold plans for the Beatles' biggest audience ever. 'He came to me and said, "Look, there's an international hook-up with all nations and the Beatles have been chosen to represent it. We'd be doing a live broadcast to 200, 300 million people in every part of the globe."'

A 'party atmosphere' was required, so, with time running out, Epstein instructed Tony Bramwell to gather suitably groovy stars for the next day's live broadcast. Bramwell decided to trawl the most fashionable clubs: the Speakeasy, the Cromwellian, the Bag o'Nails, the Scotch of St James. In the Speakeasy he found Keith Moon hurling peanuts around, 'absolutely stonkers'. Moon eagerly accepted the invitation, but turned down Bramwell's suggestion that he should first get some rest: 'If it's all the same to you, I'll just keep going.'

Bramwell found Mick Jagger in the Scotch of St James, and explained that the broadcast would be transmitted worldwide. Jagger's casual acceptance – 'No hassle' – possibly concealed a degree of envy. 'You couldn't *buy* that kind of publicity,' he said. Other clubs proved equally fruitful, with Eric Clapton and various Small Faces agreeing to turn up.

And so, on the afternoon of 25 June 1967, the beautiful people flowed into Studio One at Abbey Road: Jagger and Richards, Marianne Faithfull, Graham Nash of the Hollies, Gary Leeds of the Walker Brothers. In line with Royal Ascot, which was running simultaneously, many attendees had gone to some fuss with their clothes, not least Paul, who had stayed up all night applying psychedelic patterns to his shirt. Ringo wore a suit tailored for him by Simon and Marijke from the Dutch design group The Fool, while Eric Clapton arrived with his hair freshly permed, a striking new advance in male grooming.

Watching film of the broadcast of 'All You Need is Love' is like finding the Summer of Love in a grain of sand. It starts with trumpeters from the thirteen-strong orchestra, in regulation dinner jacket and black tie, blasting out 'La Marseillaise'. Paul choruses 'Love, love, love' sitting cross-legged on a high stool, a red flower sticking out of the headphone on his left ear. The cellists have their eyes glued to their sheet music. How do they feel about being plunged into this brave new world of free love, its music so different from their own? Do these serious musicians, these men of gravitas, resent having to kowtow to a bunch of stoned hippies, or are they exhilarated at being allowed into this magical universe where there's nothing you can do that can't be done?

John has one hand pressed on the headphone over his left ear, his eyes closed, his glasses a third of the way down his nose, two flowers sprouting from the top of his head with another popping up from his forehead like a miner's torch. He offhandedly chews gum as he sings 'Nothing you can say but you can learn how to play the game'. He appears unruffled by the idea of singing to 350 million viewers worldwide, but at the same time intent on the job in hand: he doesn't look around, or acknowledge the audience. Tony Bramwell said later that John was 'wired and speeding', but he gives a good impression of insouciance.

And so to the violin quartet, sitting in a circle, bespectacled and studious, one with a bald head bobbing in a sea of hair. The lead violinist, Sidney Sax, is fifty-four in a roomful of twenty-somethings; he also played on 'Yesterday' and 'Eleanor Rigby'.

The camera moves to a tape-machine, whirling around, then to a wider shot of the studio, decorated with flowers galore and, to add to the illusion of a children's party, hundreds of brightly coloured balloons. Aha! There's Paul's brother Mike, sitting on the floor close to John's knees, looking bored, or stoned, or possibly a bit of both. We see George for the first time, in red flares, fur coat and moustache, and there at the back the reassuring figure of Ringo, dependable as a bookend, chugging away on his drums, acting the hippy in a purple silk jacket with beads all over the place, but, despite the effort, still the obliging bus conductor.

Back to the beefy brass section, and the olden days. They are led by David Mason, forty-one, a professor at the Royal College of Music. Back in 1958 he played the flugelhorn at the premiere of Ralph Vaughan Williams' Ninth Symphony, conducted by Malcolm Sargent, in the presence of the composer.* Vaughan Williams – pupil of Ravel, friend of Holst – was then eighty-five years old, and just three weeks from death. For the first ten years of his life he had known his great-uncle, Charles Darwin. When the young Ralph had asked his mother about *On the Origin of Species*, she told him: 'The Bible says that God made the world in six days. Great-Uncle Charles thinks it took longer; but we need not worry about it, for it is equally wonderful either way.' From Charles Darwin to John Lennon in just three handshakes: the Beatles concertina time in the most extraordinary way.†

The studio is packed with so much stuff that it has an air of the set of *Steptoe and Son*: people remember the cameramen puncturing the spirit of love and peace with curses as they got caught up in all the odds and ends. In the background, a string puppet has four lettered balloons – L, O, V and E – attached to its head.

Many members of the audience stare into space, looking either bored or cool: in those days, it was hard to tell the difference. Mick Jagger sits to the front, facing away from the camera, two huge embroidered eyes staring out of the back of his jacket. Throughout, there are glimpses of oddities: as John sings 'All you need is love' for the umpteenth time, the camera floats to a bald man in a white shirt and black trousers, looking mildly cheesed-off, as though he's waiting to

---

* He also played the flugelhorn on 'Penny Lane'.

† Around this time Paul discussed Vietnam with Bertrand Russell, who remembered childhood meetings with William Gladstone; Gladstone himself used to breakfast with the elderly William Wordsworth (b.1770). So it's 'Blackbird' to 'Daffodils' in three meetings. Russell's grandfather, the Victorian prime minister Lord John Russell, visited Napoleon in exile on Elba. So, if you'd prefer, you can leap from Paul McCartney to Bertrand Russell to Lord John Russell to the Emperor Napoleon in just three bounds.

lock up. Seconds later, as John sings 'It's eea-seey!' someone who looks like Princess Margaret spins into view. *Might* she have been there? This was the Summer of Love, when the world went topsy-turvy: anything was possible.* In August, the EMI chairman Sir Joseph Lockwood was received by the Queen at Buckingham Palace. 'The Beatles are turning awfully *funny*, aren't they?' she said to him.

For some reason, George barely merits a look-in, and is not filmed at all during his brief guitar solo, once voted the fifth-worst of all time. Then the coda gets under way, the orchestra zipping through George Martin's masterly mish-mash of Bach, 'Greensleeves' and 'In the Mood', and the audience claps sluggishly along; Mick Jagger gives up halfway between claps. Where are the other members of the Rolling Stones, the Who, the Small Faces, the Walker Brothers, who were said to be there? I must have watched the video twenty-five times or more, but I still haven't caught sight of them.

Towards the end, five Beatle apparatchiks parade on, sandwich boards bearing the slogan 'All You Need is Love' in different languages hanging from their necks. They form a small, uncomfortable circle, like children forced into an Easter Parade. Tony Bramwell's board reads 'LOVE LOVE LOVE', and Alistair Taylor's 'LOVE ЛЮБОV AMOR AMORE'. Earlier in the day Taylor had been forced into a psychedelic shirt by Paul McCartney, who thought his usual office attire too square. Towards the back, someone holds a sign saying 'COME BACK MILLY', a personal message to one of Paul's aunts, away in Australia visiting her son and grandchildren.

As the song draws to a close, John and Paul start singing 'She loves you yeah, yeah, yeah,' which they first released just four years earlier, but which now breaks through the hippy fog like a hymn to lost youth.

And what of 'All You Need is Love'? Some Beatles purists find it too banal, its lyrics an odd mix of truisms – 'Nothing you can sing that can't be sung' – and untruisms – 'nowhere you can be that isn't where

---

* In April 1969 Princess Anne, wearing a navy-blue trouser suit, joined other audience members to dance onstage at the hippy musical *Hair*. 'The eighteen-year-old Princess broke into a hipswinging routine, flinging her arms in abandon,' observed the *Daily Telegraph*.

you're meant to be', the whole thing too mushy and meaningless and contradictory to be taken seriously.

Ian MacDonald describes it as 'one of the Beatles' less deserving hits', adding that it 'owes more of its standing to its local historical associations than to its inspiration'. For him, it was sloppy and slapdash: 'Drug-sodden laziness was half the problem.' His argument was as much with the zeitgeist as with the song that expressed it: the idea that anything worthwhile can be attained without effort – it's *ea-seey* – and that every single person, however dull and droopy, can count himself an artist.

Yet at the same time, 'All You Need is Love' captures the zeitgeist like no other song, which is perhaps why it is loved by such a wide range of people: the boxer George Foreman, the comedy actress Penelope Keith, the dancer Wayne Sleep and the racing driver Jackie Stewart all chose it as a Desert Island Disc. When he was Home Secretary in the mid-1990s, Michael Howard used to play the Beatles in his government car. He considers 'All You Need is Love' 'perhaps the quintessential record of the sixties'. On the other side of the Atlantic, Al and Tipper Gore played it at their 1970 wedding. In 2005 John's transcription of the verse, which he used as a crib at the recording, sold for $1 million at auction.

Brian Epstein seemed at his happiest and most relaxed that day. It was, he declared, the best thing the Beatles had ever done: 'It's a wonderful, beautiful, spine-chilling song.' He attended the session in an open-necked shirt and black velvet suit, looking unusually carefree. Maybe the song said everything he was too tortured to express. He could look through the window at the utopia beyond, but the window itself remained firmly closed. No one you can save that can't be saved; except for Brian. On that day, he had nine weeks left to live.

100

A month before his death, Brian Epstein wrote to his American business partner Nat Weiss, thanking him for his kind words following the recent death of his father.

He went on: 'The week of Shiva is up tonight and I feel a bit strange. Probably been good for me in a way. Time to think and note that at least I'm really needed by Mother. Also time to note that the unworldly Jewish circle of my parents' and brother's friends are not so bad. Provincial maybe, but warm, sincere and basic.'

He moved on, as always, to the Beatles: 'The boys have gone to Greece to buy an island … a dotty idea but they're no longer children and must have their own sweet way'.

The idea of buying a Greek island had been popped into John's head by his new best friend, 'Magic Alex' Mardas, perhaps the most fraudulent of all the Beatles' hangers-on.

Alexis Mardas was the son of a major in the Greek secret police. Arriving in London in 1965 on a student visa, he worked briefly as a television repairman before a chance meeting with Marianne Faithfull's husband, John Dunbar. Handy with a screwdriver, Mardas had constructed a box with small lights which flashed on and off at random. This was enough to convince Dunbar of his genius. The box served no practical purpose, which only added to its wonder.

Dunbar introduced him to the Rolling Stones, and Mardas seized the opportunity to pitch them a system of spotlights designed to go on and off to the beat of live music. The Stones employed the system on their next tour, though with mixed results. In Mardas's defence,

Dunbar claimed the system had worked 'some of the time' – possibly during the 'off' moments.

Having failed to convince the Stones, Mardas concentrated his energies on John Lennon. Cynthia watched as John succumbed to his charms: 'John was knocked out by Magic Alex ... He was a truly plausible person, and had the face of an innocent. His hair was as blond and as angelic as his smile. To John, who was totally ignorant of the tricks one can make with electricity, he believed that Alex really had something magic about him. He believed every word that he said.'

One morning John brought him along to Paul's house. 'This is my new guru – Magic Alex,' he said. Paul was a little taken aback, but made no comment. These were happy-go-lucky times, when scepticism was outlawed. 'We didn't really call anyone's bluff, it would have been a bit too aggressive,' says Paul. 'So we just let him get on with it.'

John regarded Mardas as a genius, and sought to reward him accordingly. On 1 May 1966 he was at Kenwood with his old friend Pete Shotton when he suddenly remembered that the following day was Mardas's birthday. 'Fuck me,' he said. 'Magic Alex is coming round tomorrow and I haven't even got anything for him. What can I give him, Pete?'

Shotton had no idea. John remembered that Mardas had purred appreciatively over the expensive Iso Grifo Italian sports car he had bought at the Earl's Court Motor Show a week before. At that time it was the only Iso Grifo in the UK. 'Let's give him the fucking Iso then!'

Pete and John wound great spools of ribbon around the car, rounding it all off with a big bow. 'The birthday boy was suitably impressed,' recalled Pete.

Mardas's adoption by the Beatles was perfectly timed. At the end of 1966 the group had been advised by their accountants to avoid an excessive tax bill by investing their money in freehold property and retail trading. They duly set up a number of companies under the umbrella of Apple Corps, among them Apple Records, Apple Films and Apple Retail (which ran their boutique on Baker Street). With the promise of far-reaching, mind-blowing inventions, Apple Electronics was given to Alex Mardas to run.

By now John was taking daily doses of LSD, which perhaps left him better equipped to appreciate the full glory he called 'one of those massive, big, sort of computerised laboratories they've been trying to invent for years'. In the months ahead, he allowed himself to be convinced by Magic Alex that generous sums of money were all that was needed to usher in a golden age of electronic wizardry.

Sitting in the studio one night, the Beatles were complaining to each other about their lack of privacy when John suggested they should create their own little kingdom, like an island, where they could build houses, and a studio, and even a school. Julian could be taught alongside the children of Bob Dylan, who would be sure to join them. At this point, Mardas's ears pricked up. There were, he volunteered, thousands of islands off the coast of Greece, and moreover they were 'dirt cheap'.

Mardas was summarily despatched to Greece to pick the perfect island. Within forty-eight hours he phoned to say he had found a cluster of Aegean islands, one of eighty acres, with a sixteen-acre olive grove and four secluded beaches, surrounded by four smaller islands, one for each Beatle. The asking price was £90,000. Mardas added that in his estimation the profits from the olive groves would pay back the total cost within seven years.

All four Beatles flew out to Greece, unfazed by the new ruling military junta's ban on both long hair and rock music, and its declarations that drug offences were to be punished with possible life sentences.

Through family connections, Mardas seems to have struck some sort of deal with the junta: in return for a form of diplomatic immunity, the Beatles would agree to pose for a series of pictures for the Ministry of Tourism. John was warned not to criticise the junta, and to behave himself. 'All I remember about the holiday is that some of us took acid, and we didn't have to go through passport control because Alex's father was so important,' recalled Pattie Boyd. As it happened, the moment he landed at Athens airport, John realised to his horror that he had left his drugs at home. 'What good is the Parthenon without LSD?' he complained. After a frantic call to the NEMS office, their willing dogsbody Mal Evans was on board the next flight with the mislaid package.

'It was a great trip,' recalled George. 'John and I were on acid all the time, sitting on the front of the ship playing ukuleles. Greece was on the left; a big island on the right. The sun was shining and we sang "Hare Krishna" for hours and hours.'

They went ahead with the purchase, against the advice of their accountants, who insisted it would place their already precarious finances in further jeopardy. Arrangements for transferring the money were made directly with the Chancellor of the Exchequer, James Callaghan. At one point the avuncular Callaghan wrote to the Beatles informing them that £95,000 was 'the absolute limit' he would allow to flow out of Britain, adding in his own hand at the foot of the letter, 'But not a penny more … I wonder how you're going to furnish it?'

This particular problem was solved by indifference. Having bought the islands, the Beatles immediately lost interest, forgot to build their utopia, and never visited them again. A year later they sold them for a profit of £11,400. Looking back, George noted approvingly that 'It was about the only time the Beatles ever made any money on a business venture.'

101

George and Pattie flew from Greece to California, where they attended a recording session by the Mamas and the Papas, dropped in on Ravi Shankar's music school, and dined out on Sunset Strip. On 7 August 1967 they flew to San Francisco in a private Learjet with Derek Taylor and Neil Aspinall to see Pattie's sister Jenny, who was living there. It is probably no coincidence that the B-side to 'All You Need is Love' is 'Baby, You're a Rich Man'.

After lunch with Jenny, George and his gang thought it would be fun to drive to Haight-Ashbury, the hippy district, where the grooviest musicians – Jefferson Airplane, the Grateful Dead, Janis Joplin – were known to hang out. On their way there, Derek passed around LSD. 'Since we were going to Haight-Ashbury, it seemed silly not to,' recalled Jenny. As they got out of the car, 'the acid kicked in and everything was just whoah, psychedelic and very … I mean, it was just *completely fine*.'

George hoped to wander around unrecognised in his blue denim jacket, psychedelic jeans, heart-shaped shades and moccasins: after all, most people in Haight-Ashbury were trying to look just like him, so who could tell the difference? Moreover, San Francisco was famous for being mellow: even if the hippies did recognise him, they would surely be too laid-back to give him any hassle.

So it came as a surprise when George and Pattie drifted into a shop, and found it immediately filling with new customers. As they left the shop and walked along the street, a crowd of people trailed behind them. Pattie could even hear them muttering, 'The Beatles are here, the Beatles are in town …'

It wasn't what George had expected. 'We walked down the street, and I was being treated like the Messiah.' How did it feel to be one of the beautiful people? At that very moment, most uncomfortable. Pattie was shaken: 'We were expecting Haight-Ashbury to be special, a creative and artistic place, filled with beautiful people, but it was horrible – full of ghastly drop-outs, bums and spotty youths, all out of their brains. Everybody looked stoned – even mothers and babies – and they were so close behind us they were treading on the backs of our heels. It got to the point where we couldn't stop for fear of being trampled.'

Hoping to shake off these hangers-on, they set off for Golden Gate Park, to the area that had recently become known as Hippie Hill. But George had become an unwitting Pied Piper. As the five of them sat down on the grass, a stream of hippies followed suit, to be joined by many more.

From the back of the gathering a guitar was produced, and passed from hand to hand to the front, before finally reaching George. It then dawned on Pattie that they wanted more from him than he was either

willing or able to give. 'I had the feeling that they'd listened to the Beatles' records, analysed them, learnt what they thought they should learn, and taken every drug they'd thought the Beatles were singing about. Now they wanted to know where to go next. And George was there, obviously, to give them the answer.'

George made an attempt to give them a little of what they wanted, demonstrating the guitar's chords – 'This is G, this is E, this is D' – rather than singing a song. A girl started yelling, 'Hey! That's George Harrison! That's George Harrison!' Hearing the cry, more hippies began to edge towards him; the crowd grew bigger and bigger.

They all started calling for a song, but George, increasingly frightened, politely handed back the guitar, saying, 'Sorry, man, we've got to go now.'

As he and his friends stood up to walk away, a hippy approached him saying, 'Hey, George, do you want some STP?' George hesitated. A week or two before, five thousand tabs of STP had been distributed at the Summer Solstice Celebration, and a large number of people had ended up in hospital. 'No, thanks, I'm cool, man,' he said, and carried on walking.

The hippy was affronted, saying, 'Hey, man – you put me down,' then turning to the crowd of followers and complaining, 'George Harrison turned me down!' The easy-going, hippy-dippy mood suddenly altered. 'The crowd became hostile,' recalled Pattie. 'We sensed it because when you're that high you're very aware of vibes.'

George and the others began to walk away slowly, before it dawned on them that their car was parked a mile away, so they picked up their pace. But as they walked faster, so did the crowd. George experienced some form of panic attack, accelerated by the LSD: 'It was like the manifestation of a scene from a Hieronymus Bosch painting getting bigger and bigger, fish with heads, faces like vacuum cleaners.'

Neil Aspinall remembered them growing ever more frantic. The drugs had made them lower their guard, putting them in the same situation they'd always taken such pains to avoid. By now, a thousand people or so were chasing them. 'In the end, we were running for our lives.'

At last they spotted their limousine, and jumped into it, slamming the doors. The crowd of hippies circled the car. 'The windows were full of these faces, flattened against the glass, looking at us.' They began rocking the car. Adulation had turned to menace, and menace to attack. Somehow, George and his friends managed to inch the car forward, and then shot away.

It was the last time George ever took LSD; never again would he place his faith in followers. 'It certainly showed me what was really happening in the drug culture. It wasn't what I'd thought – spiritual awakening and being artistic – it was like alcoholism, like any addiction. That was the turning point for me – that's when I went right off the whole drug cult and stopped taking the dreaded lysergic acid.'

102

Another guitar-playing Messiah figure on Hippie Hill that Summer of Love was also attracting a flock of devotees.

Earlier in the year, Charlie Manson had come to the end of seven years in prison for forging checks and jumping parole. During that time he had read up on the Bible, and Scientology. With his high IQ he had been fast-tracked by the authorities onto a special course studying *How to Win Friends and Influence People* by Dale Carnegie, in the hope that it would help him forge a better, more productive life. Carnegie's book certainly chimed with his key beliefs. 'Everything you or I do springs from two motives: the sex urge and the desire to be great,' wrote Carnegie.

On his release that March, Manson had headed for Haight-Ashbury, fuelled by his faith in himself as a musician, and his mission to recruit followers from the 75,000-odd youngsters set to gravitate there during the Summer of Love. Unlike Manson, most of them were in search of something – or someone – greater than themselves.

Though his time in prison lasted from June 1960, when the Beatles were still the Silver Beetles, to March 1967, when they were recording *Sgt. Pepper*, Manson had managed to imbibe their songs on prison radios, and was in the habit of telling his fellow jailbirds that one day he would outshine them.

Coloured by his paranoia, the Beatles' lyrics formed a vital part of Manson's philosophy. By combining them with passages from the Book of Revelation, he constructed an urgent message of revolution and destruction. In Haight-Ashbury he passed on his findings to the starry-eyed youngsters who gathered around him, some of them sixteen years old, barely half his age.

103

During that same period, the Beatles were in search of a guru of their own. It was Pattie Boyd who first had the idea. Browsing through the Sunday newspapers in February 1967, she chanced upon an advertisement for a Transcendental Meditation course in central London. 'Perfect. Off we went to Caxton Hall and enrolled in the Spiritual Regeneration Movement. In the course of a long weekend we were initiated and given our mantras.'

The leader of the Spiritual Regeneration Movement, Maharishi Mahesh Yogi, was a somewhat mysterious figure, either fifty or sixty years old, or somewhere in between: it was his belief that such personal considerations distracted from the universality of his message. The son of a civil servant, Mahesh Prasad Varma grew up in the central Indian city of Jabalpur, going on to take a degree in physics and mathematics at the University of Allahabad. In 1940 – the year John and Ringo were born – he became a disciple of a swami known as Shri Guru Deva, who, alone among Indian mystics, was to crop up in a Beatles song, 'Across the Universe'.

On the death of Guru Deva in 1953, Mahesh Prasad Varma restyled himself Maharishi ('great seer') and carved out a career of his own. By 1958 he had developed a ten-year plan for 'the regeneration of the whole world through meditation'. To this end he developed spiritual techniques such as levitation, or 'yogic flying', in which participants either fly, hop or bounce, depending upon their relationship with gravity. The Maharishi's promise of 'the positive experience of Heavenly Bliss' proved especially attractive to well-heeled Westerners, and in 1959 he set up a base for his Spiritual Regeneration Movement in

Hollywood, from where he embarked upon an annual worldwide tour, taking in Hong Kong and Hawaii. Far from timid, he called for a new Spiritual Regeneration Movement Centre for every million people on the planet: each of these centres would then train a thousand initiators, who would each initiate a thousand more, and so on, until all mankind had been cured of suffering.

For Pattie, his classes were 'life-changing. I couldn't wait to tell George. As soon as he came home I bombarded him with what I had been doing, and he was really interested. Then, joy of joys, I discovered that Maharishi was coming to London in August to give a lecture at the Hilton Hotel. I was desperate to go, and George said he would come too. Paul had already heard of him and was interested, and in the end we all went – George, John, Paul, Ringo, Jane and I.' The session went well. 'We were spellbound.'

The next day, Friday, 25 August 1967, the Beatles cancelled a recording session and boarded a train to Bangor, where the Spiritual Regeneration Movement was holding its ten-day summer conference. Cynthia Lennon came too, along with Mick Jagger and Marianne Faithfull and Pattie's sister Jenny. Brian Epstein had been tempted, but was already committed to hosting a house party in Sussex. To be without Brian's guiding hand made the Beatles uneasy. It was, complained John, 'like going somewhere without your trousers on'. Within hours, they realised how much they relied on him: that evening they ate in a Chinese restaurant in Bangor, only to discover that they had no money to pay the bill. Over the past few years they had grown as demanding and defenceless as infants.

That Sunday morning, they heard of the sudden death of Brian Epstein. John, Paul, George and Ringo immediately went to the Maharishi for guidance. Marianne Faithfull looked on as the Maharishi told the Beatles, 'Brian Epstein is dead. He was taking care of you. He was like your father. I will be your father now.' It struck her that the Maharishi was exploiting their grief, and she found it creepy: 'These poor bastards just didn't know. It was the most terrible thing.'

The Beatles were soon surrounded by press and TV crews, anxious to gauge their reactions. John had never been more subdued.

He seemed punctured: 'I can't find words to pay tribute to him. It is just that he was lovable, and it is those lovable things we think about now.'

Paul said: 'This is a terrible shock. I am terribly upset.'

104

GEORGE MARTIN: No one could have conceived that it would happen, and the boys were completely broken up by it. They were like a ship without a rudder. One of the awful things is that, if Brian had lived, he would have lost the Beatles. He wouldn't have survived as their manager. Because they would have split up anyway. They would probably have sought their own, younger, different people to look after their affairs. Brian, by his own design, had become too fragmented, and the Beatles were too selfish to ever have someone like that. They wanted someone who did nothing else but the Beatles. Even more than that: by that time, Paul wanted someone who did nothing but Paul, John wanted someone exclusively, and so on. So it would have become an impossible situation.

JOANNE PETERSEN, PERSONAL ASSISTANT TO BRIAN EPSTEIN: Things started to unhinge pretty quickly, almost immediately. It seemed to me that things became unstable very quickly. Brian was the glue. He held it all together, and the moment he wasn't there it was like a rudderless ship. There was no one steering the ship.

DEREK TAYLOR: Had he lived, Brian might have been more decisive and more tenacious and seen the Beatles through a lot of the things that no one else could. John had a famous quote, 'We've fucking had it now,' and to the extent that they did break up, that's true.

MARIANNE FAITHFULL: The Beatles were just fucking around, really, with the Maharishi, that's all. Brian was much more than a brilliant businessman. He was a spiritual centre. So I think what happened with the Maharishi was a betrayal of spiritual values, that's how it must have appeared to Brian. If he had met the Maharishi, he would have seen immediately that this idiotic little guy wasn't going to be able to take his place. I think everybody realised that from the minute they met him.

Here's what would have happened if he hadn't taken the overdose. They would have come back to London and Brian would have said, 'How was it?' and they would have all cracked up laughing as if it was the most ridiculous thing. The trouble with him dying at that moment was that it actually pushed them into the arms of the Maharishi, whereas if he hadn't died, it would have blown over. The Maharishi was the most ludicrous little man you could imagine. Everybody realised this, and we were all embarrassed.

Brian had an incredible antenna for sensing things. If he had been there in London when they got back from Wales and answered the phone in his silk dressing gown when John or Paul rang, the Beatles would not have gone to India and all these things would not have happened.

PAUL: Brian's death kind of opened the floodgates. It gave other people the possibility to come in whereas there had been no possibility before.

It would be too glib to suggest that the Beatles looked to the Maharishi to fill the gap left by Brian Epstein. Compared to Epstein, he was a fly-by-night. But by now the pace they had set themselves had become so rapid, their needs and quests and fads so random and restless, that perhaps they were bound to look for another hand to guide them.

John and George left Bangor so full of the benefits of Transcendental Meditation that a month later they appeared on *The Frost Report* to extol its virtues. The following week, they were invited back on the same show. Unusually, George was by far the more talkative of the two, rattling on about levels of consciousness:

> … Transcendental Meditation takes you to that transcendental level of pure consciousness, but by going there often enough, you bring that level of consciousness out onto this level, or you bring this level onto that level. But the relative plus that level becomes cosmic consciousness, and that means that you're able to hold on to the full bliss consciousness in the relative field, so you can go on about your actions all the time with bliss consciousness …

And so on; and on; and on. It says much for the awe in which the Beatles were held that the usually snappy David Frost let him drone on at such length, and on such an abstruse topic, leaving even his wildest claims unchallenged. At one point George mentioned that he had been reading a book about a yogi who lived to be 136, 'and there's another one, living in the Himalayas at this very moment … It seems pretty far out, you know, to the average person, who doesn't know anything about it. But this fellow has been there since before Jesus Christ, and he's still here now in the same physical body. They have control over life and death. They have control in everything, having attained that higher state of consciousness …'

105

On 23 August 1967, Brian Epstein had looked in on the second day of recording 'Your Mother Should Know'. Four days later he was dead. The Beatles hoped to attend his funeral in Liverpool two days later, but his family asked them to stay away, as they wanted to avoid any turmoil.

A week later, on the evening of 5 September, the four of them assembled at Abbey Road, determined to press on with the recording of *Magical Mystery Tour*. The mood was sombre. 'There was a pallor across the session that day,' recalled Geoff Emerick. 'We were all distracted, thinking about Brian.'

On his acoustic guitar, John went through a new song. 'I am he as you are he as you are me and we are all together,' he began.

Geoff Emerick wondered what on earth he was on about: 'Everyone seemed bewildered. The melody consisted largely of just two notes, and the lyrics were pretty much nonsense.'

Some of the lyrics seemed to stray beyond nonsense. When John sang 'pornographic priestess' and 'let your knickers down', George Martin turned to Emerick and whispered, '*What* did he just say?'

John finally reached the end. There was silence. John looked up at the sound box for George Martin's reaction. 'That one was called "I am the Walrus",' he said. 'So, what do you think?'

Martin was lost for words, but hesitation soon gave way to irritation. 'Well, John, to be honest, I have only one question. What the hell do you expect me to do with that?'

Nervous laughter ensued. It was evident to Emerick that John 'was clearly not amused'.

* * *

The impetus to write the nonsensical words of 'I am the Walrus' had sprung from a letter John was sent at the end of August by Stephen Bayley,* a fifteen-year-old pupil at John's old school Quarry Bank. Bayley explained that his English teacher was in the habit of playing Beatles songs in class, and getting the boys to analyse the lyrics, before weighing in with his own interpretation.

Pete Shotton, who was with John when he first read the letter, remembers John howling with laughter at the notion that his old school, which had once written him off as a failure, was now elevating his output to a set text. Shotton noticed how he saw it as a challenge. 'Inspired by the picture of that Quarry Bank literature master pontificating about the symbolism of Lennon–McCartney, John threw in the most ludicrous images his imagination could conjure.'

Trying to think of the daftest rhymes, John remembered a playground jingle. 'Pete, what's that "Dead Dog's Eye" song we used to sing at Quarry Bank?'

Pete thought for a moment, then remembered:

> Yellow matter custard, green slop pie
> All mixed together with a dead dog's eye,
> Slap it on a butty, ten foot thick
> Then wash it all down with a cup of cold sick.

Versions of this ditty were chanted by schoolchildren the length and breadth of the country in the 1950s.† It is included in *The Lore and Language of Schoolchildren* by Iona and Peter Opie, first published in 1959, alongside many regional variants. In Manchester the custard was 'splish splashy' and the pie was made of giblets; in the Forest of Dean it was 'scab and matter', and came with 'green snot pies'; in Ipswich the

---

* Bayley (1951–) grew up to be an iconoclastic cultural critic, and the author of books about cars, sex, and the Albert Memorial.

† And well into the sixties: I remember chanting it in the playground of Grove House School in Effingham, Surrey, circa 1964.

pie was at its least tempting – it was made of bogie, and served with hard-boiled snails and a dead man's eye.

John was delighted by Pete's recital. 'That's it!' he said, reaching for a pen. 'Fantastic!' He duly wrote down 'Yellow matter custard', before adding other bits and pieces retrieved randomly from childhood memories. 'He thought of semolina (an insipid pudding we'd been forced to eat as kids) and pilchard (a sardine we often fed to our cats). "Semolina pilchard climbing up the Eiffel Tower ..." John intoned, writing it down with considerable relish.' He was clearly amused by the idea that teachers would spend their time clawing away at an inner meaning. 'Let the fuckers work *that* one out, Pete,' he said.

The song was further filtered through John's childhood fascination with the topsy-turvy world of Lewis Carroll, and in particular the poem 'The Walrus and the Carpenter', which is told to Alice by Tweedledee in *Through the Looking-Glass*. Beneath its merry rhythm lies a Hannibal Lecterish tale of two exquisite psychopaths. It starts with the Walrus encouraging a crowd of young oysters to join him and the Carpenter as they walk along the shore. But once they get to their destination:

> 'A loaf of bread,' the Walrus said,
> 'Is what we chiefly need:
> Pepper and vinegar besides
> Are very good indeed –
> Now if you're ready, Oysters dear,
> We can begin to feed!'
>
> 'But not on us!' the Oysters cried,
> Turning a little blue.
> 'After such kindness, that would be
> A dismal thing to do!'

The Walrus and the Carpenter immediately change the subject, complimenting the oysters and pointing out the lovely view. The Walrus then grows sentimental:

'I weep for you,' the Walrus said:
'I deeply sympathize.'
With sobs and tears he sorted out
Those of the largest size,
Holding his pocket-handkerchief
Before his streaming eyes.

'O Oysters,' said the Carpenter,
'You've had a pleasant run!
Shall we be trotting home again?'
But answer came there none –
And this was scarcely odd, because
They'd eaten every one.

It is, as the psychoanalyst Paul Schilder pointed out some time ago, a poem of 'astonishing cruelty'. This cruelty, shielded by nonsense, clearly struck a chord with John.

As John predicted, his hotchpotch of words has indeed been subjected to all kinds of analysis – in fact, almost as much as *Alice in Wonderland* itself. Is it anti-capitalist ('pigs in a sty'), anti-academia ('expert texperts') or anti-bureaucracy ('corporation T-shirt')? You can find in it whatever you want. 'I was writing obscurely, à la Dylan, never saying what you mean, but giving the *impression* of something, where more *or* less can be read into it. It's a good game,' John confessed years later. He had, he added, written the entire song on LSD.

His dismissal of any serious intent has done nothing to staunch the flow of interpretations. And why should it? Some regard it as an attack on the police (imagining 'pilchard' to be John's near-homonymic pursuer Det. Sgt Pilcher*), while others see it as a defence of drug culture. The I-am-he-as-he passage has been interpreted as both a satirical attack on Eastern religion and an impassioned defence of it. For the Beatles' biographer Jonathan Gould, the Walrus is 'a potent symbol of John's contempt for the Beatles' idealized image as popular

* See pages 497–506.

heroes of youth'. Ian MacDonald, who considered it the high point of Lennon's songwriting oeuvre, believed the song was 'its author's ultimate anti-institutional rant – a damn-you-England tirade that blasts education, art, culture, law, order, class, religion, and even sense itself'. John's actor friend Victor Spinetti thought it an encrypted protest against family life.

Some have been keen to stake their claim to central roles in the story. 'I was the Egg Man,' wrote John's drinking partner Eric Burdon of the Animals in his autobiography. 'Or, as some pals called me, "Eggs". The nickname stuck after a wild experience I'd had at the time with a Jamaican girlfriend named Sylvia. I was up early one morning cooking breakfast, naked except for my socks, and she slid up behind me and cracked an amyl nitrate capsule under my nose. As the fumes set my brain alight, and I slid to the kitchen floor, she reached to the counter and grabbed an egg, which she broke into the pit of my belly. The white and yellow of the egg ran down my naked front, and Sylvia slipped my egg-bathed cock into her mouth and began to show me one Jamaican trick after another. I shared the story with John at a party at a Mayfair flat one night with a handful of blondes and a little Asian girl.

'"Go on, go get it, Egg Man," Lennon laughed over the little round glasses perched on the end of his hooklike nose as we tried the all-too-willing girls on for size.'

As it happens, Eric Burdon's claim has been subject to the vagaries of history, or at least historians, with many muddling up his role and making him the egger, not the egged.

John took a particular pride in 'I am the Walrus': 'It's one of those that has enough little bitties going to keep you interested even a hundred years later.' This may seem boastful, but fifty years on, it is also halfway to being true. Nevertheless, he came to think that he had made a mistake in casting himself as Carroll's Walrus. 'Later I went back and looked at it and realised that the Walrus was the bad guy in the story, and the Carpenter was the good guy. I thought, "Oh, shit. I've picked the wrong guy."' Hence, when it came to writing his self-referential song 'Glass Onion', he came up with the line, 'Here's another clue for you all – the Walrus was Paul.' But he was a slapdash reader. In the original poem there is little to choose between the Walrus and the Carpenter: both use their charm to lure the oysters away, before gobbling them up without a hint of remorse.

'What the hell do you expect me to do with that?' The answer to Martin's question was that John didn't have a clue, and nor did the others. Epstein's death had left them bewildered. At the start of the session Ringo had been close to tears, and John himself appeared to be in a state of shock. George looked beyond the here and now. 'Mr Epstein's body may be gone,' he said, 'but his spirit remains.' Not for the first time, Paul was the pragmatist: 'We just have to carry on, I suppose.'

'I distinctly remember the look of emptiness on all their faces while they were playing "I am the Walrus",' remembered Geoff Emerick. 'It's one of the saddest memories I have of my time with the Beatles.'

John told Martin and Emerick that he wanted his voice to sound as though it were coming from the moon. This left them none the wiser. Emerick set about distorting the amps to make John's voice sound both edgier and more ethereal. 'I had no idea what a man on the moon might sound like – or even what John was really hearing in his head – but, as usual, no amount of discussion with him could shed a lot of light on the matter.' The next day, John insisted on adding random sounds from the radio. George Martin rolled his eyes.

The completed mish-mash includes a snatch of dialogue from *King Lear*, and the Mike Sammes Singers* chanting 'Everybody's got one,

---

* The Mike Sammes Singers, easy-listening doyens of *Sing Something Simple*, had one of the most varied and least trumpeted careers in the history of popular music. Their voices can be heard on 'Let it Be' and 'Good Night', and they also provided backing for, among many others, Tom Jones on 'Delilah', Ken Dodd on 'Tears' and Olivia Newton-John on 'Banks of the Ohio'. They also sang the memorable theme song for Gerry Anderson's *Stingray*. The day after their 'I am the Walrus' session, they recorded a session with Kathy Kirby, and then went straight to the ATV studios to record *The Benny Hill Show*. In his days as a session musician, Elton John would occasionally work alongside them: 'Frightening isn't an adjective you would normally associate with the Mike Sammes Singers, who did backing vocals for everyone – they looked like middle-aged aunties and uncles who'd arrived at the studio direct from a golf-club dinner-dance. But if you had to sing alongside them, they suddenly struck the fear of God into you, because they were so good at what they did.'

everybody's got one', along with the playground ditty 'Oompah, oompah, stick it up your jumper.' It is both everything and nothing. It may derive, in George Martin's words, from 'organised chaos', but, like Coleridge's 'Kubla Khan', it somehow transcends interpretation to touch upon the sublime.

106

A Party:
Westbourne Suite, Royal Lancaster Hotel
Lancaster Terrace, Bayswater, London W2
21 December 1967

On 8 December 1967, the elaborately neurotic comic actor Kenneth Williams picks up his fountain pen and, in his perfect italic script, writes an enraged letter to a friend. 'Do you know those Beatles gave a private party recently at the new Royal Lancaster Hotel and their manager rang and asked if I would go along and compere their cabaret? – have you ever heard such impudence. Just cos you do it on the Telly don't mean you are available for functions does it? – the nerve of it.'

In fact, the party in question, to celebrate the completion of filming the *Magical Mystery Tour*, is not due to be held until 21 December, five days before its television transmission on Boxing Day.

Echoing the pantomime nature of *Magical Mystery Tour*, the party has a fancy-dress theme. Paul and Jane Asher come as a Pearly King and Queen, Derek Taylor as Adolf Hitler, Alistair Taylor as a matador, Tony Bramwell as a court jester, and Peter Brown as King Louis XIV, while George Martin and his wife Judy come as Prince Philip and Queen Elizabeth II. As though to emphasise their differences, John comes as a teddy boy, while Cynthia is a Regency lady in bonnet, crinoline and bows. She immediately feels overdressed, 'like the lady on the Quality Street tin.'

The party happens to coincide with one of John's brief reconciliations with his ne'er-do-well father, Fred, who dresses, appropriately enough, as 'My Old Man's a Dustman.' Earlier in the day Fred paid a real dustman £5 to swap clothes with him. Pete Shotton can't bear to be in his vicinity: 'He literally reeked of garbage, and all the other partygoers did their utmost to keep him at a safe distance.'

Even allowing for the bizarre freemasonry of showbiz, an unexpected guest is the portly comic actor Robert Morley, who arrives as Father Christmas. 'He was really sweating,' observes one guest. 'Perhaps it was a fault in the hotel's air conditioning, but he looked so uncomfortable, I couldn't believe he was doing it. I felt that perhaps his agent made him.'

Dinner is followed by a screening of *Magical Mystery Tour*. John sits at a table with his smelly father and Fred's young fiancée Pauline, dressed, just as appropriately, as a schoolgirl. At the same table are Cilla Black, dressed as a labourer, and her husband Bobby, as a nun.

There is a hiatus between the end of dinner and the beginning of the screening. 'Come on, John – do a number while we're waiting!' suggests Lulu, who is dressed as Shirley Temple, in white ankle-socks, carrying a giant lollipop, with her hair in ringlets, topped off with a bow.

'Not bloody likely,' replies John. 'How about you, Fred?'

This is a mistake. Alistair Taylor, who has organised the party, notes that Fred is 'pissed out of his head.' Consequently, when Fred leaps onto the stage he falls flat on his face.

After the screening the Bonzo Dog Doo-Dah Band take to the stage, and everybody starts to dance. John has always hated dancing, but is enticed onto the floor by the alluring sight of Pattie Harrison, who has come as a belly-dancer. Cynthia is the gooseberry, 'left sitting primly and stiffly, very much out in the cold'. Pete Shotton, dressed, like John, as a teddy boy, looks on as an unpleasant scene develops: 'Though Pattie had, undeniably, made herself especially desirable as a scantily clad belly-dancer, neither Cyn nor George were the least bit amused by John's open flirtation with her.' Upset by what is happening, Lulu, still clutching her giant lollipop, gives John a good telling-off.

At last Cynthia is asked to dance by Billy J. Kramer, who is dressed, by happy coincidence, as a Regency soldier. 'We made a lovely couple,' she recalls, 'until we tried to jive instead of waltz.' Catching her foot on her dress, Cynthia falls over, 'masses of material billowing out like a huge lavender balloon around my crumpled body'.

When John glances over in her direction, Cynthia catches his eye. 'His looks on that occasion were not of love or admiration, but pure embarrassment. I was letting him down yet again.'

107

The Beatles failed to attend the first Apple board meeting. Those who managed to make it included John's childhood friend Pete Shotton, who had been appointed even though his only previous experience of business was owning a newsagent's shop on Hayling Island, given him by John.

Shotton kicked off the meeting by saying that he didn't know anything about Apple: could the other members of the board fill him in? His request was met with silence: no one else knew anything either. Presently Clive Epstein, brother of the late Brian, piped up. 'Well, it was my impression,' he began, 'that Apple would manufacture greetings cards and the boys have agreed to write the little poems for them.'

As each board member spoke, it became increasingly clear that everyone present had a different notion of Apple's aims. Eventually, Terry Doran,* who had co-owned Brydor Cars with Brian, turned to Shotton. 'Thank God you're here, Pete. As you can see, nobody else really has much of a clue. We desperately need someone like you who can get this whole thing organised.' The meeting broke up shortly afterwards, each member saying 'Best of luck, Pete,' and 'Congratulations, Pete,' as they left.

Pete then drove straight to John's house to find out what on earth was going on. John laid out his business plan. 'In a nutshell, what's going on is this,' he said. 'The Beatles have been told that we have £3 million, which will have to be paid off in tax if we don't put it into a business. All we've really got to do, then, is just fucking spend it! So

* Sometimes credited as the 'man from the motor trade' in 'She's Leaving Home'.

why not have a go at business and have a few laughs while we're at it?'

As it happened, the laughs were few and far between. The business unrolled, and then, just as swiftly, unravelled. Early on, the music paper *Disc and Music Echo* got together with Apple to announce a nationwide hunt for new stars: 'There are hundreds of unheard-of groups who, with the right handling, could be every bit as big as today's top pop names.' Readers were asked to vote for the best groups in their area, on the understanding that Apple would despatch talent scouts to check out the winners. The six 'lucky readers' who had nominated the winning group were to be presented with vouchers for £25 to spend on clothes at the brand-new Apple Boutique.

Thousands of readers sent in nominations; almost as many posted music tapes and novels and poems. No more than a handful were ever heard or read or even opened. Instead, they were piled into cardboard boxes which were then stacked in a dark nook at the Apple headquarters that came to be known as the Black Room. Pete Shotton didn't like to think about it. 'It was really quite a heartbreaking sight, when one stopped to consider all those starry-eyed kids who had been left sitting on the edge, waiting to hear from the Beatles and to claim their Bentleys.'

In no time at all, every nutter and chancer in town was making a beeline for Apple, ready to be showered with fame and fortune. One young American who worked there, Richard DiLello, compared the office hallway to 'the waiting room at a VD clinic in Haight-Ashbury at the height of the Acid Madness of '67'. One day he was summoned to deal with a man who claimed to be able to communicate with animals, and vice versa. As proof, he produced from his pocket a poem he had transcribed at London Zoo, with alternate verses composed by himself and his friends the animals. Perhaps the only real surprise is that he was not immediately given his own department to supervise.

One of the first beneficiaries of the Apple munificence was the indomitable Japanese artist Yoko Ono, whose relationship with John was still essentially one-sided. Ono had put in an application for £5,000 to finance an exhibition at the Lisson Gallery of white objects – a chair, a table, a shoe, a hat – all cut in half. Having failed to receive the go-ahead, she waylaid John at Apple headquarters. 'I feel like only half,' she told him. 'You are my other half, and I am yours. We have been lost in space searching, and now we have found each other.'

John gave her the money, on condition that his name would not be associated with her exhibition. Tony Bramwell remembered asking him why he had agreed to it. 'To get rid of her,' John had replied. 'With women like that you have to pay them off, or they never stop pestering you.'

In this, Yoko was to prove him wrong. She immediately sent out a press release announcing a joint exhibition: 'Half a Wind by Yoko Ono and John Lennon'.

108

Parallels with the childhood of Yoko Ono may be found in that of Queen Victoria, who was said never to have looked over her shoulder before sitting down, as she knew a footman would always be there, ready with a chair. The Ono family kept thirty servants, all of whom would approach the young Yoko on their knees, and then leave on their knees, shuffling backwards. Whenever Yoko ventured beyond her family home, she was forbidden from sitting down until a servant had cleaned the seat with cotton wool soaked in disinfectant.

Yoko Ono was born on 18 February 1933 (barely thirty-two years after the death of Queen Victoria), the product of a union between two of the wealthiest families in Japan. Her maternal great-grandfather, Zenjiro Yasuda, had made his fortune in currency-dealing, going on to found the Third National Bank of Japan. Her father, Eisuke Ono, was also a banker, rising to become director of the New York office of the Bank of Tokyo.

On a trans-Pacific ship from Japan to see her father in San Francisco, little Yoko took part in a fancy-dress competition. Electing to go as Shirley Temple, she walked away with the first prize. Who knows? This early triumph may have had a lasting impact, ensuring that, for the rest of her long life, she would draw on the simple utopian messages, laced with occasional silliness, characteristic of Shirley Temple's most celebrated songs, such as 'Tra-la-la-la':

Tra-la-la-la, what a merry world we live in
Tra-la-la-la, all of it is yours and mine
So wear a smile, sing a little while it's raining
And through the clouds, ev'ry little star will shine

Clouds were also to be a mainstay of Yoko Ono's maxims for the next eighty years or so. For instance, in 'Cloud Piece', from her 1964 volume *Grapefruit*, she writes:

Imagine the clouds dripping. Dig a hole in your garden to put them in.

Four years later, bombarding John in Rishikesh with letters, she advised him:

I'm a cloud. Watch for me in the sky.

Over the decades that followed, she seemed unable to spot a cloud without drawing a moral from it. In 2019, now aged eighty-six, she put this cloud-based question to her 4.78 million Twitter followers:

When I look at clouds, I see our beauty and transcience [sic]. What do you see?

In 'Polly Wolly Doodle', Shirley Temple sang:

I came to a river and couldn't get across
Sing Polly Wolly Doodle all the day
I jumped on a gator and thought he was a hoss
Sing Polly Wolly Doodle all the day.

Similar themes of happiness gained through impossible feats are threaded throughout Ono's entire oeuvre. In one of her maxims, she advises the reader to 'Carry a heavy object on your back'; once it is in place, you should 'Dance as swiftly as you can.' In another she tells us to sit at a dock, watch the seagulls dance and 'dance with them in your mind'. We must then 'Keep dancing until you can feel their heartbeats.'

Certainly these Ono maxims:

> Carry a bag of peas. Leave a pea wherever you go.

and:

> Imagine letting a goldfish swim across the sky. Let it swim from the West to the East. Drink a liter of water.

clearly echo Temple's most celebrated song:

> On the good ship *Lollipop*
> It's a sweet trip to a candy shop
> Where bon-bons play
> On the sunny beach of Peppermint Bay

Most days, Yoko still takes the trouble to share her words of wisdom on Twitter. Their cosy optimism makes little Shirley Temple seem jaded: 'All animals feel love', 'You have infinite wisdom', 'Start by imagining a world where all of us are having good fun'.

Sometimes she is political: 'The prospect of making big money always dulls the senses of some people, even if it is very bad for the health of all living things on the planet,' she tweeted on 22 May 2019. 'We have to keep communicating the reality until these people wake up.' Her own net worth is currently estimated at $600 million.

Occasionally she stops dispensing advice, and asks for it instead. At 5.18 p.m. on 2 February 2019 she tweeted this request: 'Give us some advice that will make our lives heal and shine.'

A flood of advice followed, much of it more straightforward than she might have anticipated:

> 'Put marmite on your cheese on toast before you put it under the grill.'
>
> 'The quickest way to change lines at Green Park is to ignore all the (very circuitous) directions and head up the escalator to the ticket hall and down the relevant escalator to your chosen line. You're welcome.'
>
> 'Open a pesky bin liner with ease by giving the top of it a slight stretch.'
>
> 'Put a splash of fizzy water in your Yorkshire pudding batter.'
>
> 'Turn your tins of beans upside down when you put them in the cupboard, that way none get stuck in the bottom when you open them.'
>
> 'A decent pair of oven gloves is worth 1000 towels.'

> 'Avoid Tesco Value rice crispies. They're really horrible.'
>
> 'If you're commuting from Barnsley to Sheffield a McDonald's coffee is now 10p cheaper at Tankersley than at Meadowhall Retail Park.'

And:

> 'Don't split up the Beatles when they have a few more albums in them.'

Yoko Ono was educated at Gakushin, the most distinguished private school in Japan; the Crown Prince Akihito was a contemporary. At the age of eighteen she moved with the rest of her family to New York, to join her father, who had been appointed president of the Bank of Tokyo in the US. There, she entered Sarah Lawrence College in Bronxville; Barbara Walters and Princess Lee Radziwill (*née* Bouvier) were among her fellow students. In 1956, while John Lennon was struggling with his homework at Quarry Bank School, Yoko Ono left home to live with a young composer-pianist, Toshi Ichiyanagi, who was studying at Juilliard. The two shared a loft in Greenwich Village, and soon married. During this time she began wearing black, a habit to which she was to adhere for the rest of her life. She was always the most conservative of experimentalists.

In 1958, Toshi Ichiyanagi enrolled on a course in experimental composition. His tutor was John Cage, who introduced Toshi to Merce Cunningham, who in turn employed him as a rehearsal pianist with his dance company. Through her talented husband, Yoko met not only Cage and Cunningham but a wider group of experimentalists, including Allan Kaprow and Jim Dine. But among this bohemian set, she failed to make her mark. Her husband could play the piano, and compose, but her own particular talents were less easy to pinpoint: 'It was very hard to make people understand that I was an artist too. My husband was famous in his own circle around Juilliard and John Cage and those people ... I was having affairs and things like that to compensate, so our relationship deteriorated.'

In the winter of 1960–61 she organised a series of events in their shared loft, and managed to attract some of the key movers in the avant-garde, among them the minimalist composers La Monte Young and Terry Riley, and the Beat poet Diane Wakoski. The audience perched on orange crates. Every now and then, Yoko squeezed her way into someone else's performance, or performed something of her own. On one occasion she took a bowl of Jell-O and hurled it at a large piece of paper tacked to the wall. Having exhausted the Jell-O, she threw two eggs at the paper. She then picked up an inkpot and started finger-painting around the mess already created by the Jell-O and the eggs. Finally, she lit the paper with a match. Despite such effort, some remained unconvinced of her genius. 'I resented her calling her very bad and silly writing "poetry",' said Diane Wakoski. 'And I thought she was hustler, not artist … because she earned her living as a model, seemed to go to bed with all the men around, and in fact never seemed to sacrifice much for her "art" as all the other avant-garders that I knew did.'

In 1961, Toshi returned to Japan to pursue a musical career. Meanwhile, Yoko remained in New York, conducting an affair with a gallery owner called George Maciunas, who subsequently – or consequently – put on her first show. By this time she had nimbly embraced a form of art that centred around self-assertion bound to a single idea, no matter how pedestrian that idea might be. Her first show included a scrap of canvas laid on the floor, titled *Painting to be Stepped On*, and another scrap of canvas with a peephole called *Painting to See the Room Through*. She applied a similarly minimal technique when she staged a 'performance' at a small recital theatre adjoining Carnegie Hall, in which melody took a back seat to a medley of silence and shrieks.

Neither event proved successful, however, so she returned to Japan, where her husband was willing to take her back. She staged further conceptual events in her homeland, but they too drew reviews ranging from the lukewarm to the dismissive. Distressed by the refusal of the Japanese to acknowledge her art, she suffered some sort of breakdown, and checked into a clinic. There she was visited by Tony Cox, a young

American film-maker who had grown attached to her. In 1962 she divorced Toshi and married Cox. The couple had a daughter, Kyoko.

Yoko's strength lay in perseverance. She was unbudgeable in her instinct that in the world of art, skill would soon be edged out by audacity. In 1964 she performed *Cut Piece*, in which she sat onstage and invited members of the audience to cut pieces off her clothes. She also produced *Grapefruit*, a book of 'instructional poems' that resembled haikus, but jettisoned their rules:

> Eat your soup with a fork.
> Treasure eternity.
>
> Drop a pebble in the ocean.
> The pebble is wet.
> But the ocean is not dry.

Neither of these are by her, but they might just as well be. Her poems, to which she has devoted so much of her creative life, can be replicated in a matter of seconds:

> Cut a hole in a bag filled with seeds
> of any kind and place the bag where
> there is wind.

Actually, that one was by her.

> Empty your head.
> Pour water into your ear.
> You have become a bucket.
> Open your mouth.
> Water a flower.

Whereas that one was not.

* * *

Tony Cox devoted himself to managing and promoting Yoko's career; he also took on the responsibility of looking after Kyoko, thus leaving his wife free to pursue her art. 'I always thought of him as my assistant,' Yoko recalled years later. Gradually, she built up a reputation in avant-garde circles. In September 1966, after an English magazine published an enthusiastic piece about her – written, as it happened, by Cox – she accepted an invitation to appear at a London symposium, 'The Destruction of Art'.

Yoko performed *Cut Piece*; other artistes included a nihilist who burned a tower of art books outside the British Museum, and an Australian who mutilated the carcass of a lamb. On the strength of *Cut Piece*, the modish gallerist John Dunbar, husband of Marianne Faithfull, offered Yoko an exhibition at his Indica Gallery. The works she assembled for it included *Hammer and Nail Piece*, consisting of a hammer chained to a block of wood, with a small jar of gold-plated nails alongside it, and *Apple Piece*, a fresh apple on a Plexiglas stand, on offer for £200. *Ladder Piece* had a stepladder which led up to a card pasted onto the ceiling, with a magnifying glass dangling beside it. Viewed through the magnifying glass, the word on the card read 'Yes'.

For decades afterwards, Yoko Ono would be credited as a pioneer of conceptual art, even though Duchamp's idea that anything humdrum may be transformed into art simply by placing it in a gallery was by then half a century old. The eagle-eyed also detected a strangely hand-me-down quality to her instructional poems. 'Composition 1960 #10', by La Monte Young, reads: 'Draw a straight line and follow it.' 'Piano Piece for David Tudor # 1', also written by La Monte Young in 1960, reads: 'Bring a bale of hay and a bucket of water onto the stage for the piano to eat and drink. The performer may then feed the piano or leave it to eat by itself …' They might easily have been written by Yoko; yet they weren't. Her first book of poems, *Grapefruit*, was published four years later, in 1964.

These days, the meeting of John and Yoko at Indica has become as much a part of our island story as the meeting of Stanley and Livingstone at Ujiji, and subject to as many contradictory accounts.

Yoko has insisted that she had no idea who John was: 'I knew the name Beatles and I knew Ringo, because Ringo's easy to remember.* I never read pop magazines or pop newspapers or turned on a pop programme on the TV, you know. It's just that it never occurred to me,' she told one interviewer. When John arrived at the gallery the night before the private view, 'I thought, "What's he doing? Didn't I tell him I didn't want anyone to come until the opening?" I felt a bit angry about it, but I was too busy to complain or make a fuss … I didn't realise then who John was.' Over the years, Yoko has persisted in stating how very unimpressed she was by John's supposed status: 'When I found out I didn't care. I mean, in the art world a Beatle is, well, you know. Also he was in a suit. He looked so ordinary.' To John's biographer Philip Norman, she even claimed to have discovered John's identity only after he had left the building: 'I went downstairs, where there were several art students who were helping us. And one said, "That was John Lennon … one of the *Beatles*." I said, "Oh, really? I didn't know that."'

Others recall events rather differently. The clear-headed Beatles historian Jonathan Gould writes: 'Few things she ever said would inspire such widespread disbelief as her insistence that she didn't know John Lennon from Adam when she was introduced to him by John Dunbar.' Albert Goldman was, as one might expect, more rabid in his scepticism: 'John Lennon and Yoko Ono … were brought together not by chance but by the Coxes' relentless efforts to advance their shared career.'

Allan Kaprow remembered being surprised at how much Yoko knew about the Beatles before she left for London, which suggests she would certainly have recognised the group's leader. Tony Bramwell remembered Yoko telling Dunbar, 'John Lennon said he might come to the exhibition. Why not ask him to a private preview? He's a millionaire, he might buy something.' Dunbar said that though Yoko hadn't encouraged John to be there, she certainly knew he was coming: 'Yoko didn't want anyone to see it before it was totally finished. But we said, "He's a Beatle. He's got lots of money. He might buy something."'

---

* Incidentally, and coincidentally, 'Ringo' is Japanese for 'apple'.

It seems probable that John himself liked to believe that Yoko had no idea who he was. After three years of being lionised by one and all, he clearly found her show of indifference as bracing as a chill wind on a muggy day: 'So, I'm looking for action, you know, and I see this thing called *Hammer and Nail*. It's a board with a chain and a hammer hanging on it, and a bunch of nails at the bottom. I said, "Well, can I hammer a nail in?" and she said, "No." So John Dunbar whisks her away. He takes her in a corner and says, "That's a millionaire, you know. You know who that is?" She didn't know who I was. Anyway, she came over and said, "Five shillings, please!" So I said, "I'll give you an imaginary five shillings and hammer in an imaginary nail." She said, "All right."'

It was similar, in its way, to the meeting of the Duke and Duchess of Windsor three decades earlier. In his memoirs, the duke remembered turning to Wallis Simpson at a dinner party and, by way of conversation, asking her whether, as an American living in England, she missed the central heating.

'I am sorry, sir, but you have disappointed me.'

'In what way?'

'Every American woman who comes to your country is always asked the same question. I had hoped for something more original from the Prince of Wales.'

As accustomed to sycophancy as John was, this twice-married American's abrasiveness must have made his heart skip a beat. From that moment on, he was hers. These two sentences are as applicable to John as they are to the duke: 'From the day I met her,' he said, 'she demanded equal time, equal space, equal rights.' He continued: 'She showed me what it was to be Elvis Beatle and to be surrounded by sycophants and slaves who were only interested in keeping the situation as it was. She said to me, "You've got no clothes on." Nobody had dared tell me that before. With us, it's a teacher–pupil relationship … She's the teacher and I'm the pupil.'

Barry Miles witnessed what happened next at the Indica Gallery. 'Throughout the viewing, Yoko had linked her arm around John's as she explained the works, and when he made a move to go, she asked him to take her with him, even though Tony Cox was there. John had been up three days and was on his way back to Kenwood. He politely declined, climbed in the back of his black-glass chauffeur-driven SS Cooper Mini and sped off.'

John's chauffeur, Les Anthony, was waiting outside, but this didn't stop him offering an X-ray-vision panorama to Albert Goldman: 'Yoko took one look at John and attached herself to him like a limpet mine … She clung to his arm while he went around the exhibition, talking away to him in her funny little high-pitched voice until he fled.'

In the days and weeks that followed, Yoko Ono was the beneficiary of the trusting nature of the British media. She convinced them that she was a major artist in New York and Japan; that it was she, not her first husband, who had studied with John Cage; and that she had performed at Carnegie Hall, rather than the little recital theatre attached to it. They were happy to repeat whatever she told them, because it made for better headlines and juicier copy. No one seemed to mind that her work carried eerie echoes of other artists: like Christo, she wrapped tarpaulin around the lions in Trafalgar Square; like Warhol, she produced a film of 360 bare bottoms (giving it the po-faced title *Unfinished Film # 4*). On top of all this, she affected to be upset by the extent of her own renown. 'I despised myself for being too respected for my work, for being so highly unusual and unique,' she recalled.

Soon after her Indica Gallery exhibition, Yoko arrived at the Beatles' office, but found John absent. By chance, Ringo was in the building, so she directed herself at him instead, and began to recount her philosophy of life and art. Unfortunately, Ringo couldn't decipher a word she was saying, and exited as fast as his legs could carry him. Who knows? If she had spoken more clearly, and on more down-to-earth issues, we might now be talking of Ringo and Yoko, and it might have been not John but Ringo who posed naked on the cover of *Two Virgins*. Or would Ringo have insisted on the two of them remaining fully clothed? His influence might have been felt in her poetry, too:

> Carry a heavy object up a hill. But not for too long, or it'll do your back in.

> Sit at the dock. Watch the seagulls dance. If they come near your chips, give them a good whack.
>
> Carry a bag of peas. Pour it into boiling water. Leave for two minutes. Drain and serve.

Some have related Yoko's pursuit of John in terms of a Hammer horror, with her little black-clad figure rearing up out of the fog at any time, day or night. Tony Bramwell writes of her arriving at Kenwood uninvited, claiming to have an appointment with John. Cynthia, who had no idea who she was, told her that John wasn't there. Yoko seemed to be leaving, but 'when Cynthia glanced out of a window, she saw Yoko standing at the end of the drive … She gazed steadfastly at the house, as if willing the gates to swing open and admit her. Hours later, Cynthia looked again, and Yoko was still there … waiting for John to return. Eventually, as darkness fell, she disappeared. That was the thing about Yoko: she would appear from nowhere and then disappear … The strange visitations to Kenwood continued in all weathers.'

Once, when Yoko took up her position at the end of the drive in the pouring rain, Cynthia's mother took pity on her, and let her indoors to use the phone to call a taxi. 'Later, Mrs Powell noticed that Yoko had left her ring in the cloakroom. "I think she'll be back," she said.'

Bramwell says that letters and cards from Yoko arrived through the post daily, 'mysterious little notes with minuscule black drawings or incomprehensible one-liners'. According to him, one such parcel contained a broken white cup smeared with red paint inside a tampon box.

Cynthia herself paints a slightly less Gothic portrait, though she agrees that Yoko was no stranger to the pillarbox, posting letters to John at a furious rate. By Cynthia's account, the first time she set eyes on Yoko was at a meeting between the Beatles and the Maharishi's assistant, arranged to finalise the details of their forthcoming trip to Rishikesh. 'As we entered the main room I saw, seated in a corner armchair, dressed in black, a small Japanese woman. I guessed immediately that this was Yoko Ono, but what on earth was she doing there? Had John invited her, and, if so, why?'

Yoko sat still, saying nothing. When John and Cynthia came to leave, John's chauffeur opened the car door, 'and to my astonishment, Yoko climbed in ahead of us. John gave me a look that intimated he didn't know what the hell was going on, shrugging, palms upturned, nonplussed.' Yoko asked if they could give her a lift somewhere. She gave her address – 25 Hanover Gate – and they drove there, without another word spoken.

'What was all that about?' asked Cynthia after they had dropped her off.

'Search me, Cyn,' replied John.

Some compared Cynthia to an ostrich, but she was far from daft: 'He insisted he hadn't invited Yoko, and knew nothing of her being there, but common sense dictated that it had to have been John who had asked her to come.'

Amidst a pile of fan mail, Cynthia came across a letter from Yoko to John in which Yoko apologised for talking about herself so much, thanked John for his patience, said she always thought about him, and expressed an ongoing fear that, whenever they said goodbye, she would never see him again. Cynthia confronted John about it. 'She's crackers, just a weirdo artist who wants me to sponsor her,' he insisted. 'Another nutter wanting money for all that avant-garde bullshit. It's not important.'

109

In February 1968 the Beatles flew to the Maharishi's camp in Rishikesh, John and George ten days before the more tentative Paul and Ringo. 'They do not want publicity, fans or press,' Mal Evans informed the swarm of reporters outside the gates. 'They want to be left alone to meditate and take a holy dip in the Ganges ... They are here to meditate for three months, and there is no doubt they will remain here until the end of the course.'

The next day, the Maharishi Mahesh Yogi, no shrinking violet, boasted that 'within three months, I promise to turn Harrison, Lennon, McCartney and Starr into fully qualified teachers or semi-Gurus of Hindu meditation. George and John have progressed fantastically in the few days since they arrived here. I am not pushing them too hard at first, only a few hours of meditation a day. I am feeding them high-level philosophy in simple words.'

At first glance, it might be a school photograph. The headmaster sits in the centre, with the head prefects and the sports stars with him on the rostrum. As your eye drifts away from the bigwigs, the sitters become increasingly small-fry: the school juniors, the supply teachers, the under-matrons; the balding, the plain, the elderly, the inconsequential. These are the odd-bod civilians who had booked onto the course before the Beatles. Among them are Gunther, a Lufthansa pilot, Tony, a blackjack dealer from Las Vegas, and Nancy, the wife of a news analyst.

Only Mia Farrow is missing. From the start, the Maharishi made a great fuss of her, placing a crown on her head, strewing garlands over her shoulders and asking her to pose for photographs morning, noon

and night. Eventually she decided that enough was enough, and set off on a five-day tiger hunt instead. 'Stuff like this, it reminded her of studio calls on the coast,' explained her friend the TV actor Tom Simcox, veteran of *Bonanza* and *Gunsmoke*.

The Maharishi himself had masterminded the group shot and supervised the building of the platform, telling two of his monks exactly where to put the flowers and the potted plants and the painting of Guru Dev. He had also worked out the unapologetically stratified *placement*, with the biggest fishes to the fore. As the meditators drifted over, all in their best clothes, they were told precisely where to sit.

While the juniors took their prescribed places in the sun, the Maharishi preferred to sit in the shade of a grove of trees along with the Beatles, their partners, Pattie Boyd's sister Jenny, Mike Love of the Beach Boys and 'Magic Alex' Mardas. It was the ashramic equivalent of the Royal Box at Ascot. At last the elderly photographer, the proprietor of a small shop in Rishikesh, who had lugged his heavy, old-fashioned wood and brass 8-by-10-plate camera up the hill, announced that he was ready, and the Maharishi and his group finally joined the others in the heat of the sun.

The photographer ducked his head under a black cloth to frame and focus. Every now and then he would emerge, call, 'Ready! Everyone look happy!' and press the button in his right hand. But the Maharishi remained in sole charge, bossing the photographer about – 'You must shout one, two, three before you snap ... Any snap, you must shout!' and bellowing, 'Up higher! You don't get good scenes from there!' when he felt the camera's position was too low.

The strict order of precedence was maintained in the evenings, when everyone would adjourn to the lecture hall, described by one participant as 'a damp and hangar-like building with whitewashed walls and a floor of compressed cow dung'. The Beatles and their spouses sat on wicker chairs in front, with everyone else gathered in neat rows behind them.

'The Maharishi invariably turned up at least an hour late, nodding and murmuring praises to the Guru Dev,' recalled one participant. 'An almost coquettish smile straying across his face, he sat cross-legged on his antelope skin, often toying with a flower or a strand of beads. When he spoke to us, his voice remained gentle and soothing, as if he were speaking from someplace far away, where everything, somehow, was much simpler.'

Life at Rishikesh was far from spartan. The ashram had been built in 1963, with a $100,000 donation from the tobacco heiress Doris Duke. It is strange to think that, had Americans smoked Lucky Strike cigarettes with less gusto, the Maharishi would never have entertained the Beatles at Rishikesh, and most of *The White Album* might not have been written. Set within fourteen acres of forest, the property consisted of six large bungalows, each with half a dozen double bedrooms, plus a post office, lecture theatre and swimming pool. Peacocks wandered the grounds, squawking. The Maharishi employed a staff of forty, including cooks, cleaners and a masseuse. Before the arrival of the Beatles, new mattresses were delivered, along with new curtains and mirrors. The Beatles' rooms were equipped with four-poster beds and electric fires. 'It was back to Butlin's,' said Paul. 'You all had your own chalet.'

Every now and then a tailor would appear, to measure guests for Indian clothes. 'We all wore pyjama trousers and big baggy shirts, and the boys grew beards,' recalled Pattie Boyd.

Breakfast was served between 7 and 11 a.m., with a choice of porridge, puffed wheat or cornflakes, fruit juice and coffee, plus toast with marmalade or jam. Ninety-minute lectures took place at 3.30 and 8.30 p.m., but there was no roll-call or penalties for any absentees. These lectures covered a mixed bag of topics, including reincarnation, meditation, the nature of creativity, how to live life to the fullest and astral travelling.

Even Ringo, who enjoyed his time at Rishikesh least of the Beatles, had no complaints about its pace of life. Burdened with a weak stomach from his childhood illnesses, he had prepared for the onset of spicy, unfamiliar food by packing a suitcase full of Heinz baked beans. His foresight left him with few complaints. 'We would walk about a bit and meditate or bathe,' he recalled. 'Of course, there were lectures or things all the time, but it was very much like a holiday. The Maharishi did everything he could to make us comfortable.' He was less satisfied, however, with the sanitary arrangements. 'You'd have to fight off the scorpions and tarantulas to try to get into a bath, so there used to be amazing noise in the bathroom. To have a bath, you'd start shouting – "OH YES, WELL, I THINK I'LL BE HAVING A BATH NOW" – and banging your feet. You'd keep shouting in the bath – "WHAT A TIME I'M HAVING, YES, IT'S WONDERFUL." Then you'd get out of the bath, get dry and get out of the room before all the insects came back in.' Ringo's wife Maureen, who nursed an extreme dislike of creepy-crawlies, was particularly unnerved. John was impressed by the ferocity of Maureen's hatred of insects: he claimed that she once gave the flies in her bedroom such a thunderous black look that a second later they all dropped down dead.

As the weather turned warmer, the fly population multiplied and then settled on the food. Ringo and Maureen expressed their misgivings to the Maharishi. 'To those lost in meditation, the flies no longer matter,' he replied. Ringo was quick to spot the limitations of this aphorism.

'But that doesn't zap the flies, does it?' he replied.

110

On 25 February 1968 the Rishikesh community threw a party for George's twenty-fifth birthday. The Maharishi made his usual fuss over the Beatles and their wives, inviting them up onstage to sit on special cushions at his feet. His monks went down on their knees, ready to smudge yellow splodges on their guests' foreheads. From time to time the Maharishi stroked George's head. Meanwhile, as a monk chanted, a woman called Edna, dressed in leopardskin-print pyjamas, paraded through the audience handing out garlands of fresh marigolds. As the chanting came to an end, they all queued to hang these garlands around George's neck. At the end of this process, one observer thought George looked 'like a man in a lifejacket'.

The Maharishi launched into one of his bubbly soliloquies, gushing forth like the Ganges. Hope is alive in the world, he said: the moment he met George Harrison and his 'blessed friends' the Beatles, he knew his movement would succeed and that mankind would suffer no more. George was, he added, 'a sublime soul for whom God and all the angels give thanks'. Even for a Beatle, this was flattery on a scale unknown; just six years earlier, on the night before George's nineteenth birthday, the Beatles had been booed offstage at the YMCA in Hoylake.

The Western well-wishers of Rishikesh joined in a rousing chorus of 'Happy Birthday to You' as the Maharishi presented George with a cake topped by two candles. He also gave him a plastic globe, turned upside down. 'George, the globe I am giving you symbolises the world today,' he explained. 'As you see, it needs to be corrected. I hope you will help us all in the task of putting it right.'

* * *

Cynthia Lennon felt that Rishikesh marked a turning point in George's life. Having been, in her words, 'the most tactless, blunt and often pig-headed of the Beatles', the combination of his experiences with LSD and his time in India meant that 'He grew up very quickly, changing from a tactless youth into a sensitive, thinking individual. The rough edges were smoothed down and self-discipline became the cornerstone of his character.'

But, given time, sanctity can elongate into sanctimony; Rishikesh also brought out George's more solemn and po-faced, disapproving side. One day, when Paul casually told him that he had been thinking about their next album, George snapped, 'We're not fucking here to do the next album, we're here to meditate!' Paul was taken aback. 'It was like, "Ohh, excuse me for breathing!"'

While Pattie loved frolicking around in the Ganges, George thought it frivolous, and told her so. On the other hand, he never felt any conflict between his spirituality and his libido. Quite the opposite: in time, he came to regard them as operating in tandem, the one the handmaiden to the other. Over the course of their stay in India, Pattie noticed that George became 'fascinated by the god Krishna, who was always surrounded by young maidens'. She felt he returned to Britain 'wanting to be some kind of Krishna figure, a spiritual being with lots of concubines. He actually said so. And no woman was out of bounds.'

Paul looked back on his time in Rishikesh with a mixture of contentment and scepticism. He had meditated, but in a very English way. Whereas George extolled the benefits of meditation with evangelistic fervour – 'There's high and there's *high*, and to get really high – I mean so high that you can walk on water, *that* high – that's where I'm going. The answer's not pot, but yoga and meditation and working and discipline, working out your karma' – Paul approached it more matter-of-factly. One of his aids to meditation was, he said, to imagine someone leaning over a farm gate with a straw hanging out of his mouth – 'that feeling of being very, very calm'. Throughout it all, he hung on to the Beatles' natural sense of the ridiculous, coupled with their instinctive aversion to authority. 'Quick lads, fags out – here comes Teach!' he would say whenever he spotted the Maharishi approaching. He was even amused by the Maharishi's interest in the material world, and admired his pragmatism: one day he had asked for the Beatles' advice on the best new car. 'We said, "Well, a Merc, Maharishi. Mercedes, very good car." "Practical? Long-running? Good works?" "Yes." "Well, we should get a Mercedes then."'

John was, as usual, the most conflicted of the four, embracing or rejecting the aura of Rishikesh as the mood took him. Free of hard drugs – none were allowed or available in the ashram – he threw himself into meditation. To a fan who wrote asking him what Transcendental Meditation was all about, he replied across two pages, signing off 'jai guru dev', explaining that 'It takes the mind down to that level of consciousness which is Absolute Bliss (Heaven).' In line with this, one of the many songs he wrote in India was called 'Child of Nature'. Its hippy-dippy lyrics ('I'm just a child of nature/I don't need much to set me free') are as un-John as can be, with no trace of bite. But when he came to record the song three years later, he kept the tune but junked the lyrics. Its new title was 'Jealous Guy', and the new lyrics made it all about insecurity, loss of control, pain, spite, jealousy and remorse.

At first, Cynthia loved India – 'just peace, quiet and sweet mountain air filled with the scent of flowers. Best of all, John and I could be together for much of the time.' But after a week, things began to turn sour. Others noticed that, though the other Beatles were affectionate and tactile with their partners, and John was perfectly pleasant to everyone else, he could be very offhand with Cynthia.

'They were bright and friendly with me, but distinctly distant and cool with each other,' noted the photographer Paul Saltzman. It was not until later that Cynthia learned that John's solitary morning walks had taken him straight to the post office, to pick up daily cards from a Japanese fan he had once described to Cynthia as 'off her rocker'.

'I felt so sorry for Cynthia,' remembered Pattie. 'He received notes from Yoko in the post almost every day saying things like, "If you look up at the sky and see a cloud, it's me sending you love."' These cards were being forwarded from a Delhi hotel by the Beatle apparatchik Tony Bramwell, who was in on their secret: 'To save problems, I put these open cards in a plain manila envelope so Cynthia wouldn't be upset.'

John remembered his Indian sojourn as, above all, a time of self-doubt. 'It was that period when I was really going through a "What's it all about? Songwriting is nothing. It's pointless and I'm not talented, and I'm a shit, and I couldn't do anything but be a Beatle and what am I going to do about it?"' Was he dreading the choice he would have to make on his return?

Yet the songs poured out of him, possibly because there was not much else to do, and no drugs, or at least hard drugs, to hand: 'Julia', 'Dear Prudence', 'Bungalow Bill', 'Across the Universe', 'Cry Baby Cry', 'Polythene Pam', 'Mean Mr Mustard', 'I'm So Tired'. Some of these songs are cheerful, but filtered through John's memory they turned to gloom. 'The funny thing about the camp was that although it was very beautiful and I was meditating about eight hours a day, I was writing the most miserable songs on earth,' he recalled. 'In "Yer Blues", when I wrote, "I'm so lonely I want to die", I'm not kidding. Up there trying to reach God and feeling suicidal.'

Ringo and Maureen were the first to leave, chased away by flies and creepy-crawlies. 'The Maharishi's a nice man, but he's not for me,' Ringo informed the press. He and Maureen had nothing against meditation, but they were missing their children. 'It is not a gigantic hoax … If everyone in the world started meditating, then the world would be a much happier place.' Back home at Sunny Heights, Ringo received a postcard from John: 'Just a little vibration from India. We've got two LPs worth of songs now so get your drums out.'

Paul and Jane left after six weeks, declaring it 'a very rewarding experience'. It had certainly been fruitful for Paul musically: 'Blackbird', 'Rocky Racoon', 'Back in the USSR', 'I Will', 'Mother Nature's Son' and 'Ob-La-Di, Ob-La-Da', as well as the brief and bullish 'Why Don't We Do it In the Road?', inspired by the sight of a couple of monkeys copulating *en plein air*.

For John and Cynthia and George and Pattie, it all ended in tears. On a whim, John told the Maharishi he had a friend who could build a radio station in Rishikesh that would beam the message of Transcendental Meditation all over the world. Any spare energy could be used to light up the ashram and all the neighbouring villages. This wizard was, of course, his new Greek friend 'Magic' Alex Mardas, for whom no job was ever too large to be started or too small to leave unfinished. Mardas arrived in Rishikesh equipped with a small rucksack containing a selection of screwdrivers and a few wires. He can be spotted in the group photograph, two back from Ringo, unsmiling in dark glasses and staring directly at the camera, in a manner reminiscent of the vengeful Bruno at the tennis tournament in Hitchcock's *Strangers on a Train*.

For some reason, Mardas seems to have taken against the Maharishi. Perhaps he was jealous of the way his own shamanic place in the Beatles' hearts had been usurped by this leathery old guru with his easy promises of levitation. Or was he fearful that he himself would be unmasked as a fraud? Tony Bramwell heard it rumoured that the Maharishi, the holder of a physics degree, was asking too many questions as to how exactly Magic Alex proposed to create an international radio station out of a handful of wires and fuses: 'He asked many searching questions that Alex was unable to answer, and the young Greek panicked.'

Iago had wheedled his way into Shangri-La. Two weeks before John and George were due to leave, Mardas began pouring malice into their ears, saying that the Maharashi had made advances to a young woman, first asking to hold her hand, then suggesting an inappropriate place to put it. Not only that, but this self-styled vegetarian had been spotted scoffing chicken behind their backs. 'He seemed convinced that Maharishi was evil,' remembered Pattie. 'He kept saying, "It's black magic."'

Cynthia looked on powerless as Magic Alex's gossip took root in the minds of John and George: 'Alexis's statements about how the Maharishi had been indiscreet with a certain lady, and what a blackguard he had turned out to be, gathered momentum. All, may I say, without a single shred of evidence or justification. It was obvious to me that Alexis wanted out, and more than anything he wanted the Beatles out as well.'

Soon, John and George were coming round to the idea that their guru was up to no good. 'Why would the Maharishi want a double four-poster bed?' asked Magic Alex, and George seemed to agree, with John following suit: 'When George started thinking it might be true, I thought, "Well, it must be true, because if George started thinking it might be true, there must be something in it."'

By the end of the night they had made up their minds. By chance, Pattie had what she described as 'a horrid dream' about the Maharishi, and was now keen to leave too. 'Out of confusion and accusation came anger and aggression,' recalled Cynthia.

The next morning Magic Alex ordered taxis, and John and George and their gang approached the Maharishi. 'I was the spokesman,' recalled John, 'and I said, "We're leaving." "Why?" he asked, and I said, "Well, if you're so cosmic, you'll know why!" … He said, "I don't know why. You must tell me," and I just kept saying, "You ought to know," and he gave me a look like, "I'll kill you, you bastard." I knew then that I had called his bluff and I was a bit rough to him.'

But Cynthia saw it differently: 'I felt that what we were doing was very, very wrong. To sit in judgement on a man who had given us nothing but happiness.'

As they waited by the outside tables for their taxis, the Maharishi emerged from his bungalow and went to sit a hundred yards away, in a little wooden shelter. One of his monks walked over to the Lennons and Harrisons with a message from the Maharishi. 'He said he was very sad and wanted desperately to put things right and to convince us that we should stay,' recalled Cynthia. 'I wanted to cry. It was so sad.'

When the taxis arrived, everyone stood up and filed past the Maharishi without a glance in his direction or saying a word. It reminded Cynthia of the biblical scene in which Jesus is denied by his disciples.

* * *

By taking them on their trip to India, George had, for the first time, assumed leadership of the Beatles. In the manner of his leaving, he had allowed himself to succumb once more to the more forceful character of John. Even as they were driving away, he began to regret siding with John against his old friend and guru. On the road to Delhi, John started singing, 'Maharishi, what have you done? You made a fool of everyone.' But George objected: 'You can't say that, it's ridiculous.' To appease him, John changed 'Maharishi' to 'Sexy Sadie'.

George later came to believe that John had wanted to leave, and had seized on Magic Alex's fabrications as a perfect excuse. 'This whole piece of bullshit was invented. There were a lot of flakes there; the whole place was full of flaky people. Some of them were us.'

On their arrival back in Britain, the Beatles remained surprisingly tight-lipped over any reservations they had concerning the Maharishi. Any admission of disillusionment would have required an acknowledgement of gullibility, so perhaps they felt it best to stay silent.

For his part, the Maharishi made the most of his connection. In May of that year he embarked on a concert tour of the USA with the Beach Boys. Billed as 'the Most Exciting Event of the Decade', it consisted of a set by the Beach Boys followed by a lecture on Transcendental Meditation by the Maharishi, with time for questions and answers. Sadly, audiences tended to shout '"California Girls"!' or '"Barbara Ann"!' just as the Maharishi was explaining the more ethereal business of chakras and mantras. Following disappointing ticket sales, the final twenty-four dates of the twenty-nine-date tour were cancelled. Nonetheless, the Maharishi continued to thrive, attracting a wealth of celebrities to his Transcendental Meditation workshops, among them Kurt Vonnegut, the Rolling Stones, Major-General Franklin M. Davis, head of the United States Army War College, and, perhaps inevitably, the actress Shirley MacLaine.

The Maharishi went on to head a twenty-four-hour global satellite television channel, beaming Transcendental Meditation in twenty-two languages to 144 countries on a subscription basis. A complex network of related companies dealt in TM-related merchandise – books, CDs, spiritual consultations, massage oils. He also controlled new-age health centres, universities and charitable trusts, as well as the Heaven on Earth property company, and founded the Natural Law Party, which stood in British general elections of the 1990s on a platform of low taxes, yogic flying and a herb village in every town. He died in 2008, on an ashram in a former monastery in a small town on the Dutch–German border with the surprisingly down-to-earth name of Vlodorp.

111

Whatever happened to the Beatles? Compare their first and last press conferences in America. In the first, they are outgoing and full of joie-de-vivre; in the last, self-absorbed and world-weary. Yet barely four years separate the two.

On 7 February 1964 they arrive at Kennedy Airport looking wide awake and happy, and are whisked into a noisy press room, where cameramen jostle for pictures. Their press officer has to shout at the top of his voice for quiet. Standing behind a dozen microphones, the four Beatles remain bright and chirpy, bantering away, undaunted by the barrage of questions. They are full of fun and enthusiasm, and clearly the best of friends, delighting in each other's company, laughing at each other's jokes and finishing off each other's answers.

REPORTER: What do you think of Beethoven?
RINGO: Great, especially his poems.
REPORTER: Can you explain your strange English accents?
GEORGE: It's not English. It's Liverpudlian.
REPORTER: In Detroit, there's people handing out car stickers saying, 'Stamp Out the Beatles'.
PAUL: Yeah, well, we've got two answers to that. First of all, we're bringing out a Stamp Out Detroit campaign.
REPORTER: What do you think of the comment that you're nothing but a bunch of British Elvis Presleys?
RINGO: (imitating Elvis's gait and voice) It's not true! It's not true!
REPORTER: How many of you are bald, so that you have to wear those wigs?

RINGO: All of us.

PAUL: I'm bald! Don't tell anyone, please!

JOHN: Oh, we're all bald, yeah … And deaf and dumb too.

REPORTER: Are you for real?

JOHN: Come and have a feel.

On 10 February, the morning after their American debut on *The Ed Sullivan Show*, they give another press conference, this time in the Baroque Room of the Plaza Hotel:

FEMALE REPORTER: Who chooses your clothes?

JOHN: We choose our own. Who chooses yours?

FEMALE REPORTER: My husband. Now tell me, are there any subjects you prefer not to discuss?

JOHN: Yes. Your husband.

REPORTER: Which do you consider is the greatest danger to your careers: nuclear bombs or dandruff?

RINGO: Bombs. We've already got dandruff.

Four years later, on 11 May 1968, John and Paul are back in America, this time to launch their new organisation, Apple. Even now, in this more laid-back era, they are greeted by screaming fans at Kennedy Airport. On 14 May they sit down for a press conference in the Versailles Room of the Americana Hotel.

John never smiles. His answers are tinged with aggression. Every now and then a sprinkling of polite laughter greets one of his offhand replies. Is the laughter prompted by wishful thinking? Are these journalists hoping to be transported back to those carefree days of 1964? Sitting to John's left, Paul looks bored and distracted, and hardly joins in. Jane Asher left him a few days ago; could this be the cause of his despondency? Whatever their reasons, neither Paul nor John shows a trace of excitement at the launch of this new venture.

REPORTER: Why are you here today?

JOHN: To do this. What's it look like? What are you doing here?

...

REPORTER: Could you tell us about your newest corporate business venture?

JOHN: It's a business concerning records, films and electronics, and as a sideline, whatever it's called, manufacturing, or whatever. We want to set up a system whereby people who just want to make a film about anything don't have to go on their knees in somebody's office, probably yours.

...

REPORTER: Could you give us some idea about the capitalisation of this new corporation?

JOHN: No. We'll do it short-term, and we'll make sure we get what we want, y'know. Otherwise we won't do it. So we'll make sure.

...

REPORTER: How will you run your company?

JOHN: There's people we can get to do that. We don't know anything about business.

REPORTER: How will you set about film financing?

JOHN: We don't plan. Now we don't have any manager, there's no planning at all.

REPORTER: Tell us about your electronics division of Apple. What will it do?

PAUL: There won't be any gimmicks. But we won't say what it is until it's out.

The most complete, or least incomplete, statement of the aims of the new organisation comes from Paul: 'We're in the happy position of not needing any more money. So for the first time the bosses aren't in it for the profit. If you come to me and say, "I've had such and such a dream," I will say, "Here's so much money. Go away and do it."' Their aim, he says, is to create 'a beautiful place where you can buy beautiful things, a controlled weirdness, a kind of Western communism'.

But his tone – offhand and morose – is at odds with his message. The devil-may-care optimism and camaraderie of 1964 have disappeared. A trailer for Apple insists that the organisation will place 'EMPHASIS ON ENJOYMENT', but there is little evidence of that here today, in the Versailles Room of the Americana Hotel.

112

Throughout John and Paul's press conference at the Americana, Magic Alex sat at John's right hand, toying with a bunch of flowers. Long-haired and bearded, he looked much like any other hippy, but he was now head of Apple's Electronics Division.

A month later, he was filmed for an Apple promotional film to be screened at a Los Angeles sales convention later the same day. The film begins with heavy guitar music, and a voiceover says: 'The concept of Apple is to bring together the artists of today with the methods and media of tomorrow.'

For the next three minutes Mary Hopkin plays guitar beneath a tree and sings sweetly, while Paul's dog Martha potters around. When she finishes, Paul walks on, and crouches beside her on the grass. 'That was Mary Hopkin – and this is Alex.'

The scene switches to a room full of boxes and machines. Magic Alex wears a white shirt and trousers beneath a white technician's coat. He is seen 'fiddling with a pile of junk', as the director of the film, Tony Bramwell, put it.

Against an insistent background clamour of *Dr Who*-ish bleepy-bloppy noises, Magic Alex walks towards the camera, picks up a microphone and says, in his heavy Greek accent, 'Hullo. Arm Alexis vrum Abul Elegtronigs. Ar, I vood like to say hullo to vall my bruzzers around the world and to all the gells around the world and to all the electronic people around the world er und er –' (points to the machines and boxes behind him) '– thad is Abull Elegronigs.'

The wacky noises continue as a blue light trails up and down across a screen, as in a low-budget sci-fi movie, or an amateur heart monitor.

The film cuts to an office. John passes a phone to Paul. Music seems to be coming out of it. Paul holds the phone to the ear of the unApple-ish figure of the Beatles' music publisher Dick James, bald and heavily bespectacled. 'Fair enough,' he says, with the tired curiosity of an exhausted parent. 'Where's that come from? Whassat? Oh, it's a radio built in.'

'Wrong,' says Paul, with a laugh. 'It's a phone. Just a little thing we have up our sleeves.'

Those of Mardas's ideas that worked were not his own, and those that were his own failed to work. In all, Apple applied for one hundred different patents for Mardas's inventions, not one of which was accepted. The telephone in the promotional video might well be the one he claimed to have invented, which had voice-recognition, and could display the number of the incoming call. But Apple lawyers were soon to discover that both of these had been patented by the Bell company some time before.

Other inventions by Magic Alex included:

a) an X-ray camera that could see through walls
b) a force-field that envelops any building in coloured air, rendering it invisible
c) a solar-powered electric guitar
d) paint that makes objects invisible
e) a house that hovers in the air, suspended on an invisible beam
f) a home heating system that runs on ordinary household batteries
g) a device for preventing records being taped off the radio by sending out a series of high-pitched squeals
h) special paint that changes colour at the flick of a switch

One of his more audacious inventions was 'loudpaper', an audible form of wallpaper. Paul listened wide-eyed as the electronics guru described it: 'He would sit and tell us of how it would be possible to have wall-papers which were speakers, so you would wallpaper your room with some sort of substance and then it could be plugged into and the whole wall would vibrate and work as a loudspeaker – "loud-paper". And we said, "Well, if you could do that, we'd like one." It was always, "We'd like one."'

But George Martin, older and wiser, was less easily impressed. 'Of all the army of hangers-on, the one I recall most vividly … was Magic Alex … who was so preposterous that it would have been funny had he not caused so much embarrassment and difficulty with me in the recording studio.' His irritation increased after he overheard Mardas boasting that he could do Martin's job so much better. 'I found it very difficult to chuck him out, because the boys liked him so much. Since it was very obvious that I didn't, a schism developed.'

Martin remained studiously undeceived. 'I confess that I tended to laugh myself silly when they came and announced the latest brainchild of Alex's fertile imagination. Their reaction was always the same: "You'll laugh on the other side of your face when Alex comes up with it." But of course he never did.'

Persuaded by Magic Alex, Apple bought two huge computers for £20,000 each. But no one could make them work, least of all Magic Alex. Before long they were moved to Ringo's garage, where they remained for years to come.

Of all Mardas's visions, the one that impressed the Beatles most, and George Martin least, was the Sonic Screen. 'I was informed of this work of inventive genius by the boys one day. "Why do you have to put Ringo with his drums behind all those terrible screens?" they asked. "We can't see him. We know it makes a good drum sound, and it cuts out all the spill to our guitars and things, but damn it, with those bloody great screens locking him in, it makes him feel claustrophobic."

'I waited silently, knowing that the problem would have been solved by a flash of Greek inspiration. And so it had. "Alex has got a brilliant idea! He's come up with something really great: a sonic screen! He's going to place these ultra-high-frequency beams round Ringo, and when they're switched on he won't be able to hear anything, because the beams will form a wall of silence." Words, I fully admit, failed me.'

Mardas started work on a flying saucer, built around two V12 engines, one borrowed from George's Ferrari, the other from John's Rolls-Royce. The Beatles also financed his scheme to create an artificial sun to light up the sky above the new Apple Boutique in Baker Street. But on opening night – 7 December 1967 – the sun failed to appear. This was, of course, not Mardas's fault: it all came down to a lack of 'energy'. Other inventions had, he insisted, been days from completion when, as luck would have it, a fire swept through his workshop, ensuring that their due date had to be postponed.

He somehow persuaded the Beatles to let him design them a new studio, the best in the world, equipped with recording consoles that were not just four-track, as at EMI, or eight-track, as in America, but seventy-two-track. For months he pretended to be busying away, constructing a studio in the basement of the Apple headquarters at 3 Savile Row, and regularly asking for more money for the task.

As autumn turned to winter, the Beatles, already fractious, began to find their Twickenham studios too cold and draughty. Their patience was ebbing away; they demanded to move into the swish, state-of-the-art new studio as soon as possible.

Magic Alex finally let them into their new studio late in 1969. It immediately proved unusable, with no studio desk or any form of soundproofing. Conversations from neighbouring rooms and footsteps from upstairs could easily be heard, while every time the building's central heating was fired up a great whooshy noise filled the studio. Geoff Emerick was unimpressed: 'Alex basically did not know what he was doing. The studio he built for them was a complete and utter disaster.' George Martin realised at once that there was no space in the wall for the cables between the studio and the control room; the only solution was to open the doors so the cables could snake along the corridor. Far from being revolutionary, the mixing console was just a sheet of plywood with sixteen faders and an oscilloscope stuck in the middle. 'It looked like the control panel of a B-52 bomber,' complained the sound engineer Dave Harries. 'They actually tried a session on this desk, they did a take, but when they played back the tape it was all hum and hiss. Terrible. The Beatles walked out, that was the end of it.'

George Martin made a frantic call to Abbey Road: 'For God's sake get some decent equipment down here!'

'He'd charged them thousands, and bought the stuff second-hand,' said John Dunbar, who had grown disillusioned with his former wunderkind. George Harrison, too, suffered a crisis of faith: 'Alex's recording studio at Apple was the biggest disaster of all time. He was walking around with a white coat on like some sort of chemist, but didn't have a clue about what he was doing.' Alan Parsons, a junior EMI tape operator, arrived with equipment borrowed from Abbey Road. He too was disappointed by Mardas's efforts: 'It had obviously been done with a hammer and chisel instead of being properly designed and machined.' But their recordings struggled on, creating what John later called, in his undainty way, 'the shittiest load of badly recorded shit with a lousy feeling to it ever'. Finally, when Allen Klein took over the management of the Beatles' affairs in 1969, he wound up Apple Electronics, and stopped all payments to Magic Alex. In the end, the famous cutting-edge mixing console was sold as scrap metal to a second-hand electronics shop in the Edgware Road for £5.

Magic Alex came to personify the hippy-dippy gullibilities of the Beatles' later years. He spent the rest of his life in Greece, selling bullet-proof cars and security devices to the wealthy and paranoid. He also made a fortune selling all the Beatles memorabilia he had managed to accumulate: in 2011 he was paid $408,000 for a custom-made Vox Kensington guitar with a plaque reading:

TO MAGIC ALEX
ALEXI THANK YOU
FOR BEEN [sic] A FRIEND
2–5–1967 JOHN

In 2008, after an article in the *New York Times* described him as a 'charlatan', he threatened to take the newspaper to court. Following two years of protracted negotiations, he agreed to drop his action on condition that the paper made it clear that by calling him a charlatan, it did not intend to mean that he was also a conman.

On his death in 2017, his obituarist in *The Times* calculated that, in today's money, Alex Mardas's projects had cost the Beatles £4 million, with no tangible return.

113

At Quarry Bank, the boys would indulge in saucy group sessions in the bushes after school. At that time they would have been thirteen or fourteen years old. 'Our fantasies, at least, were strictly heterosexual,' recalled Pete Shotton, a little priggishly. '"Right boys," someone would venture, "who should we do it to today?"' They would then take it in turns to call out the names of famous pin-ups, 'each name spurring us on to new heights of ecstasy'.

When it came to John's turn, he liked to enlist the vision of Brigitte Bardot, for whom the term 'sex kitten' had recently been coined. The French actress shot to fame in Britain after posing in a bikini at the Cannes Film Festival to publicise her relatively minor role in *Act of Love* (1953). Her career blossomed during John's adolescent years: she starred opposite Dirk Bogarde and James Robertson Justice in *Doctor at Sea* (1955), before going on to play the title role in *Naughty Girl* (1956), and then 'a demon driven temptress' in *And God Created Woman* (also 1956).*

During one of their unabashed sessions, John suddenly switched his regular call from 'Brigitte Bardot!' to 'Winston Churchill!' which had the instant effect of pouring cold water on their shared fantasies.†

---

* 'A role that will make you gasp and never forget', according to the trailer.

† Though Shotton failed to mention Paul's participation in this game, Paul certainly included himself when he shared roughly the same story with readers of *GQ* magazine in 2018: 'It was just a group of us, and instead of just getting roaring drunk and partying – I don't even know if we were staying over or anything – we were all just in these chairs, and the lights were out, and somebody started masturbating, so we all did. We were just, "Brigitte Bardot! Whoo!" and then everyone would thrash a bit more. I think it was John who sort of said, "Winston

Around this time, he started collecting a new series of photographs in *Weekend* magazine. In weekly instalments, the magazine offered a new piece of what would eventually grow into a life-size pin up of Brigitte Bardot in a swimsuit. Having collected the full set, he taped the composite poster onto the ceiling above his bed.

Paul shared John's passion for the sultry French actress. 'She was it, she was the first, she was one of the first ones you ever saw nude or semi-nude,' he recalled. 'She was a great looker, and she was French, so Brigitte for us, with the long blonde hair and the great figure and the little pouty lips, was the epitome of female beauty … It was the fact that she was thought to have loose morals; we could fantasise that she did anyway.'

John was still entertaining these fantasies about Brigitte Bardot in 1957, when he left school to enrol at the Liverpool College of Art. There he had caught the eye of Cynthia Powell, who had by chance overheard him compare one of their fellow students approvingly to Bardot. Determined to win John's heart, Cynthia dyed her hair blonde, and started wearing false eyelashes, tight black trousers and clingy sweaters. Sure enough, John began to take an interest, and they soon became a couple.

Just before the Beatles set off on their first trip to Hamburg, Cynthia received a telephone call from John telling her to come over as fast as she could. Aunt Mimi had left to visit her sister Nanny in Birkenhead: the house was free. John's first impulse was to borrow a camera. 'He insisted I try out various seductive poses while he snapped away, so I put my hair up, let it down, hitched up my skirt and thrust out my chest in an attempt to do my best Brigitte Bardot. After the photo session, we made love, then lit a fire and lay on the sofa in front of the television, eating anything we could find in the fridge. It was all the more exciting for being so illicit.'

John took these photographs with him to Hamburg. When Cynthia

---

Churchill!" … It was quite raunchy when you think about it. There's so many things like that from when you're a kid that you look back on and you're, "Did we do that?" But it was good harmless fun. It didn't hurt anyone. Not even Brigitte Bardot.'

and Paul's girlfriend Dot visited them there, John and Paul persuaded them both to wear leather skirts, just like Bardot. Many years later, Paul remembered John saying, 'Yeah, well, the more they look like Brigitte, the better off we are, mate!' Tony Barrow once went so far as to claim that during John's marriage to Cynthia 'John admitted to me that he would metaphorically shut his eyes and think of some movie star, probably Brigitte Bardot.'

Paul and John's fidelity to Brigitte survived money and fame. An early version of the *Sgt. Pepper* cover, drafted in pen and ink by Paul, shows the Beatles in their colourful uniforms standing in front of a wall of framed photographs of their idols. To their left is a pin-up of Brigitte Bardot kneeling with her hands behind her head, ten times the size of anyone else. But for reasons lost to time, she failed to make the final cover, her place being filled by Mae West and Diana Dors.

In June 1968, fantasy collided with reality when Brigitte Bardot arrived in London, and sent word to Apple that she would like to meet one or more of the Beatles. John was the sole volunteer. He boasted to Pete

Shotton that he would soon be meeting the girl of their schoolboy dreams. 'Naturally, I begged John to let me tag along, but since Brigitte had specified she wasn't prepared to meet a crowd of strangers, only Derek [Taylor] was permitted to accompany him.'

Before the big meeting, John popped round to see Taylor at the Apple offices in Wigmore Street, and asked him for some marijuana to calm him down. Taylor only had LSD, so they both took that instead. The two of them then climbed into John's Rolls-Royce and were driven the short distance to the Mayfair Hotel, where Bardot was staying. Suffering an attack of nerves, John sent Taylor into the hotel while he remained crouched on the floor of the car.

Taylor found Brigitte Bardot dressed all in black leather, surrounded by female companions. When he told her that John Lennon was in the car outside she seemed disappointed that no other Beatles had come. By this time, Taylor's tabs of LSD were kicking in, causing great waves of paranoia. He and John were in danger, he told Bardot, and they were being watched by mysterious people. Bardot didn't understand what he was saying, but suggested he ask John to come up.

John duly came to the room, but the twin traumas of LSD and Brigitte Bardot in leather rendered him speechless. With some effort he managed to say 'Hello,' but little else. Bardot said that she had booked a table in the hotel restaurant, but neither John nor Taylor were sure they could walk that far. Taylor was nonplussed: 'Suddenly everyone was standing up, ready to go. This was terrible! For a start, neither of us was capable of eating anything at all; we weren't even sure we could stand up … "Please don't think us bourgeois," we begged, "but we are both married and this is getting out of hand and" … oh Christ! What a mess!'

Brigitte, in Taylor's words, 'was not best pleased'. She and her female companions stomped off to the restaurant downstairs, leaving John and Taylor in the hotel suite. When Bardot and her entourage returned from dinner, they were surprised to find the two men still there, Taylor slumped on Bardot's bed, and John strumming a guitar, playing a selection of songs he had composed in India. Bardot's indifference quickly turned to irritation; before long she asked them to leave.

John returned to Kenwood, where Pete Shotton was staying. '"What happened, what happened?" I said breathlessly. "I can't bear the suspense another minute!"'

'Fucking *nothing* happened,' said John. 'I was so fucking nervous that I dropped some acid before we went in and got completely out of me head. The only thing I said to her all night was hello, when we went to shake hands with her. Then she spent the whole time talking in French with her friends, and I could never think of anything to say.'

It had been, he concluded, 'a fucking terrible evening'.

114

THE TURDS

The explosive truth

The atmosphere at the Bond Street offices of Rubbish Ltd. is of intense boredom enlivened by occasional surrealistic hyper-symmetry. A Turd drifts by wearing an Oriental bell-bottomed pull-over with rubberised attachments. A thin spotty girl at reception is saying, 'It's the Official Receiver. Shall I say you're out?'

Already under construction at Bond Street are the biggest television aerial in the world, eighty-nine magic lanterns and some eight patented inventions by a life-long friend of the Turds, 'Mad Sid' Saint-Beuve.

These inventions include an electric blotting-paper liquidiser, a toilet roll which plays the national anthem and a car with no wheels.

A South Croydon firm has already offered the Turds £2 to take the car away.

Turd Spiggy Topes became worried last year over the decline in sales of Turd records in the USA. With the growth of miniature tape recorders fans were taping records from the radio and not buying the records. Under Turd sponsorship, a service has been patented to prevent this happening. All Turd records will in future emit a loud wailing noise so excruciating to the naked ear that no one will listen to them ever again.

For the Turds the wailing noise makes a new departure. Their latest LP, *A Day in the Life of Ex-King Zog of Albania*, took over five years to make and includes combs and paper, the sound of the Cornish Riviera Express leaving Paddington, two million zithers, an electric hydrofoil, and the massed strings of the Tel Aviv Police Band.

Says Spiggy: 'I was always terrified of classical music. I mean to say Mendelssohn and that and all those long names. And then the other day I met this taxi driver who was reading this Mozart sheet music. "You won't like this," he frankly admitted to me, "it's highbrow." And that's what I used to think. But it's not, you know. I mean, it's exactly what's happening in pop today. We are Mozart. I mean to say Christ. We're also him, that reminds me.'

Private Eye, 13 September 1968

115

In Rishikesh, Cynthia had felt that John was avoiding her: 'I was not having the second honeymoon I'd hoped for. John was becoming increasingly cold and aloof towards me. He would get up very early and leave our room. He spoke to me very little, and after a week or two he announced that he wanted to move into a separate room to give himself more space. From then on, he virtually ignored me, both in private and in public.' Little did she know that John was receiving letters from Yoko Ono almost every day.

Two weeks after they got back from India, John suggested to Cynthia that she should join Donovan, his manager Gypsy Dave, Pattie Boyd's sister Jenny and Magic Alex on a fortnight's holiday in Greece. She and John rarely holidayed separately, so Cynthia was reluctant. 'I've got a lot on at the moment and I can't go, but you should. It might cheer you up,' said John.

On her return from holiday, Cynthia drove to Kenwood with Jenny Boyd and Magic Alex, arriving at 4 p.m. She straight away knew something was wrong: 'The porch light was on, the curtains were still drawn and everything was silent.' Normally her housekeeper, Dot, would have come out to greet her with Julian. Instead, there was silence.

The front door was unlocked. 'Where are you all?' she shouted. Were they hiding behind a door?

'As I put my hand on the sunroom door I felt a sudden frisson of fear. I hesitated for a second, then opened it. Inside, the curtains were closed and the room was dimly lit, so it took me a moment to focus. When I did, I froze. John and Yoko were sitting on the floor, cross-legged and facing each other, beside a table covered with dirty dishes.

They were wearing the towelling robes we kept in the poolhouse, so I imagined they had been for a swim. John was facing me. He looked at me, expressionless, and said, "Oh, hi." Yoko didn't turn round.'

It was clear to Cynthia that they wanted her to find them like that. She found the cruelty of John's act hard to fathom. She was so taken aback that she went into a state of emotional paralysis, behaving as if nothing were out of order, and asking him if he'd like to come out to dinner with them.

'No thanks,' replied John.

Cynthia rushed out of the room. Jenny was hovering awkwardly in the kitchen, so she asked if she could stay with her. Then she went upstairs to pack a bag. On the landing she stumbled across a pair of small Japanese slippers, placed neatly outside the guest bedroom. She looked inside. The bed was untouched.

116

Pete Shotton found himself in overall charge of the Apple Boutique, which was to be stocked with psychedelic clothes, Oriental bric-à-brac, hand-painted furniture and inflatable chairs. The three young Dutch designers collectively known as The Fool were hired to design the shopfront and provide the stock, having already applied their swirly, curly, lava-lampy decorations to George's bungalow, John's grand piano and the set for 'All You Need is Love'. Like many of those who fluttered around the Beatles, they dressed in gypsy head-dresses, great bundles of necklaces, bell-sleeved shirts splashed with stars and moons, Elizabethan jerkins and low-slung satin belts snaking around velvet 'loons'. Their dreamy personas nevertheless concealed a shrewd instinct for money – or bread, as they preferred to call it – and how best to extract it from their utopian employers. On top of their regular wages, they gently asked for a bonus on signature of contract of £40,000, or £675,000 in today's money. The Beatles' startled accountant advised the group strongly against handing it over, but they ignored him. Once this deal was done and dusted, The Fool embarked on a ten-day 'research' trip to Morocco, with all expenses paid.

The clothes they designed, all rainbows and flowers and dreamy landscapes, were poorly executed, their shapes ungainly, their seams frail, their sleeves lopsided. 'We had to find people to *make* these clothes,' sighed Pete Shotton. 'And when we finally did, the clothes were shit.'

Over a weekend – the same weekend the Beatles were recording their starry-eyed video for 'Hello, Goodbye' – The Fool gathered art students to paint the exterior of the Apple townhouse in Savile Row. The mural featured moons and shooting stars and an androgynous wide-eyed hippy figure, stretching across four storeys. The launch party – 'Come at 7.46. Fashion Show at 8.16' – attracted a mixed bag of celebrities, including John and George, Cilla Black, Eric Clapton, Victor Spinetti, Twiggy, Keith Moon and Richard Lester. A circus clown handed out apples, while a conga line of hippies played finger-cymbals and tambourines. Towards the end of the evening, rather too many people tried to squeeze into rather too small a space; as partygoers clambered outside for air, trampling half the stock underfoot, a man from the BBC fainted from lack of oxygen.

Within days the Westminster planning department were insisting on the removal of the mural, for which they had never granted permission. Further Apple money was spent on contesting the decision, but to no avail: down it went.

Pete Shotton never felt at ease in the boutique he had been hired to manage: 'Every time I caught one of the blow-up chairs with my cigarette, I would collapse in a heap on the floor.'

In the spirit of the age, clothes flew off the rails and out of the door, with no intervening trip to the counter. The staff, being cool, didn't like to insist on payment, though they themselves were happy to exit each evening carrying armfuls of bell-bottoms and Nehru jackets, with little attempt at concealment. Within seven months the Apple Boutique had lost £20,000, or £340,000 in today's money.

At the end of July 1968 the Beatles decided to close it down. The night before it shut for the last time, the four of them arrived with friends and took what they fancied. John raced around, gleefully grabbing whatever he could, apparently unaware that he was purloining from himself. The next day, shoppers piled in, attracted by the idea that there was now no need to shoplift. In under twenty-four hours Apple offloaded £10,000 worth of clothes. But this left a fresh debt with which to deal: in their haste, the management forgot that all the stock was subject to purchase tax at 12½ per cent, even if it had been given away for nothing.

Having closed the boutique, the Beatles moved Apple's headquarters to 3 Savile Row, losing their tax records along the way. Their new headquarters was turned into a free-for-all, with guests and employees alike vying to see who could charge most to Apple. Whenever John and Yoko dropped by, Yoko would order a pot of caviar costing £60; Barry Miles calculated that this was 'about five weeks' wages for one of the cooks who served it'.

The Apple phone bill came to roughly £4,000 a quarter. 'Every time you turn around there are at least half a dozen people on the phone who don't even work in the building,' noted Richard DiLello, who perused the bills with astonishment. 'Since when is there an Apple office in Katmandu? Or in Sausalito? Or Acapulco?'

Visitors and employees alike walked off with all sorts of stuff: televisions, electric typewriters, speakers, cases of wine, fan heaters. One employee removed the lead from the roof on a daily basis, soon creating leaks that caused thousands of pounds' worth of damage. Musicians and artists and film-makers sponsored by Apple refused to acknowledge any distinction between loans and gifts. 'We were giving out all that money and the cameras and equipment and half of the people we never saw again – they just went off with it,' observed Ringo.

Once in a while, management made a half-hearted attempted to rein everyone in. On 2 June 1968, Neil Aspinall sent a memo to department heads:

> Please ensure that your staff are prompt each morning. Recently, a number of people have been getting very tardy. There's no excuse. Ten o'clock should be within everybody's reach. Also, please don't put joss sticks in the typewriter carriages, please keep drunken Irishmen out of our board meetings, please tell the girl hiding in the lavatory that Paul never uses that one [and] please don't try to play jam butties on the hi-fi equipment.

Apple was a runaway horse. For a year the company employed a full-time mystic called Caleb, whose role was to steer the business with regular readings of tarot cards and the *I Ching*. 'The weirdness was not controlled at the start,' noted Derek Taylor. 'You can't control weirdness, anyway; weirdness is weirdness.' He was one to talk: in the space of a fortnight, his own press office clocked up a bill for six hundred Benson & Hedges cigarettes, eight dozen Cokes, eight bottles of J&B whisky, four bottles of Courvoisier brandy, three bottles of vodka, two dozen ginger ales, one dozen tonic waters, two dozen bitter lemons, one dozen tomato juices, three bottles of lime and four dozen lagers. Having studied the invoice, another Apple employee commented, 'Oh, they've cut back a bit then.' In an editorial in the Apple house magazine Derek Taylor said, 'We've had many guests at Apple, friends. Can't remember any of them. Very stoned, you see. Affects the memory.'

George, once so beady about money and so wary of the taxman, succumbed to the anti-materialism in the air. Only when the clouds had lifted could he see the Beatles' big mistake. 'We've been giving away too much to the wrong people,' he told Pattie. 'This place has become a haven for dropouts. The trouble is, some of our best friends are dropouts.'

In this barmy army, it didn't help that the top brass were, more often than not, out of their heads. When the Beatles finally heard the sirens wail, they had no idea which way to run. 'It's really like Vietnam,' said George, with a touch of hyperbole. 'It's escalated. It's got so big, but we can't really see the way out.'

Having woken up to what was happening, John went from stupor to panic, with nothing in between, pointing an accusing finger at everyone but himself: 'People were robbing us and living on us … Eighteen or twenty thousand pounds a week was rolling out of Apple and nobody was doing anything about it. All our buddies that had worked for us for fifty years were all just living and drinking and eating like fuckin' Rome! And I suddenly realised it. We were losing money at such a rate that we would have been broke, really broke. We didn't have anything in the bank really, none of us did. Paul and I could probably have floated, but we were sinking fast. It was just hell, and it had to stop.'

Dismayed at all the money pouring out of their money-saving scheme, John met Derek Taylor and Neil Aspinall to work out a plan of action. The three men kicked off their business meeting by taking LSD, before deciding – quite reasonably, given the circumstances – that all Apple's problems could be solved by walking down Weybridge High Street and knocking on the doors of the local bank manager and the local solicitor. 'Listen,' they planned to say, 'Apple is in a mess, but we need a simple solution: a simple bank manager who is reliable and a simple solicitor who can see his way through all this mess.'

John, according to Paul – or Paul, according to John – then called in the very same big businessmen that Apple had been founded to oppose. Sir Joseph Lockwood of EMI suggested they hire the former Conservative Party chairman Lord Poole, who in turn suggested Lord Beeching, whose 1963 report into the future of the British rail network had resulted in the axing of a third of all railway stations. Beeching examined Apple's financial records, before advising the Beatles to stick to music.

On 21 March 1969, John, George and Ringo asked the New Jersey bruiser Allen Klein, a man characterised by Alistair Taylor as having 'the charm of a broken lavatory seat', to be their business manager. In a series of deft manoeuvres, Klein had managed to persuade John that he was just the man to take charge of their affairs. He won Yoko over by promising to arrange a major show of her work in the US.* Ringo had been even more easily wooed: 'All I wanted was to be looked after. I would get off the plane or the *QE2* in New York and there'd be a guy there: a pretty stocky guy who would get me through, get me in a limo, give me a pack of money, get me a suite in a hotel – and that was it. That was cool for me. I was easily pleased. Just get me to the place on time!'

A bull in this most higgledy-piggledy of china shops, Klein charged about upsetting almost everyone at Apple, including the diligent Geoff Emerick, who was perturbed by his habit of saying 'Ker-ching!' whenever a Beatles song came on the radio. Derek Taylor compared this

* This finally took place on 9 October 1971. As Yoko had not completed enough work to fill the available space, a team of workers was hired to construct further installations. Cost overruns meant that all four Beatles were left with a bill for $80,000.

period to 'the last days of Pompeii, when the boiling shit hit the fan and sprayed over leaders and followers alike, leaving us all feeling grubby and ugly and useless.' Within days, Klein had fired most of the Apple staff, including the general manager, Alistair Taylor, who had worked for the Beatles since the day they were first signed by Brian Epstein. Taylor rang each of the four Beatles in turn to tell them what had happened, but none of them was able to come to the phone.

Many unrealised ideas, at various stages of development or undevelopment, died with Apple. John had championed Apple Limousines, a fleet of psychedelic Rolls-Royces. Paul planned to open a store selling only white products: 'You can never get anything white, like cups and all that. I've been looking for a decent set of white cups for five years.' All four Beatles envisaged opening an Apple School, offering carefree education to the children of the Beatles and their staff. Other unrealised projects included an Apple Entertainment and Shopping Centre on Regent Street, with a cinema, sauna and restaurant; Apple Cosmetics, offering a range of perfumes, lipsticks and lotions in apple-shaped containers; and an international franchise of Sgt. Pepper discothèques.

In a sense, the spirit of Apple lived on in John and Yoko. Throughout the rest of 1969 they initiated a variety of schemes more impractical and improbable than any they had just abandoned. Most came to nothing. In the autumn they wrote a long letter to Eric Clapton suggesting what they called 'a kind of "Easy Rider" at sea': a ship for thirty people, including musicians and crew, plus 'doctors, etc, in case of any kind of bother', cruising from Los Angeles to Tahiti, all being filmed and financed by EMI or a film company. 'The whole trip would take 3–4–5–6 months, depending how we all felt – all families, children whatever are welcome etc.'

Generally, John's ideas would come and go. Paul developed a technique for letting them float away on air, like bubbles. One day John suggested the two of them undergo joint trepanning: 'It's an ancient Roman thing – you have a hole drilled in your skull.' Paul ummed and erred before saying, 'You have it done, and if it's fine we'll all have it done as well.' These vaguely encouraging noises were, he had worked out, the best way to ensure that nothing happened. 'Otherwise he would have had us all with holes in our heads the next morning.'

117

One day, shortly after John had run off with Yoko, Paul drove to Weybridge to see Cynthia. He thought she might need cheering up. 'Paul was the only member of the Beatles family who'd had the courage to defy John – who had apparently made it quite clear that he expected everyone to follow his lead in cutting me off. But Paul was his own man and not afraid of John,' Cynthia remembered. She had heard nothing from Ringo or George, or either of their wives: 'They didn't want to bring John's fury on themselves, and probably didn't know what to say to me anyway.'

Julian was then five, the same age John had been when his own father left home. Paul had always been close to Julian. He had a rapport with children that was lost on John: when the Beatles went to Greece to buy their island, John spent his time reading the newspapers while Paul played Cowboys and Indians with Julian. 'He'd been like an uncle to him,' John admitted years later. 'Paul was always good with kids.'

In this respect, Paul felt sorry for John. 'I remember John coming up to me once and he took me aside and said, "How do you do it?" I said, "What do you mean?" He said, "With Julian. How do you play with kids like that?" I remember feeling a wave of sorrow coming over me … I tried to give the potted version, you know, "Play, pretend you're a kid. Play with him." But John never got it. Never got the hang of it.' Now in late middle age, Julian remembers seeing more of Paul than of his father: 'We had a great friendship going, and there seem to be far more pictures of me and Paul playing together at that age than there are pictures of me and my dad.'

Driving down to Weybridge in his Aston Martin, Paul was thinking about the consequences of the split on Julian: 'I knew it was not going to be easy for him. I always feel sorry for kids in divorces.' From out of nowhere, a song came into his head. 'Hey Jules,' it began, 'don't make it bad. Take a sad song, and make it better.'

118

In August 1968 the Rolling Stones had much to celebrate. They had completed their new album, *Beggars Banquet*, Mick Jagger had just turned twenty-five, and the Vesuvio Club, part owned by Jagger and Keith Richards, was reopening.

The party they threw at the Vesuvio was a suitably wild celebration of these three events. Moroccan tapestries draped the walls, along with giant photographs of the Stones. A helium-filled zeppelin floated up and down, vast silver bowls were filled with a mixture of punch and mescaline, and tables groaned with plates piled with hash cakes. Hubble pipes were provided, along with dainty dishes of hash, for those who preferred inhaling to ingesting.

'My only fear,' recalled the club's manager Tony Sanchez,* 'was the club's proximity to Tottenham Court Road police station. It was only three hundred yards away, and a couple of inquisitive cops would have been able to arrest just about every superstar in Britain if they had decided on a raid that night.'

Jagger arrived early, having flown from Ireland with the first advance pressing of *Beggars Banquet*. Sanchez, acting as disc jockey, proceeded to play it. It was an instant success: everyone present seemed either to be dancing to it or saying how amazing it was, or both at the same time. On top of all this, John Lennon and Yoko Ono dropped by, the

* Sanchez was the 'personal assistant' of Keith Richards, and has also been credited with the no less onerous role of preferred drug dealer to the Rolling Stones, Robert Fraser and, from time to time, the Beatles.

summer of '68's progressive equivalent of a visit from the Queen and the Duke of Edinburgh.

Arriving a little later than most of the other partygoers was Paul McCartney, fresh from Trident Studios, a short walk away in Soho, bringing with him the acetate disc of the Beatles' next single. Having greeted his hosts, he walked through the dancers to the turntables, and discreetly handed the disc to Tony Sanchez, saying, 'See what you think of it, Tony. It's our new one.'

Once *Beggars Banquet* had come to an end, and Mick and Keith were milling about, garnering praise from their guests, Sanchez slipped the new Beatles single onto the turntable.

'Hey Jude, don't make it bad, take a –'

Everyone stopped talking. For the next seven minutes eleven seconds, they remained completely silent.

'It just went – boom! – straight to the chest,' recalls Marianne Faithfull. 'It was the first time anyone had heard it, and we were all just blown away … We had a sense of everyone being in the right place, at the right time, with the right people.'

Tony Sanchez felt Mick Jagger's mood changing: 'When it was over, I noticed that Mick looked peeved.' Paul remembers Mick coming up to him and saying, 'Fuckin' 'ell! Fuckin' 'ell! That's something else, innit? It's like two songs. It's got the song and then the whole "na na na" at the end. Yeah.'

Later that night, John staggered over to Sanchez, 'looking as though his eyes were about to pop out of his head', and asked him to call a cab. All three doormen went outside to hail one, but they failed to come back. Sanchez was later to discover that the interaction of the fresh air with the mescaline and the hash had rendered the three of them insensible: they completely forgot who they were, where they were, and what they were supposed to be doing. Jagger saved the day by volunteering the use of his own Aston Martin DB6, and Tony Sanchez's cousin, acting as chauffeur, successfully drove John and Yoko all the way back to Ascot, Surrey.

119

It was late afternoon on a perfect English summer's day, 30 June 1968. Paul was in his Rolls-Royce, being driven back to London from Yorkshire, where he had been recording 'Thingumybob' with the Black Dyke Mills Band. Derek Taylor, Peter Asher and a journalist from the *NME* were also in the car. As they travelled down the M1 they decided to stop off somewhere. But where? Derek, high on LSD, suggested that Peter should take a look at the AA map of Bedfordshire, and pick the village with the most beautiful name.

After a very long time, Peter made an unlikely choice: Harrold. The chauffeur obediently wended his way along minor roads until they arrived at the village of that name. For Derek, it was like a dream come true: 'Thrushes and blackbirds sang and swallows dived into thatches and a little old mower wheezed as we walked down the only street there was.'

In the garden of Mulberry Lodge, his home on the High Street, Gordon Mitchell, a mustachioed dentist, was out in his shorts, clipping a hedge. He looked up to see three men led by Paul McCartney, who asked him the way to the river. Mitchell gave him the directions, and they went on their way. Mitchell nipped inside to tell his wife Pat what had happened: Paul McCartney had just asked him the way to the river. Together, they beetled off in the same direction, hoping to bump into Paul and his friends.

Sure enough, they found them in the Magpie pub, and fell into conversation with them. Soon they were all feeling peckish, and Pat suggested that if they came back to Mulberry Lodge she could rustle something up. 'Paul showed his humanity by visiting Pat's father, at that time an invalid in bed, and had a long chat with him,' recalled Gordon Mitchell forty years later.

They tucked into ham and rice. Gordon told Paul of the raffle he was organising for the Playing Fields Association the following weekend. Mitchell's daughter Shuna brought out a child-sized guitar and handed it to Paul, who immediately started tuning it, putting two coins under the bridge. Paul wondered if they'd care to hear a song he had just composed, and they all said yes. 'Hey Jude, don't make it bad,' he began.

'Why can't life always be like this?' sighed Pat Mitchell.

According to Gordon Mitchell, 'They were all the nicest people one could wish to meet, and great fun, and it was a very special evening.'

Around 11 p.m. someone arrived to say that though the Oakley Arms was officially closed, the landlord had agreed to reopen it, 'in your honour, Paul'. So off they went to the Oakley Arms, which, according to Derek, was packed: 'The whole village was there. Paul played the piano, including another rendition of "Hey Jude", until at three o'clock a woman stood and sang "The Fool on the Hill" and he left the piano to dance with her and kiss her on the cheek.'

In the early hours of the morning Paul and his gang set off back to London in his Rolls-Royce. A few days later, Gordon and Pat Mitchell received a thank-you letter, along with two bottles of champagne for the raffle.

120

Possibly so as to avoid wounding John's fragile self-esteem, Paul changed 'Hey Jules' to 'Hey Jude' before singing it to him for the first time. John took the song to be about him, and his need for Yoko: 'If you think about it, Yoko's just coming into the picture. He's saying, "Hey, Jude – hey, John." I know I'm sounding like one of those fans who reads things into it, but you CAN hear it as a song to me. The words "go out and get her" – subconsciously he was saying, "Go ahead, leave me." But on a conscious level, he didn't want me to go ahead. The angel inside him was saying, "Bless you." The devil in him didn't like it at all, because he didn't want to lose his partner.'

John was not alone in his solipsism. Many Beatles songs have a vague, fluid quality that pulls the listener towards a personal interpretation. The lyric of 'Hey Jude' is at one and the same time pliable and precise. On its release, some took it to be directed at Bob Dylan, who had become a recluse at his farm in Woodstock. *Time* magazine thought it was a call for commitment; *Rolling Stone* felt it was a plea for John to end his negative attitude towards women.

Aged sixteen, Douglas Adams* was queuing outside a gym when the word went round that one of his schoolmates had heard the Beatles' latest single. 'We basically held him against the wall and made him hum it to us.'

John Updike, thirty-six, flush from the success of his novel *Couples*, was enjoying an extended break in London with his family. That late

* Douglas Adams (1952–2001), author of *The Hitchhiker's Guide to the Galaxy*.

summer, the Beatles 'were very much around'. Sitting in a double-decker bus, Updike looked out of the window and there was Paul walking along the street, 'looking quite unshaven'.

In retrospect, Updike saw 'Hey Jude' as 'a great song of farewell ... farewell to London, farewell to the Beatles, as it turns out. And it mounts in a way as most of this music does to a kind of ecstasy. It really is a thrilling piece, showing the Beatles at their most adventurous and offhand at the same time.'

Aged seventeen, Gordon Brown* was in hospital, recovering from an operation to save his right eye, having already lost the sight in his left. Forever after, he would associate being in hospital with 'Hey Jude' being played over the air. For him, its message was both melancholy and optimistic: 'It's sad to start with, but actually very positive by the time it ends.'

The philosopher Raymond Tallis was twenty-one, and completing a medical degree at Oxford. More than any other tune, 'Hey Jude' made him feel the spirit of 'infinite possibility you have when you're young'.

This blank canvas of meaning was evident from the start. The first time Paul played the song to John, he was embarrassed by the ricketiness of a particular line: 'the movement you need is on your shoulder'.

'I'll fix that bit,' he assured him.

'You won't, you know,' said John. 'That's the best line in the song. I know what it means – it's great.'

But what exactly, or even inexactly, *does* it mean? Paul, something of a stickler for clarity, had two immediate objections to the line: first, he had already used the word 'shoulders' earlier in the song; and second, 'It's a stupid expression, it sounds like a parrot.' Both are true; yet for some reason, when bound to the music it does make a kind of sense. Until I started writing this book, I had always thought he was singing 'the *moment* you need is on your shoulder', which obviously means something quite different to 'the *movement* you need is on your shoulder'. Yet when I realised that I had been making a mistake for fifty

* Gordon Brown (1951–), prime minister 2007–10.

years, I was surprised to find that it made no real difference to the meaning. One makes more sense than the other, but without the music, neither of them makes much sense at all.

Sung to the music, there is something very moving about those words: in fact, they become the key lines of the verse, speaking of kindness, consolation and the need to keep going. We tend to regard music as abstract, and lyrics as concrete. But in a good song, they are indivisible. Lyrics removed from music are like fish removed from water, or butterflies pinned to a card.

You could almost say that the more sense lyrics make in print, the less power they have in song: rock works most powerfully when it is like a native chant, or a Latin hymn, its scattered meanings transformed into abstract sound, floating free of specificity. This is why the valiant attempts of Professor Sir Christopher Ricks to bolster the significance of Bob Dylan by interpreting his lyrics with the solemnity of academia are doomed. It is as though a fan of balloons tried to convey his enthusiasm by taking out a sharp pin and piercing them. Allotting three pages of his five-hundred-page book *Dylan's Visions of Sin* to the song 'All I Really Want to Do', Ricks urges the reader to 'notice Dylan's dexterity with "knock you up":

> I ain't lookin' to block you up
> Shock or knock or lock you up.

'The cunning propriety tactfully, pregnantly, separates "knock" from "you up"; for a couple of words; after all, the preceding "shock" would more suggest "shock you" than "shock you *up*"'.

Under the professor's keen eye, the line 'Why wait any longer for the one you love' becomes unfathomably complex. 'It is as though "longer" were a longer form of the word "long", and so it is, but not of this yearning meaning of the word. The feeling of longing is evoked, of longing and waiting. But how much longer?'

Explaining the end of 'If Not for You', Ricks writes: 'How does the end of "If Not for You" succeed in ringing true? The inescapable acknowledgement that even gratitude cannot be expressed for ever is brought home by Dylan's decision to depart from the song with the words "If not for you" repeated and repeated – in their beautiful simplicity – as if they, though they have got to go, could go on ad infinitum.' Hang on, Professor, you want to shout: it's called a fade-out, and is often employed in pop songs when a producer can't come up with anything better.

Do 'Hey Jude's' words really matter? After all, over the years, many listeners have misheard them, converting 'Hey Jude' to 'Hey dude', or even 'Hay chewed'. There are those who have spent their whole lives hearing 'The minute you let her under your skin' as 'Remember, there's lettuce under your skin'. Who knows? Perhaps this Rorschach method has increased the impact of the song, each listener unknowingly crafting lyrics appropriate to the particular demands of his or her own existence. Small wonder, in a way, that John thought it was all about him. These days, when Paul sings the song at concerts, he finds the line 'The movement you need is on your shoulder' particularly poignant: 'When I play that song, that's the line when I think of John, and I sometimes get a little emotional during that moment.' So John's suspicion has, to this extent, been proved right: in the mind of its composer and performer, during those few seconds, 'Hey Jude' is indeed a song about John.

The last four minutes of 'Hey Jude' are, of course, virtually wordless, all meaning subsumed by chant. The na-na-na-nanananas are a mantra, its force born of endless repetition. 'Hey Jude' was originally intended as a message of hope for the five-year-old Julian Lennon, but it soon turned into a message of hope for the world. For John Updike, the Beatles were like 'the sun coming up on Easter Morning'.

121

Joel Soroka was twenty-one in 1968. Having grown up in New York, he spent that summer travelling around Europe. It was the first time he had ever left North America. 'In early September, I found myself in a B&B off the Edgware Road. There were no showers or central heating, and we ate rare bacon for breakfast. It was all new to me.'

On 3 September he caught a bus from the Edgware Road to Piccadilly, in order to pick up mail from home. Still new to the complexities of London Transport, he caught the wrong bus back. By chance, an attractive woman sat next to him. 'We got chatting. Then, out of the blue, she asked, "Would you like to meet the Beatles?" I said something like, "Give me a break."' She told him she worked for Apple, and that the Beatles were filming a promotional film for their new single the following night. 'They were looking for a crowd, and she liked my face.'

Handing him what he describes as 'an unofficial-looking piece of paper', she told him to be at Victoria station the next day at 4 p.m: a bus would be waiting.

Joel didn't believe a word of it, but he turned up on the off-chance. Sure enough, a bus was waiting, and, along with many others, he boarded it. 'We were a mixed bag of people and ages, everyone chatting excitedly, but there was a sense that no one believed we were actually going to meet the Beatles.'

They were dropped off at Twickenham Studios, which he thought looked like a hangar, and then led into a brightly lit area, with technical people milling around a platform on which drums and other instruments had been arranged. A group of about a hundred people waited around expectantly, under the gaze of the director Michael Lindsay-Hogg. Suddenly the door opened, and in trooped the Beatles. 'I thought, "Is this really happening?" We were told to hang out while they warmed up. I was in a state of total glee. Despite being a Beatlemaniac, I'd never seen them live.'

The Beatles played 'Hey Jude' three or four times. The coachload of randomers were told to surround the stage and sing along with the chorus. Joel noted that most of them 'were so quiet and British, but I was determined to make my mark'. He wheedled himself into a strategic position close to the platform. At one point Ringo placed his tambourine on the floor and, quick off the mark, Joel seized the opportunity to climb onstage and pick it up.

'I was hoping they'd go with that take, but they did about a dozen. Each time, more and more people joined me onstage. With each take, I was obsessed with getting my hands on the tambourine. I must have been a bit of a bore.'

In between takes, he introduced himself to each of the Beatles. 'Paul was charming. John was sarcastic. I recall him saying, "You're from New York? Did you come to our concerts there?" In the spirit of sarcasm, I replied, "What, pay money to see the Beatles?" I think he liked my reply. George was silent. And Ringo was a sweetheart. "Call me Ritchie," he said.' Joel went around inviting each of the Beatles back to his bed-and-breakfast, but when filming finished they were all whisked away in a limousine.

On Joel's arrival back in New York, no one believed his story, 'but soon after, the film appeared on the Smothers Brothers' show, as well as on *Top of the Pops* in the UK. And there I was.'

In 2020, Joel turned seventy-three. 'They are just people to me now, but in 1968 the Beatles were gods. Other than my children being born, it's the most amazing thing that's happened to me.'

Tom Topping was eleven in 1968, on a month's holiday in London with his parents and his twelve-year-old sister. As they were queuing to see the film of *Yellow Submarine* in Leicester Square, a man with a clipboard approached his father and invited them all to catch a bus from

Victoria station to Twickenham the next day. 'For two kids from Los Angeles who loved the Beatles, it was an amazing adventure.'

On one of the takes, Tom managed to nip up onstage and sit next to Paul and his piano. 'I reached over and touched the red velvet dinner jacket like it was the cloak of Turin. Several young women were crowded around, and one was pinching my leg so I would get out of her way. OUCH! She meant business.'

Margaret Morel had an American pen-friend, on holiday in London, who tipped off Margaret and her flatmate Coral about the trip to Twickenham. Margaret arrived at Victoria station in a bright yellow dress. When their coach drew up outside the studios, the girls peered out and saw the Beatles watching them through a window, 'giving us smiles and waves. Everyone was very excited and happy, of course.'

Inside the studio, they were told to gather round the Beatles the second the chorus began. 'Paul helped by saying "Now" when it was time to join in.' Coral and Margaret were quick off the mark: 'My friend Coral and I got up onto the stage each time and stood next to George Harrison. I don't know how we managed to do that with all the people who were scrambling to get as near as they could to the Beatles … They filmed lots of takes of "Hey Jude" all day. We seemed to sing our na na nas dozens of times. If I remember correctly, they began filming during the morning and we finished about 10 p.m. or later. My friend's parents came to collect us with their car. We were exhausted but very happy, our heads full of all that had taken place that day.'

Unfortunately, when the film was premiered four days later, on David Frost's show, Margaret's boss happened to be watching, so he spotted Margaret in her yellow dress standing next to George. 'I was supposed to be ill that day and had taken the day off,' recalls Margaret. 'I swore it wasn't me.' Her boss graciously accepted her denial. 'He was a lovely man and just let me think he believed me.'

In the finished film, the Beatles appear to be alone in the studio until Paul leads into the chorus, at which point lots of people flood in to join them, including a man in a purple turban, a woman in a large white dress, a black man in a fancy waistcoat and a heavily-made-up blonde sporting an elaborate hairdo. They all race to grab a prominent spot beside Paul. Despite jockeying for position, they look relaxed and delighted to be there. Two young boys, one in a tweed jacket and tie and horn-rimmed specs, the other in a more groovy military jacket, secure themselves places on either side of Ringo, who gives them a broad grin. Not for the first time, he seems the happiest of all the Beatles.

Six minutes in, a toothless old geezer appears, a hippy Albert Steptoe, with large flowers tucked behind both ears. Just as bizarrely, he is holding a flat brown package of some sort. He introduces a note of jeopardy into the proceedings. Every now and then, he sees it as his duty to turn around and conduct all the others. At one point he nudges up very close to Paul, and touches him on his shoulder. For a second Paul shows a flash of irritation – the movement he doesn't need is on his shoulder – and brushes him off.

As the years have rolled by, this batty old geezer has become an object of fascination in online discussion groups.

> 'Does anyone know who the strange old guy at the end of Hey Jude annoying Paul is?'
>
> 'I don't remember his name … He was a local drunkard and possibly homeless man who was hanging out nearby, so they brought him in. He kind of ruins the video but at the same time makes it better.'
>
> 'He looks like a man who used to wander the streets of London's Soho back then (1968). We all called him "Rosie" in reference to his penchant for floral adornments, although I think he usually wore carnations as in the video. Not sure how he made it out to Twickenham though.'
>
> 'His name was Bill and he helped the Beatles with Magical Mystery Tour.'
>
> 'Where does he come from and why is there a piece of cardboard pinched under his right armpit? And what is the black object that he is raising in the air with his left hand at 6:31 and again at 6:50? Is it a bottle? Why is he showing this? This object is gone at 7:14.'

The more one looks at the 'Hey Jude' video, the more mesmerising this batty old codger becomes. Like everybody else, he is in the right place at the right time, but unlike the others, he is the wrong person in the right place at the right time. Yet he doesn't hesitate to make the most of it. Bursting with self-confidence, he edges closer and closer to Paul, orchestrating the crowd, bursting with joie-de-vivre, proudly convinced of his own indispensability.

Beatle-watchers devote an inordinate amount of time to identifying this oddball. He is, in his way, the British equivalent of the umbrella man in Dealey Plaza.

> 'Is there a connection with the red carnations and left-handed guitar made of white carnations on the cover of Sgt Pepper? What is the connection to the carnations in the booklet accompanying the Magical Mystery Tour album?'
>
> 'What puzzles me most is that he touches the right shoulder of Paul twice. First at 7:26 and again at 7:36 … And then at 7:46 he looks upwards and points his left hand forefinger to the ceiling.'

The Beatles shone so brightly that anyone caught in their beam, no matter how briefly, became part of their myth.

122

In Beatles mythology, Detective Sergeant Norman Clement 'Nobby' Pilcher looms like a bumbling avenging angel. He is Tom trying to trap Jerry, Jaws snapping at innocent bathers, Cruella de Vil sizing up dalmatians for the slaughter, or – perhaps closer to the reality – a Keystone Kop balancing a bucket of water on top of a door then forgetting all about it and getting soaked himself.

Five years older than John and Ringo, Norman Pilcher joined the Metropolitan Police in 1955, moving from the Flying Squad to the Drugs Squad in 1966, the very same year the Beatles were urging the young to turn off their minds, relax and float downstream. Pastimes such as these were far from Pilcher's agenda: he wanted to bring criminals to justice, by whatever means possible.

One of Pilcher's earliest victims, Eric Clapton, described him, not inaccurately, as 'a kind of police groupie'. He was an autograph-hunter with handcuffs at the ready. He would keep an eye out for glassy-eyed singers and musicians, then target them for immediate investigation. As a consequence, his own fame began to rise commensurately.

Det. Sgt Pilcher conducted his first celebrity raid on 11 June 1966. Some weeks previously he had taken a keen interest in *A Boy Called Donovan*, a TV documentary about the hippy lifestyle of the fey, self-styled 'troubadour', in whose most recent single, 'Sunshine Superman', he had detected clear references to blowing minds. Its B-side, 'The Trip', was even more explicit.

In the documentary, louche long-haired young men and groovy women were seen lying around on cushions, playing guitars, handing around cigarettes shaped like barrage balloons and talking about

freedom and love and ending all wars. It ended with two policemen entering one of these free-and-easy gatherings, apparently hosted by Donovan, searching about, finding nothing and leaving empty-handed. At this point Donovan gave a big, bleary wink to the camera, brazenly signalling that he himself was under the influence and couldn't care less who knew it.

Pilcher had found his next target. A few weeks later, he led nine Drugs Squad officers on a raid of Donovan's flat in the Edgware Road. There, in the bedroom of the singer's friend 'Gypsy Dave' Mills, they found a block of cannabis resin. Donovan, Gypsy Dave and a lady friend were immediately arrested and charged with possession.

George and Paul rallied around, hiring their lawyer, David Jacobs, to represent the accused. But they were found guilty, and fined £250. Eight months later, in February 1967, Pilcher sanctioned a raid on Keith Richards' house, 'Redlands', in West Wittering, narrowly missing George and Pattie Harrison, who had left just a few minutes before.

And so it continued. On 19 August 1968, Pilcher successfully raided the flat of the jazz musician Tubby Hayes, charging him with possession of diamorphine and heroin. Later that month Donovan received an urgent call from John, who said: 'I just got a call from a friend. I'm going to be busted.' Donovan and Gypsy Dave drove down to Surrey, where they found John 'swaggering like a sailor, his long hair flying, angry and ready to fight'. Donovan tried to calm him down: 'Leave it to Gyp, he knows what to do.'

On a long glass coffee table were what Donovan recognised straight away as 'three pyramids of sinsemilla', a highly psychoactive variety of cannabis, the latest of a batch delivered to John every three months by a wealthy American admirer, hidden in the wings of a Mercedes. John sat back and played a Howlin' Wolf song on his jukebox while Gypsy Dave and Donovan took charge of flushing the pyramids down the loo.

According to Donovan, they had just concluded another round of vigorous flushing when Det. Sgt Pilcher arrived. Finding nothing, he 'assembled his men in the hall and said, "Next time we will get you, Lennon, mark my words."' Donovan looked on askance. 'I thought John was going to nut him then and there, but Gyp held him back. As the cops filed out of the door John held it open for them, then crashed it shut with a "Good bloody riddance. Fuck off you bastards!" And they were gone.'

John's actor friend Victor Spinetti remembers the incident slightly differently. In his version Donovan was already at John's house, getting ready to show a film, when someone phoned with a tip-off. 'Oh God,' said John, 'there's going to be a police raid.' He scooted around the house, picking up the cannabis, throwing it down the loo and attempting to flush it: 'It took forever to float away, but then it was a silly place to put it.' John then spotted something in a box, snatched it up and buried it in the garden. 'At that moment, the police barged in, went upstairs, woke Julian, John's son, and shook out his bed, this child's bed! There was nothing hidden in it. After that they went right through the house, ransacking the place. We just sat there.' According to Spinetti the police left the house empty-handed, but not before asking John for an autograph.

Two months later John and Yoko were living in Ringo's flat in Montagu Square. One Friday Pete Shotton dropped by, only to find John hard at work with the vacuum cleaner.

'Oh Christ, Pete! Am I glad to see you! The Drug Squad's on the way!'

This time John had been tipped off by Don Short, the showbusiness correspondent of the *Daily Mirror*, who had himself been tipped off by the police. Before embarking on a raid, Pilcher liked to be sure of publicity.

John grew ever more frantic with his cleaning. 'Jimi fucking Hendrix used to live here!' he yelled as he rammed the Hoover back and forth against the walls. 'Christ knows what the fuck is in these carpets!'

While Pete and John bustled about looking for anything incriminating, John disappeared into the bedroom. Through the door, Pete heard him arguing with Yoko. It soon dawned on Pete that they were arguing about him. 'I don't want him here! I just don't want him here!' screeched Yoko. The two of them had never got along.

'Well, I fucking want him here!' replied John. 'We can use a bit of fucking help right now, and Pete just wants to help us!'

'We can handle this ourselves, John, we don't need HIM around! I don't *want* him around!'

Tactfully, Pete let himself out, taking the vacuum-cleaner bag with him. Just before midnight, six policemen and one policewoman arrived on the doorstep. Yoko opened the door for just long enough to hear the policewoman say they had a search warrant. Then, in the measured words of Det. Sgt Pilcher, 'Upon being informed that we were police officers and the reason for our visit, she ran back along the passage into the flat and slammed and locked the door.'

At the same time, an officer nipped round to the back of the building, and attempted to open the bedroom window while John held it shut, shouting, 'I don't care who you are, you're not bloody coming in here!' Then Yoko took over window duty while John got dressed.

'Just open the window! You'll only make it worse for yourself!' shouted the officer.

'I want to see the warrant!' John shouted back. The police pressed the warrant to the window, and he pretended to read it. The police then tried to force the front door. Grudgingly, John let them in.

The police contingent included two dog handlers, but for some reason they had neglected to bring their dogs. In the half-hour it took for them to arrive John rang Neil Aspinall, who in turn rang Peter Brown, who was busy shepherding Paul's latest discovery, the innocent Welsh songstress Mary Hopkin, between her various appointments. Brown raced round to find John and Yoko being formally charged with possession: the sniffer dogs, blessed with the inappropriately happy-go-lucky names of Yogi and Boo-Boo,* had apparently uncovered cannabis in a leather binocular case and a suitcase. John was mystified – in his words, 'I'm not stupid. I went through the whole damn house.'

By now, the press had assembled in force outside the building. They watched John and Yoko being taken to Paddington Green police station, where they were each bailed for £100, and booked to appear in court the next morning.

Their hearing lasted five minutes. Det. Sgt Pilcher read out the two charges against them, one for possession of a dangerous drug, the other for 'wilfully obstructing Norman Pilcher, a constable of the Metropolitan Police Force …' The case was adjourned until 28 November. On leaving the courtroom, John and Yoko were forced to wait in a scrum of journalists and photographers for their car to arrive. Never slow to turn a mishap to their advantage, they included one of these photographs on the back cover of their next album, *Unfinished Music No 2: Life with the Lions*.

Two days after their court appearance, a Labour MP tabled a written

* Or were they pseudonyms?

question to the Home Secretary, James Callaghan, drawing attention to the excessive use of manpower in the raid. In his defence, hand-delivered to the Home Secretary, Det. Sgt Pilcher explained that 'at least five officers were required because of the difficulty in gaining entry to the premises and the fact that the premises consisted of two floors with numerous rooms that were in a very untidy condition'. He had needed extra manpower, he said, because 'it is not unusual when executing search warrants for premises occupied by members of the entertainment world to find that there are large numbers of people present taking part in unusual parties. In this case it was found that only two persons were present, and both were in a state of undress.'

Two days later, Mr Callaghan was asked 'to what extent the Metropolitan Police notified the press and publicity services of their intention to raid the private residence of John Lennon'. Det. Sgt Pilcher denied he had leaked news of the forthcoming raid, suggesting that a neighbour might have been responsible. However, an internal police report later concluded that 'One thing is certain as far as this incident is concerned, and that is the press was informed by somebody.'

Five months later, Pilcher struck again. This time he chose the day of Paul and Linda's wedding to raid George's home in Esher, imagining no one would be in. But, unknown to Pilcher, Paul had decided against inviting the other Beatles and their partners. This meant that Pattie was at home, waiting for George to drop by later to take her to a party in London: 'Suddenly I heard a lot of cars on the gravel in the drive – far too many for it to be just George. My first thought was that maybe Paul and Linda wanted to party after the wedding. Then the bell rang. I opened the door to find a crowd of uniformed policemen, one police-woman and a dog.'

The senior policeman introduced himself as Detective Sergeant Pilcher, and showed her his search warrant. 'In they came, about eight policemen through the front, another five or six through the back, and there were more in the greenhouse.' Yogi and Boo-Boo came too. George was later to suspect that Pilcher named Yogi after the Maharishi – not unlikely, given Pilcher's peculiarly needy relationship with those he sought to prosecute.

Pattie rang George at Apple. Calmly, George said he would sort something out. Soon the ever-faithful Pete Shotton, who lived around the corner, arrived. As the police scoured the bungalow, Pattie poured herself and Pete a vodka and tonic. Pete pulled out a packet of Rothmans, only to remember with a start that among the cigarettes were a couple of joints. Suddenly Det. Sgt Pilcher appeared. 'Look what Yogi has found!' he said to Pattie, brandishing a block of hash.

'Are you mad?' said Pattie. 'You brought that with you.'

Pilcher denied it: 'Yogi found it in one of your husband's shoes.'

'This is a joke,' retorted Pattie, adding, with beguiling honesty, 'If we had a lump of hash like that we certainly wouldn't keep it in George's shoes. If you'd said at the start you were looking for cannabis, I would have told you it's in the sitting room on the table in a pot. But you said you were looking for drugs. I thought you meant heroin or something dangerous …'

Pilcher was not amused. 'I want to save you from the evils and peril of heroin,' he said, or she said he said.

Pattie replied that she'd never touch heroin. She then accused Pilcher once again of planting the lump of hash. There was silence.

'Now what are you all going to do?' she asked.

'Any chance of a cup of tea?' asked Pilcher.

'Well, I'm not going to make it.'

To this day, the correct etiquette in such a situation remains hazy. As it was, a policewoman boiled the kettle and handed out the mugs. The various policemen then stood around looking awkward. One asked if they could watch the television. Another tried to break the ice with a polite question: 'Have the Beatles been doing any new music?'

'Yes,' snapped Pattie, 'but you're not going to hear it.'

Pete asked them about life in the Drugs Squad. Had they ever taken drugs, just so they'd know what they were after? One of them said he'd run his finger along someone's mantelpiece and then licked it, only to find himself embarking on an acid trip.

In a while, George arrived, together with Derek Taylor and a lawyer. Taylor noted how much the police were in awe of George: at the tender age of twenty-five he was, after all, one of the four most famous men in the world: 'They stood to attention and were almost elbowing each other out of the way to get closer to him.' Calm in the face of adversity, George ascended to a higher plain. 'Birds have their nests and animals have their holes,' he said, 'but the son of man hath nowhere to lay his head.' Perhaps not catching the biblical allusion, Det. Sgt Pilcher arrested him.

George was scornful of the two pieces of evidence produced by Pilcher and his officers. His defence was both novel and, within its own limits, persuasive: one piece of dope was indeed his, 'but I've never seen this one before in my fucking life! You don't have to bring your own dope to my house, I've got plenty myself! I could have shown you where the stuff was if you'd asked me.'

Later, he explained that he was exceptionally tidy by nature: 'I keep records in the record rack, tea in the tea caddy, pot in the pot box. This was the biggest stick of hashish I've ever seen, and something I'd obviously know about if I had seen it before.'

As George and Pattie were leaving for the police station, a press photographer appeared and started snapping away, causing George to lose his cool. 'What the fuck do you think you're doing on my property? I'm going to fucking kill you, you bastard!' He chased the photographer around the garden, followed, hot on his heels, by the Drug Squad. 'I couldn't help but laugh,' recalled Pete – it reminded him of a Marx Brothers chase.

At the police station, George and Pattie were fingerprinted and charged. 'We got home feeling gloomy,' recalled Pattie, 'so George said, "Come on, let's go to the party."'

The party in question was being thrown by the talented Old Etonian painter and musician Rory McEwen. As they entered, George and Pattie bumped into Lord Snowdon and Princess Margaret. 'You can't believe what happened,' said George. 'We got busted.'

'What a shame,' said Princess Margaret.

'Can you help us?' asked George. 'Can you use your influence?'

'Oh, I don't think so!' replied the princess, with a look of alarm.

Pattie's youngest sister Paula, who was also present, failed to pick up the signs. Instead, she lit a joint, took a puff and offered it to the princess, who abruptly turned on her heels and left, taking her baffled husband with her.

At Esher and Walton magistrates' court the following March, George and Pattie Harrison were found guilty of possession of cannabis and fined £250 each, plus ten guineas each in costs. 'I hope the police will leave us alone now,' George said as they left court.

The next month, George and Eric Clapton dropped in on an early-evening party given by the drug charity, Release, but they didn't stay long. Soon after their departure, Det. Sgt Pilcher arrived with his band of officers from the Drugs Squad, demanding to know the whereabouts of Harrison and Clapton. Told that they were on their way to a B.B. King concert at the Royal Albert Hall, he sighed and left.

Like so many who bobbed along in the wake of the Beatles, Det. Sgt Norman Pilcher tried to keep up with them, but ended up lost at sea. In 1972 he resigned from the Metropolitan Police in shadowy circumstances. Towards the end of that year he boarded a liner bound for Australia, where he planned to start a new life; but on his arrival at Fremantle he was arrested on charges of perjury and conspiracy to pervert the course of justice, and extradited back to Britain.

In September 1973, Pilcher was sentenced to four years in custody. The tables had turned. 'You poisoned the wells of criminal justice and set about it deliberately,' said Justice Melford Stevenson, never chummy. 'What is equally bad is that you have betrayed your comrades in the Metropolitan Police Force, which enjoys the respect of the civilised world – what remains of it.'

Thereafter, Norman Pilcher disappears from view, though some say he retired to Kent. But his legend lives on. Time has made a pantomime figure of him: the clodhopping, evidence-planting copper, mesmerised by those he yearns to bring down, rapping on the door after his prey has skedaddled. Yet he has achieved a form of immortality. In one *Monty Python* sketch he was immortalised as a giant hedgehog called Spiny Norman, 'twelve feet from snout to tail,' who sleeps in an aeroplane hangar at Luton Airport and spies on the notorious gangsters the Piranha Brothers. In another he is Police Constable Pan-Am, bent on arresting everyone, including witnesses and victims: 'I must warn you that anything you may say will be ignored … One more peep out of you and I'll do you for heresy … I'm charging you with illegal possession of whatever we happen to have down there.' In Eric Idle and Neil Innes's spoof Beatles documentary *The Rutles*, he is Detective Inspector Brian Plant, who plants Indian tea and biscuits on a member of the Rutles.

Norman Pilcher is also often credited as the 'semolina pilchard' in 'I am the Walrus', though the dates don't support it: the song was recorded in September 1967, just over a year before Det. Sgt Pilcher first turned up uninvited on the doorstep of Montagu Square.

123

On 26 August 1968, the first four Apple singles – 'Hey Jude' by the Beatles, 'Those Were the Days' by Mary Hopkin, 'Sour Milk Sea' by Jackie Lomax, and 'Thingumybob' by the Black Dyke Mills Band – were delivered by chauffeur-driven Mercedes to HM the Queen at Buckingham Palace, HM the Queen Mother at St James's Palace, and HRH Princess Margaret and Lord Snowdon at Kensington Palace. A few days later, this letter was received:

Dear Sir:
I am commanded by Queen Elizabeth the Queen Mother to send Her Majesty's thanks for so kindly sending the four new records recently made by the Apple Corps. Her Majesty is greatly touched by this kind thought from the Beatles and their new company, and has much enjoyed listening to these recordings.

Yours faithfully,
Jean Rankin, Lady-in-waiting,
Birkhall, Ballater

124

On Saturday, 23 October 2010, a small crowd of people, among them a handful of dignitaries from English Heritage, gathered for a ceremony outside 34 Montagu Square, just five doors away from where Anthony Trollope once lived. Yoko Ono delivered a brief speech, in the precise, businesslike manner of her near-contemporary, Queen Elizabeth II.

'I am very honoured to unveil this blue plaque, and thank English Heritage for honouring John in this way. This particular flat has many memories for me and is a very interesting part of our history. In what would have been John's seventieth year, I am grateful to you all for commemorating John and this particular part of his London life, one which spawned so much of his great music and great art.'

To a smattering of polite applause, she pulled a cord, causing two red velvet curtains to swing apart and reveal London's latest blue plaque:

JOHN LENNON
1940–1980
Musician
and Songwriter
lived here in
1968

In February 1965, Ringo had signed a rental agreement on Flat 1, 34 Montagu Square, shortly before his marriage to Maureen Cox. The residents did their best to take it in their stride. 'We're a very distinguished square,' Lord Mancroft, a former Conservative minister, told a journalist, 'and I'm sure we'll welcome such a distinguished gentleman and his lady.'

The flat consisted of two bedrooms and a living room on the ground floor, with a further living room and a kitchen in the basement. 'The flat was small and impractical,' was the snooty verdict of Brian Epstein's assistant Peter Brown, 'but Ringo and Maureen insisted on it.'

Ringo and Maureen contracted Brian's designer, Ken Partridge, to decorate it. They wanted him to complete the task within a month, while the Beatles were off shooting *Help!*. Ringo returned to find the first-floor living room covered with blue silk wallpaper and furnished with the streamlined white ultra-modern chairs, tables and sofas that were all the rage. Silk curtains and lead-streaked mirrors abounded, and the fashionable picture was completed by a sunken bath in the ground floor's en suite pink bathroom.

Ringo's passion for electronic gadgets was also well represented, with a wide selection of televisions, burglar alarms and record players. Visitors recall telephones 'every four or five feet'– a bright red phone in the principal bedroom had a direct line to Mr Epstein.

Within days of the Starrs' arrival, Beatles fans were flocking to gaze at no. 34, causing much neighbourly upset. By August, complaints were coming from the Swiss embassy, which backed onto no. 34; inconsiderate fans had apparently been defacing the back wall with graffiti, much of it lewd. 'It is now very unsightly,' explained an embassy spokesman. 'Our chauffeur, who is French and took part in the First World War, says the language some of these young people use is worse than anything he ever heard in the trenches.'

In July the Starrs moved away, to 'Sunny Heights' in Weybridge, renting their Montagu Square flat to Paul, who was living with the Ashers in Wimpole Street but needed a studio. Paul immediately converted the basement room into a makeshift studio, and let his electronics technician Ian Sommerville live in the bedroom.

In those carefree days the flat fast became a fashionable hang-out, with modish figures like John Dunbar, Christopher Gibbs, Barry Miles and Robert Fraser regularly dropping by. One of the more unbudgeable visitors was Sommerville's boyfriend William Burroughs, the spindly avant-garde American author of *Junky* and *The Naked Lunch*. Burroughs was still notorious, and in some circles celebrated, for a drunken party trick that went horribly awry. One evening in Mexico in 1951, he had encouraged his wife Joan to balance a glass on the top of her head. Saying, 'It's time for our William Tell act,' he then fired his .380 automatic at it. Sadly, his aim was skew-whiff, and Joan slumped forward, dead. Silence ensued. 'Bill, I think you hit her,' observed a guest.

Joan's death was no hindrance to Burroughs' renown; in fact it proved a boon, sealing his reputation as a literary daredevil. From then on, he could expound uninterrupted on his mescaline-fuelled dreams, while retaining the interest of the hip and the cool.

Burroughs favoured 'the cut-up', a method of writing involving cutting words and phrases out of books and newspapers, then lining them up at random to, in the words of one enthusiast, 'create entirely new texts … to reveal the secret meaning of things'. In reality, it resulted in free-floating gibberish: 'Old Mother Hubbard show business went to the cupboard to get the cowboy boots dog in the family he was

known when he said that blackout falaling Christmas day slithery hood bar for the dog boots a drunk policeman.' Burroughs' influence on John was considerable, particularly in songs like 'I am the Walrus' and 'Happiness is a Warm Gun'. In return, the Beatles honoured him with a place on the cover of *Sgt. Pepper*.

He spent hours in Montagu Square experimenting on a Uher tape-recorder with 'musical cut-ups' and 'sleep recordings'. Paul was happy to allow him to use the flat in this way, even if he never felt entirely on Burroughs' wavelength. For his part, Burroughs described Paul as 'very pleasant and prepossessing. Nice-looking young man, fairly hardworking.'

After Paul bought his own home in Cavendish Avenue, Ringo, the most easy-going of landlords, let Jimi Hendrix move into the Montagu Square flat with Chas Chandler of the Animals and their respective girlfriends, Kathy Etchingham and Lotta Null. Fresh from an argument with Kathy, Hendrix composed 'The Wind Cries Mary'. On another occasion, high on acid, he hurled paint over Ringo's prized silk wallpaper. In the end, Ringo asked him to leave; after Hendrix's departure, he had the flat repainted white.

In June 1968, Cynthia and Julian retreated to Montagu Square after Yoko moved into Kenwood. Three months later they switched places with John and Yoko, who complained that they found life in the country boring.

John and Yoko proved barely more houseproud than Jimi Hendrix. In the words of one visitor, 'They existed on a diet of champagne, caviar and heroin.' Hoovering and washing up were out of the question.

One day John asked his dogsbody Tony Bramwell to set up a camera with a timer, and to teach him how to operate it. The following day he furtively handed Bramwell the film for developing: 'They're a bit risqué, you know. Don't let anyone see them, know what I mean?'

When the developed photographs arrived at Apple, Peter Brown thought they were a sick joke. 'They were so scandalous that I locked them away in my desk drawer and didn't share them with anyone.' In his fastidious fashion, he wanted to look neither at Yoko, 'smiling coyly, her breasts sagging towards the floor', nor at John, 'glassy-eyed and heroin-stoned … grinning idiotically, so proud to be exposing to the world his shrivelled, uncircumcised penis'. He was almost more upset by the state of the flat. 'The bedroom is a pigsty, a junkie's haven of rumpled sheets, dirty clothes, newspapers and magazines heaped all over the floor.'

A few days later John announced that one of these photographs, of himself and Yoko stark naked, staring at the camera, was to be the cover of their new album, *Two Virgins*. According to Bramwell, on hearing the news everyone in the office 'fell about laughing … Yoko was not a pretty sight, but she and John in the buff together were plain embarrassing. None of us thought they would go through with it.'

Up until then, John had exhibited a decidedly prim attitude towards nudity. Entering a birthday party for Allen Ginsberg in June 1965, he and Cynthia had been greeted by the hairy Beat poet wearing nothing but boxer shorts on his head and a 'Do Not Disturb' sign on his penis. John was not amused: 'You don't do that in front of the birds.'

In a strange way, John also tried to disassociate himself from the naked figure on the cover of *Two Virgins*. In a rambling interview with *Rolling Stone* later that year, he said: 'When we got the pictures back, I admit that I was a bit shocked. Of course, I've never seen my prick on an album or on a photo before. I thought, "Hello! What on earth? There's a fellow with his prick out" … You're not used to it, being naked.'

When John and Yoko showed their proposed cover to Ringo, he didn't know where to look. Searching for something to say, he pointed at a copy of *The Times* in the photograph, lying on the floor beside John's feet, and remarked, 'Oh, you've even got *The Times* in it.' But he then grew less bashful. 'I said, "Ah, come on, John. You're doing all this stuff, and it may be cool for you, but you know we all have to answer for it."'

Paul was more vehemently opposed. Peter Brown recalled that he 'hated the cover beyond words', while Bramwell saw him having 'seven thousand kinds of fits. He thought it was disgusting, and was absolutely appalled that John was seriously intending to go through with it.' According to Bramwell, Paul put the blame on Yoko: 'John had been very prudish before he met Yoko. Now, Paul argued, she had released his inhibitions, to disastrous effect. "Doesn't John realise that we're all in this together? … It might be him and Yoko, but people will say it's the Beatles who are out of their tree and getting into straight porn."'

Paul called a meeting with John and Yoko and Sir Joseph Lockwood, the chairman of EMI. Sir Joseph kicked off the discussion by saying that he didn't find the pictures obscene. It was a clever tactic, undermining John and Yoko's desire to be seen as *enfants terribles*.

JOHN: Well, aren't you shocked?

SIR JOSEPH: No, I've seen worse than this.

JOHN: So, it's all right then, is it?

SIR JOSEPH: No, it's not all right. I'm not worried about the rich people, the duchesses and those people who follow you. But your mums and dads and girl fans will object strongly. You will be damaged, and what will you gain? What's the purpose of it?

YOKO: It's art.

SIR JOSEPH: Well then, why not show Paul in the nude? He's so much prettier!

In the end, Sir Joseph declared that EMI would not distribute the album with the naked cover, though they would manufacture the record itself for their usual fee. It was eventually released on the Apple label and distributed by the Who's label, Track. It was sold in record shops wrapped in a plain brown wrapper. Inevitably, many people bought *Two Virgins* for the cover alone: for some of the Beatles' younger fans, it was to be their first ever glimpse of grown-ups in the nude.

125

Katie Green's Tale

Around the age of seven, I realised that the Beatles were watching me. I would become aware, every so often, that there were four heads lined up alongside my bedroom door or peering around the wall. The tops of torsos would be just visible, reassuringly constrained in jackets, white collars and black ties. They would make their presence felt at an awkward moment – when I was getting dressed, for instance. I would hastily rearrange my clothes, pulling pyjamas off and on through underwear, so that at no point was any flesh exposed. I thought the Beatles might be rather impressed, both by my modesty and dexterity.

Generally though, like the black mammies in old films, they were there for the big moments. When I finished a race on sports day, they were there at the touchline, clapping their hands. If I sustained an injury in the playground, they would be there, peering round nurse's door, shaking their heads and clicking their tongues, doubtless noting how brave I was being.

I wanted to contain the Beatles within my thoughts; there they would stay the same, protected from the vicissitudes of reality. Unfortunately, the real Beatles endlessly changed. The Beatles of my thoughts were usually about two changes behind. No sooner had I grown accustomed to them in casual clothes (*Revolver*) than I had to learn to visualise them in weird silk soldiers' uniforms (*Sgt. Pepper*).

I first heard *Sgt. Pepper* with my friend Fiona. My dislike of change meant I was always the last to hear new albums. And my conviction that the Beatles should have been frozen in time in 1964 was borne out by what seemed to me a downward spiral of sex and drugs. I was told of allusions to drugs in several songs; I myself came across shocking allusions to sex such as 'Girl, you let your knickers down' in 'I am the Walrus'. I was in Fiona's playroom when I examined with horror a poster of John in the nude. So that was what John *really* looked like; what he had really looked like all along. For a moment I felt duped.

I began a Lett's schoolgirl diary in 1969. After months of 'nothing much happened today', I introduced a mysterious new character, an older brother, 'Alicky'. I savoured imaginary conversations in which I revealed to my friends, under appropriate duress, the real identity of Alicky – Paul McCartney.

I pictured their expressions of amazement and admiration. Alas, despite months of intriguing entries – 'Went to Abbey Road', 'Saw John today' – nobody other than myself ever saw the diary.

When the Beatles broke up in 1970, I had a small sense of heartbreak. Noting that my friends had moved on and were indifferent, I snatched up the mantle of grief with righteous relish. I can't recall to what extent I was pretending. I know I would get a drawing ache in the chest and then remember, with a slight pang of anguish, what had gone wrong. I know I felt amazed that this change had happened without my having the least intimation of it.

But I didn't cry. This was awkward, as I felt that in order to serve honour I ought to shed tears every night. Instead, I had to lie in bed imagining certain songs in my head – 'And I Love Her' or 'Let it Be' – in order to squeeze a tear from each eye. As the long-awaited drops finally trickled over the bridge of my nose I felt sure the Beatles would be moved by my devotion.

By the time I was thirty, I wanted to embrace classical music but found the Beatles endlessly impinging. Jumbles of lyrics continued to flow through my head like so many unruly, uninvited guests: like 'rain into a paper cup'. And whenever I heard the date 18 June, I would try to prevent the association springing up – but I was never quick enough to quell the tiny, jubilant voice: 'It's Paul's birthday!'

126

Of all the intellectuals who disliked the Beatles, none did so for so long, or with such passion, as Anthony Burgess.

'I have normally only to see a photograph of the Beatles to start shivering with ague,' he wrote in *The Listener* on October 1963. '... Obviously the phenomenon will last as long as the money: there's certainly plenty of that to be made. But what, in God's name, are we going to do about these children, with their screechings as in orgasm, their distorted faces, their cutting-off of the higher centres?'

In 1968 Burgess was interviewed by Tony Palmer for his celebrated documentary about contemporary pop music, *All My Loving*. In the Crush Bar of the Royal Opera House, Burgess railed against youth culture in general, and the Beatles in particular:

'I remember an old proverb which says: "Youth thinks itself wise, just as drunk men think themselves sober." Youth is not wise; youth knows nothing about life. Youth knows nothing about anything except a mass of clichés which, for the most part, through the media of pop songs, are just foisted on them by middle-aged entrepreneurs and exploiters who should know better.'

The same year, at the age of fifty-one, Burgess published a novel, *Enderby Outside*, in which his anarchist hero Enderby nurses a hatred for Yod Crewsy, of Yod Crewsy and the Fixers, who has just made a movie in the Bahamas, and received an MBE in the Birthday Honours. Crewsy is now being enrolled as a Fellow of the Royal Society of Literature: 'There were cheers. The guests of honour had come at last, embraced and worshipped from their very entrance. Hogg stopped mixing to have a good look at them. They were, he thought, about as horrible in appearance as it was possible any four young men to be.' The four of them 'were vulgarly at home, punching each other in glee and then doing a kind of ring-a-roses round the prime minister'.

Crewsy is a plagiarist, fraud and solipsist, as well as a terrible poet. To an adoring audience, he reads a few lines of one of his poems, adding, 'Don't ask me what it means; I only wrote it. No, serious like, I feel very humble. But I put them poems together in this book just like to show. You know, show that we do like think a bit and the kvadrats, or squares which is what some of you squares here would like call yourselves, can't have it all their own way.'

Burgess's loathing of the Beatles continued long after they disbanded. 'The words of their songs, pathetic when compared with Cole Porter, are so vapid that psychedelic meanings have to be imposed on them,'

he complained. He particularly scorned those of the intelligentsia, like Kenneth Tynan, who promoted their 'twanging nonsense' over Wagner and Beethoven: 'Do they merit vitriol, even a drop of it? Yes, because they corrupt the young, persuading them that the mature world, which produced Beethoven and Schweitzer, sets an even higher value on the transient anodynes of youth than does youth itself. For this they stink to heaven.'

As he grew older, Burgess prayed that there would be a special circle of hell set aside for the Beatles, in which they would be bound to 'a white-hot turntable (45rpm for ever and ever) stuck all over with blunt and rusty acoustic needles, each tooth hollowed to the raw nerve and filled with a micro-transistor (thirty-two pop stations blaring through all eternity thirty-two worn flip-sides into their sinuses), an eternal Ringo battering the tympanic membrane'.

127

Others let their resentment simmer.

A year after the death of Joe Orton, the Beatles were still searching around for material for their next feature film. Might *The Lord of the Rings* be suitable? In February 1968 Donovan had brought Tolkien's trilogy out to Rishikesh, giving John, Paul and George each a volume to read; Ringo was no bookworm, preferring comics.

Soon after the Beatles' return to England, there were rumours in the music press that they would be starring in an adaptation of *The Lord of the Rings*. Paul would play the lovable Frodo Baggins, Ringo his loyal sidekick Sam Gamgee, and George the wizard Gandalf. John was to play Gollum. His casting might have channelled a secret empathy, as his feelings towards his group were akin to Gollum's towards the ring: 'He loved it and hated it, just as he hated and loved himself.'

With its elves, quests and magic, *The Lord of the Rings* attracted a strong hippy following. Though forged in the trenches of the First World War, it would be possible to overlay it with a dreamy, psychedelic vision derived from the recent songs of the Beatles.

As the year progressed, the talk turned to the director. Who should it be? David Lean? Antonioni? John's favourite film of 1968 was *2001: A Space Odyssey*; he said he planned to watch it every week. One day he called on the film's director, Stanley Kubrick, hoping to spark his interest. But he came away disappointed: Kubrick told him it was too large and complex ever to be adapted for the screen. John complained to Pete Shotton about Kubrick's negativity. How, he grumbled, could the guy who directed *2001* be so 'nowhere'?

Soon afterwards, Victor Spinetti, a mainstay of *A Hard Day's Night* and *Help!*, was sitting in bed at home when the doorbell rang. It was the postman, with a parcel from Apple Corps. There were four books: *The Hobbit* and the *Lord of the Rings* trilogy. He started to read them, but found the process effortful. Before he had got very far, the telephone rang.

It was John. 'Have you got the books? They're going to do a film. We'll be the hobbits and you'll be Gandalf.'

Spinetti agreed to press on, but 'it was no use. I found them turgid and twee.'

He phoned John back. 'What do you think?' asked John.

'Oh, John,' sighed Spinetti. 'I couldn't finish –'

'That's all right, neither could I. Forget it.'

Nevertheless, the Beatles persisted with the project, the only barrier being Professor Tolkien himself. Fifty years their senior, and by nature a traditionalist, he nursed a particular dislike of pop music, born of bitter experience. In 1964, at the height of Beatlemania, a local band used to rehearse in a garage close to Tolkien's home on Oxford's Sandfield Road. He had detested the racket. 'In a house three doors away dwells a member of a group of young men who are evidently

aiming to turn them into a Beatle Group,' he wrote to a friend. '… The noise is indescribable.'

Four years later, when the Beatles approached him to turn his trilogy into a film, Professor Tolkien's mind drifted back to the hullaballoo that had assailed him from that garage down the road. Thinking no more about it, he turned them down without further ado.

128

I ended my first term of boarding at Farleigh House in July 1965. The headmaster and founder of the school was Jocelyn Trappes-Lomax, a tubby man in his early sixties who was in the habit of wearing the same uniform as his pupils (grey flannel shorts, Boy Scout belt, short-sleeved shirt, Start-Rite sandals). Towards the end of those long, hot summer holidays, we were informed that Mr Trappes-Lomax had died of a heart attack in his bath.

He was replaced by a more go-ahead geography and art teacher, known as 'CJ', who must have been in his thirties. One of CJ's early acts as headmaster was to convert a disused underground cellar beneath the chapel into a club for boys in their last two years at the school, the youngest of whom would have been eleven and the oldest thirteen. It was called the Cavern, presumably in a nod to the Beatles, and consisted of three dark, slightly dank chambers, enlivened by psychedelic murals of underwater scenes painted by CJ and the senior boys. One of the chambers had a ping-pong table, another a billiard table, and the third was furnished with armchairs, a beanbag and a record player.

The Beatles' *White Album* was released on 22 November 1968, when I was exactly eleven and a half years old. It was a double album, so doubly expensive – £3.12*s*.6*d*. My parents gave it to me for Christmas, and I spent the next few months luxuriating in its pure white cover, so sleek and so shiny, studying its four-colour headshots of the freshly unsmiling Beatles, and, above all else, examining every detail of its full-length poster, which came pre-folded so it could fit into the package.

On one side of the poster were the words to all but one of the songs, from the first track on side one, 'Back in the USSR', to the last on side four, 'Good Night'. I liked following the words with my finger as the record spun round, imagining that I was somehow directing the words as they flowed off the paper and into the air.

Many of the lyrics seemed to raise more questions than they answered. What is a stupid get? How could an onion be glass? Why don't we do *what* in the road?

On the other side of the lyrics sheet was a collage of photographs, some large, others so small you could scarcely see them. Again, smiles were few and far between, and mainly on snapshots from long ago: the Beatles with Harold Wilson in March 1964, or a beaming Brian Epstein looking calm and relaxed in shirt and tie around that same time.

But generally speaking, the four of them looked sullen. If you compared the moody scowls of *The White Album* to the cheery grins on the cover of *Please Please Me*, just five years before, you would come away with a poor impression of fame and fortune. The only truly happy photograph on *The White Album* was also the most formal: the bearded Ringo Starr, spruce in black tie and dinner jacket, dancing arm in arm with a visibly delighted Elizabeth Taylor against a posh background of a chandelier and ruched curtains.

At that time, I was used to family photographs of everyone looking cheerful, or at least making an effort, which meant roughly the same. We would dress smartly, and smile when the photographer told us to ('Say cheese!'). But one of the largest photographs in the Beatles collage, top right, was of Paul lying in a murky, soap-sodden bath, with his chin stubbly and his eyes shut, rather like poor Mr Trappes-Lomax. He certainly wasn't making an effort. Towards the bottom left of the poster was a black-and-white photograph of John, naked but for his spectacles, sitting cross-legged on a bed, talking on the phone while Yoko slept, or at least pretended to sleep (her head was set at an uncomfortable angle). Nude adults abounded. Close to the centre, just along from Elizabeth Taylor, was a small photograph of Paul, also naked, standing in a bathroom with a towel around his shoulders. The shot was taken through a window: the central frame covered his private parts, but only just. Up a bit and left a bit was one of John's squiggly cartoons of himself and Yoko. They too were in the nude.

Other photographs were mysteriously shoddy: it was almost as though the Beatles had plundered their rejects box for snaps that were out of focus, or dingy, or showed them at their worst: a smudgy Polaroid of John looking as if he was about to pick a fight with the photographer; a large photograph of George – the largest of the lot – with half his face lost in an overexposed blaze of white; a blurred picture of Ringo on the drums, bored stiff.

The collage was scrappy but mesmerising – or scrappy *and* mesmerising, like *The White Album* itself. And like *The White Album* it seemed modern and cutting-edge and devil-may-care, but at the same time it came steeped in a sense of nostalgia. I now see that half the photographs are from happier days – in Rishikesh, or on the set of *Help!*, or at the Variety Club awards. Two date back to John's carefree twenty-first-birthday trip to Paris with Paul, before they were famous. In one of them – presumably taken by Paul – John is sitting up in bed wearing a black T-shirt and a bowler hat. In the other, the two of them are leaning moodily against a wall plastered with concert posters, their hands half-in, half-out of the pockets of their black jeans. The photograph itself is wonky: half of each head is cut off, and, for no reason, the camera is slanted towards their winkle-pickers.

In fancy italic lettering, a message reads: '*Order of the British Empire to our trusty and well beloved Ringo Starr (Richard Starkey Esquire).*' This too is a throwback to more innocent days.

The only other words on the poster are hand-written in red biro over the imprint of pink lips:

I love you

Who was the I and who was the you? No clue was provided. Could I be the you? I found the thought sinister.

129

With my schoolfriend Charlie Miller I would sit in the Cavern, listening to *The White Album* over and over again, reading the lyrics, staring at the collage on the poster almost as though, if we stared at it for long enough, it might yield clues to the adult world. Though much of the album was strange or threatening – the weird, screechy little 'Wild Honey Pie', the gloomy 'I'm So Tired' and 'Yer Blues' ('I'm lonely wanna die') – nothing struck us as nearly so creepy as 'Revolution 9', the only track for which the lyrics were not printed. At some point during the Easter term, Charlie and I set each other a dare: would either of us be able to sit in the Cavern by himself with the lights off, in the pitch-dark, and listen to 'Revolution 9' *all the way through*? We both tried a number of times – coming in at 8 minutes 12 seconds, 'Revolution 9' is the longest Beatles track ever recorded – but we never got to the end before flicking the lights on and rushing for the exit.

'Number 9, number 9, number 9, number 9, number 9 …' It sounded rather like James Callaghan, the then Home Secretary, but in fact it belonged to a man whose voice John had plundered from the examination tapes for the Royal Academy of Music, which for some reason were stored at the EMI studios.

The track rapidly turns into a cacophony of meaningless jabber and screeches – cars tooting, crowds chanting, machine-guns firing, instruments played backwards, people moaning and yelling – with random words spoken by anonymous human beings, culled from goodness knows where: 'Every one of them knew that as time went by they'd get a little bit older and a little bit slower.' 'Only to find the nightwatchman unaware of his presence in the building.' 'Take this brother, may it serve you well.' No slave to melody, Yoko regularly emits intermittent high-pitched hums, moans, howls and screeches, as well as the spoken words 'You become naked.'

Rolling Stone called the song 'an aural litmus of unfocused paranoia'. Less indulgently, the *New Musical Express* described it as 'a pretentious piece of old codswallop'. In his masterly book *Revolution in the Head*, Ian MacDonald at first suggests that it was somehow prophetic: 'Here, in the random interaction of scores of tape fragments – some looped, others spun backwards – is a representation of the half-sceptical, half-awake, channel-hopping state of mind he [John] liked to relax in (and which, twenty-five years on, has become characteristic of a generation).' But in the end he loosely agrees with those two eleven-year-old boys who listened to it as they sat in the dark for a dare: 'the actual experience of listening to this track, where not merely boring or baffling, often inclines to the sinister'.

Yet John remained convinced of its genius. Pete Shotton remembers him declaring, 'This is the music of the future. You can forget all the rest of the shit we've done – this is *it*! Everybody will be making this stuff one day – you don't even have to know how to play a musical instrument to do it!'

Over the course of four days, John and Yoko had raided the archives of EMI for snippets of classical music, speech, chants and random noises. On Thursday, 20 June 1968, with Paul and Ringo away, John booked all three studios at Abbey Road. While all the available maintenance engineers stood around in their regulation white coats spooling loops onto tape machines with their pencils, John and Yoko sat at the console fading the sounds in and out. Geoff Emerick was unimpressed: 'There was a good deal of resentment among the staff because the session was running quite late – well past midnight – and they wanted to go home. Many of them had been there since nine in the morning.' The track was finally completed at 3.30 a.m. on 21 June.

When Paul returned from New York, John played him 'Revolution 9'. Geoff Emerick watched his reaction: 'I could see from the dark cloud that came over Paul's face that he was totally underwhelmed …

and there was an awkward silence after the track faded out. John looked at Paul expectantly, but Paul's only comment was "Not bad," which I knew was a diplomatic way of saying that he didn't like it. Ringo and George Harrison had nothing to say about the track at all. They looked distinctly embarrassed, and you could tell that neither one of them wanted to get caught in the middle of this. "Not bad?" Lennon said derisively to Paul. "You have no idea what you're talking about. In fact, this should be our bloody next single! This is the direction the Beatles should be going from now on."'

Yoko took John's side: 'I agree with John. I think it's great.'

John and Yoko added '9' to the word 'Revolution' because they were both adherents of numerology. John had been born on 9 October 1940. His first home was 9 Newcastle Road, Wavertree, Liverpool: all three place names in that address contain nine letters, as does 'McCartney'. And 'Revolution 9' appeared on the Beatles' ninth album.

Yoko once offered a further explanation for their choice: 'It turns out to be the highest number in the one, two, et cetera. Up to nine.'

130

For Charles Manson, the Beatles' *White Album* joined all the remaining dots together. Even the pure whiteness of the sleeve served as a signal that his time had come. In Canoga Park, California, at his rented house in Gresham Street, which he painted yellow and nicknamed 'The Yellow Submarine', Manson held seminars on the album. He wanted his followers to understand that what might seem a disparate group of unrelated songs was in fact a coherent call to arms, specially encoded for his own, uniquely privileged, Family.

Manson convinced the Family that the black people of America were arming themselves, ready to rise up and kill millions of their wealthy white oppressors. This insurrection would be followed by a civil war between whites and blacks. As the slaughter took place, the Manson Family would shelter in a mystic hole in Death Valley. 'People are going to be slaughtered, they'll be lying on their lawns dead,' he promised. Then the triumphant blacks would employ their 'super awareness' to find their true leader: Charles Manson.

These prophecies were all to be found in the lyrics of the Beatles. Paul's song 'Blackbird' was an incitement to a race war. George's 'Piggies' required little interpretation: life for all the little piggies was getting worse, while the bigger piggies 'always have clean shirts … clutching forks and knives to eat their bacon'. As Ian MacDonald points out, even without misinterpretation, this is a lyric that shows 'the misanthropy at the heart of so much spiritual piousness'.

George began writing the song in 1966, and was still struggling with the lyrics while staying with his parents in Liverpool in 1968. Never a fluent lyricist, he couldn't think of a rhyme for 'backing' other than 'lacking', which he had already used. From out of nowhere his mother came up with the lyric 'What they need's a damn good whacking!' Might Louise Harrison's sole foray into lyric-writing have inadvertently contributed to the death of Leno LaBianca, who was found with a fork in his stomach, and 'Death to Pigs' daubed in blood on his living-room wall?

The Beatles themselves were the four angels charged with bringing death to mankind; the buggies on which the Manson Family rode would be their horses. From the Book of Revelation, Manson discovered that locusts would arrive 'with scales like iron breastplates' – these locusts of course being 'beetles', and their scales guitars. The Beatles would one day have a fifth member, or 'angel', who would be 'given the key to the bottomless pit': this was obviously Manson himself. Together they would wreak righteous havoc: 'Neither repented they of their murders, nor of their sorceries, nor of their fornication, nor of their thefts.'

Words conjured up as playful nonsense by the Beatles metamorphosed, in Manson's mind, into rallying cries for a battle to the death. In Britain, a helter skelter is a brightly coloured fairground slide that spirals around a central column. But it is one of those English expressions that has never made the journey across the Atlantic. Ignorant of its meaning, Manson convinced himself that it was a call to insurrection: one of his followers said that he employed the term 'Helter Skelter' as shorthand for the forthcoming race war. 'What it meant was the Negroes were going to come down and rip the cities all apart.' In *My Life with Charles Manson*, one of his followers, Paul Watkins, wrote, 'Before Helter Skelter came along, all Charlie cared about was orgies.'

At the conclusion of his murder trial in November 1970, Manson stated: 'Helter Skelter is confusion. Confusion coming down fast. If you don't see the confusion coming down fast, you can call it what you wish. It's not my conspiracy. It's not my music. I hear what it relates. It says "Rise!" It says "Kill!" Why blame it on me? I didn't write the music. I am not the person who projected it into your social consciousness.' Lyrics born of whimsy had become as menacing as machetes. Later, Manson explained that the Beatles' music was 'bringing on the revolution, the unorganized overthrow of the Establishment. The Beatles know in the sense that the subconscious knows.'

Even the lightest, fluffiest song was code for something much more ominous. In a merry mood, Paul had written 'Honey Pie', a tinkly pastiche of 1920s ragtime, as a present for his jazz-loving father. But for Manson it was all about the apocalypse, the lines 'sail across the Atlantic/back where you belong' a clear indication that the Beatles would soon be joining the Family at their ranch in Death Valley. Accused at his trial of ordering the murders, Manson replied, 'It's the Beatles, the music they're putting out. They're talking about war. These kids listen to this music and pick up the message. It's subliminal.' His followers scrawled the words 'RISE' and 'DEATH TO PIGS' in blood on the wall of their victims' home, and 'HEALTER SKELTER' on the fridge.

Listening on headphones to 'Revolution 9', Manson was sure he could hear the Beatles saying, 'Charlie, Charlie, send us a telegram.' Peter Brown and Derek Taylor later remembered getting a stream of phone calls from Los Angeles from a woman who called herself Squeaky Fromme. She kept burbling on about a guy called Charlie.

As he listened to 'Revolution 9', Charlie took to screaming 'Rise! Rise! Rise!' For him, it was just like Revelation, Chapter 9:

> And out of the smoke locusts came down on the earth and were given power like that of scorpions of the earth. They were told not to harm the grass of the earth or any plant or tree, but only those people who did not have the seal of God on their foreheads. They were not allowed to kill them but only to torture them for five months.

After Manson's arrest, Family members couldn't work out why the Beatles hadn't come to Charlie's rescue, just like Charlie said they would. 'Tell them to call. Give them our number,' they told two writers from *Rolling Stone*. Manson himself instructed his attorneys to call the Beatles as witnesses: he knew they would support him. His attorneys obeyed his instruction; but their letters went unanswered.

131

Apple Christmas Party
3 Savile Row, London W1
23 December 1968

On 4 December 1968, George circulated the following memo to all the Apple staff:

> *Hell's Angels will be in London within the next week on the way to straighten out Czechoslovakia. There will be twelve in number complete with black leather jackets and motorcycles. They will undoubtedly arrive at Apple and I have heard that they might try to make full use of Apple's facilities. They may look as if they are going to do you in but are very straight and do good things, so don't fear them or uptight them. Try to assist them without neglecting your Apple business and without letting them take control of Savile Row.*

A close reading of this breezy text might have sounded alarms – '*I have heard that they might try to make full use of Apple's facilities*' … '*they may look as if they are going to do you in*' … '*don't fear them or uptight them*'. But the mood in Apple during that prelapsarian period, before the entrance of Allen Klein, was determinedly, almost compulsorily, free and easy.

The arrival of the Hell's Angels was preceded by a call from Customs and Excise to Derek Taylor. 'Is this right? We've got two Harley-Davidsons that you're going to pay the freight duty on?'

Obeying George's order to assist the Hell's Angels, Taylor nodded it through, and also paid £250 for shipping. Presently, two Angels – Frisco Pete and Billy Tumbleweed – showed up at 3 Savile Row, along with the author Ken Kesey, a hippy called Spider, and twelve hangers-on: 'zonked, wired', in the words of Taylor's assistant Richard DiLello, 'smelly, stoned' according to Peter Brown.

DiLello witnessed this mixed bag of people 'in all their splendor, sprawled across the reception lounge; laughing, smoking and reeking of patchouli oil. There were men and women and babes in arms; leather, suede, headbands, cowboy hats, bells, sleeping bags, backpacks, beads, mountain boots, sticks of incense, flutes and guitars.' Collectively, they came to be known by the Apple staff as the California Pleasure Crew.

Snippets of the Hell's Angels' conversation recorded by DiLello mix entitlement with bullishness:

'Hey, where are the Beatles?'

'How much is ten shillings in American money?'

'I've gotta take a piss!'

'Who's got Mick Jagger's phone number?'

'Where can we dump all our shit?'

On their arrival at reception, Taylor came down to greet them, and proceeded to introduce them to everyone else as though they were visiting dignitaries, which is, in a way, what they were. DiLello transcribed Taylor's meandering greeting:

'Well, you are here and so are we and this is Sally who has just joined us and that is Carol who has always been with us and Richard you know, and if you would like a cup of tea then a cup of tea it is, but if you would rather have a glass of beer or a bottle of wine or a Scotch and Coke or a gin and tonic or a vodka and lime, then that it is because it is all here and if it is not then we will come up with something, but have a seat or have a cigarette or have a joint, and I will be back in three minutes so please don't go away because there is a lot to talk about and more to find out and stranger days to come.'

'Beer!' came their reply.

Their demanding attitude soon prompted Taylor to despatch another memo to staff:

Watch out, don't let them take over. You have to keep doing what you're doing, but just be nice to them. And don't upset them because they could kill you.

During the same period, the lounge at Apple was occupied by two American hippies, Frank and Emily, and their five little hippy children.* They had originally entered Apple explaining that, while undergoing an acid trip, Emily had received a psychic message telling her to take John and Yoko to Fiji. Consequently, she and the rest of the family were allowed to camp out at Apple until John and Yoko could spare the time to see her. No stickler for formality, Emily remained naked most of the time, which meant that Apple's two kitchen ladies, Shirley and Janet, refused to enter the room. Within days the guest lounge at Apple had developed its own distinctive aroma, a pungent mix of hashish, patchouli oil and sweat.

Meanwhile, the Hell's Angels occupied their leisure hours racing their Harley-Davidsons to the West End Central police station at the top of Savile Row, screeching to a halt, turning round, and whizzing back again. 'They knew it was a police station,' recalled Debbie Wellum, an Apple receptionist. 'I told them. But they didn't care. They tried to get me to go on the back of a motorbike with them and I wouldn't go.'

---

* On the day Taylor later referred to as 'Black Friday', other visitors to Apple included the managers of the Grateful Dead, the Beach Boys, the Radha Krishna Temple, two Transcendental Meditators from Rishikesh, Yoko Ono, a German television producer and the poet Tambi Muttu, as well as the Hell's Angels and their party and the homeless family. Recollections of the homeless family differ. Taylor thought they were called Mick and Annie, had four children, not five, and had travelled to Britain in order to persuade Paul, not John, to finance their purchase of an island near Fiji 'where the sun shines all the time'. They were convinced that their case for Paul's sponsorship was good: after all, 'Annie WAS the Lady Madonna of the song, wasn't she?' An easy touch, Taylor let them live in the third-floor waiting room until they found a home. Eventually John let them live on an island he had accidentally bought off the coast of Ireland. 'Determination pays off,' he concluded. He might have added, 'And so does money.' Chris O'Dell, working at Apple at the time, recalled that 'they set up camp on the fourth floor, ate our food and walked our hallways as if they owned the place'. On top of all this, their fifteen-year-old daughter 'kept asking Derek if she could ball George'.

The Hell's Angels were still living at Apple on 23 December, the date set aside for the company's first Christmas party. Everything had been meticulously planned. For instance, a turkey weighing forty-three pounds – billed by the butcher as the largest in the UK – had been ordered, and invitations had been posted well in advance, a typically quirky mixture of formal, casual and long-winded:

The Apple Christmas party will be held on December 23 at 2:30 in the afternoon and will go on until evening. In the middle of the party, we will be visited by Ernest Castro and April, entertainers to the Queen and Duke of Cornwall and the late Sir Winston Churchill, McDonald Hobley,† and others. Mr Castro is a conjuror, ventriloquist and children's entertainer. April is his assistant and also his wife, and she plays guitar. So the idea is that all of us at Apple will bring our children and those of us who have no children are invited to bring a couple unless they can arrange to have one of their own in the meantime. Immaculate conceptions will not be accepted. There will be a party with food and*

---

* That very same year, Ernest and April Castro – veteran entertainers of children throughout London and the Home Counties – travelled down to Westcott, near Dorking in Surrey, to entertain the Brown family. I imagine we must have welcomed them into our house first, as the Beatles' party was so close to Christmas. In our navy-blue shorts and with well-brushed hair, we were doubtless more like the Castros' usual audiences. Ernest was one of the old school. He wore a dinner jacket and black tie, while his wife April wore a glamorous, sparkly, broad-rimmed pink dress of the type often seen at the time on *Come Dancing*. I remember Mr Castro producing a doll called Lettice Leefe from a black case, and then engaging her in jaunty dialogue while we all shouted 'I can see your lips moving!' Lettice Leefe and the Castros encouraged us to sing along to a song they performed together called 'The Lettice Leefe Hop' – quite a remove from the Beatles' tracks of the time, such as 'Why Don't We Do it in the Road' and 'I'm So Tired'. Before he departed, Mr Castro gave the Brown family a glossy black-and-white brochure full of pictures of his act, as well as six copies of 'The Lettice Leefe Hop', recorded on a shiny red disc. We found it irritating, but for some reason we used to play it quite often.

† McDonald Hobley (1917–87), pioneering BBC TV continuity announcer and panel-show favourite, voted 'TV Personality of the Year' in 1954. Serving with the Royal Artillery in the Second World War, Hobley (pronounced 'nobly') had been involved in a plan to abduct Adolf Hitler and bring him to Britain. The plan was later abandoned. His post-war TV career met with only one hiccup: he once introduced Sir Stafford Cripps, the Chancellor of the Exchequer, as 'Sir Stifford Crapps'.

> *wine and children and a Christmas tree, and it will be very good. I would be glad if today you will write your name on this memorandum together with the number of children you will be bringing and hand it to Carol Paddon. It goes without saying that wives, husbands, boy and girl friends are welcome, but no more than one per person unless bigamists wish to plead a special case.*

By 9 a.m. on the big day preparations were well under way, with Prudence and Primrose, Apple's two *cordon bleu* cooks, already hard at work. By 11 a.m. the press office was filled with journalists and assorted figures from the music business, already slurping champagne. By 11.30 a.m. the Black Room was, in Richard DiLello's words, 'swollen to standing-room-only proportions with hashish smokers puffing their brains out'. Meanwhile, the front office catered for the more traditional 'Scotch and Coke' brigade. By noon, the music had been turned up loud, and the two different strands of party – drink and drugs – had merged into one.

The first gaggle of the anticipated forty children arrived at 2.15 p.m., to be ushered into Peter Brown's office, where the party was scheduled to take place. By three o'clock, according to DiLello, 'Peter Brown's office was a scene of unparalleled frenzy as more than a hundred children screamed and smashed their way through a mountain of ice cream, cake and sausage rolls, impatiently clamoring to be entertained by the ventriloquist and conjuror they had been promised.'

Ernest and April Castro launched into their splendid routine of magic, ventriloquism and barnyard imitations ('With a moo-moo here, and a moo-moo there ...') with their usual gusto, finishing the show with their trademark tune, 'The Lettice Leefe Hop'. DiLello recalled hearing 'eardrum-shattering squeals of delight' from the assembled children.

Next, less than a month since their naked appearance on the cover of *Two Virgins*, John and Yoko entered the room dressed as Father and Mother Christmas. Pete Shotton felt that John was low on seasonal cheer: 'He made for the most miserable-looking Santa I'd ever seen in

my life.' Nonetheless, he managed to mutter 'Ho ho ho' while he and Yoko handed out presents, the two of them assisted by the more Christmassy Mary Hopkin.

As the children unwrapped their parcels, the sound of barracking came from the back of the room. 'Hey man! We want some food! GIVE

US THE FUCKING FOOD, MAN!' It was the Hell's Angel Frisco Pete, at his most peckish.

'They're arranging it right now,' said John. 'It should be out very soon.'

'What the fuck is goin' on in this place!?! We wanna eat! What's all this shit about HAVIN' TO WAIT?'

At this point Alan Smith, a journalist with the *New Musical Express*, stepped in, politely asking for a little consideration. Frisco Pete promptly punched him in the face, then shouted at John, 'You got more fuckin' food in that kitchen than there are people and it's all locked up and those two fuckin' broads upstairs tell me I've gotta wait until seven o'clock just like everybody else! There's a forty-three-pound turkey in that fuckin' kitchen and I fuckin' want some of it NOW!!!'

John looked non-committal.

'I don't know where those fuckin' heads of yours are at,' continued Frisco Pete, 'but where *I* come from when we got food we feed people, not starve them!'

Peter Brown intervened: 'We have every intention of feeding you and I apologise for the delay, but I was hoping you could appreciate that the kitchen staff have been working since nine o'clock and they've been under considerable pressure. We're waiting for the caterers to finish laying the tables and it shouldn't take more than another ten minutes and then we can all go downstairs and gorge ourselves to death, but please, I beg you, be patient.'

In response, Frisco Pete shook his head and stomped out of the room.

Ten minutes later the doors to Neil Aspinall's office were thrown open, revealing tables groaning with hors d'oeuvres, cold meat, jellied fish, salads, cheese and biscuits, cakes, fruit and boiled sweets. Resplendent in the centre of the table sat the largest turkey in the country, roasted to perfection by Prudence and Primrose.

Hurtling past everybody else – staff and children, hippies, journalists, hangers-on – came Frisco Pete, who picked up the turkey, ripped off its left leg and started to gnaw on it. 'It easily weighed four pounds, and more closely resembled a caveman's hunting club than a turkey leg,' recalled DiLello.

By early January, George was starting to regret his open-house policy. Throughout the building things had been going missing, among them television sets, electric typewriters, adding machines, three hundred copies of *Two Virgins*, a movie camera, three secretarial pay packets, half a dozen speaker cones from the studio, six fan heaters, an electric skillet, several cases of wine and all the lead from the roof. George now plotted to disinvite the California Pleasure Crew. At first he issued a directive to Derek Taylor that he didn't want them round any more. 'What am I supposed to say?' asked Derek, remembering the punches that had flown at the Christmas party, and how close Peter Brown and John had come to being beaten up.

In the end it was George, stubborn George, who finally gave the Hell's Angels their marching orders. Once, when he had been in his teens, a man had come knocking at the door of his family home, trying to sell them something. George's mother, Louise, instinctively knew what to do. She went to the upstairs bedroom with a tub of water and poured it over the poor man, yelling, 'Go away!'

'I think George got his toughness from her ...' reflected Paul years later. 'She didn't suffer fools gladly – and neither did George.'

If his recent embrace of hippy mysticism sometimes led George down the wrong path, there was still a more steely part of him that knew how to get back on track. So one evening he walked into the guest lounge of Apple and simply announced, 'Hello everyone! Well, are you moving all of your stuff out of here tonight?'

In turn, the California Pleasure Crew were struck mute, astonished to be addressed in such a manner by George himself.

Spider was the first to speak. 'Hey, man. I just wanna ask you one question. Do you dig us or don't you?'

'Yin and yang, heads and tails, yes and no,' replied George, enigmatically.

DiLello noticed an immediate change in the atmosphere. 'The answer to that question completely *fucked* everyone's mind. No one knew quite what to say or how to say it.'

Eventually, it was Spider who spoke up.

'All right, man, I can dig it. We'll be outta here in ten minutes.'

132

On 30 January 1969, shortly after midday, Police Constable Ken Wharfe noticed that the blue light was flashing on the police phonebox at the corner of Piccadilly Circus. He walked over and picked up the Bakelite receiver.

It was the duty sergeant.

'Can you hear that awful noise?'

'What noise?'

'Get your men over there and go and turn it down.'

PC Wharfe replaced the handset, and turned to his colleague. 'OK, listen. Old Sarge there wants us to go and turn the noise down.'

The two of them walked down Regent Street, where they found a crowd – 'Mainly of women, I have to say' – rushing down Vigo Street. It turned out that the noise was coming from the roof of 3 Savile Row, the headquarters of the Beatles.

At the chartered accountants Auberbach Hope, on Regent Street, a junior employee called Sidney Ruback was eating a sandwich at his desk when the music started playing: 'We went to the window and we could see people playing instruments on the roof, but from that distance we couldn't make out who they were.' Together with a few young colleagues, Sidney climbed out of the window, 'and we scampered over the roof and went up a fire escape to the roof opposite, which was Savile Row. We used a drainpipe as well … We walked along and suddenly found ourselves standing about fifteen feet away from the Beatles.'

Working, or at least trying to work, at Wain, Shiell & Son Wool Merchants at 2 Savile Row, Stanley Davis was a good deal less delighted.

Within minutes of the music starting, he telephoned West End Central police station to complain that the company's switchboard operators couldn't hear to put the calls through. 'It's disgraceful!' he said. 'I want this bloody music stopped!'

PC Wharfe – still only a probationary officer – duly knocked at the front door of the Apple building, and was let in, only to discover that several other policemen were already there. There seemed to be too many to deal with a minor noise infringement, but none were prepared to leave. 'We chatted among ourselves: should we stay or should we go? But we said that we were never going to see the likes of this again, so we stayed. The fact is that nobody was going to call anybody off, because this was a unique occasion.'

Most of the police gathered that day in the Apple hallway were the same age as the Beatles or younger, and so, almost necessarily, Beatles fans. At nineteen, Ken Wharfe was nearly seven years George's junior. Small wonder, then, that they were unsure what to do. 'In fact, we were effectively trespassing there, because we hadn't been invited, not properly, so it's possible that they could have asked us to leave.'

Wharfe's colleague PC Ray Shayler tried to work out the legal situation. 'We were scratching on the subject. We were thinking that it was a breach of the peace, because while the property may be private, the effect was public. And that's how we worked it out – that's how we were going to deal with it if we needed to.'

They approached the receptionist, Debbie Wellum, and asked to see the person in charge. Debbie went to get Mal Evans, who tried to stall the police for as long as possible by sauntering down the stairs rather than taking the lift. When he finally arrived in the hall 'about ten minutes later', Debbie was all ears: 'He talked to the police. They were saying, "You can't do this," and "It's too noisy, we're getting complaints, and charges will be pressed." Mal said it would be over pretty soon, but the police insisted they go up. I remember Mal telling them that they couldn't go up, because the roof was unstable and there were already people up there. We were thinking that if they all went up there, they might have arrested a Beatle each.'

In the streets outside, traffic had ground to a standstill. 'The taxi drivers weren't happy – they were shouting and hollering,' recalls one bystander, Paula Marshall. Meanwhile, more and more office workers were scrambling up ladders and scaling fire escapes to get onto adjacent roofs, though not Paula. 'I was wearing a miniskirt, so I didn't think it would have been a good idea.'

Jimmy, the Apple doorman, finally escorted all the police upstairs. Ken Wharfe remembers arriving on the roof near the lift shaft, and finding himself next to Ringo. 'I was completely starstruck with the fact that I, like most people that age a real fan of the Beatles, had this free concert on the roof in Savile Row. Nobody from the police could work out what to do. Nobody wanted to do anything. I remember John Lennon throwing out lots of quips about being arrested or whatever, but there was a real party atmosphere.'

While the Beatles continued to play, police officers negotiated with Peter Brown. 'They said, "You can't do this," and I said, "*Why* can't we do it?" "Well, you just can't do this." And I said, "I don't see why we can't do it," and they said, "Well, does your landlord know?" And I said, "We are our own landlords. We *own* the place. So why can't we do this on the roof of our own property?" And they didn't have any answer.'

Mal Evans told PC Shayler that the Beatles had to record just one more track, and then they would be finished, and the noise would stop. 'And so I said, "If you do that, that's fine. But if you try and play beyond that, then we'll have to take action."' Hearing their conversation, one of the Beatles' technicians, Dave Harries, noticed George Martin blanching at the possibility of arrest. On the other hand, he himself couldn't help thinking, 'This is great! We're all going to be arrested with the Beatles!'

'One, two, three, four …' said George, and they launched into 'Get Back', the last song they would ever play together live. When it came to an end, the four Beatles behaved according to character: Paul apologised to the police officers; John and George refused to speak to them; and Ringo fooled around: 'I'll go quietly – don't use the handcuffs!' Later, Ringo expressed disappointment that the police had been so discreet: the film would have been so much more dramatic, he felt, if he had been hauled off his drums and clapped in irons.

When Ken Wharfe* reported back to West End Central police station, the sergeant who had phoned to alert him earlier that morning said, 'You got that music turned down, then?'

'Hey Sarge, it was amazing,' Ken replied. 'It was the Beatles on the roof down at the Apple building.'

'Let me tell you something, lad,' replied the sergeant, who was in his late forties. 'When I came to London, I was dating a girl in Holborn. Every Wednesday afternoon, duties permitting, we used to go and have afternoon tea at the Waldorf Hotel in the Aldwych and listen to music from a *proper* band. Any group of musicians that is forced to play on the roof of their office has got no future.'

---

* Eighteen years later, Inspector Ken Wharfe was appointed a Personal Protection Officer to Diana, Princess of Wales.

133

At Farleigh House, the morning's post was distributed during breakfast in the dining room, an out-building of recent construction, its walls lined with grey, pleasingly crumbly asbestos, easily extractable for playing with.

Once a week I would receive a chatty letter from my mother, talking about goings-on at home and ending 'Not long now until half-term!', or 'Not long now until the holidays!'

Parcels were a rarity, largely restricted to my birthday, early in the summer term, but in the holidays I had pre-ordered *Abbey Road* from a record shop in my home town of Dorking. For a little bit extra, to cover postage and packing, they agreed to send it to me at Farleigh House. I can now date its arrival to 27 September 1969, the day after its national release. I remember my excitement as I took it out of its stiff brown cardboard envelope with the other boys looking on, not so much amazed as bemused. Only a handful had any interest in pop music – most of them preferred football, yo-yos, the *Beezer* or the *Eagle*, making dodecahedrons out of card, or constructing Airfix models of Spitfires and Lancaster bombers.

'What's that then?' asked the Latin master, Mr Needham, as I sat there, perusing the cover of *Abbey Road*. 'Top of the Flops?' He liked speaking in puns: he called the Everett brothers 'Ever Wet', and the Brown brothers 'Hovis', after the brown-bread slogan: 'Don't Say Brown, Say Hovis'.

During the summer term I had attempted to get myself into Mr Needham's good books by pointing out that both Status Quo and Procul Harum had Latin names. Misreading my level of interest, he

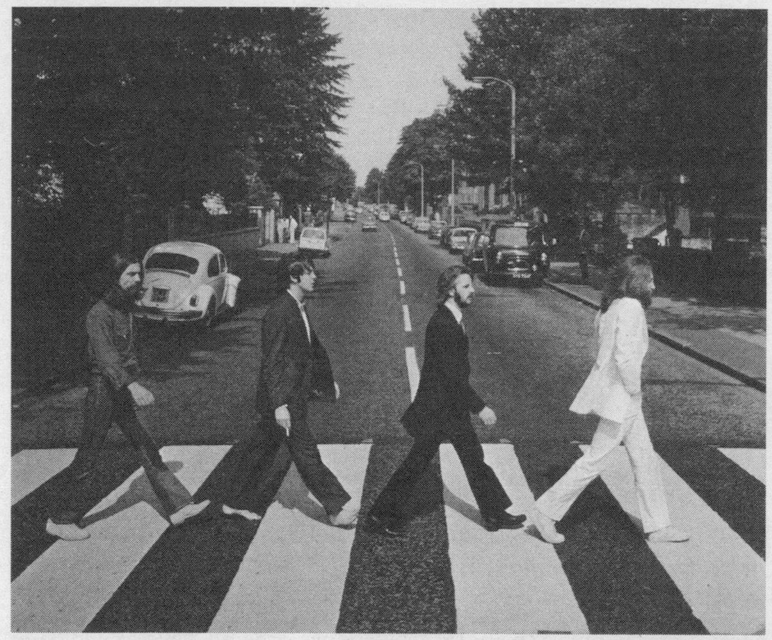

went on at tedious length about the meaning of *status quo*, and pedantically pointed out that if *procul harum* meant anything at all, it meant 'at this', which meant nothing at all. I wished I'd never mentioned it.

On first setting eyes on the cover of *Abbey Road*, I felt a keen sense of disappointment. The shiny white sleeve of *The White Album* had looked grand and luxurious, and came with all those bits and pieces inside – the colour photos, the poster which opened to reveal yet more photos and all the lyrics on the other side. *Sgt. Pepper*, too, had all those different characters standing as if for a sort of school photograph on the front, and the gatefold sleeve, and the cut-outs, and the lyrics in rivetingly small print on the back. But the front cover of *Abbey Road* just seemed dull – the four Beatles walking over a zebra crossing as though it were a bit of a chore, not even bothering to smile or look at the camera or lark about, and generally looking as if they couldn't be arsed. And the back was even duller: a dreary road sign saying ABBEY ROAD, plus something out of focus and blue swishing past. Furthermore, it was just a single sleeve, with no extras tucked inside:

no lyrics, no cut-outs, no photos. Surely, with all their money, the Beatles could have come up with something better than *this*?*

But posterity can't be second-guessed. As with the *Mona Lisa* and the Eiffel Tower and Her Majesty, time can render the dull iconic. In 2010 the British government awarded Grade II listed status to the zebra crossing on Abbey Road, on account of its 'cultural and historical importance'. And the markets took it seriously too: in 2014 a limited edition of six prints of the various Beatles/Abbey Road photographs, numbered and signed by the photographer, sold at auction for £180,000.

It is hard to think of an album cover more frequently imitated. Booker T and the MGs, Benny Hill, George Benson, *Sesame Street*, the Community of St Saviour's Monastery Jerusalem, Ivor Biggun, the King's Singers, the Red Hot Chilli Peppers, Jive Bunny, Blur and many more have released albums with cod-*Abbey Road* covers. The only time the Simpsons were featured on the cover of *Rolling Stone* it was with Lisa (as George), Bart (Paul), Marge (Ringo) and Homer (John) on the Abbey Road zebra crossing.† Paul McCartney parodied the *Abbey Road* cover for his 1993 solo album *Paul is Live*, on the cover of which he is pictured with one leg high in the air, crossing the road with his Old English sheepdog Arrow.‡

At first, the basic details of the shoot appear relatively straightforward. At 11.35 a.m. on Friday, 8 August 1969 the four Beatles spent

---

* Little did I know it at the time, but they had in fact been planning something much more ambitious. After toying with the titles 'Four in the Bar' or 'All Good Children Go to Heaven', they had decided to call the album 'Everest', with a cover photo of the four Beatles climbing the highest mountain in the world. Paul was excited by the idea of a trip to Tibet, but John and George kept changing their minds, and Ringo was dead against it, as foreign food disagreed with him. With the deadline approaching, John and George sided with Ringo. According to Geoff Emerick, a frustrated Paul said, 'Well, if we're not going to name it "Everest" and pose for the cover in Tibet, where are we going to go?' To which Ringo replied, half-jokingly, 'Fuck it. Let's just step outside and call it "Abbey Road".'

† Indeed, the cover of my own little book *1966 and All That* (2005), an update of the classic *1066 and All That*, featured a Ken Pyne pastiche of *Abbey Road*, with the parts of John, Ringo, Paul and George being taken, respectively, by Bobby Charlton, the Queen Mother (on a Zimmer frame), Sid Vicious and Winston Churchill.

‡ Offspring of the more famous Martha.

ten minutes being photographed walking across the Abbey Road zebra crossing by Iain Macmillan. But like virtually everything to do with the Beatles, even this is open to question. There are, for instance, ongoing arguments as to the exact time of the shoot: Mark Lewisohn and Barry Miles pin it to 11.35 a.m., but *The Beatles Bible* says it was 10 a.m., and Bob Spitz says it was 'some time after 10.00 a.m.'.

Most online discussion revolves around the people visible in the background, comparing the different photographs taken by Macmillan over the ten-minute period. The website of The Daily Beatle ('News and articles about the Beatles since 2008') features a long discussion about who they were, or who they might have been. The webmaster devotes a lot of attention to what he calls 'Mystery man' in a brown jacket, standing on the right, with his arms crossed. In another photo 'Mystery man' is still there, but has moved further away, and now shares the pavement with a woman in a red sweater who is looking directly at the camera.

'Here's where it gets interesting,' says the webmaster, optimistically. 'You have to look very, very carefully on the left pavement to spot her, but in the closest gateway, just behind the Beetle, is a young woman in a purple top. This is her first appearance, but she is present in three of the six frames – just one fewer appearances than "Mystery man".' In a fourth photograph 'There's no sign of "Mystery man" but there is another man in a white shirt, striding with some purpose, walking towards the camera.'

And so to photograph number five, picked for the cover because it was the only one which had the Beatles walking in step. 'On the left pavement, further back, stand three decorators, subsequently identified as Alan Flanagan, Steve Millwood and Derek Seagrove … There is no sign of the mysterious girl in the purple top.' A Mrs N.C. Seagrove writes that Derek is her husband; together with Flanagan and Millwood he was coming back from a lunch break when the picture was taken. 'They hung around just to be nosy. Derek thought if it was used, he and his mates would be edited out.'

More controversy centres around the 'Mystery man', who stands next to a police van. 'In February 2008, news was that Florida resident

Paul Cole, the man beside the police van, had died, aged ninety-three. But was he really that man? I don't think so, and here's why.' In 2004 Paul Cole claimed to have been in that spot, waiting for his wife, who was visiting a nearby museum. He said he had been starting a conversation with the driver of the police van when he spotted the Beatles. 'A bunch of kooks, I called them, because they were rather radical-looking at that time. You didn't walk around in London barefoot.' A year later, his wife, a church organist, had been given *Abbey Road* to play at a wedding. 'I saw it resting against her keyboard and I said, "Hey! It's those four kooks! That's me in there!"' Cole had never listened to the album, though he had heard one or two Beatles songs. 'It's not my kind of thing. I prefer classical music.'

But the webmaster casts doubt on Cole's claims: 'There's no museum in that part of Abbey Road. The police van was a late arrival to the photo session, as evidenced by the previous photos, so Paul Cole can't have had a conversation prior to the Beatles arriving at the scene.' He concludes that Paul Cole was a fraud. But is he wrong? There certainly was a museum nearby – the Ben Uri Gallery, dedicated to the work of émigré artists. Furthermore, Cole only claimed to have been *starting* a conversation with the police driver when his attention was caught by the Beatles crossing the road. And he was remembering events from thirty-five years before: there were bound to be inconsistencies.

'I have heard stories about people claiming to be or to know "the man on the cover" for as long as I have been a Beatles fan,' writes the webmaster. 'One of them supposedly was a gay man who died in the seventies.' He then quotes someone called Jo Pool, who writes, 'As soon as I saw the cover, I shouted, "That's my brother, Tony." Tony Staples was thirty-three and six foot four inches tall. On the day in question he was on his way to work as an administrative secretary for the National Farmers' Union.' But is this true? To my mind he looks older than thirty-three, and it seems unlikely that a secretary at the NFU would be leaning quite so nonchalantly against a wall at ten or eleven in the morning while 'on his way to work'.

The mysteries do not end there. Who is the woman in the blue dress on the back cover? Some bloggers seem convinced it is Jane Asher, though they offer no evidence. Others, tired of debating the figures on the front or back covers, seek to extend the parameters of their inquiries to those who were somewhere else. 'Does anyone know the name of the police officer who held up traffic while the photo was taken, or know anything about him?' asks Randy Ervin. But his question draws a blank.

134

A few weeks after the release of *Abbey Road*, the Apple press office began to receive calls from around the world wanting to know if Paul was dead. This type of rumour was by no means a rarity – as early as 1961, a reader of *Mersey Beat* had written in to ask whether one of the Beatles had just died in a car crash – but this one took on a life of its own, each denial acting as further confirmation of a cover-up.

The rumour of Paul's death appears to have started on 12 October 1969, when Russ Gibb, a disc jockey on the Detroit station WLNR-FM, took a call from a listener who said that Paul McCartney had died in a car accident. Tom drew Gibb's attention to the voice on 'Revolution 9' that repeated 'number nine, number nine' over and over again. The listener claimed that if you played the message backwards it said: 'Turn me on, dead man.'

Gibb broadcast it backwards. It sounded more like 'tunmyondenmum', but for anyone predisposed to believe, it offered proof galore. And so the rumour mushroomed, with everyone joining the scramble for fresh proof that Paul was indeed dead. According to one listener, at the end of 'Strawberry Fields Forever' John confesses, 'I buried Paul.' Another listened hard to the mumbles between the tracks 'I'm So Tired' and 'Blackbird' on *The White Album* and heard 'Paul is dead, man, miss him, miss him.' And so on.

On 14 October a student newspaper called the *Michigan Daily* produced a satirical spoof of these crazy rumours, illustrated with a photo of Paul's head separated from his body. Under the headline 'McCartney is Dead: New Evidence Brought to Light', the report concentrated on the cover of *Abbey Road*. The four Beatles were clearly in funeral procession, argued the author Fred LaBour. But spoofs are often mistaken for the truth – in fact, that is partly their purpose. Sure enough, the parody served only to reinforce the rumour it had set out to debunk.

Before long it seemed that virtually everything in the universe was pointing to the fact that Paul had died:

1 Paul – or rather, the man impersonating Paul – is the only Beatle to be walking barefoot on the cover of *Abbey Road*. His eyes appear to be closed, and he is out of step with the others.
2 The white VW Beetle parked on the left has the licence number LMW 28IF. LMW stands for 'Linda McCartney Weeps', and 28IF signifies that Paul would have been twenty-eight *if* he had not died. Strictly speaking, this is not so (he would have been twenty-seven) but – let's not forget! – Indian mystics date a person's real age from their conception.
3 John, dressed in white, is the preacher. Ringo, in black, is the pallbearer. George, in denim, is the gravedigger. 'Paul' is pictured with a cigarette in his right hand, but the real Paul was left-handed.
4 To the left of the road stand three men dressed in white. A single person, dressed in dark clothes, stands alone on the other side.
5 If you trace a line from the bottom of the VW Beetle through the three cars behind it, the line goes through Paul's head. Paul died of a head injury.
6 On the Australian cover there is a red stain on the road just behind Ringo and John, indicating a traffic accident.
7 On the back cover, eight dots on the wall to the left of the words 'THE BEATLES' can be joined together to form a 3 – the number of Beatles remaining after Paul's death.
8 If you turn the back cover 45 degrees anticlockwise, the shadow on the wall creates the clear image of a skull with a black gown.
9 On the night of the fatal crash, Paul gave a lift to a fan. The woman in blue on the back cover is that same fan, either fleeing the scene or running for help.

10 The signs saying 'BEATLES' and 'ABBEY ROAD' on the back cover appear to be divided into BE AT LES ABBEY RO AD. 'R' and 'O' are the eighteenth and fifteenth letters of the alphabet. Added together they make 33, which is the numerical equivalent of 'CC'. Paul is therefore buried at St Cecilia's Abbey on the Isle of Wight. Thirty-three multiplied by two, which is the number of letters, is sixty-six. Paul died in 1966.

11 On 'Come Together' John sings 'One and one and one is three'. This indicates that only three Beatles remain.

12 *Sgt. Pepper* holds almost as many clues. On the front cover, the man immediately behind 'Paul' – the music-hall comedian Issy Bonn – is holding his right hand over Paul's head. This is a symbol of death, as is the black musical instrument held by Paul. The entire cover is a depiction of Paul's funeral, with the Beatles standing around a freshly dug grave.

13 On the inside of the gatefold, 'Paul' is wearing a black armband with the letters 'OPD'. This is the Canadian acronym for Officially Pronounced Dead.

14 On the back cover, Paul is the only Beatle whose back is turned to the camera.

15 'A Day in the Life' contains the line 'He blew his mind out in a car.'

16 At the end of 'While My Guitar Gently Weeps', George wails 'Paul, Paul.'

17 The poster included with *The White Album* also contains a number of opaque references to Paul's death. The photograph of Paul in the bath – eyes closed, head floating as though separate from his body – shows what he would have looked like after the fatal crash. To the bottom right of the poster there is a small photo of Paul in white trousers, clapping and dancing. Behind him there is something blurry and unexplained. Is it the hands of a skeleton reaching out for him?

18 On 'Glass Onion' John sings: 'And here's another clue for you all – the Walrus was Paul.' In many cultures a walrus symbolises death – even if no one is quite sure exactly which cultures these are.

19 'I am the Walrus' is John's coded account of the fatal accident, which took place after Paul left the Abbey Road studio in a temper on a 'stupid bloody Tuesday'. John sings 'I'm crying' over and over again. It's an expression of grief.

20 At the beginning of the same song, two notes are repeated, making a sound similar to an ambulance siren. The 'pretty little policemen waiting for the van to come' are the police who arrived at the site of the accident. They were paid to keep quiet. 'Yellow matter custard dripping from a dead dog's eye' is a description of Paul's horrific facial injuries. 'I am he as you are he and we are all together' is an admission that the other three Beatles were involved in a conspiracy of silence. On page 557 of James Joyce's *Finnegans Wake* the words 'googoo goosth' are in the same sentence as 'them four hoarsemen on their apolkaloops'.

21 The fake Paul grew a moustache to cover up the scars of the plastic surgery he had undergone. Once the scars had healed, the powers that be let him remove it.

22 The fake Paul protested that what John was really saying at the end of 'Strawberry Fields Forever' is not 'I buried Paul,' but 'Cranberry sauce.' This is part of the cover-up.

23 On the cover of *Magical Mystery Tour*, the title is written in stars. If you turn the cover upside down, the stars form a phone number. If you call this number, you will be told the details of Paul's death.

24 In the lavish 'Your Mother Would Know' sequence of the *Magical Mystery Tour* film, 'Paul' is wearing a black carnation. The others wear white carnations.

All these signs pointed to just one conclusion: three years earlier, on 6 November 1966, Paul had died in a car crash. From then on his place had been taken by a lookalike. After all, there was no photograph of Paul for eighteen days from 6 November, and then he had been pictured with new facial hair – clearly there to cover up the scars from the plastic surgery on his lookalike. And who was the lookalike? An actor called William Shears Campbell, otherwise known as 'Billy

Shears', who had won a Paul McCartney lookalike competition and had never been seen again. Until now.

Heartbroken fans jammed the Apple switchboard. Derek Taylor contacted Paul in Scotland, and asked what he wanted to do about it. 'Nothing,' replied Paul. 'Just let it go.'

Unable to field the real Paul, Taylor's sidekick Tony Bramwell came up with a fiendish plan to scotch the rumours. Putting his own Liverpudlian accent to good use, he phoned the DJ Richie York on CING-FM in Burlington, Ontario. 'This is Paul McCartney,' he said. 'As you can hear, I'm alive and kicking.'

This aroused suspicions in two other radio stations. They immediately submitted the tape to two experts in voice recognition. Having compared Bramwell's voice with a recording of the known voice of Paul McCartney, Professor Oscar Tossey* of Michigan State University and Dr Henry M. Truby of Miami University both testified to the fact that they were not the same. This was further proof of a cover-up: Paul McCartney was, indeed, dead.

Paul was obliged to issue a written statement through the Apple press office: 'I am alive and well and concerned about the rumours of my death, but if I were dead, I would be the last to know.' This half-hearted message served only to fuel the fire. Now Derek Taylor was driven to issue a press release: 'Paul refuses to say anything more than that. Even if he appeared in public, it wouldn't do any good. If people want to believe he's dead, then they'll believe it. The truth is not at all persuasive.' Once again, the denial was taken as proof positive of a cover-up.

Two of the other Beatles stated that Paul was not dead. 'It's the most stupid rumour I've ever heard,' John said on WLNR. 'Sure, you can play anything backwards and you're going to get different connotations, 'cause it's backwards.' Ringo also pitched in, though only to explain why he wasn't pitching in. 'I'm not going to say anything,' he said, 'because nobody believes me when I do.'

* His real name.

At this stage, even some of Paul's friends began to entertain suspicions. One day Peter Blake, the designer of the *Sgt. Pepper* cover, bumped into the real, living Paul McCartney. 'He said to me, "Yes, it's true. I'm not actually Paul McCartney. You know Paul McCartney, he didn't have a scar on his mouth. I'm very like him, but I'm actually not him." I looked, and indeed there was a scar, but Paul didn't have a scar. What had happened was that he had fallen off his bike and had got a scar since I last saw him. Of course, it was Paul, and he did kid me for two minutes. And for three minutes I did believe him.'

Meanwhile the celebrated defence attorney F. Lee Bailey* had been hired by RKO to conduct a mock trial for a television special in which he cross-questioned 'expert witnesses', including Allen Klein and Peter Asher. Those defending the allegations included Fred LaBour, whose joky piece in the *Michigan Daily* had set the ball rolling. Before he took the stand, LaBour confessed to Bailey that he had perpetrated the hoax. 'Well,' replied Bailey, 'we have an hour of television to do, so you're going to have to go along with this.'

By now, four different singles on the Paul is Dead theme had been released: 'Brother Paul' by Billy Shears and the All-Americans, 'We're All Paul Bearers' by Zacherias and the Tree People, 'Saint Paul' by Terry Knight, and 'So Long Paul' by Werbley Finster,† which contained the somewhat pedestrian chorus:

> So long Paul, we hate to see you go,
> So long Paul, after making all that dough.

Later the same month, *Life* magazine sent a team of photographers and reporters to Scotland to track Paul down. Having walked four miles over marshy land to his farmhouse, they were confronted by Martha, Paul's Old English sheepdog. Alerted by Martha's barking, an irate Paul

---

* Legal representative of celebrity defendants including Albert DeSalvo ('The Boston Strangler') and, later, Patty Hearst and O.J. Simpson.

† Later revealed as a pseudonym of José Feliciano, the blind Puerto Rican singer still probably best known for his 1968 rendition of 'Light My Fire'.

emerged from his house and told them to get off his land, before throwing a bucket of water over them, an act caught by one of the photographers. As they left, Paul, ever conscious of his public image, and feeling he had gone too far, chased after them, offering an interview and photos in return for the offending photo.

Under the heading 'THE CASE OF THE MISSING BEATLE: Paul is Still With Us', the photograph on the cover of the November 1969 issue of *Life* showed the McCartney family – Paul, Linda, Heather and baby Mary – in rural bliss. In the accompanying interview Paul said, 'It is all bloody stupid. I picked up that OPD badge in Canada. It was a police badge. Perhaps it means Ontario Police Department or something. I was wearing a black flower because they ran out of red ones. It is John, not me, dressed in black on the cover and inside of *Magical Mystery Tour*. On *Abbey Road* we were wearing our ordinary clothes. I was walking barefoot because it was a hot day. The Volkswagen just happened to be parked there … The people who are making up these rumors should look to themselves a little more. There is not enough time in life. They should worry about themselves instead of worrying whether I am dead or not.'

To coincide with the interview, Apple released a triumphant and characteristically long-winded press release.

> Paul McCartney is alive. He says so. His wife says so, his children show he is. The recent photos confirm it, the new songs make it concrete, and the very fact that he is alive should be enough. If in doubt, read *Life* magazine. If still in doubt, there is nothing we can do. The Paul McCartney who wrote 'And I Love Her' still loves you, and is still alive, and has a lot to write. There are a thousand songs unwritten and much to do. Have faith and believe. He is alive and well and hopes to remain so as long as possible. If that doesn't work, then we'll start our own rumour that the public is dead from the neck up and they've been using a stand-in facsimile of a brain for the past three and a half years and then sit back and see who denies it.

Fifty years on, there are still those who believe that Paul died in 1966, and that his part is being played by a gifted impostor. In 2009 the Italian edition of *Wired* magazine published a nine-page article in which a forensic pathologist called Gabriella Carlesi and a computer scientist called Francesco Gavazenni went to great lengths to test before and after photographs of Paul, measuring differences in his teeth, lips, jaws and ears. They concluded that they were not of the same man.

A book by Tina Foster called *Plastic Macca: The Secret Death and Replacement of Beatle Paul McCartney* (2019) presents yet more evidence, including the revelation that 'the remaining Beatles and their business representatives made a pact with Paul's relatives, for a large sum of money, to keep Paul's death a secret, and hired a replacement to protect the group's image, career, popularity, and finances'.

Foster suggests that one of the initial motives for the fraud was the fear that fans would be so distraught over Paul's death that they would be driven to suicide. 'There is a precedent for this theory,' she writes. 'Shortly before Christmas 1962, a puppy named "Petra" appeared on the children's TV show, *Blue Peter*. Sadly, the dog died of distemper two days later. Rather than traumatise millions of children by revealing the puppy's tragic fate, the show's bosses found a lookalike black and brown puppy to replace the original Petra. Not a single viewer noticed.'

The book's blurb states that 'Attorney and author Tina Foster has devoted years of her life to unearthing what happened to James Paul McCartney … Recognised as an authority on the subject, Tina has been invited to speak on radio shows in the USA, UK, Canada and Australia.'

Oddly enough, Foster never explains why the remaining Beatles and their co-conspirators were so keen to give away their own secret by offering quite so many tell-tale clues to its unlocking.

135

There was lunacy in the air. Soon after the stage adaptation of John's books, *In His Own Write*, opened at the Old Vic in June 1968, Yoko Ono summoned Victor Spinetti, its director. Spinetti kept a note of their conversation.

'"Ah," she said. "I want you to direct *my* play."

'"Oh," I said. "What is it? Let me see the script."

'"No, no. No script. All audience get in bus. And allowed to go to house. Then all people in bus allowed to come and open door to symbolise awareness. Then everyone get back in bus. Then they go to other house. All allowed to come out. This time allowed to meet one person. Symbolise beginning communication. Then audience get back on bus –"'

Spinetti interrupted her monologue. 'Now wait a minute, Yoko. What's the big finish? I mean, what happens?'

'Oh, everyone go into Hyde Park and wait for something to happen.'

'Like what?'

'Like chair falling out of sky.'

At this point Spinetti glanced at John, whose face was radiating love and wonder.

'Ooh, that's fookin' great, that is, Vic, "chair falling out of sky".'

Spinetti couldn't work out whether or not John was joking. Thinking it was time to leave, he said, 'You don't want me to direct it, darling. You want to get Cook's Tours. They're great with buses.'

Yoko was not amused. 'She didn't speak to me for months,' he recalled.

* * *

Around the same time, an ambitious eighteen-year-old called Richard Branson secured a promise from John and Yoko to provide the first issue of his new magazine, *Student*, with a flexidisc recording to be attached to the front cover. On the strength of this promise, Branson had ordered an ambitious print run of 100,000 copies, commissioning the self-styled 'Man with Kaleidoscope Eyes', Alan Aldridge, to create one of his psychedelic pictures for the cover.

But as the print date drew closer, the promised recording failed to appear. In desperation, Branson instructed a lawyer to threaten to sue Apple and the Lennons for £100,000, on the grounds of breach of promise.

The threat seemed to work wonders. A few days later, Branson received a telephone call from Derek Taylor. 'Come round to Apple, Richard. We've got something for you.'

Branson was led into the basement studio at Savile Row, where he sat with John and Yoko as Taylor switched on a tape recording. Branson was all ears.

'The hiss of the tape recorder was followed by a steady, metronomic beat, like the sound of a human heart.

'"What is it?" I asked.

'"It's the heartbeat of our baby," said John.

'No sooner had he spoken than the sound stopped. Yoko burst into floods of tears and hugged John. I didn't understand what was going on, but before I could speak John looked over Yoko's shoulder straight into my eyes.

'"The baby died," he told me. "That's the silence of our dead baby."'

Taylor reassured him that it was 'conceptual art', but Branson was flummoxed. What should he do? A free recording of a baby dying was unlikely to send his magazine flying off the shelves.

'I felt unable to release this private moment as a record,' wrote Branson, with due solemnity, in his autobiography decades later. Instead, he scrapped the cover, redesigned the magazine and reduced the print order. For their part, John and Yoko had successfully side-stepped legal action. A few weeks later, the genial Taylor wrote Branson a note of apology for any trouble caused, signing off 'All you need is love'.

After Yoko's miscarriage, John stayed with her at Queen Charlotte's Hospital while she recuperated.

One morning he phoned Victor Spinetti and asked him to pay them a visit. Spinetti found Yoko sitting up in bed, typing, while John lay on the floor, looking dreadful.

'My God,' he said. 'Which one's had the miscarriage?'

John laughed; Yoko continued typing. 'I'm writing to my little daughter,' she said. 'I'm sending her a poem.' She then read out the poem: 'Do not worry, Kyoko. Mummy is only looking for her hand in the snow.'

Spinetti was taken aback. 'How old is she?'

'Five.'

'And when did you last see her?'

'Four years ago.'

'Darling – send her a doll's house,' said Spinetti.

On Spinetti's next visit, Yoko filled him in on her next venture. 'I have bought ten thousand cups. John and I take hammer. Smash cup. We sell broken cup and people all over the world will buy it and stick broken cup that John and I break, stick it together, because, you see, now we are married, we are more famous than the Burtons.' This time, Spinetti felt it expedient to keep quiet.

136

On Saturday, 14 June 1969, John and Yoko were interviewed by David Frost in London. They kicked off the show by throwing acorns to the audience, explaining that it was 'Acorns for Peace' week. Yoko then presented Frost with what she called a 'box of smile'. Upon opening it, Frost found a small mirror. He then asked them about Bagism.

JOHN: What's Bagism? It's like a tag for what we all do, we're all in a bag, you know, and we realised that we came from two bags – I was in this pop bag going round and round in my little clique and she was in her little avant-garde clique going round and round and you're in your little telly clique and they're in their … you know? And we all sort of come out and look at each other every now and then, but we don't communicate. We all intellectualise about how there is no barrier between art, music, poetry … but we're still all – 'I'm a rock and roller.' 'He's a poet.' So we just came up with the word so you would ask us what bagism is – and we'd say We're all in a bag, baby!

FROST: Well now, you've got in a bag, you've got in a sack …

JOHN: Well, we got out of one bag and into the next, you just keep moving from bag to bag.

FROST: You've got a bag there with you, what do you do with it?

JOHN: Well sometimes we get in it and sometimes other people get in it.

YOKO: You know, this life is speeded up so much and the whole world is getting tenser and tenser because things are just going so fast, you know, so it's so nice to slow down the rhythm of the whole

world, just to make it peaceful. So like the bag, when you get in, you see that it's very peaceful and your movements are sort of limited. You can walk around on the street in a bag.

FROST: Can you?

JOHN: If people did interviews for jobs in a bag they wouldn't get turned away because they were black or green or long hair, you know, it's total communication.

FROST: They'd get turned away because they were in a bag. (Audience laughter)

YOKO: Well no, if that was specified that when you interviewed the people that you wanted to employ – and you had this prejudice – and the people had to wear a bag, then you'd only judge them on what they communicated to you and you wouldn't have to think 'Oh, he's wearing black suede is he? Don't like it.'

137

From the diary of Kenneth Williams, 15 June 1969

The Beatle who is married to an Asiatic lady was on The Frost Programme. The man is long-haired & unprepossessing, with tin spectacles and this curious nasal Liverpudlian delivery: the appearance is either grotesque or quaint & the overall impression is one of great foolishness. He and his wife are often 'interviewed' from inside bags to achieve 'objectivity' and they have 'lie-ins' whereby they stay in bed for long periods & allow a certain number of people into the room. I think this man's name is Ringo Starr or something (no – it's John Lennon) but he began as a 'singer' and instrumentalist with this group called the Beatles and one searches in vain for any valid reason for his being interviewed *at all.* What this ex-pop-singer is doing pontificating about the state of humanity, I cannot imagine. It's mind-bending to listen to.

138

In September 1969, on a visit to Aunt Mimi, John stealthily removed his MBE from the mantelpiece upon which it had sat for the past four years and took it back to London without a word. He then asked his staff to enquire about the correct way of returning it to HM the Queen. Bill Oakes, Peter Brown's personal assistant at Apple, pursued the matter, and wrote this formal memo:

> The medal, with a brief explanation, should be sent to – The Secretary of the Central Chancery, 8 Buckingham Gate, London, SW1
>
> Two optional letters should be sent to:
>
> a) Harold Wilson. The main protest should be lodged here – presumably this letter would become public?
>
> b) H.M. The Queen. Solicitors advise no more than a respectful, regretful note.

On 25 November 1969, John wrote the following single-sentence letter:

> Your Majesty,
> I am returning this MBE in protest against Britain's involvement in the Nigeria – Biafra thing, against our support of America in Vietnam and against Cold Turkey slipping down the charts.
> with love
> John Lennon

He then instructed his chauffeur, Les Anthony, to deliver it to Buckingham Palace, also giving him letters to deliver to the prime minister and the secretary of the Central Chancery.

Calling a press conference at the Apple headquarters, John claimed he was always uneasy about his MBE. The Beatles had, he said, been pressured into accepting their awards by Brian Epstein: 'I always squirmed when I saw "MBE" on my letters. I didn't really belong to that sort of world. I think the Establishment bought the Beatles with it. Now I am giving it back, thank you very much …

'I had been mulling it over for a few years. Even as I received it, I was mulling it over. I gave it to my auntie who proudly had it over the mantelpiece, which is understandable – she was very proud of it. But I can't not do it because of my auntie's feelings. So I took it a few months back and didn't tell her what I was going to do with it – no doubt she knows now. And I'm sorry Mimi, but that's the way it goes.'

When Mimi found out what had happened, she was extremely upset: 'If I knew what John wanted it for, I never would have given it to him.' She clearly felt too humiliated to admit that he had taken it without asking.

139

On the Monday, Apple Records send out an invitation:

> Apple Peace/Postcard/Communication/John and Yoko and Apple Records invite you to join them on Thursday this week, July 3, to meet the Plastic Ono Band in Chelsea Town Hall, Kings Road.

But on the Tuesday, driving in the Scottish Highlands, John swerves into a ditch. The front of his car is crushed, and John, Julian, Yoko and her daughter Kyoko are all taken to hospital. John is given seventeen stitches, Yoko fourteen and Kyoko four. Julian is treated for shock, but released. 'John isn't a driving man, hasn't driven for years,' explains Derek Taylor.

John is adamant, however, that the proposed launch party for the Plastic Ono Band's 'Give Peace a Chance' should go ahead. As he and Yoko will now be unable to attend, he instructs Taylor to send a film crew to Scotland to 'tape a greeting from the hospital bed'.

On the day before the party, Taylor receives a phone call from the head of the film crew, who tells him that John and Yoko would not agree to see them; they were apparently feeling 'shitty'. So he is on his way back to London, without any film.

But the party goes ahead, with no expense spared. Chelsea Town Hall is lavishly decorated with floral arrangements and vast white banners declaring 'LOVE AND PEACE'. Tables groan with enough food and drink for five hundred guests, even though only three hundred have been invited.

They start arriving at 5.30 p.m., to be welcomed by Derek Taylor, who apologises for the absence of the hosts. 'Give Peace a Chance' is played on a loop through the loudspeakers. Hours later, after what Taylor describes as 'gargantuan amounts of alcohol' have been drunk, a conga line forms, and everyone dances out onto the street. This is the last party ever to be thrown by a Beatle, and not one of the Beatles was there.

140

The American journalist Gloria Emerson interviewed John and Yoko at the Apple headquarters on 3 December 1969. Having begun her career as a foreign correspondent in Saigon in the 1950s, she knew what she was talking about. The heated argument between Emerson and John and Yoko – notable, because Emerson was clearly no establishment reactionary – was broadcast by BBC Radio 2 a fortnight later.

JOHN: If I'm gonna get on the front page I might as well get on the front page with the word 'peace'.
GLORIA EMERSON: But you made yourself ridiculous!
JOHN: To some people, but I don't care, if it *saves lives*!
GLORIA: You don't think you –? Oh, my dear boy! You're living in a never-never land! You don't think you've saved a single life?!
JOHN: Maybe we'll save some in the future!

Eleven years older than John, and three years older than Yoko, Emerson sounds exasperated, like an adult confronted by unrepentant children.

GLORIA: What do you know about a protest movement anyway? It consists of a lot more than sending your chauffeur in your car back to Buckingham Palace!
JOHN: You're just a snob about it. The only way to make –
GLORIA: You're a fake! I mean, I know in England it's kind of smart not to be serious about everything –

Silent up to now, suddenly Yoko pipes up.

YOKO: Everything needs a smile, you know.
GLORIA: I see. The Pinkville massacre,* ha ha ha! Can't you give up something else if it –

There is an awkward silence. John looks daggers at Gloria, and starts to chew his gum much more vigorously. She, in turn, puffs on a cigarette.

JOHN: It's not the sacrifice. You can't get that into your head, can you? You've stated half a dozen times the MBE is irrelevant. I agree, it was no sacrifice to get rid of the MBE, because it was embarrassing.
GLORIA: But what kind of a protest did you make?
JOHN: (raising his voice) I did an ADVERTISING CAMPAIGN FOR PEACE! DO YOU UNDERSTAND THAT?
GLORIA: No, I can't.
JOHN: – a very big advertising campaign for peace!
GLORIA: I think it shouts of self-aggrandisement! Are you advertising John Lennon or peace?

John begins shouting at her. If she is treating him like a child, he is treating her as a bourgeois flibbertigibbet. Perhaps he doesn't know that she is a war correspondent; if he does, he seems to have forgotten.

JOHN: If you want nice middle-class gestures for peace and intellectual manifestos written by a lot of half-witted intellectuals and nobody reads them! That's the trouble with the peace movement!
GLORIA: Well, it just seems a never-never land. I mean, I can't think of anyone who seems more remote from the ugliness of what's happening than you. I do see you getting up on a Tuesday morning and thinking, 'Let's see, what shall we do today, what war is on?'
YOKO: But that's your imagination!

---

* The notorious My Lai massacre (March 1968) was originally known as the Pinkville massacre, 'Pinkville' being the US Army's name for the area in which it took place.

JOHN: Why don't you make a film while you're at it?

GLORIA: I'm someone who admired you very much.

JOHN: Well, I'm sorry you liked the old moptops, dear, and you thought I was very satirical and witty and you liked *Hard Day's Night*, love. But I've grown up, and you obviously haven't.

GLORIA: What have you grown up to?

JOHN: Twenty-nine.

GLORIA: Yes.

At this point she becomes quieter, more conciliatory. Perhaps she has only just realised quite how young he is, so finds his naïvety more forgivable.

GLORIA: How was Greece?

YOKO: Beautiful.

JOHN: We did a nice war protest on the army TV while we were there. I suppose you didn't like us going to Greece, eh? You think we shouldn't go to a fascist country like Greece where it's all right to live in a fascist country like Britain or America, is it?

Emerson is unruffled, looking to the ceiling for a second and taking stock before continuing.

GLORIA: I think America's a good place to live right now because I mean if you were interested or committed OR not too cowardly you might conceivably make a difference by what you did.

JOHN: Well, we've been trying to go to America to do something for the last seven or eight months, but I can't get in.

GLORIA: You don't understand how they protest, my dear –

JOHN: Tell me, what were they singing at the moratorium, the recent big one? They were singing 'Give Peace a Chance'! And it was written specifically for them!

GLORIA: Where are we and what is this and what do you have to do with the moratorium? So they sang one of your songs! Great song, sure. But is that all you can say about that?

John wags his finger at her.

JOHN: You were saying that in America (starts imitating her accent) 'they're so serious about the protest movement but they were so flippant that they were singing a happy-go-lucky song' which happens to be one I wrote and I'm glad they sang it and when I get there I'll sing it with them, when I get in, and that was a message from me to America or to anywhere that I use my songwriting ability to write a song that we could all sing together and I'm PROUD that they sang it at the moratorium. I wouldn't have cared if they'd sang 'We Shall Overcome' but it just so happens they sang that and I'm PROUD of it and I'll be glad to go there and sing with 'em!

GLORIA: Make it jolly.

JOHN: I WILL make it jolly.

Yoko now gives her only long speech. She speaks in a peculiarly childish voice, almost as though reading a children's book.

YOKO: We have to make it jolly because if we make it jolly maybe we might stop the war because the thing is when you're happy and when you're smiling you don't want to kill someone, do you, you know, it's when you're very serious you start to think about violence and death and killing. I mean, have you ever seen a person killing somebody with a smile on his face and being happy? No! Killers are unhappy people and they're violent because they're so unhappy and so damn serious.

Emerson picks up her bag.

GLORIA: Mr and Mrs Lennon, we're boring each other, so I'll go away. Thank you. Goodbye!

JOHN: Well, I think that's what you wanted!

Emerson leaves the room, without another word.

YOKO: (to John) The last point was a good point and she didn't want to respond to it.

JOHN: She didn't hear anything.

The following year Gloria Emerson returned to Saigon, saying she 'wanted to go back to write about the Vietnamese people and the immense unhappy changes in their lives, not a subject widely covered by the huge press corps who were preoccupied with covering the military story'. In her first reports she exposed the false American body counts, and the use of hard drugs by GIs. Years later she said that, by the end of her time there, she had lost count of the number of young American soldiers she had comforted in their final moments.

Nineteen years later, in the December 1988 issue of *Q* magazine, Yoko spoke to the journalist Tom Hibbert about the legacy of the bed-ins, in which she and John had stayed in bed 'for peace'.

HIBBERT: Are those bed-ins something you look back on with pride?

YOKO: Oh yes. Pride and great joy. Those things we did were blessings. At the time we were doing it people used to sort of laugh at us – we were hoping that they would laugh *with* us but it didn't work out that way. But in the end, you see, it did have an effect. Last year when Reagan and Gorbachev had their summit and shook hands, I sort of felt, well, John and I did have an effect.

141

On 6 December 1969 my father was about to enter the Bull Hotel in Long Melford, Suffolk, when he found his way blocked by John and Yoko, who were trying to exit.

To a child – I was twelve at the time – the difference in age between my father and John Lennon was a century or more. It's odd to think that in reality only twenty years separated them: my father (b.1920) was then forty-nine, and John (b.1940) was twenty-nine. Oddly enough, my mother (b.1930) was, and remains, only three years older than Yoko Ono (b.1933).

My father had come to Suffolk to shoot pigeons. John and Yoko had come to Suffolk to shoot a film, *Apotheosis no. 2*. It involved a hot-air balloon rising from the square of the pretty medieval village of Lavenham. As often happened in those days when they were the centre of attention, John and Yoko were also being filmed while filming, on this occasion for a BBC documentary called *24 Hours: The World of John and Yoko*.

You can still see them on YouTube, checking into the Bull Hotel (as 'Mr and Mrs Smith'), then having tea in bed, before being driven through the snow from Long Melford to Lavenham in their white Rolls-Royce. Eerily, at the beginning of the film, lying in another hotel bed, John reads out a letter to Yoko:

> Dear Mr Lennon,
> From information I received while using a Ouiji [sic] Board, I believe that there will be an attempt to assassinate you. The spirit that gave me this information was Brian Epstein.

John and Yoko both laugh.

In Lavenham, they sit on a bench in the snow, staring into space, shrouded in black, with only their eyes and noses visible. A vast orange hot-air balloon floats up into the air as they look on. I remember seeing a video of them and their balloon on the BBC's *Top of the Pops*, as a backdrop to their single 'Instant Karma'.

The doorway of the Bull Hotel was broad enough to allow my father to enter, or John and Yoko to exit, but not all three at the same time. 'I stood my ground,' my father told me when he got home. In the end, John and Yoko had moved to one side – but, his triumphant tone implied, not without a struggle.

In those days the generation gap was often an issue, especially when the talk turned to John and Yoko. The older generation knew they were up to no good: they were getting away with something, though no one knew quite what. In the *Daily Telegraph*, my future father-in-law, Colin Welch (b.1924), attempted to articulate these suspicions. 'It was as if the Beatles and the young had in common a secret language, incomprehensible to others, yet full of dark meaning to them,' he wrote years later. For him, by the end of the sixties the Beatles had turned into 'not just entertainers but avatars and prophets, heroes and philosophers of a whole generation, exemplary in their meretricious triumphs, political posturings, shallow "thinking" and sentimental feeling'. They were, he said, Pied Pipers leading children away from their parents. 'From this world, certain boring virtues are completely missing. All the military and marital virtues, all fidelity, restraint, thrift, sobriety, taste and discipline, all the virtues associated with work, with the painful acquisition of knowledge, skill and qualifications. All these give place to a decadent self-expression, in which nothing is expressed because nothing has been cultivated to be expressed.'

The great divide was, of course, the Second World War. At the age of nineteen, John was having fun playing skiffle with the Quarrymen in the Casbah. At the same age, my father had enlisted in the Cameron Highlanders. For the next six years he had been off at war, wounded at Normandy, losing his only brother at Salerno. Aged twenty, Colin was also fighting in Normandy: his battalion of the Royal Warwickshire Regiment lost a staggering 170 per cent of its original complement in the ten months after D-Day. 'The smell of Normandy was death … a gigantic abattoir, bodies everywhere, human, animal, theirs, ours, French, no chance to bury them, all stiff and hideously swollen, covered with white dust or mud, faces blown away or dreadfully distorted, crawling with flies, rotting, giving off that terrible sweet-sour stench which, once smelt, is not forgotten.'

The war affected both men deeply; how could it not? 'The fragility and preciousness of civil society, as also the dire consequences of its collapse, were indelibly impressed on us,' wrote Colin. 'In a way, we all became profoundly conservative, keenly aware of what had been lost, desperately anxious to preserve what remained.'

Aged twenty, John was playing the Cavern, set to embark on a life of phenomenal freedom, singing and playing to adoring audiences all over the world, rewarded with every luxury and indulgence life can offer. Small wonder, then, that so many of those of the war generation viewed his life with a mixture of bemusement, frustration and – who knows? – perhaps a little envy.

142

It must have been hard, too, for the generation in between. Ross MacManus* was thirty-five in January 1963, and singing with the Joe Loss Orchestra. At that time an arrangement existed between the BBC and the Musicians' Union that only five hours of recorded music could be played on the radio each day: beyond that, everything had to be performed live. The Joe Loss Orchestra plugged this gap, learning the latest hits by other artistes in a matter of days, then replicating them over the air.

MacManus's nine-year-old son Declan listened as his father learned the latest hits by playing them time after time, and singing along. 'I was used to my father's voice coming from the front room where he was practising new songs. It rattled the pane of frosted glass in the door to the hallway.'

In January, MacManus had been told to learn a song called 'Please Please Me', by a new group, the Beatles. Young Declan listened intently to the disc as his father played it over and over again. He was startled by the vocal harmony line: the second singer seemed to be singing the same note repeatedly against the lead singer. 'I knew that my dad's colleagues, Rose and Larry, would be answering his "C'mon" and probably find the whole thing a bit daft, but I couldn't hear enough of that

* Ross MacManus (1927–2011). On YouTube you can see him and the Joe Loss Orchestra performing 'Please Please Me' in 1963. MacManus looks very like his son, and wears the same uncompromising spectacles. His dancing to the Latin-American rhythms is remarkably free-form, almost experimental, and makes the Beatles' stolid jigging seem a little creaky. In 1970 his version of 'The Long and Winding Road' reached number 16 in the Australian charts.

crescendo, especially when it broke into the title line, with a little falsetto jump on the first "Please".'

Declan asked his father if he could have the record when he'd finished with it. 'He laughed and handed the record to me.' As the year went by, and the fame of the Beatles increased, Declan looked forward to his father bringing home each new Beatles single, knowing that it would soon be his. They arrived hot off the press: many had a label printed in red reading 'DEMO DISC' and 'DICK JAMES MUSIC LIMITED'.

At the beginning of November, Ross MacManus was booked to sing 'If I Had a Hammer' with the Joe Loss Orchestra at the Royal Variety Show. To Declan, the idea that his dad would be sharing a bill with the Beatles was infinitely more exciting than performing before royalty.

The morning after the big day, Declan tried to play it cool, asking matter-of-fact questions.

'Did you see Steptoe and son? … And Dickie Valentine?'

But before long he could hold out no longer.

'Did you actually meet the Beatles?'

His father mumbled that yes, he did, and very nice lads they were too. 'Then he reached into a jacket slung over the back of his chair and pulled out a sheet of thin airmail paper and handed it to me. I unfolded it, and there were the signatures of all four of the Beatles on one page … The ink seemed barely dry.'

Declan's autograph book was too small to hold the entire sheet of paper, so he cut around each signature, lopped the 'e' of the 'The' in 'The Beatles', and pasted in the four severed scraps.

Ten years later, when Declan was embarking on a career in music, Ross advised him never to tell a soul that his dad had sung with the Joe Loss Orchestra, or they wouldn't take him seriously. Declan MacManus added to the subterfuge by changing his name to Elvis Costello. 'When I think about it, he was thirty-five. It must have been tough for him to go up to these twenty-two-year-olds and say "I want an autograph for my boy."'

143

Every Christmas Day throughout her reign, Queen Elizabeth II has broadcast a Christmas message to the people of Great Britain and the Commonwealth. She delivered her first Christmas message in 1952, ten months after she acceded to the throne. She was twenty-six years old.

'Each Christmas, at this time, my beloved father broadcast a message to his people in all parts of the world,' she began. 'Today I am doing this to you, who are now *my* people.'

She went on to ask her subjects 'to keep alive that courageous spirit of adventure that is the finest quality of youth'. Looking towards her coronation, she concluded her broadcast by saying, 'I want to ask you all, whatever your religion may be, to pray for me on that day – to pray that God may give me wisdom and strength to carry out the solemn promises I shall be making, and that I may faithfully serve Him and you, all the days of my life.'

Among the many millions who heard her words over the wireless that Christmas was the ten-year-old Paul McCartney, who had passed his 11-Plus exam earlier in the year. A few months later, he entered Liverpool's Coronation essay competition. Sure enough, he won a prize, which was presented to him at a special ceremony in the city's Picton Hall.

'On the Coronation Day of William the Conqueror, senseless Saxon folk gathered round Westminster Abbey to cheer their Norman king as he walked down the aisle,' began the neatly-written essay by 'Paul McCartney, age 10 years, 10 months'. 'The Normans thinking this was an insult turned upon the Saxons killing nearly all of them.' It continued on a more reassuring note: 'But on the Coronation of our lovely young queen, Queen Elizabeth II, no rioting nor killing will take place because present day royalty rule with affection rather than force.'

Eleven years later, Paul and his fellow Beatles gathered at the EMI studios for the recording of the first of their own Christmas messages, to be posted on flexible discs to members of their fan club. This was to become a tradition, continuing up to Christmas 1969, just before the four members of the group went their different ways.

Each of their seven Christmas recordings can now be seen as a strange sort of counterbalance to the stiffer, rather more traditional form of message delivered by Her Majesty.

1963

Queen's Christmas Message

'Since my last message of Christmas greetings to you all, the world has witnessed many great events and sweeping changes, but they are already part of the long record of history' (an oblique reference to the assassination of President Kennedy in November). 'Now, as ever, the important time for mankind is the future.

'Humanity can only progress if we are truly ambitious for what is good and honourable.

'We know the reward is peace on earth, good will towards men …'

The Queen closes by reminding her subjects that 'much has been achieved, but there is still much to do', adding that 'All my family joins me in sending, every one of you best wishes for Christmas, and may God's blessing be with you in the coming year.'

Beatles' Christmas Message

'Good King Wenceslas' is sung by all four Beatles, complete with larky variations on the original words, e.g. 'Brightly shone the boot that night, on the mossy cru-el …'

John: 'Hello, this is John speaking, with his voice. We're all very happy to be able to talk to you, on this little bit of plastic … This time last year we were really chuffed because "Love Me Do" had got into the top 20 and we can't really believe that so many things have happened in between already.' (Sings: 'Gary Chrimble to you, Gary Nimble to you!')

Paul: 'Everything John said goes for me too.' (Halfway through thanking the fans for their cards and parcels, he is pinched by somebody – presumably John – and yelps 'Ow!' before bursting into laughter.) Paul goes on to say that, having once mentioned that the Beatles loved jelly babies, 'We've been getting them in boxes and crates and anyway we've gone right off jelly babies.' However, 'we still like peppermint creams and chocolate drops and dolly mixtures'.

The Beatles end by singing 'Happy Christmas' in a loose version of German, but with confident accents, a reminder of their many months in Hamburg. They then sing 'Ringo the Red-Nosed Reindeer'.

1964

Queen's Christmas Message
'All of us who have been blessed with young families know from long experience that when one's house is at its noisiest, there is often less cause for anxiety …' The Queen makes a direct appeal to young people: 'Upon you rests our hope for the future. You young people are needed; there is a great task ahead of you – the building of a new world. You have brains and courage, imagination and humanity; direct them to the things that have to be achieved in this century, if mankind is to live together in peace and prosperity.'

She ends by saying, 'God bless you and a very, very happy Christmas to you all.'

Beatles' Christmas Message
The music is 'Jingle Bells', and then they all chorus, 'I don't know where we'd be without you!' to which John adds, 'In the army, perhaps.'

Even at this early stage, they are showing signs of nostalgia. 'We are taping this little message in Number Two studio at EMI,' says Paul. 'The same studio we've used all along since the old days of "Love Me Do", many years ago, it seems.' 'Oh, those were the days,' adds John.

John mentions his new book – 'the usual rubbish but it won't cost much. That's the bargain we're going to strike up.'

The Beatles end by singing 'Oh, You Can Wash Your Father's Shirt', before shouting 'Happy Christmas' over and over again.

1965

Queen's Christmas Message
'There is overwhelming evidence that those who cannot experience a full and happy family life for some reason or another are deprived of a

Beatles' Christmas Message
Each year the Beatles' message becomes looser and more impromptu. 1965's starts with an ad-hoc rendition of 'Yesterday', sung

great stabilising influence in their lives … Cynics may shrug off the Christmas message as a waste of time, but that is only the gloomy side of the picture; there are also brighter and more hopeful signs.'

She finishes: 'To each one of you I wish a very happy Christmas, and if throughout the Commonwealth we can all make a sustained effort, perhaps Christmas next year will be a much happier one for many more people.'

off-key, followed by banter.

John employs a rapid succession of accents, including broad Scottish – 'We be-lang to Edinburgh! Bannie Christmas!' At one point he slips into singing the Four Tops' number 'It's the Same Old Song', until he is cautioned by Ringo: 'Copyright, Johnny!'

1966

Queen's Christmas Message

A new stridency creeps into Her Majesty's tone: 'This year, I should like to speak especially to women … It is difficult to realise that it was less than fifty years ago that women in Britain were first given the vote.' It has been women, she says, who have 'breathed gentleness and care into the harsh progress of mankind'. She ends with: 'God be with you, and a very happy Christmas to you all.'

Beatles' Christmas Message

It opens with Paul improvising a song on the piano: 'Everywhere it's Christmas!'

This year the Beatles take a day off recording their epic 'Strawberry Fields Forever' to broadcast a makeshift Goon-style pantomime.

The storyline is hard to fathom. 'Our story opens in Corsica,' says John. 'Meanwhile, high up in the Swiss Alps, two elderly Scotsmen munch upon a Swiss cheese …'

The Beatles bring their message to an end with a song called 'Please Don't Bring Your Banjo Back, I Don't Know Where it's Been'.

1967

Queen's Christmas Message

Her Majesty celebrates Canada's centenary: 'Canada has every reason to feel proud.'

She also pays tribute to the 'great feat of seamanship' of Sir Francis Chichester, who has sailed *Gypsy Moth* single-handed around the world.

Closer to home, she says, 'Let there be no doubt that Britain is faced with formidable problems, but let there also be no doubt she will overcome them.' In the end, 'determined and well-directed effort by a people who for centuries have given ample evidence of their resources of character and initiative, must bring its own reward'.

She ends: 'I hope and pray that, with God's help, this Christmas spirit of family unity will spread and grow among our Commonwealth family of nations.'

Beatles' Christmas Message

This is their last to be recorded all together as a group: their final couple of messages will be spliced together from individual recordings. Things have become more fragmented since Brian Epstein's death in August. On Boxing Day, *Magical Mystery Tour* is broadcast, leading to much bemusement among viewers.

In this message, a linking song, 'Christmas Time is Here Again', links a bizarre melange of Goonish voices, orchestral breaks, applause, sound effects, mock advertisements, quiz-show banter ('And what prize have you got your eyes on?') and greetings delivered in a sarcastic tone ('We'd like to thank you for a wonderful year'). The effect is psychedelic, hallucinogenic, meaningless and disquieting, to some extent a prototype for 'Revolution 9', recorded a year later.

1968

Queen's Christmas Message

The theme this year is the brotherhood of man, words that 'have a splendid ring about them'.

Beatles' Christmas Message

Of the four Beatles, the closest in character to Her Majesty is the stolid Ringo, whose voice is the first to be

However, 'this should not remain a vague thought nor an abstract idea. Each of us can put it into practice by treating one another with kindness and consideration at all times and in spite of every kind of provocation.'

Unlike the Beatles, Her Majesty speaks of peace. In a foretaste of John Lennon's song 'Imagine', she says: 'Philosophers and prophets have concluded that peace is better than war, love is better than hate, and that mankind can only find progress in friendship and cooperation … We should not be obsessed by material problems.'

She ends: 'Christmas is the festival of peace. It is God's will that it should be our constant endeavour to establish "Peace on Earth, Goodwill towards Men". I hope you all have a very happy Christmas and every good fortune in the New Year.'

heard. 'Hi, this is a big hi and a sincere merry Christmas from yours truly, Ringo Starr.'

He is followed by a burst of 'Ob-La-Di, Ob-La-Da' from the recently-released *White Album*, a speeded-up snatch of 'Helter Skelter', and bursts of opera, telephone pips and random screams ('I think it's insAAAne!'), all unevenly stitched together by John, celebrating his recent romance with freewheeling gobbledegook. 'Once upon a time there were two balloons called Jack and Yono, they were strictly in love bound to happen in a million years they were together man unfortunatimetable they seemed to …'

More traditionally, George offers greetings 'to all our faithful beloved fans all over the world', and Paul sings a little.

Finally, George announces, 'We have a special guest here, Mr Tiny Tim.' The high-pitched Tiny Tim then sings 'Nowhere Man' to a ukulele accompaniment.

1969

Queen's Christmas Message

'In a short time, the 1960s will be over, but not out of our memories.'

This is not the Beatles talking, but the Queen. She, at least, is keeping it together. She reminds everyone that in July the first men 'reached beyond our own planet and set foot on the moon, but each one of us will have our own special triumphs or tragedies to look back on'.

She says that her own thoughts 'are with my older children who are entering the service of the people of this country and the Commonwealth. It is a great satisfaction and comfort to me and my husband to know that they have won a place in your affections.

'We are all looking forward to our visit to Australia and New Zealand for the Cook bicentenary celebrations, and also to Fiji and Tonga. Later next year we hope to see something of the fascinating development of Northern Canada …'

She adds that 'It is only natural that we should all be dazzled and impressed by the triumphs of technology, but Christmas is a festival of the spirit.'

Her Majesty concludes by saying that 'At this time our concern is

Beatles' Christmas Message

It may seem peculiar that in the closing weeks of 1969, in their advanced stage of disintegration, the Beatles should have recorded any sort of Christmas message for their fan club – or indeed that in those hippy times they still ran a fan club. Yet the Official Beatles Fan Club not only survived, but outlasted them by nearly two years.

Once again, their contributions are recorded individually. John is walking around his garden, chatting with his new wife, who steers him. 'You are strolling in Ascot garden with your wife Yoko,' she reminds him helpfully. 'But do you have any special thoughts for Christmas?'

'Well, Yoko, it is Christmas, and my special thoughts tend towards eating …'

Yoko emits a girlish giggle. 'So what do you like to eat?'

'I like cornflakes prepared by Parisian hands and I'd like it blessed by Hare Krishna mantra.'

George wishes everyone a simple happy Christmas; Ringo sings 'Good evening to you gentlemen, happy to be here', Paul sings in a high voice, 'This is to wish you a merry new particularly for the lonely, the sick, and the elderly. I hope they will all feel the warmth and comfort of companionship and that all of you will enjoy a very happy Christmas with your families and friends. God bless you all.'

year,' and says that he wishes everyone 'a good fortunate, happy new year'. John asks Yoko about the new decade. 'Everyone will just be flying around,' she says.

'I'd like a big teddy!' says John. 'Oh, thank you, mommy!'

'You're a good boy, John,' says Yoko.

144

Daily Mirror front page, Friday, 10 April 1970

The end for the Lennon–McCartney song team

PAUL IS QUITTING THE BEATLES

by Don Short

Paul McCartney has quit the Beatles. The shock news must mean the end of Britain's most famous pop group, which has been idolised by millions the world over for nearly ten years.

Today, twenty-seven-year-old McCartney will announce his decision, and the reasons for it, in a no-holds-barred statement.

It follows months of strife over policy in Apple, the Beatles' controlling organisation, and an ever-growing rift between McCartney and his songwriting partner, John Lennon.

In his statement, which consists of a series of answers to questions, McCartney says,

'I have no future plans to record or appear with the Beatles again. Or to write any more music with John.'

Last night, the statement was locked up in a safe at Apple headquarters in Savile Row, Mayfair – in the very rooms where the Beatles' break-up began.

The Beatles decided to appoint a 'business adviser'. Eventually they settled for American Allen Klein.

His appointment was strongly resisted by Paul, who sought the job for his father-in-law, American attorney Lee Eastman.

After a meeting In London Paul was out-voted 3–1 by John, and the other Beatles, George Harrison and Ringo Starr.

Since the Klein appointment, Paul has refused to go to the Apple offices to work daily.

He kept silent and stayed at his St John's Wood home with his photographer wife Linda, her daughter Heather, and their own baby, Mary.

Close friends tried to pacify John and Paul. But August last year was the last time they were to work together – when they collaborated on the *Abbey Road* album.

Films

There were other elements that hastened Paul's decision to quit. John Lennon, on his marriage to Yoko Ono, set out on projects of his own, Ringo went into films, and George stepped in as a record producer.

Today McCartney will reveal his own plans for a solo programme.

Early today an Apple spokesman denied reports that Paul McCartney had left the Beatles.

But he said that there were no plans 'at the moment' for any more recordings.

145

It was John who first said, 'I want a divorce.'

In the autumn of 1969, Paul began to feel nostalgic for the days when the Beatles were at their happiest. He felt that the only way to restore their lost sense of camaraderie was to go back on the road, turning up unannounced to play small halls in out-of-the-way places: 'I thought, "That's what I miss, and what they miss too – playing."'

He mentioned his plan to Ringo and John. Ringo appeared to go along with it, but John replied, 'You're daft,' adding, 'Anyway, I'm leaving the group. I want a divorce.'

John had in fact been talking about the end of the Beatles, on and off, ever since the days of 'I Want to Hold Your Hand'. 'Sometimes I feel I'd like to try something completely different, like film directing,' he told a journalist from *Rave* magazine in February 1964, just as they were conquering America. '… There'd be less of the limelight, but I wouldn't mind.' Two years later, he gloomily told Maureen Cleave: 'We can't go on holding hands forever. We have been Beatles as best as we ever will be – those four jolly lads. But we're not those people any more. We are old men.' At that time he was twenty-five years old.

Yet for all their hyperbole, John's words contained a bizarre truth: the Beatles had aged with an almost macabre rapidity. In the five years from 1964 to 1969 they matured at a rate of knots, not only in the range and depth of their music, but also physically. Look at this shot of them in 1964:

and this one, taken in 1969:

Comparing these photographs, just five years apart, it's as though they have been crushed by the weight of the world's adulation. Such talent, so many dreams, such joy – and now they just looked trapped and bruised. Within the space of those five years they went from innocence to experience, from hope to *weltschmerz*. It reminds me of the terrifying climax to Rider Haggard's *She*:

> Oh, how beautiful she looked there in the flame! No angel out of heaven could have worn a greater loveliness. Even now my heart faints before the recollection of it, as she stood and smiled at our awed faces, and I would give half my remaining time upon this earth to see her once like that again.
>
> But suddenly – more suddenly than I can describe – a kind of change came over her face, a change which I could not define or explain, but none the less a change. The smile vanished, and in its place there came a dry, hard look; the rounded face seemed to grow pinched, as though some great anxiety were leaving its impress upon it. The glorious eyes, too, lost their light, and, as I thought, the form its perfect shape and erectness … And her face – by Heaven! – *her face was growing old before my eyes!*
>
> … 'Oh, *look! – look! – look!*' shrieked Job, in a shrill falsetto of terror, his eyes nearly dropping out of his head, and foam upon his lips. '*Look! – look! – look!* she's shrivelling up! she's turning into a monkey!' and down he fell upon the ground, foaming and gnashing in a fit.

Pictures of them around this time could almost accompany cautionary tales, or act as illustrations of the famous observation by St Teresa of Àvila: 'More tears are shed over answered prayers than unanswered prayers.'

By the end, their world had soured. Intimacy and friendship curdled into irritation and recrimination. Despite his increasing reputation as a songwriter, George felt that John and Paul were still treating him as the little boy who tagged along. 'John and Paul did allow him the occasional track on the Beatles' albums – but only in the same grudging spirit as one might throw a dog a bone to keep him quiet,' observed Geoff Emerick. He remembered George snapping, 'Look, I don't have to listen to you!' when Paul offered him advice on 'Here Comes the Sun'.

John also resented being bossed around by Paul; in turn, Paul was frustrated by John's inertia, his sneery refusal to join in.

Meanwhile, Yoko's continued presence in the studio, crouching silently, all in black, set them all on edge, not least the prickly John, on red alert for any tremors of antipathy towards her: as Paul sang 'Get back to where you once belonged', John convinced himself that he was shooting nasty looks in her direction.

John's paranoia on this score was not entirely delusional. Paul, George and Ringo resented Yoko being in the studio. 'John's in love with Yoko and he's no longer in love with the three of us,' Paul confided to a journalist at the time. George later recalled, 'The vibe I picked up was that she was a wedge that was trying to drive itself deeper and deeper between him and us.'

Tony Barrow witnessed Yoko's early days in the studio. 'The first time Yoko spoke out at full volume during a recording session it was to convey some relatively trivial word of advice to John about whatever he was singing at the moment. The other Beatles looked around, straight-faced, startled, stunned. There was a moment's dead silence that was broken by Paul: "Fuck me! Did somebody speak? Who the fuck was that?" Of course he knew full well who had spoken. The others joined in: "Did you say something, George? Your lips didn't move!" "Have we got a new producer?"'

Regardless of Yoko, the atmosphere between the four had grown fractious and scratchy. Whenever they could, they worked separately from each other. Harmonies were few and far between. At different times, George and Ringo both stormed out of the studio in reaction to perceived slights and stayed away for several days.

As it happens, this was Ringo's second day back at work: two weeks before, while they were recording 'Back in the USSR', he had walked out, saying, 'I'm going on holiday.' Everything had come to a head: like Paul and George, Ringo resented Yoko's presence in the studio; he worried that his drumming wasn't up to scratch; and he felt that the other three were treating him as an outsider. The final straw came when Paul, at his most bossy, ticked him off for fluffing the tom-toms. In Sardinia, Ringo received a telegram saying 'YOU'RE THE BEST DRUMMER IN THE WORLD. COME ON HOME. WE LOVE YOU.' When he finally reappeared, they had decorated the whole studio with thousands of flowers to welcome him back. 'And that was a beautiful moment for me.'

Ringo had come to believe that the others looked down on him: 'I … felt that the other three were really happy and I was an outsider. I went to see John … I said, "I'm leaving the group because I'm not playing well and I feel unloved and out of it, and you three are really close." And John said, "I thought it was you three!" So then I went over to Paul's and knocked on his door. I said the same thing: "I'm leaving the band. I feel you three guys are really close and I'm out of it." And Paul said, "I thought it was you three!"'

Working as an assistant engineer on *Abbey Road*, the eighteen-year-old John Kurlander noticed how hard the group found it to be in a room together: 'When just one of the Beatles was on a session it would be absolutely great; with two of them it would be OK; with three of them the atmosphere would get a bit tense; and when the four of them were together it would occasionally be unbearable.'

And they were at war over money: after they split up, their multitudes of legal actions went on almost as long as the group itself. For his part, George Martin considered it odd that they lasted as long as they did: 'They were in each other's pockets as prisoners, virtually, for eight years, and they didn't lead individual lives. They just wanted to lead their own normal lives, with wives and families, and they were eventually able to do that, and I think it was quite right that they should do.' But he acknowledged that their split was also caused by more worldly struggles: 'Money gets in the way of things … There's bound to be differences when there's so much money involved. And it was more than that. It was a question of control, too.'

The day after Paul's announcement, Derek Taylor gave an interview to the *Daily Sketch*. 'It is almost as if they have divorced each other,' he said.

146

Cressida Connolly's Tale

I was born in 1960 and the Beatles were an integral part of my childhood. They were never not on the turntable of my older half-siblings' record players, so that their songs really did seem to be the soundtrack to life itself. The gaps between the release of their records – in some cases as little as only months apart – seemed interminable, as distant and as longed-for as the beginning of the school holidays appeared to be, on the first day of a new term.

I was the sort of child who had an imaginary friend. This perhaps explains why I thought of Paul and John as essentially a second mum and dad. Or it could be a case of extreme narcissism. In any case, my real-life father was a bespectacled writer and could be difficult, preoccupied and a bit grumpy: John shared these characteristics. Paul, though, was cosy and round-faced and chipper; all qualities you'd want in a mother. I felt that, if Paul was my mum, all the children in my class would want to come back to mine for tea. He'd whistle along with the kettle and flash his cheeky grin and everyone would think my family were the nicest, happiest family.

All children long for their parents to love each other, and so it was with me and Paul and John. When they came on the telly, I was hungry for evidence of their mutual affection – and there it was: the complicit smirking, the suppressed giggles; like Dud and Pete with guitars. Dad/John was cleverer than Mum/Paul, and even a bit sarky sometimes; but Mum/Paul could handle him, coax him towards good humour.

I didn't really know that they wrote songs separately until *The White Album* came out and my half-brother told me that John had written 'Julia' about his own, dead mother. This brought up feelings too complicated to be easily managed. How was it possible that there were things about John/Dad I didn't know? In real life, too, there was a paternal grandmother I had never known, so this was at least feasible. But why had I never seen a photograph of John's mother, when she was, in a sense, my own grandmother?

My main concern was how it could be possible that Paul and John wrote songs apart when they were indivisible. Lennon/McCartney: one entity. On the other hand, this revelation did make sense of quite a lot of their output. Clearly, Paul/Mum was thinking of the family when composing such child-friendly tunes as 'The Fool on the Hill', 'I Will', 'Martha, My Dear' and – of course – 'Your Mother Should Know'. Whereas John/Dad had obviously gone off to sulk in his writing room and compose peculiar stuff like 'I Am the Walrus'. This had its equivalent in real life, where my actual father would be in the library thinking about the Cantos of Ezra Pound while my mother was in the kitchen tapping her foot to Fred Astaire singing Cole Porter.

The news of their split, which came in April 1970, was cataclysmic. (Decades later, my own daughters would take the news of Geri's departure from the Spice Girls with the same horror and disbelief.) A divorce! Breaking up the family! It wasn't possible, surely? Could it be legal, even? Someone would stop them and bang their heads together and tell them to think of the kids – wouldn't they?

And then, with a sickening inevitability, came the step-families. At least Linda had a kind face and obviously made Paul/Mum happy. But she did bring her daughter, Heather, into the new family; which meant that Paul/Mum now lived with an actual little girl of his own. Competition, a usurper. Whereas Yoko … well, John/Dad didn't look at all OK. He was pale and unshaven and remote. (The fact that Yoko had a daughter too didn't register until I was a grown-up.) Also, why did she have to be around, ALL THE TIME? How would I ever get a minute alone with him, now? These puzzles and resentments and sorrows went on for at least two years, possibly three. Then in time I became a teenager and forgot all about my parents and only thought about the Jackson Five and the Bay City Rollers and how to style my hair like Suzi Quatro.

147

Theme park, *wheeler-dealer* and the *beehive* hairdo entered the language in 1960, the year the Silver Beetles changed their name to the Beatles and set off for Hamburg.

The next three years saw the arrival of *life-style*, *Purple Heart*, *Chelsea boots*, *trendy*, *no problem* and *mind-expanding*. New trends gave rise to new words: *flares*, for bell-bottomed trousers, first appeared in 1964, along with *gonk* and *disco*. *Swinger*, *topless* and the phrase *beautiful people* heralded a less hidebound age.

In 1964, the Liverpudlian writer Alun Owen coined the adjective *grotty* in his script for *A Hard Day's Night*. Owen peppered the dialogue of the film with a number of words he thought the Beatles might use, such as *dig*, *fab* and *drag*. He had been under the impression that *grotty* was standard Liverpool slang, so was surprised to find that none of the Beatles had ever heard of it. 'We thought the word was really weird,' recalled John. 'And George curled up with embarrassment every time he had to say it.' But the film's popularity ensured that by the end of the year *grotty* had become part of the language.

Mini-skirt arrived in 1965, together with *go-go dancer*, *teeny bopper*, *loon*, *zit*, *downer*, *women's liberation* and *chat show*, as well as the injunctions *freak out* and *turn on*. They were joined in 1966 by *freaky*, *peacenik*, *centrefold*, *suss out* and *blow-dry*. *Transcendental Meditation* was mentioned in print for the first time that same year, though it was not until 1967, when the Beatles first met the Maharishi Mahesh Yogi, that it came into common parlance, along with *love-in*, *rave*, *encounter group*, *hype*, *groupie*, *generation gap*, *mind-blowing* (a late companion for *mind-expanding*), *flower power* and *flower people*.

Vibes also first appeared in 1967, though its first recorded use by a Beatle came the following year, when George caught Yoko eating one of his ginger biscuits without asking and snapped, 'You give off bad vibes.' 1968 also gave the English language *paparazzi*, *druggy*, *permissive society*, *granny glasses*, *phone-in*, *love beads*, *tank top*, *unisex* and *no way*, in its meaning of 'Can't be done.'

1969 gave birth to *ego trip*, *one-parent family*, *alternative society*, *jet lag*, *bovver boot*, *missionary position* and *roadie*; four years too late, *turn on* was joined by its antonym, *turn off*. On 25 March that year, at the Hilton Hotel in Amsterdam, John and Yoko simultaneously coined and demonstrated the neologism *bed-in*, a horizontal variation on *sit-in* (which had, perhaps surprisingly, already been around for forty years). A week later, at a press conference in Vienna, they introduced *bagism*.

The Beatles disbanded in April 1970, just as *hot pants*, *counterculture*, *right on*, *lava lamp*, *upfront*, *pop festival*, *full-frontal* and *let it all hang out* were coming into being. By the end of the year these words and expressions had been joined by *noise pollution*, *microprocessor*, *property developer* and *chicken brick*, each one the harbinger of a drabber, more prosaic age.

148

The most successful pop group of the twentieth century was formed in Liverpool in 1959 by Gerry Marsden and his brother Fred. Together with Les Chadwick and Arthur McMahon, Gerry and the Pacemakers built up a huge local following in their home city, while fine-tuning their talents in Hamburg, West Germany.

Many books have been written about Gerry and the Pacemakers, their origins, their influence, and their sociological and artistic impact on the 1960s. Different periods of their lives – from their early days rehearsing at the Cammell Laird shipyard at Birkenhead to their

eventual break-up – have been turned into movies, the most recent starring Ryan Gosling as Gerry Marsden.

Why did Gerry and the Pacemakers succeed in overtaking musical rivals like the Dave Clark Five, the Searchers, the Beatles and the Swinging Blue Jeans to become four of the best-known faces in the world of pop?

For a start, their repertoire was broader than their rivals': by 1960 they had built up a repertoire of 250 songs, from rockers like 'What'd I Say' to ballads such as 'Will You Love Me Tomorrow?' Contemporary Merseybeat groups like the Beatles, who met with similar success in the early years, never possessed quite the same range. Moreover, the Beatles lacked a front man, so had no focal point. It's hard to imagine, but had things gone differently, the world might now be talking of John, Paul, George and Ringo (the first names of the Beatles) instead of Gerry, Fred, Les and Arthur.

Their success was rapid. In January 1962 Gerry and the Pacemakers were voted number 2 in the *Mersey Beat* readers' poll when the Beatles were number 1, but this proved a blip. Historians now see the Beatles' decision to turn down the hit song 'How Do You Do It?' as their greatest mistake. It had been offered to them by record producer George Martin, but instead they insisted on releasing one of their own songs, 'Love Me Do'. This left 'How Do You Do It?' to be snapped up by Gerry and the Pacemakers. And the rest is history: the song reached number 1 in the national charts, leaving 'Love Me Do' languishing at number 2. Gerry and the Pacemakers' next couple of singles, 'I Like It' and 'You'll Never Walk Alone', also went to number 1. To this day, they remain the only artists to have achieved the number 1 slot with each of their first three singles.

For some reason, Gerry and the Pacemakers managed to catch the sixties zeitgeist in a way that no other group could. Nevertheless, the Searchers, the Beatles and the Swinging Blue Jeans enjoyed perfectly lucrative careers as mainstays in sixties revival tours throughout the 1980s and 1990s. Their surviving members still regularly appear in documentaries about Gerry and the Pacemakers, and are happy to make personal appearances at Gerry and the Pacemakers conventions.

In the second half of the 1960s, Gerry and the Pacemakers became strongly identified with the hippy movement. In 1968, having fallen under the spell of the Maharishi Mahesh Yogi, they spent several weeks studying Transcendental Meditation in Rishikesh, India. They returned to Britain with many new songs, which they included on their famous *Black Album*, released on their own Orange label. Around this time, Gerry Marsden was taken up by the Japanese conceptual artist Yoko Ono, and went to live with her in New York. In 1980 he was shot dead outside their apartment by a deranged fan.

But what became of the Fab Four's early rivals, the Beatles? George Harrison died of cancer in 2001, following a successful career as a session musician. John Lennon and Paul McCartney toured Britain last year with their 'Tribute to Gerry and the Pacemakers' show, thrilling audiences up and down the country with their exact rendition of 'You'll Never Walk Alone'. Touchingly, they still perform one or two of their own numbers – 'Yesterday' and 'A Hard Day's Night' – in each set. 'We sneak 'em in, even if no one wants to hear 'em!' quips John.

Ringo Starr retired from the music business in 1966 to pursue an earlier ambition. He now owns and manages a successful chain of hairdressing salons throughout the North-East.

149

Eleanor Roosevelt once said that the only two hotels worth staying in outside the USA were the George V in Paris and the Adelphi in Liverpool. In its heyday, Noël Coward, Frank Sinatra, Winston Churchill and FDR all came to stay at the Adelphi. On one occasion, Roy Rogers rode his horse Trigger down the Adelphi stairs.* Throughout his time as leader of the opposition and prime minister, Harold Wilson – MP for the Liverpool constituency of Huyton – used it as his campaign base.

These days, the Adelphi is past its prime. The carpets and curtains are dank. The mock-Grecian swimming pool in the basement displays a sign saying 'No Knives'. What was once an elegant cocktail bar now advertises two-for-one deals on lager during Happy Hour. In 2019 an American couple, Jane and Cliff Maugham, complained to the *Liverpool Echo* of vomit stains in the corridor outside their room, the ceiling of which was so riddled with damp that 'it looked like it could come down at any minute. The bathroom was filthy and the beds in the bedroom were awful. You couldn't open the windows as they were filthy and the curtains were half hanging off.'

Despite it all, the vast hall of the Adelphi was pullulating when I arrived at mid-morning on the Sunday of the annual International Beatleweek. Hundreds of memorabilia stores were crammed in, with more spilling out into neighbouring rooms. Most items were on sale for roughly 150 times their original price. A bath towel (US 1964) decorated with unrecognisable drawings of the Fab Four in Edwardian

* And presumably up them, too. Or did Trigger use the lift?

bathing suits was £140; a tin of Beatles talcum powder (UK 1964) £210; a 'Mega Rare Nearly New' Beatles pencil case (Germany 1965) £920; a *Hard Day's Night* bubblegum box 'with one original uncut wax bubblegum wrapper' £420; a 1967 Beatles jigsaw puzzle £250; a Beatles calendar (UK 1965) £360; a Ringo Starr bubblebath (USA 1964) £140; a Paul McCartney bubblebath (USA 1964) £240; a *Yellow Submarine* lunchbox (USA 1968) £235; a Beatles wallet (UK 60s, 'excellent condition') £175; a Beatles reversible headband ('suits all head sizes') in original plastic bag £45; a red Beatles coinholder £85. And so on.

At a stall towards the back, I came across a small sheet of George V Hotel notepaper. Next to it stood a typed letter headed 'BEATLES AUTOGRAPHS'.

> To Whom It May Concern
> The purpose of this letter is to serve as an authentification of the signatures of John Lennon, Paul McCartney and George Harrison. These signatures are found on a sheet of note paper from the Hotel George V in Paris, France. The Beatles were in Paris for several weeks just prior to their first visit to America, performing a residency at The Olympia Theatre, playing 18 days of concerts, ending on February 4th – just 4 days before they flew to America for their first historic visit. While there in Paris, they stayed at the Hotel George V. All three have autographed a sheet of George V note paper beautifully, with John and George using a red felt tip marker while Paul has signed in black felt tip, additionally adding 'Best wishes from the Beatles'. It is also signed for Ringo Starr in his absence.
>
> It is my professional opinion that the aforementioned sheet of signed hotel note paper is authentic, as described. I base this opinion on over 31 years of study and experience with Beatles signed and handwritten material.
>
> Sincerely,
> Frank Caiazzo

The asking price for what turned out to be the autographs of just three of the four Beatles was £6,000.*

At another stall, I chanced upon what seemed like a bargain: the 45 rpm single 'That's My Life' recorded by Freddie Lennon, with backing vocals by the Ladybirds, in mint condition. It was selling for £10, which was about £100 cheaper than the next cheapest item. I handed over my £10, half-expecting the dealer to say 'There's been some mistake,' but he took it with a smile. It was only later that I noticed the small print:

> This track has been digitally remastered from an original 1965 single kindly supplied by Freddie's manager, Tony Cartwright.

This meant that I had just paid £10 for a brand-new single.

The man behind one stall was raising money for the Brian Epstein Statue Project. 'Our vision is to realise a world first: a statue of Brian, the Fifth Beatle, and one of the world's great creative individuals,' read the flyer. 'He united the world in the most powerfully sustaining way, and his impact is overwhelmingly positive. His legacy is also largely unseen, even though his impact on popular culture is incalculable. Yet his smiling face is unknown to so many around the world. This is why we need this memorial in his honour. He needs to stay amongst us and will be a truly collaborative work [sic]. By the people, for the people. WE will make Brian, together …'

I wandered in and out of the various neighbouring rooms. The Bluebeetles from Brazil were playing 'For the Benefit of Mr Kite' in Crompton's Bar, where Noël Coward might once have sipped a dry martini. In the Wave Bar a Finnish group called She's Leaving Home

---

* A snip, compared to some of the items offered by Frank Caiazzo at his New Jersey base. These include a brief letter written by John to a fan in early 1963, beginning 'Dear Dawn, Thanks for your letter, glad you liked the show,' and signed 'Cherrio [sic] love John Lennon X', which is selling for $19,500, and a 'Rare Important and Revealing John Lennon Handwritten Letter' from Rishikesh to a fan called Beth in February 1968, signed 'God Bless You – jai guru dev. with love John Lennon', which is selling for $75,000. In an introductory message to his online store, Mr Caiazzo notes that 'handwritten material represents a very special intimate part of the Beatles' lives that were seldom imparted to the public in any way. To acquire even one of these treasures is indeed quite an accomplishment for any fan or collector.'

were playing 'Lovely Rita'. In the Crosby Suite, I half expected to find a group called Lovely Rita playing 'She's Leaving Home'. Instead, Abbey Road from Spain were singing 'Come Together', and in the American Bar the Fab Twins, an acoustic duo from Bristol, were singing 'Here, There and Everywhere'.

I began to feel engulfed by so many Beatles collectors and vendors and lookalike musicians, almost to the point of claustrophobia. Was I going to pass out from Beatlemania? Looking for somewhere to take a breather, I darted up a staircase off the main hall. To my surprise, half-way up the stairs I heard a voice cry, 'Craig!' An elderly man, sitting on one of the steps, was beckoning me over. I had no idea who he was, or how he knew who I was.

'Stevie T told me to look out for you!' he said. 'Bill Smith!'

As we shook hands, I remembered that Stevie T, the tour guide from the day before, had told me to keep an eye out for Bill Smith, who was one of the original Quarrymen.

'You know the history, right?' said Bill. I said yes, but of course I was bluffing. I find it hard to get to grips with the Quarrymen. Their endless comings and goings seem to me as demanding as the Wars of the Roses, or the Schleswig-Holstein question. As far as I can work out, there were at least nine different line-ups from summer 1956 (when Bill was with them) to October 1959 (when Paul and George and someone called Ken Brown had joined, and all the others had left, apart from John). Around that time – are you still with me? – the Quarrymen changed their name to Johnny and the Moondogs, then to the Beatals, then to the Nerk Twins, then to the Silver Beetles, and finally, on 12 August 1960, to the Beatles. But even this list is incomplete: at various other stages, they were also the Silver Beats, the Beetles and Long John and the Silver Beatles.

And that is only Module One on the beginners' course. A real Beatles buff could rattle off at least two thousand words on each incarnation of the Quarrymen, and would happily sit up all night arguing over whether the young George Harrison first met the Quarrymen at the Wilson Hall on 7 December 1957, as Barry Miles says, or at the same venue on 6 February 1958, as Mark Lewisohn says, or at the

Morgue Skiffle Cellar on 13 March 1958, as the Quarrymen drummer Colin Hanton says, or at a local chip shop on an unknown date, as George's mother Louise always maintained.

Encountering Bill Smith on that Adelphi staircase transported me back into another age. I might just as well have bumped into a junior member of Mr Gladstone's cabinet. What should I ask him? Happily, Bill was keen to talk unprompted. He said that he and John had been at Quarry Bank School together. 'We were always mucking about. For instance, one of us would whistle when the teacher's back was turned. And he'd turn round, but wouldn't know who'd done it. Then someone else would whistle, and he'd turn round again. Still nothing. And so it would go on. We sent him mad! And then John landed Pete Shotton in it by saying out loud, but as if it were under his breath, "Hey! Pete! You'd better stop now! I think he suspects!" And so thanks to John, Pete took the blame!'

John had the idea of forming a group in 1956. He persuaded his best friend Pete Shotton to be a member, and together they started trying to make instruments. Pete found a washboard in his father's shed, and thought playing it looked easy. Then John invited Bill, who stole a tea chest from the school woodwork room, rode away with it on his bike and turned it into a bass by putting a broom handle through it. Together with their classmates Eric Griffiths (guitar) and Rod Davis (banjo), they formed a group to play skiffle songs. What to call them? 'I came up with the Quarrymen, because we all went to Quarry Bank. John didn't like the name. He said, "No, I don't think that's much good." He probably thought it was too "Establishment", but Pete said, "No, it's good," and Eric agreed, and John couldn't think of anything else, so the Quarrymen it was.'

I found Bill very genial. Unlike so many who have rubbed shoulders with the Beatles, he was a man with no illusions. He didn't try to big himself up. He told me he hadn't been a Quarryman for long: 'My father wanted me to get on in life. We had exams to pass. Then two of us Quarrymen joined the merchant navy, and Pete joined the police. Of course, John had no father, so when he left school he idled away his time at art school.'

He said he had no regrets about leaving the group, and oddly enough, I believed him. 'I've had a good life, ups and downs of course, like anyone, but it's been a good life.' But then one regret did come to mind. 'When I left the group, I took my tea chest with me. I put it in my dad's garage. But John and Len Garry stole it. So I went and stole it back. And when I stole it back I found John had drawn all over it, cartoons and things. I sometimes wonder what it would be worth now. But my dad only went and threw it out!'

Bill had a book in his hand. I spotted that it had the word 'Beatles' in the title, so I asked what it was. 'Don't ask!' he said. He told me he had just bought it at one of the stalls. He passed it to me: *John, Paul & Me Before the Beatles: The True Story of the Very Early Days*, by Len Garry. Before long, I wished I hadn't mentioned it.

'True story, indeed! True story! Absolute CODSWALLOP! It's not as if I even wanted to buy it! I saw Len's wife the other day, and she said, "Have you read Len's book yet?" and I said, "No, I'm not a reader," and she said, "Oh, but you must," and she went on and on at me, so I bought one off her daughter, who was sitting behind one of those desks over there, with a big pile of them. It was £15, so I gave her a twenty and she said she didn't have any change. So she kept the twenty and gave me a free CD, which I never even wanted in the first place! And I was browsing through Len's book just now, and look where the page opened – just look!'

He flicked through to page 75, which was headed:

Chapter Five
Pete Shotton, John Lennon and the Tea Chest Bass
Thursday 11th November 1956: Time – 3:30

I obediently read the offending passage:

> John Lennon and Pete Shotton, the two members of the newly formed Quarrymen Skiffle Group collected their respective bicycles from the shed at Quarrybank School. It was a relatively warm afternoon for mid November and so they took their time.

'Listen John, why did you let Bill Smith join the group? He never turns up to any of the rehearsals and I can't stand the guy anyway.'

'Well, Pete, he was keen enough to join in the first place, but perhaps we should be looking to replace him because he's so unreliable.'

'What about Len Garry? You know he can sing, and he has a good sense of humour.'

'Yeah, Len sounds like just the man.'

Sixty-three years on, Bill was seething. He thought it an appalling misrepresentation of what had happened. 'Load of crap! Utter rubbish! He wasn't even there, so how does he know what they said? I left the group of my own accord! I had other things to do! And Len came much later! He wasn't even in our class! Complete and utter codswallop! And to think he's charging £15 for this load of crap!'

Bill hadn't intended to come to the Beatles Convention, and had only turned up because Stevie T told him he owed it to history. I got up to go. 'Stevie T told me not to mention Brexit to you!' I said as a parting shot. His eyes lit up. Half an hour later, Bill Smith, founder member of the Quarrymen, was still holding forth about the iniquities of the European Union.

150

Later, after the funeral and the inquest, Brian's secretary, Joanne Newfield, goes to his house in Belgravia. His brother Clive has asked her to clear out some of Brian's papers. She doesn't want to, but she feels it is her duty.

The house is empty. She goes up to Brian's bedroom, where she found him. It is eerie: she somehow feels his presence.

She wants to pick everything up, throw it all into bags, and get out of the house. She comes across a large book in which she used to leave letters for Brian to sign. Inside it, she comes across two suicide notes, one to his mother, Queenie, the other to Clive. Curiously, they are both dated several weeks before his death.

They are very short, covering barely a page. Later, she remembers them saying something along the lines of: 'Don't be sad. Don't be unhappy. I'm OK. Take good care of yourself. I love you.'

Maybe Brian had forgotten they were there.

8 September 1967

At the inquest, Dr R. Donald Teare, consultant pathologist, reports that there were 168 milligrams of bromide in the blood of the deceased. Bromide is contained in the sedative Carbrital, but such a large figure could only have been reached by taking Carbrital over a long period. 'The stomach saturation suggests six capsules. The blood concentration about nine capsules, but not taken as a single dose.' Dr Teare says that Mr Epstein was 'approaching a state of bromide intoxication. To achieve the blood bromide figure would have taken weeks rather than days.' He adds that raised blood bromide might result in a man becoming careless and injudicious.

Dr Flood, Brian's psychiatrist, tells the inquest that 'With regard to drugs, the patient had for at least five years been taking amphetamines in large doses and he had also been regularly smoking marijuana. He had also experimented with heroin but was not addicted. At times, and in particular over the last two years, he drank excessively and had a tendency to take excessive doses of any drug.' He adds that the patient, who had 'always shown some signs of emotional instability', was also homosexual, and 'had been unable to come to terms with this problem'.

29 August 1967

They bury Brian close to his father in the Jewish Cemetery at Aintree. His father died just six weeks ago. Brian had sobbed uncontrollably in the car on the way home. Now it is Brian's turn to have others grieve.

Fearful that the crowds would get out of hand, Brian's mother Queenie has asked George and the other Beatles to stay away, so it is relatively quiet. Brian's business partner Nat Weiss disregards the Jewish rule of no flowers at funerals, and drops a single sunflower on top of Brian's grave. It is what George asked him to do.

At the synagogue in Greenbank Drive, Liverpool, the officiating rabbi, Dr Norman Solomon, suggests that Brian's death is 'symbolic of the malaise of a generation'. This strikes many in the congregation, including Nat Weiss, as unjust: 'How can a man who filled stadiums, who literally was the catalyst for the greatest musical event of the twentieth century, be treated as a malaise?'

Cilla Black is so overcome with grief that Queenie Epstein gives her a Valium.

28 August 1967

John, Paul, George and Ringo go to Chapel Street to pay their respects to Queenie Epstein. She thinks they are 'like four lost children'. In fact, she is not far out: Ringo, the oldest, has just turned twenty-seven.

George, the youngest, is twenty-four. They are all very distressed. They tell her they will do anything she wants about the funeral. She tells them she would prefer it if they didn't come: she dreads it turning into a circus.

John says, 'Come to India with us and meditate.'

What, she asks, do they actually *do* when they meditate?

'Well, you think of something – like, say, a carrot,' replies John.

Queenie's reply is characteristically straightforward. 'Whenever I think of a carrot, I think of tomorrow's lunch.'

The obituaries are full of praise. 'In all his dealings, he was completely honest and trustworthy,' says *The Times*. 'By his presence and success in the pop world, he not only transformed its power and stature, he made it more respectable.'

27 August 1967

In the late afternoon, Paul has taken a break from the Transcendental Meditation gathering in Bangor, Wales, organised by the Maharishi Mahesh Yogi. He is chatting to a friendly reporter from the *Liverpool Echo*. In the background, a telephone won't stop ringing. Paul says he'd better go and see who it is. The reporter watches him pick up the receiver. He hears Paul saying, 'Oh no. Oh God, no. Oh no. Oh no.' Paul puts down the receiver and runs upstairs to where John, George and Ringo are. Some time later, he arrives back downstairs and says to the reporter, 'Brian was found dead in his bed this morning. It's an overdose of sleeping tablets or something. I don't know anything really. We've got to get back to London right away.'

John is scared. 'I knew that we were in trouble then. I didn't really have any misconceptions about our ability to do anything other than play music, and I was scared. I thought, "We've fuckin' had it now."'

Early on the Sunday afternoon of that bank holiday weekend, Alistair Taylor has just arrived home from California when the phone rings. It is Brian Epstein's secretary, Joanne. She is with Antonio and Maria,

Brian's household staff in Belgravia. They are worried: Brian hasn't appeared since late on Friday, and his bedroom door is locked. They have knocked on it, but he hasn't responded. Joanne says she is afraid to go in alone.

Alistair takes a cab to Chapel Street. Twice in the past, both times on a Sunday, Brian has phoned him to say he is going to commit suicide. 'Oh, Alistair, I've had enough now. I am just ringing to say goodbye.' Both times, Alistair has rushed over, to be greeted by an indignant Brian: 'Oh, don't be stupid. I was just a bit down. Leave me alone.'

On his arrival at Chapel Street, Alistair finds that Joanne has already summoned a doctor. The doctor forces the door open with his shoulder. Alistair follows him in. Brian is in bed. 'He looked as though he was asleep, but I knew straight away that he was dead. A wave of almost indescribable pain swept over me.'

The doctor says, 'I'm afraid he's dead.'

Alistair feels numb. He has a sense of everything, including himself, existing in slow motion.

He looks around. On one side of the bed sits a pile of correspondence, on the other a plate with three chocolate digestive biscuits. A glass and a half-empty bottle of bitter lemon are on the floor. Eight bottles of pills are on the bedside table. 'He lived on pills – pills to wake him up, pills to send him to sleep, pills to keep him lively, pills to quieten him down, pills to cure his indigestion.' All the bottles are full, and have their caps on. None of them are empty.

Together with the doctor, Alistair searches the room. There is no note, no sign of disturbance. In a drawer, Alistair finds an enormous ready-rolled joint. He slips it quietly into his trouser pocket. The two of them go downstairs. Alistair tells Joanne that Brian is dead. The doctor rings the coroner's office. Alistair braces himself and rings Brian's brother Clive.

'You're *lying*. You're *lying*,' says Clive, and hangs up.

13 May 1967

After his psychiatrist, Dr John Flood, diagnoses 'insomnia, agitation, anxiety and depression', Brian checks himself into the Priory hospital in Roehampton. They keep him in an induced sleep for just under a week.

Upon waking, he receives a stream of visitors. They find him crotchety and slightly paranoid, but he has the odd moment of emotional release. In the middle of a business visit from Robert Stigwood and Nat Weiss, an enormous bouquet of flowers arrives. He opens the note, and reads it out. It is from John. 'You know I love you, I really do.' Brian breaks down in tears. His two visitors retreat to the hallway. 'He's not in his right mind,' says Stigwood.

Paul writes Brian a four-page letter, a sweet but uneasy mix of admonishment and encouragement: 'Your BIGGEST TROUBLE IS YOU TAKE IT ALL TOO SERIOUSLY!' He cuts a headline – 'WHO CARES?' – out of a newspaper and sticks it to the third page, adding, in his own writing, 'Some people do, friends, and the time has come to listen to them.' He ends the letter, 'THINK FINE, keep your pecker up, and speedy recovery.'

The Beatles ask Peter Brown to bring a portable record player and an early copy of their new album to the Priory. Brian sits up in bed and listens to *Sgt. Pepper's Lonely Hearts Club Band* for the very first time.

Spring 1967

Brian's behaviour is becoming increasingly erratic. Once so prompt, he is seldom on time. He cancels appointments at the last minute. At business meetings, he fails to make any general sense, but will latch on to some little detail, and make a terrible scene about it, shouting and screaming, 'Why hasn't this been done??!!'

28 February 1967

Brian is staying at the Waldorf Towers hotel in Manhattan. He is about to set off for a radio interview with Murray 'The K' Kaufman at WOR-FM when Nat Weiss drops by, and finds him slurring his words. It emerges that he has taken a handful of Nembutal barbiturates, and is set to take more. Weiss wrestles him to the floor, and throws the bottle out of the window. He then plies him with coffee and, on Brian's insistence, drives him to the interview.

Weiss sits close to him in the studio, to prevent him from slumping over. For the first few minutes Brian mumbles incoherently while Murray The K fills in with DJ babble. But soon the stimulants kick in, and Brian springs back to life.

Whenever he is in Manhattan, Brian's favourite pastime is to sit by himself in the back of a chauffeur-driven limousine. Then he likes to dip into his silver cigarette case for a joint, pre-rolled by one of his staff, while being driven around Central Park. He always asks for the same music to be played over and over again on the car's stereo system: 'It's the Same Old Song' by the Four Tops.

Late January 1967

In a reversal of the usual order of things, the Beatles are concerned about Brian. 'Eppy seems to be in a terrible state,' John tells his friend Pete. 'The guy's head's a total mess, and we're really worried about him.' His concern is as much professional as personal: 'We just don't know what the fuck we can do about it. It's time for us to go off in our own direction, and that's that.'

John puts on a tape recording, which Pete later describes as 'barely recognisable as that of a human voice, alternately groaning, grunting, and shrieking – and occasionally mumbling words which, even when decipherable, made no apparent sense whatsoever'.

Pete asks who it is.

'That's Brian,' replies John. 'He made this tape for me in his house. I don't know why he sent it, but he's trying to tell me something, fuck knows what. He just can't seem to communicate with us in the usual way any more.'

Mid-January 1967

Brian asks Paddy Chambers, a Liverpool musician, to Chapel Street. 'I've got a surprise for you,' he says.

Paddy finds the four Beatles there with their wives and girlfriends. Brian vanishes, and returns carrying a big silver tray with a little sugar cube on it. 'I've got to see someone tripping for the first time,' says John. It emerges that everyone else has already taken one.

Within two hours, everyone is ripping up newspapers and flinging them around. Brian produces more and more newspapers until they are knee-deep in them.

Late November–December 1966

Now that the Beatles have stopped touring, they have less need of Brian, and less time for him too. Their studio engineer, Geoff Emerick, senses that they don't really like him hanging around in the studio. Brian misses his daily contact with them. With less and less to do, his flight from boredom grows more and more reckless.

29 August 1966

In San Francisco, just hours before the Beatles play Candlestick Park, Brian seems dejected. He has decided not to attend the concert himself. Instead, he stays in his suite in the Beverly Hills Hotel in Los Angeles. He says to Nat Weiss, 'This will be the last Beatles concert ever.'

He tells Nat that his old lover John 'Dizz' Gillespie has popped by; in fact, they spent the afternoon in and around the hotel swimming pool. 'He's changed,' says Brian.

'He hasn't changed,' says Weiss. 'Get rid of him.'

'Oh, you don't understand … he really loves me.'

Brian insists that the Beatles like Gillespie. Weiss knows this to be untrue: they have made their dislike known. Brian appears to be sexually excited by insolence and aggression, though in everyday life there is nothing that upsets him more. While the Beatles are playing what will, indeed, be their final concert, Brian and Nat go out to dinner. They return to find that Gillespie has run off with their briefcases. Brian's black Samsonite briefcase contained contracts for the Beatles tour, a bottle of illegal Seconal barbiturates and $20,000 in cash.

Later, Gillespie sends them a blackmail-cum-ransom note, demanding $10,000 for the return of their cases. Brian tells Nat to 'let it go', but by now Weiss's dislike of Gillespie has curdled to hatred. Once Brian is back in England, Weiss hires a private detective to meet Gillespie at a railway station. He has set a trap for him. Gillespie is arrested, and Brian is reunited with his briefcase and half the money it contained.*

But Brian regards Nat's action not as heroic or sensible but as a breach of trust: he had instructed him to leave Gillespie alone, and Nat had disobeyed him. 'He was very depressed by the whole thing,' reflects Weiss years later. 'The whole betrayal is what really destroyed him.'

7 August 1966

Brian is in New York, trying to calm the furore that has greeted the news that, earlier in the year, John said the Beatles were 'bigger than Jesus'. By chance, Nat Weiss notices that Brian has a row of tiny little pockets tailored into the inside of his jacket. Brian explains that these are his 'pill pockets', stocked with amphetamines and tranquillisers in ascending order of strength.

6 April 1966

After a party to celebrate Cilla Black's opening night of a three-week residency in the Persian Room of the Plaza Hotel, Brian tells Weiss that he has a problem. Dizz Gillespie is in New York, and has been in touch. He says he wants to see Brian again. Brian feels powerless to resist, but at the same time he lives in fear that Dizz will do something to embarrass the Beatles.

Nat agrees to help, and invites Gillespie to his office. The moment he walks through the door he recognises his type: 'the garden-variety hustler'.

Gillespie insists he loves Brian. 'I don't want anything from him. I just want to see him.'

'Good. Because you're not going to get anything from him, and you're not going to see him. I want you to stay away from him.'

---

* Fifty-three years later the briefcase was sold at auction in Los Angeles, 'accompanied by a letter of authenticity from Epstein's nephew, Henry Epstein', for £3,437.50.

'Well, then. Brian's got lots of money. If he wants me to stay away … well, if I had a car I could go away.'

Weiss relays Gillespie's demands to Brian, but advises him against agreeing to them, saying, 'He'll only come back for more.' But Brian tells him to give Gillespie $3,000 for a car. Before he hands over the money, Weiss tells Gillespie he must agree to remain locked in a room at the Warwick Hotel, under guard, until Brian and the Beatles have left town.

1965–66

Brian frequently dines with the *NME* journalist Chris Hutchins at Overton's restaurant in St James's. He seldom eats much. Instead, he spends time poring over the menu, choosing his dish with great care, telling the waiter exactly how he wants his vegetables cooked, and so on. Then he swallows a handful of pills, before passing some to Hutchins, insisting he joins him in enjoying what he calls 'our little helpers'. These are uppers, which have the effect of suppressing the appetite. By the time the food arrives, neither of them wants it. Time after time, the lobster and fillet steak dishes are sent back to the kitchen with 'Mr Epstein's compliments to the chef'.

17 August 1965

The American journalist Larry Kane, who has grown close to the Beatles after travelling with them throughout their first US tour, observes a notable change in Brian. He has become volatile. One minute his face is beaming, the next it bears 'a look of outright depression'.

March 1965

Brian's new boyfriend, Dizz Gillespie, has a capacity for violence. Brian and Dizz spend their evenings ingesting uppers washed down with cognac. These evenings often end in fierce arguments, involving smashed vases and mirrors. One night, Gillespie gets in such a rage that Brian orders him to leave the flat. Gillespie grabs a kitchen knife, holds it to Brian's jugular and extracts money from Brian's wallet.

Spring 1965
Paddy Chambers visits Brian in his Knightsbridge flat. Chaos confronts him: 'He just totally wrecked the whole, very expensive flat, ripped all the drapes down, smashed the cocktail cabinet to bits ... For some strange reason, and I suppose it had to be drugs, he was "off his cake"'.

February 1965
Someone gouges the word 'QUEER' with a key onto the door of Brian's Bentley, parked in the mews behind his new house in Chapel Street.

January 1965
On the telephone to his parents, Brian sounds so peculiar that they rush over to his house. They find him heavily hung over, unable to face the day. He confesses his love of Gillespie. His mother, Queenie, insists that he try to forget about him by taking a holiday in the south of France with Peter Brown. That afternoon, Brian and Peter set off for a hotel in Cap d'Antibes. On his return, Brian sells the flat that has been the scene of so much unhappiness and buys a five-storey Georgian house in Chapel Street, Belgravia.

December 1964
Brian Epstein is now the most successful manager and impresario in Britain, perhaps the world. Earlier this year the Beatles occupied the top five positions on the *Billboard* Hot 100.

Other artists under his management have also achieved extraordinary success. In March, Gerry and the Pacemakers reached number 1 with their debut single, 'How Do You Do It?'. In June, Billy J. Kramer and the Dakotas reached number 1 with their debut single, 'Do You Want to Know a Secret', written by Lennon and McCartney. And so it goes on: Gerry and the Pacemakers back at the top in July with 'I Like It', followed by Billy J. Kramer in August with 'Bad to Me', and Gerry and the Pacemakers back again in November with 'You'll Never Walk Alone'. By the end of the year his various artists have had eight number ones.

Brian's staff are surprised when he adds an actor to the agency's roster of talent: John 'Dizz' Gillespie.

6 November 1964

Brian appears on BBC radio's prestigious *Desert Island Discs*. Apart from a version of 'All My Loving' by the George Martin Orchestra and 'She's a Woman' by the Beatles, his choices are broadly classical: Bach's Brandenburg Concerto Number 5, Sibelius's 2nd Symphony, Bruch's Violin Concerto. Asked to choose one book for his desert island, he picks *Elected Silence*, the autobiography of the Trappist monk Thomas Merton.*

With hindsight, this unexpected choice seems peculiarly significant. 'What can we gain by sailing to the moon if we are not able to cross the abyss that separates us from ourselves?' asks Merton in one memorable passage. 'This is the most important of all voyages of discovery, and without it, all the rest are not only useless, but disastrous.'

October 1964

Brian meets Dizz Gillespie, a young American in his early twenties with, in the words of one associate, 'dark hair, mischievous eyes and an impish, upturned nose'. Gillespie is keen to become an actor or a singer, or both. 'There's something special about him,' says Brian. 'Something I can't name.'

Brian pays off Gillespie's debts, gives him an allowance from his personal account, signs him to NEMS on a £50 a week retainer, and buys him a new wardrobe. The newspapers announce that he is Brian's latest discovery.

15 September 1964

The Beatles appear at the Public Auditorium in Cleveland, Ohio. Their fans have never been more fervent. A police cordon encircles the Sheraton Hotel where they are staying. A young boy is discovered hiding in a packing case, hoping to be smuggled into the hotel. A

* First published in America in 1948 under the title *The Seven Storey Mountain*.

young girl pretends to faint outside in the street, then refuses to receive first aid unless she is taken inside.

During the show, the local disc jockey Jim Staggs climbs a two-hundred-foot lighting scaffold, hoping to get a better view. Halfway up he looks over his shoulder, only to see Brian Epstein climbing up behind him. 'Jim!' he shouts. 'You wouldn't be taping this performance, would you?'

Larry Kane, covering the tour for the Miami radio station WFUN, is impressed by such tenacity: 'The fact that he put himself at risk to make the climb was proof positive that Brian Epstein would do anything to protect the artistic sanctity – and profitability – of his Beatles.'

July 1964

The British Clothing Manufacturers' Federation presents Brian Epstein with a silver plaque, citing his 'exemplary standards in the choice and wearing of clothes', and adding that 'His sartorial taste hits the mark as surely as his eye for talent.'

Brian favours made-to-measure suits, Burberry raincoats, polkadot cravats, Christian Dior silk ties and gold cufflinks. His personal valet keeps everything in pristine order. Brian's client Cilla Black thinks he cuts quite a dash: 'He was immaculate from head to toe, like Cary Grant … He was everything you wanted a posh fella to look like.'

'He always looked as if he'd just stepped out of the bath,' says his Liverpool tailor George Hayes. 'He would always be polite and appreciative, but also demanding.'

17 May 1964

Brian is interviewed by the *Observer*'s star interviewer, Kenneth Harris, who asks him how long he thinks the Beatles will go on. 'Indefinitely,' he replies. 'They are bound to. There's so much talent there. Each one is a remarkable man.' Asked what they have got that other people haven't, he says: 'They've got this astonishing naturalness, this freedom from *un*naturalness. In private they are unspoiled, unaffected, sincere – themselves all the time, and to *everybody*, regardless.'

Brian talks about his shyness, and his unhappiness at school. Harris asks, 'So the Beatles solved your problem for you?'

Brian replies: 'Yes, it's a funny thing, and I've never thought about it that way before. But it's quite true. Everything about the Beatles was right for me. Their kind of attitude to life, the attitude that comes out in their music and their rhythm and their lyrics, and their humour, and their personal way of behaving – it was all just what I wanted. They represented the direct, unselfconscious, good-natured, uninhibited human relationships which I hadn't found and had wanted and felt deprived of. My own sense of inferiority evaporated with the Beatles because I knew I could help them, and that they wanted me to help them, and trusted me to help them. Then the success I registered in social and money terms was important. It didn't matter much to me in myself, but it mattered to other people. My parents were impressed that I had shown good judgement and initiative, so I felt I hadn't let them down. So my tensions and frustrations all went. I've got plenty of problems. But I'm not pulled down by them any more.'

14 January 1964

The Beatles begin a series of eighteen concerts at the Olympia Theatre in Paris. After one of the shows Brian says, 'They didn't know it but I cried tonight, I really did. They never noticed, but I cried.'

December 1963

The Beatles end the year as the most famous pop group in Britain, having had three number 1 hits – 'From Me to You', 'She Loves You' and 'I Want to Hold Your Hand'. Brian is now carefully plotting their arrival in America, where they remain an unknown quantity.

January 1963

In the *NME* annual readers' survey, the Beatles finish in joint 111th place. They share their position with Mike Berry,* the Clyde Valley Stompers† and Norman Vaughan.‡ In the 'British Small Group' category, they gain 743 votes compared to the Shadows' 45,951. They end up in eighth position, between the Temperance Seven§ at number 7 and Sounds Incorporated¶ at number 9.

---

* Mike Berry (1942–), singer. His single 'Don't You Think it's Time' reached number 6 in January 1963. In 1981 he was cast as Bert Spooner in the eighth season of *Are You Being Served?*, remaining with the show until 1985.

† The Clyde Valley Stompers, trad jazz band, formed in Glasgow in the 1950s. 'Before Beatlemania erupted, there was Stompermania' – *The Scotsman*. The Clyde Valley Stompers reached number 25 in August 1962 with their jazzed-up version of 'Peter and the Wolf', but achieved no subsequent chart success.

‡ Norman Vaughan (1923–2002), all-round family entertainer, actor (*No Sex Please, We're British*) and game-show host (*The Golden Shot*, 1972–73).

§ The Temperance Seven, trad jazz band known for their zany humour. Their 1960 hit with Peter Sellers, 'Ukulele Lady', was produced by George Martin. Their song 'You're Driving Me Crazy' reached number 1 in 1961.

¶ Sounds Incorporated, instrumental group. They signed to Brian Epstein's NEMS in 1963, and reached number 30 in the charts with 'The Spartans' in April 1964, and number 35 with 'Spanish Harlem'. They achieved more success in Australia with their version of 'The William Tell Overture', which reached number 2. They were the Beatles' opening act at Shea Stadium in August 1965, and broke up a year after the Beatles, in 1971.

7 June 1962
Having listened to their demo disc, George Martin from EMI calls the Beatles in for a test recording, but without much enthusiasm: during their session he pops out for tea and biscuits in the canteen. He sees no reason to pay special attention to 'four berks from Liverpool'. Once their audition is over he remains sceptical, particularly about their self-written songs. He is 'quite certain that their songwriting ability had no saleable future'.

But chatting to them afterwards in a café, he is struck by their magic: their quick wits, their cock-snooking banter, their devil-may-care energy.

'The next fifteen to twenty minutes was pure entertainment. When they left I just sat there saying, "Phew! What do you think of that lot then?" I had tears running down my face.'

Broadly speaking, it is on the strength of their personalities, rather than their music, that he decides to offer the Beatles a contract.

8 May 1962
Brian has been to so many record companies that he has run out of demos, so he goes into the HMV shop in Oxford Street with a tape of the Beatles' rejected Decca recordings, and pays £1 to transfer it to disc. The disc-cutter, Jim Foy, tells him that the group sounds 'not at all bad', and asks if they have a contract. 'No, I've been trying everywhere and everyone,' says Brian.

Foy takes him upstairs, and introduces him to EMI's music publisher, Sid Coleman. Sid asks him if he's tried EMI, and Brian says he has: 'I was told no go.' Sid asks him if he saw George Martin.

'Who's he?'

'He runs Parlophone.'

Brian feels that he has now really hit rock bottom: for him, Parlophone is a non-event, a dustbin for comedy and jazz.

May 1962–December 1961
Brian keeps taking time off work to go up to London, travelling from record company to record company with the Beatles' demo.

He doesn't want his father to know about these trips. 'Don't tell Daddy,' he says to his assistant Alistair Taylor whenever he sets off. 'If he comes in the shop, don't tell him where I've gone.'

Waiting for him to return from each trip, Paul and John always sit in the same coffee shop in Lime Street station. As Brian walks towards them, they look at his face to see if it's good news or bad. It's always bad.

Touting the demo around, Brian always carries a brief explanatory note about the Beatles. It reads: 'These four boys, who are superb instrumentalists, also produce some exciting and pulsating vocals. This is a group of exceptional talents and appealing personalities.'

He tells everyone he meets that the Beatles will be bigger than Elvis. He continues to say it even after he has been turned down countless times. Deep down, observes a friend, Brian thinks of himself as a man of destiny.

Four

February 1962

Fans at the Cavern are struck by the change in the Beatles' appearances and general demeanour. What has happened? A fifteen-year-old schoolgirl, Shelagh Carney, is 'hit like a brick' when she sees them. 'They had looked so rough until then. Suddenly they looked steam-cleaned, from their skin and shiny hair to their fingernails and their clothes.'

Nobody can understand how Brian Epstein has managed to get them to conform. 'How Epstein ever persuaded Lennon to put on a suit I shall never know,' says a local musician, Rod Pont.

Three

1 February 1962

For a fee of £18, minus Brian's commission of 10 per cent, Brian's new group plays the Thistle Café in West Kirby, ten miles from Liverpool. This is the first booking he has made for them.

Earlier that same day, the Beatles sign a contract with Brian Epstein for a five-year period. Brian is to receive 10 per cent of the group's income up to £1,500 a year each, increasing to 15 per cent thereafter.

Two

29 January 1962

Brian pays off the Beatles' £200 debt, accumulated from hire-purchase agreements for guitars and amplifiers. He takes the boys to Beno Dorn, his tailor, who kits them out in smart dark-blue mohair suits with narrow lapels. They keep insisting that they want their trousers narrower. Brian bargains Dorn down from 28 guineas to 23, telling him that the Beatles will be big, and so he'll get more orders.

Brian's assistant, Alistair Taylor, comes too: 'Brian embarked on a total clean-up job on the four boys. Haircuts followed the suits, and complete new wardrobes of shirts, ties, shoes, everything followed. Brian asked them face-to-face if they had any objections to his plans, and there wasn't even a murmur of dissent. Just as Brian believed in the Beatles, it was clear from the very start that the Beatles believed in Brian.'

Brian insists that they smarten themselves up. He gives them each firm directives, typed on top-quality paper: 'Onstage, there must be no drinking, no smoking, no chewing gum, and especially no swearing. The audience is not there to talk to you so don't chat to the pretty girls while you're onstage. Be punctual. If you're scheduled to arrive at a certain time, make sure you arrive when you are meant to. Remember that you are professionals now, with a reputation to keep up.'

The most troublesome member of the group, John Lennon, is impressed. Later, he recalls how 'Brian put all our instructions down on paper and it made it all seem real. We were in a daydream 'til he came along … We stopped chomping at cheese rolls and jam butties onstage.'

One

9 November 1961

One.

Two.

Three.

Four.

In their neat black suits and ties, Brian Epstein and his personal assistant Alistair Taylor make their way down the eighteen steep steps into the sweaty basement on Mathew Street. Brian finds it 'as black as a deep grave, dank and damp and smelly'. He wishes he hadn't come. Both he and Taylor would prefer to be attending a classical concert at the Philharmonic, but curiosity got the better of them. Four young musicians saunter onto the stage. Brian recognises them from the family record shop he manages: they are the ones who lounge around in the booths, listening to the latest discs and chatting to the girls, with absolutely no intention whatsoever of buying a record.

Between songs, the three yobs with guitars start yelling and swearing, turning their backs on the audience and pretending to hit one another. Taylor notices Brian's eyes widen with amazement. Taylor himself is undergoing one of the most shocking experiences of his life – 'like someone thumping you' – and he is pretty sure Brian feels the same.

After the show, Taylor says, 'They're just AWFUL.'

'They ARE awful,' agrees Brian. 'But I also think they're fabulous. Let's just go and say hello.'

George is the first of the Beatles to spot the man from the record shop approaching.

'Hello there,' he says. 'What brings Mr Epstein here?'

'Does anyone seriously believe that Beatles music will be an unthinkingly accepted part of daily life all over the world in the 2000s?'

Bryan Magee, philosopher and politician, article in The Listener, *February 1967*

ACKNOWLEDGEMENTS

Thanks to: Stephen Bayley, Antony Beevor, Vicky Bippart, Eleanor Bron, Alistair Brown, Jack Chalmers, Cressida Connolly, Seraphina D'Arby, Alastair Dougall, Cathy Drysdale and everyone at *Desert Island Discs*, Cecily Engle, Edel Eustace, Ian Hislop, David Jenkins, Mary Killen, Robert Lacey, Naomi Mantin, Charles Miller, Sheila Molnar, Omega Auctions, Nicholas Pearson, John Preston, Zoe Shine, Maxine Sibihwana, Bill Smith, Jack Smyth, Robin and Liz Summers, Hugo Vickers, Francis Wheen, Felix White, and, most of all, my wife, Frances Welch.

SOURCES

Many good books have been written about the Beatles: in fact, the general standard is much higher in terms of style and honesty than those dealing with my last subject, the royal family. For a microscopic account of their early lives, *The Beatles: All These Years – Tune In Special Extended Edition Volumes 1 and 2* by Mark Lewisohn is indispensable. I have also relied on *The Beatles* by Hunter Davies; *Beatles '66: The Revolutionary Year* by Steve Turner; *The Beatles: The Biography* by Bob Spitz; *Shout!: The True Story of the Beatles* by Philip Norman; *Can't Buy Me Love: The Beatles, Britain and America* by Jonathan Gould; *The Beatles Anthology* by the Beatles; *The Complete Beatles Chronicle* by Mark Lewisohn; *The Complete Beatles Recording Sessions: The Official Story of the Abbey Road Years 1962–1970* by Mark Lewisohn; *The Beatles Diary: An Intimate Day by Day History* by Barry Miles; *Love Me Do: The Beatles' Progress* by Michael Braun; *The Beatles Off the Record* by Keith Badman; *The Beatles: Paperback Writer – Forty Years of Classic Writing* edited by Mike Evans; *The Beatles in Their Own Words* compiled by Barry Miles; *The Beatles: A Day in the Life* compiled by Tom Schultheiss; *Ticket to Ride: Inside the Beatles' 1964 and 1965 Tours that Changed the World* by Larry Kane; *The Rough Guide to the Beatles* by Chris Ingham; *The Beatles Encyclopaedia* by Bill Harry; and the ever-thrilling *Revolution in the Head: The Beatles' Records and the Sixties* by Ian MacDonald.

Particularly useful have been two works dealing with more specialist aspects of the Beatles: *You Never Give Me Your Money: The Battle for the Soul of the Beatles* by Peter Doggett, a wonderfully clear survey of their complicated finances; and *Riding So High: The Beatles and Drugs* by Joe Goodden, an equally clear survey of their equally complicated drug lives. Other specialist books include: *The Beatles and the Historians* by Erin Torkelson Weber; *The Beatles on the Roof* by Tony Barrell; *The Beatles Lyrics: The Unseen Story Behind Their Music* by Hunter Davies; *The Walrus Was Ringo: 101 Beatles Myths Debunked* by Alan Clayson and Spencer Leigh; *How the Beatles Rocked the Kremlin: The Untold Story of a Noisy Revolution* by Leslie Woodhead; *The Beatles Are Here!* by Penelope Rowlands; *The Beatles Sent to Coventry* by Pete Chambers; *Dear Beatles* compiled by Bill Adler; *Dreaming the Beatles* by Rob Sheffield; *The Greatest Beatles Stories Ever Told* edited by Luis Miguel; *Beatles Hamburg: A Tour Guide to Beatles Sites in Hamburg* by Mark A. Schneegurt; *The Beatles in India* by Paul Saltzman; *The Beatles' Gear: All the Fab Four's Instruments, from Stage to Studio* by Andy Babiuk; *A Day in the Life of the Beatles* by Don McCullin; *Get Back: The Unauthorized Chronicle of the Beatles'* Let It Be *Disaster* by Doug Sulpy and Ray Schweighardt; *John, Paul & Me Before the Beatles: The True Story of the Very Early Days* by Len Garry; *The Quarrymen* by Hunter Davies; *The Beatles in Hamburg* by Ian Inglis; *The Beatles' Liverpool* by Ron Jones; *Plastic Macca: The Secret Death and Replacement of Beatle Paul McCartney* by Tina Foster; and *Beatlemania! The Real Story of the Beatles' UK Tours 1963–1965* by Martin Creasy.

Many books by and about individual members of the Beatles have come in very useful, among them *Paul McCartney: The Biography* by Philip Norman; *Paul McCartney: Many Years from Now* by Barry Miles; *Paul McCartney* by Alan Clayson; *Conversations With McCartney* by Paul du Noyer; *Sixties: Portrait of an Era* by Linda McCartney; *George Harrison* by Alan Clayson; *I Me Mine* by George Harrison; *Ringo Starr* by Alan Clayson; *Lennon and McCartney* by Malcolm Doney; *Being John Lennon: A Restless Life* by Ray Connolly; *John Lennon: The Life* by Philip Norman; *John Lennon* by Alan Clayson; *John Lennon in His Own Words* compiled by Barry Miles; *The Lives of John Lennon* by Albert Goldman; *John Lennon: One Day at a Time* by Anthony Fawcett; *Memories of John Lennon* introduced and edited by Yoko Ono; *The Penguin John Lennon*; and *The John Lennon Letters* edited and with an introduction by Hunter Davies.

Works by family members include Cynthia Lennon's two interesting if sometimes contradictory biographies of John: *A Twist of Lennon* (1978) and *John* (2005); *Imagine This: Growing Up With My Brother John Lennon* by Julia Baird; *Thank U Very Much: Mike McCartney's Family Album*; *George Harrison: Living in the Material World* by Olivia Harrison; *Wonderful Today* by Pattie Boyd with Penny Junor; and *Daddy Come Home: The True Story of John Lennon and his Father* by Pauline Lennon.

Virtually everyone who ever worked in any capacity for the Beatles seems to have put pen to paper, or to have had others put pen to paper on their behalf. Many of these books are full of fascinating bits and pieces, among them my favourite, *The Beatles, Lennon and Me* by Pete Shotton and Nicholas Schaffner; but also *As Time Goes By* by Derek Taylor; *The Love You Make: An Insider's Story of the Beatles* by Peter Brown and Steven Gaines; *All You Need is Ears* by George Martin with Jeremy Hornsby; *Magical Mystery Tours: My Life With the Beatles* by Tony Bramwell with Rosemary Kingsland; *With the Beatles* by Alistair Taylor; *The Man Who Gave the Beatles Away* by Alan Williams and William Marshall; *The Cutting Edge: The Story of the Beatles' Hairdresser Who Defined an Era* by Leslie Cavendish; *The Longest Cocktail Party* by Richard DiLello; *Here, There and Everywhere: My Life Recording the Music of the Beatles* by Geoff Emerick and Howard Massey; and *John Paul George Ringo and Me* by Tony Barrow. Particular mentions should be made of *Beatle!: The Pete Best Story* by Pete Best and Patrick Doncaster, and a biography of the ill-fated Jimmie Nicol, *The Beatle Who Vanished* by Jim Berkenstadt.

I particularly enjoyed two fine biographies of the troubled, enigmatic figure of Brian Epstein: *In My Life: The Brian Epstein Story* by Debbie Geller, edited by Anthony Wall; and *Brian Epstein: The Man Who Made the Beatles* by Ray Coleman.

Part of the fun of writing a book about the Beatles lies in the extraordinary number of colourful characters who surrounded them. Biographies and memoirs of these figures include: *Tearing Down the Wall of Sound: The Rise and Fall of Phil Spector* by Mick Brown; *Miss O'Dell* by Chris O'Dell with Katherine Ketcham; *I'm With the Band* by

Pamela Des Barres; *Walking Back to Happiness* by Helen Shapiro; *I Read the News Today, Oh Boy* by Paul Howard; *Groovy Bob: The Life and Times of Robert Fraser* by Harriet Vyner; *Allen Klein* by Fred Goodman; *The Day Elvis Met Nixon* by Egil 'Bud' Krogh; *Victor Spinetti Up Front* by Victor Spinetti; *King of Clubs* by Peter Stringfellow; *Freddie Starr Unwrapped* by Freddie Starr; *Christine Keeler: The Truth at Last* by Christine Keeler and Douglas Thompson; *Me* by Elton John; *The Hurdy Gurdy Man* by Donovan; *Be My Baby: How I Survived Mascara, Miniskirts and Madness* by Ronnie Spector with Vince Waldron; *King of the World: Muhammad Ali and the Rise of an American Hero* by David Remnick; *Can You Tell What it is Yet?: My Autobiography* by Rolf Harris; *I Am Brian Wilson: A Memoir* by Brian Wilson with Ben Greenman; *Catch a Wave: The Rise, Fall and Redemption of the Beach Boys* by Brian Wilson; *An Affectionate Punch* by Justin de Villeneuve; *House of Nutter: The Rebel Tailor of Savile Row* by Lance Richardson; *East End, West End: An Autobiography* by Bernard Delfont; *Faithfull* by Marianne Faithfull; *Memories, Dreams and Reflections* by Marianne Faithfull; *What's it All About?* by Cilla Black; *Eric Clapton: The Autobiography* by Eric Clapton with Christopher Simon Sykes; *Don't Let Me Be Misunderstood* by Eric Burdon with J. Marshall Craig; *Careless Love: The Unmaking of Elvis Presley* by Peter Guralnick; *Elvis Meets the Beatles* by Chris Hutchins and Peter Thompson; *Sinatra: The Life* by Anthony Summers and Robbyn Swan; *Frank: The Making of a Legend* by James Kaplan; *My Father's Daughter: A Memoir* by Tina Sinatra and Jeff Coplon; *Parcel Arrived Safely: Tied With String* by Michael Crawford; *Tom Jones: A Biography* by Stafford Hildren and David Gritten; *Redeeming Features: A Memoir* by Nicholas Haslam; *Long Drawn Out Trip: A Memoir* by Gerald Scarfe; *Wild Tales* by Graham Nash; *Losing My Virginity* by Richard Branson; *The Harder Path* by John Birt; *Grapefruit* by Yoko Ono; *Chronicles: Volume One* by Bob Dylan; *Mick and Keith* by Chris Salewicz; *The Stones* by Philip Norman; *Life* by Keith Richards; *Stoned* by Andrew Loog Oldham; *Brian Jones* by Laura Jackson; *Sympathy for the Devil* by Paul Trynka; *Up Against It: A Screenplay for the Beatles* by Joe Orton; *The Orton Diaries* edited by John Lahr; and *Prick Up Your Ears: The Biography of*

Joe Orton by John Lahr. Rereading, and re-rereading, *The Pillowbook of Eleanor Bron* has been a particular delight.

Other works from which I have drawn include: *Wondrous Strange: The Life and Art of Glenn Gould* by Kevin Bazzana; *The Odd Thing About the Colonel and Other Pieces* by Colin Welch; *The Virgin's Baby: The Battle of the Ampthill Succession* by Bevis Hillier; *A King's Story* by The Duke of Windsor; *The Mountbattens: Their Lives and Loves* by Andrew Lownie; *Shirley Temple: American Princess* by Anne Edwards; *R.V.W.: A Biography of Ralph Vaughan Williams* by Ursula Vaughan Williams; *Born to Run* by Bruce Springsteen; *Unfaithful Music and Disappearing Ink* by Elvis Costello; *This Boy* by Alan Johnson; *My Life, Our Times* by Gordon Brown; *Let Me Take You Down: Inside the Mind of Mark David Chapman* by Jack Jones; *Manson: The Life and Times of Charles Manson* by Jeff Guinn; *My Life With Charles Manson* by Paul Watkins; *It Could Have Been Yours* by Jolyon Fenwick and Marcus Husselby; *The People's Music* by Ian MacDonald; *Uncommon People: The Rise and Fall of the Rock Stars* by David Hepworth; *Revolt Into Style: The Pop Arts in Britain* by George Melly; *The People's Songs: The Story of Modern Britain in Fifty Songs* by Stuart Maconie; *Stardust Memories: Talking About My Generation* by Ray Connolly; *Hunting People: Thirty Years of Interviews With the Famous* by Hunter Davies; and *Who the Hell ...?* by the remarkable Tom Hibbert. The first book I ever read about pop remains one of the best, even though its author is not a wholehearted fan of the Beatles: *Awopbopaloobop Alopbamboom: Pop from the Beginning* by Nik Cohn.

Diaries and letters are always my favourite sources. I greatly enjoyed plundering: *Philip Larkin: Letters to Monica* edited by Anthony Thwaite; *The Letters of Kingsley Amis* edited by Zachary Leader; *The Letters of Noël Coward* edited by Barry Day; *The Noël Coward Diaries* edited by Graham Payn and Sheridan Morley; *The Kenneth Williams Letters* edited by Russell Davies; *The Kenneth Williams Diaries* edited by Russell Davies; *Like it Was: The Diaries of Malcolm Muggeridge*; *Rub Out the Words: The Letters of William S. Burroughs, 1959–1974* edited by Bill Morgan; *The Kenneth Tynan Letters* edited by Kathleen Tynan; *The Kenneth Tynan Diaries* edited by John Lahr; *Out of the Wilderness:*

Diaries 1963–67 by Tony Benn; *The Castle Diaries 1964–1976* by Barbara Castle; and *The Macmillan Diaries Vol. II* edited by Peter Catterall. Also: *All What Jazz* by Philip Larkin; *Philip Larkin: Collected Poems*; and *Philip Larkin: A Writer's Life* by Andrew Motion.

Books I have raided for intriguing information about other movements, personalities and events in the sixties include: *Modernity Britain: Opening the Box, 1957–59* by David Kynaston; *Modernity Britain: A Shake of the Dice, 1959–62* by David Kynaston; *The People: The Rise and Fall of the Working Class 1910–2010* by Selina Todd; *Never Had it So Good: A History of Britain from Suez to the Beatles* by Dominic Sandbrook; *White Heat: A History of Britain in the Swinging Sixties* by Dominic Sandbrook; *The Great British Dream Factory: The Strange History of Our National Imagination* by Dominic Sandbrook; *The Sixties* by Francis Wheen; *1966: The Year the Decade Exploded* by Jon Savage; *1963: Five Hundred Days* by John Lawton; *Our Times: The Age of Elizabeth II* by A.N. Wilson; *The Bad Trip: Dark Omens, New Worlds and the End of the Sixties* by James Riley; *The Neophiliacs* by Christopher Booker; and *The White Album* by Joan Didion. For the chapter comparing the Christmas messages of the Beatles and the Queen, *Voices Out of the Air: The Royal Christmas Broadcasts 1932–1981* was invaluable.

Random works mentioned in *One Two Three Four* include: *Through the Looking-Glass* by Lewis Carroll; *Aspects of Alice: Lewis Carroll's Dreamchild as Seen Through the Critics' Looking-Glasses* edited by Robert Phillips; *The Lore and Language of Schoolchildren* by Iona and Peter Opie; the *Just William* books by Richmal Crompton; *She* by H. Rider Haggard; *A Word Child* by Iris Murdoch; *Iris Murdoch as I Knew Her* by A.N. Wilson; *1066 and All That* by W.C. Sellar and R.J. Yeatman; *The Goon Show Scripts* by Spike Milligan; *Enderby Outside* by Anthony Burgess; *20th Century Words* by John Ayto; *Dylan's Visions of Sin* by Christopher Ricks; and the lovely *A Complete Book of Aunts* by Rupert Christiansen.

The world of pop music continues to amass a library of reference books that now seem to be outpacing those about religion or politics. I have spent many enjoyable hours consulting: *The Guinness Book of British Hit Singles*; *The Sound and the Fury: Forty Years of Classic Rock*

Journalism edited by Barney Hoskyns; *The* Rolling Stone *Encyclopaedia of Rock & Roll* edited by Jon Pareles and Patricia Romanowski; *The* Rolling Stone *Interviews 1967–1980*; *The Book of Rock Lists* by Dave Marsh and Kevin Stein; Time Out *Interviews, 1968–1998* edited by Frank Boughton; *Teenage Idols* by Frank Clews; *The Faber Companion to Twentieth-Century Music* by Phil Hardy and Dave Laing; *Whatever Happened to ...?* by Bill Harry; *The Faber Book of Pop* edited by Hanif Kureishi and Jon Savage; and *The Best of* Rolling Stone edited by Robert Love.

Online reference works are equally valuable, perhaps more so, as they are so up-to-date. Billboard.com offers an omniscient view of the American charts; rocksbackpages.com gives access to the best music papers; and The Beatles Bible strikes me as the single best source of information on all aspects of the Beatles: often, after I had patted myself on the back for discovering some particularly arcane fact, I found to my irritation that it had been in The Beatles Bible all along. My book has also benefited from research in the archives of the *New York Times*; *Los Angeles Times*; *New Yorker*; *British Medical Journal*; the Margaret Thatcher Foundation; *The Listener*; *Private Eye*; *Desert Island Discs*; *Daily Telegraph* obituaries; *Daily Mirror*; *Liverpool Echo*; *Saturday Evening Post*; *National Review*; *Seattle Times*; *GQ*; *Life*; *New Statesman*; Britishnewspaperarchive.co.uk; rollingstone.com; Omega Auctions; *Queen*; *Independent* obituaries; thisamericanlife.org; and beatlesinterviews.org.

I have spent many hundreds of hours on YouTube, watching old interviews, videos, press conferences, news footage and documentaries, such as *24 Hours: The World of John and Yoko* from the BBC, and *A Boy Called Donovan*. My chapter on the rooftop concert was greatly helped by a BBC Radio 4 documentary, *The Beatles' Final Concert*. Finally, a word of thanks to virtually everyone to whom I have spoken over the past year or two: rare is the person who does not have a favourite Beatle, or a favourite Beatles album, or an anecdote about meeting one Beatle or another, or strong opinions on the Maharishi, or the Rolling Stones, or the sixties in general.

ILLUSTRATION CREDITS

Page 22: The National Trust Photolibrary/Alamy Stock Photo
Page 24: Author
Page 39: Popperfoto/Getty Images
Page 43: K & K Ulf Kruger OHG/Getty Images
Page 64: Michael Ochs Archives/Handout
Page 78: Pictorial Press Ltd/Alamy Stock Photo
Page 83: David Redfern/Getty Images
Page 108: John Pratt/Stringer
Page 117: John Downing/Stringer
Page 125: Fox Photos/Stringer
Page 132: George Freston/Stringer
Page 137: Lefebvre André/Getty Images
Page 144: Gilles Petard/Getty Images
Page 156: CBS Photo Archive/Getty Images
Page 168: Hulton Deutsch/Getty Images
Page 173: Harry Benson/Getty Images
Page 191: Tracksimages.com/Alamy Stock Photo
Page 214: Icon and Image/Getty Images
Page 226: Lebrecht Music & Arts/Alamy Stock Photo
Page 231: Hulton Deutsch/Getty Images
Page 253: Victor Blackman/Stringer
Page 257: PA/PA Archive/PA Images
Page 260: Kent Gavin/Stringer
Page 268: Trinity Mirror/Mirrorpix/Alamy Stock Photo
Page 293: The Estate of David Gahr/Getty Images
Page 300: Courtesy of Omega Auctions
Page 306: William Vanderson/Stringer
Page 314: Rolls Press/Popperfoto/Getty Images

Page 325: Dennis Oulds/Stringer
Page 333: Robert Whitaker/Getty Images
Page 337: John Pratt/Stringer
Page 341: Keystone-France/Getty Images
Page 378: Tracksimages.com/Alamy Stock Photo
Page 381: Mirrorpix/Getty Images
Page 402: Trinity Mirror/Mirrorpix/Alamy Stock Photo
Page 407: Bettmann/Contributor
Page 423: GAB Archive/Getty Images
Page 424: Keystone Features/Stringer
Page 432: Imagno/Getty Images
Page 444: Keystone Features/Hulton Archive/Getty Images
Page 468: Sunset Boulevard/Contributor
Page 498: Mirrorpix/Getty Images
Page 510: Loomis Dean/Contributor
Page 512: Blank Archives/Getty Images
Page 518: Marvin Lichtner/Contributor
Page 521: Haywood Magee/Stringer
Page 537: Fox Photos/Stringer
Page 546: sjvinyl/Alamy Stock Photo
Page 563: Keystone Press/Alamy Stock Photo
Page 579: Keystone/Stringer
Page 591: (top) Max Scheler – K & K/Getty Images; (bottom) Trinity Mirror/Mirrorpix/Alamy Stock Photo
Page 600: David Farrell/Getty Images
Page 622: Keystone Press/Alamy Stock Photo

LAURA WILSON

A Capital Crime

Quercus

First published in Great Britain in 2010 by Quercus
This paperback edition published in 2011 by

Quercus
21 Bloomsbury Square
London
WC1A 2NS

A CIP catalogue record for this book is available from the British Library

ISBN 978 1 84916 310 1

This book is a work of fiction. Names, characters,

Prin ... es plc

To George, with love

1950

Chapter One

METROPOLITAN POLICE TELEGRAM

30-11-50

THE FOLLOWING TELEPHONE MESSAGE RECEIVED FROM POLICE, MERTHYR TYDFIL (TELE. 541). BEGINS:-

A MAN NAMED JOHN WILFRED DAVIES HAS COME TO THIS STATION THIS AFTERNOON AND STATED THAT ON 7-11-50 AT 10, PARADISE STREET, W.C., HIS WIFE HAD A MISCARRIAGE AT THAT ADDRESS, AFTER SHE DRANK SOME LIQUID WHICH HE OBTAINED FROM A LORRY DRIVER SOME TIME PREVIOUS AT A CAFE IN IPSWICH. DURING THE NIGHT OF 8-11-50 BETWEEN 1AM AND 2AM HE DISPOSED OF HIS WIFES BODY DOWN A DRAIN OUTSIDE THE FRONT OF THAT ADDRESS. HE HANDED HIS 14 MONTH OLD CHILD TO A MAN NAMED NORMAN BACKHOUSE AT THE SAME ADDRESS WHO STATED HE COULD HAVE THE CHILD TAKEN CARE OF. HE ALSO SOLD THE FURNITURE AND LEFT THE ADDRESS. WILL YOU PLEASE CAUSE ENQUIRIES TO BE MADE. A WRITTEN STATEMENT HAS BEEN TAKEN FROM DAVIES. ENDS.

FORWARDED FOR NECESSARY ACTIONS ON DIRECTIONS OF CH/SUPT

Detective Inspector Stratton closed the door of his superior's office. He stood for a moment, staring at the piece of paper, and then he looked out of the window, where the end-of-November morning sun was struggling, feebly, to shine through a sooty yellow blanket of smog that had turned the West End sky the colour of a dirty duster. Over four years after the war's end, sunshine seemed to be rationed, in line with pretty well everything else apart from the grime and drizzle through which the weary citizens moved, herd-like and damp-macintoshed, or shuffled, grumbling, in perpetual queues.

Stratton felt every day of his forty-four years, and then some: he'd had a cold since the middle of October, his chilblains were itching like buggery, and the last thing he wanted was a walk. If only he could lay hands on a pair of shoes that kept out the wet . . . He scanned the telegram again, shaking his head, and went to find Sergeant Ballard.

The sergeant was at the front desk, attempting to calm down an obviously drunk woman, whose ravaged face, beneath the rouge, had an ominous greenish pallor, and who was missing the high heel of one shoe. Spit flew from her mouth as she berated motherly Policewoman Harris, who'd brought her in, the words spilling out loud but sloppy: 'Take your hands off me, you lesbian!'

'What's the problem?'

'It's Iris, sir,' said Ballard. 'She's been making a nuisance of herself again.' Despite the fact that his face was scratched and his dark suit was smudged with chalky powder where the woman had stumbled into him, he still managed to look as smart as paint. That, thought Stratton, was also how you could describe most of the local tarts, who were certainly better dressed than the rest of the female population – except for the odd one like Iris Manning, who was clinging on, by ragged fingernails, to the Soho beat she'd had since before the war. Iris was one of their regulars: drunk, disorderly, soliciting and, once, wounding another girl in a fight over a punter. Hearing Stratton's voice she turned unsteadily, supporting herself on the desk, and tottered in his direction. Stratton, detecting the odour of decay and stale perfume, stepped smartly backwards.

'Inspector, you'll help me, won't you? I haven't done nothing. It's all a mistake. Won't you help me? I'll make it up to you.'

Shuddering inwardly at the idea of this ghoul – drunk at that – being let loose on his private parts, he said, 'That's very nice of you, Iris, and I appreciate it, but I'm afraid it's out of the question. You'll be much better off here.'

'But it's *her*,' Iris wailed, pointing a grubby, trembling finger at the policewoman. 'She's always had it in for me.'

'No, she hasn't.' Stratton exchanged glances with Miss Harris. 'She's got your best interests at heart. Now, you be a good girl and go quietly and I'm sure' – he grinned encouragingly – 'that she'll make you a nice cup of tea.'

Behind her, Harris grimaced, and Stratton made an apologetic face at her. Iris Manning, still looking mutinous, allowed herself to be led away, limping.

'Thank you, sir,' said Ballard, as they left West End Central. 'That was getting nasty.'

'Poor old Iris.' Stratton peered through the fog for the police car that was to take them to Paradise Street. 'She's not been the same since the Yanks left.' It was too thick to see very far down the street, but they could hear the hiss and splash of tyres in the wet, a shouted curse, and a lot of coughing.

'Paradise Street's next to the goods yard off Euston Road,' he told the driver as they climbed in.

'On Mother Kelly's doorstep . . .' sang Ballard, *sotto voce.*

'That's Paradise *Row,*' said Stratton. He handed over the paper for Ballard to peer at.

'What's he doing in Wales, sir?'

'Dunno. Name's Davies, so he's Welsh, I suppose. Wife dies and he goes back home to Mum.'

'A drain, though . . . three weeks . . .' Ballard made a face.

'Look on the bright side – it's not the middle of summer. And it seems pretty straightforward – as long as we can find the baby, that is.'

'Seems a bit odd just handing the kid over like that, sir.'

'That's what I was thinking, but as long as it hasn't come to any harm, it should be plain sailing. We can fetch out the body, fetch Davies up from Wales and have it sorted out by the end of the week.'

A fleet of lorries loaded with building materials – destined for the Festival of Britain site on the South Bank, Stratton guessed – was blocking Regent Street, so they went through Piccadilly Circus instead. Peering out of the window through the smoggy air, Stratton just managed to make out the oversized Bovril advert and the dramatic 'Export or Die' sign beneath it. Men in the unvarying civilian uniform of drab demob macs and trilby hats hurried along the pavements beside the car before being swallowed up by the fog, but occasionally Stratton caught a glimpse of something more colourful as a man pushing a grocer's barrow or a woman in a bright coat went past. The sootily looming Victorian buildings thinned out somewhat as they neared the Euston Road, broken up by bombsites untouched except, in the summer months, by swathes of purple rosebay willowherb.

They drove past shops selling second-hand clothes – a lot of grey stuff that looked suspiciously like demob suits, and war surplus in bundles of khaki and air-force blue; and rows of skinny, dilapidated three-storey houses with crumbling windowsills and walls that soaked up the damp like blotting paper. It was unusual enough to see a freshly repaired and painted building even in the fashionable parts of London; here, it would be a miracle, and Paradise Street seemed even more dingy than the rest. It was a cul-de-sac, ending in the back wall of the goods yard; a Victorian horror of blackened brick and rotting woodwork, one of the end houses shored up by a temporary plank buttress rising from a sea of mud that must once have been a garden. The terraced houses looked as if they had the plague, and the inhabitants, such as could be seen, didn't seem much better. The doors opened straight onto the street, and a grubby little girl of about six with scabs around her mouth, clad in a worn coat and a pixie hood and sitting on a front step, looked up as they passed. 'Sssh . . .' she admonished, one finger to her lips, then pointed to an equally filthy doll lying in her lap.

'Is your dolly asleep?' asked Stratton, bending down to her.

'No,' replied the child in a matter-of-fact tone. 'She's dead.'

Chapter Two

Diana Calthrop stared out of her bedroom window and watched the hunched, elderly form of Reynolds the gardener making his slow progress down the weed-strewn gravel that surrounded the soggy, untended parterre. Looking past him to the woodlands and fields beyond, she thought, I shan't miss any of it – not the vast, dank garden or the enormous draughty mausoleum of a house.

Sighing, she turned to resume her packing. Despite several years of wartime practice making up parcels for the WVS, she was too sad and distracted to make a decent job of it – clothes were strewn across the double bed and hanging over the backs of chairs, and cosmetics and scent littered the dressing table. They hadn't had a maid since Ellen left in 1944, and asking Mrs Birkett, the irritable, arthritic cook who was the last remaining member of the indoor staff, to help her, was out of the question. Besides, there wasn't really a great deal *to* pack – not much to show for fifteen years of marriage, when you came down to it. Not even a child. Five miscarriages had seen to that – and what was worse, she hadn't really minded. Emotionally, she'd felt only dull resignation, never the sharp grief of loss. The only thing I was bred to do, and I couldn't even manage that, she sneered at herself. One of the miscarriages hadn't even been her husband's child, but the result of a wartime affair with a fellow agent while she was working at MI5. Guy had no idea of this, but her vengeful mother-in-law, Evie, who reigned supreme over both the house and her son, did, and had enjoyed making frequent, if mercifully oblique, references to it.

For the last few months, though, Evie – without bothering to hide the fact – had been grooming Diana's successor, the daughter of a local worthy. Round-faced, sweet-natured and undoubtedly virginal, Genevieve Collier was younger, more malleable, and altogether less tarnished than herself. Guy seemed happy enough to go along with his mother's plans for his future, but then, Diana thought sourly, he always had, hadn't he?

A tentative knock produced the subject of her thoughts, standing uncomfortably in the open doorway and bearing a fistful of white hellebores. Diana stared at him, bewildered. She hadn't seen him since the previous day's stilted and painfully formal exchange when she'd finally announced the inevitable. In any case, it was a long time since they'd felt easy in each other's presence, and an even longer time since they'd entered each other's bedrooms without knocking. The war – Guy had spent almost three years as a prisoner in Malaya and returned rail-thin, plagued by nightmares and a silent, corrosive fury – and Evie, who somehow managed to be present even when she wasn't actually in the room with them, had seen to that.

'I thought' – the oak floorboards creaked as Guy advanced a couple of hesitant paces towards her – 'that you might like these.'

Diana gaped at him, unsure if she wanted to laugh or cry. 'I haven't got anywhere to put them,' she said, gently. 'They'll die.'

'I thought . . .' Guy stared at the flowers in his hand as if he wasn't sure how they'd got there, and continued, lamely, 'I just wanted . . .' He shook his head. 'I don't know.'

'I *am* leaving, Guy,' said Diana. 'It's finished. We both know that.'

'Yes . . .'

'I was too young.'

'Yes . . .'

'The war . . .'

'Yes . . .'

'I'm sorry.'

'I'm sorry, too.'

It's hopeless, she thought. There's too much to say, and, at the same time, there's nothing at all. Guy crossed the room towards her, coming so close that, fearing he was about to embrace her, she flinched slightly. The movement was small and involuntary, but Guy was aware of it, his fingers fluttering against her upper arms for a second before he turned away to deposit the flowers in the wastepaper basket by her feet. For a moment, they both stared down at the pretty, discarded blooms, trying to pretend that it hadn't happened, and then Guy said, abruptly, 'I did love you, you know.'

'I loved you, too.' As she said it, Diana wondered if it had ever been true. When she looked back, she'd come to the conclusion that her marriage, at nineteen, six months an orphan and caught up, as she'd thought at the time, in a whirlwind of romance, had been entirely orchestrated by Evie.

'What will you do?' he asked.

'Oh, you know,' Diana tried to keep her tone light, 'there's lots of things I can do. I can type, and organise . . . I can even cook a little. I'm sure I can make myself useful to somebody.'

Guy nodded. 'You're different, now.'

Yes, thought Diana, I am: older, wiser, tougher and more practical. A small voice in the back of her mind warned her that the toughness and practicality remained to be tested – war-work was one thing, a peacetime job quite another.

'You are different too,' she said. 'It isn't surprising.'

'I suppose not.' Guy stared at her with a sort of miserable wonder. 'You're very beautiful, you know. I've always thought that.' He's trying to tell me I'll find another husband, Diana thought. Right at the moment she wasn't at all sure that she wanted one. 'I'm sorry I can't give you more money, but . . .' Mentally, Diana completed the sentence – *but Evie won't allow it.*

'It's all right, Guy,' she said. 'The first thing I'm going to do is go up to Gloucestershire and see what can be done with Hambeyn House, now that the army's finally decided to relinquish it.'

'These big places . . .' said Guy doubtfully. He didn't need to complete that sentence, either, as both of them knew that Diana's childhood home was unlikely to fetch more than the small amount that a builder would pay for the raw materials. 'Well . . .' He glanced around the room. 'I can see you've got things to do, so I'll make myself scarce.'

'It might be best,' said Diana, glancing at her wristwatch. 'The taxi's due in half an hour.'

Guy acknowledged this with a nod, but made no move to leave. After a few moments, looking more awkward than ever, he cleared his throat, said, 'Well. . .' again and held out his hand. Mechanically, she held out hers, and they shook for what felt like an age. Then the sheer absurdity of the gesture, coupled with the desire to make it clear that she was well aware of her mother-in-law's machinations, got the better of her, and looking Guy straight in the eye she said, 'I'm sure that you and Genevieve and Evie will be very happy.'

Blushing, he jerked his hand free of hers. 'Yes, well . . .' He swallowed. 'No hard feelings, I trust.'

'Not at all.'

Conscious that in this exchange at least she was the victor, Diana watched him squeak his way back across the room. He paused in the doorway and turned back, an almost beseeching expression on his face. 'You will say goodbye to Evie, won't you?' he asked.

Diana, who had asked herself several times in the past twenty-four hours if it were possible to slide away without saying anything to her mother-in-law, treated Guy to what she knew was her haughtiest expression. 'Of course.'

When he'd gone, closing the door behind him as gently and quietly as if someone had died, she thought, with a rush of confidence, I shall say goodbye to Evie, but I shall do it with my head held high. Suddenly, she found herself looking forward to the encounter, and with swift, sure movements, set about finishing her packing.

Chapter Three

Number ten was at the end of Paradise Street, hard against the wall of the goods yard, with a manhole directly outside the downstairs bay window. At a nod from Stratton, Ballard squatted down and tried to lift the lid. After a few moments he looked up, shaking his head. 'Sorry, sir. Can't move it. It doesn't look as if it's been disturbed recently, does it?'

'Not really, no.' Stratton, kneeling beside him, put his fingers under the rim and heaved, but, try as they might, the two men couldn't budge the iron slab. 'It's no good,' said Stratton, finally, standing up and easing his back. 'He'd have to be Charles Atlas to get that up on his own.'

'Perhaps someone gave him a hand,' said Ballard, mopping his face.

'Mmm . . .' Sensing that he was being watched, Stratton turned towards number ten. The curtains were closed but a face was peering round them, a bald-pated, feeble-looking middle-aged man in a cardigan, blinking through pebble glasses. 'Him?' said Stratton derisively, jerking his head at the window.

The man made a curious sideways sucking motion with his mouth and withdrew his head. 'He does look a bit of a maiden aunt, doesn't he?' said Ballard.

'We'd better have some help,' said Stratton. 'Take the car back to the station and get some reinforcements. Try and find someone with a bit of muscle, like Canning. And a crowbar.'

Ballard went off to telephone, leaving Stratton outside the house. A semicircle of neighbours, mainly putty-faced women and children, had gathered to stand at a discreet distance. The women, several of whom had their hair in curlers, wore cretonne overalls, and the children, snotty-nosed, concave-chested and wearing an assortment of ill-fitting clothing and gumboots, trailed skipping ropes, sticks, and a broken tennis racket. The constant rumble of trains travelling along the line to Euston was counter-pointed by an assortment of hollow, tubercular coughs and the thin, high wail of a baby, but no one spoke. Instead, they watched warily, ready to back away and scatter, reminding him of a herd of cows.

When Stratton turned back towards number ten he saw the man again, standing in front of the still-drawn curtains, this time with a cup and saucer held in a dainty manner, little finger slightly raised. Ballard's description of a maiden aunt was spot on, he thought. The man blinked at him for a moment, then withdrew.

Stratton wondered if that were Norman Backhouse, the man who'd taken Davies's baby into his care, and why he did not come out to see what was going on outside his home.

Time enough for that later – the contents of the drain must come first. He squatted down once more to look at the manhole cover. Nobody was *that* strong, thought Stratton. Six foot three, broad-shouldered and a former boxer, he wasn't exactly a weakling, and neither, despite his slimmer physique, was Ballard. It would take at least three men, maybe four, to lift the thing. He lit a cigarette and wondered how many people lived in Paradise Street. They were little more than doll's houses, really – there couldn't be more than two rooms per storey, with one out the back on the ground floor – but he'd have bet that each building was inhabited by at least two families, plus the usual assortment of jobless ex-servicemen, part-time prostitutes, and forlorn elderly widows who eked out their meagre pensions in tea and bread and marge.

Ballard returned after ten minutes, followed by the towering, barrel-chested form of PC Canning, who was holding a crowbar, with old Arliss, the station's most incompetent policeman, grumbling along in the rear. Stratton issued instructions, but even with the four of them (not that Arliss did much more than complain about his back) it took a lot of grunting and heaving before they were able to move the cover aside sufficiently for Canning to shine his torch down the hole. When he looked up, he was shaking his head.

'What's up?' asked Stratton.

'See for yourself, sir.' Canning handed him the torch.

Stratton leant over the opening and looked. The shaft was empty. 'I don't believe there's ever been a body in there,' he said.

'There aren't any other drains nearby,' said Ballard.

Stratton turned to look down the road and found himself, instead, looking into a pair of round, pale-blue eyes, blinking rapidly behind thick glasses. 'Sorry, sir,' he said, stepping back smartly. 'Can I help you?'

The man, who Stratton now recognised as the chap who'd been watching them from inside the house, gave a soft cough. 'I think, Inspector,' he said in a voice so quiet that Stratton had to strain to hear it, 'that it might be more a question of how *I* can help *you*.'

'I see.' Wondering why he hadn't heard the man approach, Stratton looked down and saw that he was wearing plimsolls. Must have crept up behind us, he thought.

The man made the peculiar sideways movement with his mouth that he'd noticed before. Up close, it was accompanied by a small wet sucking noise. He looked, Stratton thought, like a bad ventriloquist. 'My name's Backhouse. I saw you through the window. Of course, I didn't want to obstruct you in the course of your duties – I know all about that because I was a special. In the recent war. Volunteered in nineteen thirty-nine and served for several years at West End Central. In fact . . .' he ducked his head, modestly, 'I had the honour to be commended on two occasions.' He stopped, clearly expecting a response. When none was forthcoming, he said, 'I wondered . . . are you looking for something?' During the course of this little speech, Backhouse's voice had risen in volume, so that by the end it was almost normal. He had the vestiges of a northern accent – Yorkshire, Stratton thought – eroded, like his own Devonian one had been, by years of contact with Cockneys, and spoke with exaggerated precision, taking great care with his consonants.

Stratton introduced himself, and then, drawing Backhouse to one side, said, 'Perhaps you can help us with some information about the Davieses.'

'They're not here now,' said Backhouse. 'They've left.'

'When was that?'

Backhouse considered this for a moment. 'The second week of November. I remember that because we had workmen here. The last time I saw them was the Tuesday of that week.'

'And you haven't seen them since?'

'Not Muriel – Mrs Davies, that is – or the baby. They went off then, you see, to stay with some friends in . . . Bristol, I think it was. That's what he told us.'

'Mr Davies told you that?'

'Yes, that's right. He said they were going for a holiday, and he was joining them later in the week. He told me he was going to find a job up there. Has something happened to them, Inspector?'

'That's what we're trying to find out.'

'Well, you'll not find them in the drain.' Backhouse spoke as if it were a perfectly normal place to look for someone, such as their home or the local pub.

'No,' agreed Stratton. 'Did Davies leave the baby with you at any time?'

Backhouse stared at him in surprise. When he spoke, it was barely more than a whisper. 'No. My wife used to listen out for her from time to time if Muriel went out, but that was all.'

'So you didn't tell him you'd find someone to look after the baby?'

'Tell him . . .? I'm sorry, Inspector, I don't understand.'

'Mr Davies made a statement to the police in Wales, saying you told him you'd find someone to look after the baby.'

'Find someone? That's nonsense.' Backhouse cleared his throat and continued at normal pitch, 'He left some of her things with me, but that was all . . . but I don't understand. You said he'd made a statement?'

'Yes. He said he'd put his wife's body in the drain.'

'Oh, dear . . .' Backhouse shook his head. 'Well, I don't know anything about that. I'm sure we'd have noticed, if . . . There was nothing like that. He just gave me the things to look after. He'd sold the rest of his furniture, you see, before he left.'

'All of it?' asked Stratton, remembering the telegram.

'Yes. A man came for it a few days later.'

'Did Davies collect the baby's things?'

Backhouse shook his head. 'We've still got them. Would you like to see?'

'Yes, please.'

Stratton told the others to put the drain cover back in place and followed Backhouse inside number ten.

'Lucky I was here,' he said. 'I'd normally be at work, but I suffer with my back. It's so bad now I've had to have a certificate from the doctor.' Ignoring this, Stratton peered down the dim hallway. It was narrow, with a solitary gas bracket for lighting and a flight of stairs halfway back with a passage alongside which led to the back door and, adjacent to that, the door of what Stratton guessed must be Backhouse's kitchen. Glancing through a half-open door on the right, he caught sight of the corner of a table with a dark bobble-edged cloth on it and the edges of a couple of framed photographs. Faded sepia, he imagined, dead Victorians in all their dour glory. He was proved right about the kitchen when a plump, large-bosomed woman stepped out of it, tea towel in hand. Clad in a flowered cretonne overall, she had a placid, almost bovine expression. 'What is it, Norman?' Her accent was Yorkshire, too, but more pronounced.

'This is my wife,' explained Backhouse. 'It's the police, Edna. The ones who were looking down the drain.'

'Inspector Stratton,' added Stratton, by way of introduction.

'Is there something wrong with the drain?' Mrs Backhouse looked worried. 'Only we've not touched it.'

'There's nothing wrong with it, but I'd like to see the things that Mr Davies left with you, for the baby.'

'Why? What's happened?'

'As I explained to Mr Backhouse,' said Stratton, feeling foolish, 'we aren't really sure at the moment.'

'Oh dear . . .' Mrs Backhouse put a hand over her mouth. 'They're in the kitchen. But they're not ours, so I don't know if–'

'Don't keep the inspector waiting, Edna,' said Backhouse. 'He's got to do his job.'

The Backhouses' kitchen was a cramped, cluttered room, no more than ten feet square, containing a gas stove, a range, a stone sink, shelves, a table and two chairs and an odd-looking deckchair, its canvas replaced by a home-made sling of knotted ropes. Mrs Backhouse opened a wooden cupboard door in the back wall. 'It's all here,' she said. 'We haven't interfered with it.' Peering inside, Stratton saw an alcove stretching back about six feet, which, by the looks of it, had once been used to store coal. Now, it held a pram, a baby's high chair, and two suitcases. Lifting the nearest case out, Stratton set it on the floor and, kneeling down, opened it. Inside was a grubby cot blanket, and underneath that, baby clothes.

'Do you recognise these?' he asked Mrs Backhouse, who was peering over his shoulder.

'Yes. That's one of Judy's frocks.'

Stratton took out his notebook. 'Judy's the baby's name, is it?'

'Yes.' Mrs Backhouse frowned. 'But I thought you knew . . . I mean, if you're looking for them.'

'We don't have much information,' said Stratton. 'We just want to make sure she's safe.'

Mrs Backhouse shook her head. 'Poor little thing . . .'

'If there's anything more we can do to help, Inspector,' said Backhouse, 'you've only to ask. As I said, I was with the police during the war, so I know–'

'If I might have the other case,' said Stratton, cutting him off. The way the man was toadying was downright creepy.

The second case contained a feeding bottle, napkins and yet more baby clothes – a surprising amount, Stratton thought, for just one infant. Perhaps Backhouse thought so too, because he said, 'Davies's mother bought most of Judy's things. She's always done a lot for them, hasn't she, Edna?'

'Oh yes. She's very good to them.'

'Could Mrs Davies be looking after Judy?' asked Stratton.

'I suppose so,' said Mrs Backhouse. 'I don't know. Muriel didn't say anything to me.'

'She didn't even tell you they were going, did she, Edna?'

'No.'

'Edna was quite upset about it, her not saying goodbye. We've always tried to be good neighbours, Inspector. Always looked out for them. They're very young, you see.'

'Yes,' said Stratton, wondering why, if Mrs Davies was looking after Judy, she hadn't collected her things. Surely the baby couldn't have even *more* of them? And even if she had, Mrs Davies would certainly need the pram ... He lifted up the baby's stuff to see what was at the bottom of the case, and found what was clearly a woman's blouse and a cotton dress.

'Those are Muriel's,' said Mrs Backhouse. 'Summer things.'

That, at least, made sense, thought Stratton. She'd hardly need them at this time of year. 'Did Mr Davies say anything about picking these up or sending someone for them?'

'No,' said Backhouse. 'I assumed he was waiting until they were settled.'

'And he left when, exactly?'

'About a week after Muriel and the baby, wasn't it?'

Mrs Backhouse nodded.

'So that would be about a fortnight ago.'

'That's right. That's when he sold the furniture, and he'd given up his job. He came back about a week ago.'

'And he didn't say anything about taking these?' Stratton indicated the contents of the alcove.

Backhouse shook his head. 'The thing was, you see . . .' He tailed off, blinking rapidly.

'Yes?'

'I didn't think I ought to say anything . . .' Backhouse's voice had gone quiet again, 'but he told Edna that Muriel had walked out on him. Didn't he, dear?'

'Yes.' Mrs Backhouse looked awkward, and when she spoke, her voice, too, was hushed. 'I asked him how she was, and he said she was all right, but she'd left him.'

'In Bristol?'

'Well . . . I suppose it was. I don't know.'

Backhouse, who appeared to be staring at Muriel's clothes, made the strange sucking sound with his mouth again, then cleared his throat and said, 'To be honest, Inspector, I can't say we were very surprised.'

'Oh? Why's that?'

'Well, they argued a lot, didn't they, dear?'

'Oh, yes.'

'A lot of shouting,' said Backhouse. 'Violence, sometimes. Muriel told my wife about it on several occasions. She told Edna she was afraid of him.' Mrs Backhouse nodded in confirmation of this. 'Not that we needed telling,' Backhouse continued. 'You could hear it quite clearly. So could the neighbours, I'm afraid. They were known around here for fighting.'

'Do you know what they fought about?'

'Debts, I think. It's hard for a young couple these days,

and she wasn't very good with money, I'm afraid. And there was Davies's behaviour. He went off with a woman once. A friend of his wife's, too – she was stopping with them, you see, upstairs. I told them the tenancy agreement didn't allow it, but . . .' He shook his head. 'A dreadful business, shouting and screaming . . . Mrs Davies – his mother – came over to try and keep the peace, but the police were called in the end. Davies and the girl left, but he came back – the next day, I think it was. The girl had thrown him out, and he was in a terrible temper. Threatened to run her over in his van – he's a driver, you see, deliveries. He worked in the goods yard, just the other side of the wall here. You don't like to interfere, but . . .' He shook his head again. '"I'll smash her up." That was what he said. "I'll smash her up." The whole thing was most regrettable.'

'When did it happen?'

'Sometime in August. There was a lot of rowing. I heard him threaten to throw Muriel out of the window on one occasion. And then there was the drinking. He was always in public houses. And I'm afraid he got a name as something of a liar. Telling stories. In fact, we've sometimes wondered if he isn't a bit mental.'

'I see.' Stratton rose, dusting his trouser legs.

'As I said,' concluded Backhouse, 'we weren't surprised when he said she'd left him.'

'Thank you,' said Stratton. 'You've been most helpful. Just one more thing – Mrs Davies' address. Do you know it?'

'It's nearby – twenty-two, Garton Road.'

As Stratton was taking his leave, Mrs Backhouse laid a

hand on his arm. 'You will . . .' she began timidly and then, seeing her husband's frown, she stopped.

'Yes?' prompted Stratton.

'Just . . . you will tell us, won't you? About the baby, I mean. I – we – were very fond of her.'

The street was empty but for Ballard, who was waiting for him. 'Arliss says he remembers Backhouse being a special,' he said. 'I think I do, too.'

'Do you? I don't.'

'Well, you didn't really have much to do with them, sir. If he is the chap I remember, and I'm pretty sure he is, he was good, but a bit officious. Overdid it.'

'The power of the uniform, you mean?'

'Something like that, sir,' said Ballard wryly. 'And he *was* commended. Did you get much in there?'

'Well, there's no indication that any crime's been committed, but Davies did leave some baby things with the Backhouses, which tends to back up his story that Judy – that's the kid's name – was going to be looked after by somebody other than his wife. The Backhouses say they don't know anything about it. They also said that Davies and his wife rowed a lot, and that he told them she'd upped and left him.'

'Odd that she didn't take the baby, sir, if that's the case.'

'That's what I thought. But she might be with Davies's mother, so we'd better go round there and see.'

'Righty-ho, sir.'

'I'll fill you in about the rest on the way. Backhouse said

that Davies had a bit of a reputation for telling stories, so I suppose it's not impossible that this is one of them. Seems a bit drastic, though.'

Ballard raised his eyebrows and gave a silent whistle. 'You can say that again, sir.'

Chapter Four

'I don't know what's going on.' Mrs Davies, neat and upright, with tight grey curls like steel wool, looked baffled. 'Muriel and Judy were supposed to be stopping with her father in Brighton, that's all I know about it.' Her voice was a Welsh sing-song, and as she spoke she rubbed her hands down the sides of her overalled hips. 'John told me, but I know that's not right because I wrote to Mr Binney – that's Muriel's father – and he says she's never been near the place. I've hardly slept since I had his telegram, I can tell you. I've no idea where Muriel is, or the baby – and she could write to me, even if John can't.'

'He can't write?'

Mrs Davies shook her head. 'Not much more than his signature. Missed a lot of school, you see – he was poorly when he was a boy, in and out of hospital. I can't understand why Muriel's not been in touch. I've always been good to her . . .' Seeing that her eyes were wet, Stratton hastily averted his own, looking around her neat, comfortable front room – the perfectly squared antimacassars, the symmetry of ornaments and photographs on the mantelpiece – while she collected herself. Her matronly dignity and obvious pride in her home reminded him of his mother-in-law, Nellie – dead now, like Jenny his wife. He'd been deliberately circumspect about what he'd told Mrs Davies, with no mention of bodies put down drains, but it was obvious that she was already both desperately worried and very angry.

'I've done my best to help them both, but I'm at the end of my tether. Why would John say that Mr Backhouse had taken Judy off somewhere? It doesn't make any sense, and I don't know anything about these people John says are looking after her. I had a letter from my sister saying he's been stopping with them in Wales since the fourteenth. I wrote and told her she's welcome to him. It's like I told her, I've no idea where Muriel and Judy have gone to. If she's left him and taken the baby, nobody's told me about it. And I've had all sorts of people coming up here, saying John owes them money. I put my name down, guarantee for the furniture, and this is what I get . . . His name stinks round here, I can tell you, and I'm sick of his nonsense. I'm sorry, Inspector, but that's the truth.'

'When you say "nonsense", Mrs Davies,' said Stratton, 'what do you mean?'

'Making up stories – like this business about Mr Backhouse and the baby. He's always doing it. Telling people his father was an Italian count and he's going to have a Rolls-Royce and an aeroplane and heaven knows what else. All lies and boasting. You don't want to believe a word of it. Never had the education, see? We've done our best for him. And as for saying that about Judy, even if Muriel has gone off and left him . . .' Mrs Davies spread her hands in a gesture of hopelessness.

'When was the last time you saw Muriel, Mrs Davies?'

'A Saturday, it was. The beginning of November. We went shopping with John. I bought a little chair for Judy and a pram for the new baby.'

'Muriel is expecting, is she?'

'Yes, she is, so I don't know what she thinks she's playing at, going off like that.' Mouth pursed in condemnation, Mrs Davies shook her head.

'And she didn't say anything to you about getting rid of the baby?'

'Oh, no.' Mrs Davies looked shocked. 'Nothing like that. I really don't know what to say, Inspector. I'm ashamed of John, and that's the truth. I'd have looked after Judy if he and Muriel were having difficulties, he knows I would. It's been nothing but arguments between them for I don't know how long. John's got a temper on him all right, ever since he was a boy, but the fault's not all on his side, mind – Muriel's a nice girl, but she's terrible with the housekeeping. Always asking John for more . . . I'm not saying she was spending the money on new things for herself, but she never seemed to have enough. She's very young, of course, and not having had a mother so long I suppose she never had anyone to set an example. John should have been more patient with her. You don't like to speak ill of your own, but . . .'

'Poor woman,' said Stratton as, having secured a photograph of Muriel – pretty and delicate, with brown hair and doe eyes – they clattered down the stairs and into the street. 'Obviously at the end of her tether.'

'I don't blame her, sir. Sounds as if Davies isn't quite right in the head.'

'I don't know about that, but he certainly seems to have trouble telling the truth . . . We need to find that baby. I'll make another call to Merthyr Tydfil – perhaps they'll be able to shed a bit more light on the situation.'

'How's your nipper?' asked Stratton, as the car took them back to West End Central. 'Still giving you sleepless nights?' Ballard, married two years before to Policewoman – now former-Policewoman – Gaines, had a six-month-old daughter.

The sergeant's face lit up. 'You should see her, sir. She's a smasher. And she's sleeping a lot better now.'

'Bet that's a relief,' said Stratton.

'You can say that again . . . How are yours, sir? Your boy'll be called up for National Service any day, won't he?'

Always a good working partnership, their relationship had, since Jenny's death at the hands of a madwoman, included regular enquiries about each other's families. Stratton, who had never before shared any information about his home life with a colleague, rather liked it – or some of it, anyway. He thought that Ballard did too, or at least pretended he did. At any rate, he always seemed to remember what Stratton told him about Monica and Pete.

'Went last week,' said Stratton. 'And Monica's just got herself a new job. At a film studio, of all things. Make-up and so forth – they're going to train her up a bit.'

'You don't sound very sure about it, sir.'

'Well . . . All those arty types . . . Mind you, she says I think the worst of everyone.'

'You've always said she was very sensible, sir.'

'She is. Takes after her mother.' That, he told himself, was no more than the truth. Every day, it seemed that something about Monica – her common sense, her kindness, even the way she laughed with her hand in front of her mouth – reminded him of Jenny. She looked like Jenny, too, the same curvaceous figure and creamy skin. The only thing that was different was her black hair, inherited from him. And, unlike Pete, he could talk about Monica, and think about her, without feeling guilty. The problem was his failure to engage with the boy – not that Pete ever seemed to want to be engaged with – or even, really, to 'get on' with him, in the six years since Jenny died.

Feeling that some of this might somehow have communicated itself to Ballard, he hastily changed the subject.

'Nothing?' echoed DC Williams, on the line from Merthyr Tydfil.

'Not a thing. And what's more,' added Stratton, 'it took four of us to lift the manhole cover.'

'Well, this one couldn't do much by himself. I'd say he's no more than five feet five inches high, and puny with it.'

'Obviously makes up in imagination for what he lacks in height, then.'

'*Arglwydd Mawr . . .*'

Stratton, taking this to be the Welsh equivalent of 'Good

God', sympathised entirely with the man's heartfelt tone. There followed some further exasperated muttering, and then Williams said, 'Well, I'd better see what he's got to say for himself. The strange thing is, he was desperate to talk to me. Said he couldn't sleep and wanted to get it off his chest. Tell you the truth, I'm not sure he's all there ... Seems a bit of a simpleton to me.'

Satisfied that there was nothing further he could do for the present, Stratton spent the next few hours writing up reports on, variously, a receiver who'd been found in possession of knocked-off goods ranging from whisky to tinned salmon; an inside job on a warehouse which had resulted in the theft of 20,000 pairs of nylons; and a disturbance at a Wardour Street club during which a Maltese pimp had been stabbed.

At five o'clock, Ballard put his head round the door of the office. 'Williams is on the line,' he said, 'from Wales. Says Davies has changed his story.'

Chapter Five

Stratton hung up the telephone receiver. 'Well,' he said to Ballard, 'Miss Harris will take down the full statement, but now the gist is that Davies is claiming he lied to protect Backhouse. He says Backhouse volunteered to abort Muriel but it went wrong, and when he got back from work Backhouse told him she'd died. He says she was bleeding from the mouth when he saw her, which makes bugger-all sense. And he says Backhouse showed him some sort of medical book beforehand and said he'd had some training as a doctor so he knew how to get rid of the pregnancy . . .' Stratton paused to consult his notes. 'Says he helped Backhouse carry the body downstairs to the first-floor flat, which was empty, and Backhouse told him he was going to put the body in the drain, and that he'd take the baby to some people in Euston who'd look after her . . . Claims that Backhouse told him to sell all his furniture, get rid of Muriel's clothes to a rag dealer, and bugger off back home to the valleys, so that's what he did. Williams is going to have a word with the relatives he's been staying with – it's his aunt and her husband, a Mr and Mrs Howells – to see if they can shed any light on things. Williams is of the opinion – and I can't say I blame him – that Davies is off his head.'

'Sounds very much like it, sir.'

'Either that or he's buggering us about for some reason. Williams said when he first spoke to Davies and told him the body wasn't in the drain, Davies couldn't believe it. Kept insisting it must be because he'd put it there. Then he said he'd lied about the lorry driver in the café giving him the stuff for Muriel and he wanted to make another statement. Not that this one sounds any more plausible ... Oh, and Williams says he seems to be illiterate, apart from signing his name. Had to have his statement read back to him because he couldn't manage it himself.'

'His mother said that too, sir.'

'She did, didn't she? Perhaps Muriel's run off with another chap and it's sent Davies round the bend. Stranger things have happened, after all.'

'Then why not leave the baby with his mother, sir?'

'She'd have asked questions, wouldn't she? "Where's Muriel? Why isn't she here?" And if he didn't want to admit that she'd left him ... Mind you, Williams also said that Davies wanted us to ask Backhouse the name of the people who'd taken Judy, so that doesn't really add up.' Stratton sighed. 'So, we still don't actually know if any crime's been committed, but we've got to find that child.'

'That seems about the size of it, sir. Back to Paradise Street, is it?'

*

There were only two lamps in Paradise Street, but faint yellow gaslight could be seen through the thin curtains hanging in the windows. All the children had gone indoors. Apart from the trains, any noise now was coming from the goods yard on the other side of the wall at the end. Revving and bawled instructions – 'Go on, right hand down, straighten 'er up . . . Whoa!' – as the twelve-ton lorries were parked, and heavy thumps as goods – Stratton imagined rows of unidentifiable lumps shrouded in canvas – were loaded up for the night's run.

Backhouse poked his head round the door of number ten in the manner of a tortoise expecting attack. Seeing Stratton and Ballard he gave a weak cough and said, in a voice barely above a whisper, 'Inspector?'

'If we might come in for a moment, sir? This is my sergeant, Ballard.'

'Of course. Always glad to help.'

'We'd like to have a look at the Davies's flat, if you don't mind, and then we've got a few questions.'

Backhouse frowned. 'Well, I don't know . . . I don't mean to be obstructive, but there's the matter of—'

'It is rather urgent, Mr Backhouse,' said Stratton. 'I'm sure that, having served in the police force yourself, you'll understand that Judy's safety is paramount.'

As Stratton had hoped, this comradely appeal to Backhouse's vanity did the trick, and he stood back to let them enter. 'On this occasion, I don't suppose . . . It's the top floor. The flats aren't separated – no front doors – so you'll have no trouble.'

'Who lives on the first floor?' asked Stratton.

'Mr Gardiner. An elderly gentleman. He's in hospital at present – been there for the past two months.'

'Has the flat been empty during that time?'

'That's right. I shan't accompany you, Inspector.' He rubbed his back. 'I think I may have mentioned – I suffer with fibrositis.'

At least, thought Stratton, as they went up the stairs, what Davies had said about the first-floor flat being empty was true – the first thing, as far as he could see, that actually was. 'It's a bit bloody dark up here,' he said, as they got to the top landing. Seeing the shape of a gas bracket protruding from the wall, he pulled his matches out of his pocket and felt for the tap. He turned it, but there was no hiss of escaping gas. 'Looks like we'll have to put a shilling in the meter.'

He opened the door to the room at the front of the house. The curtains were open, and, even by the faint glow that reached them from the street lamp, they could see that the room was entirely empty. The back room was the kitchen. Stratton located the meter and dropped a coin in the slot, and Ballard put a match to the gas mantle. They saw a sink, an Ascot water heater, a gas stove, and a few shelves, which were bare of everything except a couple of saucepans, a vase and a clock. On the other side of the room was a fireplace. Whatever else had been in the room – table, chairs – had been removed. Dusty, battered wooden boards covered the floor and a thin patterned paper, greyish, torn in places or sagging, lined the walls. It was darkened in the cooking area by spots of grease, but Stratton could see its original cream colour from a lighter rectangle over the mantelpiece, where a mirror or picture had been removed. The bottom half of the single sash window at the back was covered by a grimy net curtain. Raising it, Stratton made out the backs of the terrace beyond, and was staring down into the garden below when Ballard said, 'There's a briefcase here, sir, and there's some newspaper cuttings on the mantelpiece.'

'Oh?' Stratton lowered the curtain.

Ballard opened the briefcase and rummaged inside. 'Just a few bits of paper in here. Looks as if it belongs to a Mr G. Parker . . . there's an address. Nicked, would you say?'

'Possibly. I can't imagine why a van driver would need a briefcase. We'll find out if it's been reported as stolen. What about the cuttings?'

'Four of them, all about Setty. You know, the torso murder last year.'

'Let's just hope we don't find bits of Mrs Davies all over the Essex marshes, then.'

'It's a bit odd, though, sir, when Williams said Davies is illiterate. Why would he keep cuttings if he couldn't read them?'

'Perhaps his wife was interested – or she read them to him. Any dates?'

'Can't see any, sir, but it happened in October, didn't it, and if Mrs Davies left here three weeks ago, that would be about the ninth of November–'

'So it's possible,' concluded Stratton. 'Mind you, if he was working as a van driver he must have been able to read labels and road signs and things, mustn't he?'

'Perhaps he can do individual words but not a whole lot together.'

'Perhaps.' Stratton sighed. 'Well, wherever his missus has got to, she's not here now.'

'And if she's not here . . .' Ballard continued his train of thought, 'then presumably she's not lying dead somewhere in this house, sir.'

'I should think the Backhouses would have noticed a body on the premises, wouldn't you? And he said they'd had builders here, too, remember? No, I think she's gone off somewhere. Let's just hope she's taken the baby with her.'

Mr and Mrs Backhouse were in the kitchen. Backhouse was sitting in the deckchair – Stratton saw Ballard's eyes widen slightly when he saw the knotted-rope sling – and beside him, curled up on a rag mat, was a black-and-white mongrel.

'Is it yours?' asked Stratton.

'Yes,' said Backhouse, looking fondly at the animal, which thumped its tail on the floor. 'Dora, her name is.'

'Friendly, is she?'

'Oh, yes.'

Stratton crouched down to pat the animal, which responded, delighted, by rolling over so that he could rub her belly.

'We were just about to have a little cup of tea. Would you like one?'

'No, thanks.' Stratton stood up and smiled at Mrs Backhouse, who was standing in front of the sink, twisting a tea towel in her hands and looking agitated. 'Just a couple of questions, and we'll leave you in peace. We found some newspaper cuttings about the torso murder. Do you know why they would be there?'

'He was interested in that sort of thing,' said Backhouse. 'He couldn't read much himself, but his wife used to read them to him, didn't she, Edna?' Before Mrs Backhouse could respond, he continued, 'You'll excuse me not getting up, but my back's been playing me up again. We're both very worried, Inspector. This whole thing is very regrettable—'

'The baby,' Mrs Backhouse interrupted, with a force that surprised Stratton. 'Have you found her?'

'Not yet,' said Stratton. 'But we're doing everything we can.'

'Edna's very upset,' said Backhouse. 'We both are.'

'Of course. Were you aware, Mrs Backhouse, that Muriel was pregnant?'

Again, Backhouse got in first. 'There was something – I wondered if I should have mentioned it this morning. Muriel did tell my wife that she was pregnant, and she wasn't happy about it. With only the two rooms, she couldn't see how they were going to manage, and she was worried about money. She told Edna she'd been using pills and syringes trying to give herself a miscarriage, didn't she, dear?'

Mrs Backhouse, looking more distressed than ever, made a noise that sounded as if a sob was locked in her throat, and nodded.

'We both told her to stop acting so silly,' said Backhouse. 'She was making herself a physical wreck.'

'When did she tell you this?' Stratton asked Mrs Backhouse.

'I think . . . a couple of days before she left . . .' She stopped and looked at her husband for confirmation.

'It's all right, dear ... You can see how upset it's made her,' Backhouse reiterated. 'Muriel was in a bad way. She promised she wouldn't do anything silly, but I don't know–' He broke off, wincing, and bent forward to rub the small of his back.

'Did you suggest to Davies that you could help his wife to get rid of the baby, Mr Backhouse?'

Backhouse blinked several times before saying, 'I'm sorry, I don't understand what you mean.'

'Davies alleges that you showed him a medical book, and said you could help his wife abort her pregnancy.'

'That's nonsense,' said Backhouse, firmly. 'He's making it up.' He pursed his lips, then took off his glasses and began to polish them, slowly, with his handkerchief.

'Have you ever trained as a doctor?'

'No.'

'Did you tell Davies you'd trained as a doctor?'

'Certainly not. It's a lie.'

'Did you show him a medical book?'

'No, Inspector, I did not.'

'Do you have any medical books?' asked Stratton.

Backhouse thought for a moment, then said, 'I have a manual from the St John's Ambulance. I had it when I did first aid, during the war. I also,' he added, with a touch of pride, 'have two certificates. But I don't see . . .' Turning to Mrs Backhouse, he said, 'Would you have shown the book to Davies for some reason?'

Edna Backhouse shook her head in bewilderment. She was, thought Stratton, on the verge of tears.

'This is all made up,' said Backhouse. 'I don't know why he's saying these things.'

'I understand,' said Stratton soothingly. 'I'm sorry we had to disturb you, but that's everything – at least for the time being.'

'It's no trouble, Inspector.' Backhouse began to struggle out of the deckchair, but Stratton put up a restraining hand.

'Don't worry, we can see ourselves out.'

'Thank you, Inspector. If there's anything else, we're always glad to oblige.'

'Nice dog,' said Stratton, as they made their way back to the station. 'Didn't see her before. You certainly couldn't hide a body in there for three weeks without *her* knowing about it. Even if you buried it in the garden she'd have it up in no time.'

'Unless she's lost her sense of smell,' said Ballard. 'If that's possible.'

'Never heard of it,' said Stratton. 'What do you think of the Backhouses?'

'She seems a bit cowed by him, doesn't she?'

'Well, he certainly did the talking for both of them, but that's not unusual – not where we're concerned, anyway – and she's obviously pretty bothered about the whole thing, which is understandable. What a mess ... I don't know about you, but last time I looked at a St John's Ambulance handbook, it didn't say anything about how to perform an abortion.'

'Another fairy story, sir.'

'Seems like it. Anyway, we need to know what the hell is going on, and I think it's high time we brought Davies to London. We can have him for that briefcase, if nothing else – I'd be willing to bet a hefty sum that it's been pinched. I'll speak to DCI Lamb when we get back.'

Ballard grimaced. 'Best of luck with that, sir.'

'Thanks,' said Stratton. 'I've a feeling I'm going to need it.'

Chapter Six

DCI Lamb let out a gusty sigh. Stratton was familiar with the man's repertoire of noises indicative of exasperation and forbearance, and recognised this one as meaning that the person in front of him – in this case, himself – was arsing about, wasting time, and generally testing his superior's patience to the limit. Lamb, whose resemblance to George Formby seemed actually to be increasing as he grew older, took any deviation from by-the-book policing as a personal insult, and had long regarded him, Stratton, as the chief culprit. In his lighter moments, Stratton had often wondered if what his superior would really like would be for him to arrest himself, lock himself in a cell and beat himself up while he was at it.

'Let me get this clear,' said Lamb. 'You've no idea where this woman's body is – assuming that she is actually dead – and, more importantly, the baby's disappeared and you have no clue as to where she is, and everyone you've spoken to, including his own mother, thinks that Davies is off his head. Besides which, the chances of Backhouse and his wife failing to notice that they are sharing a house with a corpse are – to say the least – slender.'

'That's about the size of it, sir.'

'And Backhouse was a special constable, for God's sake! If *he* says Davies is off his rocker . . . Incidentally, Stratton, I hope you're treating him with a bit of respect.'

'Of course, sir.'

Lamb sighed again, looking more put-upon than ever. 'Nothing's ever straightforward with you, is it, Stratton?'

'With respect, sir–'

'Yes, yes, yes.' Lamb waved a hand in irritable dismissal. 'Let's just get this sorted out as soon as possible, shall we? You say that the briefcase has been reported as stolen, so get Davies up here for that.'

'Right away, sir.'

'Wait. On second thoughts, I'll send someone else to Merthyr Tydfil for Davies. You're to search the house, and for God's sake make sure you do it thoroughly.'

'Now, sir?'

'Yes, now!'

'It's going to be difficult in the garden, sir. In the dark.'

'Take a bloody torch, man. I want a full report on my desk before Davies is brought in.'

'Yes, sir.' Stratton tried to compose his features into a semblance of eager obedience.

'Don't stand there making faces – get over to Marlborough Street for the warrant.'

Going down the corridor to collect Ballard, Stratton relieved his feelings by singing 'When I'm Cleaning Windows' in a voice that he judged to be almost – but not quite – audible in his superior's office.

Having secured an emergency warrant from the magistrate's court, Stratton and Ballard made their way back to Paradise Street. By the time they reached number ten, it was after nine o'clock. 'Let's hope the poor sods aren't having an early night,' said Stratton grimly as they waited, stamping their feet in the cold, for the door to be answered.

When Backhouse answered the door he was dressed, as before, in a collarless shirt, and trousers held up in the old-fashioned way with braces and a belt. He did the bad ventriloquist thing with his mouth, then took off his pebble glasses and polished them on a handkerchief, blinking myopically. Behind him, in the gloom of the hallway, stood Mrs Backhouse, who had taken off her overall to reveal a dark-green frock.

'Sorry to call back at this late hour, Mr Backhouse. We have a warrant to search the premises.'

Backhouse jammed his glasses back on his nose and stared at the two of them. 'Now?'

'I'm afraid so, sir.' Stratton produced the paper. 'May we come in? We're anxious to get this matter cleared up – as I'm sure you are.'

'It's all very unpleasant.' Backhouse grimaced and rubbed the small of his back with both hands. 'My wife's nerves . . . she was just about to take a sleeping pill and go off to bed.'

Behind him, Edna Backhouse nodded in tearful confirmation of this.

'We'll be as quick as we can, I assure you,' said Stratton soothingly.

They started at the top of the house, in the two rooms which had been the Davies's flat, then moved downstairs to Mr Gardiner's flat on the first floor. Sparsely furnished, it yielded nothing apart from the fact that its tenant had once worked on the railways and was a staunch supporter of the Conservative Party.

They returned down the narrow staircase and, watched in silence by Backhouse and Edna, they inspected first the ground-floor living room, which faced the street – utility furniture, a radiogram, a few books and a dejected-looking plant, as well as the framed first-aid certificates Backhouse had mentioned and a photograph of him, smiling proudly, in his police uniform – then the bedroom at the back, and finally, the kitchen. There was, as Stratton had predicted, nothing at all to suggest that Muriel Davies had ever been there, alive or otherwise. 'Now, if you don't mind,' said Stratton, turning to Backhouse, 'we'll need to see the garden. Is the back door unlocked?'

Backhouse looked puzzled. 'Yes, it's always unlocked, but there's only the lavatory and the washhouse out there, and there's no light. I can assure you–'

'I'm sorry,' said Stratton firmly, 'but we do have to look.' He pulled his torch from his overcoat pocket. 'If you'll keep the dog inside for the time being . . .'

The 'garden', which consisted of a yard and a muddy patch of lawn strewn with broken bricks and the corrugated-iron remains of an Anderson shelter, was no more than thirty feet by twelve. By the light of the torch, Stratton made out a lopsided washing-line post, the rusty shell of a dustbin, old newspapers, some gnawed bones that looked like chops, a lot of weeds, some dusty-looking bushes and the sooty wall of the goods yard. On the top of it a cat, disturbed by the noise and light, fled with dainty tightrope-walker's steps into the darkness beyond.

Stratton checked the lavatory and, finding it empty, turned his attention to the fractionally larger washhouse beside it. 'These are used by all the tenants, are they?' he asked Backhouse, who was walking up and down the yard, rubbing his back and biting his lip as if in pain.

'That's right.'

'Bit stiff.' Stratton tried, and failed, to open the washhouse door.

'It gets jammed,' said Backhouse. Turning to his wife, who was standing on the threshold of the back door, shoulders hunched and arms crossed against the cold, he said, 'Fetch a knife, Edna.'

Edna Backhouse disappeared and returned a moment later with a kitchen knife which she inserted into the lock, and, after wiggling it for a few moments, managed to open the door. Shining his torch in, Stratton saw a room of about five feet square with an old copper covered by a plank of wood on which stood several tins of paint and varnish, presumably left behind by the builders Backhouse had mentioned. Next to it was a square stone sink with a single tap. A row of battered-looking planks of wood was propped up vertically in front of it.

'Those are from the hall,' said Backhouse. 'The builders gave them to me for firewood.'

Stratton nudged the plank a few inches and peered into the copper, but saw nothing except dust. 'We don't use the washhouse any more,' Backhouse explained. 'Only for storing things and emptying slops . . . there's nothing more to see.'

Stratton pulled back one of the planks standing before the sink and shone his torch into the space behind. The beam illuminated what appeared to be a green-and-white-checked tablecloth, tied round with sash cord. He pulled a couple more of the planks away and saw that it was wrapped round a large parcel. Standing back, he motioned to Mrs Backhouse. 'Do you know what this is?' he asked. 'Is it your tablecloth?'

Edna Backhouse bent forward and peered at the bundle for a moment. Straightening up, she said, 'It's not one of mine. I've no idea what's in it.'

'Well, let's have it out.' Aided by Ballard, Stratton pulled the bundle – which was heavy – into the yard. 'You don't mind if we cut the cord?' he asked Mrs Backhouse.

Frowning, shaking her head, she said, 'No. I told you, it's not mine.'

Stratton took out his pocket knife and, his torch held steady between his teeth, cut the sash cord. As soon as it was loosened, one end of the green cloth raised itself up and, with jerky acceleration as of some ghastly mechanical toy, a pair of female feet and legs slid out onto the cement of the yard.

There was a sharp indrawn breath from Edna Backhouse, then silence, thick as a fog. After a long moment during which no one moved, spoke or even seemed to breathe, Ballard's voice came from inside the washhouse. 'That's not all, sir. There's a baby.'

Chapter Seven

Diana's high heels echoed on the stone floor as she walked into the hall of Hambeyn House, startling a pair of wood pigeons so that they flapped upwards and away through the broken window at the top of the main staircase. The lower windows – those that had retained their glass – were opaque with dirt, and their decorative plasterwork surrounds were yellowing and crumbly like stale cake icing.

Shivering, she pulled the collar of her fur coat close around her neck and skirted the evidence of the birds' occupancy – by the look of things, there had been more than just two pigeons – to stand at the bottom of the staircase. The curved iron banister looked like the ribs of a dinosaur and, halfway up, a thin ray of winter sunlight illuminated an obscenity scrawled across the khaki-painted wall – left there, presumably, by a departing soldier. The words, Diana thought, were indicative of the fact that her childhood home, and what it symbolised, were obsolete in the new, post-war world.

Sitting in the train on the way up to Gloucestershire, the burst of confidence she'd felt on leaving Guy had ebbed away, and, in an attempt to lift her spirits, she'd convinced herself that somebody – a school, a nursing home, even an asylum – would want to buy the place. This hope had been all but demolished when the driver of the station taxi, hearing her destination, had looked aghast and said, 'You sure, miss?' Even so, she hadn't expected it to look quite so derelict. The house was a wreck, and she'd heard enough tales of woe from the owners of other properties requisitioned by the forces to know that whatever compensation she might be awarded would be too little to do much about it. Besides, it seemed to her that it was already too late.

It was hard to believe she'd ever lived here. The place was like an abandoned stage set for a play so long out of fashion that it was impossible to imagine how anyone could have enjoyed it. Not daring to go up the stairs, she recrossed the hall and walked down the corridor to the dining room, where she found more khaki and grey paint, loose – and in some places, missing – floorboards and heaps of rubbish in the once magnificent fireplaces. Gingerly, she made her way over to the windows and stood looking out over the terrace. Weeds had sprung up between the flagstones, and piles of cigarette ends in the bowls of the long-disused ornamental fountains had combined with rainwater to create a few inches of brownish nicotine soup. The lawn beyond was rutted with tyre tracks and the flowerbeds claimed by banks of nettles.

Hambeyn House was dead. Nothing – not repairs or fresh paint, even supposing these could be got, nor the joyful barking of dogs or even the laughter of children – could bring it back to life. At least, thought Diana, I don't feel sentimental about it. Being a lonely only child – her sole sibling, a boy, had not survived babyhood – with a distant father, an aloof mother and a series of nannies with cold, perfunctory hands had seen to that. She dredged her memory for anything that would kindle a spark of feeling, but nothing came. At least, she thought, turning away from the window, there are no death duties, because there's certainly no money to pay them. Her spendthrift father, who'd sold off parcel after parcel of land in his lifetime, had left her only a few thousand pounds, and as for what she'd get from Guy . . .

But I don't want to depend on anybody, she thought. For the first time in my life, I want to stand on my own two feet.

She would go to London. When she was dreaming of escape from Guy and Evie, that had always been her plan, but now, for the first time, she began to give it a practical form – impossible before, as Evie had a nasty habit of opening other people's letters 'by accident' and Diana knew, from bitter experience, just how vengeful her mother-in-law could be.

At least she'd had the good sense to ask the taxi to wait. She'd return to the station, collect her bags, and telephone to her friend Lally before she boarded the train. Lally, who'd been a fellow MI5 agent during the war, and was now married to another old colleague, Jock Anderson, would surely let her stay while she found herself a job. Jock, who still worked for the Secret Service, might be able to help her with that. There was their former boss, too, Colonel Forbes-James – he might know of something. She'd find herself a small flat like the one she'd had in Tite Street during the war, and she'd make a brand new start.

Chapter Eight

'A well-nourished adult woman, five feet two inches in height, estimated weight seven and a half stone. The body has been tied up in a tablecloth. It is dressed in a blue woollen jacket, a spotted cotton blouse and a black skirt. The skirt has been disarranged so that the lower parts are exposed. Knickers and stockings are absent . . .'

Dr McNally, the pathologist, looked like a clergyman – spare and ascetic in his white gown and rubber apron, with spectacles perched on his nose – and as he solemnly intoned the words, dictating to his secretary, Miss Lynn, he sounded like one, too. The Middlesex Hospital mortuary, to which both bodies had been removed, was a cold, low-ceilinged abattoir, its tiles and metal and porcelain surfaces gleaming in the harsh overhead light. It smelt of a mixture of decomposition and disinfectant. A tap dripped, and bronchitic coughing could be heard, intermittently, from somewhere in the basement corridor outside.

The pathologist turned to his assistant, a wizened little man called Higgs, who had been there for as long as Stratton could remember, working for McNally's predecessor, Dr Byrne, who had been murdered in 1944. 'You may begin removing the clothes.' To Stratton, he said, 'You'll be making a list, I trust.'

'That's correct.'

Ballard produced his notebook and pencil, and wrote down each piece of clothing as it was removed. Finally naked, lying flat on the slab, neck resting on a wooden block and head tilted back on a white towel, the woman – confirmed as Muriel Davies by the Backhouses, but not yet formally identified – looked as though she were snarling like a dog. The woman in the older Mrs Davies's photograph had been quite a looker, but now her upper lip was puffy and slightly drawn back from the teeth and there was a dark area – bruising and dried blood – around her nose and mouth. That, thought Stratton, explained the 'bleeding from the mouth' comment in Davies's second statement – the bastard had thumped her first. Her eyes were closed, and one was blackened. Stratton could see that her neck was bruised, and that the body contours were beginning to disappear. There were maggots clustered on the mound of her left breast, as if suckling. Averting his eyes from this, Stratton noticed that her left hand was unadorned. 'You didn't remove her wedding ring, did you?' he asked Higgs.

The assistant shook his head. 'Never touch nothing till I'm told.'

'She *was* married, was she?' asked McNally.

'So we understand,' said Stratton. 'Perhaps she'd taken it off for some reason. Sorry to interrupt. Please . . .' He gestured at the pathologist to continue his work.

*

McNally had been dictating for some time, medical terminology, most of which Stratton didn't understand, letting it wash over him and deliberately keeping his eyes off the baby, who, lying on the slab next door to the mother, made a pathetically small shape under the white sheet. Ballard, he could see, was doing the same. Worse for him, thought Stratton, with a baby daughter himself. Something McNally said caught his attention. '. . . There are a series of abrasions three and a half inches long on the right side of the throat, varying from one and a quarter inches in width to three-eighths of an inch. On the left side of the back of the neck is another group of abrasions . . .'

'So she was strangled?' asked Stratton.

'It would appear so,' said McNally, 'but I can't be certain until I've finished. Would you like me to move to the child now, and do the internal examinations later?'

'Please. If you don't mind.'

McNally finished his dictation, then motioned to Higgs to cover up the body. When the baby was unveiled, Stratton saw that its face was swollen and bluish. It was wearing a fancy knitted cardigan and a dress, and had a large white handkerchief wrapped around its neck, but its legs and feet were bare. The sight of the tiny, wrinkled soles was almost more than Stratton could stand, and he turned away, blowing his nose.

'The body is of a well-nourished baby girl. Height is thirty-three and a half inches . . .' McNally held up his hand to indicate that Miss Lynn should stop writing. 'Start removing the clothes, please, Higgs.'

The procedure was repeated, with Ballard noting down the items. After taking off the top clothes, Higgs fumbled at something stuck inside the vest. 'Something in here, sir. Aha ... here it is. One toy duck.' He held it up for Ballard and Stratton to see. It was a small, cheap thing, but, judging by its worn appearance, much loved. Stratton felt a lump rise in his throat.

'One ... toy ... duck,' repeated Ballard in a choked voice, writing in his notebook. Then he looked up, and Stratton saw that there were tears in his eyes. Clearing his throat, he said, 'If you could excuse me for a moment, sir ...'

'Of course.' Stratton took the notebook and pencil. 'Get yourself some air.'

Ballard left the room in a rush and, after a moment's silence, Higgs continued, 'One white handkerchief.'

'One white handkerchief.' Stratton wrote it down and kept his eyes on the page, waiting for the next item. A sharply indrawn breath made him look up and he saw that tied tightly round the baby's neck was a man's tie. 'Strangled,' he said.

'Certainly looks like it,' said McNally. 'Poor little thing.'

After a moment, Higgs said, 'Shall I carry on, sir?'

'Yes.'

'One vest.'

'One ... vest.'

'One nappy.'

'One ... nappy.'

'One nappy pin.'

'One ... nappy ... pin.'

'You all right, Mr Stratton?'

Unable to speak further, Stratton simply nodded.

'If you need some air . . .' Higgs continued.

Stratton swallowed. 'Yes. I'll be . . . outside.'

As he left the room, McNally was saying, 'Decomposition is most advanced in the upper part of the body . . .'

'Sorry about that, sir.' Ballard was in the yard, white-faced and leaning against the wall.

'No need to apologise. Cigarette?'

'Thank you.'

They smoked in silence for a moment before Stratton, feeling that he ought to say something, no matter how inadequate, said quietly, 'Terrible business.'

'Yes.' Ballard, staring down at his feet, shook his head. 'Just . . .'

'I know. Doesn't do to dwell on it.'

'Hard not to, sir.'

'Yes, it is.' Stratton allowed his hand to rest, momentarily, on the sergeant's shoulder. 'Never gets any easier, unfortunately.'

'Katy's got a little duck like that. Sleeps with it tucked in next to her . . . Duck and Teddy. She has to have those, or she can't settle.'

'Mine were the same at that age.'

'You can't help remembering, can you, sir?'

Stratton shook his head. 'Wouldn't be human if you didn't. The mother's about the same age as Monica.'

'Makes you sick.' Ballard shook his head again, then said, 'Someone's going to have to identify them formally.'

'Yes, they are. I suppose we'll have to ask Mrs Davies tomorrow. Poor woman.'

'How could he do it, sir?' Ballard burst out. 'Davies. How could he strangle his own daughter?'

'I don't know,' said Stratton. 'It's not as if we haven't had cases of people killing their own children before, but not like this. I suppose he must be off his head.'

'The bodies are in very good condition, considering the length of time,' said McNally later, as they sat in his office.

'Which was?'

'Approximately three weeks, I'd say.'

'For both of them?'

'Yes.'

'I certainly didn't notice a smell when we opened the wash-house,' said Stratton. 'Did you, Ballard?'

'No, sir. Nothing at all.'

'It would have been pretty cold,' said McNally, who'd been called to view the bodies *in situ*. 'Not refrigeration conditions, but not too far off, otherwise the decomposition would be far more advanced. Incidentally, the woman was pregnant – a male foetus, about sixteen weeks along.'

Reminded instantly and vividly of Jenny, Stratton swallowed hard before he spoke. 'Any sign of interference?'

'No. A small amount of bruising to the . . .' McNally looked at his notes, 'posterior wall of the vagina, but that's not indicative. Just to clarify – you said that the woman has been provisionally identified as Muriel Davies, aged nineteen, and the child is . . .'

'Judy Davies. According to our information at the scene of discovery, she's fourteen months old.'

'That seems about right.' McNally wrote it down at the top of his notes. 'Both strangled by ligature – the tie, in the case of the infant.'

'And the mother?'

'Well, there was nothing on the body, so one can't be sure. A piece of cord, perhaps—'

'The sash cord used to tie up the blanket?'

'Possibly. Or a scarf or even a stocking. As I said, it's impossible to be certain. There's enough decomposition there to muddy the waters, I'm afraid. There's some bruising on the legs . . .' McNally looked at his notes once more, 'the inner aspect of the left thigh, four inches above the knee, and the inner aspect of the left calf directly below the knee, so it's possible she might have been held down – if someone had knelt on her legs, or something of that sort. And, as I'm sure you saw, there were blows to the face. She was only a slip of a thing, and as for the baby . . .' The pathologist shook his head in disgust.

Chapter Nine

Lally hadn't changed much in the last eight years, Diana thought. Tall, elegant and blonde – people had often commented on the similarity in looks between the two of them – she was curled up in one corner of the brocade sofa, smoking a cigarette. The baby having been duly admired and removed to bed, and Jock not having arrived home from work ('some Ministry shindig, darling – frightfully important and bloody annoying because we've got people coming for dinner'), they had their first chance to talk. Since Diana had returned to Hampshire in forty-one they'd communicated mainly by letter, with face-to-face contact restricted to social chit-chat at the occasional party when Diana came up (or rather, was permitted by her mother-in-law to come up) to London.

Lally and Jock Anderson had a large house in Albemarle Street, off Piccadilly. 'It's falling apart,' Lally wailed, as they sat drinking sherry. 'I know the furniture's lovely, but it's all bashed about, and with income tax at nine and six in the pound we can't afford to repair the place – and even if we *could* we'd probably never find anyone to do it. Jock says the roof's in such a state that it won't be long before we're putting out pails to catch the drips when it rains. But we'd love it if you'd stay. Just so long as you've brought your ration book – I'm utterly terrified of upsetting Mrs Robinson in case she decides to retire to her sister's at Bexhill. She's the only help we've got – well, apart from the nanny – and I still can't cook to save my life.'

'I've got it here.' Diana smiled and patted her handbag. Although Lally's flighty breeziness masked a very good brain and Diana would have been happy to bet that she was a lot more competent than she let on, it was clear that, after the excitement of the war, she hadn't settled well, even after five-odd years, into the duller routine of being a wife.

'Oh, good. Anyway, never mind all that. It's too boring for words. What about you? Are you and Guy . . . Is it still awful?'

'We're getting divorced, if that's what you mean.'

'Oh, darling . . . I did wonder when you asked if you could stay. Why on earth didn't you tell me?'

'I wanted to, but it was so difficult to telephone – I couldn't use the one in Guy's office, and Evie was so absolutely hawkish about the house telephone that I became quite neurotic about thinking she'd overhear . . . And she used to open my letters. The ridiculous thing was, I know that she wanted to see the back of me just as much as I wanted to leave, but if she'd thought I was planning it – you know, that it was my idea – she'd have . . . Well, I don't know what she'd have done but she'd certainly have made my life even more unpleasant than it was already. In the end, I managed to get Guy to agree to present it to her as a fait accompli, and he's agreed to let me divorce him, which means that he's got to go through the ghastly charade of being caught with a tart or a barmaid or something. I'm told it may take a while to arrange, but Guy's found someone else – or rather, Evie's found someone else for him, which amounts to the same thing. Local squire's daughter. She's young – about twenty-five – and completely awed by the pair of them. I'm sure they'll have lots of children, which is something I don't seem to be able to manage, but I don't envy her in the least. In fact, I'm quite grateful to her – she means I don't have to feel too guilty about it all. She doesn't know what she's getting herself into, poor thing.'

'With Evie, you mean?'

'Yes. Guy's as much under her thumb as ever. More, I think. I was absolutely astonished when he finally agreed with me about the divorce.'

'It sounds hellish. But he had a bad time, didn't he, being a prisoner? I don't suppose one ever really gets over that sort of thing.'

'He's never spoken about it, but I think it was pretty grim. One was always told not to ask, so I didn't. A lot of nightmares, and he'd never seem to want me to comfort him, or . . . or *anything*, really. He seemed almost to hate women – apart from his bloody mother, that is.'

'It must be hard, though, coming back from *that* and everyone expecting you to get on with things just the same as before.'

'Yes, but Guy *wants* things to be the same as before, and

they're not. I've changed. He's changed. We've all changed – all except Evie.' Diana made a face. 'She's like a . . . I don't know, a monument or something. So sure of herself – as if she's determined not to change, or allow anything to affect her views. Perhaps that's why Guy loves her so much. But I've thought for quite a while that perhaps we were always destined to fail and it would have happened anyway, without the war.'

Lally sipped her drink and looked at Diana intently. 'You're not hoping to run into our old friend Claude Ventriss in London, are you?'

'No!' It came out too loud and vehement, and Diana was horribly aware that she was blushing. Claude – impossibly handsome, with velvet brown eyes – was the agent with whom she'd had the affair during the war.

'Really?' Lally sounded sceptical. 'Because if you are, you're in for a disappointment. The last Jock heard he was in Palestine.'

'*Palestine*? What for?'

'Looking for another war, darling. That's what men like him *do*. He isn't marriage material.'

'I know that! Anyway, it's all in the past.'

Lally raised a warning finger. 'Just as long as it stays there. Claude can cast a very long shadow – believe me, I've seen it happen before. You're better off without him, Diana. Honestly. You're not the first woman to be stupid about Claude—'

'Don't I know it,' said Diana, ruefully.

'—and you won't be the last. But if you really must have

someone to be stupid about, there's plenty of choice. *Everyone's* in London – Peter Calvert, Felix Hyde Thompson, Johnny–'

'I don't want anyone to be stupid about, Lally. I want a job. I thought I'd ask Colonel Forbes-James.'

Lally raised her eyebrows. 'I had the impression that you two parted company on . . . well, less than friendly terms.'

'Yes,' said Diana impatiently, 'but that was *ages* ago. Surely now it's all–'

'Don't be too sure, darling. F-J's wonderful, but he can certainly hold a grudge, and he's in a difficult position. After that business with Neville Apse . . .'

'Don't remind me. I was the one who found him, remember?' Diana shuddered, recalling Apse's body, suspended from the banisters of a fire escape by a pair of braces and hanging like a sack, with bulging eyes, mottled blue cheeks and a swollen, blackened tongue protruding obscenely from his mouth.

'F-J's got a great deal to lose,' said Lally.

'How do you know?' Diana had never discussed F-J's proclivities with anyone apart from Inspector Stratton, and that was back in 1940.

'Jock mentioned something once that made me wonder.'

'But surely,' said Diana, 'it isn't *generally* known?'

'I think it is and it isn't, if you see what I mean. As Jock says, everyone knows everyone. And most of them,' Lally added pointedly, 'went to the same schools. The point is, Diana, that F-J might not be too pleased to see you.'

'Why? I'm no threat to him.'

'That isn't the point, and in any case, he probably won't see it like that.'

Remembering Claude's words when she'd told him about Apse – *That's the thing about buggers, darling. Blackmail. Very simple and very effective* – Diana said, 'But I'm not a . . . I don't know . . . a Russian spy, for goodness' sake.'

'Of course you're not, darling, but you might know – even if you don't know that you know – a man who is.'

'Claude, you mean?'

'I didn't, but I suppose it's possible. He's in Palestine, and Jock says the Soviets are giving the Israelis an awful lot of help.' Lally rolled her eyes. 'Trying to get them to join the club . . . Would you like another drink, darling? It's jolly good, isn't it? Jock knows a lovely wine merchant . . .' She made a dramatic finger-to-lips gesture.

'Thanks.' Diana held out her glass.

As Lally got up to refill it, she said, 'Can't remember if I told you, but he's written a book. Naval history – all very learned. I've been reading bits of it, but it's terribly hard going because his handwriting's impossible.'

'I can type it for him,' said Diana, eagerly. 'I had lots of practice in Hampshire. A woman from the village taught me properly, so I could help Evie with the WVS and billeting and things.' Seeing Lally's raised eyebrows, she added, 'Oh, she was in her element, with the chance to boss so many people around. Honestly, Lally, I'd be delighted to help Jock. It's so good of you to put me up at such short notice – it would be wonderful if I could do *something* in return.'

'I should think Jock would jump at it, but I don't suppose

he'll be back for ages, so why don't–'

Hearing the sound of the front door, Lally stopped. 'That's odd. It can't be anyone else, but he told me–'

She stopped again as Jock Anderson walked into the room, an unhappy tension about him that was a world away from his usual urbane and cheerful self.

'Darling!' Lally sprang off the sofa. 'I thought you were out being grand.'

'Something came up,' he said with heavy irony, dumping his briefcase on the floor and sitting down in the space that Lally had vacated, head in hands. He rubbed his face for a moment, said, 'Christ!' and then, spotting the visitor, 'Evening, Diana. Didn't expect to see you here.'

'She's staying with us, darling.' Lally went to the tray. 'Have you had an awful day? You look as if you could do with a drink.'

'Thanks. Scotch.'

Sensing that she might be surplus to requirements, Diana said, 'Why don't I go and unpack or something?'

Jock put out a restraining hand. 'Thanks, but no need to be tactful. You might as well know. It's F-J.'

'We were just talking about him, weren't we, Lally? What's happened?'

Jock stared at her for a moment, as if he hadn't seen her properly before, and Diana noticed that the muscles in his jaw were clenched. 'He's dead.'

Chapter Ten

'Dead?' Diana echoed the word in disbelief. 'F-J?'

'I'm afraid so. The housekeeper found him this morning, at his flat in Dolphin Square. He'd hanged himself.'

'My God.' Lally handed Jock his drink, her face blank with shock. 'Why? Did he leave a note?'

Jock sighed, a long, uneven sound like a last exhalation. 'He didn't need to explain. He'd been arrested.'

'Arrested? When? For what?'

'Yesterday evening, for importuning.' Jock sounded weary and disgusted. 'In a public lavatory. Chap turned out to be a plain-clothes policeman.'

'I don't understand,' said Lally. 'What was F-J doing there in the first place?'

'Presumably,' said Diana, keeping her tone brisk to disguise her horror and embarrassment, 'he wanted to relieve himself.'

Jock shook his head. 'The place is known for that sort of thing, apparently.'

'But why go in there?' asked Diana, bewilderment giving place, with horrid clarity, to understanding. 'I mean, surely

F-J doesn't – didn't – have to ... well, you know ... Go into public places like that.'

Jock sighed. 'It appears that was the attraction. Meeting a ... a certain type of person. Excitement outside one's social circle. Like a married man who visits a prostitute, I suppose. Really, Diana,' he added irritably, 'I don't understand it any more than you do, but that's what happened.'

Diana thought of the night in Apse's flat during an air-raid when, hidden inside a cupboard, she'd overheard his conversation with the male tart he'd brought home, the unlikely coquettishness in his tone, and the rhythmic noises of their congress.

'F-J said he was a fool to think he could get away with it,' said Jock. 'Mind you, he said the policeman came up to him first, but the policeman said it was the other way round, and of course there's no doubt as to who would have been believed.'

'Do you mean,' said Diana, 'that there are policemen who specialise in that sort of thing? Trapping people?'

'Handsome young policemen,' said Jock. 'And this one,' he added, viciously, 'will doubtless be commended for behaving like a male prostitute. F-J gave a false name, but even if no one had recognised him, he wouldn't have been able to carry on working for the Service – too much of a risk. He was due in court this morning. God ...' Shuddering, Jock took a large gulp of his drink. 'It was horrible, seeing him like that. Blank. As if he'd been stripped naked. He talked about it afterwards. How he put it was that men like him have two sets of friends. Two lives. He said he'd always been afraid that they'd collide and that he'd tried to leave it alone, but the loneliness ... impulses – and sooner or later he'd always fall back into his former ways. He said that was a relief at first, not having to pretend all the time, but then the shame ...'

'What about his wife?' asked Lally.

Jock shook his head and looked into his glass – now empty – then went to the drinks tray and poured himself a second Scotch. His back to them both, he said, 'I telephoned her. Someone had to tell her. It was ...' Lally went to him and put a hand on his shoulder.

'I'm sure you were kind,' she said.

'She made it easy for me,' said Jock. 'When I'd told her how he'd died, she didn't ask me why he'd done it, or if he'd left a note, or anything.'

'Well, they did lead fairly separate lives, darling. Perhaps she knew about him.'

Gently, Jock pushed Lally's hand away and turned to face them. 'I don't know ... If she did, she certainly didn't want to hear me say it. I can't blame her for that ... F-J talked about her, too. He said that if things had been different, he would have told her what sort of man he was when he proposed, but he couldn't. He said, when he married her, he honestly thought he could begin again – wipe out the past.' Jock paused and looked directly at Diana, and a dull flush spread across his face. 'He told me he was ...' he grimaced, '*in love* with Ventriss.'

'I know,' said Diana. 'I overheard them talking once.' She took a sip of her drink and lit a cigarette in order not to have to look at Jock, remembering how she'd stood outside the door of F-J's office and heard Claude taunting him. *Apse did it because he thought he could get away with it. After all, most of his friends do, don't they, Charles? At least I'm honest. I don't use women as camouflage . . . You made damn sure that Evie Calthrop got to know about Diana and me, didn't you, Charles? But I don't think you're in any position to preach morality, are you?* She remembered, too, the conversation she'd had later with lovely Inspector Stratton. He'd been so kind and understanding when she'd blurted out about Claude's hold over F-J and her suspicion that Apse's death was not, as officially recorded, a suicide . . .

'He said something about that – thinking they were alone and hearing the door of the flat close. He wondered if it was you.'

'Yes, it was.'

Although she was only about six feet away from Jock and Lally, the silence between them, as the implications of this sank in, felt like an immense void. She stared down at her shoes, knowing that she'd never be able to talk to them about it, even if it were allowed.

The chime of the hall clock made them all jump. 'Oh, Lord,' said Lally. 'We've got the Tremaines coming to dinner in half an hour. Does Davy know?' Davy Tremaine had been a colleague of Jock's since the war years.

'Yes.' Jock drained his glass and set it on the tray. 'Better go and dress, then.'

Sitting at the dressing table in her room, Diana brushed her hair mechanically. She could picture F-J quite clearly, as if it was his face reflected in the mirror and not her own – the round, dark eyes with their long lashes and the squashy button nose that gave him the slightly querulous charm of a pug. The first time she'd met him, she'd been tempted to pat him, despite his formidable intellect. She remembered his flat-cum-office in the monumental Art Deco grandeur of Dolphin Square, with its strange mixture of sturdy Edwardian brass-and-wood masculinity and the feminine delicacy of the *toile de Jouy* and petit point she'd assumed had come from the wife that no one ever saw. And that strange painting of the naked boy bather that had been a gift from Neville Apse . . . She thought of his desk, always – in contrast to his dapper appearance – so untidy, and of how, after one of her first successes gathering information, he'd given her a jar of bath salts. That was when she'd trusted him. That was before his jealousy about her and Claude had led him to take steps to ensure that Evie got to hear of their affair, and before he'd arranged, quite deliberately, that she be the one to find Apse's body. It had been his way of warning her – telling her that he knew she knew about him and she'd better keep her mouth shut, or . . .

Now, she found that she felt no anger towards him, only pity. All his precautions had come to nothing because, in the end, he'd betrayed himself. Setting down her hairbrush, Diana began powdering her face. Why on earth had he done it? Thinking of Claude, and the reckless way she'd behaved over him, she supposed she did understand, a little . . .

*

The Tremaines arrived and everyone acted, in an exhaustingly resolute and determined way, as if it were an entirely ordinary evening ('Our Mrs Robinson's such a treasure, she can conjure the most marvellous food out of thin air . . .'). Sitting over drinks, then dinner, trying to talk normally, was like being caught up in a bizarre nightmare. Jock and Davy discussed China and Mao Tse Tung. They even had an argument about it, but it seemed manufactured, a repetition of familiar positions without conviction or passion. Jean Tremaine and Lally nodded, asked occasional questions and looked interested, and no one said a word about F-J. Diana stared glassily at her plate, toying with her food – which was anything but marvellous, being the colour, texture and, probably, the taste of Thames mud – and, pleading tiredness from travelling, went up to bed as soon as she decently could.

Lying on her back, staring into the darkness, she thought that, in the end, F-J had lived up to the 'code' of behaviour that bound them all. Just like all those Romans he must have learnt about at school . . . She tried to imagine him as a boy, inkily cramming at his books, reading about senators ordered to commit suicide by emperors, doing the classical equivalent of the decent thing. We flatter ourselves that we've progressed so much, she thought, but we're just like they were: impaled, like butterflies are in display cases – not by belief in the system of things but by the *necessity* for that belief, whether we like it or not. Then, as now, it meant war and treachery and casualties, but it was immutable. We must think the same, say the same, *be* the same, and if, in any way, we find ourselves unable to conform, we must pretend. Hard on the heels of that idea came another: I've spent my life trying to conform and pretend, and I've failed. I don't want to try any more. I want to change.

Chapter Eleven

It was well after one in the morning when Stratton and Ballard, accompanied by the piles of clothing removed from the bodies, returned to West End Central in a police car brought to the Middlesex for the purpose. The car nosed its way slowly through the acrid, sooty smog that swirled around it, reducing visibility to a few feet, despite the street lamps and the headlights of occasional passing vehicles.

'Message for you from DCI Lamb, sir,' said Cudlipp the desk sergeant, when they arrived. 'DI Grove and DS Porter went down to Merthyr Tydfil to collect Davies. They ought to be there now – they're awaiting your instructions, sir. Shall I place a call?'

'Yes, please.' Stratton blew his nose. It came out black. 'A real pea-souper out there,' he said, shoving the handkerchief back into his pocket. 'And if you could put these,' Stratton indicated the piles of clothing brought in by Ballard and the driver, 'in the Charge Room, and rustle up a spot of tea . . . We'll be in my office.'

'Right you are, sir. That their clothes, is it? Her and the nipper?'

'That's right.'

'This Davies sounds a right one.'

'You can say that again.'

'This came through, too. From Constable Williams in Wales, sir. Statements of a Mr and Mrs Howells.'

'Thanks.'

'Right.' Stratton put down the receiver. 'Grove and Porter will bring Davies back by the early train. They'll say nothing to him about finding the bodies – as far as he knows, it's still just the briefcase we want him for. The train gets into Paddington at ten past ten, so we'll need to organise a car to meet it. I'll go along. We'll need the formal identification first thing, and once we've interviewed Davies, which we'll do straight away, we need to get the Backhouses in to make separate statements. Then there's the workmen. Backhouse said they were at the house three weeks ago, which means they must have been around when Muriel and the baby were killed. We need to find out who they are and have a word with them, sharpish. Presumably the bodies weren't in the washhouse before they arrived, or they'd have spotted them – they seemed to have used the place for storing paint and whatnot. And we need to find out when they gave Backhouse those floorboards for firewood, assuming that's where they came from.'

'I was wondering why he hadn't used them, sir. After all, it's been pretty nippy recently.'

'Perhaps he was using up his coal,' said Stratton. 'The thing that's still puzzling me is the dog. I know that *we* couldn't smell anything, but you'd think it would have been scrabbling against the door and making no end of a fuss.'

'Perhaps they didn't let it into the garden, sir.'

'I didn't see any evidence of it – well, except for those bones, but they might have put them out there afterwards. Looked like they used the garden as a rubbish dump, didn't it?'

'It was in a bit of a state, sir.'

'Let's see what Davies's aunt and uncle have to say for themselves.' Stratton scanned the statements. 'Mrs Howells said that Davies arrived unexpectedly on the fourteenth of November at six thirty in the morning. They hadn't seen him for three or four years, apparently. Said his employer's car had broken down in Cardiff and could he stay with them while it was being repaired ... Left his suitcase at the station in Cardiff – Mr Howells said he saw a cloakroom ticket and that Davies told them Muriel and Judy were staying in Brighton until after Christmas ... Left on the twenty-first and came back on the twenty-third with a suitcase. Told them Muriel was at their flat when he went back but she walked out without a word and left him holding the baby ...'

'Sounds like our boy all right, sir.'

'It certainly does. He told Mr and Mrs H. he'd given Judy to some people who'd look after her and paid them fifteen pounds to do it. When they asked why he hadn't taken her to his mother he said it was because she was out working ... hadn't thought to bring the baby to Wales with him, apparently ...

Seemed quite contented throughout his visit, went to the pub with his uncle, enjoyed himself ... This is a bit odd ...'

'What's that, sir?'

'Says Davies bought a present for Judy – a teddy bear.'

'To throw them off the scent, sir?'

'Doesn't sound like he's bright enough for that. I'd say it's more likely he was trying to pretend to himself he hadn't done it – that would fit with the statements he made, wouldn't it? Anyway ... Mrs H. had written to Mrs Davies about him and got a letter back two days ago – which tallies with what she told us – telling her that Davies had sold his furniture and people were dunning her for cash. When Mrs H. confronted him about it, he said his mother was lying and the furniture was still in the flat. Very upset, apparently, couldn't finish his breakfast, and then he went to the police station. Well, it's all of a piece, isn't it?'

'Yes, sir. Beats me how he thought he could get away with it.'

'He probably didn't think at all ... Just made it up as he went along. Right. We'll need a statement from Mrs Davies. She said she'd not seen him since the beginning of November, didn't she? Now, I'd better get cracking on this report for DCI Lamb, but if you want to get some kip ...'

'Don't think I could, sir. Honestly.'

'Well, ask Cudlipp to set up a couple of camp beds for later, anyway. And why don't you see if you can find us a drink? For medicinal purposes, of course. I'm sure there's a bottle knocking around.'

Left alone, Stratton started bashing out a report for Lamb

on the typewriter with two fingers, concentrating like fury in an attempt to keep at bay the pathetic image of Muriel and little Judy lying side by side on their respective slabs. Ballard returned half an hour later, bearing a half-full bottle of brandy. 'All done, sir.' As he spoke, he produced a tea cup from each pocket. 'Shall I? Couldn't find any glasses, I'm afraid.'

'Why not?' Stratton took his fag out of his mouth and picked a shred of tobacco off his lower lip. 'I'm nearly finished.'

Ballard poured and pushed a cup across the desk towards him. Stratton swallowed and made a face. 'Filthy.' He held out the cup for more. 'Don't know about you, but I could have done with that a couple of hours ago.'

'Me too, sir.'

'Oh, *Christ* . . . Jenny was pregnant when she died. Not so far gone, but . . . They thought it would have been a boy.' It occurred to him then, for the first time, that Jenny might not have told him of the existence of the baby not only because she was afraid he'd be angry – they'd agreed to stop at two – but also because she'd been trying to get rid of it, as Muriel Davies had. That couldn't have been the case, could it? Jenny loved children, she'd been the best of mothers, she wouldn't . . . would she? But if she'd been afraid of giving birth with the doodlebugs, of the world she'd be bringing the child into . . . Stratton put his hands over his face. 'I just wish she'd told me,' he muttered thickly.

'I'm sorry, sir.'

Stratton jerked his head up. 'No, Ballard, *I'm* sorry. I shouldn't have mentioned it. I don't know why I did. But with something like this, it brings it back. You know, I've never told anyone – not even the children – only the lady who took them when they were evacuated. When Dr McNally said Muriel Davies definitely *was* pregnant, I felt as if I'd been punched. And Davies killed his wife . . . I'd give anything to have Jenny back, and the baby. Be five and a half years old, now, if he'd lived . . . Going off to school. Still . . .' Stratton rubbed a hand over his face. 'No use dwelling on it. Doesn't do a bloody bit of good.'

'I suppose not, sir, but it's rough, all the same. Drop more brandy?'

'Thank you. You'll have all that to come, your nipper learning to talk and walk and all the rest of it . . .'

'Unlike poor little Judy.'

'Yes . . . Too late. Best we can do is nail the bastard that killed her.'

'I'll drink to that, sir,' said Ballard, with fierce solemnity. 'I'll certainly drink to that.'

Chapter Twelve

Davies was white-faced, haggard, and very small. Next to DI Grove, who was a large, avuncular type, he seemed like a pygmy, and the top of his head barely came up to Stratton's shoulder. The camel hair overcoat he wore looked too large, so that he looked like a boy in man's clothing. Grove had told Stratton on the telephone that Davies was twenty-four years old, but he looked younger. Constable Williams's description of him as 'puny' was spot on, thought Stratton, as the four men walked down the platform at Paddington Station towards the waiting car.

'All right, was he, on the way back?' Stratton asked DI Grove as DS Porter and the driver settled Davies in the back seat.

Grove removed the pipe he habitually chomped on and, wiping a hand over his droopy moustache, stained cinnamon with nicotine, said in his distinctive phlegmy rumble, 'Didn't talk much. Mind you, neither did we. I'm not sure the lad really understands what's going on. He's hardly the brightest – to be honest, I don't think he's all there. He asked if his mother'd got in touch with the people looking after his daughter.'

Stratton, aware of a slight ache behind his eyes – he and Ballard had polished off what was left in the bottle before they'd turned in – endeavoured to collect his thoughts.

'Well, he's not been told we've found the bodies, so perhaps he thinks it's a good idea to keep on with his story.'

'I suppose so. Oh, and he told us he didn't pinch the brief-case, but he didn't say who did.'

'I'm surprised he didn't say it was Backhouse. He seems to be blaming him for everything else.'

They rode to West End Central in silence, Stratton in front beside the driver and Davies, flanked by Grove and Porter, in the back.

Ballard met Stratton in the lobby. 'Mrs Davies has identified the bodies, sir, so there's no difficulty there. She's made a statement, too. There's not much new, although she did tell us that there's some insanity in the family. Her grandfather and an uncle died in asylums, and her father was violent.'

'I suppose it's not surprising. Grove and Porter are bringing Davies in now. Tell Cudlipp I want him taken straight through to the Charge Room. I'll be waiting.'

Once in the Charge Room, Stratton arranged the two piles of clothing on a desk so that the tablecloth and the sash cord were on top of Muriel's, and the tie – still tightly knotted, but slit at the back in order to remove it – on top of Judy's. Then he took his notebook out of his pocket and positioned himself beside the table. After a few minutes, the door opened and Davies appeared, escorted by Ballard and Porter. On seeing the clothing Davies blinked several times, opened his mouth, then closed it again, and looked at Stratton in bewilderment. Bang to rights, chum, thought Stratton. Bang to fucking rights.

Opening his notebook in case he needed a prompt, he said, 'At nine thirty p.m. yesterday I found the body of your wife, Muriel Davies, concealed behind timber in a washhouse at ten Paradise Street, also the body of your baby daughter Judy concealed in the same outbuilding, and this clothing was found on them. Later I was at the Middlesex Hospital mortuary, when it was established that the cause of death was strangulation in both cases. I have reason to believe that you were responsible for their deaths.'

Davies stared at him, jaw hanging slack. Then he reached forward, picked up the tie, then dropped it back onto the pile of baby clothes. When he looked up, Stratton saw that his eyes were wet with tears. 'Yes,' he whispered, and then again, more loudly, 'Yes.'

Chapter Thirteen

'John Wilfred Davies, I am arresting you for the murder of your wife, Muriel Davies, and your daughter, Judy Davies. You are not obliged to say anything, but I must warn you that anything you do say will be taken down in writing and may be given in evidence against you.'

Stratton stared across the desk at the tiny man who sat beneath the naked light bulb in the interview room. There were deep troughs of exhaustion under his eyes. His coat removed, his over-large jacket stood proud of his shoulders as if there were a hanger still inside, and his grubby white shirt stood a quarter of an inch clear either side of the skinny column of his neck. Whatever else he looked like, Stratton thought, it wasn't a monster. 'Do you understand what I am saying to you?' he asked.

The man's prominent Adam's apple bobbed up and down as he swallowed, working saliva into his mouth. 'Yes.'

'Good. Please sign here.' Stratton pushed a pen and the paper with the caution statement across the scarred wooden table. Davies glanced at it, then looked up, bewildered.

'Sign?'

'Your name.' Stratton tapped the bottom of the paper. Davies picked up the pen awkwardly, as if he wasn't used to handling such an object, and turned it round in his fingers several times before writing his name in a series of cramped, upward-sloping loops.

'Thank you.' Stratton nodded to Ballard, who sat beside him, pen poised, and, turning back to Davies, said, 'Why did you strangle your wife and child, Mr Davies?'

'Why?' echoed Davies. Eyes narrowed, he peered intently round the room as if hoping to find an answer there.

'You killed them,' said Stratton, flatly. 'You've just told us that. Now we want to know why you did it.'

'I . . .' Davies didn't look directly at Stratton. His gaze hovered somewhere between the two policemen's shoulders. 'I done nothing wrong.' The Welsh melodiousness in his voice was discernable for the first time.

'Mr Davies.' Stratton's voice was deliberately loud. 'So far, you have given us a cock and bull story about putting your wife's body down a drain. You told us that your baby daughter was being looked after by people who turn out not to exist. You told your mother that your wife and child were in Brighton. You told your neighbours, the Backhouses, that they were in Bristol. Then you told us that Backhouse was responsible for your wife's death and that he told you *he* was going to put her body in the drain. Now you're telling us that you had nothing to do with any of it. It's been a tissue of lies from start to finish, hasn't it?'

'I done nothing,' repeated Davies, sullen now, like a schoolboy caught out in a falsehood.

'What you have certainly done – consistently, I grant you – is to tell lies. We know that you killed your wife and child. You've just told us that yourself. Now,' Stratton, resting his palms on the desk, pushed himself upwards and forwards across the table so that his face was barely six inches from Davies's, 'I suggest that you start telling the truth.'

Davies shrank in his chair, his white, creased brow beaded with sweat. 'But I didn't . . . I never . . .'

'Mr Davies.' Stratton leant backwards and folded his arms. 'You have no choice but to co-operate with us. If you don't . . .' He left the implied threat hanging in the air between them for a full thirty seconds, then uncrossed his arms and continued, in an eminently reasonable tone, 'Fortunately for you, we're patient men, and of course we have plenty of time. And I imagine,' he said in a kinder tone, 'that it will be quite a relief to get it off your chest. That's what you told the policeman in Wales, isn't it? You told him you couldn't sleep for worrying. If you tell us all about it, we can help you. If not . . .' Stratton sighed, sorrowfully, 'then – much as we'd like to help you – we can't.'

Davies cowered, seeming to collapse from within; hunched over in his chair he looked even smaller than before. Stratton could almost smell his fear, and with it the scent of victory. He leant forward, elbows on the table. 'Well?'

Once more, Davies's eyes darted about the room, frantic this time. Watching him twist uncertainly in his chair, Stratton thought, there's no escape, chum – just get on with it. '*Well?*' he barked.

'I'll tell you about it.' Eyes flitting from Stratton's face to

Ballard's and back again, he was speaking fast, with terrified eagerness. 'It was the money, see? Muriel took the money off me, from my job, and she kept spending it, and she was always asking me for more, so I killed her.'

That's more like it, thought Stratton. Now we're getting somewhere. 'How did you kill her?' he asked.

'I strangled her, see?'

'With what?'

'What . . .?' Davies looked momentarily confused, then said, 'A rope, wasn't it?'

The way he said this gave Stratton the impression that it was something he'd learnt, or tried to learn, by heart and was now repeating. 'Was it?' he asked.

Davies screwed up his face, as if trying to remember something, and Stratton felt an odd and wholly unexpected twinge of uncertainty.

Davies's eyes half closed, so that his pupils were partly hidden beneath his eyelids, and Stratton had a sudden image of a lift stopped between two floors which, for some reason he was unable to pinpoint, increased his uncertain feeling. For Christ's sake, he told himself, the man's told so many lies that he's probably having trouble remembering the real version of events.

Davies's eyes popped open again, and, as if satisfied by some inner voice of confirmation, he said firmly, 'Yes. A rope.'

'Where did you get the rope?'

Davies stared at him as if this were not a question to which he could reasonably be expected to know the answer. 'I . . . I don't know. I think I had it off my van.'

'So you brought it in with you?'

'Yes.' He sounded more confident this time, and looked at Stratton expectantly.

Feeling that some sort of encouragement was due, Stratton said, 'Good ... You brought it in with the intention of murdering your wife, did you?'

'I . . .' Davies's tentative smile of acknowledgement changed to a frown. 'No ... No!' He was irritated now, his voice a peevish semitone higher. 'It was a row, see? Like I told you.'

'So why did you bring the rope up to your flat?'

'I . . . Well, I was tidying up, wasn't I? Tidying the van.'

'Tidying the van,' Stratton repeated in tones of disbelief. 'I see. And what did you do then – after you'd strangled her?'

'I took her down to the flat below.' The reply came quickly this time, without any doubt.

'Why?'

'Well . . . Because it was empty, see? Mr Gardiner was in hospital.'

'Then what?'

'I waited a bit, and took her down to the washhouse when Mr and Mrs Backhouse were asleep.'

'And this was when?'

'The start of November.'

'Can you remember the date?' asked Stratton, leafing through his pocket diary.

'No.'

'The seventh?' asked Stratton, remembering Backhouse's words about the workmen. 'That was what you told the police at Merthyr Tydfil.'

'It must have been the seventh, then.'

'Fair enough. What did you do afterwards?'

Davies blinked in bewilderment. Thinking he hadn't understood the question, Stratton clarified it. 'I'm asking what you did after you'd taken the body downstairs.'

'Well, then . . . Then I went to sleep.'

'And when you woke up?'

'I fed my baby and went to work.'

'When did you strangle the baby?'

'Later. Two days. When I came home from my work. I strangled her with my tie. I took her downstairs at night.'

'And you put her in the washhouse?'

'Yes, that's right.'

'Who was looking after the baby when you were at work?'

Davies looked indignant. 'I fed her all right. I done it when I come in.'

'Yes . . .' Wondering about this – surely any infant left alone and unfed for so long would have bawled its head off? – he said, 'Why did you kill her?'

Davies stared at him for a moment, his face a mask of stupid incomprehension, before tears came into his eyes and, closing them, he lowered his head, shaking it slowly from side to side. When he opened his eyes, his expression was one of utter defeat. His mouth worked for a moment, apparently trying – if his blank look was anything to go by – to frame words independently of his mind. Then he said, in a whisper, 'I don't know,' and, putting his head in his hands, began to sob.

At least, thought Stratton, he's got enough decency left to feel remorse. After a moment he said, 'I think we'll leave it there,' and nodded at Ballard, who finished writing and slid the statement towards him.

'Would you like to read it?' Stratton asked Davies, who looked up, wiping his eyes and nose on his sleeve.

'You read it to me,' he said, sniffing. 'I'm not very educated, see?'

'Very well.' Stratton picked up the paper. '*Muriel was incurring one debt after another and I could not stand it any longer, so I strangled her with a piece of rope . . .*'

Davies's blank look whilst listening to the statement caused Stratton to wonder how much he'd actually understood of the proceedings, but he concluded that it was because the words were not actually his, and, the language being rather more sophisticated than his own, he may not have understood it all. However, he felt satisfied that it was as good a summary of what Davies had said as any, and Davies seemed to feel the same way because he made no comment, but picked up the pen once more and signed his name carefully in the place Ballard had indicated.

'Now,' said Stratton. 'Let's have a cup of tea, shall we? Smoke?' He fished his cigarettes out of his pocket and nudged the packet over to Davies. Ballard went to the door to request tea from the policeman standing outside. Reaching over to give Davies a light, Stratton said, 'That's better, isn't it?'

'Oh, yes.' Davies inhaled greedily. 'It's quite a relief, I can tell you.'

Chapter Fourteen

'Something's puzzling me.' Having left Davies in the interview room under the eye of PC Arliss, Stratton and Ballard were finishing their tea in the office.

'What's that, sir?'

'The Backhouses said that Muriel and the baby went away on the seventh of November – to Bristol, as they thought – when the workmen were in the house, didn't they?'

Ballard consulted his notebook. 'Yes, sir. And that Davies left about a week later.'

'Well, if the workmen were using the washhouse for storage, how was it that they didn't notice the bodies?'

'They were behind the floorboards, sir.'

'Nevertheless . . . And we need to find out when those floorboards were taken up, too.'

'The thing that's bothering me, sir, is the baby. If she was left alone for the best part of two days while Davies was at work, she must have howled a bit, and that's a small house . . .'

'Yes, I was thinking about that.'

'The Backhouses didn't hear anything – well, they thought she'd gone with the mother, didn't they? So if they had heard a baby crying you'd think they'd have gone to investigate.'

'Unless they thought it was coming from next door. I can't believe the walls are very thick.'

'That's true, sir.'

'Or the baby didn't make any noise. I suppose that's possible.' Ballard – the memory of interrupted nights evidently still fresh in his mind – looked dubious. 'And,' Stratton continued, 'I still can't understand about that bloody dog . . . Even if it's not allowed into the garden, the workmen must have left doors open, bringing things in and out, so why the hell didn't it start sniffing around?'

'Perhaps it did and nobody noticed, sir. Or Davies got the dates wrong. It was a few weeks ago, and it's hard to remember . . . And it's obvious he's not too bright.'

'You can say that again. I found myself feeling a bit sorry for the poor little sod, actually.'

Ballard nodded. 'So did I, sir. He seems so . . . well, harmless.'

'Probably is, when he's not strangling his family. Obviously lived in a bit of a fantasy world, and now it's all coming home to him.'

'He does seem to be having a job disentangling fact from fiction, sir.'

'Yes, I noticed that. And there's something else that's bothering me a bit – the way he didn't seem to know *why* he'd done things. Apart from strangling Muriel because of the row over money, I mean . . . He was pretty quick to agree with the things we put to him, but that business about the rope, and why he killed the baby . . . It was as if he genuinely didn't know what to answer.'

'Well, he's got a fair old temper, hasn't he? Even his mother said that. I can't imagine he thinks too much before he acts.'

'Loses his head, you mean. Actually, I don't suppose he thinks much *at all*, apart from making up stories.'

'That's his problem, sir – he's fine when he's making things up, but as to reality . . .'

'Yes,' said Stratton thoughtfully. 'That makes sense – in as much as anything does.' He read through the statement once more, looking for inconsistencies. 'The timing's the real bugger, with the baby alone for two days, but I'm sure we can sort it out when we interview the witnesses. Still . . .' he swilled down the rest of his tea and stood up, stretching, 'so far so good, eh? Come on, let's get back downstairs.'

They found Davies sitting quite still, head in hands. Arliss, standing behind him, hastily levered himself away from the wall and adopted what Stratton assumed was supposed to be an expression of observant obsequiousness, which merely succeeded in rendering him even more of an eyesore than usual.

Davies turned to look at him and Stratton saw that he had been crying. He bent down and put an arm around Davies's thin shoulders. 'It's all right,' he said, benevolently. 'You're doing well.'

Davies made noisy gulping sounds, then looked up at Stratton with eyes full of hope. You pathetic, inadequate little bastard, thought Stratton. He'd seen this look before – bloody awkward it was, too, when you were busy putting a noose round a man's neck and he started regarding you as some sort of saviour because you hadn't knocked him about . . . In his mind's eye, Stratton saw once more the tiny, crinkled-up soles of the baby's feet, heels resting on the cold mortuary slab, so utterly defenceless. The man was as guilty as hell, simple as that. And, Stratton reminded himself, he was doing his job and if that meant getting murderers to regard him as a guardian angel, then so be it. Abruptly, he took his hand off Davies's shoulders, marched round the table, and took his seat.

'Now, let's start from the beginning.'

Davies wiped his nose with the back of his hand, and blurted out, 'The money was the cause of it. I was working driving a van for Murchison's, off the Euston Road. Muriel kept asking for more money, so I borrowed twenty quid from the guv'nor. She had it off me, and I told the guv'nor to take it from my wages. She never told me who she owed the money to, see? Started a row whenever I asked about it. I borrowed off all different people to get more for her, but she never let up . . . We had a letter from the furniture people about money owing, and Muriel told me she never paid it. I went round there and gave them thirty bob, and then I told her she must pay every week what we owed . . .'

'That's the hire purchase?'

'Yes. Benfleet's, it is. After I done that I found she was behind with the rent, and that's when I blew up – she was wasting the money going to the pictures all the time, leaving the baby, and saying I never gave her enough. I wasn't going to stand for that.'

'When was this?'

'It was a Sunday. November, I think, early on. I had a row with her and then I went to the pub dinner time, and then the pictures. I come back about seven o'clock. I was listening to the wireless, but Muriel wouldn't stop about the money and the rent, and when we got up next morning she started arguing again. She told me she was going to Brighton with Judy, but she never, she was there when I come home from work. She said something about how she never went there because I'd have a good time while she was gone. I lost my temper and told her if she didn't pack it up I'd slap her face. She picked up a milk bottle – she was going to throw it at me – so I grabbed the bottle off her. I'd had enough of it, so I washed and went off to the pub.'

'Which pub?'

'The Horse and Groom in Great Portland Street. I stopped there till about ten o'clock, I think, and then I come home. Muriel started a row again, so I told her, "I'm going to bed." When I got up in the morning–'

'That was the Tuesday, was it? The seventh?'

'That's right. Well, I got up, and she never took no notice, so I went straight out to work. I come in at about six thirty, and she went at me again about the money, so then I lost my temper and hit her in the face.'

'How did you hit her?'

Davies's face clouded, and the familiar bewildered

expression came back for a moment before he said truculently, 'I don't know. I just hit her, didn't I?'

'Did you punch her, or hit her with the flat of your hand?'

'My flat hand. I hit her, and she hit me back so I took this piece of rope I had from my van and strangled her with it.' Davies looked at Stratton expectantly, as if hoping for approval.

'What did you do then?'

Davies's face clouded once again. 'Then?'

'Yes. After you killed her.'

'I told you that,' said Davies, irritably. 'Don't have to go into it again, do I?'

'Yes.' Stratton leant forward, arms on the table. 'We need the details.'

'Details?' echoed Davies. 'I just . . . I put her on the bed.'

'Was the rope still round her neck at that point?'

'I don't know. I think so. I covered her with the eiderdown, see. Then I carried her down the stairs to Mr Gardiner's flat, like I told you.'

'What time was that?'

'Half past ten, I think. Well, about that time.'

'And then?'

'I came back upstairs. Had to feed the baby, see? Then I put her to bed.'

'And?'

'Well, I had to wait, see? Till it was quiet. I sat in the kitchen and had a fag. I was waiting . . . Then I took her downstairs to the washhouse.'

'How?'

'I just told you,' said Davies, impatiently. 'I took her downstairs, through the back door and into the garden. I carried her.'

'You wrapped up the body first.'

'Wrapped it?'

'In a tablecloth, Mr Davies.'

Davies blinked, and passed a hand across his face. 'Yes . . .'

'Was it your tablecloth?'

'I don't know.'

'Was it the one you saw in the Charge Room?'

'It must have been . . . I took her downstairs when it was quiet.'

'And you concealed her behind the boards in the washhouse?'

'Yes. Concealed her.'

'Under the sink?'

'Yes.'

Stratton and Ballard exchanged glances. Davies was tiring visibly, and his defeated air made Stratton feel that if he suggested that the man had put his wife's body in a hot air balloon, he'd agree to it in order to get them off his back. It wasn't unusual, and they'd both seen it before, many times. 'What did you do then?' he asked.

The strain of extreme effort on his face, Davies said, 'I locked the door.'

'Of the washhouse?'

'Yes, the washhouse. Then I went back upstairs. My baby was asleep then, so I went and laid on the bed until it was time to go to work. I made a feed of milk and cereal for Judy in the morning and gave it to her, then I changed her, and I went out to work. She was asleep when I come back. That was half past five.'

'So Judy was alone all day?'

'Yes. I fed her when I come in, and changed her. Then I sat with her in the kitchen. I had a cup of tea and a smoke. I made her another feed before I put her to bed, then I sat by the fire till I gone to bed. I don't know what time … Midnight, I think it was. I got up at six–'

'This was on Thursday?'

'Yes, it must have been. Thursday. I fed the baby and changed her and put her clothes on, then I had a cup of tea and went to work.'

'So the baby was on her own?'

'I didn't like it,' said Davies, defensively, 'but I had to, see? I wrapped her up,' he added. 'I put her back in her cot.'

'And then?'

'I done my day's work, then I asked the guv'nor for money on my wages. He said what did I want it for, and I said to send to Muriel, so he asked me where she was and I said she'd gone to Bristol with the baby. He paid me the money but then he said he'd had enough of it–'

'Enough of what?'

'Me asking for money, he said. I was always asking before I done the work. He said I could come back tomorrow for my cards. I went home then. I didn't know what to do, see?'

Davies's face was creased, as if in pain, and Stratton could imagine the turmoil in his dull mind – caught like a rat in a trap, panicked and scrabbling for a way out – which had led to what surely must have been his next action. 'Was that when you strangled the baby?' he asked.

Davies blinked rapidly, holding back tears. 'Yes. With my tie. She was in the cot, so I left her there and I went into the kitchen. I made a cup of tea. I was waiting, like before. I took her downstairs later and put her in the washhouse.'

'What time was that?'

Davies looked at him with wet eyes. 'I don't know. It was later. Mr and Mrs Backhouse was asleep. I come back upstairs and lay down on my bed. Then I went to see a man to sell the furniture.'

'This was the next morning?'

'Yes, next morning. He come to my flat later, and offered me forty quid for the lot.'

'What was his name?'

'Mr Lorrimer. Got a shop in Ingersoll Road, see? He asked me why did I want to sell it, and I told him I was going to Bristol. I said I had a job up there. He said the driver would come for it on Monday. They took all the furniture and lino, and he paid me for it then, and I put my things in my suitcase and went to Paddington for the train.'

'To Wales?'

Davies nodded. 'I went to Cardiff, then I found a lift to Merthyr Vale.'

'To your aunt?'

'Yes . . .' Davies slumped still further, pathetic and vanquished, his face, drained of colour, given a greenish cast by the harsh light of the naked bulb. 'Now you know all what happened,' he muttered.

Chapter Fifteen

At home in Tottenham, Stratton sat in his favourite armchair, slippers on his feet and the *Daily Express* in his lap, and wished he didn't feel so tired. Not that he particularly wanted to read about the possible suspension of Marshall Aid to Europe, but he felt he had barely enough energy to drink his tea or have a smoke. Glancing at the cup and the ashtray on the small table beside him, he was reminded of Davies's litany of domesticity punctuated by violence – wife- and child-killing with breaks in between for tea and fags. Honestly, the whole thing was like a gruesome real-life rendition of a Punch and Judy show. 'That's the way to do it,' he murmured, opening his paper and shaking it into position in an attempt to convince himself that he did have the desire to read the bloody thing, otherwise why buy it in the first place?

'What's that, Dad?' Stratton looked over the paper to see Monica standing in the doorway and was struck, as he often was when he saw his daughter, by how attractive she was. It wasn't only her face and figure that made her lovely, he thought, but her animation and the way she presented herself.

Now, she was carrying a slice of Victoria sponge on a plate. 'One of the girls brought a cake to the studio – it was her birthday – and I saved my piece for you.'

Stratton, touched beyond measure as he always was by her small acts of kindness – so like Jenny – said, 'Don't be silly. It's yours.'

'No, really . . .' Monica deposited the plate on the little table and flopped down on the sofa.

'Well, at least have half.'

'All right, then. You first.'

'Had a nice day?'

'Mmm . . . Busy. I spent most of it painting scratches.'

'Scratches? Don't they have a Works department for that sort of thing?'

Monica rolled her eyes in mock exasperation. 'No, Dad. It was a scene – two girls having a scrap. Hair-pulling, fingernails . . . a real cat-fight. One of them kept getting it wrong, so they had to do it again. Everyone says she's the producer's mistress and that's the only reason she's in it. I shouldn't be surprised if it's true, because she's rotten.' Before Stratton could register dismay that was only partly comical at such worldly sentiments so calmly uttered by his innocent child, Monica added, 'I did my first bruise, too. It was a jolly good one, if I do say so myself. Just here.' She tapped her left cheekbone.

'Pleased with it, were they?'

'Not half! Aren't you going to eat your cake?'

'All right, then.' Stratton picked up the plate. 'Bossyboots.'

'I'm not!'

'I know. I only said it to make you indignant.'

'I'm not indignant!'

'Yes, you are,' said Stratton.

'Ooh . . .' Monica pursed her lips and picked up a magazine from the sofa.

'Jolly good, this,' said Stratton, through a mouthful of cake. 'What's for supper?'

'Rabbit stew. At least, I think that's what it is. Auntie Lilian left it.'

'Ah.' Stratton raised his eyebrows. Lilian's cooking wasn't a patch on Doris's, but as her offerings were not only kindly meant but essential, he never complained. On the whole, he was grateful for the way in which his two sisters-in-law had taken over the domestic arrangements. His home might be shabby (wasn't everybody's, nowadays?), but, largely thanks to Lilian and Doris, it was comfortable and clean. Less appreciated were their efforts, in the past couple of years, to find him a wife. These had, so far, resulted in the unwanted attentions of a droopy but persistent widow, a fading but excruciatingly girlish spinster, and an ugly woman with a sniff whose husband, still listed as missing in action, had, in Stratton's view, simply buggered off sharpish while he had the chance. Worse than all these, however, were the advances of another local widow, mercifully unencouraged by either Doris or Lilian on the grounds that they found her common. Over-rouged, with hands like grappling hooks, she had taken the opportunity, at a party the previous Christmas, of manoeuvring him beneath a bunch of mistletoe and, to his appalled amazement, making a grab for his scrotum, causing him to jump backwards and upset a tray of tea. The memory of it still made his toes curl, and he had avoided her ever since.

He could see that Doris and Lilian meant well – and that having him off their hands would make their lives a lot easier – but he wished they wouldn't bother. He didn't want to get married again. The pricks of anger and resentment at the sight of other couples that he'd felt for several months after Jenny's death had given way to a numbness which still remained deep within him, so that it was impossible to contemplate that sort of intimacy with anyone else. He supposed that Doris might have a point when she said it was because he hadn't met the right person, but he wasn't at all sure whether there would ever be another 'right person', or even if he *wanted* there to be one.

'Dad?'

'Mmm? Oh . . . Sorry, love.' Stratton held out the remains of the cake, but Monica shook her head.

'Not that. I asked if you'd had a good day at work.'

'Oh. You know. Tiring.'

'It's just that I thought you must be doing something important because you didn't come back last night.'

'Too much to do . . .' Stratton hesitated, then said, 'New case. Chap killed his wife and child.'

'Oh, *Dad*!' Monica looked stricken. 'How horrible for you.' She put the magazine aside and stood up. 'It seems so . . . unfair . . . your having to do something like that.'

'It's the job, love.'

'I know, but . . .' Stratton knew what Monica was trying

to say, but was glad she seemed unable to articulate it. Instead, she looked at his now empty cup and said, 'Can I get you anything? More tea?'

'I'm fine. I suppose you might put the supper on . . .'

'All right.' Monica stood looking down at him, obviously trying to think of something to cheer him up. 'I think there might be some cocoa left. We could have it afterwards, if you like. And,' she added, 'why don't you finish the cake? Silly for me to have it – there's only a mouthful.'

Chapter Sixteen

Washing up after supper, Monica paid particular attention to her favourite plate, which was an old one, decorated in blue willow pattern. It wasn't just that she liked the colour and design, but she also thought of it as being friendly, somehow, unlike the cracked yellow one, which was definitely unfriendly – spiteful, almost. One of these days, she supposed, they'd be able to get some new china, and then everything would match and washing up wouldn't be the same at all. From childhood, she'd thought of everything in the house, from the largest items of furniture down to teaspoons and table mats, as having particular characters. It was a feeling – and not the only one, either – that, she strongly suspected, had persisted long after she ought to have grown out of it. If I were to tell anyone about these things, she thought, they'd say I was mad.

Having finished the drying up, she thought she ought to look in on Dad in the sitting room, just to see if he wanted anything, but he was fast asleep with the newspaper in his lap. He was obviously exhausted. Whatever he'd said about it just being his job, she still thought it was pretty unfair of them to give him a case where a man had killed his wife, after what had happened to Mum. It might have been five years ago, but all the same ... She stood looking down at him for a moment, the sensation of fierce protectiveness welling inside her chest as it always did at such times, before going upstairs to her bedroom. A girl at the studio had lent her some fashion magazines to read – well, not read, exactly, because several of them were French, but look at – and she'd spent most of the day in happy expectation of a couple of hours by herself, immersed in a world of glamour and sophistication and colour. Not that there wasn't plenty of that at work – she still couldn't believe her luck in getting the job – but it certainly wasn't much in evidence elsewhere ...

Flopping down on her bed, she opened the first magazine and began working her way through pages of long-necked beauties with perfectly arched eyebrows, high cheekbones and expressions of serenely haughty composure, clad in gorgeous creations that, despite the ending of clothes rationing, you still couldn't buy in the shops even if you did have the money. Stroking the swathes of shining material that gleamed from the pages like soft jewels, she imagined the texture of the cloth beneath her fingertips. Her fingers moved, seemingly of their own accord, from a gorgeous drape of satin to the model's upper arm, and she found herself imagining how that might feel, were she to be touching it. It was quite impossible, of course, that she could ever find herself, in real life, stroking the skin of such a loftily beautiful woman, but all the same ...

Her hand strayed to her own breast, and she stared down at the photograph, and then closed her eyes, imagining that the woman was touching her – and then the sound of a passing car recalled her, abruptly, to the present. She jumped, suddenly on fire with shame, and slapped the magazine shut. What was *wrong* with her? Other people didn't have thoughts like that. She stared down at the magazine's front cover where the model, chin raised, looked disdainfully away from her, as if in reproach. Whatever this feeling was, and its exact nature wasn't something she could bear to dwell on in any specific detail, she knew for certain that it wasn't – couldn't possibly be – shared by anyone else, anywhere. Perhaps she really *was* mad. All the girls she knew talked about boys and got soppy over the male film stars. Her cousin Madeleine was always asking about the actors, what they were like and if they ever talked to her. She knew that Madeleine was disappointed by the lack of information and shared confidences, but, no matter how hard she tried, Monica could never think of anything interesting to say on the subject.

She used to think that her problem, like the silly business of believing that plates and cups had personalities, was to do with being young, and that, when she grew up, things would be straightforward. But she was grown up, wasn't she? She was twenty, with a proper job and everything, and the whole business of feelings seemed to be more complicated than ever.

She'd had boyfriends, for heaven's sake – well, one boyfriend anyway, last year. And it wasn't as if boys never asked her to come out with them, because they did, and fairly often. She didn't particularly mind the things they tried to do, all the kissing and stuff – the thing was that she didn't *feel* anything while they were doing it. It wasn't horrible or frightening or anything like that, it just wasn't . . . well, it wasn't anything at all, really. Other girls, judging from their conversation, seemed actually to like it – or they said they did. She'd tried to persuade herself that she enjoyed it, too, but she didn't. Not unless she was thinking of something else, anyway. Once or twice with Leonard she'd got quite passionate, but that was because she was imagining he was Lucy, the farmer's daughter she'd been friendly with when she was evacuated in Suffolk. When he'd put his hand on her breast she'd imagined it was Lucy's hand and things had got quite interesting for a bit, until Leonard had started talking to her and she couldn't pretend any more.

Taking the magazines off the bed so that they wouldn't get creased, she lay down on her back with her hands behind her head and stared up at the damp patch – also friendly, because it was crescent-shaped, like a smile – on the ceiling. Her future, in so far as she imagined it, had always involved – ideally – sharing a flat with another girl. And carrying on working at the studio, of course, either in Make-up or designing frocks – or perhaps even making special props, assuming they let women do that. It would be lovely if she could share a flat with Lucy, or someone like her . . . She'd liked being with Lucy so much – well, that was normal, because everyone enjoyed being with their friends, otherwise they wouldn't *be* friends with them in the first place – but the peculiar hot feeling she'd had inside, the sort of pleasant mild ache that she'd thought, aged fifteen, must be the effect of too much sun, was, in retrospect, disturbing. It wasn't until Madeleine had mentioned something similar, in connection with a boyfriend, that she'd realised that it was actually *bad*. Not bad like, say, Hitler, or even bad like her cousin Johnny, who'd stolen things and got involved with the wrong sort of people, but definitely wrong and not normal at all. At work, surrounded by half-dressed actresses in Make-up, so casual about their nakedness, she kept her eyes averted for fear that one of them might spot her staring. And supposing she were to betray, somehow, what was going through her mind, nobody would ever speak to her again and she would lose her job . . . She might even end up in a mental asylum.

Even thinking about it like this was dangerous; it made her feel all morbid and just . . . not *right*. She'd put the whole thing out of her mind and she wouldn't look at the magazines any more. She sat up, swung her legs over the side of the bed and looked at her watch: twenty to ten. She'd promised Dad some cocoa, hadn't she?

But she must do something else first – something ordinary, to put a barrier between her thoughts and going downstairs. If ever Dad, the person she loved and admired more than anyone else in the world, got to know about her problem . . . No, it was unthinkable. She'd rather be dead.

She must pretend to be normal, even if she wasn't. Perhaps, if she pretended for long enough, the strange feelings would go away, like the constant and terrible grief she'd felt when her mother had died. No one need ever know she'd been ‘different’. Glancing round her room, she spotted an old jigsaw. That would do. Grabbing the box, she upended the pieces onto the rug and, kneeling down, began feverishly assembling the picture of a fallow deer in a woodland clearing.

Chapter Seventeen

The following morning, Stratton spent half an hour with Lamb, who, having been away from the station the previous day, needed to be put in the picture before Davies was taken to the magistrates' court at Marlborough Street. 'This is more like it,' said the DCI, when Stratton had taken him through Davies's statements. He wasn't quite rubbing his hands together, but Stratton thought he wasn't far off it. 'The thing's open and shut. Get your case straight, and for God's sake try not to complicate matters in your usual fashion, and we'll be home and dry. Bring Mr and Mrs Backhouse in here as soon as you can. I'll ask Grove and Porter to help you with interviews to speed things up. I must say, this man Davies sounds a thoroughly nasty piece of work.'

'As a matter of fact, sir,' said Stratton, 'I thought he was rather pathetic.'

'Yes, well . . . as long as you don't let him fool you. Unusual for you, Stratton,' – here, Lamb gave a disconcertingly roguish leer – 'it's generally the women who pull the wool over your eyes, isn't it?' Stratton tried not to wince as one side of his superior's face screwed itself up in a wink. 'I know you've always been rather susceptible to the ladies . . .' This patronising attempt to be chummy, never before seen, was far worse than Lamb's normally irritable demeanour. Stratton managed to excuse himself before any more gruesome bonhomie came his way and, once in the corridor, shook himself like a dog after a swim to rid himself of what felt like an all-over coating of embarrassment before returning to his office.

Sitting beside Stratton in the back of the car en route to the magistrates' court, Davies looked smaller than ever. Silent and hunched inside his overcoat, he stared straight ahead for most of the short journey and then, just as the car rounded the corner into Marlborough Street, he turned to Stratton and said, urgently, 'There's something I forgot to tell you.'

Automatically, Stratton began to caution him, but Davies, plucking at his sleeve, cut him off. 'No, I meant to tell you before, and I want to get it off my chest. I took Muriel's wedding ring and I sold it.'

Staring into his eyes, Stratton saw the same hope of approval one might see on the face of a child and, to his surprise, felt pity for the inadequate little man. He said encouragingly, 'It's good that you told me. Was that after you killed her?'

Davies blinked at him for a moment, then nodded. 'After. I got six shillings for it from a jeweller in Merthyr Tydfil.'

'Do you remember the name?'

'No.' Davies looked crestfallen. 'It was some shop . . . I feel bad about it, Mr Stratton. I shouldn't have taken it off her.'

The car stopped and the driver walked round to open the back door nearest the kerb. They scrambled out, Stratton first and Davies, handcuffed to him, close behind. 'Here we are,' said Stratton.

Davies looked up at him. 'Are you going to stay with me?'

'For the time being,' said Stratton. Seeing some flecks of dandruff on Davies's shoulders, he batted them away with his free hand. 'Come on. It's just a few questions this morning.'

'Questions? But I've told you—'

'Nothing like that. Just your name and occ— your job. That sort of thing. Just remember to speak up when you're asked.'

Davies looked at him again, the boy eager to please. 'Yes,' he said. 'Thank you, Mr Stratton.'

The hearing was over in minutes. Davies was remanded, given a legal-aid certificate, then led away to be taken to Pentonville. The last glimpse of him Stratton had was a strained white face, as Davies twisted round to look back at him between the solid, dark-blue shoulders of two burly policemen. Whatever Lamb said, he thought, 'pathetic' was the right word for Davies. He'd dealt with people of low intelligence before – plenty of them, including a couple of murderers – but he'd rarely felt moved by them, and certainly not by anyone who'd killed a child. Davies obviously hadn't understood the consequences of his actions. How anyone could think that if you strangled a baby it might still live was beyond him, and yet Davies's remarks to Grove on the journey from Wales showed that it was exactly what he *had* thought. What a sad little family,

Stratton thought, and trudged back to West End Central to continue the process of putting a noose around Davies's neck.

Chapter Eighteen

Sergeant Ballard and Mr Backhouse were waiting for Stratton in the lobby, Backhouse standing up very straight and staring about him with an air of self-important concern. 'Of course we came at once, Mr Stratton,' he said. 'We want to help in any way we can. Edna – Mrs Backhouse – well, she can't sleep with the worry of it.'

'Where is she?' asked Stratton.

'In the interview room with DI Grove and DS Porter,' said Ballard, drawing him aside. 'They've taken her to identify the clothes, sir. We thought it made more sense – women tend to notice more what other women wear.'

'We'll need to ask Backhouse about the tie, though. Davies said it was his, but we ought to make sure. Right, then,' Stratton turned to Backhouse. 'Let's go through to my office, shall we?'

'You've been most helpful already, Mr Backhouse,' said Stratton, as they pulled up chairs around his desk.

Backhouse glanced about him with, Stratton thought, some

satisfaction, clearly pleased to be taken to Stratton's own office and not some anonymous interview room. He'd seemed thoroughly at home as they'd walked down the corridor, joking that, despite the circumstances, it was nice to be 'back in the old place'. 'Well,' he said, 'anything I can do to help you with this . . .' he pursed his lips prissily as he deliberated over his choice of word, '*regrettable* matter.'

Stratton thought that, as understatements went, 'regrettable' was masterly, and wondered why he couldn't feel any kinship with the man, even though he was a former special. 'Now,' he said, 'you've given us quite a bit of information already, but we need to make sure of the specific details. When was the last time you saw Muriel and Judy Davies?'

The answer came fluently, with no hesitation. 'I saw Muriel on the Tuesday – that would be the seventh – she was going out to empty some slops. The last time I saw the baby was Monday.'

'The day before?'

'That's correct,' he said, smartly. Then, wetting his lips with the tip of his tongue and making the strange sideways sucking motion with his mouth, he continued, 'I did remember, after we spoke before, that Edna and I heard some odd noises on the Tuesday night.'

'What time was this?'

'Around midnight, I should think. There was a bump that woke us up. I did wonder if it wasn't the Davieses arguing again, and I thought I might go upstairs – I've had to do that before, on a number of occasions, to ask them to keep the noise down, for the neighbours – but my wife said she thought it sounded like someone moving furniture.'

'And that was definitely the night of the seventh?'

'Oh, yes. I remember that because I'd been to the doctor, and I always go on a Tuesday. For my fibrositis. I've had to take rather a lot of time off work recently. I'm afraid to say I've been rather troubled by diarrhoea, as well . . .' Here Stratton, trying not to grimace at the mental picture this created, stole a glance at Ballard, but his head was firmly down and he was writing busily with the air of one giving total attention to his work. 'The doctor had given me a compound,' Backhouse continued, 'which I took so as not to have to get up during the night and wake Edna.'

'Of course,' said Stratton, hastily. 'What is your occupation, Mr Backhouse?'

'Ledger clerk. For the British Road Services.' This was said more quietly than before, and Stratton had to strain to hear it. The whispering and the finicky precision of the voice were beginning to get on his nerves.

'Would you mind speaking up a bit, Mr Backhouse?'

Again, the tongue moistened the lips. After more sucking and swallowing, Backhouse said, 'I'm sorry. I have a quiet voice. It's from being gassed during the war. It affected the larynx.' He put his hand up and fiddled with the knot of his tie, as if to illustrate this.

'The last war?' asked Stratton, incredulously.

'In nineteen seventeen. I lost my voice entirely for a couple of years, and I'm afraid it still affects me from time to time.'

'That's a pity,' said Stratton, sorry for the man but not

liking him any more than before. 'Did you see Davies on the seventh?'

'That was when he told us that Muriel had taken the baby to Bristol for a holiday. It was about seven o'clock, I think.'

'In the evening?'

'That's right. He said he was going down later to visit them.'

'And when did Davies leave?'

'On the thirteenth, after the van came for the furniture. We'd seen him on the Thursday, too, the ninth, in the evening, and he told me he'd left his job. "Packed it in," he said. He told me he'd asked for his cards back, and he was going to see about a job in Bristol. I saw him again on Friday the tenth – I remember telling him to be careful because of the flooring being up in the hall.'

'That's what the workmen were doing? Replacing the boards?'

'Yes. Some of them were quite rotten. They did some repairs in the washhouse, too, and the toilet.'

'So they would have had no reason to go upstairs?'

'Oh, no. There was nothing to do up there.'

'Did Davies say anything else to you on the Friday?'

'Yes, he told me he was selling his furniture. He said he wouldn't be able to take it with him to Bristol.'

'Did you see him again before he left?'

'On the Monday,' said Backhouse promptly. 'He said that the man had given him sixty pounds for the furniture. He had a suitcase with him, and he said he was going to Bristol.'

Interesting, thought Stratton, that Davies had told him

he'd got forty pounds for the furniture. He was obviously unable to resist telling lies, even about something as pointless as that. 'Did you see Davies after that?' he asked.

'Yes, I did.' Backhouse's voice had descended once more to a whisper. 'Nine or ten days after, I think. He said that Muriel had left him and taken the baby, and he couldn't find a job. He said he'd been travelling about a lot and he'd just come from Wales. I told him he should go back there and try and get himself some work. When I said he should find a place to stay and use the sixty pounds from the furniture to tide him over he told me he'd spent most of it.'

'Did he say how?'

'Travelling, he said. I took it to mean that he'd been going to public houses, and visiting . . .' Backhouse fingered his tie again, ran his tongue round his mouth and added, in an even quieter voice, so that Stratton had almost to read his moist lips, '*prostitutes*.' He shook his head with an air of pious disgust.

'Did he tell you that?' asked Stratton.

Backhouse screwed his mouth to the side once more, and said, 'Not exactly, but it was of a piece with his previous behaviour. I told him he was being foolish, and he left soon after. I did wonder if he'd gone to see Shirley Morgan. That's the friend of Muriel's I told you about. She lives nearby.'

'That's not very likely, is it, if he'd threatened to . . . what was it you said? "Run her over in his van"?'

'Well . . . she did come back to the house, you see. On the Monday, I think.'

'Which Monday?'

'The sixth. I told her to clear off, because it would only upset Muriel, and there'd been quite enough rowing as it was. My wife and I live very quietly, Inspector. My health is poor, and Edna suffers with her nerves. We didn't like all the upset.'

'So she didn't see Muriel?'

'Not as far as I know. She'd been up and knocked on the door, and I heard her calling out, but Muriel evidently wasn't answering.'

'Was Muriel there at the time?'

'I don't know. I think so.'

'Did you hear the baby at all during that week?'

'Not that I can remember. Edna used to listen for her, if Muriel was going out, but we thought they were in Bristol.'

'But you didn't know that then, did you? You said the last time you'd seen Muriel and the baby was on the seventh, and that Davies told you a few days later that they'd gone away.'

'Yes . . .' Backhouse dropped his voice again. 'That's right. But we didn't hear anything, so we thought all was well and Muriel was up there with her.'

'So – and I apologise for asking this again, Mr Backhouse, but we need to include it in your statement – you did not, at any time, tell Davies that you could help his wife to get rid of a baby?'

Backhouse blinked and licked his lips. 'No, I did not.'

'Davies said you'd showed him a medical book, and said you could help his wife abort her pregnancy.'

'That's nonsense,' said Backhouse firmly. 'He's making it up.'

'Did you ever tell Davies you'd trained as a doctor?'

'Certainly not. It's not true.'

'Did you show him a medical book?'

'No, Inspector, I did not. As I told you, the only medical book I have is a St John's Ambulance manual.' Backhouse shifted in his chair. 'Would you mind if I stood up for a moment? If I sit too long, it's a strain on my back.'

'Of course,' said Stratton. 'Please . . .'

Grimacing, and with great care, Backhouse stood up slowly and rubbed the small of his back. 'I suppose that Muriel might have spotted the book and told him about it . . . I really don't know, Inspector, but that's all nonsense.'

'He told the police in Wales that you helped him to carry the body.'

'Inspector . . .' Backhouse rubbed his back once more, 'that is ridiculous. My fibrositis has been so bad that I have to get on my hands and knees to pick something up from the floor. I certainly couldn't lift anyone.' He shook his head, slowly. 'I don't understand why John is saying these things about me.'

'It must be upsetting for you,' said Stratton. 'Did you visit the washhouse during the week of the sixth of November?'

Backhouse blinked for a moment, then shook his head. 'I don't believe so. I wasn't at all well . . .'

'But you would have visited the washhouse at some time in the following week?'

'Oh, yes. I remember that, because I went to get some wood to light the fire and I noticed the timber stacked in front of the sink. That was on the Monday – the thirteenth.'

'What time was that? Do you remember?'

'Early in the day. About half past seven in the morning, I think.'

'I see. And did you notice your dog paying particular attention to the washhouse at any time? Nosing around, scrabbling at the door, anything like that?'

'No, nothing like that. But then, Inspector, I was in bed a lot of the time, because of my back.'

'I see. Just one more thing, Mr Backhouse, and then you're free to go. Sergeant Ballard, would you mind fetching the exhibit?'

Ballard was back in under a minute, bearing a tray on which lay the tie that had been found around the baby's neck. Twisted, it looked like a flat red-and-black-striped snake. All three men eyed it as if it might begin to writhe at any moment.

'Do you recognise this?' asked Stratton.

Backhouse's tongue popped out once more to moisten his lips, which it did with a slow turgidity that repulsed Stratton who noticed, out of the corner of his eye, that Ballard had averted his face from the man.

'That isn't mine,' said Backhouse, finally.

'Do you know who it belongs to?'

Backhouse cleared his throat. 'I'm not certain, but I think I've seen John wearing a tie very like that one.'

'Fair enough.' Stratton stood up. 'Thank you, Mr Backhouse. You've been most helpful.'

'I'm sure he means well,' Stratton said to Ballard when he'd returned from seeing Backhouse out, 'and he *is* very helpful, but he makes my flesh crawl.'

'Me too, sir. DI Grove says he'll be along in a minute. They've finished – Mrs Backhouse was waiting in the lobby.'

'Right. Whatever we think of Backhouse, it looks like an open and shut case.'

'That'll please DCI Lamb, sir.'

'Let's hope so.' Stratton rolled his eyes, then sprang up to open the door as a heavy tread, which could belong to nobody except DI Grove, echoed in the corridor. Grove paused on the threshold, chewing his empty pipe thoughtfully.

'Mrs Backhouse identified Muriel Davies's clothes,' he said, plonking himself heavily on the nearest chair. 'She recognised the baby's cardigan, too, and the little frock. Nice woman – very distressed about the kid. Said that although they'd never been blessed, she'd looked after little Judy a lot and thought of her as almost like her own.' Clamping his teeth angrily round the pipe and grimacing so that they showed up to the roots, he added, 'When I think of what that bastard did . . .' Leaning forward for emphasis, he chomped the pipe into the corner of his mouth and continued, 'My girl came round to see us last night, with my little granddaughter. God, I'd like to get hold of that murdering little shit for five minutes . . .'

Grove was a kindly man who, despite years in the police force, rarely said a sharp thing about anyone, but now his rage seemed to reverberate around the walls of the little room, unchecked and raw. Stratton saw his own anger and incomprehension reflected in Grove's eyes and saw, also, from Ballard's face, that he felt exactly the same way.

Grove cleared his throat and opened his notebook. 'Mrs

Backhouse said she saw Judy on Monday the sixth – looked after her when Muriel went out. That was the last day she saw either of them. Shirley Morgan came to the house on the same day. Backhouse told her to clear off, apparently. And . . . she said they've got a medical book – St John's Ambulance – but when I asked her about Backhouse training to be a doctor she said Davies was making it up.'

'He seems to have done a lot of that,' said Stratton.

Grove nodded, chewing his pipe. 'Said she knew Mrs Davies was pregnant, but that she and her husband were moral people and wouldn't help anyone to get rid of a baby . . . Seemed quite genuine. Said they didn't know of any childless couple who wanted a baby in Euston or anywhere else . . . She saw Davies on the seventh, in the evening, and he told her that Muriel and the baby had gone to Bristol. Said she was surprised because Muriel hadn't said anything about it to her. Davies told her that Muriel hadn't told his mother, either . . . Also said she heard a bump in the night of Tuesday the seventh of November. Sounded like furniture being moved about. She saw Davies at about quarter to seven on the evening of the ninth, when he came downstairs and told Backhouse he'd given up his job . . . Then she saw him a few times on the Friday when he came in and out, because he wasn't working then . . . Didn't see him at all after that. She said she'd been in and out of the washhouse since the seventh of November, as usual, getting water to rinse the slop-pail . . . There were some bits of wood in there, stacked in front of the sink . . .'

Stratton nodded. 'That tallies with what Davies said about concealing the body. Backhouse said he'd noticed planks stacked in front of the sink on the thirteenth – the same ones, presumably.'

'She said she didn't notice anything out of the ordinary,' Grove continued. 'No smell or anything out of place. There's not much more, really . . . they were married in nineteen twenty, in May . . . they've lived in Paradise Street since thirty-eight . . . came to London in twenty-three . . . Halifax before that . . . she was away for a while during the war, stopping with relatives in Sheffield, and came back in forty-four . . . never had any trouble . . .'

'A model citizen, in fact,' said Stratton. 'I mean, you've seen the man. Anyway, the accounts seem to fit, so it's just the workmen and the tradesmen and the Morgan woman and then we're home and dry.'

Chapter Nineteen

'So,' said Stratton, when Grove had gone, 'we'll need to see the men from the building firm. The name's in Backhouse's statement somewhere, isn't it?'

Ballard scanned the document. 'Kendall's, sir. Premises in Drummond Street, off the Hampstead Road. There's Mr Kendall, and the plasterer's name's Walker, according to this, and the chippie – if you can believe it – is called Carpenter.'

'Sounds like Happy Families,' said Stratton, scribbling in his notebook.

Ballard grimaced. 'We wouldn't be doing this if it were, sir.'

'Quite,' said Stratton, hastily. 'Take PC Canning and round them up, tell them exactly why we want them, and don't take no for an answer. Get hold of the time sheets for the job while you're at it. Then we've got the bloke from the hire-purchase place, Benfleet's, and the chap who bought the furniture . . .'

'Lorrimer, sir,' said Ballard. 'They're both on the telephone. I have the numbers here.'

'Good ... and there's Davies's boss at Murchison's van company, and that woman Backhouse was talking about – Muriel Davies's friend.'

'Shirley Morgan.' Ballard found the relevant page in the statement. 'Says here "she lives nearby".'

'I'll do that. Shouldn't be too hard to find out where she is. And I'd better get someone to speak to the owner of that briefcase, too, although I can't imagine he's got anything to do with it.'

'That's a Mr Parker. Address in Everton Buildings. I think that's somewhere off the Hampstead Road, too, sir.'

'In that case, maybe you can kill two birds with one stone. Canning can escort Kendall's lot back here, and you see if you can get Parker to come and identify the thing. And,' he added, getting heavily to his feet, 'while you're doing that, I'll go and tell DCI Lamb what we've been up to.'

Twenty minutes later, Stratton unlaced his shoes and spent several minutes rubbing his feet violently against each other to ease his itchy chilblains – Lamb ('for God's sake make sure it's watertight') seemed to have had a bad effect on them. Somewhat relieved, he lit a cigarette and picked up the telephone. In short order, he spoke to Mr Benfleet from the hire-purchase outfit, and to the furniture dealer, Lorrimer, requesting their presence at the station, then ascertained Shirley Morgan's address and packed an unwilling Arliss off to fetch her. He'd just spoken to Davies's former employer, Murchison, when PC Canning put his head round the door and summoned him to the lobby, where he found Kendall,

Walker, and the carpenter called Carpenter sitting in a depressed-looking row.

Stratton and PC Canning started with Kendall, a lugubrious man with a soggy roll-up glued to his lower lip. 'I don't like this,' he said, unhappily. 'Don't like it at all. It's nothing to do with any of my men. Been working for me for years, they have, and we've never had nothing like it.'

'I'm sure you haven't,' said Stratton. 'But we need to clarify a few things. When did you begin the work at Paradise Street?'

'We started the job on the Tuesday – that was the seventh of November. We'd have gone in on the Monday' – here, the fag drooped disconsolately – 'but the weather was bad. I give your bobby' – Kendall nodded righteously at Canning – 'the time sheets for Walker—'

'That's the plasterer?'

'That's right. There's time sheets for Walker and Carpenter there.'

PC Canning produced a sheaf of time sheets from his tunic, and Stratton peered at the scrawl, trying to make sense of it. 'It says here . . .' he indicated Walker's first sheet, dated 7 November, '"taking material to job" . . . and he was working there until Friday the tenth. Where would this material have been stored?'

'In the washhouse. Same as Carpenter, for his tools, only he come later.'

This, thought Stratton, was going to be more difficult than he'd imagined – Davies had told them he'd put Muriel's body in the washhouse on the night of the seventh, and there was the Backhouses' description of the noises in the night . . . 'So

Walker would have been in and out of the washhouse from Tuesday until Friday?'

'Yes. Well, he had to, see?'

'You're absolutely sure about this, are you?'

'Well,' said Kendall, with exaggerated reasonableness, 'he would, wouldn't he, if that's where he was storing things? Mind you, I wasn't there so much, only in the beginning, and when we cleared out the tools and that on the Friday.'

'And you didn't notice anything unusual about the washhouse during that time?'

'Can't say I did.' Kendall scratched his chin with a thumb and forefinger stained cinnamon by nicotine. 'And I don't reckon Walker did neither, or he'd have told me.'

'Did you see any wood in there – planks?'

Kendall shifted the limp dog-end ruminatively from side to side. 'Can't say I did.'

Stratton sighed. 'I see. Did you see this woman at any time?' He pushed the photograph of Muriel Davies across the table.

'Is that the girl who was killed?'

'Yes.'

'Poor lass.' He shook his head. 'Nice-looking, too . . . I didn't see her. I'd remember if I had.'

'Fair enough,' said Stratton. 'Now, let's look at Carpenter's time sheets, shall we?' As Stratton read the scribbled notes his heart sank: Lamb wasn't going to like this one little bit. 'They say Carpenter pulled up the rotten joists and flooring in the ground-floor passage on the Thursday afternoon and the Friday, and laid new flooring on the Saturday. He fitted the new skirting on Monday the thirteenth, and then he'd finished the job, had he?'

'That's right.'

'So you're saying there wouldn't have been any timber stacked in the washhouse until Friday the tenth?'

'No. There wasn't nothing to put there, was there?'

'What about the stuff taken up on the Thursday?'

'Well, he had to loosen it first, see, so he'd have done that then . . . Even if he'd started taking it up, I doubt there'd have been much to move.'

'What about the new flooring?'

'I picked that up myself, on the Friday, and he collected it on the Saturday, before he started.'

'Mr Kendall,' said Stratton, 'as I'm sure you understand, it's very important that we get a clear picture of what happened.' Here, he looked hard at Kendall, who waggled the remains of his roll-up solemnly in response. 'These time sheets,' Stratton indicated the grubby pages, 'would you say that they give an accurate picture of what happened and when?'

'Well . . .' Kendall pinched the fag end out of his mouth, and gave a deep sigh. 'It was a contract job, see, so what's on the sheets is a bit . . . Well, put it this way, what it is, I have to make sure that the work's done in the time allowed.'

'So you wouldn't check them?'

'I'd have a look, but unless the bloke's put down that he's at another site where he shouldn't be, or he's doing a job that's not in the contract . . . then I'd have to have a word, because that's a mistake, see? I mean, the time sheets aren't really a timetable for the job, as such.'

At least, thought Stratton, that gives us a bit of room for manoeuvre. Nevertheless, after Canning had escorted Kendall from the room, he shook his head gloomily. Lamb was going to go berserk, even with dodgy time sheets. It was more likely, he thought, that Davies had muddled up the dates, but that said ... Stratton pulled the telegram towards him to check – the date of the seventh was the one thing he'd been consistent about right from the beginning. Backhouse had said the seventh was the last time he'd seen Muriel, so perhaps it was possible that Davies had killed Muriel later on the same day, as he'd said, and brought her downstairs on the evening of the tenth. Or that there'd been two lots of wood ... but in that case, surely Kendall would have noticed? He'd have to ask Carpenter.

Stratton leafed through his notebook. Backhouse had said Davies had left 'about a week' after the seventh and Davies himself said he'd gone to Wales on the Monday, which was the thirteenth, and that he'd put the baby's body in the wash-house on the night of the ninth ... 'Balls!' Stratton flipped his pencil across the desk. Providing the timings were right, and that Carpenter had put the timber in the washhouse on the tenth, as Kendall said, it might still fit ... It might even explain the noises in the night, if Davies had moved his wife's body down one flight of stairs into Gardiner's flat instead of right down to the ground floor. But if that was the case, why not say so? A mixture of confusion, fear and wanting to please might muddy the waters, he supposed, especially with someone as feeble-minded as Davies clearly was – and with such difficulty telling the difference between fiction and reality.

PC Canning put his head round the door. 'Next one, sir?'

'Yes. Let's have Walker.'

The plasterer was an elderly man with a red face, a thin white moustache which reminded Stratton of a milk mark on a baby's upper lip, and a defensive air. His account tallied with Kendall's in every respect, until Stratton pushed the photograph of Muriel under his nose. 'Did you see this woman at any time?'

'Is that the one who . . .?' Walker tailed off, shaking his head, as Stratton nodded. 'And her kiddie, too. Terrible business. I did see a woman on the Tuesday, going out. Never saw the face, so I don't know.'

'Did she have a baby with her?'

Walker shook his head. 'I just saw her go out the front door, that's all.'

'And it wasn't Mrs Backhouse.'

Again, Walker shook his head. 'No. I saw Mrs Backhouse several times, and this woman was younger. Quite a bit younger, I'd say.'

'Can you describe her?'

'Well, I didn't pay much attention . . .'

'Fat? Thin?'

'I suppose . . . about sort of medium-sized really. A woman.'

'How old?'

'Youngish, I'd say. Hard to tell.'

'Do you remember what time?'

'In the daytime. I mean, it was light . . . but morning or afternoon, I couldn't say.'

*

Walker's statement taken, Stratton told PC Canning to fetch Carpenter, who was a solid chap, heavy and square. He gave the impression of immovability – he wouldn't go out of his way to swat a fly, but neither would he step out of the way of a charging bull. Hoping fervently that this was just his appearance and not his character, Stratton fixed him with a basilisk stare, thinking, you're my last hope, you fucker. Don't let me down.

Chapter Twenty

'Lamb'll have my guts for garters,' said Stratton, gloomily, when Carpenter left half an hour later.

'It's not all bad news, sir,' said Ballard. 'The Brighton police have telephoned a statement from Muriel's father, Mr Binney.'

'Oh? What's the gist of that?'

Ballard scanned the sheet in his hand. 'Says Muriel told him she wanted a divorce and asked if she could take Judy and go and live with him . . . She told him Davies never gave her any money and spent most of his free time in the pub.'

'Useful, I suppose, but it doesn't help us sort out this mess with the timing. That was like trying to dig a hole in cement with your fingers.'

Carpenter hadn't seen Muriel and he'd been adamant that he'd left the pulled-up boards on the stairs on the Thursday and Friday evenings, and only put them in the washhouse on the Monday, and, when shown a photograph of the boards *in situ*, he'd been equally positive that they were the ones taken up from the passage.

'If the boards were in the passage all weekend, it's odd that no one else mentioned it, sir,' said Ballard.

'Bloody odd. Apart from anything else, it's a nuisance. Of course, the only person it would have really affected is Davies, especially if he was taking a body, or – if he's got the dates for Muriel wrong – two bodies, downstairs . . .'

'Or maybe Backhouse moved some of them into the wash-house over the weekend – but then, of course, he'd have seen what was in there.'

'And the furniture bloke, sir. Lorrimer. He'd have noticed wood on the stairs, wouldn't he?'

'That's true. Except he only valued the stuff, didn't he? He didn't actually take anything away till the Monday, according to Davies.'

'Well, we'll have to see what he's got to say for himself. But the Backhouses must have seen the planks on the stairs, mustn't they? And they didn't mention it.'

'Well, we didn't ask them, but all the same . . .' Stratton passed his hands over his face.

'Of course, the workmen don't have to be called to give evidence, sir.'

'I suppose not. Let's see if we can get something sensible out of the Morgan woman, at any rate.'

Shirley Morgan was a lumpy girl in her late teens with a poor complexion and an air of cheerful incompetence which Stratton found surprising, given the circumstances. Charitably, he decided that it must be because disengagement and inanity were her response to everything and she was simply incapable of behaving in a different manner. ‘Funny,’ she said, brightly, ‘I thought it was the Tuesday I went round there.’

‘The seventh of November?’

‘Was it? I don’t know. I’m no good at remembering things. It might have been the Monday, for all I know. It’s a while ago, isn’t it? I can barely think what I was doing yesterday . . .’ Here, apparently involuntarily, she gave a grating, shrieky laugh. ‘Mr Backhouse was very funny with me.’

‘In what way?’

‘Well . . .’ She leant forward conspiratorially. ‘He said I shouldn’t come round again because my clothes were so nice,’ she smoothed her skirt complacently, ‘they made Muriel jealous. I mean, what a thing to say!’ She shrieked again.

Stratton winced. ‘Where was this?’

‘Where?’ Another shriek. ‘Oh, I see what you mean! Yes. On the landing. I’d gone up to knock on the door of Muriel’s kitchen, you see . . . Oh, no, wait, that was afterwards . . . or was it before? I’m all confused – I told you I couldn’t remember things. Oh, dear, I’m not being much help, am I?’

Stratton felt like slapping her. ‘It’s important that you remember, Miss Morgan. Please try to keep calm.’

‘Oh!’ The single syllable came out on a high, squealing note. It sounded like the rending of metal.

‘This is a murder enquiry,’ he said, in his most soothing voice, adding, mentally, ‘you silly bitch.’

‘Oh, I know . . . of course . . . oh, dear . . . I don’t know what to say.’

‘When did Mr Backhouse tell you not to come round?’

'Because of my clothes, you mean?'

'Yes. Was that before or after the sixth or seventh of November?'

Shirley Morgan thought for a moment. It looked like quite a strain. 'Before,' she said, finally. 'About a month, I think. I remember now . . . there'd been some trouble, you see. I'd stopped there for a few nights, and John – that's Muriel's husband – didn't like it, because we were in the bed and he had to sleep in the kitchen. He didn't like that at all.'

I don't blame him, thought Stratton. Half-deafening a bloke with that laugh and then turfing him out of his own bed . . .

'Muriel wanted me to stay because John was going to work somewhere foreign. Something to do with aeroplanes, I think he said. It turned out to be one of his stories . . . The second night I was there they had a row. John hit Muriel, so she got hold of the bread-knife. He said he'd push her out of the window. I've heard him say things like that before to Muriel – "I'll do you in," that sort of thing . . . Well, it got very nasty. Mr Backhouse came up, and he told me to leave.'

'You left with Davies, didn't you?'

'No, he came after me. He was always giving me the eye. That was after Mr Backhouse said those things about my clothes. He shut the door in my face and told me not to come back, and then a minute later John came out and suggested we go somewhere together. Well . . .' She gave Stratton a meaningful look. 'I didn't know what to do – I didn't have anywhere to go, so we walked around . . . Miserable, it was. Cold. I said I was going to get lodgings, but I didn't want him coming with me. He was Muriel's husband,' she added, as if this might not have occurred to Stratton. 'John said to pretend we were married, but I said what if we were found out, so then we had a row about it and he got nasty again . . .'

For Christ's sake, thought Stratton, wondering if – given the trouble she was having with a sequence of fairly drastic and important events – it would actually have registered if Davies had beaten the living daylights out of her. 'What happened then?' he asked.

'Like I said, we walked around and sat on benches. I found some lodgings. That was the next day . . . I suppose he must have gone home, because I didn't see him again. I went to see Muriel because she's my friend, and she was feeling poorly, with the baby coming.'

'You knew she was pregnant.'

'Yes.' Shirley's dull eyes registered surprise. 'She told me.'

'Did she tell you she was trying to get rid of the baby?'

'Get rid of it?' Surprise was replaced by incomprehension. 'Why would she tell me that?'

Good question, thought Stratton. You'd be a fat lot of use. Poor Muriel, surrounded by idiots. 'What happened,' he asked, 'when you went back to see her?'

'Well, I didn't see her, did I? I knocked on the door, but there was no answer. I thought she must be in there, so I said if she didn't want to see me, she'd only got to say so.'

'Why did you think she was in there?'

'I don't know. I just thought she would be, I suppose. I tried the kitchen door, but it wouldn't open.'

'Did you hear anything?'

Shirley shook her head. 'No. I just had a feeling she was, because when I tried the door, it wasn't as if it was locked—'

'Are you sure about that?'

'Yes, because it gave a bit. I thought that was because she was pushing against it to stop me opening it.'

'Leaning on the other side, you mean?'

'Yes. That's when I said if she didn't want to talk to me, she should just say, and I'd go. I was quite upset about it, because we were friends.'

Except that you'd just gone off with her husband, thought Stratton. 'Did you see anyone in the house?'

Shirley shook her head, then said, 'No, but I think Mr Backhouse was there, because I heard something when I went downstairs.'

'Why *Mr* Backhouse in particular?'

'Because it was a very quiet noise. I couldn't really tell where it was coming from. I suppose it could have been Muriel, if she was there, but I thought it was him because he's always creeping about in those plimsolls of his.'

'Frankly,' said Stratton, when Shirley Morgan had been shown out by PC Canning, 'that young woman struck me as pretty half-witted, so I think we'd better take Backhouse's word for it that she visited on the Monday and not the Tuesday. Of course, it could have been her that Walker saw, but Muriel was still alive then, and she could have popped out for something, couldn't she? And Backhouse saw her on the seventh as well, so that seems more likely.'

PC Canning appeared at the door. 'DI Grove is talking to

Mr Benfleet now, sir, and Mr Lorrimer's here. Shall I bring him in?'

Lorrimer, a small man who looked as if he'd been kept under the stairs for a number of years, wore a flat grey cap that gave him the appearance of a mushroom and had a palm so damp you could have grown mustard-and-cress on it without much difficulty. 'Davies come into my shop on Friday the tenth. Said he wanted to sell his furniture because he'd got a job abroad, so I said I'd come and have a look later and give him a price for it. I offered him forty pounds for the lot, and I sent my boy round Monday to collect it and give him the money.'

'When you went to look at the furniture, did you see any wood on the staircase? Floorboards?'

'Yes, there was something. A few boards, I think. In a pile. Wasn't much room to get past. I remember thinking my boy'd have a bit of a job if they weren't moved.'

'And how did Davies seem to you?'

'Well, I don't know the bloke, so that's a bit difficult. He seemed like he was in a bit of a hurry, but he'd told me he'd got this work abroad so I thought he wanted things sorting out, you know . . . He wanted me to take all the stuff except the baby's things. Said the bloke downstairs was keeping them for him until he'd fixed up a place for them to live.'

'Did you see the baby?'

Lorrimer shook his head. 'Didn't see no one except him.'

'More lies,' said Stratton, after Lorrimer had gone. 'That tale about working abroad.'

'And about the money, sir,' said Ballard. 'He told Backhouse he'd got sixty pounds for the furniture.'

'Yes, I remember that . . . It's odd that he didn't include the baby's things. I mean, he sold his wife's wedding ring, didn't he? He doesn't strike me as the type to see the consequences of his actions.'

'You mean looking suspicious, sir?'

'Yes. Mind you, I suppose he had to have something to tell Backhouse, and asking him to keep the baby's things would have put him off the scent, at least.'

'That must be it, sir. It's the only thing that makes sense. Pity about the wood on the stairs.'

'Yes . . . he said a few boards – perhaps some of them had already been put in the washhouse.'

'Not a long passage though, is it, sir? I mean, you'd only need a few.'

DI Grove's pipe-bowl appeared round the door, followed, in short order, by the rest of him. 'Here you are,' he said, proffering a piece of paper. 'Benfleet's statement. Davies sold the furniture on before it was paid for. Said they were behind on payments – forty-eight pounds, he owes – and Benfleet's had been dunning the mother for the money.'

'Yes,' said Stratton. 'She said something of the sort to us.'

Grove grunted. 'I saw Murchison, as well, from the van company, and one of the drivers who was a pal of his. Murchison said Davies was always asking for advances on his wages, and when he wouldn't give him any more Davies told him to stuff the job because he had a better one lined up. That was on Thursday the ninth of November. Murchison paid him off, and that was that. Said he wasn't sorry to see him go because he'd been mucking things up – he'd had people complaining the orders weren't delivered. The other bloke – McAllister, his name is – said that Davies was always complaining about his wife spending too much money and he'd told him that he wished he'd never married her.'

Ballard, who'd been scanning through Backhouse's statement, looked up and said, 'That all fits, sir.'

'That's a relief,' said Stratton. 'Now I suppose I'd better go and report all this to DCI Lamb.'

Grove grimaced. 'Best of British luck,' he murmured, as Stratton left the office.

'I thought I told you,' said DCI Lamb, stabbing his forefinger on his desk for emphasis, 'to make sure it was watertight.'

'Yes, sir. But, as I've explained, there's a discrepancy between when Davies says the bodies were put in the washhouse and when the workmen say the floorboards were put there. If they weren't stacked in front of the bodies, it would have been obvious that something was there, even if it just looked like a bundle of stuff wrapped in a tablecloth. That washhouse is tiny, sir, and those workmen were in and out all the time for their tools. We can't just ignore it, sir.'

'You're sure about this, are you?'

'Yes, sir. All three statements – Kendall, Walker and Carpenter. Walker swept out the washhouse on the morning of Wednesday the eighth, when, according to Davies, Muriel's body was in there, and he says he saw nothing at all. And

Carpenter says he left the pulled-up boards from the hall on the stairs on the Thursday and Friday, and only put them into the washhouse on the Monday—'

'Get them back in here, Stratton. I'll see them myself. Not Carpenter, just the foreman and the plasterer – they'll do.'

'But Carpenter's the one who moved the—'

'Stratton!' This time, it wasn't a forefinger but a fist that pounded Lamb's desk. Realising that the offer of any more elaboration would be met with an apoplectic response, Stratton decided that his best bet was to say as little as possible and let his superior get it out of his system.

'Look,' said Lamb, making an obvious effort to restrain himself and adopt a reasonable tone. 'Your man's confessed, hasn't he?'

'Yes, sir.'

'Well then. There's no point in overcomplicating matters. What we need to do – what you should be doing – is make sure that there aren't any weak links in the chain of evidence.'

'Yes, sir.'

'And – as I believe I've already reminded you – Mr Backhouse was a Special Constable. You couldn't have a better witness if you'd invented him, man. His word's going to weigh more than some dullard of a workman – and you've just told me that even the foreman admits that what's on the time sheets is poppycock.'

'He didn't quite say that, sir.'

'As near as dammit! For God's sake, man, stop wasting my time! Just get out of here and fetch those witnesses. You'll be present, but I don't want you sticking your oar in unless I tell you. And I'll need all the statements you've taken on my desk as soon as you can.'

'Yes, sir.'

Having delivered the statements, Stratton sat down at his own desk and closed his eyes. Feeling Jenny's presence so strongly that she seemed almost to be physically there beside him, he kept his eyes shut so as not to dispel the illusion. 'Stay with me for a moment, love,' he murmured. 'It's going to be a very long day.'

Despite his resentment at Lamb's mental armour-plating against any new, unfamiliar idea, Stratton knew that his superior was right. It *wasn't* going to be anyone else: in cases of domestic murder, spouses or lovers were, invariably, responsible. Besides which, there were no other suspects, just a problem with consistency. Lamb's words about Backhouse – *You couldn't have a better witness if you'd invented him* – echoed in his mind. He thought of Shirley Morgan's shudder of disgust when she'd talked about Backhouse padding around in his plimsolls and giving her the willies. Half-witted she might be but Stratton, remembering the first time he'd met Backhouse – the way the man had sidled up behind him, the soft cough, the quiet precision of the speech, the blinking eyes behind the thick glasses, the general creepiness – knew exactly how she felt. Perhaps they ought to look into Mr Backhouse. After all, if something seemed too good to be true, then it probably was. He'd ask Ballard to check Backhouse's background. It was pretty unlikely, Stratton thought, that he would turn up anything, but it was best to be on the safe side, especially with Lamb on the warpath.

Chapter Twenty-One

At half past seven the next morning, Stratton and Ballard stood side by side in the Gents' at West End Central, staring bleary-eyed into the mirror and wearily scraping razors across their chins. By the end of Lamb's interviews, first with Kendall, and then with Walker, Stratton had been almost as desperate to get out of the room as the witnesses themselves. For a total of five hours, Lamb had first made the workmen wait, then alternately threatened and cajoled, thumping the table and shoving mortuary photographs of Muriel and the baby under their noses, until, in the end, he'd got what he wanted. Although Stratton had witnessed Lamb in action often enough – and he was bloody good, you had to give him that – and he had used similar methods himself on numerous occasions, he'd felt increasingly uneasy, despite the fact that both the Backhouses had, independently of each other, given statements that the wood had been stacked in the washhouse during the week. What really bothered him was that he couldn't put his finger on quite *why* he felt so uneasy.

Lamb had backtracked, gone in circles, insisted and generally muddied the waters until the workmen began to question their recollections of events. Stratton had seen the uncertainty in their eyes – reality, as they saw it, assuming different shapes until, finally, it became unrecognisable. Their statements now suggested that there may have been planks of wood and dead bodies in the washhouse but they'd somehow failed to notice them; even, in the case of Walker, when sweeping the place – not, of course, that workmen were ever very good at cleaning up after themselves . . .

With Carpenter out of the picture altogether, the timings were certainly looking more solid, but nevertheless . . . And as for Lamb telling Walker that they had ten witnesses who'd seen planks in the washhouse during the week . . . 'Talk about entering the realms of fantasy,' he muttered.

'We seem to have been there from the beginning, sir,' said Ballard, rubbing his chin. 'What with Davies's first statements from Wales, I mean.'

'That's true. Mind you, Davies wouldn't recognise the truth if it bashed him on the nose. If it wasn't for the Backhouses saying they heard bumps in the night of the seventh, I'd think he'd got the dates wrong.'

'He's been consistent about the seventh throughout, though, sir – it's practically the only thing that's been the same in all the statements: that she died sometime on that day.'

'Well, the business with the bumps couldn't have just been a case of Edna Backhouse backing up what her husband said, because she told Grove about it when she made her statement. She said the wood was in the washhouse before the workmen did, too, and of course *she* was up and about the place – Backhouse said he'd spent a lot of time in bed for his back, remember? Mind you, it's still a bit of a mess, what with the muddle over days and the baby being left alone all that time and not crying . . . not to mention the dog. I don't know what to think.'

Ballard looked surprised. 'We *have* got a case, sir.'

'Oh, yes . . .' Stratton rolled his eyes. 'We've got one of those all right.'

The sergeant's surprise turned to incredulity. 'Do you mean, sir, that you think Davies *isn't* guilty?'

'Course he is,' said Stratton. 'I just wish it were a bit clearer, that's all. Have you got any hot water?'

Ballard shook his head. 'Tepid, sir.'

'So's this.' Stratton leant on the edge of the basin. He did feel bloody tired, but it wasn't just that. The inconsistencies nagged at him, as did the thought that Davies might well hang as a result of partial evidence. The other capital cases he'd worked on had been, on the face of it, a lot more complicated than this one, but there was just something . . . 'You know,' he said, 'Monica brought back a book from the library a few months ago. Abstract paintings – Cubism and what-have-you. All the pictures had names telling you what they were – *Still Life With a Newspaper* or something – and I could see that was what they were supposed to be, but not how they fitted together, or why anyone would want to paint them like that in the first place. This whole business is a bit like that. Mind you, I don't know anything about art and paintings, and they were in black and white . . .' And, he thought, no one got hanged at the end of it.

As he'd said this, Stratton had been staring at the porcelain tiles, but, looking up, he saw the worried expression on the sergeant's face. Hardly surprising, thought Stratton, with him talking a lot of bollocks like that. 'Sorry, Ballard. You must think I'm going off my head, too.'

'No, sir, but are you sure you're all right?'

'Fine. I'm tired, that's what it is. Those bloody camp beds . . . You'd get a better night's sleep on a park bench.' He unplugged the basin. Watching the scummy grey water gurgle away, he thought, I must be even more tired than I feel.

His job was to uphold the law, not to question it. That was the reason – well, one of them, anyway – that he'd joined the police force in the first place. It's the best justice system there is, he told himself, and then reflected that he didn't actually know that because, without knowledge of other places, he wasn't in a position to make comparisons. He adjusted the towel on its roller and turned back to Ballard, who was still regarding him with some concern. 'Do you think,' he asked, 'that British justice is the best there is?'

Ballard raised his eyebrows. 'That's a pretty big question, sir. I don't really know. I don't suppose any system in the world is perfect – ours isn't – but it's reckoned to be the best by people who know about these things.'

'Wiser heads than ours, you mean.'

'Well, yes, I suppose so.'

'Just as well there are some wiser heads, then. Wiser than mine, anyway. Tell you what, let's see if we can get some breakfast, shall we? Round the corner – I don't know about you, but I could do with getting out of here for a bit. Oh, and it's on me.'

Fortified by a cooked breakfast and several cups of strong tea, he felt much better, and things improved still more when the sun began to come out as they returned to the station, where he took a telephone call from Dr Sutherland, the Principal Medical Officer at Pentonville. Stratton, who'd had previous dealings with Sutherland, pictured him in his office – a man with suspiciously luxuriant hair and the square, determined jaw of the sort of film actor who stands about radiating quiet strength before performing heroic and morally impeccable acts. 'You'll be glad to know that Davies is fit to plead,' said Sutherland. 'We went through the family history, personal history and so on . . . He spoke quite freely. Told me he'd killed his wife on the seventh, and the infant on the ninth, and put the bodies in a washhouse at the back of the property.'

'He said that, did he?' Stratton was surprised. Sutherland's job was to make sure that Davies was fit to plead and stand trial, not to take confessions.

'Yes. I didn't question him about it – in fact, I warned him I'd have to report it, but he carried on . . .' Sutherland paused, and Stratton wondered if he was radiating a spot of quiet strength at the fixtures and fittings. 'Davies said it distressed him to think about it, but he seemed more shocked than distressed to me. Understandable in the circumstances, I think. He seemed worn out, which again is understandable.

Low intelligence quotient – sixty-eight, and I'd estimate a mental age of about twelve to thirteen years.'

'Is that all?'

'I'd say so. That seems to be largely an educational defect and not an innate one – he missed a lot of schooling because of an infected foot – but it's an inadequate personality, psychopathic in the sense of wanting his own way, acting without thought, and a clear lack of understanding about the consequences of his actions, coupled, of course, with an absence of reasoning power. However, there are no insane impulses or delusions, and observations made on the ward suggest that he's reasonably cheerful and talkative, gets along with others and so on. I'll put it all in the report, anyway.'

'Do you think,' asked Stratton, 'that he was telling the truth?'

Another pause – for a bit more radiating, presumably – and then the doctor said, 'Yes. I believe he was. He did show some emotion talking about his daughter. I had the impression he loved her very much.'

IQ 68, Stratton scribbled in his notebook. *Mental Age 12–13 years.* That meant that if Davies were found guilty, they'd be hanging someone who was, in all but years, a child. He tried to remember what Monica and Pete were like when they were twelve or thirteen, and found it surprisingly difficult. That was probably, he thought dully, because they'd been evacuated and he hadn't seen much of them. Maybe that was why he and Pete never seemed to hit it off – they'd missed some vital stage that could never be got back . . .

Grove appeared and rumbled over to his desk, followed closely by Ballard with a cup of tea and a sheaf of notes, both of which he deposited under Stratton's nose. 'Thought you might need this, sir.'

'Oh? Why? And what's that lot?'

'Backhouse's record, sir. Turns out he's not the golden boy we took him for.'

'That's all we need. What's he done?'

'Well, in nineteen twenty-one he was sentenced to three concurrent terms of three months for stealing postal orders, and in nineteen twenty-nine he assaulted a prostitute. He was living with her, apparently, in Battersea, and–'

'Hold on. What about Mrs Backhouse? He'd been married a few years by then, hadn't he?'

Raising his head from his paperwork, Grove said, 'She was away. Up north, staying with relatives, and he was down here. She was away during the war, as well.'

Stratton flicked through his notes. 'Assaulted the woman with a cricket bat – must have been pretty bad, because he got six months' hard labour.'

'You're sure it's the same bloke?' asked Grove.

'Afraid so, sir,' said Ballard. 'He told the court he was just practising his strokes. You know, the sort of thing that could happen to anyone.'

'I'll bet Dennis Compton does it all the time.' Remembering Backhouse's smug gentility, Stratton added, 'Dishonesty *and* violence – what a pious little hypocrite.'

'There's more, sir. In nineteen thirty-three he stole a car. From a Roman Catholic priest, of all people.'

Stratton groaned. 'Tell me you're joking.'

'Sorry, sir. He got three months for it, but the good news is, he's been straight ever since. Wife came back to him after – maybe that had something to do with it.'

'Sounds like it, doesn't it? Why the hell didn't they find out about this when he applied to be a special?'

'I suppose they didn't check, sir, and he wasn't going to tell them, was he? And what with everything else going on, I suppose it got overlooked.'

Stratton groaned again, louder. 'Bloody hell! It would have only taken one telephone call . . . I'll have to tell Lamb about this – it was this station, so I shouldn't be at all surprised if he somehow comes to the conclusion that I'm personally responsible for not checking. Type it all up, could you?'

'Yes, sir.' Ballard scooped up the papers and left.

Stratton could easily imagine Backhouse going to a prostitute – the usual dreary story of the reserved, cautious man, seeking to gratify a timid itch for amorous adventure, guilty in anticipation, remembering halfway through the fumbled act all the dire, lurid warnings he'd ever heard about chancres and insanity, and becoming impotent and creeping apologetically away . . . All that he could see happening, but *living* with – and therefore, presumably, *off* – a prostitute? And *hitting* her? That was an entirely different kettle of fish . . .

'Grove?'

The older policeman looked up and, with a deft movement of his jaw, transferred his – currently unlit – pipe from one side of his mouth to the other. 'Mmmph?'

'You don't think it's possible that Davies didn't do it, do you? Just,' Stratton added quickly, seeing Grove's normally placid features take on an exasperated cast, 'for the sake of argument, I mean . . .'

Grove took his pipe out of his mouth, then peered at it and poked the bowl with his finger before applying a match. 'You're thinking about Backhouse walloping that tart, aren't you?' he asked, between puffs.

'Yes . . .'

'Bit of a turn-up, I grant you. Not the sort of thing you'd expect.'

'Not really, no.'

Squinting at Stratton through a dense cloud of smoke, Grove said, 'Surprised me, too. But when all's said and done, it was over twenty years ago, and he's been as good as gold for the last . . . what? seventeen-odd years. No reason for him to start murdering people, is there?'

'I suppose not, but I was just thinking . . .'

'I can guess what you're thinking. You can't help liking Davies – or at least feeling sorry for him, in spite of what he's done – and you don't like Backhouse.'

'Something like that, yes.'

'I found myself liking him, too. Davies, I mean – when we were bringing him back. Same as the kids we get in here sometimes, the delinquents. You know they're villains all right, but you can't help feeling sorry for the little sods. And from what I've seen of Backhouse, well . . . I don't know if you remember him from when he was a special, but I had a few dealings with him and he was a proper little Hitler, I can tell you. Uniform went straight to his head.'

'I don't remember him, but Ballard said something similar.'

'Well, he's right. I shouldn't be at all surprised if he'd taken a few favours off a few of the girls, but nothing more–'

'Well, apart from bashing one of them senseless.'

'Yes – years ago. But it doesn't mean he'd suddenly strangle his neighbour's wife for no reason at all. He's a nasty piece of work, but he's not a murderer. You've got your case: Davies is bang to rights and what's more, he's confessed. Apart from anything else, you start suggesting that to Lamb–'

'I wasn't going to,' said Stratton hastily.

'Good. Because if you did, he'd have your head on a plate and you know it. And he may be an irascible old ... you know ... but in this case, he'd be right. You take it from me, mate. I've seen it all.'

'You're right, of course.' Stratton sighed. Grove *was* right. Not only that, but he was as sensible a copper as you could hope to find. It was him, looking at things cock-eyed – he was as bad as those blokes who'd painted the pictures in Monica's book. There *was* no reason for Backhouse to have killed either Muriel or the baby, whereas *Davies* ... In any case, Backhouse having a record wasn't a disaster. Far from it. As Grove had pointed out, the man had been as good as gold for years, and any half-decent barrister would have no trouble at all in presenting their best witness as a man who'd learnt from his mistakes and was now firmly on the straight and narrow.

Grove was right about Lamb, too. For all his faults, the man had done a bloody good job, and people who lived in glass houses ... because he wasn't exactly a saint when it came to coercing witnesses, and neither was Grove or any other copper he knew, come to that. If you found a weak link in the chain of evidence, you replaced it with a stronger one – that was how things were done. Davies was guilty of a hideous, unforgivable crime and if the witnesses weren't perfect, so be it. They were, Stratton thought, good *enough*, and that was what mattered.

Chapter Twenty-Two

Nineteenth-century Baker Street was rotting in the damp December air – much, Diana thought, like its real, twentieth-century counterpart. At the end of the row of quaint but peeling shopfronts stood a guillotine and, beside it, a weather-beaten pile of canoes which were leaning against what surely couldn't be – no, actually was – a baby Sphinx. To the right stood a grey platform topped with a funnel-like structure, which Diana guessed was the upper part of a submarine.

Her guide was a young man with a chalk-white face haloed by orange curls which, combined with a skewed, upstanding collar and expansive gestures, made her think of a painting she'd once seen of Queen Elizabeth rallying the troops at Tilbury. 'We do try to economise,' he said, 'but we can't re-use everything, and there isn't room to store it all in the Scene Dock. The backlot's over there by the river,' he added, flinging out an arm so near Diana's nose that she flinched involuntarily. 'That's for exterior stuff. We had two hundred Zulus camped out there last week – not real ones, black sailors from Cardiff. Mayhem! We've got fifteen stages –

they're so big you can't miss them. The workshops,' Queen Elizabeth, whose name was really Alex McPherson, gestured again, this time at a row of boxy, flat-roofed buildings across a concrete causeway, 'are there – carpentry and so on – and the Cutting Rooms, where film is edited – you'll see that later – and then there's the Dressing Rooms and the Art Department and Viewing Theatre and what-have-you over to the right. The producers have offices in the old house, that-a-way,' he spun round and waved a hand at a Victorian mansion, bits of which were visible behind a row of trees, 'and the bar is there, as well.' Alex raised his eyebrows. '*Most* important, as you'll soon find out. The restaurant is in there, too. That's for the units, of course. Extras and clerical staff and groundsmen and people like that eat in the big canteen,' he spun round again, and jerked out a thumb, 'down there.'

While he was talking, several girls in pink tulle hurried past, shivering, followed by a boy carrying an elaborate Regency wig on a stand, and another in overalls, hauling on the leash of a goat which kept craning its neck to try and eat the wig, sending little puffs of powder into the air each time its nose brushed the horsehair curls. Bringing up the rear was a ludicrously handsome man in tails, his hair held in place by kirby grips. Seeing Diana's slack jaw and following her gaze, Alex said, 'Oh, those won't be in the shot. It's just so it stays in place.'

'And the goat?'

'Background. They're shooting a Victorian melodrama on C Stage. Humble farmer's daughter, lusty young squire – doomed love affair with picturesque haystacks and beasts of the field dotted about the place. You know the sort of thing . . . Actually,' Alex lowered his voice, 'it's been rather awful because Robert Monckton – that's the leading man – has got this absolute horror of watching women eat. God knows why, but it's holding everything up because there's all this stuff with Jessica Miles biting into apples and things. You know, ripeness and bountiful nature and all the rest of it . . . So poor old Jessica is nibbling away, take after take, and he's meant to be looming over her, all dark and brooding, but instead he looks as if he's going to throw up at any moment. They had to do separate reaction shots in the end.'

'Oh dear,' said Diana.

'Not really,' said Alex. 'They're supposed to be madly in love, but they can't stand the sight of each other and it doesn't half show. Anyway, come and see the costumes.'

Rounding a corner and ducking under a precarious-looking balustrade, complete with a swathe of artificial ivy, they entered a warehouse the size of an aircraft hangar, where, suspended from a hundred rails, Nazi uniforms cosied up to crinolines and poke bonnets and yokels' smocks were crushed against angels' wings and sailor suits. 'Extraordinary, isn't it?' said Alex. 'Well, that's really the end of the outside tour. I'd better show you the stages.'

'If it's not too much trouble,' said Diana. She was feeling rather giddy – there was so much to absorb, and most of her attention seemed to be taken up in keeping out of the way of Alex's flailing arms.

'Not at all.' Alex raked a hand through the orange curls so that they sprang up even higher. 'Follow me. You've got to get to know your way around if you're going to work for Mr Carleton. You're jolly lucky, you know. Most people get thrown in at the deep end, but I was told to take special care of you.'

The job with Mr Carleton, a film director at Ashwood Studios, was Jock Anderson's idea. She, Jock and Lally had been amongst the few who'd attended F-J's funeral the week before. It had been an unconvivial affair, the hymn-singing faltering and the mourners avoiding each other's eyes. The whole thing was conducted at a forced, slightly desperate pace, as if everyone present feared that the thin ice of distant politeness might give way between them at any moment. Mrs Forbes-James was absent, and after the service the congregation dispersed hastily, in the guilty manner of conspirators.

At dinner afterwards, Jock, who'd been impressed by the speed and efficiency with which she'd typed his manuscript, had told her that he'd arranged a meeting for her with an old acquaintance, Julian Vernon, who was head of Ashwood Studios. Diana had liked Mr Vernon, but had left with only the vaguest idea of what she might be expected to do as assistant to Mr Carleton, whom she had not yet met, and Alex, who was Mr Vernon's assistant, hadn't enlightened her. 'Supposing Mr Carleton doesn't like me?' she'd said to Lally after the meeting. 'And what if I can't do whatever it is I'm meant to do?' Lally'd just laughed and told her she'd pick it up, adding that it was probably just fetching cups of coffee and looking decorative.

*

Diana's apprehension about being up to the job – whatever it turned out to be – took an instant and vertiginous hike when they entered the enormous studio where she'd be working. Inside, beyond a painfully brightly lit area which appeared to be where the action was about to take place, everything was dark and shadowy, but the entire building echoed with the din of a dozen men in brown overalls who were manhandling pieces of heavy ornate furniture, laying cables, getting in each other's way and shouting almost continually. Thirty feet above her head were more shouting men, some perched precariously on rails angling giant lamps, while others lowered a vast, glittering chandelier into place. Still other men fussed over two enormous cameras on tracks, and groups of people in old-fashioned clothes stood in the shadows, patiently, like cattle. 'Extras,' murmured Alex, propelling her forwards. 'Another Victorian melodrama, I'm afraid. We've had rather a run of them recently and they're very tiresome. Lots of nonsense about historical accuracy when all they really want is grand clothes and a lot of flouncing about.'

Diana laughed. 'What's it called?'

'*Trial at Midnight*. I ask you!' Alex rolled his eyes. 'It's about a bloke who's trying to drive his wife mad so he can get his hands on her money. That's him, there.' He flapped a hand at an exhausted-looking individual in a frock coat who was slumped in a chair at the side of the set being fussed over by a make-up girl in a white smock. He appeared to take no notice of her at all, but sat listlessly, arms hanging down. His face, shiny with greasepaint, looked like a drying death mask, with the eyes like two black marbles pressed into wet plaster.

'He looks ill.'

'He is. His doctor forced him to go on the wagon a few months ago, and it doesn't suit him.'

The young make-up girl, apparently flustered by the direction of their gaze, looked up, dropping her sponge as she did so. 'Then why is he doing it?' asked Diana, turning away slightly to spare the girl's embarrassment.

'No choice,' said Alex. 'Not if he wants to stay alive, anyway. Although,' he added sardonically, 'I'd say that's debatable at the moment.'

Shocked by this flippancy, but trying not to show it, Diana said, 'I meant, why is he doing the film?'

'Last chance saloon. Five other actors turned it down because they're sick and tired of moustache-twirling parts, and he's turned down so many things himself that the studio threatened not to renew his contract. They won't anyway, but . . .' Alex shrugged.

'Poor man.'

'Poor man who's wasting everyone's time and the studio's money. It's a pity, because he used to be good.'

'Who is he?'

'Anthony Renwick.'

'*Really*? But he's . . .'

'I know. Taller, slimmer, better-looking . . . Mind you, it's always odd the first time you see film actors in the flesh, whatever shape they're in. One's so used to seeing bits of them vastly enlarged on screens that one imagines they must actually be the size of hills or something. Anyway, mighty fallen, and all that. It'd be a mercy to give him a drink, really – might improve his performance, at any rate.'

'Excuse me, miss.' Diana turned to see an electrician behind her with a lamp on wheels.

She stepped smartly backwards, tripped over a length of cable, and would have fallen if Alex hadn't rescued her.

'Don't worry, happens all the time.' He took her arm. 'We should get back a bit,' he murmured. 'They're about to go. That's the second assistant director, marshalling the extras.' Diana saw a group of women in ball gowns being herded across the floor by a slight, nervous-looking individual. 'Oh,' added Alex, *sotto voce*, 'and that's Mr Carleton, sitting under the camera. I'll introduce you when they break for lunch.'

Following his gaze, Diana saw the profile of a dark-haired man in a grubby open-necked shirt, sleeves rolled up, elbows on knees, staring intently in front of him. At his side was a thin woman in a plain black frock, her expression permanently fixed at surprise by the high arches of her pencilled brows. 'Who's that?' she whispered.

'Marita Neill. She's the continuity girl. Makes sure all the shots match up and nobody's wearing a wristwatch and so forth. You need eyes in the back of your head, and she's the best in the business. Been here for *ever*.'

Diana jumped as a hugely amplified voice boomed, 'Quiet, please!' A sudden silence, so tense that it was almost palpable, filled the studio.

'That's the first assistant director,' Alex muttered in her ear. 'You'll meet him later.'

'Scene Five, Take One,' said the voice. Mr Carleton and the continuity girl moved away from the camera as the clapper boy dashed forward, snapped his board in front of the camera, and beat a hasty retreat.

Mr Carleton, hands on knees and leaning so far forward that Diana felt he might topple over at any moment, shouted, 'Action!'

There was a buzz of conversation from the extras, and Anthony Renwick, side by side with another frock-coated man, strolled through them towards the camera, which retreated before them on its tracks. Renwick's face lacked animation, even when he began to speak, and he was gripping a champagne glass with a white-knuckled immobility that looked actually painful. The exchange of dialogue completed, leaden on Renwick's part, with desperate over-compensation in both energy and emphasis by his companion, Mr Carleton shouted, 'Cut!'

'Not so much acting as an endurance test,' Alex muttered into the wave of noise which enveloped them as suddenly as had the silence before. Glancing at his watch, he said, 'Quarter to one. I'd say we've got at least an hour before there's any hope of lunch, so you might as well see round the rest of the place.'

They returned just in time for the final take. To Diana's eyes, it seemed no different to the first, but Mr Carleton said, 'Print that one – it won't get any better. Reserve, take three.'

As Renwick walked off the set, his head sunk between his shoulders like a tortoise retreating into its shell, Alex murmured, 'Better than yesterday, at any rate. He had to slap Anne Chalmers – she's the leading lady, by the way. Took the *entire* afternoon, and she got very fed up. At one point she asked him if he was actually awake.'

They waited while Mr Carleton had a complicated exchange with the continuity girl about playing time and footage. Close to, he seemed to radiate waves of energy, like heat, and when he stood up she saw that he was tall, thin and scruffier than she'd expected. Also younger – thirty-five or -six, perhaps – but anyway, not much older than she was. His face, aquiline, with the beginnings of cragginess, was screwed up in concentration, and the words seemed to rush from his mouth, falling over each other as if he couldn't quite keep pace with his thoughts. Dismissing the continuity girl, he stared into space for a moment, rubbing the back of his neck, apparently oblivious to their presence until Alex coughed, making him shy like a nervous horse.

'Mr Carleton, this is Mrs Calthrop,' said Alex.

Mr Carleton raised his head and looked at Diana. Staring into his muddy-brown eyes, she experienced a physical jolt inside that made her catch her breath.

'She's come to work for you,' prompted Alex.

'Oh . . . yes. Yes, of course. That's . . . yes . . .'

Diana was aware of opening her mouth, but could think of nothing to say, and closed it again. Her brain seemed to have stalled like an engine refusing to fire up. It was a moment before she realised that Mr Carleton was holding out his hand and then, after staring at it for what seemed like a full minute – *what was wrong with her?* – she took it and felt a tingle shoot up her arm like a small electric shock. 'James Carleton. Pleased to meet you.'

'Yes . . . Diana Calthrop.'

'Well, Mrs Calthrop–'

'Diana, please.'

Mr Carleton raised his eyebrows fractionally, and to her horror, Diana felt herself beginning to blush. Why was she behaving like a schoolgirl? Not only would she not be up to the job, whatever it turned out to be, but she was making a fool of herself. Why him, she thought desperately. Why now? Perhaps she should just excuse herself and leave, before she did something really stupid . . . 'I feel,' she began, 'that I'm here under rather false pretences. Mr Vernon only gave me a job as a favour to a friend, so if you don't want–'

Mr Carleton held up his hand. 'But I *do* want,' he said, seriously. 'I want very much. If you'll come with me, I'll tell you what I want over lunch.'

'Thank you. It's very kind–'

'No it isn't.' He put his head on one side and stared at her, intently. 'Welcome, *Diana*, to the place where nothing is real.'

Chapter Twenty-Three

'I trust you, Inspector. I don't trust the others, see? But I trust you.' Davies's words echoed in Stratton's mind as he brushed earth off the parsnips he'd just dug up and laid them down on a sheet of newspaper. It was Saturday afternoon and he'd been at his allotment for over four hours, harvesting carrots and potatoes, preparing earth, tidying up, and then pottering about and making work, even though it was getting too dark to do anything really useful. Although he'd told himself it was because he ought to make the most of his severely limited free time – and it was entirely true that, in the past week, he'd barely been home except to snatch some sleep – he was deliberately stretching things out until darkness fell at teatime because he wanted to be on his own and outside. There were still times when being in a Jenny-less house felt like solitary confinement. And although working on the allotment was a great improvement on sitting in an armchair and staring at the empty one opposite, the fresh air hadn't blown the thoughts of Davies out of his mind in the way that he'd hoped.

Especially those last few words of his. They'd been uttered in the car, on the return journey from the committal. Staring down at the parsnips – feeble things, not a patch on last year's crop – he shook his head. Grove was absolutely right – he must not let his emotions get in the way of his work. Davies might have a mental age of twelve, but he'd killed his wife and child and been judged fit to stand trial and that was all there was to it. Hanging him wouldn't bring back Muriel or the baby, but justice would be served. And if he, Stratton, wasn't doing his job to the best of his ability, he might as well give it up and go and be a market gardener or something. Not that he'd be much good at that on the present showing, he thought, fingering one of the pathetic-looking parsnips.

He thought back to the chats he'd had with Davies in the car to and from the committal hearing, of the slight, childish form beside him, hunched inside the overcoat. 'I want to tell Mam what I done, but I can't do it, Mr Stratton.'

'You should tell her the truth. Tell your family, and your legal advisors. It's the best way.' Davies had reminded him of Pete when he was younger and caught out over a falsehood or a broken window – right down to the mumbled responses, the chin glued to the chest and the sharp tang of boy sweat. Then the excuses, 'I was married too young, see? Never had any money, that was my trouble. I could have made a bit of money if I hadn't married, then I'd have managed all right, see?' Then he'd talked about what he'd done on occasions when he did have money – football matches and going to the dogs, this with improbable boasts about the quantity and frequency of his winnings, followed by equally improbable – and inappropriate – boasts about his sexual conquests. Stratton could easily imagine him saying these things in a pub and engaging in banter with other men – he'd be able to hold his own in that company, or with his fellow van drivers at work. He had been cheerful and talkative, as Dr Sutherland had said, even to the extent of eliciting from Stratton that he supported Tottenham Hotspur, and teasing him about their recent poor performance. His under-developed mind, Stratton thought, did not allow him to dwell on his predicament for long. When they'd parted, Davies had shaken his hand and asked when they'd meet again. Stratton remembered the little man's face falling in dismay as he'd explained that it would be on opposite sides of the Court, and how Davies had gripped his hand once more and said that he was sorry . . .

'Dad! There you are!' Stratton looked up to see Monica standing over him in the near-darkness. 'Are you all right?'

'Oh . . . Yes, love.'

'You were all hunched over, snapping parsnips in half and talking to yourself.'

'Was I?'

Monica knelt down next to him, and pointed at a heap of broken vegetables. 'It doesn't matter – Auntie Doris will only cut them up anyway. Are you going to come back now? It's gone six.'

'I lost track of time.'

'*Are* you all right, Dad? *Really?*'

'I'm sorry, love. Just feeling a bit blue, that's all. Nothing to worry about.'

'I thought I'd better come and fetch you. It's way past teatime.'

'I didn't mean to put you out.'

'You didn't. Anyway, I wanted to tell you – I met someone you know.'

'Did you? Where?'

'Yesterday, at work.'

'Work?' echoed Stratton, trying to imagine what on earth anyone he knew could possibly be doing on a film set.

'Yesterday. Her name's Mrs Calthrop.'

Thank God she can't see my face properly, thought Stratton. 'Diana Calthrop?' he asked, in what he hoped was a neutral tone. He hadn't thought about Diana – well, not much, anyway – for a long time. Not consciously, at least. He'd dreamt about her quite a few times in the years since they'd met and now, in Monica's presence, the sudden and excruciatingly detailed memory of those dreams made him hot and uncomfortable.

'That's right. She said to give you her regards.'

'What was she doing at the studio?'

'She's just started there. She's working on Mr Carleton's picture, same as me. She asked if I was any relation to you.'

'I don't understand. How did she know who you were?'

'She said she'd heard someone calling my name.'

Stratton couldn't remember ever telling Diana about his family, but he supposed that he must have done. Either that or, Diana's world being what it was – everyone knowing, or knowing *of*, everyone else – she'd simply made an assumption. 'But why is she there?' he asked. 'She lives in Hampshire, and she's married. She's got a family.'

'I don't know, Dad. I could hardly ask, could I? It would have been rude. It was jolly strange as it was. She said she'd met you in the war, and asked how you were. Then she said it was only her third day so she was still finding her feet.' Rising, Monica tugged at Stratton's elbow. 'Come on, Dad. Your supper'll be all dried up.'

They walked in silence for some minutes, Stratton cradling his package of vegetables, his mind a whirl of questions. What was Diana doing working at a film studio? Perhaps her husband had died – or she'd left him . . . but in that case, what about the children? Colonel Forbes-James had definitely said she was starting a family. Perhaps her child was Ventriss's after all, and she'd run away with him. Not married him, though, or she wouldn't still be called Mrs Calthrop. Besides, he thought sourly, Claude Ventriss wasn't the marrying kind, baby or no. She'd had a war job, but that, for her class, was simply doing one's bit with well-bred courage and county phlegm and all the rest of it – a normal, peacetime job, with connotations of *having* to earn one's living, was an entirely different kettle of fish. There were a dozen questions he wanted to ask Monica: how did she look, what did they talk about, did she seem happy, was she wearing a wedding ring . . . But he couldn't. Not without her getting the wrong impression – an impression as absurd as it was unthinkable. Because it *was* unthinkable. He was just a copper, and Diana was . . . was . . . Well, she was *Diana*. She belonged to a different world – not his, and not Monica's, either. But then, what was she doing working at a film studio?

'She's nice, isn't she?' said Monica, as they turned the corner into Lansdowne Road. 'I mean, terribly posh and cut-glass and everything, but she's not stand-offish at all. How on earth did you meet her, Dad? I didn't like to ask in case it was something awful.'

Stratton hesitated. 'Well . . . she wasn't a suspect, if that's what you mean.'

'Can't you talk about it?'

'Not really, love. Not allowed to.'

'Oh.' Monica sounded disappointed. 'Oh, well . . .'

Stratton decided to change the subject before he said something he'd regret. 'Aren't you going out tonight?'

'No. I was going to the pictures with Madeleine, but we said we'd help Auntie Doris with the mending instead. I thought I'd keep you company – I haven't had supper yet – and go round later.'

'That's nice of you,' said Stratton, pushing open the gate of number twenty-seven, 'but you shouldn't have waited. What's Auntie Doris left for supper?'

'Cheese pie and tomatoes.'

Stratton had tried growing tomatoes for the first time in the summer. The experiment had gone well – a bit too well, in fact, because they'd ended up with a glut, and, having been bottled by Doris, they appeared with monotonous regularity. Stratton stabbed the largest one with a fork, causing a gout of warmish liquid to spurt across the plate. He realised that he couldn't actually remember the last home-cooked meal – breakfast included – that hadn't involved the bloody things. Shoving the deflated tomato to the side of the plate so that it wouldn't turn the cheese pie, which he rather liked, into a soggy mess, he wondered what Diana was doing. Eating, perhaps? Stratton glanced up at the kitchen clock. Half past six. Too early. She'd be having drinks somewhere, or getting dressed up to go out to a party, or even—

'Dad? I said, I've left it on the mantelpiece.' Monica's raised voice shattered a wholly inappropriate image of Diana clad in nothing but camiknickers.

'Left what?' he asked.

'Honestly! Pete's letter, of course.'

'Oh. When did that come?'

Monica rolled her eyes. 'This morning. I just told you.'

'Sorry, love. What's the news?'

'Only that he's fed up and so's everyone else, and the sergeant can't even be bothered to sound properly fierce when they do their bayonet drill, whatever that is.'

'Charging at straw-filled sacks and stabbing them and bawling a lot, like this.' Stratton lowered his knife and fork, thrust his head forward, and emitted a blood-curdling yell.

'Blimey, Dad. You'll give yourself indigestion, doing that.'

'Your Uncle Reg used to do it up at the football ground with the Home Guard. It wasn't a pretty sight.' Stratton winced – not entirely theatrically – at the memory of his brother-in-law, pop-eyed and bulging in khaki, wheezing as he launched himself at a stuffed sack hanging from a gibbet.

'I can't imagine Uncle Reg charging at anything.' Monica giggled.

'Don't try, or you'll be the one with indigestion. What else did Pete say?'

'Just that when they're not doing the charging, they're doing silly things like polishing belt brasses on the insides and that he's skinned his palms trying to get round the assault course. That's it, really – except that he's coming home for Christmas.'

'That's good, anyway.' Stratton pushed his plate away. 'I'm sorry, love, but I don't feel very hungry.'

'It's the tomatoes, isn't it?'

''Fraid so.'

Monica put her knife and fork together. 'I'm not that hungry, either. I won't tell Auntie Doris if you don't. Can I have a cig? I've run out.'

'If you make me a cup of tea before you go.' Stratton stood up. 'I'm going next door to have a look at Pete's letter.'

After a cursory glance at the letter, which said no more than Monica had reported, Stratton sat down in his armchair to read the paper. In the five minutes before his tea arrived, he managed to concentrate fairly well on a piece about whether all the money spent on the Festival of Britain wouldn't be better put towards rehoming people, but as soon as he heard the front door close he let the paper fall and, leaning back, closed his eyes and allowed the image of Diana back into his mind. After a few moments of this, an obscure feeling – he mentally skirted the word 'guilt' – that despite being alone he really ought to give the appearance of doing something else, made him get up and turn on the wireless. Returning to his chair, he settled back and let his thoughts take him where they would.

Chapter Twenty-Four

Clutching her notes to her chest, Diana stared down at her shoes. She'd been told that they were days behind schedule, and Anthony Renwick had spent the morning – it was now quarter past eleven – stumbling through take after take, disorientated and constantly forgetting his lines, until nobody could bear to look at him. Now, the unit were avoiding each other's eyes, too, ashamed at being part of a disaster. Only Carleton kept on staring at Renwick with pinpoint concentration, as if he were trying to force a performance from the actor by sheer willpower.

'Action!'

Diana glanced up in time to see a look of consternation momentarily animate Renwick's otherwise immobile features. A second later, he let out a long, wailing fart.

'Cut! Cut!' Carleton jumped up and strode towards him. 'For Christ's sake, Tony . . .'

The crescendo of laughter – a release of tension, if not actual merriment – stopped abruptly when Renwick burst into noisy, gulping tears. Carleton put an arm round his shoulders – 'Break, everybody! Ten minutes!' – and escorted him outside, motioning Diana to follow. She'd been working at Ashwood for two weeks now, and while she felt she'd never be on top of the myriad jobs involved in assisting Marita Neill, the continuity girl – it turned out that Mr Carleton had a perfectly good secretary already – she was at least beginning to understand how things worked. And, when she wasn't worrying about missing something or getting it wrong, which was still quite a lot of the time, she was enjoying herself a great deal. The other good thing was that, although his attraction was undeniable, she was managing not to be openly stupid about Mr Carleton (as Lally – who'd guessed immediately, much to her chagrin, from the way she spoke about him – had put it).

Anthony Renwick stood in the feeble winter sunlight, shoulders heaving, with Carleton wiping his nose for him as if he were a baby. As Diana approached Carleton broke away and took her by the arm. He seemed so supercharged with tension that it was like being inside an electric force field. 'Get him a drink.'

'But he's not supposed to–'

'For Christ's sake, Diana, *look at him*!'

'You'll kill him. His doctor–'

'His doctor hasn't got the studio breathing down his neck. Just go across to the bar and get him a bloody drink,' Carleton hissed. 'You can get one for me, too, while you're at it.'

Seeing that it was useless to argue, Diana said, 'What would you like?'

'Anything! Just make sure it's strong.'

Renwick, who'd been staring into the middle distance somewhere over Diana's left shoulder during this exchange, suddenly said, with more firmness and clarity than he'd managed all week, 'Brandy. I want brandy.'

'There you are,' said Carleton. 'He wants brandy, and I'll have the same. Now go!'

Dismissing her, he returned to Renwick and steered him back towards the studio. 'Come on, Tony,' she heard him say. 'Pull yourself together. You'll be all right now.'

As she walked down the causeway, Diana felt very doubtful that Renwick would ever be 'all right'. Certainly, judging from the way in which Mr Vernon had harangued Carleton the previous evening – she and Marita had been in Carleton's office when he took the telephone call, and his feelings, if not his actual words, had been excruciatingly obvious – Renwick wouldn't be working for Ashwood again. Whether Carleton himself would, having told Mr Vernon in no uncertain terms that he hadn't wanted Renwick in the first place, also seemed open to question.

As she entered the old house, Diana was nearly knocked off her feet by a young lad with an armful of paperchains and a grin so wide that it threatened to meet itself at the back of his head. There were people up ladders tacking coloured streamers to the gallery and the whole place had an atmosphere of bustling, anticipatory festivity.

The restaurant, in contrast, was deserted, except for a few waitresses laying tables and the old barman who, on seeing Diana, raised his eyebrows so high that they all but disappeared beneath his toupee. 'You're on G Stage, aren't you, miss? I thought it couldn't last.'

'It's just the one,' said Diana, defensively, taken aback by the man's familiarity and instant summing-up of the situation. 'Well, just the two, anyway. Brandy.'

The barman picked up two balloons, and looked pointedly from the one in his left hand to the one in his right. 'For Mr Carleton, is it?'

'Mr Renwick,' said Diana, assuming that he must know about the actor's problem.

'*Both* of them?'

'Well, no. The other one's for Mr Carleton.' Diana wondered why she was explaining this – after all, what business was it of his?

'Is it indeed?' The barman's tone was arch, but he turned away too quickly for Diana to read his expression, busying himself with the optics. 'Can't say I'm surprised.' He turned and slid a tray across the polished surface. 'Would you like a siphon?'

'Yes, please,' said Diana, briskly.

'Right you are.'

'Thank you.'

As Diana picked up the tray and turned to leave, the barman said, 'I'll see you later, miss.'

'Naturally,' said Diana, with hauteur. 'I shall return the tray.'

'Of course, miss.' To her astonishment, the barman closed one eye in a deliberate, conspiratorial wink.

She returned to G Stage to find Carleton and Renwick

huddled at the side of the building, smoking in silence. Ignoring the soda, Carleton picked both balloons off the tray and held one up to Renwick, whose eyes followed it with a precision of focus Diana hadn't seen from him before. If he were a dog, she thought, he'd be slobbering. 'There you are,' said Carleton. 'Just what the doctor didn't order.'

As they clinked their glasses, Diana saw a look pass between them, a strange mix of solemnity and devilment, as of a secret shared. Obviously, Carleton had supplied Renwick with illicit drinks before. But surely, she thought, he can't really believe that everyone inside hasn't guessed what Renwick's doing out here? And even if they don't, they're bound to smell it the moment the two of them walk back in.

Renwick drank greedily and returned the glass to the tray with a flourish. 'Bless you, my child,' he said, giving her a mock bow.

'That,' said Carleton, tossing back the remains of his own brandy, 'should get us through till lunch, at any rate.'

Two hours and three scenes later, Diana was forced to admit that the brandy – and the second helpings she'd fetched an hour later, to the unconcealed amusement of the barman – had done the trick. Renwick was a changed man and the alteration infused the unit with new energy. As he seemed almost to blaze before her, Diana felt herself lit up by the presence and the vitality that had made him a star. Now, everyone was looking at him. He didn't draw your attention so much as actually drag it to him, so that you barely noticed any of the other actors. But we're watching him die, she thought, remembering what Alex had told her about the doctor's warning. If he carries on with it, then he really *will* die. And she'd got him the brandy, hadn't she? And, she thought ruefully, she would again if Carleton requested it. She not only needed the job, especially as Hambeyn House was still on the market and she was looking for a flat – despite their protests to the contrary, she felt she'd imposed herself on Jock and Lally for quite long enough – but she loved working at the studio.

Only obeying orders, she mocked herself, that's what I'm doing. Would Renwick, she wondered, have cracked if Carleton hadn't suggested the brandy? He could have refused it, of course, if he'd had the mental strength, but anyone could see how weak he was.

As if he could read her thoughts, Carleton beckoned her over during a pause for set-dressing and said, 'There's no option, Diana. It's him or the picture.'

When they finally broke for lunch, and Carleton and Renwick strolled off towards the restaurant, arms round one another's shoulders, Diana, too disturbed to be hungry, decided to take herself off for a walk. It was a desire to be elsewhere, rather than a conscious decision, that led her in the direction of Make-up, where, peering through a half-open door, she caught sight of Monica Stratton. Kneeling on the floor beside a supine and almost naked actress, who was unconcernedly smoking a cigarette, the policeman's daughter was occupied in painting a delicate lacework of what was obviously meant to be blood across the young woman's legs.

'We've got company,' said the actress, raising her head fractionally from its cushion. 'Can I get up now?'

'No, you've got to dry ... Oh!' Monica half-turned and, catching sight of Diana, blushed.

Hoping the girl hadn't thought she was eavesdropping – she certainly hadn't overhead anything – Diana felt uncomfortable. 'I didn't mean to disturb you,' she said, lamely.

'Can I help you?' asked Monica, getting to her feet.

Diana, having only talked to her briefly on the previous occasion they'd met, now had the chance for a proper look at her. Despite the severe hairstyle and unbecoming overall, her fresh complexion and bright-green eyes made the languid sophisticate who sprawled before them on the floor in her *maquillage* and silk underwear seem tawdry and stale.

'I was just getting a breath of air,' she said. 'Wandering about, really.'

'Oh . . .' Monica, too, seemed at a loss for what to say. 'Well, it's a nice day, for a change.'

'I am sorry if I disturbed you.'

'Oh, no. I wouldn't mind some fresh air myself. We're starting again in ten minutes, and I've missed lunch, so . . .'

'Do you fancy a quick walk?' Honestly, thought Diana, anyone would think they were a boy and a girl at their first dance, tongue-tied by proximity and etiquette.

Monica looked down at her paint brush. 'I'll have to wash this first, or it'll get hard.'

'What about me?' asked the actress.

'You'll have to stay put till we start again,' said Monica. 'I'll finish you off on set. It's all right, I'll put a notice on the door so no one'll come in. It's for a Donald Colgate picture,' she explained to Diana. 'I'm not supposed to be doing it, but one of the girls is off with chickenpox.'

'I'm just the legs,' added the actress. 'Still, at least I'll be able to tell everyone I've been killed by Donald Colgate. It's practically a rite of passage.'

'Is it?'

'Oh, yes,' said Monica placidly, from the basin, 'he's always playing men who murder their wives – they get him if they can't have James Mason.'

She put on her coat and scarf and the two of them wandered down the causeway. Despite Monica's remark, it wasn't a 'nice day'. It wasn't raining, but above them, dark clouds were beginning to conjoin so that the sky resembled an ominously heavy grey eiderdown. Turning her collar up, Monica said, 'I told Dad about meeting you.'

'Oh . . .' Diana, gratified by this – she'd thought the girl might have forgotten – asked, 'What did he say?'

'He remembered you.' Another grin, quick this time. 'Very well, I think – although he didn't say that.'

Diana, wondering what to make of this, said, 'He was very kind to me.'

'That sounds like Dad.' The girl stared at Diana for a moment, then blurted, 'I'm worried about him,' and stopped abruptly, looking alarmed.

Surprised, Diana said, 'Why?'

Monica looked as if she wished she hadn't said anything.

'It's probably nothing, but he's gone sort of quiet. Gone into himself.'

'Perhaps he's worried about something ... a case.'

Monica nodded. 'I know he is,' she said, more enthusiastically this time. 'It's a man who killed his wife, and it's horrible for Dad because of Mum.' Before Diana could say anything, she added, 'Mum was killed, you see.'

'During the war?'

'Yes, but it wasn't a bomb. It was a woman that Mum and my Auntie Doris were looking after when she was bombed out, and she went sort of mad and attacked Mum ... stabbed her. It happened while I was evacuated. Dad feels guilty because he thinks he should have saved her, but he wasn't there in time. He's never told me that, but I know he does. I've known for ages. And I know he keeps on remembering what happened, and it's this case, making it all worse ... He misses her like mad. We all do, but ... I'm sorry, I don't really know why I'm telling you this. I don't normally talk about it.' Monica huddled into her coat, and Diana had the impression that she was battening down the hatches.

'I'm not surprised.' Seeing Monica's stricken face, she hurried on, 'I just meant it must be very hard for you, that's all. But you can tell me, if you like.' She smiled encouragingly. 'I'm quite good at listening.'

Monica considered, biting her lip, then said, 'I didn't really think about it until recently – or I suppose I didn't notice – but it's as if his life has sort of stopped. His memory, I mean. Sometimes he tells me things, stuff from the past ... It's always me he tells, never Pete – that's my brother – because he won't talk about Mum at all, and anyway he's not at home any more . . . But when Dad says things, it's always stuff from when Mum was here.'

'Perhaps he thinks those are the things you want to hear about.'

'Yes, I do, but . . . The years between then and now are like a big . . . *nothing*, as if there's only what happened today, or yesterday, and then before that it was nineteen forty-four, before Mum died. I mean, I don't want him to forget about her, but I think he should start living properly, not just going to work and his allotment and reading the paper as if he's just pretending, because that's how it seems. Auntie Doris and Auntie Lilian think he should get married again.'

'What do you think?'

'I don't know. I don't think I'd mind if it was someone nice, but I don't see why he should have to if he doesn't want to. Look, I really am sorry for telling you. It's just that I really can't talk about it with Pete, or Auntie Doris, or my cousin Madeleine, and you're . . . you're . . .'

'I'm . . .?' Diana prompted.

'You're so . . . *different*, I suppose – sorry, I hope that doesn't sound rude or anything.' Monica paused for a moment, frowning at Diana, then added, 'Was your husband killed in the war?'

'No,' said Diana. 'Why do you ask?'

'Well . . .' The colour in Monica's cheeks intensified.

'Go on. I shan't be offended.'

'Working here, for one thing. And it was what came into my mind when I first saw you – that you'd had a loss. I mean,' she said, 'I suppose it could have been anything,' Monica gave an awkward little laugh, 'but it seemed as if you'd lost something important.'

Although taken aback – Monica was clearly as observant as her father – Diana found that she didn't in the least mind the girl's frankness and found herself willing to repay one confidence with another. 'I did lose my husband in the war – just not in the way you thought. We're divorcing.'

Monica's blush was now a vivid scarlet. 'I really didn't mean to pry, Mrs Calthrop. I'm terribly sorry.'

'I'm not,' said Diana. 'I left him. Not,' she added hastily, 'that I'd like it generally known.'

'No. No, of course not. I shan't tell anyone.' She put her hand on her chest and said, 'Not a soul – cross my heart.' The childishness was deliberate, put-on, but the sincerity was real enough.

'Thank you. And please . . . tell your father how very, very sorry I am.'

A few minutes later, Monica set off back to her drying actress, mimicking 'At least I'll be able to tell everyone I've been killed by Donald Colgate!' with surprising accuracy, and leaving Diana to contemplate the sheer magnitude of grief, in all its forms, in everything that the girl hadn't said. A sudden image made her wince and blink as if avoiding something real: the picture of a prim, rigid little woman, lace handkerchief dangling from one sleeve of her cardigan, who said, 'I beg your pardon,' and set about gouging at Monica's cowering mother with a pair of sewing shears. Ridiculous, she thought. She had no idea what Mrs Stratton was like, or the woman who'd killed her. She had, in fact, no idea about Stratton's home life at all, except that it must now be lonely and, judging by what Monica had said, haunted by the spectres of guilt and regret as well as his murdered wife. Poor, poor man . . . She hoped he'd got somebody he could talk to – if he wanted, that was, because men very often didn't. He'd been so understanding – a good friend to her, when she'd needed one. It would be nice, she thought, if she could do the same for him – comfort, perhaps, or just listen. But I shall probably never see him again, she thought sadly – after all, she wasn't likely to meet him socially, was she?

Diana found Marita in the restaurant, huddled with Alex McPherson in the corner. The tables around them were deserted, but across the room, in the middle of an appreciative coterie of studio staff and partially costumed actors, was Anthony Renwick, declaiming, brandy balloon held aloft. 'Don't mind me,' said Alex. 'I'm on a spying mission for Mr Vernon. Management needs to keep tabs on the Means of Production, and I shall have to report that one of the Means has dined not wisely, but a bit too well. And,' he added, glancing at his watch, 'we'll have the unions on our backs if this sort of thing keeps happening.'

'Mr Renwick was wonderful this morning,' said Diana.

'So I gather,' said Alex wryly. 'Let's just hope he gets a few more takes under his belt before he falls over. Coffee?'

'Thanks.'

'Have this,' said Marita, pushing a full cup towards her. 'I haven't touched it, and I need to get back.'

When she'd gone, Alex said, 'So . . . Mr Carleton is making quite a pet of you, according to Marita. Taking you under his wing, so to speak.'

'He's been very . . . kind,' said Diana carefully, realising, as she said it, that these were the exact words she'd just used to Monica about Inspector Stratton.

'So I understand.'

This seemed so pointed that Diana found herself saying, 'Marita hasn't taken against me, has she? She certainly hasn't said–'

Alex held up one hand like a traffic policeman. 'Marita,' he said, 'never "takes against" anyone. She may look like a human exclamation mark, but she's as tender as a lamb. Except where the interests of the studio are concerned, and frankly, my darling, it's not you that's likely to incapacitate the Means of Production. In fact,' he raised an eyebrow, 'you may have quite the opposite effect, so–'

Whatever else he'd been going to say was lost in a bellow of laughter from the other side of the dining room. This seemed to signal the end of Renwick's performance, because a moment later people began to leave. Alex glanced at his wristwatch and stood up. 'The triumph of hope over experience,' he murmured. 'Well, he can't say we didn't warn him.'

'Mr Renwick, you mean?'

'Mr Vernon. Sorry, Diana, got to dash.' He loped off, waving his arms at someone at the far end of the room.

As she gulped the remains of her coffee, Diana wondered what on earth Alex had been talking about. Still, he'd seemed to have implied that she was an asset to the picture and not the reverse, which was obviously a good thing. Anyway, it couldn't have been all that important, or he'd have stayed and elaborated. . .

Diana looked up as a shadow fell across the table. Mr Carleton was standing beside her. 'My rudeness this morning was unforgivable,' he said. 'I've come to apologise.'

Jolted by this, Diana said, 'Really, there's no need.'

'Yes, there is. There's every need. In fact, I was wondering if you'd like to have dinner with me. . . By way of apology, of course.' His expression, as he looked down at her, was solemn, but there was a light in his eyes that made her heart jump inside her chest.

'Well, then,' she said, in a deliberately measured tone. 'By way of accepting your apology, I accept your invitation.'

'Does tomorrow suit?'

'It does.'

'Wonderful. I'll take you to one of my favourite haunts.' He tapped the face of his wristwatch. 'Drink up, then. We start in five minutes. Oh, and talking of drinking . . .' He pulled a silver hip flask out of his pocket. 'Would you mind asking the barman to fill this up? I fear that neither Mr Renwick nor I will last the distance without it.'

Chapter Twenty-Five

Reg, who was carolling away fit to bust in ill-fitting suit and bulging knitted maroon waistcoat, had his back to the fire and his arms around the restive shoulders of Monica and her cousin Madeleine. It was extraordinary, thought Stratton, how his brother-in-law managed to look as if he, personally, had orchestrated all the Christmas festivities. In fact, it was Doris and Lilian who had, between them, managed to obtain everything from turkey to tangerines, and then knocked themselves out in Doris's steaming, fragrant kitchen to produce a feast. Monica and Madeleine had livened up the place with holly, ivy and berries, provided along with the vegetables by Stratton, and Donald had fashioned ingenious decorations from newspaper and coloured inks. All Reg had done was fiddle with the wireless and give unnecessary advice to the people doing the actual work, accompanied by infuriating jabs of his pipe.

Still, there was nothing like being warm and full of grub, with a bottle of beer at your elbow, new leather slippers (from Lilian and Reg) on your feet and two new jazz records (from Doris and Donald) to listen to later, for putting you in a forgiving mood, and he had to admit that Reg ('Joy-ful all ye nay-shons ri-ise') did have a very nice baritone. Don wasn't bad, either – he'd been in a church choir as a kid – and even Pete, who was on leave from Catterick for forty-eight hours, could sing a bit. He, on the other hand, couldn't hold a tune in a bucket and, not wishing to give anyone a chance to comment on this, kept his mouth shut on such occasions. He thought of all the previous Christmases he'd had to miss when Jenny was alive – and now here he was, and she wasn't. The nipper would have been getting old enough to appreciate it now, too, and they could have filled the stocking together and crept into the bedroom, Jenny shushing and giggling as Stratton put his hand on her bottom on the way upstairs and then pretended to drop things, just as he had when Monica and Pete were little . . .

The whole family hadn't been together for a while, and looking round the room, Stratton noticed that the older members were definitely showing signs of age. Don's sandy hair was pepper-and-salt now, but at least, unlike Reg, who admittedly had several years on both of them, he'd still got quite a lot on top – although not as much, Stratton thought with more satisfaction than he'd have cared to admit, as he himself had. And his hair was still, except for a few bits near the temples, almost entirely its original black. He was pretty much the same shape that he'd always been, too, whereas Reg and Don seemed to be growing fatter and skinnier at equal rates and Lilian and Doris appeared to be following their husbands' examples. He supposed they couldn't help it. Jenny, he was sure, would have kept her figure, which had, in any case, been better than either of her sisters'. But she never had the chance to grow old, he thought, so I'll never know . . .

Wrenching his mind away from the subject, he found himself wondering what Davies was doing in Pentonville. Last time he'd been there at Christmas, the eye-catching jollity of a big painted sign – Merry Christmas To All! – suspended over the counter in the reception had struck him as gruesome in the extreme. He knew that the food rations in prison became smaller in the weeks before Christmas as the cooks saved up for a big, rich blow-out, but that was all. Christmas in prison, he thought, must be much the same as Christmas was for him nowadays: a milestone. In his case, it was a measure of time passing since Jenny died; for a prisoner, it would be a measure of how near (or far away) was the release date, or, in Davies's case, the trial. Remembering what Sutherland the prison doctor had said, Stratton doubted that Davies was much aware of this. Like an animal not knowing that it was destined for the abattoir . . . It was, he supposed, a symptom of the unease that he still felt about the whole thing that it continued to nag at him, even at a time like this.

'Dad?' Stratton jumped. The singing had ended and Monica was bending over him. 'Nodded off,' he lied. 'Sorry, love.' Seeing the lavish-looking box of chocolates in her hand, he added, 'Where did those come from?'

'A present.'

'Got a boyfriend, Monica?' Pete looked up from poking the fire. 'Took your time about it, didn't you?'

'No, but Madeleine has – as you very well know,' said Monica, speaking with exaggerated patience. 'He gave them to her.'

'You want to get yourself a boyfriend, too.' Pete put the poker back on the stand, then getting to his feet, added with studied casualness, 'Or perhaps you don't.'

Seeing Monica's face flush, and feeling that if anyone was going to interrogate *his* daughter about having admirers it would be *him*, and in private if at all, Stratton said, 'Leave her alone, Pete. It's none of your business.' Monica shot him a look of gratitude. She'd had a boyfriend some time back, Stratton remembered, but he didn't think it had lasted very long. He had no idea why it had ended – Monica hadn't been forthcoming and he hadn't wanted to pry – but as far as he could recall, she hadn't seemed particularly upset by it. Or maybe she had been, because that was evidently what Pete was alluding to.

He stopped listening and considered his son. Pete was, he thought, already bigger, stronger and fitter-looking than when he'd left. Unlike Monica, who'd been straight up and down like a boy until she was at least sixteen, Pete had looked adult early on and, compared to him, other National Servicemen Stratton had seen seemed puny and not fully formed. Pete's build was just like his own, although he was – Stratton felt a flicker of surprise that he'd never really noticed this before – considerably better-looking; handsome, in fact, with thick, conker-brown hair and pale skin that was just like Jenny's. He was cruder than before, though, with an undercurrent of belligerence that showed itself in an abruptness of manner, a tendency – as just now, with Monica – to talk out of turn, and the generally rough way he moved about the place. The latter, of course, could be because he was still growing – Stratton had painful memories of his own clumsiness at seventeen and eighteen. The crudeness, he supposed, was hardly surprising, as he must be billeted with a lot of young chaps wanking and boasting about girls, with all the talk ritualised into mocking, joking and one-upmanship as they probed for one another's weaknesses. It was all too easy to imagine the fetid atmosphere of the barracks, farts and arse-scratching and sweaty armpits and meaningless obscenities . . . He suddenly realised that he had no idea whether or not Pete was still a virgin. Not that he particularly wanted this information, but it was another indication of the boy moving even further away from him, and more especially because he himself had never served in the forces. He wondered if Pete might hold this omission against him. Donald hadn't fought, either. Only Reg, the family buffoon, had; the trenches in the Great War and then – if you could count it, which Stratton supposed you had to – the Home Guard.

Later, when the women went to prepare a supper of ham and salad and the men were left alone, the conversation turned – or rather, Reg turned it – to army life. After they'd listened to a lot of guff, so familiar that Stratton knew the phrases off by heart, about shaping an efficient fighting force and a fine body of men and all the rest of it, Donald asked, in a suspiciously neutral tone, 'So what do you think, Pete, about the *modern* army?'

'It's all right, I suppose, except there's no bloody privacy, unless you're asleep. And even then the bloke next to me keeps having nightmares and shouting. The sergeant told him he was going to be shot for some breach of regulations and the stupid berk actually believed him – he's a bit simple, you see. The sergeant even had him dictating a last letter to his mum, and he was bawling his eyes out.' To Stratton's horror, Pete laughed. 'It's about the only fun we've had. If you're not exhausted, you're bored stupid. We do all these war exercises – outside for hours, freezing your arse off, and then they tap you on the shoulder and tell you you're dead. Still, as long as I don't get shipped out to Korea . . .'

Reg, his voice quivering under the weight of betrayed courage and despairing patriotism, said, 'Don't you want to fight for your country–'

'It wouldn't be for my country,' said Pete, mildly. 'I wouldn't mind getting stuck in, if I thought there was something to fight *for*.'

'You'd be fighting against Communism,' said Reg.

Pete shrugged.

'You won't get very far with that attitude. What about the Selection Board?'

'Selection Board? I'm not *officer* material, Uncle Reg. That's for the public school types. They only let blokes like me make up the numbers in wartime.' Pete wasn't aware of it, but this was so entirely the reason that Reg had been made a captain in the Home Guard that Stratton almost choked trying to turn a laugh into a cough. 'Look,' Pete continued, 'I don't mind the drill and all that, and most of the chaps are OK, but they never let you think for yourself.'

Stratton was about to point out that this was pretty much true of any job when Reg declared, in a professorial tone, '*I* think that you haven't understood the fundamental aim of a fighting force. A good soldier must accept rules and regulations. Discipline' – here, the pipe stem did its stuff – 'is vital on a battlefield.'

Stratton felt that this was a bit rich coming from someone whose son, turned down for active service during the war on health grounds, had such a lack of regard for rules and regulations that he'd narrowly avoided Borstal. Johnny having left straight after their meal, Stratton thought of mentioning him, but was prevented by a warning grimace from Donald. It wouldn't be fair – Lilian had been very upset by her son's abrupt departure. In any case, Stratton thought sourly as Reg carried on pontificating, he knew perfectly well what Johnny was doing: working for a very dodgy car dealer in Warren Street. Having had to deal in an official capacity with his nephew before, he frequently and fervently hoped that next time Johnny got into trouble, some other poor sod would get there first.

He had resisted the temptation to say anything, but was fairly sure that Pete, who was beginning to look irritated, might not. Seeing that this could be the beginning of a row – Pete calling Reg a warmonger and Reg calling him a Communist – Stratton decided it was high time he left the room.

He could do with a breath of fresh air. He went down

the passage and let himself out of the back door. It was bloody cold – although, thought Stratton, it wasn't a patch on the winter of forty-six, when the pipes froze again and again and your breath was visible even inside the house and no matter how many clothes you wore, in bed or out of it, you never seemed to get warm. Peering into the almost darkness, he could make out the shapes of Donald's apple and plum trees at the bottom of the garden. He stamped his feet a few times, trying to keep warm. He didn't want to go back inside with the others – at least, until there was a good chance of any row having blown over. He'd had enough of Reg anyway, and, if he was honest, he wasn't really sure what to say to Pete.

This was partly, he supposed guiltily, because – aside from what he could glean by observing – he actually had very little idea about the sort of man his son was becoming. A callous one, judging by what he'd said to Monica and his reaction to the poor simple sod who'd been so tormented by the sergeant – or maybe that was the effect of the army, with its brutal ideas about toughening people up. But either way, at that precise moment, he wasn't even sure he *liked* his son very much.

He found himself wondering about the boy's taciturn reaction to Jenny's death – he'd assumed it was grief and that the lad had simply found the subject too painful to talk about. Stratton had been six when his own mother had died, but that was expected – tuberculosis – and he couldn't remember ever discussing it with his father or his brothers. He'd assumed that, even though the circumstances were entirely different, Pete must have had similar feelings to his own about losing his mother, but now he wondered if that were the case. Perhaps Pete simply hadn't cared all that much. Or perhaps Jenny's death had begun an inexorable hardening process within him.

Jenny'd once told him that she'd like Pete to have an office job, although he couldn't remember if she'd said what sort. Maybe she'd meant an accountant or something like that – something that involved wearing a suit, anyway. The other thing she'd said, which he *did* remember clearly, was that she didn't mind what the children ended up doing as long as they were happy. Pete's papers had come through soon after he'd left school, where he'd done surprisingly well, especially in science and mathematics. Perhaps some sort of conversation about his future was in order – although of course any future would have to be postponed until he'd done his National Service – but Stratton felt that this would need, if not actual preparation, then certainly a bit of thought.

Had he, after all, been so different to Pete at eighteen? He pictured himself, slimmer and fresher faced, marching down the endless corridors of the police-training school – shiny green and cream paint – and remembered the smell of disinfectant, sometimes so strong that it seemed to permeate the food. The army was probably quite like that, he thought. Unlike Pete, the training school was the first time he'd been away from home, and for a long time he'd missed his family and the sights, smells and sounds of the Devon farm where he'd spent his childhood. Somehow, he doubted that Pete had been very homesick. After all, he'd been evacuated, and he seemed too self-contained, too assured . . .

Perhaps Pete's confidence was a bluff, too. Stratton had never tried very hard to find out. The truth was that he'd been afraid of being rebuffed, and was still afraid. Jenny wouldn't have been. He suddenly remembered their honeymoon, walking hand in hand across sand dunes covered in scrubby grass and rabbit holes, and the hotel – the first time either had stayed in one – their awkwardness in the big, echoing dining room with its stiff napery and even stiffer waiters, and their giggly relief afterwards, finding themselves alone in the bedroom. How her beautiful green eyes had shone as she turned her face up to his for a kiss . . .

Hearing a tapping noise, he swung round and, seeing the same eyes looking out at him from behind the glass panel in the back door, he thought, for a split second, that—

'Dad! Tea's ready!' Monica opened the door. 'What are you doing out here? You'll catch your death.'

To his absolute horror, Stratton felt tears pricking at his eyelids and he turned away from her, squeezing his eyes shut. For God's sake, he told himself, get a grip. Monica stepped out and put a hand on his sleeve. 'Were you thinking about Mum again?' she asked.

'Yes, love. Stupid, really . . .'

'No, it's not. It's normal.'

Stratton put his arm round her and they stood for a moment in silence. Then she said, 'I meant to tell you before, but I forgot.'

'What's that?'

'About Mrs Calthrop. I bumped into her again – well, she was walking past the Make-up Department . . . Anyway, we had a chat. I was telling her about Mum, and she was ever so nice, and then–'

'Do you often tell people about Mum?'

'No, but ... I don't know why I told her, really.' Monica sounded embarrassed. 'Anyway, she told me that she and her husband are ... well, they're divorcing. I wasn't being nosy or anything, but she just said it, and ... It was an odd conversation all round, really.'

'Must have been,' said Stratton. 'I suppose that's why she's working at the studio.'

He wasn't sure that he wanted to continue this conversation. Hearing about Diana Calthrop, especially from Monica, made him distinctly uncomfortable. An image of Diana as he'd first seen her came into his mind: the slender, glacial beauty, the gorgeous long legs, the expensive perfume ... she'd exuded an air of exclusivity so strong that she might as well have had a label attached to her reading 'Not for the likes of you ...' Although, of course, that was quite out of the question, him being married, and–

Oh, to hell with it. 'Let's go in,' he said. 'No sense in both of us freezing.'

'Mrs Garland'll be here in a minute,' said Monica, as she bent down to bolt the back door behind them. To stop me running away, Stratton thought, with an inward shudder. Mrs Garland was the latest in the line of war widows who were very much, according to his sisters-in-law, *for* the likes of him, and was obviously about to be paraded before him as a potential wife. Unnervingly small, with kittenish blue eyes, her main tactic was, he remembered, to get him to talk about his work and pretend to be fascinated while he did so. It was a sort of game, he supposed, but not one that he felt like playing, especially with Doris and Lilian monitoring every word. He had hoped – obviously foolishly – that on Christmas Day he'd be safe from that sort of thing.

Monica straightened up. 'Auntie Doris invited her for tea. Don't look like that, Dad. She's quite nice, really.'

'I'm sure she's delightful,' said Stratton, who wasn't sure of any such thing. 'It's the *reason* your aunt invited her that I'm not so keen on.' Talk about going from the sublime to the ridiculous, he thought.

'You should look on the bright side, Dad.' Monica giggled. 'It could be Miss Trew.'

'Oh, very funny.' Miss Trew was a tough old bird with iron hair and a kippered face who'd been in charge of the local Girl Guides for as long as anyone could remember. 'Come on then, let's get it over with . . .'

Chapter Twenty-Six

Monica rubbed her hands vigorously, trying to dry them on the thin towel that hung on the back of the scullery door. The fabric had barely any nap left to absorb moisture. All the towels in the house were like that. Unlike hard things, she didn't categorise them as good or bad, friendly or unfriendly – they were simply worn out. The previous week, she'd gone into the dressing room of a visiting American star, who must have brought her own towels because they were thicker and fleecier than any she'd ever seen. She'd been sent in there to fetch something, but she'd lingered, touching them and marvelling at how luxurious they were – much more so than the ones they used in Make-up, which were scarcely better than the ones at home.

She stepped back quickly as the door was shoved open. Dad had gone straight up to bed when they'd returned from Auntie Doris's, and she'd thought Pete had done the same – or hoped he had. It was late – almost eleven – but she wasn't tired enough to go to bed. She just wanted to be by herself for a while. She certainly didn't want to talk to Pete, after he'd embarrassed her this afternoon, talking about boyfriends in front of everyone, but here he was, lounging in the doorway. 'Got a cig, Monica? I've run out.'

'In my bag. Wait a minute.'

Pete followed her into the kitchen. 'Fancy making us a cup of tea?' he asked, when he'd lit up.

'At this hour?' said Monica, even though she'd been thinking about making some tea for herself.

'Why not?' Pete plonked himself down at the kitchen table. 'I'm not ready for bed yet.'

'Oh, all right.'

'What about that Mrs Garland?' said Pete, when she came back from filling the kettle. 'Ooh, Mr Stratton . . .' He launched into a cruel but accurate impersonation. 'Your work must be *so* interesting . . . Do tell me *all* about it. Honestly, I'm surprised she didn't jump into his lap.'

'Oh, stop it.' Monica lit the gas. It had been an uncomfortable evening, with Mrs Garland being embarrassingly skittish and Dad, who'd obviously hated every minute of it, almost painfully polite.

'Mind you,' said Pete, 'he could do a lot worse. She's not a bad-looking woman . . . for her age, I mean.'

'He's not interested,' said Monica. 'In case you hadn't noticed, he still misses Mum.'

'Oh, yes,' said Pete, narrowing his eyes. '*Mum*. Now there's a subject . . .'

Knowing what was coming – the few conversations she and Pete had had about their mother since her death had ended in rows – and determined not to be goaded, Monica said, 'Not now, Pete. I know what you think, but you're wrong. It wasn't Dad's fault.'

'Of course not,' said Pete, sarcastically. 'She was murdered by a lunatic with him standing two feet away, but let's not blame him.'

'I'm not going to argue about it.' Monica turned her back on him and began taking the tea things out of the cupboard.

Pete blew smoke at her. 'You're a real daddy's girl, aren't you? You think the sun shines out of him.'

'Pete, I'm not–'

'That why you don't have a boyfriend, is it? Can't find anyone as good as your precious Daddy?'

'Stop it!' Close to tears, and furious not only with him, but with herself for letting him upset her, Monica dumped two cups on the table. 'Why do you always have to be so horrible? You can't even start a conversation without turning it into a fight or insinuating something – like you did this afternoon.'

'This afternoon?' Pete asked, pretending innocence. 'I don't know what you're talking about.'

'You know damn well what I'm talking about.'

Pete shook his head. 'You're imagining things. Or,' he regarded her shrewdly, head on one side, 'you've got a guilty conscience.'

'Oh, rubbish!' Monica whirled round and threw the saucers down on the table so that they spun and clattered.

'Steady the buffs.' Pete put a hand out to still the wobbling china. 'Well, it must be one or the other,' he added, 'because as I said, I've got absolutely no idea what you mean.'

'You know exactly what I mean – that stuff about boyfriends.' The moment the words were out of her mouth, Monica knew she shouldn't have said it. Pete was nodding, a smug expression on his face, as if she'd blurted out something incriminatingly significant.

'What did you think I was *insinuating*?' he asked, folding his arms. 'Because that was the word you used.'

'Nothing! Stop it!' she raged at him, furious at having fallen into his trap. 'Just . . . stop bullying me!'

'You'd better stop shouting or you'll wake Dad,' said Pete, in tones of exaggerated reasonableness. 'And I wasn't bullying, I was asking a question, so . . .?'

'I don't want to discuss it,' said Monica. 'You were being horrible this afternoon and you're doing the same thing now.'

'Oh, come on, Monica,' said Pete, in a wheedling tone. 'It was a joke. I wasn't suggesting anything.'

'Weren't you? It certainly sounded like it.'

'What could I have been suggesting?' The tone of mock innocence was back again.

'I told you, I don't want to discuss it.' The kettle was boiling. Monica grabbed the cloth and went over to the stove to take it off the gas. At the same moment, Pete stood up and then, just as she'd begun to lift the kettle, took hold of her arm so that she jerked and a few drops of hot water splashed on her hand.

'Ouch!' She let go of the kettle and shook her sore fingers. 'What the hell do you think you're doing?'

'Trying to make you answer the question. Be fair, Monica. You can't keep telling me that I've *insinuated* things and *suggested* things and then not say what they are.'

Monica suddenly felt as if she couldn't breathe. 'But you know bloody well what they are!' she burst out. 'You were suggesting I wasn't normal and you said it right in front of everybody and–'

'They wouldn't have understood,' said Pete, dismissively. 'And anyway,' he said, 'it *was* a joke. I wasn't really suggesting that you were . . . you know . . . one of *them*. Here, give me that,' he took the cloth from her, 'and I'll make the tea. You sit down.'

Monica sat down. Watching Pete as he made the tea, she wondered if he had meant it as a joke. If it really was a joke, then why had he just done all that business pretending he didn't understand what she was talking about? She knew why he was making the tea – because he knew he'd gone too far and upset her and he was trying to make up for it. Or perhaps he was doing it because he'd got what he wanted – even though she hadn't actually admitted anything . . . or not in so many words, anyway. With a sinking heart, she thought, he's being nice *now*, but he'll never leave the subject alone – sly digs, little comments that couldn't be understood by anyone else . . . She should never have said anything. Of course, he might have carried on doing it anyway, but now that he knew she knew what he was getting at, he'd be impossible.

She'd only found out what 'one of *them*' meant a couple of weeks ago, when Anne, her best friend in the Make-up

Department, had referred to a woman who worked in the Ashwood administration block in that way. Monica knew the woman in question, though not her name; she stood out because she was mannish, with cropped hair and a deep, fruity voice, and stomped about in severely tailored suits and brogues. When she'd asked Anne what it meant, Anne had giggled and said, 'You know, one of Nature's mistakes. A woman who wants to be a man.' When Monica asked, 'How do you mean?' Anne said that she was more attracted to other women than she was to men. She'd heard people laughing about the woman behind her back, or speaking about her in pitying tones or worse, contempt.

Monica had been thinking about the woman on and off ever since. I'm not like her, she kept telling herself. I'm not like her because I don't want to be a man. In fact, she couldn't think of anything she wanted less. Men did get more opportunities to do things, but if she'd been a boy she'd have had to do National Service, and she didn't fancy that at all. Imagine having to spend all your time with a lot of blokes like Pete! It wasn't that she disliked men – after all, Dad was a man, and she loved him, and so was Uncle Donald, and he was lovely, and . . .

She didn't want to end up like the woman at work, with everyone laughing behind her back. But they would if she carried on making a fool of herself as she had with Mrs Calthrop. Since that awful afternoon when she'd blurted out all of that stuff about Dad and being worried about him and Mum dying, Monica had avoided her. It was impossible not to think about her, though: she was so unbelievably beautiful, just like the women in the magazines. Being anywhere near her made Monica feel breathless. When she was actually with her, she felt that she couldn't even have told anyone her name, let alone anything else, and then she'd suddenly found herself jabbering about her family. She glanced at Pete, who was taking his time stirring the pot, and realised how odd it was that, despite the embarrassment and the rest of it, it was far easier to talk about Mum to Mrs Calthrop, a virtual stranger, than it was to talk to her own brother. She wished she didn't blush so easily, though – that was a dead give-away.

Taking her tea upstairs – she'd had more than enough of Pete for one day – she decided, as she very often did nowadays, that it would be all right to think about Mrs Calthrop for, say, five minutes before she went to sleep. She'd fallen into the habit of asking herself permission to do this, which she usually granted, but only for short periods – and only *thinking*, nothing more – as otherwise it was almost impossible to wrench her mind onto a different subject. She felt an agonising sense of guilt about doing it at home, because Dad was clearly keen on Mrs Calthrop himself, and the thought of him somehow picking up on her imaginings was horrifying. And with Pete here as well, it felt even less safe than usual, but tonight, she felt, she deserved it. In any case, Monica reasoned, Dad was bound to be asleep by now, and Pete would soon follow, so it would be – sort of – like being alone in the house.

Even if she did, by and large, manage to avoid Mrs Calthrop at the studio in the sense of staying out of her way, it had become impossible in the last week to avoid the subject of her. Speculation about her and Mr Carleton was rife, and there was a different rumour every day – almost as many as the rumours about how Mr Carleton had fallen off the waggon. It was a shame, Monica thought, because everyone said he was the best director working at Ashwood. She supposed Mrs Calthrop must be aware of it. If Mr Carleton was in love with her, Monica thought, and she with him, that would be enough to make anyone stop drinking, wouldn't it? Not that other people in the studio thought so. There's so much, she thought as she cleaned her teeth, that I don't understand.

In spite of her anxiety about seeing Mrs Calthrop, she was half-hoping she'd be working on Mr Carleton's next picture. This was partly because it would be fun and partly – well, mainly – because Mrs Calthrop would be on the set.

Monica took off her clothes, put on her nightdress, and got into bed. Closing her eyes, she indulged – for twelve minutes, rather than the allotted five – in a fantasy of telling Mrs Calthrop about Mr Carleton's drinking, and Mrs Calthrop thanking her and looking into her eyes and pressing her hand in gratitude . . . And then, feeling – temporarily at least – a great deal happier, she fell asleep.

1951

Chapter Twenty-Seven

'You're going to marry me, darling,' said James Carleton. 'The moment you're free.'

Diana laughed. 'Are you sure you haven't had too much champagne?' It was the beginning of February, and they were walking through the Green Park mist after celebrating her imminent move into her own, albeit rented, flat by lunching at the Ritz so lavishly ('Always be extravagant when you're in funds, darling – you never know when the chance'll come again') that it was almost possible to believe that rationing had ceased to exist.

'There's no such thing as too much champagne,' said James solemnly. 'Left hand, please. And close your eyes.' Still thinking that he was joking, Diana did so and, presenting her hand, felt something being slid onto her third finger. 'You can look now.'

Whatever she'd expected, it certainly wasn't a ring with diamonds and sapphires twinkling in an art-deco setting. It was old-fashioned, but so lovely that it almost took her breath away. In the two months since their first dinner together, they'd seen a great deal of each other – most evenings as well as every day at the studio – and James, as Diana had admitted to a sceptical Lally, had swept her off her feet. She'd never met a man who *knew* so much: films, the theatre, classical music, poetry, philosophy, mathematics, jazz . . . His knowledge and zest for life made her giddy. He'd opened new worlds to her – things she'd never thought about or barely knew existed – and she listened, rapt, to his explanations, devoured the books he recommended and listened to the records, bombarding him with questions afterwards. 'I'm not intelligent enough for you,' she'd told him, and he'd replied, 'Yes you are, you just don't know it yet.' And it was true that she'd felt her senses heightened, not only by falling in love, but by all this new information, as if she could suddenly see and hear things that weren't apparent to other people. Lally, despite her initial caution, had taken to him immediately when they'd met at Christmas, and so, Diana thought, had Jock, although he hadn't said as much. But then, as Lally'd pointed out, you could hardly expect him to gush, and the nature of his work did tend to make you suspicious about people, even when there was no need to be.

Unlike Claude Ventriss, James was devoid of cynicism, and, also unlike Claude, he hadn't yet attempted to get her into bed. Part of Diana was glad about this, but another part was rather offended. Remembering Guy's hands-off behaviour during their courtship, she worried that it might not bode well for the future. 'Are you serious about this?' she asked.

'Don't you like the ring?' James's tone had an uncertainty

she'd never heard before. 'It belonged to my mother but we can get it reset, if you don't like–'

'It's not the ring, darling. That's perfect – beautiful . . . It's . . .' Diana looked down at her hand and then back at James. 'It's just that you . . . you . . . Oh, I'm being stupid again.'

'Of course I'm serious, Diana. I love you. Don't you love me?'

'Yes . . .'

'Then say it.' James made his hands into a loudspeaker and said, 'Cue lights . . . Turn over . . . and . . . Action!'

Squaring her shoulders, Diana looked him straight in the eye and said, 'I love you, James Carleton.'

'Very good. Almost believable, in fact.'

Confused, Diana said, 'But I do–'

Laying a finger on her lips, James said, 'That was a *joke*, darling. People make them from time to time. I believe you.'

'Oh.' Diana took a step back, not quite sure whether she wanted to laugh or cry.

'Then why didn't you think . . .' James stopped and regarded her, head on one side. 'Ah *ha*! You're worried because I haven't pounced on you. That's it, isn't it?'

'No!' It came out too shrill, too vehement. 'That wasn't what I–'

'Oh yes, it was.' James's hand closed around her wrist, and she was aware of the pressure of his thumb against her racing pulse. 'VSITPQ as the debs used to say. You remember . . . Yes, you do, you're blushing. "Very safe in taxis, probably queer",' he declared in the clipped tones of Noël Coward. 'Well, I'm not.' His hand moved up her arm, pushing back the sleeves of her fur coat and dress so that his thumb was now massaging the soft flesh of her inner arm, hard enough to hurt. Diana stood and let him do it. There was nothing particularly intimate about an arm, and James's face wore a casual expression, as if completely unaffected by what he was doing. How can he be? she thought. It was one of the most sexual things she had ever experienced, and the sensation was so intense that she was aware of nothing else but a fierce erotic warmth that seemed to overtake her entire body.

It stopped abruptly when he removed his hand in a single movement so sudden that he almost tore the material of her dress, then grabbed her round the waist and pulled her towards him, whispering, 'I'll take you behind that tree and ravish you right now if you want me to prove it.'

Diana gasped, and, flustered, tried to right herself, pushing him away. 'That won't be necessary,' she said, primly. 'My mother always told me that once the season's over, ravishing should take place indoors or not at all.'

'That's better! Come here . . .' Gathering her to him once more, James ran his thumb down her cheek as if he was sculpting her, then, in a swift movement, tilted up her chin. 'I'll settle for a kiss.'

It lasted a long time. At the end of it, Diana felt as though they were already lovers.

'I'd better not wear this ring, you know,' she said later, when they were strolling towards Hyde Park Corner. 'I'm not yet divorced.'

'I've never cared much how things look, but you're right. You can wear it in private. We mustn't spoil your reputation.'

'I don't think I've got one to spoil,' said Diana, ruefully. 'Not any more.'

'You did the right thing, you know,' said James. 'You'd have gone mad with frustration and boredom stuck out in the country. Anyway, I need you, and now I've got you I'm certainly not going to let you go.' He stared around him. 'Extraordinary, isn't it, the way that history is crumbling into dust before our eyes. Mutability ... the way bombed-out places' – he pointed at the hulk of a huge wrecked building in the distance, its harsh outlines rising, softened, out of the mist – 'look like the ruins of ancient castles from a distance, especially in this light. We could be in a fairytale.'

'Until we get close to it and see the nettles and the rubbish and the stray cats,' said Diana.

'That's no way for a princess to talk. Especially in one of my fairytales.'

'Well, what happens next in your tale, then?'

'Well, the princess is so beautiful that everyone is madly in love with her, down to the castle's lowliest scullion and kitchen-maid—'

'Rubbish!'

'Stop interrupting. In any case, it's perfectly true. Even that little make-up girl. I've seen how she looks at you.'

'What little make-up girl?'

'The one you're always sneaking off to chat to. In fact, I've been wondering whether I shouldn't be starting to get jealous . . .'

'You mean Monica Stratton?' asked Diana, incredulously.

'Never heard of a schoolgirl crush, my dear?'

'I didn't go to school. That's why I don't know anything.'

'I wouldn't say that.' James leant over and kissed her cheek, squeezing her bottom at the same time. 'Well, not quite ... Anyway, where was I?'

'Everyone's in love with this wretched princess.'

'Oh, yes. Well, the prince – that's me, in case you're wondering – being possessed of infinite sagacity as well as the courage of a lion, a countenance like the sun, and a ... oh, you know, all that other stuff that princes have ... Anyway, he leads the princess to a nice little place where an aged crone peps them up with the elixir of life.'

'But we've only just had lunch.'

'The tragedy of this particular prince, my darling, is that he was born several drinks behind the rest of the world and is doomed to spend his life catching up ... And we've got to celebrate. This is the beginning of a real adventure, my darling.' His eyes were shining, his excitement almost palpable. 'And apart from anything else, it's bloody cold out here. Come on!' He began to run across the grass, tugging her behind him.

Much later, alone in the taxi on the way back to Jock and Lally's, she closed her eyes and rested her head against the back of the seat. Flushed, tipsy and languorous, with a delightful tingly pain between her thighs, she felt as though she actually had been making love all afternoon. When she arrived at Albemarle Street, a disapproving Mrs Robinson was waiting for her with a note from Lally. 'Mr and Mrs Anderson were waiting,' she said, and Diana remembered, with a guilty pang, that she'd agreed to accompany the two of them to a performance of choral music at St James's Church in Piccadilly with a reception afterwards.

Despite the housekeeper's ill-concealed censoriousness, Lally's note was breezy.

Waited for you as long as we could – you're obviously gadding about somewhere with gorgeous Mr Carleton (don't blame you at all – much more fun!). Hope you enjoyed yourselves. Jock brought back a letter for you from F-J. He found it when he was going through the last of F-J's papers and thought you ought to have it. It's on yr bed – I thought you'd prefer to read it in private. See you as soon as we can get away, L.

Diana carried the cup of tea, grudgingly produced by Mrs Robinson, up to her room. Picking up the letter, she sank into the armchair without bothering to remove her gloves or coat and sat turning the envelope over in her hands. It was neither addressed nor sealed, so clearly someone – Jock, perhaps – had already read its contents. Given the nature of F-J's work and the manner of his death, she decided, that was inevitable.

The juxtaposition of these thoughts with the events of the afternoon made her feel uneasy, guilty about her new-found happiness, and she couldn't help wondering if it would last. Had F-J ever thought he could be happy, she wondered, or had he merely hoped to escape detection?

The letter inside the envelope was scrawled so that the words were ugly tangles, hard to decipher, with minimal punctuation, degenerating into a list of sentences down the page. Diana wondered if F-J had been drunk when he wrote it. Perhaps, she thought, it was just some notes towards a letter he'd been planning to send her, but had never got round to finishing. Anyway, why did it matter? It meant he'd thought of her, didn't it?

Dear Diana,
I owe you an apology. I am sorry not to be able to deliver it in person.
I deeply regret my behaviour over Neville Apse. I hope that you can now forgive me.

He must have known what he was going to do when he wrote it, Diana thought – he'd never have set those words down on paper otherwise. 'I do forgive you, F-J,' she murmured. 'Of course I do.' From her cocoon of happiness, she could have forgiven anything.

That slate is clean at least.
Perhaps the only one, who knows?
I hope you will be happy.
Remember what I said about Ventriss. You are the natural prey of an unscrupulous man (as I was)
If in trouble, you might contact Edward Stratton
I am sure you remember him. He is a good man

*

It wasn't signed, but at the bottom of the page there was an address – somewhere in north-east London, with a street name Diana couldn't read, but which she supposed must be where Inspector Stratton lived. F-J's trying to provide me with a guardian angel, she thought. The fact that she didn't now need one made it, somehow, all the more touching. Perhaps F-J had guessed how unhappy she was in Hampshire, and had thought that Stratton might be able to save her from Claude Ventriss at some unspecified future time . . . Diana glanced at the letter again. *The natural prey of an unscrupulous man.* The words leapt at her as if they were written in crimson ink. But James wasn't unscrupulous, so she had nothing to fear. A tiny flare of alarm, like some misshapen thing glimpsed out of the corner of the eye and not quite recognised, flickered in her mind, then died. Regretfully, she tugged James's ring off her finger and bent down to put it into her handbag. Nothing must be said before the divorce, not even to Lally. The gesture made her remember how she'd taken her wedding ring off in the war years, working for F-J. Even in the depths of his despair, about to take his own life, he had thought of her . . .

'You were a good man too, F-J,' she said aloud. 'You *were*, and you didn't deserve this.'

Later, lying wakeful in bed, she found herself clutching at the sides of the mattress as if the room were about to start shifting around her. Everything seemed to be mutating so much that really, there was no reason for the furniture –

the very house – not to move as well. All the old values, the ones she'd grown up with, must be re-examined, weighed in the balance. Never, she thought, had life seemed so precious, and so fragile.

Chapter Twenty-Eight

From the witness box, Stratton looked down at the sea of wigs in the Old Bailey's Number One Court. The greyish-white curls reminded him, as they always did, of cauliflowers with the leaves cut off, and they seemed incongruous, bobbing about amidst the wood and leather of the heavy, dark furniture and the rolls of paper tied up with pink tape. He looked round at the jury, upright and self-consciously solemn in their box, at the press in the well of the court, and then up at the gallery, which was packed with the usual array of ghouls. They all looked the same, somehow, with dull hair and dun-coloured faces, leaning down, mouths agape, as if they had all been cut out of the same piece of damp wool. So far, February had been very cold and very wet, and periodically the ghouls broke the silences with salvos of bronchitic coughing, so that Stratton imagined a thickening cloud of germs hanging in the air above the lawyers and clerks.

He looked across at the judge, Lord Justice Spencer, seated on his elaborate throne. He was an ascetic-looking man, who reminded Stratton of newspaper pictures he'd seen of Sir

Stafford Cripps. He wore half-moon spectacles and, staring at Davies over the top of them, he could have served as a symbol for the unwavering and pitiless scrutiny of the law.

Some criminals Stratton had seen in the dock seemed to have a sense of their celebrity, a consciousness that they were the focus of attention. Davies wasn't one of them. Standing in the pen that was easily large enough to hold ten or even twelve people, he seemed smaller and more insignificant than ever. Tidy, in a clean shirt, with hair so neat and shiny that it might have been creosoted, he stood quite still, eyes down, while behind him the seated guard doodled with a slightly open mouth and the absorbed air of a child with a crayon in its fist. For Davies, it was the difference between life and death; for the guard, it was the rather dull means of putting food on the table, regardless of the impressive surroundings.

And they were impressive – everything about the Old Bailey was meant to intimidate, from the high ceilings and the paintings of varnished darkness on the walls to the unassailable might of the law in all its pomp and ceremony. Stratton had given evidence at the Old Bailey a fair few times in his career, but still found it unnerving enough to get an actual sensation of discomfort in his scrotum; what it must be doing to Davies was anybody's guess . . .

August Ronstadt, for the Crown, was a man with the sort of fine-grained portliness that looked as though it came from beef and good wine, whose appearance exactly matched his rich, plump voice. He strode about the court – no mere walking for him – and, even though he was on their side, Stratton's instinctive dislike of all lawyers, but especially ones like this, made him wonder sourly if the man ever merely ate, drank or farted, either. Not for him such ordinary animal functions – he would devour, imbibe, and blast like a celestial trumpet afterwards. Although Stratton had put hundreds of dullards in the dock and witnessed equal numbers of barristers smashing their evidence to pieces, the immense gulf between Ronstadt and Davies – in stature, intellect, opportunity, entitlement, and every other possible thing – impressed him as never before.

The Crown had decided to proceed on the indictment charging Davies with Judy's murder, rather than his wife's. It was easy to see why, although there had been a sticky half hour's wait earlier on while council argued whether evidence about the death of Muriel was admissible. Hearing that it was, Stratton uttered one of the most heartfelt Thank Christ's of his whole career, and hearing that none of the workmen would be called and that Davies would be the only witness for the defence had made him feel even better.

Of course, if Lord Justice Spencer had deemed the evidence inadmissible, the Crown could simply have gone ahead with the indictment for Muriel's killing, but it was much more likely to be plain sailing this way round – as, so far, it had proved. Dr McNally the pathologist, Backhouse, Edna Backhouse, Mrs Howells and the Welsh policeman Williams had so far been called for the prosecution, and August Ronstadt had done a splendid job. The judge had helped, too. As Ballard had remarked, *sotto voce*, 'Well, he's on our side.' Despite the business of Backhouse's previous convictions, Ronstadt, with a surprising amount of assistance from the judge, had done a very good job of painting the chief witness as a reformed character, a hero of the Great War and a man struggling valiantly against ill health. Lord Justice Spencer had even asked him if he'd prefer to give his evidence sitting down, and when the time came for the defence lawyer Humphrey Shillingworth (less richly plump than Ronstadt but, in Stratton's opinion, well on the way there) to suggest that Backhouse had had something to do with the baby's death, it looked like simple bullying. Shillingworth himself clearly found the task distasteful. His unease had been evident when he'd questioned Backhouse; he'd hedged the allegations round with semi-apologies to a degree that Stratton couldn't remember ever having heard before. After all, given what they did for a living, expecting sincerity from barristers was as unreasonable as expecting genuine passion from prostitutes. It was appearance that counted, which was why Shillingworth's obvious lack of appetite for his work had made an impression on him, and, Stratton thought, the jury.

Given that there was no medical evidence whatsoever to back up Davies's cock and bull story about Backhouse killing Muriel in the performance of an unsuccessful abortion – not to mention a single reason why Backhouse should want to kill the baby – Stratton was surprised that nobody had tried to talk the little man out of issuing instructions that would be bound to fail, but he could see that they had bugger-all else to go on.

The questions from Ronstadt were a piece of cake. After a

brief pause, filled with a lot more coughing and wheezing from the gallery, Shillingworth stood up and started taking Stratton through the statements Davies had made at West End Central, with a lot of questions about the timings and who'd said what to whom and when. Stratton could see the point of these – Shillingworth was trying to find out if they'd put words into Davies's mouth about the circumstances in which the bodies were found. This had given him a couple of sleepless nights before the trial started, but when it came to the point it was all pretty straightforward and he hadn't needed to check his notebook once. This wasn't something he liked doing, because it called up the image of the comedy plod, shuffling and thumb-licking, and the bloody lawyers were quite condescending enough already, thanks very much, without all that.

After that, Shillingworth started on the timber used to hide the bodies from view. 'He told us he'd concealed his wife's body behind timber in the washhouse, sir.'

'He said that, did he?' asked Shillingworth. '"Concealed behind timber"?'

'Yes, sir.' The moment he'd spoken he realised that he wasn't actually sure that Davies had used those words – in fact, he had a distinct memory of saying them himself when he'd cautioned the man – but Shillingworth moved on to another question and it was too late to go back. Not that he wanted to go back, of course, and besides, Davies had known about the timber because of the workmen, hadn't he, so . . . Trying to clarify it all in his mind, Stratton failed to hear Shillingworth's next question and had to ask for it to be repeated. Bloody well *concentrate*, he told himself. Just get through the next ten minutes without landing on your arse, and we're laughing.

Chapter Twenty-Nine

After a break for lunch, during which Stratton and Ballard, who'd followed him into the witness box, toyed with two pieces of very dead plaice, they sat together at the back of the court. They'd found, on checking their notebooks, that Stratton *had* mentioned the timber in the caution, but, Ballard having agreed with him that Davies knew about the timber because he knew about the workmen, he'd felt reassured. In any case, the moment had passed, and it was only one tiny thing . . . Something in the back of his mind told him that that wasn't the only incidence where they'd put words into Davies's mouth, but it had been so bloody hard to untangle the truth from all the lies the man had told. And he'd confessed, hadn't he? So why did he, Stratton, feel the need to justify his actions? Why did it bother him? Irritable with himself, he put the thoughts from his mind and concentrated on Davies, who was giving evidence.

Shillingworth was taking Davies through the statements he'd given in Wales, his allegations about Backhouse, and the stuff about selling his furniture. Standing alone in the dock, clutching the rail with white knuckles, Davies looked more insignificant than ever, as if struggling against the onslaught of some remorseless force of nature against which he was powerless. This, thought Stratton, was entirely true, even if the bloke was supposed to be acting for him. As for when Ronstadt got to his feet . . . Stratton scribbled 'What do you think?' in his notebook, tore out the page and pushed it towards Ballard. After a moment, the answer came back. 'Hasn't got a prayer.'

'What happened when you got to West End Central police station?' asked Shillingworth.

'Inspector Stratton told me my wife and baby were dead, sir.'

'Did he say where?'

'Yes, sir. At number ten Paradise Street in the washhouse, and he said he thought I'd done it.'

'Did he say how it appeared they died?'

'Yes, sir, by strangulation.'

'Did he say with what?'

Puffy-eyed and squinting with concentration, Davies said, 'With a rope, sir, and my daughter had been strangled with a tie.'

'Did I say she'd been strangled with a tie?' whispered Stratton to Ballard.

The sergeant looked through his notebook. 'No, sir, but the tie was in the Charge Room with the rest of the stuff.'

'Was anything shown to you at that time?' said Shillingworth.

'Yes, sir. The clothing of my wife and daughter.'

'Before Inspector Stratton told you, had you any idea that anything had happened to your daughter?'

'No, sir. No idea at all.'

Stratton and Ballard exchanged glances, and Ballard grimaced and rolled his eyes. Taking this line, Stratton supposed, was a bit like the business of accusing Backhouse. Shillingworth was bound to take Davies's instructions, even if they were ridiculous.

'Did he tell you,' continued Shillingworth, 'when he said the bodies had been found in the washhouse, whether they had been concealed or not?'

'He told me they had been concealed by timber.'

Stratton and Ballard exchanged glances again.

'When Inspector Stratton said he had reason to believe that you were responsible for the deaths of your wife and daughter, what did you say?' asked Shillingworth.

'I said, "Yes".'

'Why?'

'Well, when I found out about my daughter being dead, I was upset. I didn't care what happened to me then.'

'Was there any other reason why you said "Yes" as well as the fact that you gave up everything when you heard that your daughter was dead?'

'Yes, sir. I was frightened at the time.'

'Why were you frightened?'

'I thought that if I did not make a statement the police would take me downstairs and start knocking me about.'

'Did you then make this statement saying that your wife was incurring one debt after another: "I could not stand it any longer so I strangled her with a piece of rope"?'

'Yes, sir.'

'And later that you had strangled the baby on the Thursday evening with your tie?'

'Yes, sir.'

'Is it your tie which is Exhibit Three in this case?'

'No, sir.'

'Had you ever seen the tie before you were shown it by the Inspector?'

'No, sir.'

'That's nonsense, sir,' murmured Ballard to Stratton. 'He told us at least twice that he'd strangled the baby with it.'

Stratton nodded, and would have dismissed the matter, but something occurred to him. 'Did we ever ask him to identify the tie?' he whispered.

Ballard shook his head. 'Not after he'd seen it in the Charge Room. He picked it up, remember? But then he's a great one for changing his mind . . . Anyway,' he added, after a moment's thought, 'Backhouse identified it for us, didn't he?'

'That's true enough.' But, thought Stratton, Davies had never been able to explain to them *why* he killed the baby, had he? Oh, pull yourself together, he told himself – it wasn't as if it could have been anyone else, and you're a policeman, not a bloody trick cyclist. Rubbing his face, he suddenly realised quite how much he wanted the trial to be over and done.

'Is it true that your wife was incurring debts?' asked Shillingworth.

'Yes, sir.'

'But untrue that you strangled her?'

'Yes, sir.'

'Why, if you had not committed these murders, did you say that you had?'

'I was upset. I don't think I knew what I was saying. I was afraid that the police would take me downstairs.'

'Is that why you told a lie to them?'

'Yes, sir. I was upset pretty bad. I had been believing my daughter was still alive.'

Davies was doing surprisingly well, thought Stratton. In fact, his part in these exchanges was so prompt and fluent that it must surely have been rehearsed many times. All the same, he couldn't help thinking it was a bit daft of Shillingworth to try and let Davies have it both ways – it was one thing if the man hadn't known what he was saying because he was upset, but quite another if he had deliberately confessed because he'd been scared. Which, Stratton thought, he had been – after all, he'd been caught, hadn't he?

'Trying to have his cake and eat it,' whispered Ballard, confirming his thoughts. In the hiatus that followed when Shillingworth had concluded and the prosecution was readying itself, Ballard added, 'Ronstadt's going to make mincemeat of him.'

Stratton looked round the courtroom and, after a moment, picked out the neat, upright form of Davies's mother from the rows of people in the gallery. What must she be thinking? Her baby granddaughter was dead and her son was a murderer twice over – three times, if you counted the baby Muriel had on the way. For a moment, the elderly woman's pinched little face became Jenny's, and Stratton, blinking rapidly, looked away.

The Backhouses were sitting together on the other side, a solid, respectable unit of two. Edna Backhouse, in a dark coat with a matching hat firmly planted on her head, had her lips pursed and her hands primly folded over the capacious bag in her lap. Backhouse, next to her, bent over to polish his glasses, the light reflecting off his domed, bald head. Stratton hadn't warmed to the man, and he certainly thought he was laying it on with a trowel about his various ailments, but the sort of ordeal the poor sod had been through in court was something you wouldn't wish on your worst enemy, never mind the fact that he and his wife were having to live in a house where murder had been committed.

Feeling that he was staring, he lowered his gaze. In the dock, the author of all the misery looked smaller and more pitiful than ever.

Chapter Thirty

'Is it true,' began Ronstadt, 'that on five different occasions at different places and to different persons you have confessed to the murder of your wife and to the murder of your child?'

Stratton raised his eyebrows at Ballard. He couldn't see how he'd arrived at *five* different occasions and thought that Shillingworth must be straight on his feet, but there was no objection.

'Well . . .' Davies hesitated, a baffled look on his face. Finally, he said, 'I have confessed it, sir, but it isn't true.'

'But you did confess five times?'

Again, Stratton looked towards Shillingworth, but he remained in his seat.

Davies looked completely lost. Stratton could well imagine how lost – caught up in the vast tangle of the lies he'd told, he was trying to work out how to answer, and, of course, he wouldn't have been able to rehearse any of this.

After some hesitation and in the voice of one giving up

on an insurmountable challenge, Davis said, simply, 'Yes, sir. I was upset.'

'Are you saying,' Ronstadt asked, in tones that rang with disbelief, 'that on each of these occasions you were upset?'

'Not all of them,' said Davies, who now appeared to have taken the five occasions as gospel, 'but the last one I was.'

'If you were not upset on all of the five, why did you confess to wilful murder, unless it was true?'

Davies blinked rapidly several times, then said, 'Well, I knew my wife was dead, but I didn't know my daughter was dead.'

Ballard murmured, 'Still sticking to it, then. Surprised he can remember, after all he's said.'

'You say you didn't know your daughter was dead,' said Ronstadt. 'What had that got to do with it?'

'It had a lot to do with it.' Davies sounded petulant.

'We're on our way . . .' Ballard murmured.

'Is that a reason for pleading guilty to murder, that you are upset because your daughter is dead by someone else's hand?'

'Yes.'

'Is it?' It wasn't only Ronstadt's voice that was heavy with disbelief now, but the very air in the courtroom, as if all those present had somehow exhaled their thoughts.

'Do you think that's possible?' Stratton asked Ballard out of the corner of his mouth.

Ballard, looking at him as if he'd suddenly grown an extra head, gave a firm shake of his own. 'Sir, he's making it up as he goes along. Look at him – he hasn't got a clue what he's saying.'

That was certainly true. Davies, in the dock, looked as if he barely knew where he was, let alone anything else. 'Yes,' he repeated, after a long pause.

'I see,' said Ronstadt, making it clear that he didn't, at all. 'Let's just look at those occasions. You voluntarily went, did you not, to the police on November the thirtieth after having had read to you a letter from your mother to your aunt?'

'That's right.'

'It was because in the letter your previous lies were exposed that you decided to go to the police, was it?'

'It was not because of the lies,' said Davies, suddenly truculent. 'I was getting worried about my daughter.'

Ronstadt raised an elegant eyebrow. 'Are you seriously telling the jury that you went to the police and confessed to murder because you were worried about the whereabouts of your daughter?'

At this, Shillingworth did get to his feet. 'With respect,' he said, 'there was no confession of murder. He said, "I have disposed of my wife. I have put her down the drain."'

'It sounds very like murder,' said the judge, dismissively.

'Blimey, sir,' whispered Ballard, in the short silence that followed. 'That's going a bit far.'

'Blimey indeed,' murmured Stratton. Despite the niggling worries, things were going better than he could possibly have imagined. Lamb, he thought, was going to be delighted.

'I will amend my question,' said Ronstadt, with an exaggerated air of patience. 'Because you are upset about your daughter, who so far as you know is perfectly well, you go to the police and confess to the disposition of your dead wife's body. Is that right?'

After a moment, during which Stratton wondered if Davies knew what 'disposition' meant, he said, 'Yes, sir.'

Might as well give him a spade and tell him to dig his own grave, thought Stratton, scanning the jury members' faces and seeing expressions that ran the gamut from incredulity to revulsion.

'I see,' said Ronstadt. 'So that is your defence, that you confessed to the murder of your wife and child because you were upset . . . And therefore you make an allegation through your counsel against a perfectly innocent man that he caused the murder.'

Again, Shillingworth got to his feet. Save your breath, chum, thought Stratton. You're on a hiding to nothing with this one. 'Is that the proper way of asking the question, with the greatest respect? "You make an allegation against a perfectly innocent man" can only be a statement based on the assumption that his witness is innocent and mine is not. My friend has no right to make a statement describing Mr Backhouse as "a perfectly innocent man".'

The judge looked perplexed. 'Why not?'

'Well, it can only be done for the purpose of prejudice.'

'I crave leave,' said Ronstadt, in a voice that dripped with irony, 'not to have to believe that everything the accused says is true.'

'Bloody hell,' muttered Ballard.

There followed some to-ing and fro-ing over statements, during which Davies appeared to get into a complete muddle about which one was being discussed. By the end of it, the picture of a man whose past was rapidly and remorselessly catching up with him was clearer than ever. 'So,' concluded Ronstadt, 'you are saying that, out of the four statements you made, three of them were lies, and only the second statement from Wales – the one in which you accuse Mr Backhouse – is true?'

'Yes.' Davies sounded surer now.

'So, would it not be right to say that you are a person who is prepared to lie or tell the truth at your convenience?'

'Why should I tell lies?' Davies burst out angrily. His eyes were bright with panic, and for a moment Stratton had the impression of some tiny, furtive animal, flushed into the open and then cornered, twisting frantically this way and that to escape its captors. Stratton glanced at Ballard, and guessed from the flinty, set expression on his face that the sergeant was thinking exactly what he was: Shame you didn't consider that before you murdered a woman and a helpless baby. He felt no sympathy now, just the excited anticipation of watching a fellow hunter using all his skills and training to go smoothly for the kill. The rest of the court felt it too; where there had been disbelief, there was now a different undercurrent – almost a thrill, as, necks craning and mouths agape, people leaned forward as if straining to catch Ronstadt's next words.

'After you made the first statement at the police station in London – that's Exhibit Eight, which is the short statement of confession – you told the police, "It is a great relief to get it off my chest." That's correct, isn't it?'

Stratton raised a questioning eyebrow at Ballard, who tapped his notebook by way of confirmation.

'Yes.'

'So it was a relief to you to tell the truth at last to the police, which was a confession of murder?'

Davies looked puzzled. 'It wasn't the truth,' he said at last. 'It was a lot of lies.'

'You are telling us that it was a relief to tell a lot of lies?'

'I was upset,' said Davies, doggedly.

'Do answer the question,' said the judge, testily. 'Was it a relief to you to tell a lot more lies?'

'I . . .' Davies paused, mouth agape. 'No,' he said, 'it wasn't a relief.'

'Now,' said Ronstadt, 'you've told us that the second of your statements, in which you accuse Mr Backhouse, is true. Is that right?'

'Yes, sir.'

'You've said that Mr Backhouse commits an abortion on your wife so that she dies of it, and that knowing that he is responsible for her death, he organises the disposition of her body and the removal of your child to some other place? Is that right?'

'Yes.'

'And then he comes along here and commits perjury against you? Is that what you are saying?'

'Yes, sir.'

'I see. Let's look a little further at what I suggest is your habit of lying to suit your convenience. You lied to the Backhouses, didn't you, about your wife being away?'

'I lied to Mrs Backhouse, yes.'

'You lied to Mrs Backhouse. And you lied to your aunt down in Wales, didn't you?'

'Yes, sir.'

'You then told half a dozen separate, distinct and deliberate lies to the police, inventing any story that came into your head, didn't you?'

'Not any story, sir,' said Davies, desperately. It didn't really matter now, thought Stratton, what he said. Ronstadt's hammering home of the words 'lied' and 'lies' were so effective and so final that they might as well have been nails in the little man's coffin.

'Well, you began by lying about putting your wife's body down the drain. That wasn't true, was it?'

'No, it wasn't true.'

'You lied about helping Mr Backhouse carry your wife's body downstairs, didn't you?'

'No, I didn't. That was true.'

'Do you not realise from what you have heard today,' said Ronstadt, with the air of patient, even compassionate, explanation, 'that he was physically incapable of doing that, or even of carrying the baby?'

'I still say I helped him carry my wife's body,' said Davies stubbornly.

Ronstadt sighed audibly. The sound managed to convey a dozen things unspoken – regret, sorrow, dismay at such a blatant show of mendacity . . . Despite his antipathy to the man, Stratton was impressed. There was no coughing now, no stirring or rustling, just a taut silence.

'I suggest,' said Ronstadt, 'that that is another lie. You lied to your employer, didn't you?'

'Yes.'

'Another lie. You lied to Mrs Backhouse, your aunt, the police, and your boss.'

'Yes. I did it because Mr Backhouse told me to.'

'Mr *Backhouse* told you to lie to all these people?'

'He said that if anyone asked about my wife and daughter I should say they'd gone on holiday.'

'I see.' Ronstadt half-turned from Davies and then, swivelling back on the balls of his feet with the dexterity of a matador about to administer the *coup de grâce* in a bull ring, said, 'And now you are alleging that Mr Backhouse is the murderer in this case? Perhaps you can suggest *why* he should have strangled your wife?'

Davies opened his mouth, then closed it again. Unblinking, Ronstadt stared at him, waiting, a predator about to spring.

'Well,' he said uncertainly, 'he was home all day.'

'I asked you,' said Ronstadt, 'if you can suggest *why* he should have strangled her?'

Davies looked dazed, and appeared to shrink a little more, as if squashed by the air itself. The silence seemed to be quivering with electricity, and Stratton felt the blood pounding in his ears. As if in slow motion, Davies bent, then raised, his head, then looked around the court as if he might find an answer there. When he finally answered, it was in the thick voice of a man waking from a dream. 'No,' he said, 'I can't.'

'Well,' said Ronstadt, in tones of the utmost reasonableness, 'perhaps you can suggest why he should have strangled your daughter.'

Davies shook his head, defeated. 'No,' he said.

With elaborate courtesy, Ronstadt said, 'Thank you, Mr Davies,' and, striding across the courtroom, resumed his seat. As he did so an audible exhalation, like a sigh, went round the court, and, the tension evaporating, people began to shift about and murmur to one another.

Shillingworth rose. 'My lord,' he said, wearily, 'that is the case for the defence.'

'I think that must be the shortest closing speech from a prosecuting council I've ever heard,' said Stratton, when they emerged at the end of the day.

'Caught Shillingworth on the hop, didn't it?' said Ballard. 'He looked as if he wasn't expecting to have to do anything till tomorrow.'

'Yes, he did. Mind you, it's not going to make any difference – not unless the judge changes his mind overnight. I've got to get back to the station – DCI Lamb'll be waiting with bated breath, I shouldn't wonder, but why don't you cut off home?'

'I'd like to, sir, if it's all right. See the nipper before she goes to sleep.'

'Don't blame you.' For want of a more intimate gesture, Stratton clapped Ballard on the back. 'Off you go, then. Give my best to your missus, won't you?'

'Course, sir. And . . . you know . . .' Ballard's grin became lopsided in the effort to hide his embarrassment, 'thanks.'

Chapter Thirty-One

Listening to the judge's summing-up the following day, Davies, dead-eyed, looked more like some sort of grotesque, outsized man-doll than a human being. Stratton wondered how much of the arcane language he understood. Behind him, the warder had stopped doodling and was alert, head on one side, rather in the manner of an attentive dog. Looking about him, Stratton thought that he was the only one whose focus had sharpened – compared to the previous afternoon the atmosphere in the court was calm, the silence no longer twanging with anticipation. No cut and thrust here – this was a formality, and it was going pretty much as they'd expected – Mr Justice Spencer, bless his ermine socks, was restating the case for the prosecution with as much, if not more, righteous ire, than Ronstadt. After insisting to the jury in no uncertain terms that Davies had 'lied and lied and lied', he told them, almost as an afterthought, that of course they had to make up their own minds about whether he was telling the truth. Stratton, scanning their twelve faces, decided that they'd done that already.

*

'It's in the bag,' he said, as the jury, armed with copies of Davies's statements, filed out of the court.

'Seems so, sir,' said Ballard.

'I almost felt sorry for him . . .' Stratton said. Now it was almost over, it was much easier to dismiss the nagging, unfocused worries that had been bedevilling him. They were, he told himself, a consequence of trying to do a good job, and nothing worse than anything he'd experienced with other cases. 'Talk about a poisoned chalice,' he added.

'We didn't need to worry about the stuff we never got straight, after all.'

'Can't dot all the i's and cross all the t's every time,' said Stratton, easily. 'Always one or two little mysteries. Still,' he added, 'the judge did everything but tell them to convict him.'

'He convicted himself, sir. The jury won't have believed him any more than we did.'

When, after only forty more minutes, they were told that the jury were about to return, Stratton knew they'd been right about the conviction. As he followed Ballard into the courtroom, he tried to stabilise himself, mentally, against the conflicting rush of emotions that he remembered all too clearly from the handful of capital cases he'd worked on. There was something horribly primitive about the soaring sense of triumph that overcame him, but it was, at least, undermined by his shame for feeling it and blunted by his pity and sorrow for Davies's victims – who were, after all, going to be given some form of revenge. Not of course, that it would do them any good, but all the same . . . Still, Stratton supposed, feeling those things was better than being indifferent, because that would mean one didn't care.

'Members of the jury,' intoned Mr Justice Spencer, 'are you agreed upon your verdict?'

The foreman, a dapper individual who looked as if he might work in a gents' outfitters, stood up. 'We are.'

'Do you find the prisoner, John Wilfred Davies, guilty or not guilty of the murder of Judy Davies?'

There was a second's silence and Stratton felt a tightness grip his chest, as if a collective intake of breath had robbed the air of oxygen, and then the foreman said, 'Guilty.'

A hastily stifled cry came from the gallery. Davies's mother, thought Stratton. In the dock, Davies who'd been standing with his head bowed, jerked like a marionette being twitched into life on invisible strings, his face as taut as a mask.

'You find him guilty and that is the verdict of you all?'

'It is.'

'John Wilfred Davies, you stand convicted of murder. Have you anything to say why the court shall not give you judgement of death according to the law?'

Davies's expression did not change, but his voice quavered as he said, 'No, sir.'

An usher, as sombre and reverent as if he were serving at an altar, laid the black square on Mr Justice Spencer's head and, backing slowly away, returned to his seat. Get on with it, for God's sake, thought Stratton. He'd seen this before, a couple of times, and it never got any better. There was something terrible about the way that the ceremony of it all, the pauses, the sheer theatricality, cloaked desire for retribution and the sheer barbarism of putting a man to death, no matter how much he deserved it. Turning it into a spectacle like this was sickening, and the repulsed fascination he felt about it disgusted him.

Straightening his back, the judge turned to the dock and spoke. 'John Wilfred Davies, the jury have found you guilty of wilful murder and the sentence of the court upon you is that you be taken from this place to a lawful prison, and thence to a place of execution, and there to suffer death by hanging, and that your body be buried within the precincts of the prison in which you shall have been last confined before your execution, and may the Lord have mercy upon your soul.'

Stratton saw Davies take a deep breath, as though preparing for a dive, and close his eyes. Startled by a sudden, harsh sob from the other side of the court, he turned to look and saw that Backhouse, head in hands, was weeping.

Emerging into the street, Stratton and Ballard were distracted from their conversation by shouts just ahead of them. Moving quickly to the site of the disturbance, they heard a female voice: 'Murderer! You've killed my son!'

It was Mrs Davies. No longer small and neat, she was shrill and vengeful, eyes popping and fists clenched in rage, and yelling at the top of her voice with a hatred so palpable that everyone close was backing out of range. She was screaming at Backhouse who, vacant with shock, was staring at her.

Just as Stratton and Ballard reached the pair of them, Edna Backhouse, goaded from her habitual meekness, sprang in front of her husband and, handbag clutched in front of her like a shield, shouted into the other woman's face, 'Don't you dare say that! He's a good man!'

As Ballard moved forward to take Mrs Davies's arm and lead her away, Backhouse caught sight of Stratton and registering, through pink-rimmed eyes, who he was looking at, gave the discreet, complacent smile of one firmly re-established on the moral high ground.

Chapter Thirty-Two

Doris gazed at the dish of meagre-looking chops. 'Tuppence off the meat ration – again,' she said, wistfully. 'I do wish they'd end it.'

'Plenty of greens, anyway,' said Donald, nodding approvingly at the khaki-coloured mound of spring cabbage, which was all that Stratton's allotment was capable of producing in such a relentlessly wet April as this one.

'Nature's policemen, those,' said Reg, helping himself. 'Shouldn't eat too much meat, anyway. Bungs you up.'

In order to forestall any enquiry as to the state of everyone's bowels – Reg, who'd recently taken to studying the 'Home Doctor' book and now fancied himself an expert, was quite capable of it and he could see the fear in Lilian's eyes – Stratton turned to Doris and said, 'You decided to go to the Festival, then, when it opens?'

Before she could reply, Donald said, 'The whole thing's irresponsible, if you ask me. Eleven million pounds on a bloody carnival–'

'Don!' Doris glared at him.

'Sorry, love, but that's what it is. Eleven million quid on that when there's people still need homes to live in – the government must want their heads seeing to.'

Stratton, who'd momentarily forgotten Don's feelings about the Festival of Britain in his attempt to steer Reg away from bowel movements, said mildly, 'Well, now we've got the thing, it might make a nice day out for the girls. I know Monica's keen, aren't you, love?'

Monica, her mouth full, nodded enthusiastically. Swallowing, she said, 'Madeleine wants to go, too.'

'Waste of money, if you ask me,' grumbled Don.

'Ted didn't ask you, he asked me,' said Doris. 'And I want to go, too. I'd say we could all do with a day out.'

'Well, I shall certainly be attending,' said Reg, making it sound as if the aldermen of London were going to turn out *en masse* to greet him. 'I think it's a very good thing all round – "a tonic to the nation" as it's been said.'

'Opium for the nation, more like it,' muttered Don.

'Well I, for one, will be very interested to see these new scientific developments they've been talking about. It's important to keep abreast of these things.'

After a brief pause, during which Doris looked daggers at Don and Stratton kept his eyes firmly on his plate so as not to have to look at him at all, Monica said, 'What about you, Dad? Can you come?'

'I'll do my best.' Stratton grinned at her. At least he got on with one of his children, he thought – Pete, taciturn and sullen throughout most of his Christmas visit, had hardly written since. 'If you're sure you want your old dad tagging along, that is . . .' Monica made a face at him. 'Now things have calmed down a bit at work, I should think–'

'Oh, Dad, I nearly forgot . . . Was this your man?' Monica produced a folded sheet of newspaper from her pocket and passed it across the table to Stratton.

'Reading *The Times* now, are we?' asked Reg. 'Very clever.'

'Somebody had it at the studio, and I asked if I could take the cutting.' Stratton unfolded the sheet and saw:

MURDERER HANGED

John Wilfred Davies, 25, lorry driver, of Paradise Street, Euston, London W.C., was executed yesterday at Pentonville for the murder of Judy, his 14-month-old daughter, on November 10, 1950. Davies was sentenced to death at the Central Criminal Court on February 13.

'Yes,' he said, 'that was him.' He'd known it was going to happen, but since he'd heard that Davies's appeal had failed, he'd been trying not to think about it, and especially not about Davies's mother. It was all too easy to imagine the woman's pitiful hope of a reprieve, and how she must have felt when that had failed, as the inexorable days, and then the minutes, ticked away towards the bag on the head, the yank on the lever, the sudden drop . . . He pushed away the remains of his lunch.

'Aren't you going to finish that?' asked Reg, leaning forward, fork poised to spear the remaining bits of meat.

Stratton shook his head. 'Help yourself.'

'Let's have a look at the cutting,' said Don. 'Nasty . . . Looks like he got what he deserved.' The piece of newspaper was handed around until, to Stratton's relief, Doris announced that hanging wasn't a suitable subject for the dinner table and removed it.

'I'm sorry, Dad,' said Monica, as they walked up to the allotment together after lunch. He hadn't been looking for company but she'd volunteered to help him carry some flowerpots.

'What for, love?'

'That cutting about your murderer. I was trying to change the subject because I thought Uncle Reg and Uncle Don were going to have a row. I didn't mean to upset you.'

'You didn't, love.'

'Dad, I could see your face.'

'Yes. I suppose . . .'

'But he did do it, Dad, didn't he?'

'Oh, yes. He did it.'

'Why? Who would kill a baby?'

'We never got to the bottom of that. Davies was a pretty simple creature – it's hard to understand how these people's minds work.'

'Well, I think it's vile. He must have been horrible.'

But he wasn't, thought Stratton. In many ways, he was rather likeable. 'Let's talk about something else, love, shall we? What are you up to at work?'

'I started work on a new picture this week – *The Belle of Bow*. It's a comedy, but I don't think it's going to be very good. It's got the wrong people in it.'

'Who's that, then?'

'Donald Colgate. He's very good at brooding and

smouldering and slapping women, but he can't do jokey stuff at all. He says the lines as if he doesn't understand why they're supposed to be funny. It's driving Mr Carleton mad. He's the director. Oh, and your friend is working on it, too. They're getting married.'

'Who is?'

'Mrs Calthrop and Mr Carleton.' As she spoke, Stratton went cold, the unexpectedness of it jolting him like an icy shower. 'Nobody's meant to know they're engaged, but of course everyone does, and the whole studio's been talking about them for weeks, because Mrs Calthrop isn't divorced from Mr Calthrop yet.' Monica talked on, about other people in the film's crew, but Stratton barely heard her. For Christ's sake, he told himself. Stop being ridiculous. What do you care about Diana Calthrop? It's not as if you'll ever see her again – and even if she wasn't going to marry this other chap, she'd hardly look at you, would she?

It was an enormous relief when, on reaching the allotment, Monica took off back home and left him to his thoughts and – despite what he'd been telling himself – his disappointment.

Chapter Thirty-Three

James Carleton nodded at the row of slot machines on the promenade. 'That's how much we see of the outside world,' he said.

'What do you mean?' asked Diana.

Linking arms with her, he said, 'I mean, my darling, that film directors have a very narrow view of things. The studio isolates us and we don't see everyday life.'

'You're seeing it now. All this.' Diana waved a hand at the fountains and bandstand and the people dancing with the neon shining behind them in the inky twilight waters of the Thames.

'It's a show, my darling. The Festival of Britain is simply a vast advertisement for things we can't have because we're exporting them all.'

'But it's lovely all the same. And as far as *things* are concerned, we're luckier than most.'

'Well, I am, because you're going to marry me. Not sure it's such a fortunate arrangement from your point of view, having to put up with me for the rest of your life . . . But you're right about the things – you've done wonders with your new home. I'd no idea you had such a practical streak.'

'Neither did I.' Diana had spent every spare moment since she'd moved into her flat in redecorating; discovering, and revelling in, skills that she'd had absolutely no idea she possessed. Finding no wallpaper or paint to her liking in the shops, she'd taken to pestering the studio's technical department for advice, and soon learnt how to mix up the colours she wanted and how to apply them. Once she'd persuaded the painters and carpenters that she was serious, they'd been very helpful, even lending her a brown overall which she wore over an old summer dress. Wearing sandals, her face, hands and bare legs flecked with paint, she'd spent whole evenings transforming the place into somewhere bright and welcoming. It was so much nicer than James's cramped rooms that they'd decided to make it their home after they were married.

'And you've got a good eye,' said James. 'You could be a designer if you were trained up a bit.'

'Do you really think so?'

'Yes, I do. Don't look so surprised. Do you remember when you said you weren't intelligent enough for me and I said you were but you just didn't know it?'

Diana nodded.

'Well, this is the same sort of thing.'

'I suppose so,' said Diana. 'But when you're happy you feel as if you could do anything, don't you? And I've got lots more ideas from looking around today.'

'Darling . . .' James pulled her into his arms. 'At this rate, you're going to run out of house. I don't suppose they've got any vacancies in the Design Department right at the moment, but we could find out. I'd hate to lose you, but . . .'

'But you've got me at home.'

'That's true. And as long as you fetch my slippers and bring me drinks I shan't mind. Well, well, well . . .'

'Well what?'

'Over there – your little friend from the Make-up Department.'

Following his gaze, Diana saw Monica and, following just behind – she blinked, but it was, it really was – Inspector Edward Stratton.

'Must be her father,' said James. 'They obviously haven't seen us, so let's—'

'No, please,' said Diana, delighted. 'I know him.'

'*Do* you? How?'

'Tell you later.' As she called out to Monica, Diana decided to tell James she'd met Stratton when her handbag had been pinched in the blackout. That was plausible enough – it must have happened to lots of people.

As they came towards her, she thought that, apart from a few grey hairs, Edward had hardly changed at all. The same impression of strength and calm, the broad shoulders and strong face, the broken nose and the wonderfully kind eyes . . . They really were the nicest eyes, she thought disloyally, of anyone she'd ever met. Realising that she was staring, she hastily stepped forward and made introductions. After a spot of handshaking and awkward remarks about it being unexpected and so on, no one seemed to know quite what to say until James started talking about the Dome of Discovery, which they all agreed was wonderful.

When they parted a few minutes later – Edward saying gruffly, 'Mustn't detain you' – James said, 'Another conquest, I see. Father as well as daughter. You obviously made quite an impression on him – and he on you, judging from the way you were looking at each other.'

'Don't be silly, darling.' Diana could feel that she was starting to blush, although, she told herself sharply, there was no reason for it. I shouldn't have called out to Monica, she thought. I should have let them go past us. 'In fact,' she added, hastily, 'I'm surprised he remembered me at all. We only met because—'

'I suppose you must have come across quite a few policemen during the war,' said James, matter-of-factly. 'Oh, don't look so alarmed – I'm not going to ask questions. I guessed you must have been a spy as soon as I met your friends the Andersons.'

'What nonsense! Jock's a civil servant, and I certainly wasn't—'

James laughed. 'Oh, it's all right. But even if you weren't exactly a spy, I know you can't talk about it, whatever it was. Woman of mystery . . .' He swung round to face her and put his hands on her shoulders. 'Just adds to the attraction, my darling.'

'Well,' said Diana defensively, disengaging herself, 'you've never said anything about *your* war, either.'

'I was a junior member of the Crown Film Unit. Propaganda – very unheroic and not the least bit hush-hush. All very dull, which yours evidently wasn't.'

'I–'

'Look, Diana, even before I met the Andersons, I knew that *something* must have happened to you, or you'd still be mouldering away in Hampshire, opening fetes and giving out cups at gymkhanas.'

'I didn't–'

James put a finger on her lips. 'I don't want to know. It's the past. Over and done. All this' – removing his finger, he flung out his arms – 'is the future. *Our* future. And you are so beautiful. Utterly radiant. Would you care to dance?'

'Why not?' At that moment, flooded with relief, everything seemed so exciting and momentous that, with a waltz striking up in the background, Diana felt as though she were in a musical.

'Come on, then.' James took her hand and led her into the dancing throng.

Chapter Thirty-Four

Stratton wrenched off his tie and flung it down on the bed. He couldn't ever remember feeling such a complete and utter idiot. Seeing Diana like that, and not knowing what to say . . . what an ass she must have thought him. Mr Carleton, too – he'd caught the amused look on the man's face as he'd stammered and fidgeted and generally behaved like an imbecile.

He sat down on the bed, his head in his hands. Seeing Diana again, in his mind's eye, he recalled the sensation of breathlessness, as if he'd just been walloped in the solar plexus, the feeling that suddenly, nothing else existed in the world but her. She was even more beautiful than he remembered. All he could think of to say – Oh, God, he hadn't actually said it, had he? – was '*You*. It's *you*.' Everything seemed to go into slow motion, and the touch of her hand, cool and soft, had seemed to go on for ever as, dry-throated, he'd mumbled a few words.

She'd only called out to them to be friendly, and had obviously begun to regret it when he couldn't manage to string two sentences together, and they'd stood there, awkwardly, until Carleton had said something about the exhibition. God knows what he'd said in reply – he couldn't remember. He couldn't even remember what the bloody man looked like. Young and fine-featured, damn him, and clearly intelligent and well-educated and witty and all the rest of it, otherwise he wouldn't be directing films, would he?

It was all too easy to imagine the conversation afterwards, the two of them laughing at his ineptitude – he'd not dared to look back – what a clumsy, slow-witted creature, what a clod, what a big lummox . . . Even his *own daughter* was embarrassed for him. She hadn't looked at him once, never mind spoken to him, the entire way home.

He wondered how Diana would have explained knowing him – 'The war, darling . . . One ran into *all sorts* of odd people . . .' That was all he was to her – a curious memory of a strange time, with no place in her world.

He lifted his head and looked around at the cheap furniture – the wardrobe and the bedstead, the shoddy bedside table with its barley-sugar legs and the utility dressing table which didn't match any of the other bits – at the curtains, faded with washing and several inches too short for the window, and at the rag rug on the lino. This is where you belong, chum, he told himself, and don't you forget it.

Diana belonged – would always belong – with a man like Carleton, and he was a fool to waste his time mooning after a woman he could never hope to have.

Chapter Thirty-Five

'. . . and she keeps complaining that Mr Hotchkiss has shaved off her eyebrows – as if it's my fault!' said Anne.

'Never mind. It's nice to be outside.' Monica and Anne were leaning against the back wall of the department, enjoying the May sunshine after a hectic morning making up dancers as chorus girls for one of *The Belle of Bow*'s music-hall scenes.

'Yes, isn't it? Ooh, I forgot to tell you – I saw Raymond Benson this morning. He's gorgeous, isn't he?'

'Yes, very handsome,' said Monica, wearily. She was sick and tired of hearing about Raymond Benson. She could see that he *was* handsome, with his corn-coloured hair and insolent blue eyes – looks that had got him a score of parts playing wayward but ultimately decent young men who saved the day and won the heart of the girl whilst being terrifically modest and self-deprecating – but honestly . . .

'Shame we're so far away from D Stage.'

'Yes, isn't it?' Benson was working in a picture about Bonnie Prince Charlie. Every single woman in the studio, it seemed to Monica – as well as several of the men – was sneaking over there every chance they had to catch a glimpse of him prancing about in a kilt like something off a McVitie's biscuit tin.

'He's just my type,' said Anne, dreamily.

Thinking that if she had to listen to any more she might not be able to stop herself screaming, Monica changed the subject. 'What about your boyfriend?' she asked. 'You said you were going to the Festival with him, and Kenneth's *real*.'

'So's Raymond.'

'You know what I mean. Did you go?'

'Yes. I did enjoy it, but there was so much of it – we kept getting lost. Have you been yet?'

'Yes, on Saturday. We had a family outing.' Seeing Anne's look of pity that she didn't have anyone else to go with, Monica said, quickly, 'It was wonderful, wasn't it? Pity they didn't have much in the way of fashions, but the crafts were really interesting – all those people making things – and the fabrics and furniture . . .'

'Those funny spiky legs?' Anne made a face. 'I bought a nice tea caddy for Mum, though, and a scoop. One of those red, white and blue ones. She was ever so pleased.'

'We bumped into Mr Carleton and Mrs Calthrop. My dad knows her – he met her during the war. It was a bit odd, really. Nobody quite knew what to say.'

'I'm surprised they even saw you. They never seem to have eyes for anybody but each other. Oh, sorry, Monica. But you know he's spoken for.'

Anne's constant references to her being keen on Mr

Carleton were irritating, but Monica played along because it saved her from questioning. It was expected that she'd have a crush on someone, and her reticence on the subject had led to Anne choosing a candidate for her. Carleton, she knew, had been arrived at because he was often spoken of in the same breath as Mrs Calthrop, and Anne had misinterpreted her reactions – or rather, the person to whom she was reacting. But Dad had reacted to Mrs Calthrop, all right. Monica didn't think she'd ever seen him so stiff or tongue-tied – stammering, almost. She hadn't known what to say to him afterwards. Not that it had been a problem, exactly, because he'd hardly said a word for the rest of the day. She wondered if Mr Carleton had noticed – awful if he had, and even more awful if *she* had given herself away, somehow. The whole thing made her feel sick with shame – at least Dad, even if he was *Dad*, was feeling something entirely normal, whereas *she* . . .

Glancing at her wristwatch, Anne said, 'We've still got a few minutes left. I think I'll go for a walk in the direction of D Stage . . . You coming?'

Monica shook her head. 'You *are* stuck on Mr Carleton, aren't you?' said Anne. 'You can finish my cig if you like. Here . . .'

'Thanks, Anne. Don't be late, will you?'

'For your precious James?' Anne winked. 'I'll be back, never fear.'

Left alone, Monica slumped back against the wall, and turning her face up to the sun, closed her eyes. I must stop this, she thought. It's horrible. I'm horrible. And, after all, it had been a thoroughly enjoyable day, even with Uncle Reg talking nineteen to the dozen about scientific advances and the shape of things to come all the way round the Dome of Discovery. There'd been a funny moment when Uncle Donald, dragged along by Auntie Doris against his will and grumbling all the way, had tapped an 'Out of Order' sign on one of the exhibits and said that *that* was the shape of things to come. He and Uncle Reg were still arguing when they stopped to eat their sandwiches by the fountains, but then he'd cheered up a bit and taken some snaps of them standing in front of the Skylon. She and Dad had gone off by themselves after that, which was a lot more fun. He'd wanted to see the farming exhibition, which had been quite interesting – except the new battery cages for hens, which anyone could see were cruel – and then they'd had a ride on the Water Splash at the funfair and had a look round the Mississippi Steamboat that was moored on the promenade . . .

Hearing her name called, she opened her eyes. Mrs Calthrop was waving to her as she crossed the lawn on the other side of the causeway. Self-conscious and aware of her heart beating like a tom-tom, she waved back, then stared after Mrs Calthrop until Anne's cigarette, which she'd completely forgotten she was holding, burnt her fingers.

1953

Chapter Thirty-Six

Alone in the Make-up Department, Monica sat in front of the line of mirrors, sponging foundation over her face and rubbing it in, careful not to overdo it. She'd kept her promise and hadn't told anybody where she was going, even Anne. Actually, especially not Anne, because she knew that if she did she'd never, ever hear the last of it. They'd agreed to meet in the lane around the corner from the main gates, to minimise the chance of anyone seeing – which, Monica thought, was pretty unlikely at seven o'clock in January. She'd told them at home that she was working late. She'd been promised a ride back, so at least she didn't have any worries on that score, and she could get out of the car a few streets away from Lansdowne Road . . .

On just about every other score, though, she felt more agitated than she could ever remember. Her hands, so deft when applying cosmetics to other people, were nervous and clumsy. Putting down the sponge, she picked up a pencil and began darkening her brows. Her elbow nudged something on the work surface and the pencil slipped, leaving a line down her cheek. Scrubbing at it, she decided it might be better to give up and just put on some lipstick – she didn't want to go out looking like a clown.

Brushing her hair, she wondered, for the thousandth time, if she were doing the right thing. Despite all her efforts to change, her feelings and inclinations were exactly the same as they'd ever been – more so, if anything. In desperation, she'd been on lots of dates with local lads, but each had proved more disastrous than the last, and only served to cement the fact that she simply wasn't attracted to men. The problem wasn't the lack of offers – rather the reverse, if anything – but after so many failures on her part to feel anything at all, she'd given up hoping that she'd wake up one morning and think differently about them. Her cousin Madeleine was engaged to be married, now. So was Anne, and both of them were madly excited about it, so that all the chat, both at home and at work, was of very little else. Monica made a face at her reflection; Anne certainly would be talking about something else if she got wind of what happening this evening . . .

I must do this, she told herself. I must try . . . After all, if she couldn't manage to fancy Raymond Benson, who was everybody's heart-throb, what hope was there for her?

Tilly was Raymond Benson's fourth film for Ashwood Studios, and the first in which he'd been given top billing. Monica, now promoted from extras and occasional retouching to full make-up for supporting actors and actresses, was also working on the picture. It was the story of an aristocratic widow who, discovering that her wheelchair-bound son – Benson – had secretly wed a dancer, tried to prevent them from consummating their marriage. In the end, the dancer faked a drowning accident in order to demonstrate that her husband's inability to walk was all in his mind – which it proved to be when he leapt into the river and saved her. Originally, Mr Carleton had been the director. He'd had a great deal of time away from the studio in the past six months, and there was a rumour that he'd wanted to do a project of his own – a drama about life in the slums of Liverpool or somewhere – but the studio wouldn't let him. What was definitely not a rumour, but a horribly obvious reality, was that, despite the fact that he was now married to the person Monica still could not help thinking of as her ideal woman and the loveliest in the world, he was drinking very heavily indeed. This, and his disgust at having to work on yet another costume picture – *Tilly* was set in Edwardian times – had made him uncharacteristically savage, so that everyone on the set had been walking on eggs for weeks.

Carleton had been sacked a couple of months ago, after an incident on E Stage. As the film got further and further behind schedule, the atmosphere on the set had grown ever more tense and miserable. The final straw came when Carleton, enraged by what he saw as interference by the studio head Mr Vernon, had taken a swing at his assistant, Mr McPherson, causing him to stagger backwards into the make-up trolley, knocking it over and breaking his wrist in the process. Carleton had stormed out after that, leaving poor Mr McPherson on the floor, cradling his arm.

In the confusion that followed, nobody quite seemed to know what to do, but all the same she'd been astonished when Benson, who'd been lolling in his wheelchair nearby, had got up and begun to help her gather the bits and pieces scattered across the floor. She'd noticed him watching her a few times – at first, she'd thought she must have imagined it, or that perhaps it was the way he looked at all women, but she kept catching him eyeing her. Not so much her face, but the rest of her, in an intense, speculative way that made her feel unpleasantly self-conscious.

She'd righted the trolley, pushed it into a dark corner to be out of the way and was just beginning to rearrange the things when he came up behind her. Depositing a handful of stuff on the top, he'd said, standing so close that she could feel his breath on the back of her neck, 'I've been watching you.'

Monica had frozen.

'Has anyone ever told you how attractive you are?'

She'd felt his hands on her shoulders, and he'd turned her round to face him. 'Don't worry, we can't be seen. I've been wanting to talk to you alone ever since we started this wretched picture.'

'Have you?'

'Don't sound so surprised. As I said, you're very attractive. I've been thinking I'd like to get to know you better.' He'd stared down, quite unashamedly, at her breasts.

'I . . .' Amazement that the film's heart-throb should be making a pass at her, and the fact he was uncomfortably close and she couldn't move because of the trolley behind her, had made her falter. 'I don't know.'

'Don't you like going out and having fun?'

'Well, yes, of course I do, but I don't really . . .'

'Don't really what?'

'It's just . . . I'm not very good at all that sort of thing.'

'That's only because you haven't met the right person.' She'd stared at him, hypnotised, as, locking his eyes on hers, he put up a hand and stroked her cheek. 'You think about it. I've been feeling very lonely on this picture.' He'd gazed pointedly over her shoulder, and Monica, turning her head, saw that he was looking in the direction of the actresses playing his mother and his wife, who were standing in the gloom beyond the arc lamps. 'Not exactly a bed of roses, if you know what I mean.'

'No,' said Monica. It was common knowledge that the three stars didn't get on well, which compounded the already strained atmosphere.

He'd patted her on the shoulder, then stepped back. 'Why don't you think about it, hmm?'

Relieved, she'd gabbled, 'All right, yes. I'll think about it.'

She had thought about it. In fact, she'd thought of little else for the next three weeks, during which Benson didn't come anywhere near her, so that she wondered if he'd forgotten about it or gone off the idea. Perhaps he hadn't liked her not saying yes immediately. He certainly seemed to assume that she'd find him irresistible – but that, she supposed, was because women did find him irresistible. And when he'd finally asked her to come out to dinner, she'd agreed.

In the end, what had persuaded her was thinking about *Tilly*. Of course, it was only a film, but all the same, if something as physically serious as paralysis could be shown to be all to do with the mind and therefore conquerable, surely something that was emotional might respond to the same treatment? Going out for the evening with Raymond Benson wasn't like jumping into a river to save someone from drowning, but in this situation it seemed, as an incentive, to be on a par with it. And he could have chosen *anybody*, couldn't he? But he hadn't. He'd chosen her, Monica Stratton, lowly make-up girl.

Fluffing up her hair, Monica put on her coat and gloves and set off down the causeway towards the main gate. Even at this late hour there were lorries and things rumbling up and down, so she didn't hear anyone come up behind her and the shout of 'Monica!' somewhere near her ear almost made her jump out of her skin.

Turning, she saw that it was Mrs Carleton, standing under one of the roadside lamps and looking pale, but – if possible – more lovely than ever. She'd been working in the Design Department for the past year, which meant that Monica hadn't had to avoid her because she'd seen very little of her anyway. Now – especially after what had happened with Mr Carleton – she couldn't think of anything to say.

'I thought it must be you,' said Mrs Carleton. 'I recognised your coat.'

For a second, Monica experienced a sensation of mad happiness that she'd committed such a detail to memory – but then she realised that, working in the design department, Mrs Carleton would be bound to notice what people were wearing, even if it wasn't good quality or anything. After all, *she* noticed those sorts of things, didn't she? In that way, they were alike . . . Staring into the beautiful blue eyes, she was lost until Mrs Carleton, frowning slightly, said, 'Is there something wrong, Monica?'

'Oh, no, no . . . I'm sorry . . . Sorry about Mr Carleton, I mean.'

'Yes,' said Mrs Carleton, in a matter-of-fact way. 'So am I. Are you going home now?'

'Yes.'

'Let's walk, then – it's freezing out here. I'm going home, too, but I've got to go back to Design first.'

'He was really good,' said Monica, after they'd walked in silence for a moment. 'Everyone thought so. And everyone liked him.' Percival Addington, who wasn't half so good as Carleton, had taken over the reins.

'I know,' said Mrs Carleton. 'But these things happen.' She sounded tired.

'It wasn't really his fault,' said Monica. 'The picture was behind schedule, but there were lots of other reasons–'

'No, Monica. It's very kind of you, but it isn't true and we both know it isn't. While we're being honest,' she smiled wistfully, 'I don't know how much longer I shall be working here myself. So I just wanted to say – in case I don't see you again – that it was nice meeting you, and do please give my regards to your father, won't you?'

'Yes. It was nice meeting you, too.' As she said this, they reached the turning for the Design department.

'Goodbye, Monica,' said Mrs Carleton, 'and good luck.'

'Good luck to you, too,' said Monica, with more daring than she'd thought she possessed.

'Thanks.' Mrs Carleton walked off at a fast clip and Monica stood watching until she merged with the darkness.

Monica supposed that Mrs Carleton must be leaving because of Mr Carleton, which seemed pretty rotten. She hadn't told Dad about what had been going on at Ashwood. Even though the incident at the Festival of Britain was almost two years ago, it was still, in her mind, excruciatingly vivid – the clumsy, fumbled handshake, the way his eyes had never left hers, the fact that his behaviour seemed to mirror, so exactly, the turmoil inside her . . . Just thinking about it made her squirm with embarrassment. But she ought to pass on Mrs Carleton's regards, really, if she could bring herself to do it. It would be so much easier, she thought, if Dad had met somebody else, but his heart wasn't in it, any more than hers was.

Still, there was time enough to worry about that. Now, she must put Mrs Carleton right out of her mind and concentrate on the evening ahead of her. Stomach churning with apprehension, she continued walking towards the main gate, and Raymond Benson.

Chapter Thirty-Seven

'That's the way to do it!' Inside the red-and-white-striped booth, Punch, with his glazed pink face, hooked nose curving down to meet jutting chin, battered Judy about the head with his cosh.

We should be laughing, thought Diana, shoving her hands deeper into the pockets of her coat in an attempt to keep warm. The bright weather promised for the end of April had failed to materialise, and the Brighton sky and sea were the matching dull grey of old saucepans. It was mid afternoon and, but for a solitary child running aimlessly about while her mother stood by and a couple of scruffy-looking donkeys with drooping heads, the beach was deserted.

In front of the booth, deckchairs were scattered about at odd angles, some upside down, giving the al fresco auditorium a dismal, abandoned air. Apart from the attendant, who was lying in one, apparently asleep despite the puppets' distorted shrieking, she and James were the only audience. It had been he who'd wanted to see the show, not her. He'd persuaded the professor, a lugubrious individual who'd been packing up his wares when they'd arrived, to perform for them, with a story about scouting for a Punch and Judy show for his next film. Judging from the racket and the vigorous jerking of the figures, the man was giving his all, but there was, in fact, no next film to cast. Although James had made light of her reaction when he'd told her, all that time ago, that he was born several drinks behind the rest of the world and was doomed to spend his life trying to catch up, Diana knew now that it was no more and no less than the truth. No matter how much he drank, he never could catch up, and his intake had increased to such a degree that he was not only bankrupt but unemployable.

Shivering on the damp deckchair, Diana recalled, as she often had in the last six months, the demeanour of the barman at the studio when she'd gone to fetch the brandy in that first week. She'd assumed that the man's comment about thinking the sobriety couldn't last was aimed at Anthony Renwick, but now she knew that wasn't wholly the case. After all, who would know better than a barman? It was certainly true that James had encouraged Renwick to drink because he needed to finish the film, but it was also because he was slipping off the waggon himself and wanted an excuse. She remembered, too, what Alex McPherson had said to her in the restaurant, about warning Mr Vernon. Now, she understood that what he – and probably others, too – had warned Mr Vernon about was putting two drunks on the same picture, but she hadn't known that at the time. Or had she? Perhaps her subconscious had known it, but being in love, she'd failed to acknowledge that anything could be wrong. And it was certainly true that the highly visible nature of Renwick's problem had masked James's, because he held his drink well, and it was only in the last few months that he'd started slurring words and lurching unsteadily into the furniture. This, and the covert nature of his drinking, and the fact that, apart from that terrible last week at Ashwood, he'd never become aggressive – and, she had to admit, her own tendency to deny that the problem existed – were the reasons why it had taken her so long to face up to the extent of it. Anyone who'd worked at the studio for any length of time had known but, because James was well liked, they'd covered up for him repeatedly. And none of them had warned her. But then, she thought resignedly, I wouldn't have listened even if they had.

Despite the initial appearances, a mocking chime in the back of her mind had been telling her for some time that this was history repeating itself. It was Guy, her first husband, and then Claude Ventriss, all over again. She'd been impetuous, rushing headlong into love, refusing to let her feet touch the ground and never stopping to reflect, and pain and shame had followed. How much, in the past year, had she hung onto the memory of her whirlwind romance with James, even as it had become – first slowly, and then with escalating speed – as destructive as a hurricane that raged about them both and would not set them free? Drying out had only resulted in shaking hands and hallucinations so bad that they'd led, at one stage, to a straightjacket. The doctors hadn't let her see him then, but she remembered all too well his terror of the huge cockroaches that crawled over his skin and the hideous crippled lobster that followed him around, dragging one giant claw along the floor.

As Punch gleefully hurled the baby out of the window and massacred Judy in a rain of blows, Diana felt as though she was in one of those hallucinations now. Beside her, James was rapt as a child, revelling in the anarchy of the performance.

He'd been the one who suggested coming to the coast. A spot of sea air to blow away the cobwebs, he'd said. They'd arrived the previous day and spent the evening wandering up and down the promenade, too cold and dispirited to talk. Besides, what was there to talk about any more? They couldn't even find refuge in a hotel bar, because James was in a 'drying-out' period, aided by some medicine that was supposed to make him sick if he so much as smelt alcohol. Diana found these times actually worse than when he was drinking – the wait for the inevitable fall off the waggon, hoping against hope and against experience, was agonising. She'd stayed because, in spite of everything, she still loved him – and even if she hadn't, the burning shame of having to admit another failure at marriage was too terrible to contemplate – but she was beginning to wonder if she actually had any choice in the matter.

She knew, now, that the drinking wasn't his fault. At first, she'd been angry – wasn't she, on her own, with her gift of love, enough to make him stop? *He* had thought she would be. He'd told her that, but it seemed, after all, that the urge to drink was stronger. Then she'd tried drinking with him. It had seemed easier than the torment of watching, coldly sober, while he destroyed himself. That had been a disaster – she'd lost her wonderful job in the studio's Design Department, and with it, their only income and the flat which had been her pride and joy. She'd tried to get other work, but every time she declared this intention, James, sodden in the armchair in their pokey, chilly new home, a blanket round his heaving shoulders, had groped for her hand and sobbed, 'Don't go, darling, don't leave me.' If she did go out, he'd manage to scrape together enough to buy more to drink, and, in the end, she'd given up and they'd settled into a dreary, never-ending game of hide-and-seek as she searched the place for hidden bottles and emptied their contents down the sink, while James alternated between defiance and remorse.

She'd gradually lost touch with Lally and Jock and her other friends, so that they were now marooned, a wrecked island of two, afloat in a sea of alcohol. Lally and Jock had given her enough help already, and such pride as she had left would not allow her to call on them yet again.

How Evie would love this, she thought. She'd heard through the grapevine that Guy's mother finally had the grandson she'd always wanted – the one Diana hadn't been able to give her. If Evie could see her now, she'd think she'd got her come-uppance, all right.

The hangman was fixing the noose around Punch's neck. 'It's the end for you, Mr Punch. Say your prayers.'

Punch ducked his head and, cackling in gleeful self-satisfaction, sent the hangman flying with one swipe of his cudgel. 'That's the way to do it!'

Diana closed her eyes to block out the sight of the malevolent doll as it twirled and flailed in a triumphant dance. The small amount of money raised by the sale of Hambeyn Hall and what she'd managed to save from the allowance Guy had given her – and which had stopped when she remarried – was gone, much of it on 'cures' for James, and such inheritance as she had, that she'd thought might buy a flat for them, had been plunged, instead, into a disastrous film that had never, in the end, been completed. Why the hell, she thought, didn't I have the sense to hold onto it – or at least to keep some of it back? Now – she groaned at the thought – they were already weeks behind with the rent and the landlady was growing restive.

Diana clapped half-heartedly as the puppets took their bows. James did not join in, and when she turned to look at him she saw that he was sitting quite still with tears coursing down his cheeks.

'What is it, darling?'

He shook his head. What had started him crying? The sausages, the policeman, the crocodile? Lost in the tangle of her own thoughts, she hadn't noticed. The Punch professor, emerging from behind his booth, looked first mystified and then downright annoyed when James, noticing him, rose from his deckchair and walked hastily off down the beach. 'What's his game?' he asked Diana. 'He might have told me himself if he didn't like it. I've gone to all this trouble . . .'

'It's not that,' Diana assured him. 'He's always like this when he's working. When he gets an idea he needs to think about it immediately. Doesn't want to break his concentration. You've obviously given him an idea.'

'Oh.' The professor sniffed, but seemed to accept this. 'I suppose that's all right, then. Now,' his tone became wheedling, 'seeing as I did it special for you, shall we say—'

'Two shillings,' said Diana quickly, naming the smallest sum she felt would be acceptable. She'd thought that James's story would suffice but the man clearly expected payment for the show and she didn't feel she could refuse. She looked around for James, but he was heading down the beach towards the flight of steps that led up to the esplanade. The man stiffened, his doleful face becoming taut with angry disgust. She had no idea how much he usually got from holidaymakers, but he'd obviously hoped for a lot more from film people. He looked her up and down – the tight-fisted bitch in the fur coat. He wasn't to know that nowadays the thing often did duty as a blanket as well as a garment.

'I'm sorry,' she said, 'I—' Unable to complete the explanation, she took her purse out of her handbag, scrabbled for the coins and pushed them into his hand saying, 'Here you are,' and walked away as fast as she could with her heels sinking into the pebbles.

She caught up with James at the bottom of the steps, grabbing hold of his arm and yanking on it to make him stop. She saw, as he turned to her, that his face was blurry and smudged with tears. 'What are you doing, James? I had to give him two shillings, and I'm not sure we've got enough money to get home without—'

'Diana!' He took her by the shoulders, crushing her to him in an embrace. 'I'm sorry. I'm so sorry. Please forgive me.'

As he drew her towards him, she became aware of a hard, flat shape bumping against her leg. Pushing him away from her, she said sharply, 'What's that in your pocket?'

'Nothing, darling. You're imagining it.'

'No, I'm not.'

She made a grab for it and this time he shoved her away, hard, so that he lost his balance and sat down with a bump on the bottom step. Swiftly, Diana bent down and before he could stop her yanked the half-bottle out of his coat. It was whisky, and the seal was unbroken, which explained why she hadn't smelt it on his breath. 'When did you get this?'

'This morning. When you were buying stamps.'

The postcard to Anthony Renwick, who was now in hospital, had been his idea. At the time, she'd been encouraged by the thoughtfulness of the gesture, but now she saw that it was merely a ruse to get her out of the way. It also meant that they had even less money than she'd thought.

'I'm sorry, Diana.' As he held out his hand for the bottle, she looked down at his face and saw the forlorn hope of the beggar. 'Please. I can't manage–'

'You'll have to bloody manage.' Stepping backwards, she turned and, holding the bottle above her head, elbow bent, was about to hurl it away from her as far and as hard as she could, when she heard a crunch of pebbles behind her and felt something tugging at the hem of her coat. Looking down, she saw that James was stretched at full length on the ground, dragging himself on one arm in a horrible parody of a parched man in a desert, blood trickling down his wrist from a cut on a sharp stone and soaking into the exposed cuff of his shirt. He wasn't looking at her: his eyes were fixed on the bottle.

'I'll walk into the sea,' he said, quietly.

'It would certainly be quicker than drinking yourself to death,' said Diana, acidly. What was the point? If she threw the bottle and it shattered on the stones, there would only be another, and another, and another . . . 'Oh, for God's sake. Get up!' She went back to sit down on the step and broke the seal on the bottle. Averting her eyes from James, who was half-walking, half-crawling, to join her, she thrust the whisky at him. Not wanting to see the abject expression and the relief on his face as he took a greedy pull on the bottle, she stared straight in front of her at the indistinct line of the horizon.

'Bless you, darling.'

'James . . .' She couldn't bring herself to look at him.

'Wait.' James took another drink. She heard him set the bottle down carefully on the far side of the step so that she could not reach it, and begin rooting in his pocket for cigarettes.

'I can't do this any more,' she finished.

James fumbled with the matchbox, opening it upside down so that the matches fell out, scattering around their feet. He scrabbled after them with trembling hands, dropping as many as he collected. She watched him with growing impatience and then, unable to bear it any longer, bent down to help. They grovelled about in silence until all the matches were restored to the box, then James, leaning his elbows on his knees to steady himself, managed to light two cigarettes.

'You should go,' he said, handing one over. Beneath the red blotches his face was a sickly greenish-white. 'Go home.'

'And leave you here to kill yourself? Anyway, what home? In case you've forgotten, we haven't paid the rent in over a month.'

'I know. I'm sorry.'

'Stop saying that!'

'It's all I can say.' James turned his head away, as if he couldn't bear to look at her, either. 'I've dragged you down far enough, Diana. We both know it's hopeless. You said so yourself – that you couldn't do it any more. If it's any consolation, you can't be half as sick of me as I am of myself.'

Wearily, Diana got to her feet. 'It isn't.'

James didn't look up at her. His shoulders sagged, and she wanted to bend down and put her arms around him. This charming, intelligent, talented man who had such appetite for all that life had to offer . . . No, said a small, cold voice inside her head. She must recognise, as he did, that there was, quite simply, no more to be said or done. She stood for a moment, staring down at James's bowed head, and then, very slowly, began to walk up the steps to the esplanade.

'I love you,' he murmured. Diana turned, but he wasn't looking at her – the words were addressed to the sea.

As she reached the top, a torn newspaper borne on the light wind slithered round her ankles like a cat, so that she had to shake it off. Apart from a couple of spivs, jacket shoulders as wide as yokes, talking together, there was no one around. From one of the peeling shopfronts, their garish colours faded by sea-spray and long neglect, she could hear the rumble of distant, placid voices intoning numbers after the bingo caller, like responses in church.

Standing on the top step, she heard a retching sound from below and, turning, she looked down and saw James, still sitting where she'd left him, bent forwards from the waist. Her last sight of him was a heaving back and vomit splattering the cold, grey stones of the beach.

Chapter Thirty-Eight

A battered chocolate box with grey ash scattered across the empty waxed paper casings; a bottle of powdery aspirins; a cup of cold tea, scummy white on the surface; an open pot of face cream; a plaster model of an Alsatian dog with its tail snapped off; a broken carriage clock, and a lot of dust: Iris Manning's mantelpiece. The rest of the room was no less depressing – dingy wallpaper, filthy windows, and shoddy, chipped furniture. It stank of stale cigarette smoke and unwashed clothing. Standing on the stained rug and trying not to breathe too deeply, Stratton stared down at the tangle of grimy blankets on the bed. On the off-chance, he knelt down to look beneath the sagging frame, but found nothing except an enamel chamber pot lined with a foul-smelling crust of dried urine.

Stratton doubted if Iris had ever conducted any business in this room. As far as he knew, she'd always worked outside. There was nothing high-class about her: ten bob for a wank; fifteen for a plate; thirty for the lot. Stratton knew her from way back. They all did. She'd been living and working on their patch since she'd absconded from reform school in 1938 or thereabouts, and no matter how many times they'd taken her back, she'd always returned. Now she was missing and had been for five days, and there was nothing amongst her belongings to indicate why, or where, she'd gone. Her sister, who'd decided to look her up after a separation of five-odd years, had reported it.

Missing tarts were not exactly top of the station's list of priorities at any time but at the moment, with yet another spate of car thefts – there'd been a steep increase in the three years since petrol had come off ration – and Lamb's obsession with the preparations for the Coronation in June, they were very low indeed. Stratton himself had not taken the news of Iris's disappearance too seriously, his initial reaction being that she'd got behind with her rent and scarpered, but now he was beginning to wonder. If she had done a midnight flit, she'd surely have taken such clothes as she owned with her, but the presence of a battered valise on top of the wardrobe and several frocks inside it suggested otherwise. Bugger the Coronation, he thought: I should have got here sooner.

A loud thump and several shouts from the stairwell suggested that Policewoman Harris was not having an easy time with the house's other occupants. Stratton clattered downstairs and found a slovenly creature in a soiled dressing gown barring the way to the kitchen. 'You know your trouble,' she was shouting at Harris, 'you've never had it!' Seeing Stratton, she added, 'Why don't you have a bash at her, take that expression off her face?'

'That's enough, Bessie,' said Stratton mildly, recognising her as a tom who'd been hawking herself around Soho for nearly as long as Iris.

'It's not my turn,' whined Bessie. 'You done me last week and I paid the fine. And you have to nick me on the street or it don't count. I know the law.'

'We're not here to take you in,' said Stratton.

Bessie stuck her chin out aggressively. 'Well, what you poking around for, then?'

'Iris is missing, and we need to have a look round.'

Bessie, who didn't seem at all bothered by this news, sighed and moved away from the door. 'Oh, go on then.'

The kitchen was in an even dirtier state than Iris's bedroom. Stratton, shifting his feet on the sticky lino, tried not to recoil as he caught sight of mouse tracks in the congealed fat of a frying pan. He could tell by the stiffness of Policewoman Harris's back and shoulders as she looked in the cupboards that she was doing the same. Bessie pushed the remains of a meal to one side, and, perching on one end of the newspaper-covered table, began examining the soles of her bare feet. They were, Stratton noted, hard and yellow, with deep splits in the heels that made him think of cheese left in the air for too long.

'When did you last see Iris?' he asked her.

'I told *her*,' Bessie let go of her foot long enough to jerk a dismissive thumb at Policewoman Harris. ''Bout a week ago.'

'Where did you see her?'

'Here. She was on her way out.'

'Did she say where she was going?'

Bessie shrugged. 'I don't know, do I?'

'Do you think she was going to work?'

''Spose so.'

'Do you remember what she was wearing?'

'Well, she'd have had her coat on, but apart from that . . .' Bessie shook her head.

'Where did she go when she was working?'

'All over.'

'Didn't she have a regular patch?'

'Not any more. Got taken over, didn't it? She hangs round the cafés and pubs, mostly.'

'Which ones?'

'The Panda Café, mostly. And she goes into a lot of the pubs round here, but the Champion's her favourite.'

'Does Iris have a current man friend – someone who looks after her?'

Bessie shook her head. 'He's long gone – six months or more. Gave up on her and found himself something better, didn't he? She was always saying how skint she was. Even tried to borrow some money off me. I told her, I'm not *that* stupid.'

'You thought she wouldn't pay you back?'

'*Iris?* Not likely.' Clearly feeling that there was no more to be said on the subject, Bessie pulled a grip from her hair and began poking at the grime beneath her toenails. Averting his eyes, Stratton spotted an advert, torn from a magazine, tacked to the opposite wall: a drawing of a model draped in tulle and lounging on a sofa surrounded by eager suitors, accompanied by the legend 'Charm and Beauty

Course – Change your life for just 50 guineas'. A clip round the ear and a bar of carbolic soap would be a better bet, thought Stratton. Feeling that they were on a hiding to nothing, he coughed a discreet enquiry to Policewoman Harris and, receiving a shake of the head in return, thanked Bessie for her trouble and left.

The elderly proprietor of the Panda Café had a ravaged look, as though he were in the grip of some ferocious and terminal illness. His cheeks had collapsed and his teeth – which to Stratton's surprise were clearly his own – seemed to have grown as his gums shrank so that his mouth was always slightly open, sticky white saliva clogging its corners.

His customers didn't look much better. Such rays of sunlight as had managed to penetrate the dirt and steam on the windows and the fug inside illuminated dandruff on shoulders, ingrained dirt on necks and clumps of bristles on imperfectly shaved chins. In one corner, an old woman was muttering to herself from behind a copy of the *Daily Mail*. Peering across at the masthead, Stratton saw that the newspaper was over three months old.

The proprietor studied the photograph Stratton had produced. Swollen-eyed and truculent, Iris Manning glared back at him. 'I know her,' he confirmed, 'but I haven't seen her for a good bit.'

'How long, would you say?'

'Week, ten days . . . Something like that. She comes in quite a lot. I've had to speak to her about trying to pick up men in here.'

'Did you have any conversation with her the last time you saw her?'

'If I did I can't remember. Nothing out of the ordinary, at any rate. What's happened to her, then?'

'That,' said Stratton, 'is what we're trying to find out.'

They got the same story in the Champion, and the rest of the pubs yielded no further information, except for the fact that she'd been barred from both the Red Lion and the Dover Castle for drunken and abusive behaviour. The man on the desk at the Pontefract Hotel, a flyblown and seedy establishment that rented rooms by the hour, gazed at them with watery, disillusioned eyes and told them he hadn't seen Iris in a fortnight and didn't care if he never saw her again because she was nothing but trouble.

'You don't think she could have gone off with a customer for a few days, sir?'

They'd come in a full circle and were now standing once more at the top of the street where Iris Manning lived. Stratton stared down the row of soot-blackened terraced houses, their windowsills crusted with pigeon dung, towards Tottenham Court Road. A black cat which had been sniffing around a jumble of rusty dustbins on the pavement shot him a filthy look and slunk away to merge with the shadows in a nearby alley.

'She's not the type for that,' he said. 'Not nowadays, anyway. Strictly short-time. If she'd left a note in her room I'd have seen it. Don't suppose you gleaned anything, did you?'

Policewoman Harris shook her head. 'The other girls were

just as unhelpful as Bessie. Couldn't remember when they'd last seen her, and didn't care. One of them said good riddance because Iris had borrowed ten bob off her last month and still hadn't paid it back.'

'Both parents are dead, according to the sister, and there aren't any other relatives,' said Stratton, 'so that's out. Let's get back to the station.'

As they arrived, Sergeant Ballard was escorting a slight, fair girl of about eighteen out of the door. 'Be right with you, sir,' he murmured as they passed. The girl detained him for a moment, talking earnestly, a look of anxious entreaty on her face, before he caught up with them. 'Any luck, sir?'

'Not a dicky bird. I don't suppose that she,' Stratton waved a hand in the direction of the departed girl, 'had any information, did she?'

'Not about Iris Manning, sir. She came in to report another missing girl. Brought this with her.' Ballard produced a small photograph of the head and shoulders of a woman who was both younger than Iris Manning, and, with her big almond-shaped eyes and full lips, considerably more attractive. 'Kathleen McKinnon. Gone missing, according to her chum. Brown hair and eyes, about five foot three.'

'Tom, is she?' asked Stratton. Ballard nodded. 'Can't say I recognise her,' said Stratton, and Harris's shake of the head told him that she didn't, either. 'Must be new.'

'She is, sir. Only been here a few weeks.'

'Well, she's obviously got a friend, which is more than you can say for poor Iris.'

'They often work together, sir. That's why she came in. I asked if she could be sure McKinnon hadn't gone off for a holiday or to visit relatives – got a kiddie up in Scotland, apparently, her mother looks after it – but she said no, they'd had an appointment with some chap who wanted to photograph them together, and she never turned up. That was three days ago, and she's not seen her since. Told me they usually meet up for a drink before they start, but she didn't appear, and she hadn't said anything about going away.'

'Let's just hope there's not a spate of them,' said Stratton gloomily. 'Lamb'll go spare.' With the Coronation procession passing so near their manor, the DCI was determined to eradicate all vestiges of crime and vice from the streets surrounding Piccadilly Circus, so that the huge influx of people expected could enjoy their day's outing without being propositioned or having their pockets picked. Stratton, who, like most of the station, viewed Piccadilly Circus as the centre of an Inferno-like series of concentric circles, each with a denser and more dangerous concentration of corruption, vice and crime, had remarked after the pep-talk that he hoped it would keep fine for him.

'Wouldn't be the first time we've had someone killing tarts, sir,' said Ballard.

'That's true. Did you ask this . . .'

'Joan Carter, sir.'

'Did you ask her if she knew Iris?'

'Said she'd never heard of her. Sorry, sir.'

'And the chap with the camera?'

'Told her his name was Charlie, but she didn't have an

address. They met him in the Red Lion, and they'd made an arrangement to see him there again. She said he was going to take them off somewhere to do the pictures.'

'Try asking in the pub. Perhaps McKinnon met him on her own.'

'Yes, sir. This is Miss Carter's address, and that's McKinnon's – round the corner from each other.'

Glancing at them, Stratton recognised the streets. More sagging rows of houses chopped up into dismal single rooms, with a pervasive atmosphere of damp, mould and rot. If failure had a smell, Stratton thought, that was it: ambitions and desires unfulfilled and, in the case of these girls, lives spoiled and broken before they'd got properly started. All of them somebody's daughter . . . He thought of Monica – lively, happy, sensible – and shuddered inwardly. 'Come on,' he said to Policewoman Harris. 'Let's take a look.'

Chapter Thirty-Nine

They'd moved twice in the past few months, each time to cheaper and poorer accommodation, and this flat was . . . A refuge, anyway, thought Diana. A shabby, threadbare cocoon where she could hide away until she could think straight about what to do next. But not now. In order to save money, she'd walked from Victoria station, over a mile, and she was exhausted, too tired even to scratch up a meal from whatever remained in the cupboard. All she wanted was to lie down. Dragging herself up the stairs, she didn't think she'd ever been so glad to be home.

There was a note pinned to the door. Diana's heart sank as she recognised her landlady's handwriting. *Dear Mrs Carleton, I have taken your belongings in place of the rent which you have not paid for seven weeks . . .*

Grimacing, she crumpled up the paper and pushed her key into the lock. She'd find the money somehow, and redeem their things, but, right at the moment, she just wanted to get inside, away from everything. She turned the key, and jiggled it, but the door remained firmly closed. After a couple of minutes' desperate pushing and rattling, she gave up and, leaning against the wall, closed her eyes. This isn't how it's supposed to be, she thought. Random images from the past flickered behind her eyelids: the morning of her wedding to Guy, bright-faced with anticipation in the mirror while the maid dressed her hair; lying in Claude's arms on the mattress beneath the improvised shelter in his flat during an air-raid; her mother-in-law's venomous face; the despoiled desolation of her childhood home; running through Green Park with James. Shaking her head in a sort of hopeless wonder at her situation, she remembered James's words about walking into the sea. I could go down to the river now, she thought; it isn't far. What difference would it make?

Wearily, clutching the banister, she went back downstairs and out into the street. There was no point trying to talk Mrs Pritchard into letting her back in, and anyway, she couldn't face it. She walked down the road to the corner. It was twilight, and she stood, swaying slightly on her feet, just outside the spill of light from the open door of the pub. From inside she could hear laughter and the clink of glasses as the evening's business got under way. All down the street, people coming home from work were turning in to their front doors. Lights were being turned on and curtains drawn against the gloom. They'll soon be having supper, Diana thought, settling down for the evening. Hats and coats will be removed, slippers will replace shoes. The wireless and the paper. The children, the cat, the dog. Life carrying on.

Was that what she wanted, life to carry on? If you wanted something badly enough, you were supposed to get it, weren't you? Perhaps she hadn't wanted James to stop drinking badly enough. Perhaps he hadn't wanted it himself. Or perhaps it didn't work like that after all.

The river was to her left. Only a short walk . . . She'd be able to manage it. If she turned right instead, she would eventually, after several miles – provided she didn't get lost on the way – arrive at Lally and Jock's house. Overwhelmed by the thought of the distance, all the streets, squares, road-crossings, turnings off, the sheer effort of placing one foot in front of another, she took a few, faltering steps to her left. As she did so, a man emerged from the shadows by the wall of the pub, fumbling at his fly buttons, and grinned at her. For a moment, their eyes met. Then, with an impetus born of pure disgust, both with him and with herself, she turned right and began the long walk to Albemarle Street.

Chapter Forty

By the time she reached Piccadilly, Diana, though light-headed with tiredness, felt a new clarity of purpose. She'd decided not to die, hadn't she? Now, with the cold rationality of a chess player, she must calculate her next move. One step at a time. The first was to smarten herself up a bit. Bad enough to present herself on Lally's doorstep without warning, which, without even the tuppence needed for a telephone call, was what she'd have to do. She did, however, have one penny left, and that could be spent smartening herself up in the Ladies' at Piccadilly Circus. Clutching it, she marched down the stairs to the Underground.

The attendant, an elderly crone with a long nose and a flat chest, was chatting, mop in hand, to a couple of heavily made-up women, their conversation punctuated by the sound of dripping. Diana walked to the furthest basin and stared at herself in the mirror above it. The harsh electric light and white tiled walls gave her face a pallid, sickly look, and she must have been crying without being aware of it, because her eyes were pink-rimmed and there were the tracks of tears down her cheeks. Her hair, which she hadn't touched since her walk on the beach, was dishevelled. I look like a madwoman, she thought.

She was rummaging in her bag for a comb to repair the damage when a rasping Cockney voice said, 'Hello, dear.' Turning, she saw that the attendant, footsteps muffled by carpet slippers, had come over and was smiling encouragingly. 'New here, are you?'

'New?'

The two women eyed her from across the room. They didn't look half as friendly as the attendant, and it took her a moment to realise why. Her stomach contracted in fear, and she heard herself give a jittery little laugh as she turned back to the basin.

'You going to be sick?' asked the attendant, not so welcoming now. 'Cos if you are, you can go outside and do it.'

'No . . .' Diana found her comb and held it up. 'Just tidying my hair.'

'Been to a party, have you?' asked one of the women. The tone was menacing.

Feverishly, Diana began to smooth her hair. Both women were advancing towards her now. Unable to bolt, she carried on combing mechanically, not paying attention to what she was doing, staring into the mirror and seeing only the two hard slabs of their faces and the red gashes of their mouths, one on either side of her own.

'Somewhere nice, was it?'

'I haven't been to a party.'

The woman looked her up and down. 'Going to one, are you?'

'No . . .'

'You've torn your stocking,' said the other.

Had she? 'Oh . . . I didn't know.'

'I didn't know,' repeated the woman in mocking imitation. She had a smear of lipstick, like blood, on her top teeth.

'Nice handbag,' said the other. Diana shrank from her, clutching the straps tightly. The woman looked down at her shaking hands and said, 'You haven't told us where you're off to.'

'Nowhere,' said Diana, backing away. 'A friend . . .'

'Oh, a *friend*. Give you that, did he?' The woman took a quick step towards her and clamped a hand on her arm, gripping it so that Diana could feel the nails through her fur coat. 'You want to watch yourself,' she said.

Diana felt as though she might stop breathing at any moment. The room was beginning to spin. She looked round for the attendant, but the old woman had shuffled away into a corner and was doing something with a pail. 'Yes . . .' she heard herself say. 'Please, I'm sorry . . .'

'Bitch!' Diana felt a warm spray of spittle land on her face before the woman released her, shoving her backwards. She tottered for a moment before regaining her balance, then she grabbed her bag and fled, mocking laughter echoing behind her, back up to the surface.

She stopped at the stop of the stairs to catch her breath. Everything around her was moving: traffic, neon signs, blurry bright, dancing in front of her eyes, and streams of people moving purposefully forward, rushing past her. Where were they all going?

She made her way down Piccadilly to Albemarle Street. Everyone seemed to be going in the opposite direction. It was as though she had become invisible – however much she tried to avoid the oncoming crowds, people kept knocking into her, pushing her from side to side so that she struggled to remain upright. Keep going, she told herself. Nearly there . . . nearly there. And then she was there, standing in front of the Andersons' front door.

All the windows were pitch dark. What would she do if they weren't at home? She hadn't thought of that. There were waiting rooms in railway stations . . . perhaps she could go there. Or ask a policeman? She had no idea, and without her address book, which must be amongst the belongings purloined by her landlady, she had no idea of anyone else's address or telephone number either. Heart thumping in her chest, she lifted the heavy brass knocker and brought it down sharply, twice. They must be there, they *must* . . .

After what seemed like an age she heard footsteps in the hall and Mrs Robinson, looking more monumental than usual and very suspicious, opened the door a couple of inches. Her eyes widened on seeing Diana, and for a moment she did not speak, but stared, taking in her disordered appearance, almost bristling with disapproval. 'Good evening, Mrs *Carleton*.' The words were grudging and Diana's heart sank. She'd obviously heard about the divorce. People in the film community might be more accepting of – or at least, more used to – people divorcing, but Mrs Robinson, upright and cantilevered in her stiff black frock, was a true Victorian. She hadn't seemed to like Diana much before, but now . . .

For a second, Diana thought the door was going to be slammed in her face, and involuntarily extended an arm to keep it open. 'Good evening, Mrs Robinson.'

'Mrs Anderson's not here at present,' said Mrs Robinson. 'She didn't say she was expecting any visitors.'

'I'm sorry,' said Diana humbly. 'She wasn't expecting me.' She added, as casually as she could, 'May I come in, do you think?'

Mrs Robinson looked her up and down once more, then pursed her lips, as if this request merited careful consideration. 'Well,' she said, after a long pause, 'I don't know when they'll be back.'

Abandoning the pretence, Diana said, 'Please, Mrs Robinson. I need to speak to her.'

There was no light in the housekeeper's eyes, no flicker of sympathy, but she stepped back to let Diana into the hall. 'Shall I take your coat?'

Suspecting that the fire wasn't, and wouldn't be, lit, Diana said, 'I think I'll keep it on, thank you.'

Once in the sitting room, Diana sank into an armchair and inspected her legs. The woman in the toilet had been right – one stocking was laddered, badly. Mrs Robinson, who'd followed her, stood mute and unwelcoming in the middle of the room. Seeing that she was to be offered nothing, Diana said, 'Do you think I might have some brandy?'

Expressionless, but still managing to radiate hostility, Mrs Robinson stalked over to the drinks tray and poured a very small amount of brandy, scarcely more than a trickle, into a glass. Handing it to Diana, she left the room quickly, as if to remain might contaminate her in some indefinable way.

Tired almost beyond thought and profoundly relieved to be alone at last, Diana drained the glass, leant back in her chair and closed her eyes. She imagined James's hand sliding up her arm, massaging the flesh as he had that day in Green Park. The feeling was so strong that she felt he was there, in the room, leaning over her, his breath warming her cheek. Then, as drowsiness overcame her, James's face seemed to melt and reform into that of Edward Stratton, eyes smiling and lips moving as though he were trying to tell her something, but she couldn't hear him . . . And then she slept.

Chapter Forty-One

'A *third* one?' said DCI Lamb. 'Are you *sure*?'

His superior's expression was George Formby at his most gormless and imbecilic, and for a second Stratton was tempted to say, 'No, I'm just larking about.' Aloud, he said, 'I'm afraid so, sir. Name's Mary Dwyer. Boyfriend reported it this morning. She promised to meet him three days ago but she didn't turn up and he hasn't seen her since.' He slid the photograph – head and shoulders, showing an angular face, handsome rather than beautiful, surrounded by a cloud of dark curls – across Lamb's desk, where it was given the briefest of glances before being flicked back to him.

'The first one's been missing quite a few days now, hasn't she?'

'Ten, sir.'

'And you've got nothing at all?'

'We're still making enquiries, sir.'

'And the second?'

'Nothing to go on yet, sir.'

Sighing, Lamb let him go with instructions to 'find out

what's happened to these wretched women as soon as possible'. As if he thought I was going to take Ballard and Harris on a coach outing to the seaside instead, thought Stratton irritably. Lamb was right about one thing, though – 'Wretched' was what the three women were, all right – they were amongst the lowest and least successful of their kind. Dwyer and her boyfriend didn't even have a permanent address.

The next two days were spent traipsing round interviewing toms, from adolescent, gawkily provocative girls to aged whores, beneath a succession of hand-tinted pictures of Princess Elizabeth and Prince Philip in rooms that smelt of mice. When they weren't doing that, they were trudging round cheerless pubs with engraved mirrors and curly brass ornaments, showing photographs to staff and drinkers in the hope of jogging someone's memory. Such places had a regular clientele, but they also functioned as a sort of no-man's-land for a certain type who, impelled by randiness or curiosity, made a foray to pick up a tart, throwing off the shackles of respectability for a brief time before retreating in self-disgust to his daily life.

At the end of the second day, Stratton dispiritedly bade Ballard and Harris goodnight and went off home, reflecting that the whole thing had been a waste of time, and tomorrow didn't look as if it was going to be much better. *Tomorrow*. He'd completely forgotten. Pete was coming home, and Monica had reminded him, several times, that Doris was making a special dinner and he must be sure to be back in time. Much to Stratton's surprise his son, despite his initial reservations about the army, had decided to stay on when he'd finished his national service. Stratton thought that, although Pete had never said as much, the boy had come to enjoy the uniformity of it all – the drilling, the rules, the ranks. He had avoided thinking too deeply about this, because it smacked too much of Reg. Not, of course, that Reg was a blood relation, whereas he himself, being in the police force . . . He couldn't quite put his finger on exactly *why* it should make him so uncomfortable, but it did. If only he found it easier to talk to Pete . . . but, if anything, the gap between them had widened. When something that smacked of introspection or emotion reared its head, they both took refuge in hearty good humour until the danger had passed off.

He suddenly wondered if Pete went with prostitutes. It would be nice to feel sure that the answer was no, absolutely not, but he didn't. There were always plenty of girls in garrison towns, and if his pals went along . . . Anyway, Stratton told himself, angry for speculating, it was a bloody sight better than promising the moon and stars to some innocent young girl when all you wanted was . . . but for all he knew, Pete had done that, too. It was yet another thing they'd never discussed, and that was *his* job, not Jenny's – even if she were here – and he'd failed.

He supposed that there had been prostitutes in the local towns when *he* was growing up, but he'd never encountered one until he started working in London. His first sexual experiments had been with the Ellens and Doras of neighbouring villages. There'd been no broken promises, no anguished wranglings, just good fun. Of course, there'd been plenty of gentlemen's daughters who went hunting and attended county balls, but they'd filled him with awe, not lust, and it wouldn't have occurred to him to raise his sights so high. In fact, he couldn't remember ever speaking to one of these lofty creatures. Here, the spectre of Diana, smiling in welcome as she had when they'd met at the Festival of Britain and he'd made a prize idiot of himself, flitted across his mind. Wincing, he pushed it away.

What he needed was a quiet pint, but he didn't get it. In the pub, Donald and some of the neighbours were engaged in a discussion about clubbing together to rent a television for the Coronation, and his opinion was immediately solicited as to where the viewing should take place. After suggesting the church hall, he withdrew to a table in the corner and left them to it. He'd be working, but, judging from what he'd seen of television through the windows of showrooms, he didn't think he'd be missing much: everything on the little screens looked to him as though it were taking place in a snowstorm. He regretted his lack of enthusiasm, but there it was – he wished the new queen the best of luck and all that, but he had other things on his mind: Pete's visit and the three missing women. If only they could make some progress . . .

Some hope, thought Stratton sourly, as he and Ballard sat in the detectives' office at West End Central the following morning, reviewing their progress – or rather, the lack of it.

'We'll need to widen the search, sir,' said Ballard. 'That's everything in Conway Street, Warren Street, Grafton Mews–'

A knock on the door produced Policewoman Harris with two cups of tea. 'There's a call, sir,' she said. 'Urgent. Cudlipp's putting it through.'

Stratton gestured at Ballard to pick up the telephone and went back to studying his list of informants. The obvious ones had proved useless, but perhaps—

'What number?' Something sharp in Ballard's tone made him look up. His sergeant's handsome face had turned rigid, a blank-eyed mask. He took the receiver away from his head and was staring at it as if it were about to disgorge a stream of poison. Stratton stared as, collecting himself with a visible effort, Ballard returned the telephone to his ear and said, 'Don't touch anything, sir. We'll be there right away.'

Putting the telephone down, Ballard stared at Stratton. The air between them was static with unspoken, and very bad, news. Stratton swallowed. 'What is it?'

'That was the new tenant of the ground-floor flat at number ten, Paradise Street.' The sergeant's voice was expressionless. 'Just moved in this morning. He's found a woman's body in the kitchen alcove.'

Chapter Forty-Two

Stratton's shoes echoed on the dusty boards of the kitchen floor. The small room was empty, but for the range and the deckchair with its sling of knotted rope that he remembered from when they'd visited the Backhouses. Then, in the company of the table and chairs and other domestic paraphernalia, it had looked merely odd; now, on its own in the middle of the room, it was downright sinister. Stratton sniffed. There was a smell of decay – what one might expect, perhaps, from a dead mouse or rat under the floorboards – but, although unpleasant, it wasn't overwhelming. He could see the gap in the wall where the new ground-floor tenant, Mr Maynard – currently being interviewed by Ballard – had torn the paper away, revealing the ragged tops of rough wooden boards. Stratton remembered that these formed the door of the alcove cupboard where the Backhouses had stored baby Judy's things.

Don't jump ahead, he told himself. It must be coincidence. It has to be. In the ten minutes that had elapsed between the telephone call and their arrival at the house, he'd mentally repeated this over and over again, like a prayer, trying to hold at bay the panic, the dread of what he might find. Feeling as precarious as a man on a high wire with no safety net, he pulled the torch from his jacket pocket and switched it on. As he did so, he noticed, quite objectively, that his hands were trembling. Could this really be happening? Couldn't the man have made a mistake – seen something that merely looked like a body, a dummy or doll, perhaps, somebody playing an evil practical joke, or–

There was no mistake. The moment he pushed the torch through the aperture, the beam illuminated a knobbly backbone beneath grey, grimy skin, bisected by the strap of a brassiere. The body appeared to be seated on something and was leaning forward facing the back of the alcove so that the head was almost between the knees, dark hair flopping around it. Something thick and grey – a blanket, Stratton thought – had been looped through the bra strap. Following it with his torch beam, he saw that it was attached to something lumpy and wrapped in another grey blanket, and that this was part of a larger parcel – human-sized, in fact – which appeared to be fastened with a cord, and that behind it was a second one.

I cannot believe this is happening. Stratton blundered back into the hall and found Ballard talking to Mr Maynard who was sitting, ashen-faced, on the bottom step of the stairs. Leaving the unfortunate man in the care of Policewoman Harris, he led Ballard outside. 'Get down to the box. We'll need a photographer as well as the pathologist. I think there's three of them.'

'Think they're our girls, sir?'

'I don't know. Two of them are wrapped up and I can't see the other one's face. What did he,' Stratton jerked his head towards Maynard, 'have to say for himself?'

'Says he's only been here once before, sir, and that was yesterday, with the landlord. That's a Mr . . .' Ballard checked his notes, 'Morrison. Says they looked round together, and he agreed to take the flat, but apart from this morning, he's not been here on his own at all. In any case, Morrison told him the previous tenant had tried to sub-let the place without his knowledge and he wanted him to know he wouldn't stand for it.'

'And the previous tenant was . . .?'

'He didn't know, sir, so I sent Policewoman Harris next door to find out . . .' Ballard faltered.

Feeling that the world was disintegrating around him, Stratton said, 'And . . .'

'Still Mr Backhouse, sir,' said Ballard, apologetically. 'The lady told Harris Mrs Backhouse had gone up north a few months ago, to stay with her sister, and she'd not seen *him* for a few days so she thought he must have left. Said he'd told her he'd given his notice at work because he'd got the offer of a job up there.'

'Oh, Christ. I just hope . . .' Stratton didn't complete the sentence. He could see that Ballard knew only too well what he just hoped, because he was hoping the same. It didn't need spelling out. Just as well, he thought, because he didn't think he could bring himself to say it. 'Go down to the box and talk to Lamb. We've got to find the fucker.'

Ballard opened his mouth, and Stratton saw, from his expression, that he was about to offer a palliative lie, but then he seemed to decide against it and merely nodded. Speech temporarily defeating him, Stratton clapped the sergeant on the bicep. His stomach seemed to be filled with cold ash, so that he felt hollow and sick. His legs felt unsteady and, if Maynard hadn't been sitting on the bottom step of the stairs, he'd have sat down on it himself. As it was, he leant against the adjacent wall. Policewoman Harris, who'd been carefully avoiding his eyes since the telephone call came, continued to do so, staring grimly down at the floor.

The kitchen was crowded with coppers but, beyond the brief acknowledging nod of greeting, nobody looked anyone else in the eye. The unexpressed sympathy, curdled by the beginnings of blame, made the atmosphere even more uncomfortable, but Stratton knew that he mustn't leave the room. He was meant to be in charge – to desert his post, even for a moment, would be taken for either cowardice or admission. The pathologist, McNally, busied himself with his bag and gloves, and the rest of them watched in thickening silence as PC Canning removed the remains of the wallpaper from round the alcove and then pulled open the wooden door, stopping at each stage of the operation for the photographer to do his work. The man's bright lights seemed to illuminate the splintered kaleidoscope of hideous pictures inside Stratton's head: the baby's tiny, curled feet on the mortuary slab, Muriel's legs sliding out of the bundle they'd dragged from the washhouse, and worst of all, Davies's haggard face as he stared into infinity . . . He put a hand over his eyes to try and block them out, but it was useless.

'Sir?' Ballard was beside him, a hand on his arm. 'Can we move the body now?'

Stratton nodded dumbly then forced himself to watch as Canning and Ballard manhandled the corpse, arms and legs flopping, out of the narrow space and across the passage where, following McNally's instructions, they laid it on the floor of the now empty back room.

The face, despite its discolouration and bulging eyeballs, was recognisably that of Mary Dwyer. She looked pathetic – a human object used and then, just as callously, discarded. Her wrists tied together with a handkerchief, and dressed only in a brassiere, stockings and suspenders – the knickers were missing – she was a pitiful sight: jutting hipbones and ribs clearly visible, the skin flashing a hideous greenish-white in the harsh glare of the photographer's bulb. The only thing that wasn't greenish-white was the groove of the ligature, the brownish-red of raw liver, that circled her neck.

Chapter Forty-Three

Stratton swallowed, trying to work saliva into his mouth. Aware that everyone was watching for his reaction, he opened his mouth to ask a question, but McNally got there first. 'The rigor's passed, but she's not been there long. Forty-eight hours, perhaps.' The gentle tone and the expression of sympathy on the man's face were far harder to take than the usual rebuke for wanting answers before a proper examination had been carried out at the mortuary. 'You know her?'

Stratton wondered how McNally had deduced this. 'Possibly . . .' Taking refuge in professional language, he added, 'There'll have to be a formal identification, of course.'

McNally nodded solemnly, a priest taking an unspoken confession. 'Of course.'

Stratton followed Dwyer's sheeted body as it was carried out to the ambulance on a stretcher. He stopped just inside the door. He could hear the crowd that was gathering in the street, but he didn't want to see them – the eager faces, agog with excitement, reminding each other of the events of two and a half years earlier. 'Newspapers, too, sir,' said Ballard, behind him. 'They'll be here shortly.'

McNally, crouched inside the alcove, was running his gloved hands over the blanketed objects. Turning round to come back out he said, with an apologetic grimace, 'Three's a crowd . . . The one at the back's standing on her head. That's assuming it's a woman, of course.'

Canning goggled at him. 'You mean she's upside down?'

''Fraid so.'

Canning's face contorted, and barging past the others he shoved open the back door and almost fell into the garden. They listened in silence as the sound of loud retching followed by liquid splattering told them that he was being violently sick.

'Sorry about that, sir.' Canning returned looking slightly sheepish and wiping his mouth with his handkerchief. 'Think I'll be fine now.'

'It's all right,' said Stratton, catching a faint, sour whiff of vomit as the big policeman edged past him. 'Ready to go again?'

Canning nodded. With Ballard's assistance, the second body was carried across the passage and laid on the floor of the back room. McNally, kneeling, began to loosen the knots that held the hideous parcel together. 'Must have been a Boy Scout,' he said grimly. Finally, a pair of legs was revealed, then some sort of flannelette garment bunched up between the thighs like a diaper, then the stomach, which was covered in rough-looking white patches, and the torso, small breasts beneath a grubby white cotton vest, one strap secured lopsidedly by a safety pin. Finally, the head emerged, covered entirely by a pillowslip which was secured around the neck by a tightly knotted stocking.

McNally looked up at Stratton, who nodded assent, and began removing the pillow case. As it was pulled upwards, Stratton saw that there was a piece of flowered material fixed across the mouth, like a gag, some tendrils of brown hair trapped underneath on either side. When that was removed, Stratton could see that the blackened end of the tongue was sticking out from between the teeth.

'Think it's McKinnon, sir?' asked Ballard, beside him.

'Could be.' Stratton didn't turn to look at the sergeant. What had they done, he thought. What had *he* done?

The skin of the face looked dried and the eyeballs were distended, the irises a dull brown. As McNally removed the stocking, Stratton saw the pressure marks on the neck. 'Is that from keeping the pillowslip in place?' he asked.

McNally shook his head. 'Too deep. Probably strangulation. I imagine that's why the . . .' he gestured at the wadded material between the woman's legs. 'Fluids.'

'Can you say how long she's been dead?'

Again, no rebuke for the question. The pathologist said thoughtfully, 'Not sure. She's in pretty good condition, all things considered – must be the dehydration. Not more than a week, I'd say. Ten days at the outside.'

'There's not much of a smell.'

'Decomposition hasn't really got going. The weather's not

been that warm, and although that cupboard wasn't entirely airtight, with that wallpaper, and being wrapped . . . that would certainly have helped retard it.' McNally pointed at the face. 'Heading for partial mummification, I'd say. There's mould, though. From spores and such.' He pointed to the area below the vest. 'She's ready to move.'

The third body appeared, at first sight, to be fully clothed in a dress and cardigan. She was fatter than the others, and there was a towel wrapped around her head, and another between her legs, visible where her skirt and slip had become disarranged. McNally peered down. 'This one's not wearing knickers either.'

Hearing this, Ballard murmured, 'Muriel Davies wasn't wearing any knickers, sir, remember?'

'Wasn't she?'

'No, sir.'

'We can't jump to conclusions, Ballard.'

The sergeant stared at him for a moment, eyes widening with irony, then said, 'No, sir.'

'For God's sake,' snapped Stratton, 'we don't *know*. But Backhouse is obviously out of control – judging by what we've found, it's only a matter of time before he does it again. I doubt he's bothered about being caught . . .'

'I shouldn't think he'd have left the place like this if he was, sir.'

'Exactly. He's got beyond that point – doesn't care any more. Still, if it makes him reckless, he should be easy to catch, which is something. As soon as McNally's finished here, we're going to take this fucking place apart. Brick by brick, if necessary. We'll need some men for the garden, too, so you'd better go back to the box – but not Arliss. I don't want him anywhere near the place. Then you better take Canning, and . . . how many men are out at the front?'

'Three, sir.' Ballard's neutral expression betrayed no reproach, but Stratton felt both guilty and, perversely, irritated by the man's sympathetic demeanour.

'I'm sure two can manage, so take one of them and start on that bloody washhouse and the toilet, and if you don't find anything there you'd better get cracking on the floorboards. Don't do anything else. We'll need to get the surveyors' department in for that – don't want the place falling down round our ears.'

'Right, sir.'

'And, Ballard . . .'

'Sir?'

'I'm sorry.'

'No need, sir.'

'Yes, there is,' snapped Stratton, goaded by Ballard's understanding tone. 'There's every bloody need. This is a fucking nightmare, and it's my fault.' He turned his back on the sergeant and fixed his eyes once more on the body on the floor.

'Shall we have a look at her now?' asked McNally. Again the voice was soft, hesitant.

Stratton nodded, gritting his teeth. For Christ's sake stop *humouring* me, he thought. Just get it *done*.

Again, the distended eyeballs, congealed and purple skin bleached in the glare and flash of the photographer's bulb, the black tongue protruding. White mould on the skin around the mouth, and a stub of white stalactite, like a horn, sticking out of one nostril. Was it Iris Manning? He thought so. Unlike the others, he'd known her in life, but in this condition . . . We could have saved her, he thought. I should have. I should have saved all three of them.

'She may be pregnant,' said McNally, gently. The words seemed to hover somehow in the air of the dismal room, reverberating so that Stratton heard them not once, but several times over. Dragging his eyes from the ruined face, he saw that the pathologist was feeling the belly with the palms of his gloved hands, as delicately as if she'd been a living woman. 'There's something here, quite bulky. Could be something else, but . . .'

'How far gone, if she is?'

'*If* she is, I'd say four or five months.'

Stratton, well aware that it was normally impossible to extract such speculation from McNally or any other pathologist, suddenly wondered if he knew about Jenny. He hadn't conducted the post-mortem himself, but he would surely know the man who had, and perhaps... McNally's expression wasn't telling him one way or the other. The pathologist was staring at him with intense concentration, as if willing him to focus on the job. Grasping for some sort of logic, he said, 'Do you think either of the others might have been pregnant?'

'Won't be able to tell that until we get back to the mortuary.' Until they were cut up, Stratton thought. 'Won't know if this one's been interfered with yet, either. The pregnancy, I mean – if that's what it is.'

'Muriel Davies's pregnancy wasn't interfered with.'

'No,' McNally looked away. 'It wasn't.'

No one had said anything about Iris Manning being pregnant. Perhaps she hadn't told anyone. Perhaps Backhouse had offered to get rid of it for her, enticed her in . . .

A thump from outside made him turn his head in the direction of the back yard, and he saw that Ballard and the others were trooping back inside and down the passage to the front room. Nothing in the washhouse then, this time, but there was always the garden . . .

McNally was saying something. '. . . move her now?'

'Yes. You can take her away.'

As they stood back for the sheeted corpse to be removed, McNally said, 'Do I take it that you'd like me to stay?'

'I'm afraid so. Pulling up the boards shouldn't take long. Would you excuse me for a moment?'

Averting his eyes from the drying puddle of spew where Canning had voided the contents of his stomach, Stratton stared around the small back yard. It seemed even more untidy than it had been in 1950 – but then, he thought, they'd only seen it by torchlight. The wrecked Anderson shelter was still there and the twisted chicken wire, the old tin cans, crumpled newspapers, broken bricks and odd tufts of grass sticking out of the dry mud, as well as a surprisingly vigorous mock orange and another bush that he didn't recognise. Seeing a small bone, gnawed white, that looked like the remains of a chop, Stratton wondered where the dog was. Had Backhouse taken it with him?

Unless it wasn't an animal bone, of course . . . Some human bones were small and a dog, knowing no different, would enjoy chewing one of those as well. Human remains could fertilise plants. They did in graveyards. Was he looking at a graveyard now? And if he was, had there been women buried here when they found Muriel and Judy Davies? For Christ's sake, he told himself, you were only looking for Muriel and Judy, not a lot of dead tarts. There was no reason then – *none whatsoever* – to think that anyone else had been killed. And certainly no reason to think that Norman Backhouse, with his fibrositis and his diarrhoea, his visits to the doctor and his old-womanish ways . . . No reason to think that Backhouse the former police Reservist, the reformed man . . . No reason to think that Backhouse, who had a nice quiet wife and a nice quiet life – except that *he shared his nice quiet home with Christ-knows-how-many dead whores . . .*

If Davies was innocent, why had he confessed? Because he felt guilty about what had happened to his wife? Guilty that he hadn't protected her?

'Jesus Christ!' He smashed his fist against the wooden panels of the washhouse door. He, of all people, should have understood about the guilt. But it was Jenny's death, Jenny and their unborn child, that had made him pursue Davies with such certainty; resentment against a man who, it appeared, had had a pregnant wife and killed her, and who'd killed a baby, when he'd have given anything, anything at all—

'Yes.' That's what Davies had said when he'd shown him the clothing at West End Central. He'd reached forward and picked up the tie that was used to kill his child, and he'd said 'yes'. Then he'd wept. And Stratton had been *absolutely sure* that he'd got his man. 'Yes.' One word: it could mean everything or nothing.

And the stupid bastard had lied about practically everything else, hadn't he? No one, not even his mother, had believed a word he said . . .

'Sir?' Ballard stuck his head round the back door.

'Found anything?'

'Not yet, sir. Canning and Tillotson are getting started on the floorboards in the back room.'

'That was their bedroom, wasn't it?'

'Yes, sir . . . And there are a couple of things you ought to see.'

'Oh?'

'A length of rubber tubing, and a bulldog clip. We found them by the fireplace in the front room. And there's this, sir.' Ballard took a small object wrapped in a handkerchief out of his pocket. When he laid it on the scabby, flaking paint of the windowsill, Stratton saw that it was a rusty tobacco tin: Old Holborn.

'It seems he took souvenirs, sir.'

'Sou– Oh, *Christ*.' The lid open, Stratton could see four separate clumps of short, coarse hair, which had been carefully teased out into ringlets so that they looked like nests for miniature birds. 'Pubic?'

'I think so, sir, yes.'

'Where did you find that thing?'

'Medicine cabinet in the kitchen. Behind the door, sir.'

'Anything else in there?'

'Lot of tablets, sir. Tonics and sedatives and God knows what else. Harris is making a list. And the other tenants are back – the ones who live on the top floor. Young coloured couple.'

'See if you can't get one of the neighbours to make them a cup of tea. What about the ones on the first floor?'

'It's the same chap, sir – Mr Gardiner. He's back in hospital, so I don't think—' Ballard was interrupted by a discreet cough from the direction of the back door, now blocked by the burly form of PC Canning, claw hammer dangling from one meaty hand. 'Found another one, sir.'

Chapter Forty-Four

The floorboards from the centre of the room were stacked in front of the fireplace. Looking down, Stratton saw that one of the joists had been sawn away to make room for body number four, which was encased in a flannelette blanket, lashed at each end and covered with a dusting of earth. When the photographer had finished, Canning and Tillotson removed the body with an effort and stood back for McNally to do his work.

'Definitely a Boy Scout . . . Safety pins as well, this time. Perhaps he ran out of rope.'

Like the previous two, the head was wrapped, this time in what looked like part of a sheet. The body, which was considerably stockier and heavier than the others, was naked apart from stockings. It was covered on top by a nightgown, with what appeared to be a dress lying beneath. McNally lifted the nightgown, exposing the heavy breasts and belly. The skin was hard and mouldy like the outside of a cheddar cheese. As with the other two bodies, there was a garment of some sort stuffed between the legs. 'That first one . . .' said

McNally, 'he must have been interrupted before he could do all this, so he just stuck her in the cupboard as she was. This one's a good bit older than the others,' he added. 'Both in terms of age and of how long she's been here.' Ballard and Stratton exchanged glances as he began unwrapping the material from the head. Suddenly, the reek of putrefaction hit Stratton like a blow to the face, making him gag.

'Damp air getting in somewhere,' said the pathologist in a matter-of-fact voice, as if giving a lecture. Forcing himself to turn his head, Stratton saw that while the right side of the woman's face was dry, and covered with the same mould as her body, the left side was decomposing wetly so that the features appeared to have slipped and melted down the side of the cheek.

Fighting rising nausea, Stratton turned to look at Ballard who, although so pale in the face that he was almost translucent, seemed steady enough on his feet. He could feel the stink wrapping itself around him, clinging to his clothes like smoke. Better you smell of dead women than live ones, Jenny'd once said, in an unusual moment of black humour – except she wasn't there to care what he smelt of . . . Still, he'd better give himself a good scrub before— Oh, Christ. The bloody party. Pete. He'd never be able to get back in time – he'd have to telephone Doris later. Pete would understand.

'Cause of death?' he asked the pathologist.

'Not sure yet. There are some grooves here,' McNally pointed to the neck, 'but the condition of the skin . . .' He shook his head.

'Can you say how long?'

'At least a couple of months, I'd say.'

'The neighbour said Mrs Backhouse had been away for about three months, sir,' said Ballard quietly.

As they followed the draped and stretchered corpse outside to the ambulance, Stratton was aware of a low, expectant hum, which stopped as Canning stepped backwards out of the front door with his end of the load. Following with Ballard, he stopped on the threshold and stared out at the crowd of mainly women and children who stood in a half circle around the ambulance, three and four deep. They were being kept at a distance by two policemen, helmeted and wearing overcoats, who were watching over the vehicle with the proprietorial air of shepherds guarding a flock.

Judging by the numbers Stratton thought it was a fair bet that, as well as neighbours, the usual collection of ghouls were present, who'd thrill to carnage and catastrophe of any kind. In fact, Stratton often thought that given the speed with which they turned up in such situations, they must somehow be able to sense it. You could tell who they were by their gawping; they were avid and shameless. The other faces bore degrees of shocked or guilty fascination and some of the kids had a slightly distracted look, as if they couldn't concentrate wholly on what was unfolding because they had to be on the lookout in case their parents caught them at it. They needn't have worried: from what Stratton could see most of the parents – the mothers, at least – were in the crowd as well. Some of them, he realised, must have been here when they'd come for Muriel Davies; but if anybody did recognise him, they were keeping it to themselves, which was a relief.

Still, you couldn't blame the neighbours for coming to see what was going on. I'd be out here, too, if I lived next door, he thought, I'd want to see what the next turn-up would be. And that, he thought, as a police van pulled up in front of the goods yard wall and men in overalls began unloading spades, sieves and stacks of wooden boxes, was anybody's guess.

Scanning the crowd once more, he spotted, towards the back, an anxious-looking coloured couple who must be the ones from the top flat. Several feet away, a slatternly woman whose hair was quilted by metal curlers stood talking to a couple of solid-looking men in fawn mackintoshes. Coarse-faced, they had a brazen look about them which, in Stratton's experience, meant one of two things. Either they sold stuff on commission or – far more likely in the circumstances – they were journalists. Well, they could whistle for it, because they weren't getting a peep out of him.

He looked past the crowd, down the short length of the street with its row of mean, bay-windowed front rooms surrounded by grimy brickwork. As the day started to draw in, a glum, grey pall seemed to shroud everything in view.

'Paradise Street,' said Ballard wryly. 'Evidently someone's idea of a joke.'

'Ha-bloody-ha.' Stratton was standing right beside the side pane of the smeary front window of number ten, and, as he spoke, he peered into it, almost expecting to see Backhouse's face, bespectacled and ghostly, hovering behind the net curtain.

To his left, he could hear the monotonous thrum of traffic and to his right, chugging and clanging from the railway tracks; the sounds of life continuing as normal. 'It's ordinary,' he said. 'Ordinary life in an ordinary street. I keep imagining him pottering around this house, brewing tea and taking bloody ... *kaolin and morphine* for his diarrhoea, and all the time ...'

'Do you think Mrs Backhouse knew, sir?'

'Back in nineteen fifty? She was very much under his thumb, so ...' Stratton shook his head wearily. 'I just don't know. The whole thing is just ...' Unable to think of a word that would accurately describe what it was, he illustrated it with a small, hopeless gesture.

'Inspector, if I might just ...' Turning, he found himself confronting one of the journalists, who must have edged around the back of the crowd. Close to, he recognised the man as one who'd badgered him before, sidling up and offering to buy him a drink (or, as he put it, 'a gargle') on a number of occasions, always in the creepily confidential manner of a false friend. Now, the voice was goading, aggressively cheerful. 'What about Davies now, Inspector? Still think he's guilty?' Revolted by the brutal breath and the predatory eyes, the man's whole air of gorging himself on misery, Stratton said, 'I've got nothing to say.'

'But surely, Inspector–'

'Piss off.' Stratton turned his back and, muttering, the man went to rejoin his colleague.

He shouldn't have said that – the man was bound to find some way of sticking the knife in ... 'Stupid,' he said to Ballard. 'You should never lose your temper with them.'

'Quite understandable, sir, in the circumstances.'

'Yes, but he won't see it like that . . . It's all very well for them,' Stratton added, sourly. 'For them it's just the next sensation. Here and then gone, and they never have to worry about the consequences.'

Ballard was staring past him down the street. 'I think DCI Lamb is about to arrive, sir.'

Following the sergeant's gaze, Stratton saw the official car nosing its way round the corner. 'That's all we bloody need. I'd better go and meet him.'

He'd assumed that Lamb would insist on arriving with a great fanfare of horn-honking, and was surprised when the car pulled up almost immediately and his superior emerged from the back seat unaided. Stratton, who was bracing himself for the full performance from righteous anger to bravely borne resignation, taking in disappointment and endeavouring to rise above it and Christ knew what else in between, reflected that at last there was no convenient surface for the forefinger-jabbing that always accompanied a high-grade bollocking. Unless – Stratton winced – Lamb was going to use his chest and prod him backwards down the length of the cul-de-sac. I'll strangle him if he tries that, he thought savagely. I'll put my hands round his neck and shake him till his eyes pop out, and then I'll–

'How many?'

Stratton blinked. Lamb's voice was so quiet it barely reached him, and he looked not only defeated but stupefied. Watching him, Stratton's dismay and anger was transformed into the same intensity of amazement. It was as disconcerting as if a dummy had suddenly reached out a real, flesh-and-blood hand. 'Sir?'

'In the house – how many?'

'Four, sir, so far. I'm fairly certain that at least one of them is one of our missing girls. It's possible that the other two are there as well, but it's a bit hard to tell at the moment . . . We also think that the fourth body – we found her under the bedroom floor – might be Edna Backhouse. They're making a start on the garden now, sir. It's the usual drill – removing soil to a depth of two feet and sieving for evidence. I don't imagine they'll be able to finish today, but we'll station constables front and back overnight, and—'

'This is a fucking shambles.' Lamb shook his head in disbelief and Stratton, who had never heard his superior swear so harshly before, was as astonished by this as by finding himself entirely in sympathy with the man.

'Right.' Pulling himself together with a visible effort, Lamb said, 'I suppose I'd better have a look.'

'Yes, sir. This way.'

'Any reporters yet?'

'A couple, sir.'

'For God's sake don't speak to them. I'll have something sent out for tomorrow's papers. If they persist, tell them to contact the station.'

'Yes, sir. Thank you.'

Lamb was silent throughout the short tour, merely nodding at Stratton's explanations. Finally, as they stood outside the washhouse, watching the team of men dig and sift in the garden, he said, in a tone of baffled wonder, 'He was a special.'

Stratton, feeling it would be inappropriate to offer condolences of the anyone-can-make-a-mistake variety, and uncomfortable with the memory of enjoying a quiet gloat about Lamb being hauled over the coals after Backhouse's criminal record came out, settled for, 'Well, he was commended, sir.' He knew, even as he said it, that he should have kept his mouth shut, but Lamb didn't appear to have heard. Instead, he was staring at one of the diggers, who was gesturing from the far corner of the garden.

'Something here, sir. Could you take a look?'

The digger was pointing to the corner where the rickety wooden planks of the back fence met the brick wall of the goods yard, and Stratton, approaching, saw something dirty white sticking out of the earth. Squatting down beside it, he saw that beneath the soil and grime was the smooth, rounded end of what looked like a thigh bone. Judging by its fleshless condition, it had been there for some time and it was, he thought, too large to belong to a cat or dog.

'He must have been at it for quite some time, sir,' said the digger. 'This must have worked itself loose somehow or other, because he's been using it to prop up this end of the fence.'

Chapter Forty-Five

'Those women in the lavatory at Piccadilly,' said Diana. 'They thought I was one of them. A tart.'

'Why on earth didn't you tell me what was happening, darling?' Lally was sitting on the end of the bed, looking worried. 'You were in such a dreadful state last night – a sort of faint. We didn't know what to think . . . And the last time we saw you, you seemed so *happy*. I know that was some time ago, but I had no idea. I thought you were just . . . well, busy.'

'I'm sorry, Lally. I didn't mean to cause . . . you know. But I couldn't tell you. You've been so kind to me. It wasn't fair to keep on running to you for help, and I thought it would be disloyal to James.' Diana lay back on the pillows. At some point the previous evening, Lally and Jock had returned and persuaded a reluctant Mrs Robinson to make up a bed for her. She'd been so exhausted that she scarcely remembered Lally leading her up the stairs and helping her into bed. Looking down, she saw that she was still wearing her underclothes. 'I didn't know what to do. I thought I could help him, but . . . He *told* me to leave him, Lally. I didn't want to

– or maybe I did. I don't know any more. I'm just . . . just . . . It's all such a failure. Guy, James, everything. My whole life. I should never have got married again – or not so quickly, anyway.'

'I did wonder, when you told me you were going to marry him,' said Lally. 'But you seemed so in love and so *sure* and these things often do work, so . . .' She made a face. 'But you're not hopeless, and it isn't your fault. James's drinking wasn't your fault, and neither was the rest of it.' Lally's tone was sharp, and Diana was surprised to see that her face was white with tight-lipped anger. 'It's the way we were brought up. We weren't taught to think for ourselves. Beauty, compliancy, *complaisancy* . . . That's all that's ever been expected. No useful skills and precious little education – beyond what we've managed to scrape for ourselves, that is. What the hell *are* you supposed to do if you're a cross between a . . . a . . . brood mare and an ornament? Especially as half the men our generation of girls married – or were supposed to marry – were killed in the war, and all those big houses we were supposed to run have either been knocked down or sold off as boarding schools or something because nobody can afford to live in them any more.'

Taken aback by her friend's vehemence, Diana said, 'It's not that bad. And you seem to manage pretty well.'

Lally shot her a rueful look. 'Sorry. I suppose that was a bit about me. But not everything in the garden is roses, you know.'

'Better than no garden at all. I was thinking about those things – what you just said – when I was up at Hambeyn

Hall . . . You've put it much better. We're dinosaurs, really, and it's hard to be any different, no matter how much you want to. You'd think, with the war, one would adapt one's thinking, but somehow one just goes back – behaves as if nothing had changed . . . Or perhaps that's just me. God knows . . . Anyway, thank you, darling, for letting me stay.'

'Don't be silly.'

'Mrs Robinson doesn't like me much, does she?'

Lally grimaced. 'I suppose she's another kind of dinosaur – a Victorian one. Divorced women not allowed across the threshold . . . She's been with Jock's family for about five hundred years. But don't worry, I'm sure we'll manage to get round her somehow. Now, you look absolutely shattered, and I forbid you to set foot out of bed until you've revived a bit. When you're better, Jock will take you to see your landlady and sort out the rent.'

'Are you sure? I don't know when I'll be able to repay you.'

'Don't you get any money from Guy? I don't mean to pay us back – you mustn't worry about that – but to live on.'

Diana shook her head. 'I was getting a small allowance, but it stopped when James and I married. We ploughed what was left of my money into James's projects, but none of them came to fruition, so . . . That's it, really.'

'What about James's family?'

'All dead. The close relatives, anyway. There are some others somewhere – abroad, I think, but I don't see why they should help me. In any case, I hate the idea of leeching off people. I need to find a job.'

'Well, what about the film studio?'

'I doubt they'd have me back.'

Lally frowned. 'You won't know until you try. I shan't open the curtains – you need to rest. You can have a bath later.'

'Thank you, Lally. I really am grateful.'

'Listen, darling . . .' Lally stood up. 'It may feel like the end of the world, but it isn't – not really. "If at first you don't succeed, try, try, try again," as Nanny used to say.'

'Mine used to say, "Those who ask don't get,"' said Diana, glumly. 'And she said, "You're so sharp you'll cut yourself." Or perhaps that was a different nanny. I had quite a procession of them. I was always told they wouldn't stay because I was such a naughty little girl. It was only years later that I realised they'd all fled because Pa used to take liberties.'

'My nanny was obviously a better philosopher than all of yours put together – and I'd have backed her against your Pa any day.' Lally adopted an outraged tone, chin up and hands on hips. 'None of your sauce, my man!' Bending to smooth the bedclothes, she added, 'I may have reconciled Mrs Robinson to your presence, but I certainly won't be able to change her mind about the decadent implications of sitting on beds. Now then,' she wagged her finger, 'good night, sweet repose, lie on your back, and not on your nose.'

I've fallen flat on my nose, Diana thought when she'd gone. How shall I ever recover? *Try, try again . . .* To succeed at what? She stared up at the smooth white emptiness of the ceiling. The same as my future, she thought with dread: nothing there.

Chapter Forty-Six

Waking with a start as the front door slammed, Stratton realised that he must have fallen asleep in the armchair. Stiff-necked and befuddled, with a foul taste in his mouth, it was a few seconds before he remembered: Pete's dinner. Oh, hell. He'd meant to telephone Doris to apologise as soon as he got in, and he'd only sat down for a moment . . .

What time was it? Past eleven. The footsteps in the kitchen were heavier than Monica's, so it must be Pete. She must have come in already and gone upstairs to bed. Why hadn't she woken him? The sitting-room light was on, so she must have realised he was there.

He was just about to get up and go through to the kitchen when Pete appeared, larger and beefier than ever. He was still in uniform with a bottle in his hand and a loose co-ordination to his movements which – together with his general air of beery belligerence – suggested that he was, if not actually drunk, then certainly well on the way.

'Hello,' said Stratton, cautiously. 'Pete, I—'

'Hello, Dad. Want one?' Pete held up the bottle in one

hand, and attempted to point to it with the other, but missed.

Stratton, realising that he did very much want one, and deciding that it couldn't make a bad situation worse, and might even help a bit, said evenly, 'Yes, thanks.'

Pete withdrew and, after some banging about, returned with a second bottle. Positioning himself once more in the doorway he lobbed it, underarm, at Stratton, who lunged forward and caught it just in time to field the bottle-opener that followed. 'Steady on, old chap!' Stratton placed both objects on the sideboard. 'Why don't you sit down? I'll fetch a glass.' Pete, he noted, hadn't bothered with one, and was swigging straight from the bottle.

He took a glass from the kitchen cupboard, then went into the scullery and splashed his face with water. Standing in front of the sink, wet hands resting on the wooden draining board either side of the porcelain rectangle, images crowded his mind: the bodies in the alcove, Davies's face, the baby lying on the slab, the squalid terror of the women's last moments . . . He shook his head violently and began to count to ten. Deal with the situation in hand. Pete was clearly in a dangerous mood. He must have been to the pub after leaving Doris's, Stratton thought. All the guilt that formed the undertow of every thought he'd had about his son since Jenny died seemed to wrench itself upwards like a shipwreck breaking through to the surface: his preference for Monica; not loving Pete enough or even, in truth, liking him all that much; his utter failure to communicate with the lad . . .

At least, he thought, he could go back in there and apologise properly for not being home – wait until they were both settled so that the words could be given – and, he hoped, received – with the weight and importance that was due. Taking a deep breath, he picked up his glass and returned to the sitting room.

'Thought you weren't coming back.' Pete was slumped in 'his' armchair, legs outstretched, and Stratton noticed that he'd almost finished his beer. Concealing a flash of irritation – you're not in the bloody NAAFI now – he sat down opposite his son.

'Well,' he said, 'as you can see, I'm here.'

Pete nodded as if confirming this fact and then, peering down at his feet as if from a very great height, bent forward so suddenly that he almost fell on the hearthrug and began unlacing his boots with a series of savage jerks. This done, he heeled them off, punted them in the direction of the empty fireplace and looked up at his father expectantly.

'I'm sorry,' said Stratton. 'I got held up at work. New case.'

Pete waved a dismissive hand. ''S'all right, Dad.'

'No, it isn't. But it was unavoidable and, as I said, I'm very sorry that I wasn't there. Did you have a nice time?'

'Uncle Reg bored us all stiff with a lot of guff about the Coronation, but the food wasn't bad.'

This would ordinarily, given the trouble that Doris must have gone to, have deserved a rebuke, but Stratton felt that this was neither the time nor the place. 'Went down to the Swan after,' Pete continued. 'Some pals from school . . . One of them's working in an abattoir, out Woodford way. Kept going on about how they kill the cows. Wouldn't get off it. Even worse than listening to Uncle Reg.'

'You should have asked him if he can't get us a bit of meat off ration.'

Ignoring this feeble attempt at levity, Pete said, 'So, this case that kept you, this *unavoidable* case ... What was it, then?'

'You don't want to hear about that.'

'Yes, I do,' said Pete aggressively. 'I want to hear *all* about it. Got to be more interesting than anything else I've heard this evening.' Widening his eyes so that his face became a horrible parody of an eager child's, he added, 'Go on, Dad. Give us a bedtime story.'

'All right, then ...' Stratton, thinking that actually enunciating the whole wretched business might help him clarify things a bit – and that, given the state of Pete, he'd be talking mainly to himself anyway – said, 'Well, it started a few years ago, when—'

'Hold on.' Pete was pawing at his top pocket. 'Lemme get a fag going.'

Not wishing to witness the owlish fumbling with matches that was bound to ensue from this, Stratton lit two of his own and passed one across. 'There you are.'

Pete sucked in the smoke hungrily, then leant back and shut his eyes. 'Go on, then, Dad. Once upon a time ...'

Stratton began to talk. He spoke for some time, trying as best he could to relate the events in chronological order and as objectively as possible. All the while, at the back of his mind, he was conscious that he was looking for things to salvage from the mess in order to reassure himself ... of what, he wasn't entirely sure. The possibility that Davies might, after all, be guilty, that he'd done his job to the best of his ability, that . . . he didn't know. A leaden numbness had settled on him, burying all his previous reactions beneath its weight. 'So,' he finished, 'that's why I wasn't there tonight.'

Pete's eyes remained closed and, for a moment, Stratton thought that he must have fallen asleep. He lit another cigarette and sat staring into the empty grate. Why had Pete asked him about it all, anyway? He was about to suggest going to bed, when Pete opened his eyes. 'Looks like you hanged the wrong man, then.'

'Well, the investigation's barely started, but–'

'But you hanged an innocent man.'

'We don't actually know that he was–'

'Don't you?' Pete leant forward. 'Don't you, Dad? After all, two stranglers in one house – taking coincidence a bit far, wouldn't you say?'

'Yes, I would, but–'

'But what, Dad?'

'But it's not that simple.' Aware of how feeble that sounded, and aware, too, that Pete was staring at him with an intensity of scorn he'd only ever seen him direct at Reg, he struggled for something to say that might redeem him in his son's eyes. What? *I'm not perfect?* Pete was only too well aware of that, and, in any case, he was of a generation who, given the events of the last sixty years, had every right to condemn both parents and grandparents. It was bad enough having colleagues at work solicitously monitoring his failure, without attacks from his own family as well. 'We all make mistakes, I'm afraid.'

'As *mistakes* go, Dad,' said Pete with heavy sarcasm, 'I'd say this one rather takes the biscuit.' This was said in a derisive parody of an upper-class accent – the voice, Stratton imagined, that he used for mocking officers behind their backs. Before he could reply, Pete continued, switching back to his normal voice, 'When you felt so sure that Davies was guilty, was that because of Mum?'

Stratton stiffened. This was almost the first time his son had mentioned Jenny in his hearing since she'd died. There was an almost demonic shrewdness in his eyes. He'd meant the question to strike home, and it had. In as calm a voice as he could manage, Stratton said, 'One tries to keep one's emotions out of these things, but I suppose that might have had a bearing on it. With that sort of crime – a mother and child – it's hard not to think of your own family. And usually, with a case like that, it is the husband who's responsible.'

There was a moment's silence – Pete was tipsy enough for it to slow his reactions – before his son said, quietly, 'Yes. Isn't it just?'

Stratton took a deep breath, biting back his instinctive reaction – you're drunk and you don't know what the hell you're talking about. There was no ducking this. Useless to pretend he hadn't understood, because he could see from Pete's expression that his own face had already betrayed him. In any case, he told himself, Pete doesn't know Jenny was pregnant. He's angry, and he's lashing out: don't rise to it.

'I do feel guilty about your mother,' he said evenly. 'I should have been there to protect her. Not a day goes by when I don't think about that . . . and when I don't miss her. I loved her very much. You do know that, don't you?'

'Oh, yes,' said Pete. 'I know that. But perhaps,' he leant forward, gripping the arms of the chair, and Stratton saw a flash of malicious triumph in his eyes, 'if you'd been thinking a bit less about that and a bit more about a few other things that are under your nose . . .' He stopped, jerking backwards as if tugged by an invisible thread, a flush of guilty confusion flooding his face, cockiness evaporating so that he seemed like a small boy conscious of blurting out more than he'd meant to say.

'What do you mean, *under my nose*?'

'It's nothing.' The tone was sullen, defensive. 'Doesn't matter.'

'It obviously does, or you wouldn't have said it.'

'It's none of your business.'

Pete was looking furtive now, seeking a way out. Sensing that he was about to get up, Stratton rose and took a step towards him. 'If it's happening in this house, then it *is* my business. Tell me.'

Shrinking back in his chair, Pete stared up at him, wide-eyed, shocked into sobriety by fear. Stratton placed his hands on the arms of Pete's chair and glared at him. 'Just bloody tell me!' he roared.

'All right.' Pete reared back even further, holding up his hands in a gesture of surrender. 'But stop shouting. Sit down, for God's sake.'

Stratton, backing off, complied. 'I'm sitting down. Now, what's going on?'

With a visible effort, Pete gathered himself together. 'It's Monica.'

'What about her?'

Now he'd made the decision to speak, Stratton saw Pete's former bravado returning in leaps and bounds. 'You really have no idea, have you? Well, let me enlighten you.' The officer-mocking tone was there, and then, in the next second, gone. The look in his son's eyes was a challenge, brutal and direct. 'She's pregnant.'

Chapter Forty-Seven

Dressed in borrowed finery and bejewelled at wrists and neck, Diana fiddled with her fork and wished she felt like eating. She'd already had two glasses of wine on top of quite a lot of champagne and she knew she ought to attempt to soak it up with food, but she was far too jittery to be able to do more than toy with what was on her plate. Lally and Jock had taken her to Ciro's in an attempt to cheer her up, and she was trying her best to *be* cheered up, but it wasn't working. All the shining silver and glassware sparkling in the light cast by the rows of chandeliers, the dazzling white napery, the bright music and the alcohol could not dispel her heavy, dull despair, and knowing that she was worrying Lally and boring Jock didn't help.

Jock's manner had been brusque the previous day, when they'd driven over to pay her landlady the arrears on the rent. The wild hope she'd had of finding James waiting for her on the steps outside had crystallised into an almost-certainty on the journey, so that finding that he wasn't there plunged her more deeply into gloom even than before. Jock had insisted that she stayed in the car while he sorted things out, and, hating herself for her passivity, she'd waited miserably until he returned with a new key to the second-floor flat.

Jock hadn't been able to disguise his disgust as they walked into the cheerless sitting room. 'It's not normally as bad as this,' Diana said, defensively. 'She's packed away all our things.' They'd been stacked in the hall, in suitcases and wooden boxes.

'Is this everything?' Jock had asked incredulously, surveying the small pile. 'Or has she taken some away? She told me she hadn't, but . . .'

'I think so,' said Diana. 'I'll check later.' She knew she wouldn't have to check – one or the other of them had already pawned all the larger or more expensive items.

'Well,' said Jock awkwardly, 'if there's nothing else, I'd better be going.'

'Yes . . . Thank you, Jock. For everything.'

'Oh, that's all right. No need to make a fuss.'

When he'd gone, Diana opened the first suitcase and, finding that it contained her clothes, began unpacking in a mechanical fashion. The second suitcase contained what was left of James's wardrobe. She was about to lift out a pile of shirts and underclothes when it occurred to her that it was pointless to go through the charade of hanging them up or folding them away in drawers if he wasn't coming back.

He must come back, she thought. Surely, he would. He couldn't leave her like this, so alone. Then with agonising clarity came the image of him as she'd last seen him, grovelling at her feet on the beach, the poached eyes staring past her to the bottle she'd been holding in her hand. He's not coming back, she thought. He's not capable of it. She closed the suitcase, snapped the locks, and pushed it into the hall cupboard, closing the door.

The books and ornaments – those that were left – would keep until tomorrow. She went into the kitchen where she found a tin of soup and a bottle of sherry with half an inch left that must, somehow, have escaped James's notice. She placed them side by side on the draining board and got as far as putting a saucepan on the stove before realising that she had neither the energy, nor the desire, to cook or eat even this simple meal.

Wandering into the bedroom, she glanced at herself in the mirror over the mantelpiece. The face that looked back from behind the light coating of dust was dazed and cloudy. Turning away, she kicked off her shoes and lay down on the bed with all her clothes on, including her fur coat, which she hadn't felt warm enough to remove. As she closed her eyes, she thought detachedly, I ought to be afraid, but I'm not. I'm too tired, even for that. It seemed to her that somewhere, somehow, she had lost the instinct for self-preservation. Had she ever thought that her life would, at some point, turn out right, and she would be happy? Or had she always known this would happen? She couldn't remember.

She'd remained in bed, getting up sometime in the middle of the night to undress to her underclothes, for over twenty-four hours, until a sharp tapping on the door compelled her to rise. Pulling back the curtain, she saw that it was dark outside and the streets were lit. Dressing hastily, she found Jock and Lally, dressed in evening clothes, waiting on the landing.

'Surprise, darling!' Lally's voice seemed excruciatingly bright. It's started already, thought Diana bleakly: the pity. 'We're taking you out to dinner, darling. I thought you needed a bit of a cheer-up. I've brought you some things to wear,' she indicated a suitcase held by Jock, who looked markedly less enthusiastic, 'so you can't use that as an excuse, and there's jewellery and things in there.' She pushed a dressing case into Diana's arms. 'Aren't you going to let us in?'

Diana blinked at her, bleary-eyed. 'I don't think . . . I mean, I'm not . . .'

'We know you're not, darling,' said Lally, 'and that's why you need some fun. Now, come on . . .' She advanced towards the sitting room and, looking round at its dusty anonymity, said, 'Heavens, this is all very . . . *bijou*, isn't it?'

'I think,' said Diana, 'that "small" is the word you're looking for. And "dismal".'

'Nonsense. Once you've got your things sorted out it'll be fine. Smaller places are so much easier than great barns like ours, anyway. You can make it really modern.'

She meant well, but the vehement optimism was more than Diana could bear. 'I haven't anything to offer you,' she said, ungraciously.

'Doesn't matter, darling. Why don't I come and chat to you while you get ready? Jock can wait here.'

Jock was standing in the middle of the room, a look of detached politeness on his face. Clearly, thought Diana, all this was Lally's idea, and she had a strong suspicion that Jock had tried to talk her out of it. 'It's very kind of you,' she said, 'but I really don't feel ... As you can see, there's an awful lot to do here, and I don't suppose I'd be terribly good company, so . . .' But Lally had overridden all her protests and borne her into the bedroom to change and dress her hair, and now, an hour and a half hour later, they were all three sitting in sumptuous surroundings like strangers in a railway carriage who have started a conversation out of politeness and exhausted all subjects of mutual interest. Jock wore an expression of thin-lipped endurance, and Lally, who was facing the door, had begun discreetly searching the room for anyone they might know who could be persuaded to come over and enliven things. Laughter and chatter rippled the air all around them, and Diana felt lonelier and more hopeless than ever. 'I'm sorry,' she said, when Jock excused himself, 'but honestly, everything just feels like a dream at the moment. Everything since the war, really . . . No, since I went back to Hampshire. None of it seems real – as if I'd . . . I don't know . . . *died* or something, somewhere along the line. Or part of me has.'

'I know, darling.' Lally reached across the table and patted Diana's hand. 'But things will get better.'

'Will they?'

'Of course they will!'

Diana sighed. 'I shouldn't have come out,' she said. 'This is all so kind of you, but I feel like the ghost at the feast.'

'There'll be dancing soon,' said Lally. 'That's bound to cheer you up. Do you know, I'm sure I spotted Phyllis Garton-Smith just now. You remember she was at Bletchley Park during the war – of course, you told me you'd seen her when you went there with F-J. Well, she's engaged to the *strangest* man – his family are something to do with shipping, but apparently he didn't want any part of it, so he went off and became an explorer.'

About halfway through this speech, the focus of Lally's gaze had switched to somewhere past Diana's left shoulder. When she stopped talking – clearly too distracted by whatever she'd seen to keep up the flow of chatter – Diana turned to see what had caught her friend's eye and, almost immediately, caught her breath. Lounging long-limbed and elegant in the doorway, louche in immaculate evening dress and, nine years on, more absurdly handsome than ever, was Claude Ventriss.

'Diana . . .' Lally's voice was low, warning. '*Diana* . . .'

Diana caught her breath. Claude was scanning the room. She couldn't work out from his expression whether or not he was looking for someone in particular. The arrogant tilt of his lazy, half-closed eyes suggested that every woman in the room was available to him and he was just deciding which one to snap his fingers at . . . Presumptuous as ever. Smiling involuntarily, Diana shook her head.

'Diana . . .' said Lally, again. 'For God's sake! Stop staring at him.'

Claude's gaze swept past Diana and, for a second, she thought he hadn't noticed her. Just as she was wondering if this was genuine or deliberate, his face seemed to break open in recognition, and his glowing, velvet-brown eyes looked directly into hers.

Chapter Forty-Eight

Unable to sleep, Monica leant over and fumbled for her bedside lamp. Turning it on, she saw, from her alarm clock, that it was quarter past three in the morning. All her nights had been like this recently – lying awake, her thoughts going fruitlessly round in circles, the imagined outcomes growing worse each time. At first, it hadn't been too bad, because she'd been able to tell herself it would be all right in the morning, or, if not then, during the day, or the following morning – that her period would come, must come, soon. Now, such wishful thinking was impossible.

It wasn't as if she'd *wanted* to have intercourse with Raymond. They'd seen each other a lot over the past months, always travelling miles from the studio to spend evenings at little, faraway places because – or so he'd told her – he didn't like being recognised by fans. He never had been, although he'd made plenty of nervous jokes about it. She'd thought, then, that it was just the inconvenience of people asking for autographs or gushing over him when he wanted to be alone with her. She was so taken up in playing the part of his girlfriend that she'd never even considered that there might be another reason.

The really idiotic thing was that she could see it would be a whole lot worse if she'd been in love with him. She'd found that she quite enjoyed his company – it didn't matter that he talked mostly about himself, because it was interesting, and he had lots of funny stories to tell about the plays and films he'd done. He'd had an off-screen romance with Patricia Regal, who was one of her favourite stars, and she'd wanted to know so much about it that he'd teased her for being jealous. Which she was, of course – just not in the way he'd thought . . .

When he'd suggested that they spend a night together somewhere, she'd agreed. Not immediately, of course, but when she considered the matter, she'd come to regard it in the same heroic, desperate light as Tilly's action in the film, when she'd pretended to be drowning in order to show her husband that he wasn't really crippled at all. It would be like a cure for her, because if she could bring herself to do *that*, then perhaps there would be a normal future for her, after all. Following a couple of days' consideration, she'd come to regard it as a perfectly sensible – in fact, an almost scientific – course of action.

They'd only done it three times, and she must have made the right noises, or done *something* right, anyway, because he'd seemed very pleased afterwards. The odd thing was, it hadn't been as bad as she'd feared – more uncomfortable than anything. She'd kept her eyes tight shut all the time so as not to have to look at him, but he had been gentle, especially the first time. He'd probably had heaps of practice because he wasn't at all awkward about it, and he hadn't seemed to mind her shyness one bit. When he'd told her that intelligent, sophisticated women didn't believe in saving themselves for marriage, because it was vulgar to use virginity as a bargaining chip, she'd seen his point immediately, because women ought to be equal with men.

Except that it was obviously more for men than for women – she really didn't see how they could get any fun out of it – and men didn't have babies, did they? He'd said he'd take care of that side of things – and obviously thought he had done so, because he'd been appalled and furious when she'd told him. That was when he'd told her he was married.

She wondered, pointlessly, which of the acts had conceived the baby. Not that it mattered. She wasn't going to have it, was she? She'd argued when Raymond insisted, but, thinking about it – and she'd thought of practically nothing else since she'd missed her period – she didn't have much choice in the matter. She hated the idea of an abortion, but, as Raymond said, the baby was hardly there yet, just a collection of cells, a nub of a thing, and – although she hadn't admitted it to him – she certainly didn't feel any connection with it. Sometimes, when she was busy at work, she'd manage to forget about it for minutes together and then, suddenly remembering, she'd be struck by the sheer unbelievability of her situation. Now, she was struck by the feebleness of her arguments. She couldn't have a baby – of course she couldn't. As if to underline this, there was a faint noise from behind her head. Dad. He sees this sort of thing all the time at work, she thought: abandoned infants, runaways, tearaways, girls cast out, prostitutes, married women who'd tried to pass off a cuckoo in the nest with disastrous consequences . . . She'd heard the tales often enough. Not that he'd ever preached morality at her, but sometimes, when she asked him how his day had been, the stories had come out, the pathetic, sordid lives, the single, impetuous acts that led down the road to ruin . . . Clearly, he pitied them, but he would think her no better. Why should he? After all, they hadn't had her advantages, or her luck.

No. It was out of the question. She was going to do as Raymond told her. He'd seemed to know all about that, too, fixing it up. He's done it before, she thought. There'd been another – maybe several other – stupid girls like her, easily wooed, easily used and just as easily discarded. But she'd lied to him, too, hadn't she? Or not told the truth, anyway. And if it was a question of using people, didn't that make her as bad as he was? Worse, in fact, because his desire was natural, and hers was not. And why had she told *Pete*, of all people?

What a stupid question. She got up and lit a cigarette, breaking her self-imposed rule about not smoking in her bedroom. Pete had taunted her, as he always did, goaded her until she'd got so blazingly angry she'd heard herself blurting it out. She'd seen horror replace the malice in his eyes, and he hadn't said much at all after that – except for agreeing not to tell Dad. Now she'd just have to trust him . . . After all, he'd promised, hadn't he?

Chapter Forty-Nine

The television, encased in a wooden cabinet and crowned with a doily and a china shepherdess, had pride of place in the stuffy, cluttered front room of number eight Paradise Street. 'We're the only one in the street,' said Mrs Anson proudly. She was a sensible, bulky woman whose frock and cretonne overall hid all but the very top of a monstrous chasm of cleavage. 'We've had quite a few of the neighbours in to watch. Mrs Backhouse used to come every Thursday. She'd get her book from the library and then she'd come in to see the children's programmes. That's what she liked – *Andy Pandy* was her favourite, and *Prudence Kitten*. I think . . .' Mrs Anson leant forward conspiratorially, lowering her voice, 'she'd have liked kiddies herself, but they were never blessed. Still,' she added, 'that's probably just as well, isn't it?'

'So you saw quite a lot of her?' asked Stratton.

'A fair bit, yes, up until she went away a few months ago.'

'Did she tell you she was going?'

Mrs Anson thought for a moment, then said, 'No, it was Mr Backhouse who told me. To be honest, I was a bit surprised she didn't pop in to say goodbye. Of course *now*, with all those bodies . . .' Eyes widening, she added, 'She wasn't in there, was she?'

'We don't know yet,' said Stratton. 'We're still making inquiries.' They hadn't heard anything from McNally, but a telephone call to Edna Backhouse's relatives in Sheffield had revealed that the family hadn't seen hide nor hair of her for at least six months, although they had had a card from Backhouse saying he was writing on Edna's behalf because she had rheumatism in her fingers. As it seemed increasingly likely that the poor woman *was* their fourth body, her brother was coming down to see if he could identify her. 'So,' he continued, 'she said nothing about going away the last time you saw her?'

Mrs Anson shook her head. 'She was on her way to the laundry, I remember that. Just passing the time of day. I thought she seemed quite cheerful – more than usual, in fact.'

'How do you mean?'

'Well, she was always a nervy sort, and the last few months she'd got a lot worse. Said the darkies upstairs were getting on her nerves. They seem nice enough to me – always very friendly, and you never hear any noise – but she was quite frightened of them. Mr Backhouse told me she was terrified of him going out and leaving her alone in the house with them.'

'I see.' Stratton hadn't actually 'seen' anything all morning, and feared he wasn't doing a very good job of hiding this fact from Ballard. Pete had gone straight up to bed after the previous night's revelation, refusing to discuss it any further. Unable to sleep, his son's words in all their vicious triumph echoing over and over again in his head, he'd woken late to find that Monica had already left for the day so he'd not been able to find out whether or not they were true.

In the absence of any definite information, the torrent of speculation that had been flowing through his mind for the last twelve hours continued to torment him, fuelling his sense of frustration and helplessness. Why had Monica chosen to confide in her brother and not him? Or why not Doris or Madeleine, or even *Lilian*? Unless, of course, they knew and were deliberately keeping it from him . . . And who was the father? Was he going to marry her? Or was he – God forbid – married already? Visions of a cravatted Lothario from the film studio, all suede shoes and glib sophistication, seducing his innocent child with false promises, goaded him to an inward, impotent fury, all the worse for being inexpressible. Monica had never really talked about any boyfriends apart from that chap a couple of years ago. If only Jenny were here now, none of this would have happened. He'd assumed that she – or Doris or even Lilian – must have explained the facts of life to Monica, but he'd never asked. But he shouldn't have *needed* to ask about a thing like that – it was women's business, not his.

Pete's behaviour the previous night was troubling, too. The circumstances of the war had made his fathering a passive, rather than an active affair, removing his power to shape his children's lives. But it was no good casting around for excuses. The brutal fact was that he'd failed both his children. And they weren't the only ones: Muriel, little Judy, Davies himself and all those poor women, who'd still be alive if he'd got the right man . . .

'Sir?' Ballard's anxious tone cut across his thoughts, and he wrenched himself back to the present. Mrs Anson was looking at him askance, and, realising he was glaring at her, he hastily adjusted his features to an expression of professional concern.

'I said, he told me he'd had letters from her,' repeated Mrs Anson.

'Mr Backhouse said that?' asked Stratton.

'That's right. He said she was getting along well now she wasn't being bothered by the negroes. I told him I was surprised they'd taken the upstairs flat in the first place, after what happened – who'd want to live in a place like that? – but I suppose they don't get a lot of choice, poor things, all those notices you see saying they won't let rooms to coloured people . . . Mr Backhouse didn't like them, either. Said he was going to write to the council to see if he could get them put out. Said they'd been pestering him to use the garden and it wasn't part of the tenancy agreement. I thought it was just prejudice, but now we know why, don't we? Mind you, he was always on about that garden. Poor Muriel told me she'd asked if she could put the baby out there to get a bit of air, and he'd said it was against the regulations.'

'Did you see the dog out there much?'

'Not often. I suppose it must have done its business there sometimes, although he did take it for walks. Twice a day, more often than not. Whatever's in that garden,' she added, narrowing her eyes, 'he didn't want it disturbing. And I'll tell you something else, too – several times I've seen him going about with Jeyes Fluid, sprinkling it in the hall. He told my husband it was because of the blacks and their dirty habits. We thought that was a bit strange at the time – I mean, you can see they're not dirty from the way they're both turned out – but of course *now, well* . . .'

'When was the last time you saw Mr Backhouse?'

'Four days ago. I know that, because Mr Anson always goes to the British Legion on a Monday, and I remember telling him about it when he came back. Mr Backhouse had had a van come for his furniture, and when I saw that I asked him if he was leaving and he told me he was going to live in Sheffield with Edna. Said he'd got a job up there. I saw a suitcase in the hall, so I thought that must be his clothes.'

'Did you go into the house when you spoke to him?'

'No, we were just outside.'

'Do you remember what he was wearing?'

'Let me think . . .' Mrs Anson's forehead crenulated in a frown. 'Well, he had his overcoat on, and his hat . . . I remember that because it made me think he must be leaving at once, but when I asked him he was a bit foggy about it. You know, vague . . . but he must have been going somewhere, otherwise he wouldn't have had the coat on.'

'What colour was it?'

'Dark blue. A double-breasted one, with a belt. And the hat was a trilby, dark brown. He'd got a tie on, so I suppose he must have been wearing a suit. Suit trousers, anyway. Grey, I think.'

'And this van – was it from a removal company, do you know?'

'No, it was the second-hand place, Lorrimer's. I don't suppose they paid much. I wouldn't have given you tuppence for any of it. That mattress! Absolutely filthy, it was – and crawling, I shouldn't be surprised. Probably blamed those poor darkies for that, as well. Mrs Backhouse always did her best to keep things nice . . .' She paused for a moment, hitching up her bosom for emphasis, then said, 'I'm surprised at him. He seemed such an *educated* man. A cut above most people round here. Used to give people advice, you know.'

'What sort of advice?'

'Well, if they needed help with anything – a legal matter, or something like that. With him having been in the police during the war – not that he ever let you forget it. He was always telling people, anybody new . . . And about the St John's Ambulance. Had the certificates up on the wall, all framed. Just goes to show you can't judge by appearances. And,' she added shrewdly, 'he fooled you lot, didn't he?' Before Stratton could say anything, she nodded, sagely. 'Yes, he did. And now we've got all sorts coming here gawping, newspaper men poking their noses where they're not wanted. My husband went out this morning and got this to read about Queen Mary's funeral, and look what's there, right next to it on the front page!' She brandished a copy of the *Daily Mail* and Stratton saw the headline, *FOUR WOMEN DIE IN MURDER HOUSE*, and, in smaller type underneath, *Police Dig in Garden*, illustrated by a photograph. Mrs Anson stabbed at it with a chunky finger. 'You know how they got that picture, don't you? Mr Pyle upstairs. He's been renting his back room out to the photographers from the papers. He had two pounds off them yesterday, and he told me they'll be coming back later for more. I don't think it's right, making money out of those poor women like that, and I'm certainly not reading *this*,' here, she gave the paper a little shake, like a terrier with a rat, 'thank you very much.'

Stratton and Ballard interviewed Backhouse's upstairs neighbours, Mr and Mrs McAndrew, who, as Mrs Anson suspected, had only taken the flat because they couldn't get anything else and were now embarking, in horrified bewilderment, on what was very likely to be a fruitless search for a different place to live. They confirmed the business about the Jeyes Fluid, but had little else to add.

'Poor sods,' said Stratton, when they'd left the house and were out of earshot of the clutch of reporters stationed outside who were watching the procession of men ferrying out boxes of debris from the garden. 'Imagine coming to a country where you stand out like a sore thumb and the reception's as cold as the bloody weather.'

'It seems to me,' said Ballard thoughtfully, 'that you're always reading stuff in the papers about whether there ought to be a colour bar, but from the way they get treated, there might as well be one already. As far as I can see, they're no dirtier or worse behaved than anyone else.'

Policewoman Harris was waiting for them in the corridor outside the Middlesex Hospital mortuary. 'Positive identification of Mary Dwyer by Mr Fleet,' she said briskly. 'He was the man friend who reported her as missing – and Iris Manning's been identified by her sister Mrs Cartwright. DI Grove's taken their statements, and DS Porter's gone to fetch Joan Carter to see if the other one is Kathleen McKinnon. Mr Foulds – that's Mrs Backhouse's brother – is due here this afternoon.' Still she wouldn't look him in the eye.

'That's some progress, anyway,' said Stratton, writing notes. 'And I've got a spot of information that might help with the description of Backhouse, if you wouldn't mind relaying it to the station . . .' He passed on what Mrs Anson had said about the clothing and they went to find McNally, who was in his office dictating a letter to his secretary, Miss Lynn. 'Do have a seat. This is for the lab at New Scotland Yard,' he explained. 'Blood samples and stomach contents and so on. There's also the matter of the pubic hair. Our initial analysis tells us it's from four different women, so we're sending samples from each of the bodies so that the lab can try to match . . . I take it they're aware of the urgency.'

'I imagine my superior's had a word with them,' said Stratton, adding, wryly, 'And if he hasn't they'll have read all about it in the papers. What can you tell us?'

'Well,' McNally pushed his spectacles up his nose, 'from the tests we've been able to do here, I can tell you that spermatozoa were present in the vaginas of the three women in the cupboard, but not in the one under the floorboards. None at all in the swabs taken from the rectum . . .' Pulling a sheaf of typewritten notes towards him, he continued, 'The body under the floorboards is of a well-nourished woman, height five feet, three and a half inches, between fifty and sixty years old, death caused by asphyxia due to obstruction of the air passages . . . No pregnancies – ovaries quite atrophic, in fact, so I don't suppose that was ever on the cards. Certainly no sign of any disease that could have caused her death.'

'How long?'

'Twelve to fifteen weeks.'

Stratton made a note. 'What about the others?'

'Well, asphyxia was the cause of death in every case. Number one – that's the first one we removed – she's now been identified as . . .'

'Mary Dwyer,' supplied Stratton.

'Yes . . . Twenty years old, I gather. Never been pregnant. She was the only one who wasn't covered up, and she didn't have a diaper, either. Number two – not identified yet – was between twenty-five and twenty-seven years of age and had had at least one pregnancy at some stage, but not at the time of death. She'd been dead for between seven and eight days. Number three–'

'Iris Manning.'

'Yes. Thirty-two years old – I'd estimated slightly older, but that was the sort of life she'd led, I'm afraid. Approximately six months pregnant – a male foetus, not interfered with in any way that I can see–' Stratton, who was staring intently at the floor at this point, heard Ballard catch his breath. 'Dead for around three weeks.'

'Do you think they were put into that alcove immediately after death?'

McNally considered this for a moment and then said, 'I can't say "yes", because I don't know, but I can see nothing to indicate any other sequence of behaviour. Now, about the findings from the garden . . . What we do know for certain is that there are two of them, and they're both women, but at this point I'm afraid we know precious little else. I've enlisted the help of a colleague from the department of anatomy and our professor of dental surgery – he's getting rather excited about an unusual type of crown . . . Perhaps you'd like to come and have a look?'

In one of the mortuary's side rooms, two partial skeletons, one with a skull, were being painstakingly assembled on slabs side by side, with other bones scattered randomly on a third slab, and all of it surrounded by wooden boxes full of bits and pieces from the garden at Paradise Street. An intense young man with a pale face and a forelock of black hair who Stratton thought looked more like a poet – or a certain type of artist's idea of a poet, anyway – than a doctor, was standing between them, weighing what looked like a kneecap in one slender hand. Higgs was behind him, scrabbling around in one of the boxes.

'Dr Gilpin – Inspector Stratton – DS Ballard.'

Gilpin put down the patella and held out his hand. 'Pleased to meet you. I'm sure you know Higgs, Dr McNally's extremely capable assistant. He's quite something – better at anatomy than most of my students.'

Higgs grinned. 'Learnt it in the war, Dr Gilpin. Always doing these sorts of jigsaws, we was – only the pieces mostly had flesh on 'em.' Seemingly embarrassed by his outburst, he ducked his head and applied himself once more to the contents of the box.

'Miss Lynn's been getting to work with her coloured pencils,' said McNally, gesturing at two diagrams pinned to the wall, one showing two skeletons with various bones shaded in different colours, and the other showing the areas of the garden divided into squares. The hard blocks of red, blue, green and yellow made them look like a grotesque version of a children's board game.

'That's pretty well everything. All the bones are coded to show which part of the garden they came from. Those,' McNally added, pointing at the small piles on the third slab, 'are animal bones. That garden seems to have been a quite a rubbish dump.'

'It was a fair old mess. Probably Backhouse's dog. The neighbour said it didn't go in the garden much, but all the same I was a bit surprised it hadn't dug up those bodies before. If it had smelt them, I mean.'

McNally looked thoughtfully at the boxes. 'I should think with all the other stuff in the garden, there was plenty to keep it occupied without digging them up . . . And perhaps Backhouse didn't let it out there for long enough to have a really good crack at them.'

'I suppose so. Can you tell me anything else about them?'

'Well,' said McNally, 'this one here was on the tall side for a woman – five feet eight or nine inches, and we think she was about twenty years old. The other was five feet two. She was older – twenty-eight or -nine. We do have her skull, but there's been some attempt to burn it. There was part of a dustbin recovered, with evidence of burning, so that might have been used for the purpose. We've sent it to the police lab. We have this' – McNally gestured towards a makeshift table on which lay a mass of brittle-looking dull brown hair, one side of it held with a rusting metal kirby-grip – 'and these,' he pointed at some fragments of rotted cloth which lay beside the hair, 'which appear to be portions of clothing. We'll be sending them along for analysis as well. There were a number of small bones – fingers – mixed up in it.'

Stratton applied himself to the diagrams, rubbing his eyes. Hot with tiredness, they felt as if they were cooking in their sockets. 'Just a moment,' he said, looking at his notebook. 'I'd like to make sure I've got it all clear . . . The first body from the alcove – we'll call her Body One. She . . .' he glanced at the page, 'has been identified as Mary Dwyer. She's twenty years old, never been pregnant, she'd been dead around forty-eight hours when she was found and there were traces of spermatozoa inside her.'

'That's right,' said McNally.

'Body Two,' Stratton continued, 'who may or may not be Kathleen McKinnon, has been dead for between seven and eight days. She was between twenty-five and twenty-seven years old, and has been pregnant, but not when she was killed. You found spermatozoa there, too.' McNally nodding in confirmation, Stratton moved on. 'Body Three, identified as Iris Manning. Dead for around three weeks, six months pregnant, thirty-two years old, body contained traces of spermatozoa . . . fine so far?'

'Yes.'

'Body Four, found under the floorboards, a woman between fifty and sixty years old, who might be Edna Backhouse. No pregnancies, no spermatozoa . . . And all of the deaths were caused by asphyxia. Is that correct?'

'Yes, that's right.'

'Good. Now, the two from the garden . . . have you any idea of how long they've been dead?'

'Impossible to say. We don't know how the soft tissues were lost – the mechanism, if you see what I mean. Unless, of course, you can establish who they are and when they went missing and there's collateral evidence and so on. The lab might be able to help with that, because there were some pieces of newspaper in amongst the debris. Quite a lot from Area Three, where the skull was found.'

'I don't suppose you've any idea of the cause of death, have you?' asked Stratton.

McNally shook his head. 'As I said, you'd need collateral evidence for that. Speaking of which, there's the matter of the four pubic hair samples in the tobacco tin. I imagine,' he said, carefully, 'that it's already occurred to you that one of them might have been taken from Mrs Davies.'

Stratton nodded. 'What about spermatozoa? In Mrs Davies's case, I mean?'

McNally shook his head regretfully. 'I've been reading through the notes. We – I – didn't check for that. I realise now that it was an oversight, but the . . . complexion, shall we say, of that case, at the time . . .'

'I understand,' said Stratton. 'We weren't looking for anything like that either.'

McNally nodded. 'When I received the telephone call, I . . .'

He tailed off, shaking his head, and they stared wide-eyed at each other, united in recognition of the catastrophic extent of the whole business, bound together by an invisible and inescapable cat's cradle of assumptions made and things left undone. Keep a lid on it, thought Stratton. He could just imagine what Lamb would say if he started talking about exhumation orders on Muriel Davies, who, together with her child, was buried in Kensal Rise Cemetery.

'I understand,' he said. 'The facts at the time . . .'

'Yes,' said McNally. Perhaps it was just because he was tired, emotional and susceptible, but the word seemed to Stratton to echo around the tiled room, bouncing off the harsh, tiled surfaces, and for a second, the pathologist's spare, ascetic features transmogrified into the docile, bewildered ones of Davies. 'Yes,' McNally repeated. 'Yes.' A single word, that could mean both everything, and nothing at all.

Chapter Fifty

Diana woke at eight. For a moment, she wasn't sure where she was. Cautiously, she levered herself into a sitting position, resting against the headboard. Her brain seemed to arrive in this upright position some seconds later than her body, and when it did, a large lump of dry, hard pain in the core of her head made her wince. God, how much had she had to drink? It was an effort even to blink. Mercifully, the curtains were pulled shut, but she could see, in the half-light, that she was in the bedroom at her flat, and that there was an evening dress – not her own – draped across the stool in front of the dressing table, and that her fur coat lay curled on the floor in the corner like a sleeping animal. Thirsty and confused, she wondered where James had got to, and then her warm, vague impression of whispers and fumbles and giggles resolved itself into an actual, cold memory – it had not been James at all, but Claude. He'd been here . . . But, judging from the dent in the pillow beside her, and – but for the distant roar of buses passing the end of the street – the silence, he was gone.

What had she done? Looking down at herself, she realised that she was naked. Where were the rest of her clothes? Dragging her body across the bed, she peered down and saw that her stockings and underclothes were lying in forlorn heaps on the rug, discarded in the progress towards the bed. Disorientated and nauseous, she dimly remembered Claude peeling them off her, his gloating face – an excited boy unwrapping a longed-for birthday present – next to hers, his hot breath on her face . . . Dredging her memory, she came up with fragments: dancing with Claude at Ciro's; him sitting down with them and ordering champagne, and then more champagne; Claude talking about the Mau Mau Uprising and Jock barely civil; feeling tipsy and reckless, not really listening to them, tapping her feet in time to the music; seeing, as though through a veil, disappointment on Lally's face, and the cold disapproval on Jock's . . . She wasn't sure how it had been decided that Claude should accompany her home. Lally and Jock had left before they had, and Diana remembered protesting against their offer of a lift on the grounds that it would take them right out of their way. The recollection of Jock's curt 'Good night' made her face burn with shame. How he must despise her.

It's all right for him, Diana thought angrily. He's a *man*. She'd known that Claude was manipulating her, and hated herself for being manipulated, but she'd let it happen because she couldn't bear the thought of going home alone to the dreary flat. After Lally and Jock had left they'd danced some more, drunk some more, and Claude had hailed a taxi and asked Diana for the address. She'd talked about F-J, then. He already knew, of course, but he hadn't seemed to care. When she said, 'He cared about you,' Claude had said, 'Yes, and a bloody nuisance it was, too – surely you weren't jealous, darling?' and laughed it off. She'd tried to impress on him how awful it was, but he'd dismissed it – 'Life goes on' – and kissed her. She should have pushed him away then, got out of the taxi, but she hadn't.

Where was he staying? she wondered. He hadn't said, only that he was going back to Kenya. He'd fit in beautifully with all those bored, promiscuous expatriates, she thought sourly. If the Mau Mau didn't get him, an irate husband almost certainly would. She remembered sitting on the sofa with him, and him producing a bottle of champagne like a conjuror – they'd drunk it out of tea cups because she hadn't been able to find any glasses – and then banging her leg on the door frame as he'd carried her across the threshold of the bedroom . . . and then, once undressed, only numbness as he'd entered her.

Had it been like that with James? She tried to remember the last time they'd been intimate, but couldn't. She supposed she ought to feel guilty, but she didn't. She didn't feel anything except sick. Gingerly, she got up, dragging the counterpane off the bed and wrapping it around herself. As she crossed to the window, her bare foot struck something hard and she looked down to see an empty champagne bottle rolling across the floor. Pulling aside the curtain, she peered out of the window, but a blast of morning sunlight hit her, making her draw back. It didn't matter – who, or what, was she looking for? Claude would have left hours ago.

Turning, she saw on the small table beside the bed a piece of paper with a short message. *Didn't want to wake you, darling. Until next time x*, she read.

As if I was just there for the taking, she thought, as angry with herself for being so as she was with him for assuming it. She screwed the note into a ball and was about to go and drop it into the wastepaper basket beside the dressing table when she caught sight of another piece of paper, folded into four – Claude must have left that, as well.

It was a five pound note.

Chapter Fifty-One

Having returned to the station and sifted through what seemed to be a small avalanche of statements taken by Canning and Arliss from the Paradise Street neighbours, Stratton was desperate for a few minutes on his own. DI Grove had telephoned to confirm that the other victims were Kathleen McKinnon and Edna Backhouse, the winnowing of the garden was now, by late afternoon, completed, and there was a large pile of reports about sightings of Backhouse on his desk – Colwyn Bay, Kettering, Berwick-on-Tweed and God Only Knew Where Else. Stratton shovelled up handfuls of them and put them aside. He needed to clear his head. With all that was in there jostling for space, he felt as if he might simply explode into pieces if he had to deal with any more people. Staying in the office meant constant interruption and the lavatory was out of the question – Arliss, who was having one of his periodic bouts of flatulence, was bound to come in and poison the air. The answer, he thought, was a walk round the block. Nothing too peculiar about that, and he'd look in at the tobacconist's while he was at it.

He set off at a brisk pace and, striding past the end of Cork Street, suddenly thought of what Higgs had said about learning anatomy from doing human jigsaws. This, in turn, made him think of a conversation he'd had with the man sometime towards the end of the war, when he'd asked him whether a former mortuary assistant might have been a bit too keen on corpses . . . Anyone who'd been in civil defence or the police in London at that time would have seen, and handled, their fair share, and that included Backhouse. Had he learned to like it then? Stratton thought of the bodies he'd seen: tattered, shattered and crushed, caked with plaster dust and grime. How anyone could have found them in any way sexually arousing – unless they were stark raving mad – was completely beyond him. Perhaps Backhouse *was* mad. In any case, thought Stratton grimly, he did seem – quite literally – to be at home with the dead. Dead women, anyway.

There'd been no spermatozoa inside Edna Backhouse, though. Stratton wondered about Muriel Davies. Presumably, nothing would be detectable after such a long time, or McNally would have mentioned the possibility.

It seemed pretty stupid to foul your own doorstep in that way, but then Backhouse had killed in his own home, and one of his victims had been his own wife. And Davies was the ideal scapegoat – like so many of the liars Stratton had encountered, he was no good at recognising when he was being lied *to*, and being a dullard made him all the more vulnerable.

If you were attracted to dead women, perhaps you couldn't get it up for living ones? That would explain the lack of children – except that McNally had said there was something wrong with Edna Backhouse's ovaries, hadn't he? Perhaps he'd killed her because she knew – or had discovered – something about Muriel and Judy. Or perhaps just to get her out of the way so he could have his murderous way with a few tarts in the comfort of his own home . . .

He passed a newspaper seller, whose board read: *MURDER HOUSE GIRL NAMED*. Presumably the rest would make the late edition, or tomorrow morning's. Nothing like a good murder, Stratton thought bitterly, and this one had it all: sex, a rising body count, a national alert for the missing killer, and all topped off with a massive police cock-up – *his* cock-up. He watched as a few discarded sheets, clawed from the pavement by a sudden gust of wind, fluttered away down the street.

As for where Backhouse actually was . . . The description had been in the newspapers twenty-four hours now, but not one of the dozens of reports that had come in so far was any use at all.

'I thought I might find you out here, sir.' Ballard, having apparently materialised out of thin air, was standing beside him.

'Just needed a breath of air.'

'Yes, sir. I thought you might like to see this.' He gave Stratton a copy of the *Daily Mail*, folded to show a photograph of Muriel Davies, captioned *Found Strangled With Her Baby*. 'Have a look at the fourth paragraph.'

'"It has been established that the tragedy has no link with the murder of 19-year-old Muriel Davies and her 14-month-old daughter Judy, who were found strangled at the same address in 1950." No, it bloody hasn't been established. Where did that come from?'

'DCI Lamb, sir. Trying to discourage speculation.'

Stratton sighed. 'Closing the stable door after the horse has gone, more like it.'

'That's what I thought, sir, although it might keep them off our backs – for the moment, at least. I've just had a word with DS Porter. He's been talking to the British Road Services.' Noting Stratton's blank look, he added, 'Backhouse's former employers, sir. Apparently, he gave his notice a month ago, and they've not seen him since. His records show that he was working as a clerk at the Ultra Radio Works before that, during the war – after he'd resigned as a special. I did a spot of checking, and it appears that one of the employees there, May Drinkwater – 29-year-old spinster – was reported missing in nineteen forty-four. Of course,' Ballard ducked his head as if ashamed at his efficiency, 'it's possible that it had nothing to do with Backhouse – might have been a flying bomb or something – but she's described as being the same height as the shorter skeleton, and she had brown hair, so . . .'

'So we ought to look into it,' finished Stratton. 'Well done, Ballard. At least one of us is on the ball.'

'Thank you, sir. And we've got this photograph . . .' he palmed it from his pocket and handed it to Stratton, 'from Mrs Backhouse's brother, to send to the papers. Obviously, it'll have to be doctored to show the overcoat.'

Stratton stared at the domed, bald head, the glasses, the

prissy mouth and the weak, sloping shoulders. 'Doesn't look like a monster, does he?'

Ballard shook his head. 'No, sir. But they never do.'

Chapter Fifty-Two

When Stratton eventually arrived home and opened the front door, he caught a glimpse of Monica in the sitting room, reading – or anyway looking at – a magazine. She called out a greeting but as she made no move to get up he went into the kitchen to make himself a cup of tea. He couldn't face her just yet – his mouth was dry and foul, and the way he was feeling, having brooded on the matter all the way home in the bus, he feared he would start bellowing accusations at her and not be able to stop. Pete was gone, back to his unit, and except for the rustle of pages the house was silent, but the very air seemed to be poised and ominous, waiting for something to erupt. It must not be him, thought Stratton. He must remain calm.

He stared down at the plate of food that had been left out for him – ham and lettuce, with two slices of beetroot bleeding over the leaves. Eating was out of the question; his stomach had contracted into a tight ball of anger. Hands trembling, he picked up the kettle and then, almost immediately, set it back down on the gas ring with a clatter. At this rate, he'd end up breaking something. He went down the passage into the scullery and cupped his hands beneath the tap, gulping some water and splashing his face.

Slowly and carefully, he retraced his steps and went into the sitting room. Monica – who, thought Stratton, certainly didn't *look* pregnant, although she seemed tired and very pale – put her magazine down and, for a long, dangling moment, during which time seemed to hover rather than pass, they stared at each other. Then she said quietly, 'Pete's told you, hasn't he?'

The feeble hope that Stratton had been nursing at the back of his mind that Pete was, for some reason of his own, lying to make trouble, crumbled. His last illusions about having control over his daughter fell sharply away, leaving him with the vertiginous sensation of standing on the very edge of a precipice. He sat down on the sofa. Swallowing, he said, 'It's true, is it?'

'Yes. It's true.'

The air seemed to tighten around him and, for a moment, he felt as though he were suffocating. 'You're certain about it, are you?'

Monica nodded miserably.

'How far . . .?'

'Two months. Well, two and a bit.'

'How did it happen?' God, what a stupid thing to say. 'I mean . . .'

'It's all right, Dad. I know what you mean.'

'It isn't bloody all right!' Stratton checked himself with an effort, biting back a torrent of stuff about you're my daughter and how dare you and I should never have let you go to work at that studio. He knew that, however much he felt all this, it was both pompous and pointless to come out with any of it. Closing his eyes for a brief moment in order to try and contain his feelings, he opened them again to find that Monica, her face set and white, was gazing at him with something a lot like fear in her eyes.

'I'm sorry, Dad.'

'It's a bit late for "sorry",' Stratton snapped. 'You'd better tell me,' he continued, 'what the hell has been going on.'

'He's an actor,' said Monica. 'I met him at the studio. I was working on his picture. He started talking to me, and invited me out, and things just . . .' Mouth wobbling and eyes blurred with tears, Monica blinked and gulped, trying to get the words out. 'Just . . . sort of . . . he just . . .'

'He's married, isn't he?' asked Stratton, grimly.

Monica nodded miserably. 'Last year. He didn't tell me before.'

'Why didn't you know? Surely, with him being in the public eye, that sort of thing is common knowledge.'

'Not with people like him. With male stars – the younger ones – the studio tends to keep quiet about that sort of thing because the fans don't like it. Oh, Dad, I don't know what to do.'

'I do,' said Stratton viciously. 'He wants horsewhipping.' Monica had fallen for the oldest trick in the book, one he'd seen dozens, perhaps hundreds, of times in the course of his work, but had never for one second imagined would be played on his own daughter. 'Who is he? What's his name?'

Shoulders heaving, face collapsed and soggy, Monica said, 'Dad, you *can't*. He said . . . he told me . . .' the next words came out in a wet rush, 'he'd pay for me to go to a clinic where it's safe . . .'

'An abortion,' said Stratton, flatly. 'That's what he wants, isn't it?'

'He said it would be for the best. He got so angry, Dad. He said I was trying to trap him and if I told anyone he'd deny he'd had anything to do with it and no one would believe me because we'd kept the whole thing secret, but it wasn't like that, Dad, it really wasn't . . . I didn't know what to say.' Monica stared at him, stupefied. 'He was like a different person.' Monica pulled her handkerchief from her sleeve and buried her face in it, shoulders heaving.

'*I'll bet he was.*' And if I ever get hold of him, thought Stratton, I'm going to tear his head off his shoulders and piss down the hole. Trying to contain his mounting fury he said again, through clenched teeth, 'Who is he?'

Monica, face still hidden by her handkerchief, shook her head. 'No . . . Dad . . . please . . .'

'He's got to face up to his responsibilities.'

'He can't, Dad. He's *married*. He said he'd never leave his wife and he thought I knew that it was just a . . . a sort of . . . game. But that wasn't what he said, not at the start.'

'I'm damn sure it wasn't. *Bastard!*' Unable to stop himself, Stratton thumped his fist into his palm. He couldn't remember the last time he'd wanted – ached – to hit someone so much. Jumping up, he began pacing up and down the room as Monica sobbed. 'Tell me his name.'

'If I do . . .' Monica paused, gulping and snuffling, 'you won't . . . do anything, will you?'

'What, thump him? No, I won't – much as I'd like to. But something's got to be done. As I said, he needs to face to up his responsibilities. He obviously thinks he can just shell out money to get rid of his mistakes and go sailing on regardless. Abortions aren't just illegal, Monica, they're dangerous. They can mess you up for life.'

'But he says it'll be safe – and that if I don't he won't have anything to do with me or acknowledge the baby or anything.'

'We'll see about that,' said Stratton, grimly. 'If he's the father, then he needs to contribute to the child's upkeep and that's all there is to it. Now, who is he?'

'His name's Raymond Benson.'

'And he's a film actor.'

'Yes. He's not one of the biggest stars, though – at least, not yet.'

'How old?'

'Twenty-eight, I think. I *am* sorry, Dad,' Monica wailed. 'I truly am. I've let you down. And Mum.'

Stratton stopped pacing and stood over his daughter who, hunched in an armchair, seemed very young and very small. 'Yes, well . . .'

Monica gazed up at him with enormous, wet eyes. 'It was an accident,' she whispered. 'I didn't mean it to happen. I wish Mum was here.'

'So do I,' said Stratton, fervently. 'So do I.' Stiffly, he reached over and patted her on the back. 'I'm sure you didn't mean it to happen, love.'

This reassurance produced more choking sobs and, without quite knowing how, Stratton found that he was standing with his arms around her and his chin grazing the top of her head. 'It's all right, love, it's all right,' he repeated, stroking her back. 'Look,' he said after some minutes of this, 'why don't you go up to bed? We can't do anything about it tonight.'

Monica disentangled herself and picked up her handbag, saying meekly, 'Yes, Dad.'

'Have you told anyone about it, apart from Pete?'

'Only Ray.'

'Who's– Oh, yes, of course. Well, it might be an idea to keep quiet about it for the time being. Until I've spoken to this man. I presume he's on the telephone, is he?'

'Yes.'

'Do you know his number?'

'Yes. He gave it to me when his wife was away once, on tour. She's an actress.'

Stratton held up his hand. He didn't think he could bear to hear any of the details, however marginal. 'What is it?'

Monica dug around in her bag and scribbled it on the corner of a piece of paper on which was printed some sort of schedule, including the name of Raymond Benson. 'Don't you need this?'

'No. The picture's finished.'

'He was in it, was he?'

Monica nodded.

'Will he be in the next picture you're working on?'

'No, but he'll be at the studio, on a different stage. He's under contract. You won't do anything to him, will you?'

'I've said so, haven't I?'

'Thanks, Dad.' Monica sniffed. The small sounds coming from her seemed to intensify the silence around them, and for a moment Stratton's thoughts boomed so loudly that he wondered if they hadn't somehow escaped from his head to reverberate round the room. Suddenly awkward, they avoided each other's eyes as they said their goodnights.

Stratton sank onto the sofa. God, he wanted to punch Benson into the middle of next week. Knock his handsome white teeth – he didn't know what the man looked like, but he was in films so handsome white teeth seemed a fair bet – right down his lying throat. He felt so helpless. It was all right when they were little, if they hurt their knees or fell out of a tree or something, because you could always kiss it better. But *this* . . . If Jenny was here, he thought, this wouldn't have happened. Or perhaps if he'd got married again after she'd died and Monica had had more of a woman's influence . . . Grief had made him selfish, and he'd assumed that because he didn't want another wife, they wouldn't want, or need, a stepmother. Maybe Doris and Lilian had been right, trying to push widows at him. In the last year, he had tried to take an interest in a couple of them. He'd even taken one out to supper, at a Lyons Corner House. It was a perfectly pleasant evening; she was sweet, and mercifully unaffected, but when he got home he found himself wondering why he'd done it. With no desire to repeat the experience, he'd written her an awkward letter, using pressure of work to cancel the tentative arrangement they'd made for the following week.

Throwing back his head and closing his eyes, he wondered if it were possible to pinpoint the exact moment when things had started to go wrong. At present, it felt as though his entire life had been a sequence of catastrophes leading up to this one, but surely that couldn't actually be the case? There must have been a specific time. Why hadn't he *known*? Why wasn't there a siren or a warning bell or something? Why was everything in his life – Monica, Davies, Backhouse – spinning out of control?

Even if he murdered this Benson bloke, it wouldn't do any good. Monica would still be pregnant. The thought of an abortion made him remember Davies's story about Backhouse volunteering to get rid of Muriel's baby, and a vision of the man's bald, sweating pate as he bent over Monica's prone body and fumbled between her legs with grimy-nailed fingers made him wide-eyed and sick with horror. Clapping a hand over his mouth, he ran into the scullery and leant over the basin. Arms braced and head lowered like a bull about to charge, he remained there until the danger was over.

Seeing the empty beer bottles from the previous evening standing on the draining board, Stratton decided something stronger was needed. Remembering that there was some Scotch in the sideboard in the sitting room, he retraced his steps and poured himself a bloody big slug of the stuff. Then, shrugging off his jacket, and jerking his tie loose in a single, swift movement, he sat down once more.

He could go and see Benson, and try to persuade him to look after his child, but beyond extorting the necessary conscience-money, there was fuck all he could do. Benson had obviously never had any intention of leaving his wife. For all he or Monica knew, they might be starting a family as well. If only he'd never agreed to Monica working at that bloody studio . . . He took a gulp of his drink. If only he'd been a better father, husband, copper – a better *person* . . .

He thought about Reg, in . . . 1940, it must have been . . . discovering the extent of his son's criminal activities and going berserk. He'd sat silently for hours at their kitchen table and then burst into fury at Stratton, calling him an interfering shit and accusing him of having cooked the whole thing up to, as he put it, 'make him look bad'. Stratton understood, now, how his brother-in-law had been feeling, although, as far as he himself was concerned, it was less to do with other people's opinions than with one's estimation of oneself. What Reg, with his unearned worldliness, would have to say about Monica's current situation, he couldn't bear to think.

Later, in the bathroom, he caught sight of himself in the mirror. Christ, he looked one step away from the madhouse. Perhaps he was going off his rocker, too. The pillow, usually comfortable, felt like a sack of potatoes under his head as he lay wet-eyed, staring hopelessly into the thick darkness of the curtained room.

Chapter Fifty-Three

Monica sat hunched over on her bed, clutching her favourite cushion, found in a bric-a-brac shop and carefully washed and mended, to her stomach. It was definitely 'friendly' – she'd thought so the minute she'd spotted it – but it wasn't doing her any good now.

What on earth was she going to do? She didn't want a baby. Now Dad had found out – and she'd known, somehow, just as soon as he'd looked at her, that Pete had broken his promise – there was no chance of her being able to go to the place that Raymond had suggested and have it taken away . . . Lying to Dad had been horrible, pretending that she had normal feelings for Raymond, and all the time knowing that the truth was a hundred, thousand times worse. Saying the words out loud, and seeing the expression on Dad's face – his disappointment and fury – had made her feel sick. Oh, God . . . Why, *why*, had she allowed Pete to goad her into telling him? She should have known he couldn't be trusted.

Dad had called Raymond a bastard. The word had been reverberating in her head ever since he'd said it. This child really would be a bastard. It wouldn't be long before her belly started to swell and then everyone would know and she'd have to leave her job. It would be like all the cautionary tales she'd heard – the knowing looks, the pointed remarks, the questions about who the father was, the shame for her family, and then having to give birth in one of those places where they humiliated you and made you scrub floors because no decent, proper hospital would take you . . .

The baby, she supposed, would have to be adopted. That would mean handing it over to strangers who might or might not love it, and that it would grow up knowing – supposing it were told – that its mother had rejected it, and it would hate her. But she couldn't keep it, could she? Here, a memory surfaced of a girl from school who'd vanished for several months and whose mother's 'late baby' had been greeted with nods and winks and tuts. She had no mother, so it would have to be Aunt Doris who pretended, supposing that she'd even consent to such a thing – and why should she? Everyone said babies were sweet and lovely and all the rest of it – she'd never thought so, particularly, although perhaps it was different if it was *your* baby – but they certainly seemed to involve a lot of looking after, and Aunt Doris had enough on her plate already.

Or would they expect her to look after it herself? After all, it was her responsibility. If that were the case, she'd never be able to go back to work, never do any of the things she'd dreamt of doing. And it wouldn't always be a baby. It would grow up, resenting her for its illegitimacy, for the taint and shame that she'd inflicted upon it. And as for her own life – that would be over before it had begun.

Chapter Fifty-Four

Wrapped in the counterpane, Diana sat on the floor beside the dressing table, her face buried in the thick fisherman's sweater James had worn for filming outside in the winter. The curtains were still drawn, and she had no idea how long she'd been there, listlessly picking through the contents of her handbag, looking for . . . what? She didn't know. Just something, anything, to hold on to, to reassure, to comfort – but there was no comfort to be had from the stubs and scrapings of cosmetics, the balled-up handkerchiefs, the tickets from pawn shops for items she'd never be able to redeem, or the pitifully thin purse. Behind her, Claude's five pound note lay on the bedside table, an accusation in black and white, evidence of her weakness, her lack of judgement, her pathetic betrayal both of James and of herself. She hadn't wanted to touch it, but she knew that eventually self-disgust would be swallowed up by necessity, and the knowledge made her hate herself all the more.

Scrabbling once more in her handbag, she fished out a tattered piece of thick writing paper, folded into four: F-J's last letter. *You are the natural prey of an unscrupulous man (as I was) . . .* Never more so than now. Diana shook her head in weary self-recrimination and scanned the rest. *You might contact Edward Stratton . . . he is a good man.* 'How can I?' she muttered, letting the paper fall to the floor. Every time she'd thought of him since that awkward meeting by the river at the Festival of Britain, she'd squirmed inwardly at her gushy, girlish behaviour. He'd been so diffident – obviously horribly embarrassed by the whole thing. The past should remain in the past, she thought, remembering the look on his face in the café all those years ago as he'd tried to warn her about Claude. 'He'll destroy you, Diana.' Well, she'd proved fairly well capable of doing that all by herself, hadn't she?

Even if she did contact him, what was there to say? 'Oh, dear, I've made the same mistake all over again, please rescue me?' How pathetic! Besides, he had his own life, and, doubtless, his own troubles, and neither was anything to do with hers ... And just the thought of doing anything was exhausting. In any case, it wasn't a matter of working out what to do next, because there didn't seem to be any 'next'. At least, she couldn't summon up either the energy, or the inclination, to work out what it might be.

She was woken, several hours later, by a loud, insistent pounding at the front door of the flat. Disorientated for a moment, she stared wildly around the room, and then remembered. Perhaps it was James! He'd come back. She scrambled off the bed. Everything was going to be all right – she'd *make* it all right, she'd do *anything* to make up for Claude, for—

Catching sight of the empty champagne bottle, she kicked it under the bed. Dragging on her dressing gown, she glanced into the mirror, hastily patting her hair. She looked a fright, but it would have to do. Dabbing the last of her perfume behind her ears, she rushed across the sitting room to open the front door.

'Darling, I–'

'Expecting someone, were you?' Her landlady, diminutive and belligerent, was on the landing. With her pinched, beaky face and pecking head movements, Mrs Pritchard had always reminded Diana of a hen left behind in the rush for scraps, but she didn't look like that now. 'I can see it wasn't me.' Bristling, she pushed Diana back inside the flat and closed the front door firmly behind them both. 'Where's your husband?'

'He . . .' Wordless in her disappointment, Diana stared numbly at the small form that seemed almost to pulsate with righteous anger.

Mrs Pritchard eyed her shrewdly. 'Gone off and left you, has he? If he was ever your husband in the first place.'

'Of course he was!'

'No "of course" about it, if you ask me. One man coming round to pay your rent, and from what I've heard there was a different one here last night, sneaking out at six o'clock this morning. I don't know what you think you're doing, but you're not doing it under my roof. I want you out of here now.'

'But–'

'I've had complaints – noise and I don't know what else

– and this isn't the first time. I told that man who paid your rent I wasn't happy about it. I was willing to give you a second chance, but now . . .'

Jock didn't mention any of that to me, thought Diana, wondering if the 'second chance' had been given in exchange for extra money. 'Please,' she said, 'I haven't got anywhere to go.'

'You should have thought of that before. There's plenty of people want rooms, you know. Decent people, who'd pay double what you do for a place like this, and they wouldn't keep me waiting, neither. People who don't want the likes of you under the same roof.'

'But you can't just–'

'Oh, can't I just? You watch me!'

'But,' said Diana, desperately, 'what about my things?'

'You can come back for those. I want you out, and that's that.'

'But–'

'Listen, *Mrs* Carleton. My husband's waiting downstairs. You can pack a suitcase and leave quietly now, or I'll call him up here and he can throw you out. It's up to you.'

Diana had seen Mr Pritchard on a few occasions when she'd gone down to her landlady's flat to pay the rent. A bull-necked hulk of a man who breathed through his mouth, he was a silent, glowering presence in her kitchen. She fled to her bedroom, and with shaking hands, dressed herself and packed as much as she could into a single suitcase. Mrs Pritchard followed her, and began to inspect the room, sniffing and tutting, running her hands over her precious fixtures and fittings as though checking for contamination. With no fight left in her to counter the accusations or stand up for her rights – whatever they might be – all Diana wanted was to get away.

Closing her case, she turned to pick up the five pounds that Claude had left beside the bed, but the little table was bare and so was the floor around it. Perplexed, she rifled her purse, but it wasn't there, either, or anywhere in her handbag. Mrs Pritchard, now standing in the doorway, was glaring at her like a gorgon, arms folded in outrage.

'There was five pounds on that table,' said Diana. 'What have you done with it?'

'Accusing me of stealing now, are you?'

'It was *there*,' said Diana, pointing. 'Now it's gone.'

Mrs Pritchard shook her head. 'You're a fine one, you are, calling me a thief. Well, I'm not going to stand here and be insulted by the likes of you . . .'

'Mrs Pritchard, that money belongs to me!'

'Yes, and we all know how you earned it, don't we? On your back!'

'So you did see the money–'

'I never saw any money. I know your game, and I've had enough of it.' The landlady took a couple of paces back and, turning towards the still open door of the flat, bellowed, 'Arthur! Come up here!'

'Please,' said Diana. 'Wait . . .'

'Wait, nothing!' Eyes glittering with malice, Mrs Pritchard advanced on Diana. 'Now you'll get what's coming to you, all right. You won't look so fine when he's finished with you, my lady.'

Scarcely able to believe her ears – surely the woman couldn't threaten her like that? – Diana ran to the window. Struggling to open it, she said, 'You can't do this. I'll call a policeman.'

'And I'll tell him you're nothing but a common prostitute. You're the one who's been stealing – what about my rent? What about that?'

Shock rapidly giving way to anger, Diana shouted, 'You've got a lot more than your rent in your pocket. You've just taken it!' She tugged desperately, breaking two nails, but the sash refused to budge. Heavy footfalls in the next room made her redouble her efforts, but the window remained obstinately shut.

'What's going on?' Arthur Pritchard's huge frame filled the doorway of the bedroom.

'Calling me a thief, now, she is.'

'A thief, is it?' Pritchard advanced on Diana, catching hold of her arm.

'Take your hands off me!' Diana clawed at him, but his grip was vice-like.

'That's enough of that!' He slapped her across the face so hard that, if he hadn't had hold of her, she'd have fallen onto the bed. She clutched her cheek. Her right eye, hot and stinging, felt as if it were about to explode. Shoving her back against the wall, and breathing beerily into her face so that she thought, for a moment, that she might be sick, he said, 'One more word . . .'

'Please,' said Diana, through clenched teeth. 'Let go of me.'

He leered at her, nose so close to her own that all she

could see was a greasy landscape of pores. 'Out you go,' he said, and jerked hard on her arm so that she cried out in pain.

Pausing only to scoop up her suitcase in his free hand, he dragged her out of the flat to the top of the stairwell. 'Now,' he said, 'get out before I throw you out.' Flinging her suitcase down the stairs with one hand, he pushed her after it so hard that she'd have fallen if her flailing hands hadn't found the banister.

Her case had burst open on impact. As she scrabbled about on the landing, trembling with humiliation and fear as she shoved her clothes back inside and struggled with the locks, her handbag, thrown from the top of the stairs by Mrs Pritchard, with a cackle of 'Good riddance!', narrowly missed her head. Watched by the triumphant pair, who stood side by side, arms folded, at the top of the stairs, she picked up her things and fled.

Chapter Fifty-Five

It was dusk. Diana dropped the suitcase on the path and sat down on the bench, watching the lights reflected in the sluggish, oily water of the Thames and wondering exactly where she was and how long she'd been walking. She wasn't even sure what she'd put in the suitcase, other than James's sweater.

Her arm still ached where Mr Pritchard had grabbed her, and so did her face, but a glance in her pocket mirror had told her that she didn't have a black eye. Something to be grateful for, she supposed. She hadn't gone to find a policeman – what was the point? Even though she was in the right about the five pounds it would be her word against theirs, and Claude *had* spent the night with her. He'd left her the money, yes, but she hadn't offered herself to him for it . . . It would, she thought, be impossible to explain. How terrible to think that one wouldn't be believed. There must be people who go through their whole lives with everybody thinking the worst of them. She'd never really considered it before, merely assumed that some sections of society must be less honest than, say, her own. Now, for the first time, she saw how appallingly unjust this was.

But it was her own stupid fault, wasn't it? Going off with Claude like that . . . After all the resolutions she'd made . . .

After leaving the Pritchards, she'd simply walked, with no idea of where she was going. Not to Lally and Jock, that was certain – they must hate her too, and with good reason. Dazed, she stared at the lights across the river until they seemed to blur into a flaring, squirming network of tubes, obliterating everything but themselves. Where was James? Was he out there somewhere, walking aimlessly in the neon maze of central London? James's welcoming words to her at Ashwood came into her mind: *Welcome to the place where nothing is real* . . . Diana stretched out her legs, trying to ease her aching feet. At least her fur coat would stop her getting *too* cold.

An hour later, chilly and faint with hunger, Diana hauled herself to her feet and went in search of a café. The coins she'd found in her purse would be enough for a cup of tea, at least – and perhaps, if she were lucky, they might stretch to bread and margarine. If only she could get fed and warm, she might be able to form a plan.

After wandering through some backstreets, she came upon an all-night place, lights shining through the steamed-up windows. Peering in, she saw from the rows of caps, mufflers and dirt-stiffened jackets that most of the customers were workmen. A solitary woman sat in the corner near the door, dabbing at her face with a grubby shred of powder puff, a limp hat perched forlornly on her head and a mangy glass-eyed fox wreathing her neck. The moment Diana pushed open the door, the painted, rocking-horse eyes locked onto her with an aggressive warning stare. Diana patted her suitcase. 'I'm not after your business,' she murmured. 'Just passing through.'

The woman relaxed, modifying her expression to mild curiosity. She wasn't the only one – Diana was aware of half a dozen pairs of eyes following her as she selected an empty table and sat down, fixing her gaze on the prices chalked on the blackboard behind the counter. It was better than she'd thought – she had enough for tea and a fruit pie. She ordered and sat waiting, inhaling the fug of cigarette smoke mixed with grease fires from the kitchen, marvelling at her degradation. This was a world away from the previous night at Ciro's, but that no longer seemed real. Realising that she'd left Lally's dress and jewellery at the flat, she was wondering how on earth she could rescue them when a workman with a nose like a prize strawberry put a newspaper down on her table. 'Here, miss. Have that, if you like. I'm done with it, anyhow.'

'Thank you.'

It was a copy of the *Telegraph*. Surprised, she looked after him, but he was gone. Perhaps someone had given it to him, she thought. Or perhaps . . . but who was she to judge? *She* didn't look as if she ought to be here, did she? At least, she hoped she didn't, but after that run-in with the two women at Piccadilly Circus, she couldn't be sure about anything. Looking down at the paper, she thought, there'll be jobs advertised. Situations Vacant – that was what she needed. Of course! Why hadn't she thought of it before? She didn't need Jock or Lally – she could do it herself. Surely someone at Ashwood would give her a reference, and then . . . Feverishly, she began leafing through the pages then stopped, abruptly, arrested by the sight of James's face smiling up at her in smudgy black and white. Instinctively, she smiled back, and then, a second later, she saw the heading: *Obituaries*.

Chapter Fifty-Six

The light penetrated her eyelids. Dazed and blinking, she gasped, 'Please ... don't–' Black spots danced in front of her in the gloom, and as her eyes adjusted she could see a solid bulk in front of her – an overcoat, trouser legs. 'Wake up, miss.'

The voice was brisk and official. Looking up, Diana realised she was facing a policeman's torch. 'I ... I wasn't asleep. At least, I don't think I was.'

Shining the beam away from her face, the policeman asked, in a softer tone, 'Do you know where you are?'

Shaking her head, Diana put her hand down and felt the cold, hard wood of a bench beneath her palm. How had she got here? She remembered sitting in the café in shocked disbelief, reading James's obituary again and again, about his achievements, his contribution – no mention of the drinking, of course – and how he'd died after being hit by a car, leaving a wife but no issue. *She* was his wife – why hadn't anyone told her? Perhaps they hadn't known where she was ... if he'd become separated from his belongings and there was no address ...

'I was in a café,' she said. 'And then ...'

'Yes, miss?'

'I'm not sure. I was walking. I got lost.'

'You can't stay here, miss.'

'I haven't anywhere to go.'

'You've got to go somewhere, miss.'

Diana shook her head. 'He's dead. That's why he didn't come back.'

'Who's that, miss?'

'James . . . My husband. He's dead.'

'I'm sorry about that. When did it happen?'

'I've only just found out.' Diana held up the newspaper. 'It's in here. It says he was hit by a car.'

'In there, is it?'

He's humouring me, Diana thought. He thinks I'm mad. 'It's there,' she said, holding up the paper and tapping James's picture. 'That's him.'

'James Carleton, film director,' the policeman read. 'That's your husband, is it?'

'Was my husband,' said Diana.

'I see.' He didn't believe her.

'He *was*.'

'Of course he was,' said the policeman, soothingly. Bending down, he took her by the arm. 'Now, why don't you come along with me, and we'll find you a bed for the night.'

Diana allowed herself to be raised to her feet. 'My suitcase . . .'

'I've got it, don't worry.'

Walking was painful – she must have developed blisters – but she hobbled along as best she could.

*

Waking before dawn, the first thing Diana was aware of was the smell: body odour, stale linen and carbolic. Then the sensation of something itchy next to her cheek: a blanket. She sniffed it, and hastily drew her head away: the rough wool was impregnated with dirt. She wasn't alone. Somebody was snoring to her left, and from her right there came a series of yelps, muffled and puppyish. Turning on the narrow bed, she felt something soft and silky twist around her waist: my slip, she thought, and reached beneath the blanket – there seemed to be no sheet – to pull it down around the tops of her legs. The next thing she was aware of was the string tied around her neck. Fingering it in the darkness, she found a metal disc. Recalling an efficient, hospital matron's voice saying, 'Fifty-five!' she thought, this is my number. She'd been sitting in the café, hadn't she, looking at the paper, and then James was dead, and now . . . now she didn't seem to have a name any more, only a number. I ought to be crying, she thought. Why aren't I crying?

Vaguely, she remembered entering the hostel, the exchange between the woman in the wire-caged cubbyhole in the lobby and the policeman. She'd wondered why the woman, upright and stiff in a suit that looked like a uniform, was in the cage. To protect her? If so, it must be from the people here. A sudden lurch of fear jerked her into a sitting position, and she stared wildly into the unpredictable darkness. As her eyes adjusted, rows of grey humps appeared down the length of the room. In the gloom, they seemed petrified, as though an earthquake had encrusted them with dust or ash and converted them into concrete. The nearest bed was barely three feet away. She couldn't see the woman's face, but a wrist and hand, knuckle joints exploded by arthritis, protruded from the blanket.

She'd seen the policeman's eyebrows telegraph his disbelief to the woman in the cage when she'd given her name as Mrs Carleton, but she was too tired to make a fuss. She'd explained that she'd spent the last of her money in the café, but the policeman must have made it all right because her suitcase was taken from her and she was escorted upstairs to the dormitory. His face, as she'd thanked him, had said it all: she was now, officially, an object of pity.

Chapter Fifty-Seven

. . . I have examined these and I found entwined in the roots of the philadelphus plant (from Area 3) a cervical vertebra and pieces of skull. There was also a mass of decaying fabric through which the roots were growing freely. From the debris labelled 'Area 3' there were found numerous pieces of burnt newspaper which appear to have been cut into strips before burning. Pieces of root similar to the philadelphus root were adhering to this paper. A date '9th July 1943' was found on one of the pieces.

In the material labelled 'Areas 2, 3, 6, 8, 9' there was found a quantity of rotted cloth. This cloth consists of 7 types of material which can be associated to form the remains of a black artificial silk crêpe dress, a black (?dark-navy) coat, and possibly a navy-blue skirt. The total quantity of clothing recovered represents a moderately extensive area of clothing . . .

Wondering what the hell 'moderately extensive' was supposed to mean, Stratton pushed the Metropolitan Police Laboratory report away from him and lit a cigarette. The lab had obviously been working round the clock, because there was an enormous pile of notes to be sifted. Stratton, who'd managed no more than a couple of hours' fitful sleep, stared at them blearily, trying to keep his mind on the job. Images from the nightmare that had woken him, shaking and dripping sweat, at half past five, kept recurring in his mind: Monica and Jenny prone on the dusty floor of Paradise Street; Backhouse, scarlet penis bursting out of his fly like some demonic jack-in-the-box as he pulled his tie over his head and snapped it taut between his fists; himself, held back by some invisible power, struggling lead-legged, unable to reach them . . .

Subdued at breakfast, Monica had avoided looking directly at him. The atmosphere was solemn, as if there had been a death in the house, and his daughter's face was pale, the skin under her eyes the translucent blue of sleeplessness. He'd wondered if he'd shouted out in his dream, and if so, whether she'd heard him. They didn't speak much over their tea and toast. Monica had given him her bacon, and he'd wondered if this was the onset of the morning sickness he remembered Jenny suffering, but said nothing. Watching her, his helpless feeling had returned, and, when he rose to leave, he'd rubbed her back and said, 'Chirp up, chicken,' just as he used to when she was small and something had upset her.

'You will keep your promise, won't you, Dad?'

'Yes, love. Just remember – least said, soonest mended. For the time being, anyway.' Except, he'd thought as he closed the gate, this couldn't be mended at all. Catching sight of the bloody man's name on an Odeon film poster from the top deck of the bus, jeering at him in bright red from beneath

Phyllis Calvert and Stewart Granger, he'd had to fight the urge to tear down the stairs and rip the thing out of its frame.

At least, he thought, Lamb wasn't breathing down his neck. The discoveries at Paradise Street had knocked the wind out of his sails to the extent that he now listened passively when Stratton brought him up to date with the revolting litany of their findings. There'd been a couple of routine exhortations to 'get on with it, for God's sake', but his heart wasn't in it. Despite the statement he'd issued about the two cases having nothing to do with each other, Stratton knew he didn't believe it.

Pulling another section of the lab report towards him, he began to read: *I have examined samples of blood taken from all four women, and found that samples 1, 2 and 3* – the women in the alcove, thought Stratton – *all contain carbon monoxide. The sample of blood (2)* – that was Kathleen McKinnon – *also contained alcohol. The amount found was 0.240%. This figure is equivalent to the consumption of 8 pints of beer or 13 fluid ounces of spirits. This figure, however, cannot be entirely relied on owing to the decomposition of the blood.*

Stratton whistled. Decomposition or not, the woman must have been blotto, or well on the way to it, when she died. Still, if it meant she hadn't realised what was happening to her, he supposed it was a blessing. *A small quantity of alcohol was found in the stomach contents of (2), and traces of alcohol in the stomach contents of (3).* That was Iris Manning. Stratton scanned the rest of the page. No traces of drugs found in any of them . . . An area of seminal staining found on the top of the left stocking from (1) – that was Dwyer – information about laundry marks found on the linen, and at the bottom, a very long list of the contents of the bottles found in the medicine cabinet, which included sleeping pills and phenobarbitone.

Hearing an alarmingly viscid throat-clearing behind him, Stratton turned to see the bulky form of DI Grove. 'Been to see the furniture bloke, Lorrimer. Says Backhouse told him he was going up to Northampton to look for a job and his wife was staying there with her sister.'

'He seems to have as much trouble with the truth as Davies,' said Stratton, tiredly. 'Judging from this lot,' he gestured at the pile of statements taken from the Paradise Street residents, 'everyone got a different story. Two of them said Birmingham – that was for a woman's operation, apparently – and the rest thought it was Sheffield.'

Perching his substantial bottom on the corner of the desk, Grove gave a sympathetic grimace. 'Well, Lorrimer gave him twelve pounds for the furniture. Said he wanted fifteen, but most of the stuff was no good. According to him, the last time he saw Mrs Backhouse – February sometime, he reckons – she was in a terrible state of nerves and terrified of her husband.'

Stratton sighed. 'Isn't hindsight a wonderful thing? Mind you, we thought she seemed pretty well under his thumb back then.'

'Yes, well . . .' Grove adjusted his backside, sweeping several papers to the floor in the process. 'The bad news is that he's been talking to the press.' Holding up his arm, he extended his thumb and fingers to frame an invisible headline. '"Did She Know?"'

'Well, she certainly didn't know about the women in the alcove, because she was under the floorboards by the time they got in there.'

'Not about them, about the Davieses. They won't say that, of course, because of Lamb putting the mockers on it, but that's what they'll imply. "Mrs Backhouse was terrified by her guilty knowledge. Eventually her killer realised that her nerves were at breaking-point and decided that he must silence her for ever." Or something like that.' Seeing Stratton's expression, Grove added, 'Still, at least the inquest tomorrow should be pretty straightforward.'

'Yes, except for the fact that we can't actually find the fucker.'

'Well, he can't stay hidden for ever. We've had a lot more sightings. Likeliest was in Bognor but it didn't come to anything. You know they even stopped a theatre performance last night – someone thought they'd spotted him in the audience. Bloke turned out to be nothing like.'

'What was the play, sir?' Ballard was listening from the other end of the room, where he'd been in conference with DS Porter.

'*Macbeth*, believe it or not. Sir Donald Wolfit.'

'Blimey,' said Ballard. 'He must have been cheesed off.'

'I don't know about that,' said Grove. 'Think of the publicity – murderer unmasked at *Macbeth* . . . You all right, Stratton?'

'Not so's you'd notice, no.' Mention of the theatre had

brought Raymond Bloody Benson sharply to mind. He wasn't looking forward to that conversation *at all*. He put his hand in his pocket and fingered the paper on which Monica had written the phone number, touching it gingerly as though it might suddenly burst into flames.

Getting to his feet with a grunt, Grove laid a heavy hand on his shoulder. 'I can imagine . . .' he said, gruffly. 'But if it's any consolation, Lamb'll be feeling a lot worse.'

'It isn't,' said Stratton, shortly.

'Oh, by the way, Backhouse seems to have forged his wife's signature to cash in her savings. We had a communication from the . . .' Grove flicked through his notebook, 'Yorkshire Penny Bank. Ten pounds, fifteen shillings and tuppence, it was. Right, I'd better get cracking – check we've got all our witnesses for tomorrow.'

'Thanks, Grove. It's . . .' Temporarily lost for words, Stratton said, 'I know you've got enough on your plate. I appreciate it.'

Two pinkish spots appeared on Grove's putty-coloured cheeks. 'This sort of thing . . .' He turned to stare out of the window for a moment, and then, tight-lipped beneath the drooping moustache, said, 'We're all in it together.' Taking his pipe from his pocket and jamming it between his teeth, he left the room.

Ballard came up to the desk, a sheaf of paper in his hand. 'We've got the name of May Drinkwater's dentist, and he's sending all her bumpf over to the Middlesex Dental Surgery Department for comparison. And Professor Anderson – he's the man in charge – says the crowns are made of some sort of alloy they use in Central Europe. DS Porter's looking into it.'

Stratton raised his eyebrows. 'Central Europe's a big place. Who was it reported May Drinkwater as missing?'

'Her brother, sir. He gave us the name of the dentist.'

'Did he give a description of what she was wearing?'

'Yes, sir.' Ballard leafed through his notebook. 'A dark-coloured dress and coat.'

'Looks like you might have hit the nail on the head.' Stratton handed over the lab report. 'We've got fabric samples from both, and some buttons – partially burnt, apparently at the same time as the skull.'

'Fingers crossed, sir.'

'You bet. Oh, and there's a scrap of newspaper with a date which might help with identifying the other one – ninth of July, nineteen forty-three.'

'I'll look in the records, sir, although what with the bombing . . .'

'I know. Just do your best.'

'Yes, sir. And there's something else. A woman came in this morning – DS Porter spoke to her, sir. A Mrs Jean Halliday. She said she was in a café in Marylebone last week and she had a conversation with a man she now thinks must have been Backhouse–'

'Hold on. Last week's not much use.'

'Not as far as locating him goes, no, which is why Porter didn't think to tell you immediately. But what's interesting is that she told DS Porter they'd got talking and he started asking her about her health . . . Well, turns out she's pregnant. Married, but she wasn't very happy about it because she's got four already, and Backhouse – if that's who this chap was – said he could help her. Told he used to be a doctor but he'd been struck off because he did a favour for a friend and got found out. He said that if she'd go round to his house, he knew a way to get rid of the baby. She said she wanted to think about it, so they arranged to meet the following day at the same café, but she got cold feet so she didn't turn up.'

'Did the man say *where* he lived?' asked Stratton.

Ballard shook his head. 'Just told her he lived nearby. And Euston's not far from Marylebone, sir. Oh, and he asked if her husband knew about the pregnancy, and when she said she hadn't told him, the bloke said there was no need to say anything because he could have it all sorted out in no time and no one would be any the wiser.'

'It certainly sounds like him,' said Stratton. 'Did she give a description?'

'She did.' Ballard found the right piece of paper and read, 'Medium height, bald head, thick glasses, grey-striped suit—'

'No coat?'

'Not according to this. But she said she'd read a description in the paper and thought it sounded like the same man, and when Porter showed her a photograph, she told him it was spot on.'

'Well, if it was him, he certainly didn't lose any time lining up his next victim after Mary Dwyer.'

'That's what I thought, sir. He's out of control – can't help himself and doesn't care about getting caught.'

'It certainly sounds as if Mrs Halliday had a very lucky

escape. And now he's left Paradise Street, he's presumably not got anywhere to take anyone . . . But if you're right – and you might well be – that he no longer cares about getting caught, that makes him even *more* dangerous. Christ! We'll just have to hope that–' Stratton stopped as Arliss's head appeared round the door, an expression of malevolent relish lighting up his normally morose features. 'A Mrs Davies at the desk, sir. John Davies's mother. Says she'd like a word, sir.'

Stratton, exchanging glances with Ballard, saw only compassion in the sergeant's eyes. Heart sinking still further, he rose and followed the constable down the corridor.

Chapter Fifty-Eight

Diana headed towards Green Park – to the spot where James had proposed to her. Now, her single objective was to be close to him, and she could think of no other way to achieve it.

The obituary hadn't mentioned where he'd died, only how. Had he returned to London, she wondered and, if so, how had he managed it with so little money? Light-headed with hunger – the hostel had not provided breakfast beyond a cup of nauseatingly strong tea – she stumbled along as fast as the painful rubbing of the raw flesh on her heels would allow, her suitcase banging against her legs, impelled by the idea of being near him.

Reawakened at half past five by a clanging fire-bell and a rough hand yanking the blanket from her body, she'd seen, as though in a dream, the grey shapes rise off their beds, scramble into their clothes and make for the door. Dazed, she'd followed them, barely able to remain on her feet in the middle of the elbowing, clattering descent down two flights of stairs to the basement washhouse. The room she'd found herself in was a wet version of hell, reeking of carbolic soap with dirty water everywhere, coursing in rivulets down the concrete walls and sluicing in soapy rivers across the floor to drain away down gulleys cut into the stone. The air was thick with shrieks and swearing, punctuated with flushing lavatories, as sixty women jostled each other for the use of three taps and fought over hanging space on the clothesline strung above their heads. Now, making her way from Victoria – where, it turned out, the hostel was situated – towards Hyde Park Corner, revoltingly detailed images detached themselves from the memory of the violent, steamy blur: a single, pendulous dug with the thick, pocked surface of orange-peel; mottled legs disfigured by bulging knots of varicose veins; a discarded sanitary towel floating in a scummy puddle . . .

Just twenty minutes later, upstairs in the ante-room, those same women had sat waiting for the doors to open at seven o'clock, silent and withdrawn from one another, adjusting their dress and pinning on the few pitiful ornaments they still possessed, the vestiges of self-respect that would enable them to face the world. She'd seen their sidelong, envious looks at her fur coat and been careful to keep her mouth shut for fear of exciting their scorn. Perhaps she needn't have worried – their lack of curiosity had suggested that, if she was there, she must be one of them.

Was she? She neither knew nor cared. All she wanted was to be with James. Wincing, she quickened her pace.

It was over two years since she'd last been in the park and, with the trees in leaf and mist still rising from the grass, it looked different to what she remembered. After five minutes' walking she stopped, blinking up into the weak spring sunlight. She was sure she was near the place where James had proposed – or rather, where James had told her she was going to marry him – and she'd definitely chosen the same entrance, but she wanted to be sure. After turning round several times, she made for a clump of trees whose shapes she thought she remembered, but felt no sense of his presence. She stopped and removed her gloves, staring down at her engagement ring that sparkled next to the thin gold wedding band.

There's no such thing as too much champagne . . . James's voice echoed in her ear and, in a warm rush, the liquid heat of desire coursed through her body, just as it had when he'd touched her arm. Dizzy now, she could feel his lips on hers, his breath on her face, and then – she spun round – they'd run across the grass . . . Oh, God . . .

Her legs seemed to have turned to water, and she leant against a tree trunk and closed her eyes. When she opened them, she knew he was gone. There's no point in being here, she thought. He's nowhere. He's dead. She buried her face in her hands, and wept.

When she straightened up, she noticed that there was a man standing on the path, looking in her direction. Seen through a blur of tears, he looked as if he'd just risen out of the mist, middle-aged and ordinary in his tweed overcoat and trilby hat, the sunlight glinting off his glasses so that she couldn't see the eyes behind them. Turning her back on him so that she was facing the tree, she blew her nose and, taking her compact from her handbag, began to repair her face. Returning the cosmetics to their place and pulling on her gloves, she turned round once more and saw that he was still there. He seemed, although she wasn't sure about this because of the sun, to be staring at her. Discomfited by the blank spaces that were his eyes, and wondering what she ought to do next, she began walking in the direction of the railings. Out of the corner of her right eye, she saw him hesitate and then, as if he'd reached a decision, square his shoulders and begin walking towards her. Thinking that he might be lost, she stopped. He approached her and, removing his hat to reveal a domed, bald pate, he blinked several times, as if uncertain, and made a curious sucking motion with his mouth. 'Good morning,' he said, in a husky, confidential tone, 'I wonder if I might be of any assistance?'

Chapter Fifty-Nine

Stratton thought afterwards that it would have been easier if Mrs Davies had cursed and spat at him. The elderly lady's quiet dignity had filled him with shame. 'When I visited my son in prison before his trial,' she said, 'and I asked him what happened, he told me it was Backhouse. "He knows all about it, he's got medical books." That's what John said. "Get Mr Backhouse, he's the only one who can help me." When I asked him why he made all those statements, he said it was because Mr Backhouse told him that things would be fine if he confessed. Then he said only one of the statements was true, and that was the one where he said Backhouse had done it. When I asked him why he signed the confession, he said that when you told him Judy was dead he had nothing to live for. Until then, I didn't know what to believe, but when he said that I knew he was telling the truth. He told you that, Mr Stratton, but you didn't believe him.'

'No,' said Stratton, 'I didn't. But he did have a reputation as a liar, Mrs Davies. You said so yourself.' Stratton forbore to point out that she'd also said, in a statement made to DI Grove, that her son had a terrible temper.

'Yes, I did. But I knew when he was telling the truth.'

Stratton doubted the veracity of this, but wouldn't have dreamt of challenging it. Death, especially in these sorts of circumstances, tended to simplify people into much better – or much worse – versions of themselves, and this black-and-white-ing process extended to their relationships with others. Bonds, especially intuitive links, such as Davies's mother was now claiming, became ever stronger as the dead person was dismantled and remade by those left behind. But if it comforted them, where was the harm?

'Do you still think he's guilty, Mr Stratton?'

Stratton hesitated. 'I don't know,' he said, finally. 'We need to complete our investigation before we can come to any conclusions.'

Mrs Davies held Stratton's gaze until he could bear it no longer and lowered his eyes. 'When John's appeal failed,' she said, in a steady voice, 'I asked him again. I told him it couldn't make any difference now – it was for my own peace of mind and because I wanted him to make *his* peace with God. He looked me straight in the eye and said, "Mam, I didn't do it. Backhouse done it."'

Stratton had a fleeting image of Mrs Davies on the morning of the execution, flanked by relatives in a neat sitting room, all of them watching as the minute hand of the clock on the mantel inched nearer and nearer to the hour. He could imagine her clutching her son's photograph, waiting for the second when the present of his life tipped over into the past, gathering herself for the invisible but all-too-well-imagined snapping of the neck as the trap was released and the bag-headed, pinioned thing that had been her boy plummeted downwards . . .

I want to tell Mam what I done, but I can't do it . . . Stratton remembered Davies's words to him in the car on the way back from the committal. Could he have been referring to something other than the murders? It didn't seem very likely. If he *was* guilty, then clearly he hadn't been able to face confessing it to his mother. But it was a very odd thing to say if he wasn't.

'What I came to tell you,' Mrs Davies continued, 'is that I'm writing to my Member of Parliament to ask about an inquiry. I've also written to the Home Secretary. I thought I ought to tell you because John said you were a gentleman. He liked you, Mr Stratton.'

This was said sincerely, without a trace of irony. Humbled, Stratton said, 'Thank you.'

'Well . . .' Mrs Davies rose and stood, straight-backed and self-contained. 'I'm sure you're very busy.'

Stratton said goodbye to Mrs Davies at the station door. As she began to descend the steps, an impulse he was unable to resist made him put a restraining hand on her arm. She looked down at it and then up at his face, frowning slightly. Removing his hand, he said, 'I am sorry. Very sorry.' He didn't – couldn't – elaborate further, but Mrs Davies appeared not to require this. With a single, emphatic nod that made her tight grey curls bounce, she turned and left.

*

Leaving West End Central that evening, Stratton felt as furtive and mortified as a man coming out of a knocking shop and onto a street where he might easily meet someone he knows. Logic told him that Davies's death wasn't solely his fault. The man had done a great deal to hang himself, Backhouse had lied, and everyone, including the judge, had considered Davies to be guilty. He wondered if Mrs Davies had, initially at least, thought so too. If that were so, he thought, then by now she'd almost certainly convinced herself she'd always been sure of his innocence. He couldn't blame her for that – in the circumstances, he'd probably have done the same. But then what about what Davies had said in the car . . .

He'd turned this over and over in his mind during the bus journey home, but reached no conclusions. The house was unlit, and turning on the kitchen light he saw that there was a note lying on the table. Assuming that it must be instructions for heating up whatever was in the saucepan on the stove, he went through to the scullery and poured himself a glass of beer. Staring out of the window into the dark garden, he tried to rehearse what to say to Raymond Benson. At least, he thought, separated by a telephone line, he wouldn't be able to clobber the bloody man, no matter how strong the urge. Imagining him, sleekly handsome and languid in a velvet smoking jacket, he clenched his fists, but he knew that, however much he wanted to break the man's neck, he'd promised Monica – and, he repeated to himself, violence wouldn't change, or solve, anything. It'd make me feel a whole lot better, though, he thought, grimly.

First things first. Supposing that he ought to try and eat

something, at least, he took his beer back to the kitchen and picked up the note. *Dad, I am sorry I have betrayed your trust and let you down, and Mum. I am going to see a friend who can help. Please don't worry about me. Love, Monica x*

Stratton felt sick. What friend? What help? The vision of his beloved daughter being mauled by some seedy struck-off doctor in a back room, or worse – appallingly, horrifyingly worse – encountering Backhouse, was so strong that he felt as if he'd been punched in the stomach. Backhouse bending over her, panting and sweating with lust, as he pawed at her knickers and . . . *Stop it!* Hands palm-down on the table and elbows locked, he took several deep breaths. He must not panic. He must find her before . . . before . . . No! He must not think about that. Monica wouldn't allow herself to be drawn into a conversation with a strange man, and certainly not someone like Backhouse – but then Monica, at present, wasn't her normal, sensible self. She was upset and desperate and he had no idea what she might do. He *had* to find her.

Where to start? His mind raced. Monica had said that she'd only told Pete, but perhaps she had talked to Madeleine as well. They'd always been close, just as Jenny had with Doris. Except, said a voice in the back of his mind, Jenny hadn't told Doris that she was pregnant, had she? Telling himself that Monica wasn't Jenny, and that the circumstances were entirely different, he strode into the hall and picked up the telephone.

'Doris? It's Ted. Is Monica with you?'

'Hello, love. We haven't seen her today . . . Are you all right? You sound a bit–'

'Is Madeleine there?'

'Yes.' Doris sounded surprised. 'She's in the kitchen. But what–'

'Can I speak to her?'

'Yes, of course.'

There was a pause as Doris handed the receiver to her daughter. 'Hello, Uncle Ted. What is it?'

'Have you seen Monica today?'

'No. Not since the night before last . . . Is there something wrong, Uncle Ted?'

'Did she say anything to you?'

'Say anything? No, we just . . . you know. Just normal things. Why?'

'If she telephones, can you let me know?'

'Of course, but . . . Is she all right?'

'I'm not sure. Do you know if she's got any particular friends at work?'

'Well, she's mentioned someone called Anne, who works with her doing the make-up, but nothing . . . I mean, just about funny things that happen, not anything important.'

'Did she mention a surname?'

'Not that I remember. She told me about Mrs Calthrop, as well – she said you knew her before, from the war – but that was ages ago. She's not talked about her recently . . . I can't think of anyone else.'

'Did she mention Raymond Benson?'

'The film actor? No. I'd remember *that*, Uncle Ted. He's dreamy.'

'I don't doubt it,' said Stratton, grimly. 'Could I have another word with your mum?'

There was another pause, as the telephone was handed back to Doris. 'What's going on, Ted?'

'I'm not sure ... Look, Doris, Monica's in trouble and I don't know where she's gone. She's left a note, but ... I'm worried she's done something stupid.'

'Stupid? What–'

'She's pregnant.'

'Pregnant?' Doris's voice was sharp. 'Do you know anything about this, Madeleine?' There was some muttering, and then Doris's voice again. 'She says she doesn't. Are you sure?'

'It's what she told me.'

'Well, it's the first we've heard of it. Is there anything we can do, Ted?'

'No ... just stay by the telephone in case she rings. I need to find her. Is there anyone local she might have gone to – a friend, I mean? Madeleine might know ...'

Madeleine came back on the line. 'I can't think of anyone, Uncle Ted. I mean, there's girls from school, but she's never really had a special friend – if she'd told anyone, it would be me.

His niece sounded both shocked and hurt, and Stratton didn't blame her. 'All right. But if she does telephone, you will tell me, won't you?'

'Of course I will! I hope she hasn't ... I mean, I hope she's all right.'

'So do I,' said Stratton. Putting the receiver down, he rubbed his face. 'Christ, so do I.' Returning to the kitchen, he picked up Monica's note once more, and read it again, trying to make it yield some clue as to where she had gone. *Dad, I am sorry I have betrayed your trust . . .* But, he thought, it hadn't been a matter of trusting her; it had simply never occurred to him that anything of this sort might happen. Monica hadn't betrayed his trust – what she *had* done was to show up, with vile clarity, his utter negligence as a father: *he* was the one who had betrayed *her*.

Chapter Sixty

Stratton fished Benson's telephone number out of his pocket and rubbed it with his thumb for a moment, staring fixedly at the thing as though expecting its owner to appear before him like a pantomime genie. Then, white-knuckled, he yanked the receiver from its cradle and, jabbing his finger into the relevant holes, began to dial the number.

'Hadley Green 521–'

'Mr Benson?' Cutting off the rich, silky tones, Stratton almost spat the words with the effort of keeping his own voice level.

'Yes. Who is this, please?'

'This is Detective Inspector Stratton. Monica Stratton's father.'

'I *see* . . .'

Stratton took a deep breath, taking in, with the air, the effortless superiority and poise of the man's tone. 'I should bloody well hope you *do* see. I'd like to kick your arse from here to Land's End.'

'Steady on, old chap.'

Old chap? Stratton took another deep breath. 'Much as I'd

like to do that,' he said, every muscle in his body taut with the strain of maintaining any degree of calm at all, 'I'm not going to, because I promised my daughter I wouldn't. The reason I'm telephoning is because Monica has disappeared.'

'She's not with you?'

'Obviously not, or I wouldn't be asking.'

'Well, she's not *here*.' Benson managed to sound as if this was the most ridiculous idea he'd ever heard in his life.

'She left a note saying that she was going to see a friend who could help her, and I want to know if you have any idea who that is.'

'No, I can't say I–'

'So you didn't give her an address, or–'

'I have offered,' said Benson carefully, 'to . . . make reparations, as it were.'

'*Reparations?* You mean you've offered to pay for Monica to have an illegal operation which may very well ruin her health for life. I need to know where she's gone.'

'I think that's somewhat of an exaggeration, don't you? There are perfectly good clinics where every care is taken to do a competent job.'

'Monica,' said Stratton through gritted teeth, 'is not a piece of machinery. She is *my* daughter, and she has feelings, and I'm very concerned that she's done something stupid. Did you, or didn't you, give her the name of an abortionist?'

'No, I did not.'

'Did anybody?'

'I have absolutely no idea.'

'What about people at the studio? Friends? Anyone she's mentioned?'

'Well, she's pally with another make-up girl, Anne, but I don't know any more than that. You'd have to ask the studio, unless Monica's left an address book or something like that . . .'

Cursing himself for not having thought of this and feeling that there was nothing to be gained by prolonging the conversation, Stratton rang off, but not before leaving Benson in any doubt that they'd be discussing the matter further and face to face, and assuring him that if anything happened to Monica then he would hold him personally responsible.

Stratton stood on the threshold of his daughter's bedroom. It wasn't territory into which he usually ventured – certainly not by himself, anyway – and he felt uncomfortable. He had a clear memory of himself in 1940, when the children were evacuated, coming in here and purloining a tiny pink scarf Monica had made for one of her dolls. Remembering the embarrassment he'd felt at this sentimentality, even though no one had seen him do it, he found himself wondering what had happened to the little scrap of knitting. If Jenny had found it in one of his pockets, she'd never mentioned it . . .

The dolls were gone now. Sketches – portraits, flowers and fruit – from the evening classes she'd attended were pinned up on the walls, and there was a Jean Plaidy novel and a film magazine on top of the small bedside cabinet, a dish of hairpins and a bottle of scent on the mantelpiece and a chiffon scarf draped over one edge of the mirror. Stratton glanced at the neatly made bed with its shiny pink eiderdown; the idea of his daughter lying in it and thinking about that bloody man, as she must surely have done, revolted him, and he turned away. Looking around the room, trying to avoid the bed with his eyes – almost impossible, as it took up nearly half the available space – he couldn't see anything that looked like an address book. As far as he knew, Monica had never kept a diary. He stared at her chest of drawers. He really did not want to search through all her underclothes and whatever else she might have in there, but . . . Perhaps he ought to ring Doris? For Christ's sake, he told himself, this is no time for pussyfooting around. Just get on with it.

Gingerly, as if the action might detonate a bomb, Stratton opened the top drawer. Finding only the usual array of underwear and stockings, he slammed it closed as if that would shut the image of Benson fingering these garments, and the corresponding regions of their wearer, out of his mind. Finding nothing of note in the next drawer, he opened the bottom one. Beneath a folded cardigan, he found a bundle of letters. Perhaps they would help . . . Recognising his own handwriting, and Jenny's, and seeing the faded ink, he realised that Monica must have kept them from the war years, when they'd written to her and Pete in Suffolk. Blinking, he stuffed them back into place and stood up, staring round the room with scalded eyes.

He looked in the wardrobe, which seemed to contain the right amount of clothing. Monica's suitcase was sitting at the bottom, which was something to be grateful for, at least. Finding that the bedside cabinet held nothing but a pair of gloves and a drawstring bag containing sanitary towels and a belt, Stratton turned his attention to the two small bookshelves. Perhaps the assorted Georgette Heyers, Daphne du Mauriers and A. J. Cronins would yield something. There were a few exercise books, too, kept from school, and an elderly jigsaw which, judging from the picture on the box, was of a deer in a woodland glade. He began with the books, flicking through the pages and shaking them before dropping them on the bed. Nothing there, and nothing hidden behind them, either. The exercise books were similarly barren, but when he opened the jigsaw box, he saw, beneath the jumble of cardboard, the corners of two letters. Scrabbling for them and sending half the pieces flying in the process, he saw that he was holding two notes in the same unfamiliar hand. Both were signed *With all my love, dearest one, R.B.* Scanning them quickly, Stratton saw that they were, underneath all the flummery and flowery language (Benson seemed to have been reading the same sorts of books as Monica), assignations, and, for his purposes, quite useless.

Stratton stuffed them back in the box and stood shaking his head and staring down at the cardboard fragments of bark and leaves scattered around his feet. He hadn't found a single clue to where she might have gone.

Chapter Sixty-One

A call to Ashwood Studio, in Stratton's official capacity, yielded the information that Anne the make-up girl, whose surname turned out to be Browne, lived in Clapham but wasn't on the telephone, and that the last-known address for Diana Calthrop, now Carleton, was in Pimlico, but there was no telephone there, either.

Recollecting that Ballard lived somewhere in, or anyway near, Clapham, Stratton picked up the telephone once more and asked the operator to put him through. If the sergeant was surprised to hear his voice, he didn't show it, and when Stratton, as succinctly as he could, explained the situation, Ballard responded with commendably impersonal efficiency and agreed to go round to Tremlett Gardens and question the girl at once.

'Shall I telephone you at home, sir?' he asked.

'No . . . I'll telephone you later on – or leave a message at the station. I'm going out. There's someone else I need to follow up, who might know where the hell Monica is.'

'Yes, sir. And, sir . . . Good luck.'

'Thanks, Ballard. Believe me, I appreciate this.'

By nine o'clock, Stratton was in Pimlico standing outside the address he'd been given for Diana, and wondering if the man he'd spoken to at the film studio had made a mistake. The tall, thin house, in the middle of a semi-derelict terrace, looked as if it was being held upright by the buildings on either side. Clearly divided into flats, it didn't look like anywhere that Diana might visit, let alone inhabit. But then, he thought, as he walked up the four steps to the front door, 'his' Diana existed only in memory. She won't be the person I used to know, he told himself, or the one I met for those few excruciating moments at the Festival of Britain, any more than she'll remain the woman she is now. Everyone changes . . . Here, a sudden vision of Monica as a little girl made his eyes burn. Childhood was only an imagined cocoon of safety, he told himself. Look at poor little Judy Davies . . .

In answer to his knock, an elderly woman who smelt faintly of mildew put her head round the door and eyed him up and down with an irritable pecking movement like a parrot adjusting its plumage. Must be the landlady, thought Stratton. Large or small – and this one appeared to be pocket-sized – they tended to be of a kind.

'I've come to see Mrs Carleton,' he said.

The landlady let out a short yipping noise. 'Not here. You another one of her *gentlemen*?' She made the word sound like the worst of insults.

'I'm a policeman,' said Stratton, sharply, producing his warrant card. 'DI Stratton, CID, and I'd like to talk to her.'

The landlady's head, still the only visible part of her, twisted to one side in a way that didn't look possible, never mind comfortable. 'Police now, is it? Well you won't find her here. I gave her notice.'

'Do you know where she went?'

'Didn't ask. I won't have that sort here.'

'What sort?'

'Well, she *said* she was married, but the husband – if that's what he was – disappeared a few weeks back, and then some other man came and paid all the rent they owed, and then she started having *visitors*, if you know what I mean. For all I know, she might have gone to live with one of those. She never had no money, or if she did I never got the smell of it. Now, if that's all . . .'

'Yes. Thank you.'

Chapter Sixty-Two

Monica sat well back, not wanting to put her arms on the sticky surface of the café table. She didn't much want to touch anything in the place, including the tea she'd ordered. She knew she was just putting off the moment, but she couldn't face it, not quite yet.

The only other customer was an elderly, toothless man who, after sucking noisily at a forkful of mince to extract the flavour, removed the resulting pulp from his mouth with his thumb and forefinger and laid it on the side of his plate. It was only when he looked up from his gummy exertions that Monica realised she must have been staring, and looked down at her lap, hoping the revulsion hadn't shown too much on her face.

She had to go through with it. The more she'd thought about it, the more obvious it was. People like her shouldn't have children, because they were abnormal and would pass on their defects. Everyone knew that: it was how you ended up with cripples and kids with awful diseases who died young. Imbeciles, too. It would be as bad as if someone with venereal disease had a child. Auntie Doris had explained about that when one of their neighbours' sons turned out to be mentally defective: the mother had told her that her husband had caught something when he was serving overseas and passed it on to her so that she, in turn, had given it to the baby.

She'd never be able to explain any of that to Dad, of course. He might, in time, come to terms with what she'd done even though it was against the law and dangerous, but never with the other thing. That was why she hadn't asked Raymond about the special clinic. Dad, she was positive, would talk to him, and it was much better that Raymond knew nothing of her plans. Dad was a dab hand at getting information out of people, and Raymond, she felt sure, would be no exception.

Instead, she'd confessed to Anne. She hadn't wanted to, but a whispered confidence about an actress who'd found herself in trouble had persuaded her that her friend did know something of such matters, and there was nowhere else to turn. Initially, Anne had thought she was joking, and it had taken most of the day to convince her, but she'd managed it without revealing that Raymond was the father, inventing a local boy instead. Now, she had a name and address in her pocket, along with every bit of the money she'd managed to save since she started working. All she needed to do was to walk round the corner and knock on the door . . .

Chapter Sixty-Three

Stratton was so completely revolted by the old woman and her insinuations that Diana had turned into some sort of prostitute that it was only after striding down the road in disgust that he stopped to consider what she'd actually said. *No money, or if she did I never got the smell of it.* The Carletons must have been badly off, and something had evidently happened to him. Had he deserted her? If she'd had any money, she'd have paid the rent herself, he was sure of it. Perhaps she'd had to borrow from a friend, and that was what had planted the idea about men and visitors in the old besom's mind. Surely, with no money, she'd have gone to stay with friends or relatives . . . in which case, she'd be impossible to find, at least at short notice. That was the obvious thing to do if one were thrown out with nowhere to go. But just in case, he'd try the women's hostel near Victoria Station. He couldn't believe he'd actually find her there – but then, he reasoned, he'd never have believed she'd have ended up in such ramshackle lodgings, either. It just went to show . . . what did it go to show? That one ought to expect the worst in any situation? No, he told himself firmly. Monica will be fine. I *shall* find her, and everything *will* be all right, somehow.

At least he was doing something. After the hostel, he'd go to West End Central and see if there was any message from Ballard about the girl in Clapham. Bound to set the cat amongst the pigeons, turning up when it wasn't his shift, but he could always make out it was something to do with the Backhouse case. As long as Lamb didn't get wind of it and start asking awkward questions . . . Walking fast in the direction of Victoria, keeping his eyes peeled for a passing taxi, he found himself wondering what his own father would have done in such a situation. He imagined the taciturn old farmer towering over the culprit, a shotgun jammed in his ribs until an early wedding was agreed upon. Except his father had had only sons – himself and two older brothers – and Benson was already married. He could just hear the wretched man bleating about his reputation . . . But film stars got divorced all the time, didn't they? In Hollywood, anyway. They weren't the same as normal people. But Benson might have children as well – they weren't to blame, and neither was his wife.

Eventually, he managed to flag down a taxi which took him to Victoria Station. Unsure of his bearings, he asked an elderly beggar whose face looked as though it had been under a harrow where to find the women's hostel.

'Down there, guv, on the right. Spare any change?'

Stratton gave him the price of a cup of tea and hurried off. The hostel was a squat, two-storey brick dwelling standing alone in the middle of a vast bombsite. In the windowless lobby, Stratton identified himself to a hard-faced woman of military bearing who sat, formidably, behind a wire grille. Unshaded, the single electric bulb gave her face a greenish cast, as if she were beginning to decompose, and behind her head, a series of metal rings hung like bizarre decorations, from lengths of coarse string. Halfway up a flight of stairs on the right, a stooped woman with an iron caliper on one leg pushed a mop backwards and forwards, punctuating their conversation with clanging noises whenever her metal support came into contact with the pail.

'Carleton?' The woman in the cage ran her finger down a list of names in a ledger. 'Yes, last night. Policeman brought her in.'

'Do you know where from?'

The woman drummed her fingers on the ledger for a moment, trying to remember. 'Oh, yes. Fur coat. Not our usual type at all. Quite confused – in fact, PC Eliot thought she might have lost her memory. Told me she'd showed him a picture of a man in the paper and said he was her husband and he'd died and she'd only found out when she'd read about it. We weren't even sure that Carleton was her real name. Well,' she added, defensively, 'it doesn't sound very likely, does it?'

'Maybe not, but it is her name. Where did PC Eliot find her, do you know?'

'One of the squares near the station. That's his beat – he often brings women in here. He said she didn't seem to know *where* she was.'

'I see. And she hasn't come back?'

The woman shook her head. 'Mind you, if she's still . . .' she tapped her temple, 'we'll probably get her back. Is she wanted for something?'

'Only information. We think she may know about a missing person.'

After telling the woman to contact West End Central if Diana did return, Stratton returned to Victoria Station and telephoned to Ballard from a public box. When the sergeant's wife, an ex-policewoman remembered by Stratton with affection, reported that he had not yet returned, he put another tuppence in the slot and telephoned Doris.

'I'm sorry, Ted. She's not been in touch.'

'Oh, Christ . . . Sorry, Doris, I didn't mean to—'

'Listen, Ted – Don's just come in. He wants to know if there's anything he can do to help.'

'It's very kind of him, but I can't think of anything at the moment . . . That girl Madeleine mentioned, I've managed to run her down and my sergeant's gone round to talk to her, but beyond that, I really don't know what to do. I'm just so . . .' Words failing him, Stratton started on another tack. 'I'm trying to find the other person Madeleine mentioned – I don't think it can be her but it's worth a go, and now I'm here . . .'

'Where are you?'

'Victoria Station. Look, I'd better go.'

'Ted, please . . . I know it sounds stupid, but try not to worry. Monica's always been a sensible girl. I'm sure she won't do anything . . . you know . . .'

Doris clearly didn't know what to say, either, and Stratton

couldn't blame her. Hopelessly, he scanned the faces of the people who passed him, the echoing noise of their heels quickly swallowed up by a cacophony of steam engines, whistles and porters trundling luggage trolleys. A needle in a haystack, a pebble on a beach . . . Why would Monica be in a bloody station, for God's sake? He'd go round to the local police and see if PC Eliot could shed any light on Diana's possible whereabouts. As he'd told Doris, he didn't really think it likely that Diana could be the 'friend' but, in the absence of any information from Ballard, he had to do *something* useful. Anything was better than going home and doing nothing.

Chapter Sixty-Four

Diana felt as though she were in a dream. The man in the park had appeared out of the mist like an omen – as if, somehow, James had sent him to her. Unprepossessing and shabby, certainly, and rather odd, but he sounded respectable enough – and he was *there*, wasn't he? Besides, what else did she have to do?

He'd offered to buy her a cup of tea, and they'd walked back towards Victoria Station, with him carrying her suitcase. He'd told her, in a husky whisper for which he'd apologised, explaining that his vocal cords had been damaged by gas in the Great War, that his name was Davies. 'I'm just passing the time,' he said. 'Since my wife died, I've had a lot of time on my hands. I'm waiting for my unemployment cards to come through, then I'll look for a job.'

'I'm sorry,' said Diana. 'It must be lonely.'

'Yes. But she'd had a long illness. I looked after her, you see – that's why I wasn't working. It was a mercy, really – terrible suffering, so hard to watch . . .'

'It must have been dreadful for you.'

'It was. She was one in a million ...' Reaching into his overcoat pocket, he pulled out a pair of earrings and offered them to her. 'Would you like these?' They were cheap, screw-on things of the sort one might buy in Woolworth's, with a large blue stone set in a circle of smaller white ones.

Taken aback, Diana said, 'It's very kind of you, but I couldn't possibly ... Did they belong to your wife?'

'Yes. I've been carrying them about. I often carry something of hers, to keep her near me. Are you married?'

'Yes. Or rather ...' And she'd found herself telling him all about James, and what had happened.

'Very regrettable. I suppose, with him being in the pictures, it's the sort of thing ... oh, dear.' He shook his head several times, then said, 'How are you off for money? I could give you a pound.'

'No, really,' said Diana. 'I couldn't.'

'Well, how are you going to manage?'

'I need to find out about James. I suppose I ought to go to the police.'

'Police?'

'Well, to find out what's happened about the body, and so on.'

'Yes ...' murmured Mr Davies, vaguely, and then, with some pride, 'I could have helped your husband, you know.'

'Helped him?'

'Oh, yes. I used to be a doctor, you see. Before the war. That's why I could look after Edna – my wife – because I know about health matters. Anyone else, of course, and she'd have had to go to hospital, but I know what to do.'

'Were you really a doctor?' She must have sounded more sceptical than she intended, because he said seriously, 'Oh, yes. I trained as a doctor, but I was struck off the Medical Register for helping a friend.'

'Helping?'

He gave her a knowing look. 'I'm sure I don't have to tell you what it was for.'

They'd had tea in a café round the corner from the hostel where she'd spent the night, which was full of workmen having breakfast and indulging in cheerfully crude banter with its slovenly proprietress. 'Not really the type of person I'm used to associating with,' murmured Mr Davies, as they took the last available table. 'Or yourself, I should imagine.'

'You've been very kind,' said Diana, when she'd drunk her tea, 'but really, I mustn't take up any more of your time.'

Mr Davies looked flustered. 'Where are you going?'

'Well, the police. I–'

'Police?' he said, sharply.

'About James. I was hoping they could tell me where–'

'Oh, there's no need to do that yet. They won't be able to find out anything about your husband until all the tests have been done.'

'What tests?'

'Well,' he said, professorially, 'when somebody dies, and it's not expected, they have to do all sorts of tests . . . on the body, you see.'

'But he was hit by a car. That's what killed him.'

'All the same, they have to take extra care. Medical negligence, you know – very serious. They're not allowed to give out information to anyone until it's all been done.'

'Not even to the next of kin?'

Mr Davies shook his head. 'Those are the rules. It's very strict. When I was in the police—'

'Police? You said you were a doctor.'

'Oh, no . . .' Mr Davies chuckled. 'This was later, during the war. We did a lot of that sort of thing with bodies that were found. It was always very thorough.' He gazed into the middle distance for a moment, caught up in some memory of his own, then said, 'So there's no hurry. Why don't you have something to eat?'

With no breakfast and very little to eat on the previous day, Diana's stomach had been rumbling ever since they'd entered the place, and, after only a token demurral, she agreed. While she ate, Mr Davies told her stories about his time in the police, about criminals he'd caught and people he'd followed – even, apparently, in his free time – and the commendations he'd been given on two occasions. She was conscious, as he spoke, that there was a lack of focus about his conversation, its clarity and direction coming and going like a faulty wireless signal. Every so often, he would stop and look round the room as if searching for something. 'They wanted me to stay on,' he finished, 'but I couldn't because of my health. I was in a car accident myself, you know, before the war. That was why I had to stop training as a doctor. It was a pretty bad injury. Caused a lot of problems for me later on.'

'But you said you'd been struck off the medical register.'

'Yes,' he said, vaguely. 'Struck off . . . That's right.'

'So . . .' Diana gave it up and concentrated on her food. Why did it matter what this strange, creepy little man said? He'd bought her a meal, hadn't he? The least she could do in return was to listen politely until she could, reasonably and without giving offence, leave. She wasn't entirely sure that she believed all the business about the police not releasing any information to anyone before the post-mortem was completed – why shouldn't they be allowed to tell her where his body was, for heaven's sake? Anyway, she'd soon find out for herself whether it was true.

Now, he was pushing an item cut from a newspaper across the table. 'I was a witness in that case,' he said. 'For the prosecution. Three, four years ago. Perhaps you remember?' Diana read the headline: *BODIES ON HIS HANDS*.

'I don't think so,' said Diana. 'What happened?' She put out a hand to take the scrap of paper, but Mr Davies jerked it away from her in the manner of someone teasing a dog and tucked it back into his jacket pocket.

'It was all a long time ago,' he said. 'Mind you, it was quite a thing at the time. Yes . . .' He glanced round the café, repeating, 'quite a thing . . .' and then, with startling suddenness, reached out and took hold of her hand, so that she dropped her fork on the plate with a clatter.

Odd, Diana thought. He looks the type to have clammy hands, but his touch was warm and dry – not unpleasant, in fact, save for the fact that she didn't want him holding her hand in the first place. 'I've got other things,' he said in an urgent tone. 'Clothes and shoes. Jewellery . . . All a bit old-fashioned, I suppose, but good quality. You could have it. And you could come and stay with me. I'd have to lock the doors because I wouldn't want the coloureds upstairs to know I had a lady living with me . . . Dirty lot, always making a noise, and I'm afraid,' here, he lowered his whispery voice so that it became almost inaudible and Diana had to lean forward to hear him, 'there's the matter of sharing a lavatory. I've written to the council to try and get them out. Edna – my wife – was terrified of them. But you could come . . .'

'It's very kind of you,' said Diana, gently withdrawing her hand, 'but I couldn't possibly impose. I'll go back to the hostel.'

Mr Davies contemplated her, his head on one side, making the strange movement with his mouth that she'd noticed when she'd first seen him. He really is creepy, she thought, with an inward shudder. 'They won't miss you, you know.'

'Miss me? What do you mean?'

'If you don't go back. It won't matter.'

'I know that, but–'

'I'm going to Birmingham soon. You could come with me.'

'Really, I don't think . . . I mean . . .'

'We could live together.'

Diana stared at him, asking herself, with a sort of miserable wonder, why on earth she was having this ridiculous conversation. It was, she supposed, just another measure of how out of kilter her life had become.

'I've got a job. They're putting me in charge of a firm of long-distance lorry drivers.'

'I thought you were waiting for your cards.'

'Oh . . .' He gave her a tight smile. 'That's just a formality. They've been wanting me to work for them for a long time. With my sort of expertise, you know . . .'

'I'm sure you'll be wonderful,' said Diana. 'Now I really must–'

He caught her wrist as she began to stand up, making her sit back down with a bump. 'Where are you going? I told you, the police won't be able to help.'

'Yes, you said. Please let go of me.'

'Oh . . .' Mr Davies looked down at his hand as if it had taken on a life of its own, and removed it from Diana's arm.

'Thank you very much,' she said pleasantly, rising again. 'Now, I really must go.' In the last few minutes, something had seemed to click in her brain and she felt a new impetus: survival. A host of possibilities raced through her mind. If she pawned some of the clothes in her suitcase she'd be able to get enough money for another night at the hostel and a meal, and then she'd leave the case at Victoria Station and find a library so that she could read the papers and see if there was any more about James. That would help her when she went to the police, and she could have a look for a job at the same time. She'd find out the address of the assistance board or whatever it was called – the librarian was bound to know – and surely they'd be able to help her when she explained her situation.

'Why don't we meet again this evening?' said Mr Davies. 'We could have a meal. There's a nice place down there,' he waved a hand in the direction of the station. 'Much better than this.'

With no intention of showing up, Diana agreed in order to be able to leave without more fuss, and they fixed on eight o'clock at a café nearby.

Dismayed at the small amount given her by the dismissive pawnshop owner in exchange for her silk blouses and dressing gown, and exhausted after her poor night's sleep, Diana dropped off over the newspapers in the library. The surprisingly kindly librarian let her be – 'I thought you looked all in, dear' – and she awoke over an hour later, her face streaked with tears. The librarian had been very helpful about the assistance board, but when Diana got there she discovered that she could not be seen without an appointment, and the soonest she could speak to anyone was in two days' time.

Hungry once more, and realising that the pawnshop money would not, after all, cover a meal as well as the night's lodging, Diana resigned herself to another dose of Mr Davies's company. Although, she said to herself, if he thinks he's getting anything else out of me than a dining companion, he's got another think coming . . . And she could go to the police station first thing in the morning.

Chapter Sixty-Five

Monica stared at the flaking paint of the front door of number three. Tregarth Row was a narrow, poorly lit alley with slippery cobblestones and four or five meagre houses huddled abjectly together, as if for warmth.

It had taken all her courage to get this far. Now she had to steel herself to knock on the door. You have to do this, she told herself. You have no choice.

She turned and looked back towards the main road. No one must see her going in . . . Not that anyone would know who she was, but if they lived nearby, they would surely guess why she was there. And the longer she stood outside, the greater her risk of being seen.

Resolved, and closing her mind as best she could to all thoughts of what was going to happen to her, she raised her hand and rapped on the door.

For a moment, there was no sound. Perhaps Mrs Lisle wasn't there. Perhaps she'd moved away, or died . . . or been arrested. Perhaps the police were waiting and it was a trap and she, too, would be arrested, and Dad would–

Hearing footsteps – only one set – from within, Monica told herself not to be stupid. It was bound to be unpleasant, but then it would be over. It occurred to her then, as she listened to the bolts being slid back, that she had no idea of what the procedure was.

The door opened a fraction and a woman with a beetroot complexion surrounded by tight rolls of greasy hair stuck her head through the gap and eyed Monica suspiciously. 'Yes?'

'Are you Mrs Lisle?'

'Who wants to know?'

Taken aback by the woman's aggression, but determined to stand her ground, Monica said, 'I do.'

'Why's that, then?'

'I understand that you might be able to . . . help me.'

'Help you?'

'Yes. I'm in trouble. I've got some money, and—'

In a flash the door opened and before Monica could think or act, Mrs Lisle had bundled her inside and shut the door. Under the gas in the hallway, she could see that the woman's face wasn't beetroot-coloured at all, but a fairly normal sort of dull pink, and that her clothes and apron looked quite clean.

'Sorry, dear,' she said briskly, ushering Monica into a small back room which was empty but for a chair and a ratty-looking chaise longue with stuffing hanging out of the bottom, 'but I can't have you telling my business to all and sundry. Now then . . .' Her face softened. 'Been a silly girl, have you?'

'Yes,' said Monica. 'I'm afraid I have.'

'Well,' said Mrs Lisle, quite kindly, 'you're not the first and I daresay you won't be the last. Got the money, have you?'

Monica nodded.

'You sit down there, then,' said Mrs Lisle, pointing to the chaise longue. 'Take off your knickers and make yourself comfy. Don't you worry, I always have a good old boil up first so it's all clean.'

Left alone, Monica did as instructed. She lay down gingerly on the lumpy, saggy cushions and stared up at the ceiling wondering how many women and girls had done the same thing before her. She must find something to concentrate on while it was happening. Unlike the spotless linoleum on the floor – a good sign, she thought, like Mrs Lisle's clean apron – the ceiling offered any number of possibilities. There were the brown clouds of damp stains in various shapes, an area by the door that was leopard-flecked with mould spores, and a cluster of frilly-edged mushrooms in one of the corners. Monica chose a damp patch that looked like a dog's face, or a shadow puppet of one, anyway, with a long nose and pricked ears. It looked like a friendly dog, with its mouth slightly open as though it were panting and smiling at the same time. She could imagine that it was real, an ally, guarding her . . . Keep looking at it, she told herself. Whatever happens, no matter how much it hurts, just keep looking.

Chapter Sixty-Six

'You're in luck, Inspector,' said the desk sergeant at Victoria Station. 'He's just brought someone in. If you wouldn't mind waiting . . .'

After about five minutes, the desk sergeant reappeared, tailed by a middle-aged man who appeared to be the size and consistency of a barn door. 'Well, sir,' he said, when Stratton had explained the situation – although without mentioning his personal involvement – 'I don't rightly know where she might have gone. I know she didn't have any money to speak of, and she didn't seem quite right in herself, if you know what I mean . . . She was all-in last night, so I don't think she could have got very far, even with a bit of a sleep, although I don't suppose you get much in a hostel. I'd say your best bet might be one of the cafés round here. I could show you the likely ones. Do you want to stop for a cup of tea first? I hope you don't mind my saying, sir, but you look as if you could do with it.'

Understanding that Eliot's offer was made out of kindness, rather than the – perfectly understandable – desire to keep the weight off his feet for a few more minutes, Stratton declined, and the two of them went out into the night.

'There's Handy's Café, just down there next to the boot repairer. The New Scala Café's in the next street, and then there's Rossi's Café down by the scrap-metal yard and the Croxley Tea Room.' PC Eliot paused to grin, then added, 'That makes it sound a lot more respectable than it is, by the way.'

'Right you are,' said Stratton.

As they made their way towards Handy's, PC Eliot said, 'Your Mrs Carleton seemed a cut above the usual type we take off the street, sir. Quite a long way above, in fact. Nicely spoken, good clothes . . . Was it some sort of breakdown?'

'I'm not sure,' said Stratton, truthfully. 'I was given her name in connection with the disappearance of this young woman' – also true, as far as it went – 'but if she is in some sort of trouble, perhaps we can get in touch with her family.'

'I had the impression,' said Eliot, slowly, 'that she didn't have anyone. And she said she'd just read about her husband's death in the newspaper.'

'Well,' said Stratton, 'we'll get to the bottom of it somehow.' Distancing himself from the whole business by treating it as though it were an official inquiry made it easier somehow and, for the first time since he'd read Monica's note, he felt as if he had room in his mind to think. He certainly wouldn't get anywhere if he kept letting his feelings get in the way. If, he wondered, he hadn't kept thinking about Jenny and the baby, would he have come to a different conclusion about Davies? Preconceived ideas meant that you were looking for evidence to support your theory, which was exactly what he

– and everyone else – had done. However much he might want to excuse himself, that was what it came down to in the end.

There was only one person in Handy's Café, a grim-faced elderly woman who was scanning the flyblown menu in her hand as though it were a casualty list. When the proprietor, who looked scarcely more cheerful, shook his head at Stratton's description of Diana, they left. The New Scala and Rossi's were both closed for the night, but a glance through the steamed-up window of the Croxley Tea Room – festoons of dusty artificial ivy nailed across faded bamboo-patterned wallpaper – showed that it was packed.

'Do you see her, sir?' asked Eliot, at Stratton's elbow.

'Not sure . . .' There were three women with their backs to him, two of whom were wearing fur coats, but the condensation and fug of smoke made it hard to tell. 'Let's go in.'

As the two men entered, rows of docile, tired faces turned in their direction. At the sight of Eliot's uniform, the murmur of conversation ceased, and a dozen loaded forks and slices of bread seemed to hang in the air, arrested in their progress towards partially open mouths. Stratton's eye took in bright, lipstick-smeared gashes, yellow teeth, glimpses of liver-coloured tongues, and then, as if led by an invisible pointer, came to rest on a bald, domed pate in the very centre of the crowded room.

He stopped in his tracks, staring in disbelief. Everything seemed to have slowed down, so that the next few moments had an unreal, almost dreamlike quality. The owner of the pate, who was still staring down at the table, was slight, and wearing a tweed overcoat. His thumb and forefinger were curled around the handle of a cup of tea, the little finger stretched out in an exaggerated show of gentility as he began to lift it to his mouth. As he did so, he raised his head, and Stratton found himself looking straight into the eyes, blinking rapidly behind their pebble glasses, of Norman Backhouse.

Chapter Sixty-Seven

'Two birds with one stone you might say, sir.' PC Eliot looked jubilant. Stratton couldn't blame him. 'Extraordinary that none of them had recognised him when he's had his face all over the papers.'

'Well, he'd changed his clothes – the description we put out had him wearing a blue overcoat, so I suppose he must have swapped it somewhere along the way. And perhaps the people in the café hadn't read the papers.' Stratton knew, as he said the last bit, that it was ridiculous. It was far more likely that several of the patrons of the Croxley Tea Room – and wherever else Backhouse had been – had seen someone who looked vaguely familiar, but, not knowing why he was familiar, had dismissed it with no more thought. But it was, by a very long chalk, the strangest arrest that he'd ever made. Eliot's gasp of recognition, the loaded, expectant silence in the café as he spoke the words, the look on Backhouse's face – something, to Stratton's astonishment, that was almost like relief – then hearing Eliot say, 'Mrs Carleton?' and then a woman's voice, small and clear, like something dropped into a void: 'Inspector Stratton?'

When he'd turned and seen Diana sitting on the other side of the table, he'd thought for a second that he must be having a hallucination and had stood, blinking and open-mouthed, until a discreet cough from Eliot recalled him to his senses. Then, turning from Diana to Backhouse in confusion, seeing that they were together but unable to make any connection between them in his mind because it seemed so unlikely – so *wrong* – he'd stood silent and appalled, and it was left to Eliot to hustle Backhouse out of the place and onto the pavement. 'We'll need a statement,' he'd told Diana abruptly, hiding a welter of feeling behind his official self. 'So if you would accompany us . . .?'

The journey to West End Central had been extraordinary, too. In the car (PC Eliot had taken Diana in a separate vehicle) Backhouse had started rabbiting on about his health as though Stratton were a doctor or something – fibrositis and enteritis and hospital and a nervous breakdown caused by persecution from the coloured tenants at Paradise Street – and he'd listened, incredulous, his mind reeling. Clearly, Backhouse wanted – perhaps even expected – his sympathy, or at least his understanding. But what the hell had Diana, of all people, been doing with him?

'Where did you meet Mrs Carleton?' he asked, cutting across Backhouse's whispered, carefully enunciated confidences about his diarrhoea and how he'd left his medicine in his suitcase at the Rowton House at King's Cross.

Backhouse swallowed. 'In the park. Green Park. We were

just having a cup of tea together. I'm afraid, Inspector, that she wanted me to ...' He cleared his throat. 'Well, she was making suggestions. She wanted me to go away with her ...'

Sensing Stratton's outrage, Backhouse fell silent for a moment and then, as if unable to help himself, continued, 'Of course, I told her I wasn't interested in anything of that sort–'

'If I were you,' Stratton said, 'I'd keep my mouth shut until we get to the station. Otherwise ...' He jerked the wrist that was cuffed to Backhouse's. 'Understand?'

Backhouse pushed his lips into an 'o' and moistened them with the tip of his tongue. 'Yes,' he whispered. 'Yes, of course.'

Stratton stared fixedly ahead. There'd be hours of this to come – unctuous, self-serving hypocrisy – but he was buggered if he was going to listen to it now, especially if it involved lies about Diana. Just occupying the same space as the snivelling little sod was nauseating enough. Ballard must have left a message by now, he thought. Surely the girl Anne must know something ...

'There's something, Inspector, it's about my wife ...'

Stratton clenched his free fist. 'I've warned you, Backhouse. No more until you're at the station.'

'But I'd like you to know, Inspector.' Backhouse blinked at him. He seemed to know that there wasn't anything Stratton could do to him in the car, no matter how much he wanted to. Stratton saw the driver's shoulders stiffening, and every single sinew of his own body seemed to throb with the desire to throttle the man. 'She was suffering so much, and I couldn't bear to see it ... I didn't want to be separated from her,

Inspector. That's why I put her under the floorboards in the bedroom, to keep her with me . . . I wanted her to be near me, you see.'

He thinks he's showing me what a loving husband he was, thought Stratton, revolted. Wound now to breaking point, he snapped. 'If you're so keen to talk, *Norman*,' he said, 'tell me this. When did you fuck them? Was it before or after you murdered them? Prefer a cold fuck, do you, *Norman*? A tart without a pulse? Why don't you tell me about that?'

Chapter Sixty-Eight

The rest of the journey took place in silence. Backhouse having been removed to the cells at West End Central – 'I'll deal with him later,' Stratton had growled at the officer in charge, 'just get him out of my sight before I do something I'll regret' – the desk sergeant appeared with a message. 'From Sergeant Ballard, sir. Came in half an hour ago. We knew you were on your way, so . . . He said you'd know what it was about, sir.'

Informant unwilling but eventually persuaded to talk, Stratton read. *Following lead Camden Town. Have alerted station there. Will call back soonest.* That was something, at least, he thought. Firmly suppressing any speculation about what might be happening to Monica if Ballard – or the local constabulary – had failed to get there in time, he made arrangements for Backhouse's suitcase to be retrieved from the doss house in King's Cross and transferred to the police laboratory. There is nothing I can do for Monica, he told himself. Ballard was a good man – the best – and could be trusted to look after his daughter and handle things at the Camden Town station with discretion. All he could do was wait for news of Monica, and for Diana to arrive. Telling the desk sergeant to let him know immediately if Ballard telephoned again, he went to the office, which proved to be full of jubilant coppers waiting to slap him on the back. There was even a message of congratulation from DCI Lamb.

Excusing himself as soon as he decently could, he made for the lavatory which, thank God, was empty. Finding coherent thought impossible, he settled for pacing up and down in front of the row of basins, trying to blot out the hideous carousel of images – Monica, Backhouse, Davies, cupboards full of corpses, soil planted with bones and teeth, stains of decomposition on clothing and bedding, and the filthy deckchair with its canvas of knotted rope – that went round and round inside his head.

Diana, dishevelled and exhausted, was slumped over a cup of tea in the interview room. She was thinner, Stratton thought, as he sat down opposite her, and, under the harsh light of the single bare bulb, her expression seemed somehow harder and more vulnerable at the same time, the cheekbones sharply angular and the enormous eyes bruised with tiredness. 'PC Eliot explained everything to me,' she said, before he could speak. 'He said you probably saved my life.'

'I think that's putting it a bit strongly,' said Stratton, embarrassed. 'I'm sure,' he added, 'you wouldn't have placed yourself in that sort of danger.' As he spoke, he realised that he wasn't sure of any such thing – Diana had put herself in danger before, with Ventriss, hadn't she? And she'd seemed so helpless, so bloody *passive*, when he'd warned her about the man, unwilling or unable – perhaps both – to protect herself. Remembering his visit to her former landlady and his feeling of outrage at the woman's implication that Diana was some sort of whore, he thought, surely she couldn't have sunk so low? People did change, but not *that* much . . . Still, there was clearly a lot more to it than met the eye.

'Those women,' said Diana, as if she'd guessed what he was thinking, 'the ones he killed, they were prostitutes, weren't they?'

Unable to look at her, Stratton said, 'Most of them. One was his wife. That man,' he said, in a lighter tone, 'makes Claude Ventriss look like an angel of mercy.' He felt, rather than saw, Diana's head jerk back as though she'd been slapped in the face, and wished he hadn't spoken. It wasn't fair, and certainly not chivalrous, to remind her of what he knew. Ashamed, he busied himself patting his pockets for his cigarettes. When he raised his eyes to hers again she was sitting upright, and – despite the dereliction of hair and make-up – was once more recognisable as the well-bred, expensive product of deportment lessons and finishing school that he'd first met thirteen years earlier.

'PC Eliot said you wanted to see me,' she said coldly. 'Why was that?'

'It's about Monica,' said Stratton. Now that she was here, in front of him, the whole thing seemed absurd, but he felt that some sort of explanation, however lame, was in order. 'My daughter. I know you both worked at Ashwood – she mentioned you. She's in some trouble, and I thought you might know . . .'

Diana was shaking her head. 'I haven't seen Monica since I stopped working at the studio. Didn't . . .' She stopped, the veneer cracking. 'I mean . . . Oh, dear. I suppose PC Eliot must have told you what happened.'

'Yes. Your husband.' Stratton tried momentarily to think of something adequately comforting to say, failed, and settled for, 'I'm very sorry, Mrs Carleton. If there's anything–'

'Diana, please. We're a bit past Mrs Carleton now, aren't we? What's happened to Monica?'

'She's pregnant. The man's married, and she . . . well, she's run off and I'm worried she might have done something stupid. I had an idea she might have . . . well, she mentioned you on a number of occasions, and I thought–'

Two hard blotches of colour had appeared on Diana's pale cheeks. 'You thought that I might have helped her arrange a backstreet abortion without your knowledge? I can well imagine what you must think of me, Inspector Stratton, but I can assure you I have done nothing of the sort.'

'Please . . .' Stratton's face felt as though it were on fire. 'I'm very worried about her, and I just . . . I didn't know what to think. My sergeant's gone to see if he can find her – she seems to have gone to see someone in Camden Town – and I'd be there myself, but it seemed like a bit of a long shot and . . . Well, I'm sorry. I'll find someone to take your statement, and then you're free to–'

'No, please!' Diana cried out, and Stratton stared at her, disconcerted by the sudden change of tone. He felt a sudden bond with her – both wretched, both unhappy in their different ways, both uncertain of the future. 'Please,' she said, 'I'm the one who should be sorry, not you. It was a perfectly fair question, and I shouldn't have reared up like that. You must be out of your mind with worry. Why don't you stay here? Unless you've got other things to do, of course – but you could take my statement about that man, Mr . . .'

'Backhouse.'

'Backhouse? He told me his name was Davies.'

'Did he, indeed?' said Stratton, grimly.

'Yes. If I tell you about him, it might help to take your mind off things, at least until your sergeant's got—'

A rap on the door heralded the desk sergeant. 'Call for you, sir – Sergeant Ballard. Will you take it in the office?'

'Sorry I've been so long, sir, but it was like pulling teeth. That girl was—'

'What's happened?'

'Well, I managed to prise the information out of her eventually, and I told the Camden lot – they were at the place by the time I arrived and they'd talked to the woman. Turned out Monica had been there, but she'd changed her mind. The woman didn't know where she'd gone – said she went out of the room and by the time she came back Monica had disappeared. I persuaded them to let her off with a warning, but they'll be keeping an eye on her from now on. They've no idea it was a . . . a personal matter . . . so there's no need to worry on that score. Do you think Monica might have gone home, sir?'

'I'll telephone my sister-in-law – she lives down the road from us, so somebody can keep an eye out. Where are you?'

'Camden Town Police Station.'

'You'd better get along home, then. Rather a lot's been happening – we've got Backhouse.'

'That *is* good news, sir. How–'

'Tell you tomorrow. It was a fluke, really, but still . . .'

'Ted? We've been frantic, trying to get hold of you – she's here. Walked in about twenty minutes ago.'

'Thank God for that. Is she all right?'

'I don't know about that. She's exhausted, poor thing, but she's safe, and that's what matters.'

'Yes . . . My sergeant tracked down that Anne girl Madeleine mentioned, and found out where she was going. Where is she now?'

'I put her to bed on the couch and Madeleine's getting her some hot milk.'

'Can I talk to her?'

There was a moment's hesitation, and Stratton could hear the sigh of his sister-in-law's breath coming down the line. Then she said, 'I don't think that's a good idea, Ted. She's upset enough as it is.'

'I don't want to upset her, just to tell her . . .' Stratton ground to a halt, a lump the size of a boulder in his throat. There was a whole mountain of things that needed saying, and he had no idea where, or how, to start. There didn't even seem to be words for most of it. 'Give her my love,' he said, finally. 'Tell her to get some sleep, and I'll see her tomorrow evening. And tell her that everything's going to be all right, and I'm glad she's home.'

Stratton replaced the receiver and sat back in his chair, weak with relief. He wanted to be with Monica now, to hug her and make her laugh and see her roll her eyes and say, in exasperated fondness, 'Oh, *Da-ad!*' and feel the unspoken bond between them like a tug on a wire that encircled his heart. At that moment, he felt an actual pain in his chest, although whether it was from emotion, release of tension, or merely slight indigestion, he couldn't have said. He was going to be a grandfather. No good – that wasn't, yet, comprehensible. He'd have to wait a bit for it to sink in – but, right at the moment, all that mattered was that his precious daughter was out of harm's way. He sat, smiling foolishly into space, for several minutes, before the memory of Davies's words, *When I knew my daughter was dead I had nothing to live for*, snapped him out of it as if cold water had been hurled in his face.

As he made his way back to the interview room, it occurred to him that he hadn't said thank you to Ballard. No matter. Such things were better done face to face – and if that didn't merit standing the man a drink, he didn't know what did. And perhaps he could help Diana, too . . . Straightening his back and thrusting out his chest, he pushed open the door.

Chapter Sixty-Nine

'Forgive me.' Diana indicated the cigarette in her hand. 'I took one from your packet. I hope you don't mind.'

'Not at all. I'll join you.' Grinning, Stratton sat down and lit one for himself.

Seeing his expression, Diana said, 'Monica ... It's good news, is it? You've found her?'

'Not me, my sergeant. She's safe.'

'So she didn't ...'

'She changed her mind. She's back home – that is, she's at my sister-in-law's.'

'She told me about your poor wife. It must have been terrible for you.' Diana gazed at him, eyes luminous with sympathy, and shook her head. 'It's ... Well, one doesn't know what to say, really.'

'Yes ...' Stratton didn't know what to say, either – he never had and knew he never would. It was yet another thing for which no words were adequate. Not wishing to pursue it, he produced his notebook and pencil and said, 'Well, let's get on with your statement, shall we?'

For a moment, Diana looked bewildered by his change of tack, then said, 'Yes, yes, of course. But really, I don't know how much help I can be.'

'You've been a lot of help already,' said Stratton. 'I found Backhouse when I was looking for you. There has,' he added gently, 'been a nationwide hunt for him, you know.'

'I'm afraid I didn't. I haven't been reading the papers recently – at least, apart from the obituaries.'

'I understand. Look . . . *Diana* . . .' Her answering smile told him that using her Christian name was not only acceptable but desirable and, reassured, he continued, 'When we're finished, do you have anywhere to go? Eliot said you spent last night in a women's hostel at Victoria.'

'That's right.'

Stratton made a sympathetic grimace. 'Not very nice, I shouldn't have thought. There must be somebody you can stay with,' he said. 'Someone who can help. If you give me a name, I'm sure we can arrange—'

'I don't think I can face going back there,' said Diana in a small voice.

'I'm not surprised. So, who should we telephone?'

'It's difficult. Lally – Mrs Anderson – she's an old friend, but we've rather fallen out. My fault, of course – she and her husband have been very kind to me, and I'm afraid I've rather thrown it in their faces . . .'

Diana recounted the events of their night at Ciro's. When she reached the part about meeting Claude Ventriss, Stratton felt a jolt of sheer rage shoot through him. 'He spent the night at my flat,' she said, miserably. 'He'd gone when I woke up. He'd left me,' she added, in a hard, self-mocking voice, 'a five pound note but my landlady took it . . . Tell me, is that the going rate?'

Stratton stared at her, aghast. 'Diana . . . But your husband . . . I don't understand.'

'James and I had already parted company,' said Diana. 'Thank you for not saying "I told you so".'

'I'd never . . . I mean, it's not my business.'

'I suppose not. But whatever you're thinking about me, you're right.'

Stratton began to deny this, but she cut him off. 'I can see it in your face. I don't blame you.'

'We all make mistakes,' said Stratton helplessly. 'I do. Everyone does.'

'Well, it's fairly put the kibosh on my friendship with Lally.'

'I'm sure that's not the case,' said Stratton. 'Does she live nearby?'

'Albemarle Street. But I couldn't bear–'

'Why don't you let me speak to her? I'm sure she'll understand. I imagine that they will have read about your husband in the papers.'

Diana sighed. 'I suppose I've got nothing to lose . . .'

'Good. Now, let's have that statement, shall we?'

'Can I ask you something before we start?'

'Fire away.'

'It was something he said – Backhouse, I mean. When I told him I'd only found out from the papers about James, I said I was going to go to the police to find out what had happened to him – to his body – and he said they wouldn't tell me anything before they'd done medical tests on him.'

'That's nonsense. It was an accident, wasn't it?'

Diana stared at him, surprised. 'How do you know?'

'PC Eliot told me. He was quite worried about you.'

'Oh, I see . . . He was very kind to me, although he must have thought I was mad or something. And,' she added, ruefully, 'I suppose he was right to think that.' With a painful little laugh, she continued, 'I don't think I know who I am any more. Perhaps I never did know . . . Anyway–' Pulling herself together with a shake that seemed to Stratton to signal the end of the subject, she said, 'James was run over.'

'And you read this in yesterday's paper, did you?' Diana nodded. 'Do you know where it happened?'

'It didn't say. But the last time I saw him was in Brighton.'

'The seaside?' Stratton was surprised. 'Was he making a film there?'

'No. He hadn't had any work for a while. He . . . Well, he drank, you see. I didn't realise at first, but then it got worse – so bad that no one would employ him. We'd gone to Brighton because he thought, with a change of scene, that things might be better.'

'But they weren't?'

Diana shook her head. 'It was somewhere he'd been happy – he'd had holidays there as a child – but it didn't work. I told him I couldn't go on as we were, and he told me to leave him, to . . . to save myself, I suppose he meant. Then he said he loved me, and . . . well, that was it, really.'

'But he loved the bottle more,' said Stratton, as gently as he could.

'Yes,' said Diana sadly. 'That's what it boiled down to, in the end. It was like a disease,' she added, defensively. 'He couldn't help it.'

Stratton wasn't at all sure about this, but he didn't challenge it. Instead, he stood up and went to the door. 'I'll ask someone to find out where he is,' he said. 'Far from not telling you anything, the police will be trying to locate you. Backhouse – for obvious reasons – didn't want you going anywhere near us.'

The woman's a magnet for unsuitable men, Stratton thought, impatient with Diana for her recklessness and almost morbid inertia in the face of certain trouble, and impatient with himself for his attraction to her. Not that he was any more suitable than either Ventriss or Carleton, but he, at least, would neither treat her like a prostitute nor succumb to alcoholism. That's probably, he thought sourly, why she'd never even look at me. She wouldn't anyway, he told himself. *He* wasn't a glamorous spy or a film director, was he? But if she could not, or would not, fit into the life that society prescribed for her, then why not? That was the only way he'd ever stand a chance. And, even tired and unkempt, she was still the loveliest thing he'd ever seen ... But she'd made herself a victim, hadn't she? She was no different to poor, pathetic John Davies.

It struck him then, so forcefully that he stopped in the middle of the corridor, that whatever she might say, she still had her sense of herself, and her courage. Look at the way she'd stood up to him over Monica! She'd made him feel about an inch high. In any case, who was he to judge her? It wasn't her fault he'd stuck her up on a pedestal. She was just another poor devil of a human being doing her limited best – and she'd just lost her husband, for Christ's sake. He was being a bloody fool.

Jock Anderson's handshake was perfunctory. Stratton had spoken to him after taking Diana's statement and, while he didn't sound exactly enthusiastic, he'd agreed, after listening to a summary of events, to collect her from West End Central. Now, standing at the station door, he said, 'We read about Carleton's death. My wife has been trying to contact Mrs Carleton. We went to the place where she was living, but we were told she'd left.'

'She was wandering about,' said Stratton. 'She's still in a state of shock.'

Anderson nodded curtly. 'We'll manage.'

'I realise that,' said Stratton, curt in his turn. 'If there is anything I can do, I'd be more than happy—'

'That's very kind of you, but I can't imagine . . .' Anderson allowed the rest of the sentence to hang in the air, leaving Stratton with no doubt that he'd overstepped the mark. He watched as Anderson greeted Diana, who was sitting on a bench in the lobby, huddled inside her fur coat. He raised his hand in a valedictory gesture as they passed, intending to leave it at that, but Diana broke away from Anderson and, standing before him, held out her hand. 'Thank you,' she said, her voice cracking. 'I don't know what I'd have done . . . Edward . . . thank you so much.'

Surprised that she'd remembered his name, Stratton took a step back.

'Aren't you going to shake hands with me?' she asked.

'Yes. Yes, of course . . .'

Retaining his hand in both of hers, Diana said, 'Colonel Forbes-James . . . I don't know if you know, but he died.'

Confused, Stratton shook his head.

'He left me a letter. He said if I was ever in trouble, I should contact you. He said you would help me . . . that you are a good man.'

His throat seeming to have sealed itself up in astonishment, Stratton merely nodded, staring at her. The liquid eyes, soft pink lips and blonde hair appeared to float before him in a sort of nimbus. Catching his breath, he said, 'Diana . . . if there's anything I can do, anything at all, please . . . I'd be delighted . . .' He stopped, realising he must sound like a fool.

'Thank you, Edward.'

Releasing his hand, she turned away and went to Anderson, heels clicking across the stone floor. As she walked through the door and away down the steps, Stratton felt as though he were watching her pass through a veil and into another world.

Chapter Seventy

'She was choking. I tried to help her, but it wasn't any good. Her face was blue. I couldn't bear to see her like that . . . I had to tie a stocking round her neck and put her to sleep.'

As though Edna Backhouse were an animal, Stratton thought in disgust. He watched Backhouse flick a speck of dust from his lapel with a fastidious movement of his thumb and finger, and fought the urge to lunge across the table and swat his hand down. He could see, from the tight set of Ballard's jaw as he bent over his notebook, that he was experiencing something similar.

'You didn't think of calling an ambulance?'

'It was too late for that, Inspector. I could see that. She was convulsing – that's the medical term, of course . . . I saw the empty bottle afterwards. Phenobarbitone. The doctor had given them to me because I couldn't sleep from all the trouble with the coloureds upstairs, but I'd only taken two, so she must have had the rest. An overdose–'

'There were no drugs found in your wife's body, Mr Backhouse.'

'Well, she'd taken them. I acted out of mercy, Inspector.'

Pull the other one, thought Stratton, it's got bells on. 'And what did you do after that?' he asked.

'I left her in bed for . . .' Backhouse paused to consider. 'Two days, I think, or three, because I didn't know what to do. Such a shock.' Here, his eyes widened and his mouth trembled slightly.

What does he expect, thought Stratton. Sympathy? Narrowing his own eyes to show that none was forthcoming, he said, 'Go on.'

'It must have been then that I remembered the loose floorboards. I knew there was a space underneath so I took them up. I put her in a blanket and I tried to carry her over there, but she was too heavy, and with my fibrositis . . .' Backhouse paused, shaking his head and then ducking it as if remembering a trial bravely borne.

'Never mind your fibrositis,' said Stratton. 'Get on with it.'

'Well, in the end I had to half-carry and half-drag her, and I put her in there and covered her with some earth. I felt,' he added, sententiously, 'that it was the best way to lay her to rest.'

Stratton glanced at Ballard, and saw that the sergeant was looking as if he might be sick. If you're determined to keep playing it that way, Sunny Jim, he thought, let's just see how you explain the tarts, shall we?

'We have identified the three bodies found in the alcove at your former home as Iris Manning, Kathleen McKinnon and Mary Dwyer,' he said. 'Can you tell us about them?'

Backhouse frowned and took off his spectacles, rubbing his forehead and pinching the top of his nose, giving the impression of one valiantly trying to solve a problem that was not of his making. 'I'll help you if I can, Inspector,' he said. 'It's hard to keep it straight in my mind.'

'Let *me* help *you*,' said Stratton. 'You killed those women and you're going to tell us how you did it. So, the first one, Miss Manning?'

Backhouse repeated the head-rubbing, nose-pinching, you-know-I'm-trying-to-help-you act. 'If you say that they were in my flat,' he said, 'then I suppose I must have had something to do with it.' Resting his arms on the table, he frowned, thoughtfully. Then, seeing that this was making no impression on his stony-faced audience, he said, 'I believe . . . yes, that's it. I met her in a café by the station. She must have come up to me . . . I think she asked me for a cigarette and then started a conversation. She mentioned that she had nowhere to live. It was some story about a friend who'd let her down – I can't remember the details.' Backhouse ran his tongue over his lips. 'I'm not sure . . . I must have mentioned that I was thinking of moving, because she asked if she could see my flat. She wanted to come that evening and have a look – that was her suggestion. I said that would be all right . . .' Backhouse tailed off and his eyes darted furtively round the room as if seeking something.

'And then . . .?' prompted Stratton.

'Well, she came along. We had a cup of tea together . . . That's right. A little cup of tea.' He indicated the littleness of the tea with his hand, accompanying it with a small, tight smile. 'She said she'd like to take the flat. I said that was up to the landlord, he'd have to give his permission. She asked me if she could stay for a few days until it was sorted out. She indicated – said to me – that we could have sexual intercourse if I put in a good word for her, about the flat. Well . . .' Backhouse leant forward, an expression of theatrically outraged horror on his face. 'I told her that sort of thing didn't interest me. She got into quite a temper when she saw there was nothing doing and said I was accusing her of things, all sorts of stuff. I told her she was talking a lot of nonsense and asked her to leave, but she wouldn't. I got hold of her arm and tried to lead her out of the kitchen, but she started struggling and then . . . then . . .' Backhouse's voice had sunk to a whisper. After swallowing several times and fingering his collar, he continued, 'It seemed that she was on the floor at one point . . . I don't know – there was something . . . it's in the back of my mind. A picture, but I'm not sure . . . Perhaps it'll come back to me. If it does,' he added, ingratiatingly, 'I shall tell you straight away.'

'Iris Manning was six months pregnant,' said Stratton. 'Did you know that?'

Backhouse made the odd sucking movement with his mouth that Stratton remembered from before. 'That is unfortunate. *Most* regrettable.' It was obvious to Stratton that what was regrettable to Backhouse was the fact that Manning was unmarried, not that he'd murdered both her and her unborn child.

'Did you offer your services as an abortionist?'

Backhouse blinked at him, his mouth silently framing

words as if trying them out, then shook his head sadly and whispered, 'Oh, no . . . As I told you, Inspector, I don't know about that sort of thing.'

Stratton contented himself with raising his eyebrows in disbelief. 'We'll come back to that in due course,' he said. 'Tell us about Kathleen McKinnon.'

Backhouse looked puzzled. 'Kathleen McKinnon,' repeated Stratton, glancing down at his notebook. 'Five feet three inches in height, brown hair, brown eyes, full lips . . . Quite a looker – when she was alive, that is. Before she became the second body in your alcove. Didn't you know her name?'

'I don't think . . .' Backhouse shook his head. 'No. She didn't introduce herself.'

Give me strength, thought Stratton, closing his eyes momentarily. Anyone would think they were talking about a fucking garden party. 'That was her name,' he said. 'Kathleen McKinnon.'

'She came up to me in the street,' said Backhouse. 'I'd gone to get some fish and chips for my dog and cat . . .' He must have seen the look of puzzlement cross Stratton's face, because he said, 'A tabby cat. I was very fond of her.' Remembering the animal he'd seen in the garden the night they'd found Muriel and the baby, Stratton nodded for him to continue.

'I was on my way home when the woman – McKinnon, you said – came up and propositioned me. I could see,' he added, reprovingly, 'that she was drunk. I don't like that sort of thing.' He paused, looking from Stratton to Ballard as if expecting agreement that they didn't like that sort of thing, either.

'I was annoyed, Inspector. I'm well known in the area and I didn't want a scene. She wanted a pound for me to take her round the corner. I told her I wasn't interested, and she began threatening me.' The upright citizen act all over again, thought Stratton, wearily. 'She followed me home, shouting at the top of her voice, and the whole thing was most unpleasant. She forced her way into the house and started fighting. I remember she picked up a frying pan and tried to hit me with it, so I got hold of her . . . There was quite a struggle, and she kept shouting that she'd get the police down to me. I must have pushed her at some point, because there's an impression in my mind that she fell onto the deckchair. There was a piece of rope – I suppose it must have been on the chair, but I'm not sure . . . I'm finding this very difficult, Inspector.' He paused; this time, Stratton thought, in search of sympathy. He stared, trying to keep his face impassive, as Backhouse polished his glasses and fussed with his handkerchief. The precise fastidiousness of the man's movements enraged him.

'How did you kill her?'

Backhouse opened his mouth and put his hand up to his throat as if trying to force sound from it. 'I don't remember,' he whispered. 'I must have gone haywire. The next thing I remember she was lying on the chair with the rope round her neck. I must have put her in the alcove, because then I made a cup of tea for myself and fed the animals.'

'Did you gas the women before you killed them?'

'Gas?' Backhouse looked perplexed.

'Their blood samples contained carbon monoxide,' said Stratton. 'All three of them.'

'Well, if . . . Yes, I suppose I must have. It's not clear in my mind.'

'You're telling us you don't remember, are you?'

'Yes. I'm not sure. If it comes back to me . . .'

'Poor Mr Backhouse,' said Ballard, when they stopped for lunch. 'Just think, all those dirty women throwing themselves at him.'

'Most regrettable,' mimicked Stratton. 'And him so virtuous. Course, he couldn't say that about a respectable woman like his wife, so it had to be a mercy killing . . . but, do you know, I think he believes it.'

Ballard looked surprised. 'Really, sir?'

'Well . . .' Stratton picked up his sandwich, which was beginning to curl at the edges, inspected it closely, then, disheartened, returned it to the plate. 'In a way, I do. He wants to be on our side, doesn't he? Former police reservist, pillar of the local community and all that. That's how he sees himself. He doesn't want to remember how he gassed and strangled those women because he doesn't want to lose his self-respect. Oh, I don't know. I'm not a trick cyclist, but that's how it seems to me . . . It's the way he talks about it, as if it doesn't have anything to do with him . . . What was it, "an impression that she was in the deckchair", or something like that?'

'Yes.' Ballard consulted his notebook. 'And when he was talking about Manning he said, "It seemed that she was on the floor." As if he were watching it happen.'

'And he didn't admit to gassing them. Or ravishing them.'

'Hardly that, sir. I mean, if they were toms, they probably agreed to it. The sex bit, anyway.'

'That's true. We'll leave the gassing for later, once he's been remanded. I've got a fair idea his account of killing Dwyer is going to be more of the same – all her fault.'

'I wonder why he killed his wife,' said Ballard. 'I mean, if she knew about Muriel Davies, why wait so long? Unless she'd found out, somehow, and was threatening to tell us.'

'Or perhaps he just wanted her out of the way. I don't think she'd have come to us even if she had suspected. Too much under his thumb.'

'She can't have had much of a life, poor woman. Remember the neighbour? She made it sound as if watching *Andy Pandy* was the high spot of her week.'

'That neighbour told us she was scared of the black tenants, didn't she? Perhaps she'd got so fed up she told Backhouse she was going back up north to wherever it was – she'd already done it once, remember, before the war. Maybe he thought that if she was with her family she might start talking about what she suspected.'

'Or perhaps she'd taken to digging in the garden.'

'You know, I still don't understand about that bloody dog . . . God, you can just imagine it, can't you? Nice cosy scene, him feeding his pets with fish and chips and a dead tart still warm in the cupboard not three feet away.'

'I've been trying not to, sir.' Ballard pushed his plate from him. But for a single bite, his sandwich was untouched.

'Not hungry?'

Ballard shook his head, then shuddered. 'He makes me

feel sick. Have you noticed, sir, that when it's something he doesn't mind talking about his voice is quite normal, but when you ask him a question he doesn't want to answer he goes all whispery?'

'Yes . . .' Stratton considered this. 'You're right. So much for the old war wound. I suppose he must have done the same when he was in court, only we never cottoned onto it.'

'Can't remember, sir. I remember him bursting into tears though, straight after.'

'Relief, I suppose. He'd got away with it, hadn't he?'

'I was thinking about that, sir. About six months ago, I was down at Pentonville – one of those safe-breakers, I think it was – and one of the warders I spoke to had been in the cell with Davies when they told him the appeal had failed. They'd been playing cards, and this bloke said that he just stared at the governor for a minute and then sat down to get on with the game. Said he wondered afterwards if Davies understood what the governor was telling him. Made me wonder how much he'd understood at all. That's not to say,' he added hastily, 'that he didn't do it, of course, but—'

'But it's not very likely, is it? That'll depend on what Backhouse has to tell us. I thought I'd leave it till last. I'd say that when he learns how much we know, he might be more likely to confess. I get the impression that he's not going to tell us anything he doesn't have to – all that stuff about wanting to help but not being able to remember. He isn't stupid . . .'

The words 'unlike Davies' hovered, unspoken, in the air

between them, until Ballard said, 'Still fancies himself with the medical stuff, doesn't he, sir?'

'When it suits him. He's strangely unforthcoming on the matter of backstreet abortions . . . Look, changing the subject for a moment, I still haven't thanked you properly for what you did last night.'

'It's nothing, sir.' The tips of the sergeant's ears had gone faintly pink. 'I hope Monica's recovered.' Apart from a brief exchange that morning, when Stratton explained that Monica was safely home, they hadn't had time to discuss it. Lamb had insisted that Stratton spoke to the press, which he hated. There were policemen who'd speak to the newspapers at any opportunity, but he'd never been one of them. It was too much like showing off and in any case, journalists were better kept at arm's length. Besides which, they seemed to regard it as a foregone conclusion that Davies was innocent and had asked a lot of questions that he was in no position to answer. He'd hardly covered himself in glory, but Lamb was so relieved that Backhouse had been caught that Stratton reckoned he'd have forgiven him if he'd recited 'Humpty Dumpty'.

'She's fine,' said Stratton. 'I hope that . . .' he stalled, realising that he had no idea what former Policewoman Gaines's Christian name was, 'your wife–'

'Pauline, sir.'

'Pauline wasn't too put out.'

'She understood, sir. If it had been Katy . . .'

Seeking to display some degree of knowledge about – and therefore interest in – Ballard's family, Stratton said, 'Walking now, is she?'

Ballard grinned. 'Walking, talking, the lot. She's three, sir.'

'Yes, of course, she would be. I wasn't thinking.'

'Actually, we've got another on the way. Only a few months, now.'

'Congratulations. Another reason for me to buy you a drink when all this is over.'

As Stratton had suspected, it was more self-justification over Mary Dwyer – this time, her clothes had become caught around her neck in the struggle. After that, they got onto the two skeletons in the garden. Backhouse confirmed that the women had been killed sometime in forty-three or forty-four, while Edna was staying with her family in Sheffield. His account of the first, whom he remembered as being called Else Kircher or Kirchner, an Austrian – which explained the foreign fillings in the teeth – was markedly similar to his stories about the other prostitutes. The second – who turned out, as Ballard had suspected, to be May Drinkwater – obviously caused him more of a problem because, not being a whore, he couldn't claim that she'd thrown herself at him. Instead, he recounted a story about luring her to the house on the pretext of treating her catarrh and getting her to inhale a mixture of Friar's Balsam and gas.

'I may have had intercourse at that time, but I'm not sure,' he finished, frowning. 'Or it might have been the other one. I can't remember . . .'

How very convenient, thought Stratton. Hard on the heels of this came the thought that it was entirely possible that a man like Backhouse might *not* remember; at least, not clearly. His desires gratified, he'd dispose of the bodies and go on to the next ... It occurred to him then, that for all Backhouse's greater intelligence, he had just as little thought for the consequences of his actions as had Davies. 'Were there others during that period?' he asked.

'Others?' came the whisper.

'Other women you killed at that time?'

Backhouse looked momentarily thoughtful, then said, 'I don't think so. That is, I can't remember. If you say I did, then ...'

In other words, thought Stratton, produce the evidence. 'We found your souvenirs,' he said. 'A tobacco tin with four samples of pubic hair. Now, assuming you didn't go around asking *living* women to help you with your collection' – Backhouse looked outraged at this idea – 'then you must have taken them from *dead* women. Women you'd killed. A little something to remember them by, was it?' Stratton deliberately kept his tone conversational, as if asking a perfectly reasonable question. 'Those tender moments when you put a stocking round their necks *and strangled them and fucked them while you were doing it?*'

The eyes glittered for a moment behind the glasses, and then Backhouse put his head into his hands. His shoulders heaved, and a snorting noise told Stratton that he was crying. 'There's something,' he spluttered, 'but I can't get it. It's forming a picture and then my head hurts and it gets all jumbled up again. It doesn't get clear, but there's something ...'

'I'll say there is,' said Stratton, ignoring the tears. 'There's Muriel Davies.'

Backhouse sat up straight. Staring at Stratton, eyes wet and blurry behind the glasses, he seemed suddenly soft-bodied, as if, boneless, he'd assumed the shape of his chair.

'Muriel?'

'Yes,' snapped Stratton. 'Muriel. Muriel Davies. Don't tell me you've forgotten *her*. And for God's sake, speak up.'

Backhouse cleared his throat. 'There is something in my mind,' he said, hesitantly, 'about Mrs Davies, but I can't quite remember . . .'

Chapter Seventy-One

'If he tells us he can't remember once more,' said Stratton, 'I'm going to knock his block off.'

'I know what you mean, sir.' The report having arrived from the police lab, they'd adjourned, and were sitting in the office.

'The ones in the garden, fair enough,' said Stratton. 'It was a while ago. But he bloody well *does* remember about Muriel Davies. In fact, Mrs Carleton said that he was about to show her an old newspaper cutting about a court case he'd been involved in, but then he changed his mind. Was it with his clothes when he came in?'

'They're checking them now, sir. I'll find out.'

'He told her he'd been a witness. And he told her that his name was Davies, too.' Mentioning Diana, Stratton was aware of concentrating on negative things, like not turning red or spilling his tea.

'She was the one with him when you found him, wasn't she?' Ballard, who didn't seem to have noticed anything amiss, spoke in a neutral tone.

'That's right.' Stratton did not enlarge on this. His feelings were too confused to enunciate, and besides, as far as Diana was concerned, he didn't want to make himself feel even more of a fool than he did already. 'You know,' he said, partly to change the subject and partly because he was genuinely puzzled, 'I don't see how he could have gassed those women. May Drinkwater, fair enough – he said he'd got some sort of device, didn't he? Presumably he put it over her nose and she let him because she thought it was going to help with the catarrh. But with the others, how did he persuade them? If he'd just left the tap open, he'd have been overcome himself, wouldn't he?'

'Perhaps if he'd opened a window . . .'

'But then the gas would have been dispelled. And surely they'd have smelt a rat if he'd suddenly stuck his head out of the window – unless he'd made some excuse, I suppose. But it's a bit odd.'

'Perhaps he persuaded them as some sort of game. We found tubing in the flat, remember, sir?'

'Well, he certainly didn't tie them up – there weren't any marks.'

'Mary Dwyer had her wrists tied in front of her with a handkerchief – *that* could have been part of a game – and McKinnon must have been pretty drunk, judging by the lab reports, so perhaps she didn't realise what was happening to her.'

'And Iris Manning was pregnant,' concluded Stratton. 'Backhouse denied offering to help her get rid of the baby, but if he had, he might have said the gas was to knock her out while he did it. That makes sense.'

'He might have done that to Muriel Davies too, sir.'

'It's possible. We didn't find anything like that device he mentioned, but he could easily have thrown it away.'

Stratton pondered this for a moment before Ballard spoke again. 'Last night, sir, when you telephoned, you said you were going to follow someone up . . . Did you find them, sir?' The sergeant's gaze was so penetrating that, for a horrible moment, Stratton thought the man must be clairvoyant and connected this to his earlier comments about Diana's statement.

'No,' he said. 'I had an idea they'd be somewhere near Victoria, but . . .' He shrugged, hoping it looked realistically off-hand. 'Anyway, turns out it didn't matter.'

Ballard looked at him carefully, a bit too much like a man who realised he'd been warned off for Stratton's liking, but all he said was, 'True enough, sir,' then bent his head to the pile of paper in front of him. 'There's a whole list of stuff from the suitcase we fetched from the Rowton House at King's Cross, sir. Ration books – his wife's as well – identity card, ticket for the doss house, seven nights' accommodation . . . That's interesting. When Canning went to fetch the case they told him that he'd only stayed for one.'

'Probably wandering about trying to pick up women,' said Stratton. 'What else?'

'Rent book for Paradise Street, marriage certificate, three pawn tickets, St John's Ambulance badge, two first-aid certificates, gloves, scarf, handkerchief – all the usual men's clothes, and there's women's stuff here, too. Nightdress, petticoat, necklace, lipstick . . .

'Mrs Carleton said he'd offered her some clothes. Said they'd belonged to his wife.'

'Charming. There's a whole list of medicines, too.'

'There would be.'

Ballard leafed through the pages. 'Lab report's right at the end, sir. Blimey . . .'

'What is it?'

'"I have examined package no. 4,' read Ballard 'and found on the trousers an area of seminal staining containing spermatozoa on the inside of the right fly opening near the bottom . . . spot of seminal staining on the lining of the left pocket . . . On the front flap of the shirt there are extensive areas of staining, semen containing spermatozoa was identified . . . On the vest there was an area of old staining with semen, the other vest shows comparatively extensive areas of staining . . . On another pair of trousers . . . On the plimsolls there were found some spots and smears of seminal staining . . ."'

'All right,' said Stratton, utterly revolted. 'I've got the picture. Is there anything else?'

'"Awaiting the clothes worn by Backhouse on arrest . . ."'

'They'll probably be covered in wank-stains as well.'

'. . . and the comparisons with the samples found in the women show that it's possible they could be from the same source.'

'Anything on the pubic hair?'

'It's a bit inconclusive, sir. It says here, "It should be pointed out that while it is possible to say that two samples of hair are dissimilar, it is not possible to say that a sample of normal hair must have come from the same source, since the range of structural and colour variations of human hair is limited and there are millions of people having hair within this range of variation.'"

Stratton sighed. 'Tell us something we don't know. Any similarities, then?'

Ballard frowned. 'It says that one of them might be from Mrs Backhouse, but there are no matches with the women in the alcove. So, if two of the samples turn out to be from the women in the garden – assuming the stuff they picked out of the earth isn't too far gone to test – that still leaves one unaccounted for . . .'

'Muriel Davies.'

'That's what I was thinking, sir. Are we going after an exhumation order?'

'Let's see what Backhouse says about her first. Then I'll talk to Lamb.'

When they returned to the interview room, Backhouse had straightened up, and looked at them with something like defiance on his face. Stratton knew immediately that they'd missed their chance.

'Muriel Davies,' he said, firmly. 'Tell me.'

There were no ticks of the mouth now, no fussing with his glasses, no blinking. Backhouse looked him squarely in the eye and said, in a clear voice, 'If you can prove it, Inspector, I'll admit it.'

Chapter Seventy-Two

Two days later, shivering in the chilly dawn air amongst Kensal Rise cemetery's thickets of marble and stone, surrounded on all sides by crosses and angels sprouting at awkward angles from the earth, Stratton and Ballard stood beside McNally and another, older, pathologist, Dr Tindall – who was to perform the second post-mortem – and watched the men digging.

It was five a.m., but despite the closed cemetery gates and the barricades and constables outside, there were dozens of reporters and photographers with stepladders lining the road. At least – apart from the odd curious early riser – the public weren't there, thought Stratton, wondering, not for the first time, why on earth people came to gawp at this sort of thing. The idea of being part of something, perhaps, in the sense of bearing witness, or hoping, misguidedly, for a glimpse of the killer – although they must, having followed the case in the papers, already know what he looked like.

Stratton saw that the newest graves were blanketed with bunches of flowers. The older ones had only a single bunch, wilting and apologetic, and the oldest of all had ivy and ragged grass. There hadn't been anything in front of the plain stone slab that marked Muriel and Judy's grave, now removed: too painful, perhaps, for the family to visit. Or maybe, like him, they didn't see the point. He'd never visited the plot where Jenny's ashes were scattered and nor, as far as he knew, had Monica or Pete. It was just a place: Jenny wasn't there.

The coffin being raised, the earth was brushed away to reveal the brass plaque. The original undertaker, McLeavy, stepped forward and nodded. 'That's the one.' The dark boards – elm, Stratton guessed – looked in good condition, with the lid only slightly warped. 'We'll need to raise the lid a little,' said Tindall. 'For the release of gases.'

The diggers unscrewed the lid and pushed it to one side. There was no smell, at least not from where he was standing, and Stratton could see nothing but darkness within. There was a short, solemn pause, as though an invisible vicar had requested a silent commemoration, and then Tindall nodded, satisfied. The lid was screwed back into place, the coffin lifted up, and the cortège, led with sombre authority by McLeavy, moved off in a hail of clicking camera shutters to the waiting van.

At the mortuary Higgs removed the coffin lid, revealing stalactites of white mould hanging down from the inside. The same white mould covered the shroud, through which the outlines of the two bodies – Muriel and the baby, Judy, who lay on her stomach – were clearly visible. Stratton, who'd placed his handkerchief over his nose in readiness, was surprised at how little they added to the usual mortuary smell of decay and disinfectant. Nevertheless, he was aware of a heaviness in the air, as though a thick cloth had been pulled around him, close and stifling. He stared down at the runnels in the concrete floor until a sudden, vivid memory of the country abattoir where his father had occasionally taken him as a boy when they were delivering stock, with its sluiced tides of blood and offal, jabbed him, making him blink and jerk his head up again.

He withdrew a little as Higgs and the other assistants began to remove the bodies from the coffin. Ballard, who'd done likewise, murmured, 'Are you all right, sir?'

'Not really,' muttered Stratton, grimly. 'It was bad enough the first time. But I'll manage.'

'Of course, sir.' From this simple exchange Stratton knew that the sergeant was remembering it, too – the horror of seeing the baby's little clothes taken off, one by one, and the toy duck, just like the one he'd said his daughter had to have in her cot or she couldn't sleep, and then sitting up late in the office afterwards, when he'd told the sergeant about Jenny being pregnant when she died and how determined they'd been to see Davies swing . . . He shuffled further away, towards the door.

Ballard followed. 'Do you suppose he ever thinks of them, sir?' he asked quietly. 'Backhouse, I mean.'

Stratton shook his head. 'Or about Davies, either. I'd like to think they all bloody haunt him, but I doubt it – I mean, you'd need to have a conscience, wouldn't you? Christ, I hope this works.'

Hearing Tindall's voice, 'Very well preserved,' they turned back to see him bending over the dun-coloured shape on the slab. 'A sample of the outer shroud, if you would, Mr Higgs . . . thank you.' They kept their distance, and Stratton glanced into the coffin, now empty save a bed of sawdust, stained brown, then watched as Tindall, bald head shining waxily beneath the electric bulb, lifted Judy, who was clad in her own separate shroud, away from her mother. The little bundle lay in his arms as he held her secure against his white rubber apron, carrying her across the room and gently laying her down.

The shroud being now removed from Muriel, Stratton could see that her face was, incredibly, almost recognisable. He nodded when Tindall looked to him for confirmation, then focused his attention on the rough line of McNally's sutures down the stomach that disappeared into the dark mound of pubic hair. The organs detached from Muriel the first time would have been crammed back inside her, he knew, like so many parcels in a bag of skin and bones . . . These were things one shouldn't have to think about, never mind *see*. She – *it* – is here because of me, he thought. I must watch, and I must not be sick. It occurred to him then that Jenny would have looked like this now, had she been buried and not cremated. The doctors of death had performed a post-mortem on her, laying claim to her flesh by cutting, removing, replacing and stitching, with others standing by, watching while she lay there, wounded, naked and forlorn . . .

At the time she'd died, he hadn't thought about those things. The heavy pall of grief had dulled him, blunting his mind, so that the post-mortem had been simply another fact, a stage in the process, not something actively imagined.

Swallowing hard, he felt Ballard's hand, gentle, on his arm. 'Sir?'

'I'm all right,' he said through clenched teeth, and moved away, keeping his eyes fixed on the corpse.

Muriel's skin was a dirty white, but there were two areas of pink on her thighs where the child had lain. 'Cherry pink,' said Tindall. 'We'll need specimens for carbon-monoxide analysis. McNally, if you would . . .'

'Of course,' said McNally, adding defensively, 'It would have been evident the first time. I'd say that patch of colouring's more likely to be post-mortem pink, but by all means . . .'

'Best be on the safe side,' said Tindall, a slight edge to his voice.

'Is it likely to show up now?' asked Stratton, mildly.

'Pretty unlikely, I'd say,' said McNally.

'Must do the thing properly,' said Tindall, in a manner which suggested it might not have been done properly before. Privately, Stratton doubted this – McNally was experienced and, from what he'd seen, painstaking and careful about his work. Besides which, even his untrained eye could see that the pink colour was slowly beginning to fade. 'Let's have a look at the pubic hair, shall we?' continued Tindall, briskly. 'Doesn't look like anything's been cut. We'll need a sample of that, too, for the lab, so if you would . . . Now, let's begin, shall we?' He held out a gloved hand. 'Scalpel, please, Mr Higgs.'

Chapter Seventy-Three

Stratton sat in the office, trying to ignore the thump and ping of a dozen typewriters from across the corridor. He was looking through the list of samples sent to the police laboratory – *Jar labelled 15, both lungs of woman, Jar labelled 16, vagina and labia of woman, Jar labelled 17, sample of sawdust from coffin* – and trying to get his thoughts into some sort of order, when a telephone call came through from Dr Sutherland at Pentonville Prison where Backhouse, like Davies before him, had been remanded in custody.

'I've interviewed him twice,' said Sutherland. 'He was physically exhausted when he arrived, and underweight. He was complaining of fibrositis in his back and shoulder, but it proved pretty mild on examination . . . I've taken a medical history, and barring the incidents during the war, which I believe you know about – loss of voice and so on – he seems to have spent his life taking refuge in minor ailments, fibrositis, diarrhoea, sleep disturbance and so forth. Quite the hypochondriac, in fact, always in and out of the doctor's surgery.'

'Yes, the first thing he did when I arrested him was to tell me about his health,' said Stratton.

'Well, I can certainly give you some more information, if that would help. I believe you're going to interview him again, about Muriel Davies.'

'That's right . . .' With the receiver wedged uncomfortably between his chin and his ear, Stratton flicked through his old notes to find the details of their conversation about Davies. Coming to something heavily underlined, he said, 'When we spoke about Davies, you were under the impression that he was telling the truth about killing his wife and child. Is that still your opinion?'

There was silence – no radiating of quiet strength or square-jawed film-actor stuff this time, thought Stratton – just the hesitation of a confused human being.

'It *was* my opinion, yes . . .'

'And now?' persisted Stratton.

'It's difficult to say. I've been looking at my notes, and I certainly was confident of it at the time. Backhouse hasn't said or indicated to me that he killed Mrs Davies. The only time he spoke of it was when I was taking his medical history and he told me he'd given evidence at Davies's trial and he'd been very much upset by it. Treated for chronic diarrhoea and insomnia afterwards, according to my notes. He was distressed that Davies had said he was an abortionist. Said Davies had mistaken his St John's Ambulance first-aid manuals for medical textbooks and jumped to the wrong conclusion. I have to say that did give me pause – judging from what I wrote down at the time, I wouldn't have said that Davies possessed the mental agility to make such a leap. He was a liar, certainly, and imaginative, but it was more in the realm of storytelling than putting two and two together to make five, if you see what I mean.'

'I think so,' said Stratton. 'What did Backhouse say about the other women?'

'Told me the wife was a mercy killing, and he showed some signs of emotion while talking about her, but I had the impression that it was more to impress me than from genuine feeling. He was very anxious to tell me how happy they'd been together. As far as the others were concerned, he tried to tell me that the women had died accidentally and then he said . . . wait a minute . . . Ah, here we are: "I must have done them, the police said I did." Distancing himself . . . Yes, again, "If I did it, I must have dismissed it from my mind afterwards."'

'Very convenient,' said Stratton, drily.

'In my experience, it's not uncommon in people accused of murder. There's also the lack of remorse – but then one can hardly regret things that one can't remember . . . That's a protective mechanism of the mind, of course. He's not going to remember something that might incriminate him. When I asked him about the evidence of the semen in the women he said, "It must have happened at the time of strangulation." I asked him if he meant he'd had sexual intercourse with them, and he said he thought it *had* happened but he wasn't clear about it. He didn't say anything about gassing them. When I asked him he said he didn't remember anything like that.'

'Well, it's a bit more than I got, I suppose . . . Do you have any idea *why* he did any of it?'

'It's always hard to say when these abnormal impulses begin. There doesn't seem to be any history of sadism – torturing animals and so forth, and—'

'Talking of animals, did he mention any pets?'

'Yes, a dog and a cat. Seemed very fond of them . . . Wait a minute – the cat died a few years back and the dog was getting very old and blind so he took it to the vet and had it put to sleep before he left his flat. Got quite emotional telling me about it. Anyway, as far as his sexual history is concerned, nothing much seems to have happened – at least, not out of the ordinary – until an incident when he was sixteen or seventeen. He used to go to a local place – that was in Halifax – he described as being "frequented by girls of loose morals" – what one might call a "Lovers' Lane", I suppose, judging from what he said. There was an occasion when he was there with a couple of male friends and was unable to have intercourse with one of these girls. He was teased about it afterwards – by the boys as well as the girls, apparently. They called him "Norman No-Dick".'

'And you think that might . . .?'

'It's possible. Hatred of women, and so on. Of course, thousands of men might have had an experience like that in boyhood, but it wouldn't affect their subsequent behaviour in such a way. He was very damning about anything to do with sex – masturbation, prostitutes, et cetera. Tendency to moralise . . . Oh, yes, and there was an incident around the same time where a local girl became pregnant out of wedlock and he told me she'd thought a lot of herself before but ... here we are: "That took her down a peg or two, she couldn't hold her head up after that, with everybody talking ..." He seemed to take a good deal of pleasure in remembering that. And he said his sisters – four of them, and one brother – were always bossing him about and he didn't like it ... Afraid of his father, told me he had a violent temper, very critical, bullied him ... He said he'd had recourse to prostitutes while he was in the forces ... difficulty with intercourse during the first two or three years of marriage. Said they'd stopped having sexual relations by mutual consent about two and a half to three years ago–'

'Around the time of Davies's trial.'

'Yes, I suppose that would be right. Both disappointed in not having children. He's physically quite normal in terms of his development. He spoke about all this quite freely – unlike his discussion of the murders. However, I ought to point out that what he says seems to depend on who he's talking to. I was told this morning that he's been quite happy to talk about the case with the other prisoners. In fact, one of the warders overheard him boasting that he'd ... where is it? Oh, yes, that he'd "done twelve of them". Those are his words, of course.'

'Twelve?' echoed Stratton.

'I shouldn't read too much into that. Probably just an attempt to impress. He's very conscious of his status – how other people view him. The other possibility, of course, is that he's beginning to form the idea of a defence of insanity. So, the more the merrier, as they say – or madder, in this case. If that's what he's doing, it's possible that he may confess to the murder of Muriel Davies in order to bolster it, although none of the staff or – so far as I'm aware – the other prisoners, have heard him mention her or the baby.'

'So you *don't* think he killed them?' asked Stratton, rumpling his hair in frustration.

'As I said, it's hard to tell. The confession – if he makes one – may be entirely genuine.'

Stratton sighed. He knew it wasn't worth asking for anything more definite, because he wasn't going to get it. 'Do you think he's insane?'

'No, I don't. The psychologist appointed by the defence may, of course, have other ideas, but in my opinion he's sane. Highly abnormal, certainly, but not suffering from mental disease.'

'I suppose that's something to be grateful for,' Stratton told Ballard at the end of the day, when they were comparing notes.

'Yes, sir . . .' Glancing at his wristwatch, the sergeant added, 'If you don't mind my saying, you look as though you could do with a drink.'

'I don't mind at all,' said Stratton, gratefully. 'But I'm buying. Come on.'

By unspoken consent, they headed for the Three Crowns, known to be favoured by policemen and therefore not too popular with villains, and found a quiet corner.

'We ought to get results with that lot,' said Ballard, once they were settled with their pints. 'All those samples . . .'

'Ballard?'

'Sir?'

'Would you mind if we talked about something else?'

'Of course, sir. Anything in particular?'

Stratton shook his head. 'Just anything that isn't *this*.'

'There's always football, sir. *We*,' Ballard grinned, 'are doing rather well at the moment.'

Stratton pulled a face. 'Perhaps not such a good choice of subject.' Ballard had a lot more reason to be cheerful than Stratton, whose team, Tottenham Hotspur, had not been enjoying nearly so much success. 'Why do you support Arsenal, anyway?' he asked. 'You live in Putney.'

'I grew up near there – the Holloway Road, up towards Archway. My dad used to take me to matches when I was a nipper. Haven't been for a while, though,' he said wistfully. 'Being so far away doesn't help.'

'I had an idea you came from south of the river.'

'Heavens, no. That's the missus. I'd have preferred to stay north – doesn't feel like proper London, somehow, being across the river – but Pauline likes it, being close to her family. My father-in-law's a Chelsea supporter, always giving me stick ... What about you, sir? You grew up in Devon.'

Stratton, detecting a faint undertone of accusation – the suspicion that he might have done the unthinkable and turned his back on a boyhood, and therefore formative, allegiance – said hastily, 'I wasn't really interested as a kid. The local team wasn't up to much, and I didn't play beyond the odd kick around. Other things to do in the country, I suppose, and my dad had us all helping on the farm as soon as we could walk.

When I was courting Jenny her dad invited me along to White Hart Lane – I think it was his way of showing his approval – and I enjoyed it, so,' he shrugged, 'I carried on going.'

Going home afterwards on the bus, aware of the three pints he'd drunk but not unpleasantly so (he'd emptied his bladder before leaving the Three Crowns), Stratton thought what a relief it was to talk about something normal. Ordinarily, he avoided the hearty confidences of pub intimacy, but this was different. He'd never given any thought to Ballard's domestic set-up – any more, he supposed, than Ballard thought about his. It was nice to have a small glimpse of the other side of the sergeant's life, he thought. It made him think of when his own children were small, before the war. Kicking a ball in the garden with Pete, Monica proudly showing him her drawings and the doll's clothes she'd made out of scraps, great big loopy stitches . . . Now that the sheer relief of knowing she was safe had worn off a bit, he wondered how they were going to manage when the baby came. She'd have to stop work, of course, as soon as the pregnancy started to show. What was she going to tell them at the studio? The truth was bound to cause all sorts of speculation, and he doubted if the girl Anne could be relied on to keep her mouth shut for long . . . He'd bet that in a place like Ashwood gossip about anyone, no matter how low down the pecking order, was valuable currency. And Raymond Benson, of course, was pretty high up the pecking order . . . What would he do if it came out? Deny it, probably, but whether he'd be believed or not was another matter.

He spent the rest of the journey with his mind tangled

in pointless hypotheses and suppositions, so that by the time he stepped off the bus in Tottenham High Road, the gentle glow cast by the chat and the pints had worn off completely, and the suffocating feeling of worry combined with failure had returned in spades. At least Monica will be home now, he thought. She'd spent the last couple of nights at Doris's, but she'd be back tonight and they could have a talk about the future.

Passing the hedge two doors down from his house, he was jerked out of his gloomy thoughts by a man's voice bellowing in anger. He couldn't make out the words, but somebody, somewhere, was having a hell of a row. He stopped and looked around but couldn't, immediately, pinpoint the source of the noise. The only thing that looked in any way unusual was a strange car, a Jowett Jupiter sports model by the look of it, parked beneath a street lamp on the other side of the road. Only three families in the street possessed vehicles – there was a Morris Minor, a Wolseley four-door saloon, and an elderly Baby Austin, none of them nearly as new or as smart as this one. Someone's wealthy relative, perhaps, come to visit? Stratton shrugged and carried on walking.

It was only when, seconds later, he got to his own front gate that a shrill scream, followed by a thud, removed in one horrible, visceral second any uncertainty about its origins.

Chapter Seventy-Four

'Monica!' Stratton jabbed the key into the lock and turned it, but the door would not open. He walloped it with the flat of his hand and it yielded, but only a small fraction, as though somebody, or bodies, were bracing themselves against the other side. 'Monica!'

Stepping back, Stratton dropped his shoulder and charged. There was a moment's resistance, and then the door flew open. Caught off balance, he toppled forward into the hall, catching himself painfully on the bottom of the banister.

'*Dad!*'

Pushing himself upright, he saw Monica cowering in the doorway of the kitchen, a livid red mark on one side of her face. Turning round, he saw a man scramble up from the floor of the corridor and make for the back door. 'Oh no you don't!' Stratton charged after him, grabbed him, and shoved him face-first against the wall.

Grunting in pain, the man made a single convulsive effort to break away from his grip and then stood, still and limp, where he was. Monica appeared at his side. 'Let go of him, Dad. Please. Don't hurt him.'

'I should have guessed,' spat Stratton, manhandling him round so that they were facing each other. '*Raymond Benson.*' He'd be handsome, all right – a real Romeo, in fact – if he wasn't about to shit himself. Grabbing him by the lapels and yanking him forwards, Stratton said, 'Well? What have you got to say for yourself? You've obviously hit my daughter – don't bother denying it. That mark didn't get there by itself. What else have you done to her, you bastard?'

'Dad.' Stratton turned his head to see Monica by the stairs, pale with fright. 'Please, you won't—'

'Don't worry,' he said grimly. 'I won't harm a hair on his pretty head, much as I'd like to. You go upstairs and bathe your face.' Turning back to Benson, he said, 'You and me are going to have a little chat.'

'Dad . . .'

This time Stratton didn't turn round. 'Upstairs, Monica. Now!'

When she'd gone, Stratton let go of Benson. 'Are you going to talk to me,' he asked in a low voice, 'or are you going to try and make a run for it again?'

'Talk,' spluttered Benson, looking as if his legs might give way at any minute.

'I thought so.' Stratton walked him into the sitting room and pointed to an armchair. 'Sit.'

Benson sat down with a bump, his eyes round with fright.

'Now,' said Stratton, standing directly in front of him. 'What's going on?'

'I wanted to see Monica. I was worried.' The rounded, silky tones were gone now, replaced by a reedy tenor.

'Like hell you were. You were shouting at her – I could hear you halfway up the street.'

'I'm afraid I . . .' Benson swallowed. 'I might have lost my temper a bit.'

'I see. You were worried about her and you lost your temper. And you hit her. What else did you do?'

'Nothing. I swear . . . I didn't touch her.'

'But you came to see if she'd got rid of your baby, didn't you?'

'Well . . .'

'Disappointed, were you? Tried to persuade her but she wouldn't listen? That's what the argument was about, wasn't it?'

Benson didn't answer, but his face said it all for him. Stratton could see the man's mind racing, the speech being prepared. 'I do appreciate your feelings,' he said at last. 'I also appreciate that I must take my share of the blame in this . . . this matter . . . I thought if I could speak to Monica, we might be able to work out a solution that—'

'—that meant you could waltz off to your next conquest and forget all about it!'

Benson swallowed, his Adam's apple bobbing convulsively. 'I really don't see what else I can do,' he said, helplessly. 'These things do happen—'

'Not in this house they don't.'

'And I do have my reputation to think of.'

'Shame you didn't think of it before you took your trousers

off,' said Stratton, acidly. 'My daughter's reputation doesn't matter, I suppose.'

'I didn't say that, Mr Stratton. All I meant was that, unlike myself, Monica is not the subject of public scrutiny.'

'I should have thought that public scrutiny, as you call it, was a very good reason to face up to the consequences of–'

Stratton was cut off by a scream from above. Whirling round, he dashed out of the room and up the stairs. On the half-landing he was stopped in his tracks by the sight of Monica standing at the top of the stairs outside the bathroom. In the weak light afforded by the bulb on the landing he saw that not only had she removed her stockings but that there was a thick, dark trickle of what could only be blood flowing down the inside of one leg towards her ankle. For a moment, he stared at her stupidly, not realising what it meant.

'Daddy, the baby . . . it's the *baby* . . .'

'Baby, yes . . . yes . . .' Mind racing, he looked wildly about him as if a solution might pop out of the walls.

'Help me . . .' Monica bent double, clutching her stomach.

'Look,' said Stratton, as calmly as he could. 'Just . . . Here . . .' He leapt up the last few stairs and put an arm round her, steering her into the bathroom and lowering her onto the toilet. 'Keep as still as you can . . . Use this.' Grabbing two towels from the rail, he pushed them into her lap.

'Daddy . . .' Monica stared at him, eyes wide and bewildered. 'The baby,' she repeated, as if he hadn't understood.

'I know. Just stay put. I'm going downstairs to telephone Aunt Doris – she'll know what to do.'

He closed the door and charged back down the stairs.

Benson was standing in the doorway of the sitting room. 'What's happened?'

'Monica – she's losing the baby.'

As he turned to pick up the telephone, Stratton caught, out of the corner of his eye, a flash of unmistakable relief cross Benson's features. Without thinking or even really knowing what he was doing, he pivoted on the balls of his feet – a move learnt in his boxing days, now unconsciously and perfectly replicated – and punched him: a single knockout blow to the jaw.

Chapter Seventy-Five

'No evidence of carbon monoxide,' said McNally. 'As I mentioned, I'm pretty sure I'd have picked it up the first time round if there had been.' The calmly professional tone didn't quite mask the pathologist's relief. Not that Stratton blamed him – the tension between him and Tindall had been obvious during the post-mortem, and it would definitely have been one-up to Tindall if any traces had been found.

Tucking the telephone beneath his chin, Stratton scribbled a note. 'Anything on the pubic hair?'

'Well . . . it's a bit complicated, this. One of the samples in the tin could have come from Mrs Davies, but not just prior to death.'

'I don't understand.'

'The problem is the ends of the hairs. Without going into too much technical detail, if the hairs in the tin *do* come from Muriel Davies, then they must have been cut at least six months before she died, and I don't suppose that the lady went around giving out samples of her pubic hair, so . . . I'm afraid it doesn't help much.'

Stratton grimaced. 'That would have gone a bloody long way to establishing that Backhouse killed her.'

'It does mean that there's at least one sample unaccounted for. I'm sorry it's not better news, Inspector. But surely it doesn't rule out Backhouse as Muriel Davies's killer? There were four samples in the tin and – assuming that he's responsible for everyone we found on the premises – he killed six, so that means he didn't always take souvenirs or you'd have found the other two samples as well.'

That's all I need, thought Stratton, replacing the receiver. For Christ's sake . . . Why couldn't anything – even pubic hair – be simple? His eyes felt prickly, as though they had sand in them, and he rubbed them with the heels of his hands, but it made no difference.

It had been a long night, made longer by the fact that, when it was over, he'd felt far too tense to sleep. Monica, now tucked up in bed after the ministrations of Doris and their doctor, had lost the baby. When questioned, she'd told them that, far from not touching her, Benson had slapped her so hard that she'd fallen across the back of a chair, and then he'd picked her up and punched her, this time in the stomach. The doctor, whose raised eyebrows had signalled disbelief at this story, changed his tune abruptly when, on examining Monica, he found the emerging bruises that confirmed it. Fortunately for Benson – and, probably, in retrospect, himself – the actor, who'd dropped like a sack of potatoes when Stratton punched him, had been brought round with a wet sponge and frog-marched, groggy and whimpering, out to his fancy car before the doctor arrived. Don, who had come round with Doris, had assisted in the process, and stood by while Stratton delivered his parting shot in a flat, menacing tone. 'Don't even think of making a complaint, chum. And if you ever come near my daughter again, I'll kill you.'

They'd left him muttering to himself and inspecting his face in the rear-view mirror, and five minutes later, hearing a car start, they'd pulled back the sitting-room curtains to see him driving slowly away.

'Let's hope you haven't damaged him for life,' said Don.

'Don't know how they'd tell,' Stratton had replied. 'Unless it was his face. Shame it won't be his balls.'

Don had produced some Scotch, and they'd sat on either side of the fireplace, drinking it while the doctor and Doris were upstairs with Monica. His brother-in-law, as always, had been a godsend, but the fact that it reminded him of sitting helpless, in the same place, while Jenny had given birth to both children upstairs, didn't help. At least, he thought, there were no yells of pain. About halfway through, Doris, emerging from the bedroom to boil water for some mysterious medical reason that neither man was inclined to question, had reported that although Monica had lost the baby the doctor thought there would be no lasting damage. When she'd gone, Stratton and Don had exchanged glances, and he'd known that his brother-in-law was thinking the same as he was; that, aside from the way it had come about, it was, in the long run – Monica's future health being assured – for the best . . .

They hadn't talked about it, just sat in silence for a while, and then Don had made a remark about something he'd seen in the newspaper to do with nuclear artillery testing in Nevada. Both men had fallen on it with gratitude and a relish that Stratton knew neither of them felt, but at least the topic was far enough away from the immediate circumstances to render it a subject for emotionally neutral conversation.

The doctor had given Monica a sedative, and she'd been fast asleep when he'd looked in on her after everyone had gone. As he'd stood in the doorway, watching her soft face and swirl of dark hair on the pillow, he'd experienced an uprush of love and anxiety so great that it took his breath away and it was all he could do not to weep. Not daring to disturb her, he'd contented himself with blowing her a kiss, and murmuring, 'Sleep tight,' before retreating, in a torrent of confused and confusing feelings, to his own bedroom.

When he looked up again, Ballard was at his shoulder. 'You all right, sir?'

'Fine.' Stratton didn't think he could bring himself to mention the events of the previous evening without hitting something and besides, it was no part of the sergeant's job to act as his nursemaid – he'd done quite enough of that already. Briskly, he told Ballard about the pathologist's findings, or lack of them, from Muriel Davies, and then the pair of them set off, in silence, for Pentonville.

Chapter Seventy-Six

'I believe I wanted to help Mrs Davies,' said Backhouse. Now washed, shaved and decked out in prison clothes, he looked a lot better than he had at the station, and – thank God – there was a lot less of the outraged-eye-and-indignant-nostril routine, too. Behind him, a warder stood impassively, like a statue, arms folded. 'It was after the business when he went off with that friend of Muriel's—'

'Do you mean Shirley Morgan?' asked Stratton.

'I think that was the name, yes. After that, Muriel told my wife that she was going to leave her husband. We talked about it and agreed that if the Davieses did separate, we'd see if we could adopt little Judy. My wife mentioned this to Muriel, but she said that Davies's mother would look after her, which we were quite sorry about, especially my wife, because she was very fond of the child, you see.'

Backhouse paused, looking very much the worthy and concerned citizen. Stratton indicated, with a curt nod in Ballard's direction, that it was all being taken down, and said, 'And then . . .?'

'Some time after that, Muriel came to me, very upset, and told me Davies had been knocking her about and she couldn't bear it any more. She said she was going to make an end of it.'

'Meaning?'

'I took it to mean,' Backhouse's voice was hushed – this time, thought Stratton, for effect – 'that she was planning to commit suicide.'

'Go on.'

'Well, it must have been shortly after that when I went upstairs and found her lying in front of the fireplace in their kitchen. She'd taken the quilt from the bed and was making an attempt to gas herself. When I saw her I knew I had to move quickly.' This was said as one modestly recounting a heroic act. 'I turned off the tap – she'd attached a piece of tubing to it, and the end was near her head – and opened the window.'

'Have you any idea how long the gas had been on?'

Backhouse shook his head. 'She'd done it before I got there. There was a lot of gas in the room – that's why I opened the window. She came round after that and I made her a cup of tea. She asked me not to tell anyone about it, and I said I wouldn't.'

'Was there anyone else in the house at the time?'

'Well, my wife was downstairs.'

'What about Davies?'

'He wasn't there.'

'The workmen?'

'I'm not sure . . . They weren't there when I went downstairs.

My head was thumping from the effect of the gas, you see, and I wanted some air. I didn't say anything to my wife about it. I was very worried about Muriel – it was playing on my mind – so I went upstairs again the following day to see if she was all right. As far as I remember, it was about lunchtime when I went up, after my wife had gone out ... Muriel told me she still intended to do away with herself. She begged me to help her – in fact, she said she would do anything if I would help her.' Backhouse gave a meaningful nod.

'What did you understand by that?' asked Stratton,

'That she ... she would let me be ... intimate with her. She brought the quilt in and put it down in front of the fireplace and lay on it. As far as I can remember, she was fully dressed ...' Backhouse tailed off, as if in a reverie, and when he spoke again his voice was almost inaudible. 'I got down on my knees then, but I wasn't capable of having intercourse because of the fibrositis in my back ... I couldn't do it. She begged me ...'

'Begged you for what?'

'To help her ... As far as I can make out, I must have turned on the gas tap and put the tubing close to her face. When she became unconscious I turned it off again. I was going to try to have intercourse with her then—'

'You weren't affected by the gas?'

Backhouse blinked, looking confused, then shook his head. 'The gas wasn't on for very long, not much over a minute.'

'Did you hit her? Punch her?'

Backhouse shook his head. 'No ... I'm sure there was nothing like that.'

'But she became unconscious in that time?'

'Yes, that's right . . . I couldn't have intercourse because I couldn't bend over her. I think that's when I strangled her.'

'What with?'

'A stocking, I think. I found one in the room. I'm not certain about it, but I think that's what I did. I left her where she was and went downstairs. I think my wife was there then, but I didn't say anything about it.'

More holes than a Dutch cheese, thought Stratton. Still, it was a confession, and probably as good as they were going to get. 'What happened after that?'

'Davies came home about six o'clock in the evening, I think. Anyway, I remember it was dark when I heard him come in. I went into the passage and told him what had happened – that his wife had committed suicide by gassing herself. He was very upset' – You don't say, thought Stratton – 'so I went upstairs with him. He picked her up and carried her into the bedroom and put her down on the bed.'

'Was the stocking still round her neck when he did that?'

'No . . . I think I took it off before I went downstairs. I must have thrown it into the fireplace – I think there was a fire in the grate.'

'A *fire*?' asked Stratton, incredulous. 'And you'd turned on the gas?'

'I'm not sure . . . The fire might have been the day before.'

'But there was even more gas then.'

'That's why I opened the window. I was worried about an explosion. Yes, it must have been the day before.'

Stratton raised his eyebrows. 'So Davies didn't know that his wife had been strangled.'

'No.'

'What happened then?'

'I made Davies a cup of tea to calm him down. I told him – I said it was likely – that he'd be suspected of having done it himself–'

'Gassed Muriel himself?'

'Yes, because of the rows and fights they'd been having. He agreed with me – he said he'd bring the van he'd been driving and take the body away somewhere. I went downstairs after that . . . I had the impression that he'd taken his wife in the van.'

'This was on the Tuesday, was it, the seventh of November?'

'I think it was.'

'And you didn't check to see if the body was still there?'

'No, I thought . . . I'm not sure what I thought. A few days later – the Friday, it must have been – he told us he was going to Bristol, and he left. He'd sold the furniture, and they came for that afterwards.'

'What about the baby?'

'I don't recollect seeing the baby again. I remember Davies saying to me that he'd fed her, but I can't remember when that was. Sometime that week, it must have been . . . Davies came back the following week, but he didn't stay long. That's when we had the conversation about the money – I told him he should be careful with it. We left the house together, because I was going to the doctor, and we got on the number seven bus. I remember, because I paid his fare . . . I got off at the doctor's and he stayed on because he was going to Paddington.'

'Why was that?'

'He told me he was going back to Wales.'

'Did you kill the baby?'

Backhouse's mouth twisted round to the side, and he closed his eyes for a moment before answering in a whisper. 'No.'

'Did you see the baby again after you killed Mrs Davies?'

'No. I didn't see her. I didn't know what happened to the body–'

'Whose body?'

'Muriel. Mrs Davies. I didn't know what happened until the police came and found them both in the washhouse.'

'Are you prepared to sign a statement saying all that?'

'Yes.'

Chapter Seventy-Seven

Monica lay quite still, eyes closed, for a long time. Although she still felt groggy and strange, she was definitely awake. The house was quiet. Perhaps Auntie Doris had gone . . . She'd definitely been there when the doctor came, holding her hand and wiping her face with a wet flannel.

Raymond had been *so* angry. When he'd arrived, she'd thought it was Dad and rushed to the door to find him on the step. When she'd told him how she hadn't gone through with the operation, he'd just exploded. He'd asked her why she hadn't come to him to fix something up, and when she'd tried to explain about Dad, and how it was Pete who'd told him and not her, he'd got even more furious. 'He threatened me!' he kept shouting. 'He dared to threaten me!'

She'd thought, for a moment, that he was going to kill her. She remembered, in a blur, him coming towards her, knowing what he was about to do but being too late to stop him, the blow and the fall, being unable to save or protect herself, her gestures as feeble as if they'd been made underwater. Then her relief when Dad had come home, and her fear that he would kill Raymond or hurt him badly, and get into trouble because of her; and then she'd gone upstairs and the pain had started. Like a cramp at first, doubling her up, and then the feeling that her insides were separating, that something was giving way, and seeing the blood . . .

She didn't remember much about the doctor's visit – hushed voices, probing hands, something soft being slid beneath her bottom, and Doris leaning over her, brushing the hair off her forehead . . .

She gazed up at her favourite damp patch that was the shape of a smile and thought about the dog's head on the ceiling of Mrs Lisle's back room. Lying and looking up at it, she'd thought that she would be attended to immediately, but as the minutes passed and she lay listening to footfalls from upstairs and Mrs Lisle still did not come, she began to experience an odd sensation. It was as if her mind or her spirit, or possibly both, had become divorced from her body so that she was looking down at herself from above. Quite coldly and dispassionately, she'd considered what might happen if she were to die as a result of Mrs Lisle's ministrations. Strangely, she'd found that she didn't mind much for herself. In fact, she'd reasoned that dying in such a manner would guarantee that her family never discovered what was – or had been – wrong with her. Then she'd thought of Dad. Dad who'd already lost Mum, and who didn't deserve to lose her as well, no matter how unsatisfactory a daughter she was.

It was this that impelled her, robot-like, to stand up, pull on her knickers, fasten her stockings, put on her coat, and leave. Moving like a sleepwalker, she'd gone down the passage, opened the door, and walked away into the night.

It occurred to her now that during all that time she hadn't thought once about the baby. But Raymond had seen to that himself, hadn't he? So things had turned out for the best after all. Even if the baby had managed not to inherit whatever it was that was wrong with her – being one of 'Nature's Mistakes' Anne had called it – it would still have been Raymond's child, and Raymond was . . .

Monica shook her head. She was too tired and confused for her emotions to be anything but a vague jumble. Grief, she certainly felt, like she had when Mum died, but for what she wasn't sure. The baby, she supposed. That must be it. The baby. But there was relief as well, and the absolute, certain knowledge that, whatever happened, she was never going to have anything to do with a man ever again.

Monica turned over and was about to drift back to sleep when out of the corner of her eye she saw a little card on her bedside table. Reaching out for it, she read, *Have a good rest. See you later. Love, Dad x*

He will forgive me, she thought. And Pete will never dare say another word after this . . . She was safe. Just as long as they never found out what she was really like, everything would be all right . . . And that was up to her – to make sure they didn't. Kissing the card, she propped it up against the lamp and then positioned her head on the pillow so that – assuming she didn't turn over in her sleep – it would be the first thing she'd see when she woke.

Chapter Seventy-Eight

'Doesn't sound very likely,' said McNally. 'The recovery Backhouse is alleging the first time Mrs Davies tried to gas herself doesn't sound possible, especially given that *he* was affected after so short a time . . .'

'The thumping head, you mean,' said Stratton.

'Yes. And as for the second time, the actual administration of the gas, he must have got quite near the outlet himself . . . And there's the business about the fire, well . . .' Stratton could imagine the pathologist, who was on the other end of the phone, shaking his head.

'I thought so.'

'I assume it's not germane, is it?'

'Not as far as the trial's concerned, no – DCI Lamb's just told us they've decided to proceed with the murder of Edna Backhouse.'

'Well, you shouldn't have any problems there.'

'That's true,' said Stratton. 'Thanks, anyway.'

*

'If he's so keen on "the more the merrier",' Stratton asked Ballard when he came into the office several minutes later, 'why hasn't he confessed to the baby?'

'Well, sir, whatever's going on in his mind, I don't think it's as straightforward as all that. He's justified all the others, hasn't he? The prostitutes were making the running, being aggressive and starting fights and so on, and Muriel and Mrs Backhouse and the woman from the factory were mercy killings.'

'Except that someone punched Muriel in the face.'

'That might have been Davies – I mean, if they'd quarrelled earlier on. But if it was Backhouse, he's not going to admit it because it won't fit his story. And how on earth could he justify strangling a *baby*?'

'Because it was in the way?' said Stratton. 'Making a noise and attracting attention?'

'Yes, but there's no way to say that without putting himself in a bad light.'

'People have killed babies for less. We've come across it a few times.'

'Parents,' said Ballard. 'End of their tether and whatnot. It's not the same – and anyway, it's no sort of defence.'

'No, you're right. It isn't. If he did, I don't believe that Edna Backhouse knew about it. And Davies had bought a teddy bear for the baby, hadn't he? He showed it to his aunt and uncle in Wales. We thought at the time he wasn't bright enough to do that to put them off the scent.'

'And the duck, sir. Remember? With the body . . . tucked into the clothes. I remember it because my Katy had one just like it.'

'You mean that it might have been her favourite toy and only a parent would have known that.'

'Yes, sir.'

'But perhaps it was just there – in the cot or wherever she was, and got caught up in the things when Backhouse bundled her up, if he was doing it quickly – but then again, he claimed not to know anything about how the bodies got into the washhouse.'

'That's true, sir. I suppose it was because it made an impression on me – it just made me wonder about it.'

Stratton leant forward, across the desk. 'But what do you actually *think*?'

Ballard looked genuinely helpless for a moment, then said, 'I honestly don't know, sir.'

'Me neither.' Stratton shook his head, remembering his son's scorn, his own pathetic attempts to justify himself, and Pete's voice, dripping with sarcasm: *As mistakes go, Dad, I'd say this one rather takes the biscuit* . . . If only Davies could be proved guilty, he thought, that would go some way to redeeming him in Pete's eyes – although nothing, he knew, could make up for Jenny's death. But wishing wouldn't make it so . . . And what one thought about the logic of the thing didn't, and couldn't, square with what he instinctively felt, which was that Davies had been innocent all along. 'Mind you,' he added, 'I suppose Davies taking the body – or bodies – off in his van would explain why no one spotted them with all those workmen about . . . But then why bring them back, especially if he'd planned to scatter the bits about, like the torso murder – remember those cuttings we found in the flat?'

If Ballard thought he was clutching at straws, he didn't show it. 'Backhouse could have planted them, sir. He's pretty keen on newspaper cuttings himself – he had quite a few in his suitcase about Davies, and there was that one he almost showed Mrs Carleton. That was about the Davies case, too.'

'Was it?'

'Arliss gave me a message from the lab – it got sent there by mistake. I asked him to bring us some tea, by the way.'

'Well done . . . Coming back to what we were saying before, I should have thought taking an adult's body downstairs and out the front door would have caused a bit of a racket, and if Davies had done it at night that would be all the more reason for the Backhouses to hear . . .'

'Here you are, sir.' Arliss shuffled in with two cups of tea, most of which seemed to have ended up in the saucers.

Hastily shoving all his papers aside as the elderly constable's unsteady hand pushed the china onto the desk, Stratton thought that Arliss's retirement, due in a few months, couldn't come a moment too soon. With ill-health, in the form of tremors, being added to his habitual incompetence, he'd become a one-man liability in the last year, regardless of how simple the task.

'Thanks, Arliss.' Stratton turned back to Ballard. 'The Backhouses said they heard him bring Muriel's body down to the washhouse, didn't they? He said he thought Davies was moving furniture . . . Of course, if the last statement's true, that means he was lying before, so . . . But somebody must have heard something, for Christ's sake, and–' Stratton, suddenly aware that Arliss was still standing somewhere over to his right, stopped and looked at him. The constable seemed suddenly alert – or rather, his usual expression of morose vacancy altered sufficiently for him to look grotesque and slightly shifty at the same time.

'Was there something else?' Stratton asked pointedly.

Arliss sucked his teeth and shook his head, as if contemplating a piece of exceptionally shoddy workmanship. 'I can't see why you're bothering about all this, sir.'

'What?'

'All this about Davies and his missus and baby.'

'Well,' said Stratton, with withering sarcasm – not that anyone as dim as Arliss could be expected to recognise it as such – 'let me enlighten you. In the first place–'

'I know Davies did it, sir.'

Oh, for Christ's sake, thought Stratton, irritably. What next? Maybe the station charlady would come and favour them with the benefit of her opinion. 'What are you talking about?'

'He told me.'

'Told you? When?'

'When he was here.'

'Yes,' said Stratton, exasperated, 'obviously when he was *here*. But when, exactly?'

'It was the morning after he come in, sir. I remember it was early, because I'd just had my tea, and I was on duty downstairs, keeping observation. We got talking because I was outside the cell. I told him I could understand him killing his wife' – Stratton could well believe this; Arliss had been blaming *his* wife, or, more accurately, her cooking, for the fact that he'd been locked in mortal combat with his bowels for years, with the results of which his colleagues were all too well aware – 'but I couldn't understand an innocent kiddie. He said it was because the crying got on his nerves and he couldn't put up with it, so he'd strangled her. Those were his words, sir – I remember it clear as day.'

'Why the hell didn't you say anything?'

'Well . . .' Arliss stared at him with an air of absorbed mystification, like a chimpanzee meddling with the workings of a watch, then said, 'you'd got the confession off him, hadn't you, sir? I never thought there was any need . . . Anyway, I say it's all a waste of time. He done it, all right. He told me himself.'

'Who in their right mind,' asked Stratton, after the constable had taken himself off, leaving him and Ballard staring at each other, 'would make a confession to *Arliss*?'

With a carefully neutral expression and tone, Ballard replied, 'A man like Davies would, sir.'

'I suppose so. Maybe he recognised a kindred spirit. I mean, they can't have been that far apart mentally.'

Ballard looked reproachful. 'Arliss was once seen to read a newspaper, sir. Or rather, he was caught turning over the pages and moving his lips at the same time, so—'

'Point taken. You know what I mean. Actually, I suppose I can see how it might have happened. For all his faults, Arliss has a good way with prisoners, especially the younger ones, and he's not threatening.'

'Do you believe it, sir?'

'Arliss obviously does, and he certainly isn't sophisticated enough to have tricked Davies into saying it, or anything like that. Perhaps he was the one person that Davies felt comfortable enough with for him to tell the truth. Or . . .' Stratton and Ballard stared at each other for a long, uncomfortable moment, 'we'd put the idea into his mind that it was necessary for him to confess it.'

'You've got to admit, though, sir, that it has a ring of truth about it. Davies must have been in terrible state of stress at the time, and . . .' Ballard broke off, shaking his head in confusion, and fiddled with a paperclip.

'And,' Stratton finished for him, 'we just don't know.'

Ballard looked up. 'No, sir. And I know it's not much comfort, but I don't believe anyone else does, either – except Backhouse, that is, and he's not going to tell us, is he?'

THREE MONTHS LATER

Chapter Seventy-Nine

Stratton stood on the pavement in Albemarle Street, looking up at the Andersons' house, which was impressively large: five floors, and a basement, and it obviously went back a good way, too. Diana had telephoned the station the previous day, asking to see him. She'd not said much, just invited him to come and see her – for tea, he supposed, as it was half past five.

He was wearing a clean shirt, which at least went some way to make up for his baggy suit and the shaving cut on his chin. As surreptitiously as he could he shone the toes of his shoes, in turn, on the calves of his trousers, before mounting the three steps to the door and raising the enormous brass knocker.

He'd been surprised when the telephone call came. After all, he reasoned, the last time he'd seen Diana, she'd been at her lowest and most vulnerable, and it was only human not to want to be reminded of that. *He* certainly didn't like being reminded of himself at his weakest points – and, in the last few months, what with the inquiry into the Davies case and Backhouse's trial, there'd been nothing but reminders. He couldn't pretend that he hadn't been relieved when the inquiry had ruled that Davies was, after all, guilty of both murders, and exonerated the police. However, judging by the furore this had caused in the press, the thing wasn't going to go away any time soon, even though Backhouse had been found guilty. There being no appeal, he'd been hanged the previous week, but instead of making Stratton feel better, it had only served to give him nightmares about the things left undone and questions unasked.

At least, Stratton thought, Monica was all right, back at Ashwood and apparently quite happy in her work. Benson, she'd told him, had gone to America. He was in two minds about this, pleased that the man was separated from his daughter by God knew how many thousands of miles, but also feeling that work in Hollywood constituted a reward for bad behaviour. As he'd said to Don, he'd have preferred it if Benson's enforced separation from Monica had been caused by, say, a fatal step in front of a bus, but, as Don had remarked, one couldn't have everything . . .

The door was answered by a large woman with a pair of vast bosoms that looked, in their casing of stiff grey cloth, like some sort of defensive fortification. Once it became clear that Stratton, who hadn't given his official title, wasn't there to repair the drains or sell a vacuum cleaner but had been invited by Diana – about which she clearly hadn't been told – she seemed unsure of quite what to do with him. She was on the point of making him wait outside when an attractive blonde woman appeared and, introducing herself as Mrs Anderson, whisked him into what he imagined must be known as the drawing room. Dark and high-ceilinged, with plenty of fancy cornicing and whatnot, it was full of the sort of furniture which was never bought, but handed down from generation to generation.

Mrs Anderson offered him a seat and a glass of sherry. He'd have preferred a cup of tea, but didn't like to say anything, so he accepted. Mind you, he thought, sipping it, it was a lot less sweet and consequently much nicer than any sherry he'd had before – clearly the real stuff. While not betraying any hint of snobbery, his hostess spoke to him – 'Diana's told us so much about you . . . I'm sure she'll be down in a minute . . . Don't mind Mrs Robinson . . .' and so forth – with an odd mixture of friendliness and impersonality. Although she was obviously trying to put him at ease, Stratton couldn't help wondering if this was how she would have spoken to an old family retainer if they'd happened to meet in unusual circumstances. All in all, he felt pretty uncomfortable, so it was quite a relief when, a few minutes later, the sound of a distant telephone bell was followed by the appearance of Mrs Robinson to say that Lady Melling was on the line.

Mrs Anderson excused herself and left, and Mrs Robinson stayed long enough to give him a look that stopped just short of telegraphing the fact that she'd be counting the spoons before following suit. Left alone, Stratton stood up and went to examine the line of silver-mounted photographs on the mantelpiece. The one in the middle showed a stately country pile; Mrs, or perhaps Mr Anderson's childhood home. Stratton picked it up, weighing the frame in his hand. Diana, he thought, would have grown up in a similar place. This was 'the other half' all right. The sheer, unassailable *poshness* of the whole thing . . . The long line of noble sperm stretching back through history and culminating around the eleventh century with Sir Somebody de Something who'd been rewarded for his services to the king – and not for roasting oxen or shovelling shit, either.

He was glaring down at the photograph when he heard a discreet cough behind him, and turning, he saw Diana standing about two feet away. 'Sorry,' he said, 'I didn't hear you.'

'That's all right.' Her smile was hesitant, but she looked far healthier than when he'd last seen her, glowing and fresh as if newly minted and wearing a smart grey suit that showed off her elegant legs. 'Hideous, isn't it?'

Confused – surely she couldn't mean what she was wearing? – it took him a second to realise that he was still holding the photograph. 'It's certainly very big. And old, of course,' he added, feeling stupid.

'Fourteenth century, I think – originally, anyway. Until it got smothered. Some Victorian ancestor of Lally's obviously told the architect to lay it on with a trowel.'

'Yes . . .' Unable to think of anything to say, Stratton stared at the photograph in silence until Diana took it, very gently, out of his hands and repositioned it on the mantelpiece with the others.

'You know,' she said when she turned round, 'that's the past. That house' – she indicated the photograph – 'it's a white elephant. Like the one I grew up in. That's . . . well, it's a ruin, really. Once the army'd finished with it . . .' She shrugged. 'I managed to sell it in the end, but it didn't fetch much.'

'But don't you . . . I mean, aren't you sorry? I mean . . . Well, you must have felt an attachment . . .' Stratton tailed off, embarrassed.

'Not really,' said Diana, moving briskly towards the drinks table. 'It's just a place. I wasn't very happy there.' Picking up the decanter, she said, 'More sherry?'

Stratton was surprised, when he looked at his glass, to find that it was empty. 'Thank you, if it's not too much trouble.' God, what a ridiculous thing to say . . . What the hell was the matter with him?

Diana refilled his glass and, pouring a glass for herself, held it up. 'Cheers!'

'Er . . . cheers!' Stratton touched his glass to hers, carefully. There was a moment's silence as they both sipped and then, as Diana didn't seem about to speak, he said, 'What . . . I mean, why did you want to see me?' God, she was staring at him – it was the wrong tone, too abrupt . . . 'I mean, I'm delighted to see you, and you look . . . you look . . . much better, and . . . If there's anything I can do . . .'

'You've been very helpful,' said Diana. Two hard spots of colour had come into her cheeks and, speaking very fast, she continued, 'I don't know what I'd have done if you hadn't . . . I mean, that man . . . I've been staying here, and Lally and Jock have been very kind. I've been doing some decorating for them as payment for bed and board.'

'Have you?' Stratton couldn't for the life of him imagine her up a ladder, wielding a paintbrush.

'Surprised?' Diana grinned.

'Yes, frankly.'

'I like doing things like that – and I'm quite good at them, believe it or not. I only discovered I could do that sort of thing quite recently. After I married James, actually – I wanted to get our flat decorated and I couldn't find anyone to do it, so I decided I'd set to and do it myself.' Stratton was relieved that she said this quite neutrally – imparting information rather than painfully reliving a memory of happier times. But then, he thought, she'd hardly do that in front of me, would she?

'I didn't think,' Diana continued, 'that I'd be able to get another job like the one I had before, so I've been taking a course in shorthand. We had to do an examination, to test our speeds.'

'Did you pass?'

'Yes! Believe it or not, I'd never taken an examination before. I haven't had much in the way of . . . well, formal education, I suppose you'd call it, and I was terribly nervous, but I practised like anything and it all went swimmingly.'

'Well, congratulations,' said Stratton, raising his glass once more.

'They're taking me back at Ashwood,' said Diana. 'The Design Department, so I shan't need the shorthand after all, but I'm glad I did it because you never know about the future . . . I'm starting on Monday. Oh, I'm sorry, I meant to ask – how's Monica?'

'Fine,' said Stratton. 'She lost the baby, but she's fully recovered. I'm sure you'll bump into her at the studio.'

'Oh, good. I mean, about seeing Monica again, not about . . . But as long as she's not hurt, physically . . . It's always so . . . I mean, I've been in that situation – losing a baby.' Diana looked down at her feet. 'Several times, in fact. It was pretty horrible, but,' looking up, she gave him an encouraging smile, 'one does get over these things, you know.'

'I'm sorry,' said Stratton, surprised by this intimacy and hoping he wasn't blushing. 'It can't have been easy for you. Any of it, I mean.'

Diana acknowledged this with a nod, then, after a second, carried on in a normal voice. 'Well, there has been one piece of luck. An aunt of James's died several weeks ago. He'd never spoken of her – in fact, I didn't even know she existed – so they obviously weren't close, but she left him some money. Her death was sudden – a heart attack – so I suppose she hadn't got round to changing her will . . . Anyway, it comes to me. It's enough for a small house or a flat somewhere. Lally's going to help me look. Oh, dear. You're looking at me as if I'm mad, and I don't blame you, but—'

'No,' Stratton protested. 'I wasn't. I'm sorry if that's how it seemed. I just . . .' He stopped, swallowed hard, and feeling that there was nothing, at this point, to lose, ploughed on. 'I just like looking at you.'

'Oh . . .' Diana gave a little laugh and turned away slightly. The redness of her cheeks seemed to have intensified. She took another sip of her sherry – quite a large one this time – and said, 'I wanted to tell you. I suppose I want you to know that

I'm not completely useless. I don't really expect you to understand or anything, but I just . . .' Shaking her head, she looked miserably down at her glass.

'I've never thought you were useless,' said Stratton, bewildered. 'Just . . . different, that's all.'

'That's it, isn't it? Different.'

'Well, you are. I mean, we are. Oh, dear. I'm not doing very well, am I?'

'Neither am I. It's just, when I saw you again, I was so glad, and . . . Well, I was glad, that's all. And,' she continued fiercely, 'I want to stand on my own two feet, and I wanted you to know that.' Her eyes blazed for a moment, as if she thought he was about to contradict her or laugh at her.

'I understand,' said Stratton, staring at her. Suddenly, the room, and all it implied, seemed to fall away and Diana herself was all he could see. 'Perhaps,' he said cautiously, 'if you can find a free evening in your new schedule, you might like to come out to dinner. Nowhere fancy, I'm afraid, but I'd like to hear how you're doing.'

Diana's eyes widened, and Stratton took an involuntary step backwards. Was she going to raise her chin and coldly ask him to leave? Scream? Slap his face?

She didn't do any of those things. Instead, she smiled, a wide, genuine smile. 'Yes,' she said. 'I'd like that. I'd like that . . . very much. Thank you, Edward.'

A NOTE ON HISTORICAL BACKGROUND

Part of the storyline of this book is based on a pair of true cases: that of Timothy John Evans, who was hanged in 1950 for the murder of his fourteen-month-old daughter, Geraldine, and that of John Reginald Halliday Christie, who was hanged in 1953 for the murder of his wife, Ethel. Both resided at the same address, 10 Rillington Place, Notting Hill Gate, London W11. Although names and places have been changed and there has been some tinkering with dates, I have stuck as closely as possible to the known facts in both cases in the writing of this book. However, it should be noted that I have treated them as a novelist, rather than as a historian. Some of the characters are, of course, based on real people, but others are entirely made up and have no resemblance to anyone either living or dead.

I first heard of these cases in the mid-seventies, from my mother. At the time, I was attending a school situated close to the street that had been Rillington Place (the area immediately surrounding it has now been redeveloped and the roads renamed). I cannot now remember how the subject came up, but my mother, a doctor, had studied the medical aspects of the cases when she trained at St Andrew's and she told me what had happened. It was the story rather than the forensic details that drew my attention, and I remember feeling desperately sorry for Timothy Evans and his family.

Many years later, considering the cases as potential material for a novel, I began to wonder about the feelings of the detectives in the Evans' case. In 1950, when Evans was hanged, everybody was sure that justice had been done – there seemed no doubt at all that he had killed not only his daughter, but also his wife, Beryl. What must those policeman have felt when, in 1953, six bodies, two of them skeletons, were discovered at the same property, in Christie's flat and in the garden of which he had sole use?

When it emerged that Evans's conviction had been, in large part, secured on the evidence of a serial killer, doubt was cast on the fairness of his trial. With a growing number of people feeling that two stranglers of women living in the same house was too great a coincidence, there were demands for an inquiry. On 6 July, a fortnight after Christie was sentenced, the then Home Secretary, Sir David Maxwell-Fyfe, announced to the House of Commons that he had instructed Sir John Scott-Henderson QC to hold an inquiry which would determine whether a miscarriage of justice had occurred in the case of Evans. Scott-Henderson interviewed not only Christie (who was hanged on 15 July), but also twenty witnesses who had been involved in one, or both, of the investigations. In his report, he concluded that

Evans was guilty of both murders and that Christie's confession to the murder of Beryl Evans was not reliable. He wrote: *I am satisfied that Christie gradually came to the conclusion that it would be helpful in his defence if he confessed to the murder of Mrs Evans.*

As Scott-Henderson had accepted, apparently without question, not only Christie's confessions relating to the other murders but also the evidence he had given at Evans's trial, many people felt that the report was flawed and the controversy over the case continued. Besides numerous articles in newspapers and magazines, several books were written on the subject. The most famous of these is *10 Rillington Place* by Ludovic Kennedy (1961), which began with an open letter to R. A. Butler (known as Rab), who was Home Secretary at the time, requesting an urgent review of the case. In this letter, he quoted a statement from the Rt. Hon. James Chuter Ede, the Home Secretary who had sanctioned Evans's execution, saying that he felt a mistake had been made.

A second inquiry, chaired by the High Court judge Sir Daniel Brabin, was held at the end of 1965. This was a longer and altogether more thorough investigation than the Scott-Henderson inquiry, which had been criticised, by Kennedy and others, for its haste and lack of proper analysis. The Brabin report included information about an apparently spontaneous confession by Evans that he'd killed the baby because 'he had to strangle it as he could not put up with the crying'. This was made to Sergeant Trevallian of the uniformed branch while the Welshman was in custody at Notting Hill police station in 1949. It is on this that I based

Davies's confession to PC Arliss, although, unlike Arliss, Sergeant Trevallian mentioned the confession to a senior officer immediately but was told that 'they knew all about it as Evans had made a statement'.

Neither of the reports reached the conclusion that the police in the Evans case had acted improperly. After examining the evidence, Brabin made the following statement about the murders of Beryl and Geraldine Evans:

. . . it would now be impossible for me to come to a conclusion in respect of the guilt of Evans beyond reasonable doubt.

The warrant under which I was appointed to hold this Inquiry does not call only for a conclusion reached with that degree of certainty, for I am called upon to report such conclusions as I may find it possible to form. If the evidence permits me to come to a conclusion on the balance of probability, I must do so.

I have come to the conclusion that it is more probable than not that Evans killed Beryl Evans. I have come to the conclusion that it is more probable than not that Evans did not kill Geraldine.

As Evans had been tried only for the murder of his daughter – the one crime, incidentally, to which Christie never confessed – the then Home Secretary Roy Jenkins recommended a posthumous pardon for Evans, which was granted in October 1966.

Although Evans had been declared not guilty of the crime of which he was convicted, there was still the matter of Brabin's refusal to accept Christie's confession to the murder of Beryl and his decision that Evans was responsible for her death. Leading pathologist Professor Keith Simpson, who had assisted with the exhumation of Beryl Evans, agreed. In his book *Forty Years of Murder* (1978), he stated: *the Brabin Report upheld the coincidence [of there being two stranglers of women living in the same house], and it never seemed to me very far-fetched. Coincidences are far more common in life than in fiction.* Books by Rupert Furneaux (published in 1961) and John Eddowes (1994) also argued the case for Evans's guilt. However, the version of events that has become generally accepted is Ludovic Kennedy's. His book, *10 Rillington Place*, was made into a film of the same name in 1970. Directed by Richard Fleischer and starring Richard Attenborough, Judy Geeson, Pat Heywood and John Hurt, it gives a vivid and persuasive account of Evans's innocence and wrongful conviction.

A pardon does not formally erase a conviction, and in 2003 Evans's family applied to the Criminal Cases Review Commission for his conviction to be re-examined. The Commission decided that, although there was what it termed a 'real possibility' that the Court of Appeal would not uphold the conviction, it would not refer the case. The Commission's report stated that the free pardon, with its attendant publicity, was sufficient to establish Evans's innocence in the eyes of the public and that the formal quashing of the conviction would bring no tangible benefit to his family and was not in the public interest. An ex gratia payment was, however, made to the family by way of compensation for the miscarriage of justice.

In the months I spent researching this book, I read everything about both cases that I could lay my hands on, including the files of the Metropolitan Police, the records of the Director of Public Prosecutions, the trial transcripts and correspondence, and the Prison Commission and Home Office files, all of which may be found in the National Archives. What do I think happened? The honest answer is that I just don't know. The forensic evidence, such as it is, doesn't point conclusively to either man. There is also the fact that, in the words of the Brabin report, *One fact which is not in dispute and which has hampered all efforts to find the truth is that both Evans and Christie were liars. They lied about each other, they lied about themselves.*

As Professor Simpson says, coincidences *are* far more common in life than in fiction. It seems to me to be pretty unlikely that Evans killed his wife and child, but it isn't actually impossible. My heart doesn't believe it, but in the course of writing this book, my head has told me time and again that one cannot entirely discount the possibility that that is, in fact, what happened. There are many things unaccounted for, such as the dog, the timing, and why, if Beryl Evans's body was in the tiny washhouse for several days while the workmen were constantly in and out, they did not notice it. There is also the fact that baby Geraldine, unattended for two days in a very small house, wasn't heard to cry – even, apparently, by Ethel Christie, who was used to listening out for her on the occasions when Beryl left her by herself. All these are mysteries that cannot now be unravelled.

It is, however, an extraordinary story, and it's certainly true that controversy surrounding the Evans case and a number of others from the same period contributed to the abolition of capital punishment in Britain. That, I believe, can only be a good thing.

Acknowledgements

I am very grateful to Tim Donnelly, Claire Foster, Stephanie Glencross, Jane Gregory, Liz Hatherell, William Howells of Ceredigion Libraries, Trudy Howson, Maya Jacobs, Jemma McDonagh, Claire Morris, Lucy Ramsey, Manda Scott, June and William Wilson, Jane Wood, Sue and Alan Young, the staff at the National Archives and Florence Mabel Basset Hound for their enthusiasm, advice and support during the writing of this book.